The Rise and Crisis of Psychoanalysis
in the United States

FREUD IN AMERICA

VOLUME I

Freud and the Americans
*The Beginnings of Psychoanalysis
in the United States, 1876–1917*

VOLUME II

The Rise and Crisis of Psychoanalysis in the United States
Freud and the Americans, 1917–1985

The Rise and Crisis of Psychoanalysis in the United States

Freud and the Americans, 1917–1985

NATHAN G. HALE, JR.

NEW YORK   OXFORD
OXFORD UNIVERSITY PRESS
1995

Oxford University Press

Oxford   New York   Toronto
Delhi   Bombay   Calcutta   Madras   Karachi
Kuala Lumpur   Singapore   Hong Kong   Tokyo
Nairobi   Dar es Salaam   Cape Town
Melbourne   Auckland

and associated companies in
Berlin   Ibadan

Library of Congress Cataloging-in-Publication Data
Hale, Nathan G.
The rise and crisis of psychoanalysis in America / Nathan G. Hale, Jr.
p. cm. — (Freud and the Americans ; v. 2)
Includes bibliographical references and index.
ISBN 0-19-504637-4
1. Freud, Sigmund, 1856–1939.
2. Psychoanalysis—United States—History.
I. Title.
II. Series: Hale, Nathan G.   Freud and the Americans ; v. 2.
BF173.F85H318   1971   150.19'52'0973—dc20
94-178643

3 5 7 9 8 6 4 2

Printed in the United States of America
on acid-free paper

For Ann, David, and Elizabeth

Acknowledgments

This book would not have been possible without the help and criticism of colleagues, friends, and family. I am particularly indebted to the hospitality, generosity, and stimulation of Sanford and Ingrid Gifford and Hildi Greenson. Dr. Gifford was an invaluable guide to sources and people, and Peter Loewenberg also contributed valuable information. I owe a major intellectual debt to Nancy Chodorow, with whom I have had the privilege of discussing psychoanalytic issues over the years. I am especially grateful for the help and encouragement, research and translations of Cornelia Levine. Frank Sulloway was a stimulating discussant of science and psychoanalysis. A section of the book was first presented to Roger Hahn's history of science seminar, University of California, Berkeley, and to Barbara Rosenkrantz's history of science seminar at Harvard. Chapters have been read by Nancy Chodorow, Paula Fass, Lawrence Friedman, Sanford Gifford, Gerald Grob, Georgine Marrott, William McKinley Runyan, Justin Simon, Frank Sulloway, Brenda Webster, and Abby Wolfson. Prof. Grob generously made available the manuscript of his book *From Asylum to Community* before publication as well as particularly helpful criticism. The entire manuscript was read and criticized by Cornelia Levine, Ann Hale, and John Burnham, and I am especially grateful for their insightful comments and suggestions. I owe a staggering debt to Ann, whose intellectual stimulation, amazing patience, and love made possible the completion of a project that grew and grew and grew. David and Elizabeth Hale were benign observers of their father's ongoing project that must have seemed endless. Finally, Sheldon Meyer, who fostered the book from its beginning, was an enduringly patient, critical, and encouraging editor, and Stephanie Sakson gave the manuscript a meticulous, helpful reading.

I am especially grateful to the American Psychoanalytic Association, the Boston, Pittsburgh, Los Angeles, and San Francisco Psychoanalytic Institutes, the Menninger Foundation, the William Alanson White Foundation, and the Freud Archives for access to their collections. Many splendid library professionals gave invaluable help, especially Sonja Kaufman of the Education Psychology Library, University of California, Berkeley; Phyllis Rubinton, Maria Astifidis, and Nellie Thompson of the New York Psychoanalytic Institute Library; Fred Bauman, James Hutson, and David Wigdor of the Library of Congress; Jane Rizzuoto Singh and Paul Bunten of the History of Psychiatry Section of the Cornell-New York Hospital Medical Center; Richard Wolfe of the Francis A. Countway Library of Medicine, Boston.

For gracious permission to cite and quote letters and papers I thank Naomi Bettelheim Pena for Bruno Bettelheim; Ruth B. Goldberg for Sigfried Bernfeld; George Bibring for Edward and Grete Bibring; the Newberry Library in Chicago for Floyd Dell; Hannah Pitkin for Otto Fenichel; Mark Patterson Associates for Sigmund Freud and Anna Freud; Frances Gitelson for Maxwell Gitelson; and Daniel Greenson for Ralph Greenson; Roy Grinker, Jr., for Roy Grinker; Mervyn Jones and the British Psycho-Analytic Society for Ernest Jones; Paul D. Byers for Edward Glover; Martha Rusnak for Ives Hendrick; the Menninger Foundation for Karl and William Menninger; Henry Nunberg for Herman Nunberg; Robert Knight, Jr., for Robert Knight; Caroline Murray for Henry Murray; Columbia University for the Columbia University Oral History Collection; Irene Soffer for Theodor Reik; George Pollock and Paul N. Crane for Franz Alexander; The Yale University Library for Mabel Dodge Luhan; Edmund Brill for A. A. Brill; Ann Kubie Rabinowitz for Lawrence Kubie; Samuel Guttman for Robert Waelder; John Wittels for Fritz Wittels. For Adolf Meyer, the Alan Chesney Medical Archives of the Johns Hopkins Medical Institutions.

Several parts of the book were first given to the San Francisco Psychoanalytic Institute and I am grateful for the criticism of its members. Research associates included Spiro Goritz and Jacqueline Reinier. Grants from the Academic Senate of the University of California, Riverside, the John Simon Guggenheim Foundation, the Grant Foundation, and the National Institute of Mental Health supported the research and writing.

Contents

The Rise and Crisis of Psychoanalysis
in the United States

Introduction

No other system of thought in modern times, except the great religions, has been adopted by so many people as an explanation of human behavior, an American critic observed of psychoanalysis in 1956.[1] Celebrating the centennial of Freud's birth, popular magazines reported that this "Darwin of the Mind," had fathered "modern" psychiatry and psychology and new approaches to child raising, education, and sexuality. He influenced the daily lives of millions in America, the adopted homeland of psychoanalysis. That rather grandiose assessment was typical of popular judgments of Freud's status in America in the late 1950s and early 1960s when I first began work in the history of American psychoanalysis.

Then, in 1975, Sir Peter Medawar, a British medical research scientist and Nobel prize winner, announced in the *New York Review of Books* that "doctrinaire psychoanalytic theory" was the "most stupendous intellectual confidence trick of the twentieth century," a terminal product like the dinosaur. Frederick Crews, a distinguished critic, renounced his Freudian allegiance arguing that not only the therapeutic claims of psychoanalysis but the presumed scientific acumen and integrity of Freud were myths.[2] These opinions could have been dismissed as additions to the polemical attacks on an ideology that had drawn opposition from its inception. However, they signaled a significant change in the status of psychoanalysis in America. I had seen this change unfold in ways I could not have anticipated, ways that added to the historical puzzle I was working on—how to account for Freud's American reception. Because the apparent decline of psychoanalysis was as fascinating a problem as its rise and pervasiveness, it seemed time for an overview that would encompass both.

How much of the rise and apparent decline could be accounted for by the nature of psychoanalysis and how much by shifts in American society? In an earlier study of the beginnings of psychoanalysis in America, I attempted to account for its remarkable early success by an unexpected fit between the two. I argued that psychoanalysis met particular American needs at a crucial historical moment. Freud's theories provided a timely instrument for dealing with two concurrent crises that were occurring in the first decade of this century—crises in sexual morality and in the treatment of nervous and mental disorder.

The first crisis entailed the breakdown of a particularly stringent version of what Freud had termed "civilized" sexual morality, a code that prevailed in Europe and America in the later 19th century. The American version not only confined sexual intercourse within monogamous marriage, but sought to assure purity of thought as well as behavior, partly through reticence about all sexuality, partly through a relatively asexual stereotype of woman.

The internalization of the "civilized" code structured the symptoms of some of the American psychoanalysts' first patients, symptoms for which the uncovering techniques of psychoanalysis and its insistence on the universal nature of sexual thoughts and needs were singularly appropriate. Recent research has modified somewhat the asexual stereotype of the late 19th-century American woman, but has not challenged the nature of the code's prohibitions, or the contention that its internalization could have structured patients' symptoms.

The "civilized" moral code was the ornament of the accepted medical authorities of the somatic style that prevailed in the treatment of nervous and mental disorder, a style that was undergoing a crisis at roughly the same time as the sexual code. Similar norms ensured sexual morality and mental health: the judicious conservation of energy, control of the lower functions of the body by the higher functions of the brain, notably by the enlightened will. This style assumed that nervous and mental disorder resulted from inherited defect and from lesions or malfunctions of the brain and the nervous system, and patients presented, accordingly, a luxuriant compendium of physical symptoms, aches, pains, paralyses. Nervous and mental disorders could be cured by such means as electric currents, diets, rest, or drugs. Theories of the localization of specific functions in the brain and the hope that specific lesions could be linked to specific forms of nervous and mental disease had aroused fervent hopes for the future among the somaticists. But toward the end of the 19th century, these hopes seemed increasingly doubtful. The match of functions with localized areas and of disorders with lesions remained frustratingly unconsummated. Little systematic attention was paid to the emotions, although it was assumed that these could influence the functioning of the brain and body. Nor did the style pay close attention to family relationships, except as these involved the impact of heredity. Perhaps most important, recovery rates for the psychoses in the United States had declined to about 25 to 35 percent.

In America reactions against "civilized" morality and against the somatic style were already under way by the turn of the century. Psychoanalysis was part of an international effort that sought alternatives to the existing difficulties of the somaticists. Freud offered the most radical of several new medical psychologies. His psychoanalysis rejected theories of hereditary degeneracy, claimed to cure a limited number of neuroses and shed light on the meaning and significance of the psychoses, and, finally and most important, stressed the role of sexuality. It offered a conception of the "unconscious" as a repository of sexual impulses and implied that the understanding and mastery of these impulses would unlock energies previously lost to repression. Americans, particularly in Boston, were developing their own psychotherapy, based largely on the theories of the French psychologist Pierre Janet, and a Boston movement that combined this new approach with religious healing was receiving national publicity.

Critics challenged not only the somatic style but also major elements of the "civilized" sexual code, particularly the requirement of reticence, and in so doing hoped to purge America of vice and prostitution in yet another campaign of Progressive uplift and social reform. By asserting the importance of repressed sexuality as a cause of neuroses, by insisting on the sexual needs of women, Freud advanced a powerful medical argument for reform, beginning with greater frankness about sexuality. Although Freud was but one factor in this change in attitudes, he came to symbolize all of them. Some educators and psychologists had begun to advocate the sexual "enlightenment" of children, who themselves had become the objects of serious study, including studies of their sexual development. The maverick president of Clark University, G. Stanley Hall, had been a major figure in these enterprises and had been following the new departures in medical psychology as well.

Thus, when, at Hall's invitation, Freud lectured at Clark University on his only visit to America in 1909, he came at a strategic moment. Expounding his theories at his most beguiling and simplistic for the "practical Americans," he united existing American concerns: a hopeful psychotherapy that rejected much of the relevance of heredity, challenges to "civilized" morality, a new emphasis on the importance of sexuality, childhood, and the role of the unconscious. Moreover, Freud presented aspects of his theories that Americans could congenially exploit: his comparative therapeutic optimism, the simplicity of his model of catharsis and cure, his truculent ambiguity about the reform of sexual customs, and, especially beguiling, his view of dreams as a key to the mysterious unconscious.

Psychoanalysis appealed to disparate groups of Americans—a few psychologists, a few neurologists who specialized in the treatment of the nervous and mental disorders of the well-to-do, and a perhaps larger number of hospital psychiatrists, some of whom were entering private practice because institutional jobs were few and competition growing. The physicians were associated with the major centers of renewal and reform in American psychiatry—in Boston, New York, and Washington.

The movement's converts among physicians were primarily native Protestants, Jews, and Jewish immigrants. Many of them were younger than most psychiatrists and neurologists, and many were upwardly mobile. They developed a version of psychoanalysis that differed from Freud's in ways that bore the stamp of values prevalent in the Progressive America of Theodore Roosevelt and Woodrow Wilson. Their version was more optimistic about treatment, applied psychoanalytic principles to the psychoses, and gave greater weight to environmental influences, particularly the impact of parents on their children. Within this general framework two approaches evolved; one was largely eclectic, with an avid interest in applying psychoanalysis to social reform and "mental hygiene." A second version, far more orthodox, was closer to Freud's ultimately tragic sensibilities, insisting on the aggressive and sexual nature of the child. Freud's ambiguity about what he considered to be desirable reforms in the control of sexual behavior gave rise to two very general interpretations of the sexual issue that can be termed "radical" and "conservative." The "radical" interpretation saw psychoanalysis as enjoining an ill-defined sexual liberation. The "conservative" interpretation tended to emphasize control and "sublimation," again never clearly defined but deployed in the service of American moralism. The concept of the will, so central to "civilized" morality, vanished from the orthodox psychoanalytic vocabulary, not to reappear for almost four decades.

By 1917 psychoanalysts in America had founded two small professional organizations, led by a few influential neurologists and psychiatrists; psychoanalysis was finding a place in textbooks as a hopeful mode of treatment for the neuroses and as contributing a new understanding of the psychoses. An eclectic "American" psychiatry and psychoanalysis grew alongside the more orthodox practice of Freudians.[3]

Within ten years of Freud's visit psychoanalysis outstripped every other variety of psychotherapy in the popular press. And these expositions exaggerated the optimism, moralism, and environmentalism of the American psychoanalysts, the simplicity and certainty of psychoanalytic therapy, and the energizing power of the unconscious.

None of the American "victories" of psychoanalysis, as Freud termed some of them, had been achieved without struggle and opposition. Controversies raged over issues that would persist in the history of American psychoanalysis: How scientific was psychoanalysis? How valid were Freud's theories of sex and gender? What kinds of evidence validated psychoanalytic interpretations? Could they be confirmed experimentally? Could there be uniform methods of reporting cases? Should not theories about children be based on direct observation rather than on retrospective data from the analysis of adults? What would happen were a single case to be studied by several different observers? How compromising for psychoanalytic validity were the problems of suggestion by the analyst or the patient already knowledgeable about psychoanalytic theories?

In 1909 Freud had been uneasy and ambivalent about what he sensed as his potential American welcome, which he appreciated, disliked, and sought to explain. At first he attributed the warm reception of psychoanalysis to a uniquely American open-mindedness and a remarkable public enthusiasm for psychotherapy which he distrusted because of its association with religion. By 1914 he seemed pleased that a few important psychiatrists had adopted his theories. In the 1920s it even seemed possible that America's prosperity and generosity might lead to funding the psychoanalytic training of social workers, for instance.[4]

By the 1930s all these advantages had become, for Freud, national liabilities. The medical enthusiasm was pernicious. Freud feared that psychoanalysis would become not the general psychology he envisaged but a mere handmaiden of psychiatry, branded in texts as a specialized therapy. Even American wealth was baneful. It did not support psychoanalysis, but rather other "scientific and pseudo-scientific undertakings." He now saw the earlier interest as an unwelcome popularity among the "lay public." American open-mindedness had led to the watering-down of psychoanalysis, which, Freud believed, lost sight of essentials and reflected a lack of scientific rigor: "They create for themselves a kind of hodge podge of psychoanalysis and other elements and boast of their doings as a sign of broadmindedness while they actually reveal thereby a lack of judgment."[5] Americans had no "emotional investment in genuine understanding," he told the young analyst Franz Alexander, who consulted him about moving to America. "They took you in in Chicago, I know from my own experience in the States that masterful way of giving lip service."[6]

Alexander, who became one of the major figures in American psychoanalysis, in his autobiography, published in 1960 and modestly entitled *The Western Mind in Transition,* rejected Freud's strictures. He found Americans genuinely curious, with a "refreshing interest in new ideas." Moreover, public pressure, rather than being a liability, had forced physicians to recognize psychoanalysis. Americans were "empirical rather than theoretical or dogmatic." Although naive about the philosophy of science, they were far more receptive to psychoanalytic research than Europeans had been.

There was, in fact, some truth in both these versions. Many of the first American psychoanalysts were open-minded but also incorrigibly eclectic, mixing and matching theories without much regard for their internal logic or consistency. Above all, they were pragmatists, concerned with practical matters of therapy and with the application of psychoanalysis to psychiatry and to social problems.

Neurologists and psychiatrists found the psychoanalytic focus on the emotional relations of love and hate among family members revealing and important, probably because they reflected the changing structure of American family life. John Demos has suggested that the increasing role of the mother in raising children in the smaller American family beginning in the late 19th century created fertile ground for the development of intense and sometimes pathological emotional relationships centering on the Oedipus complex.[7] Some of the first American psychoanalysts were alert to the overly close ties of the mother to the only child and, like Freud, advised that the child be not smothered with too much love or sensual stimulation. Charting the emotional relationships within changing family structures has been an important continuing theme of psychoanalytic observation.

There were also structural reasons why neurologists and psychiatrists were open to psychoanalysis. American medicine was highly decentralized, and borrowing from Europe was commonplace. For example, German and Viennese medicine had provided influential models in the development of programs at American medical schools and their prestige was high.[8] Then, too, no entrenched conservative figures hostile to psychoanalysis dominated the new centers of psychiatric research and reform.

American conceptions of science in medicine, which would change radically over time, then were close to Freud's. Physicians still relied, as did he, on the clinical judgment of data observed in the individual case. Laboratory science and experiment were compatible with this approach. Epidemiology and medical statistics, which might have suggested other models, were just gaining a foothold, and academic laboratory psychology still was largely irrelevant to treatment. Finally, like most American medical specialties, psychiatry and neurology were in their formative stages and would not develop national standards of competence and national boards of review, thus cementing criteria of acceptable and unacceptable knowledge, until the 1930s.

Within a decentralized and open medical establishment, American psychiatry sought to cloak itself in the scientific authority of medicine by insisting that psychoanalysis conform to prevailing canons of the scientific, a demand that would become increasingly important in the 1930s and beyond. It was also one reason why psychoanalysts insisted that those in their profession be medically trained. This seemed all the more necessary because the role of the psychiatrist was beginning to change from administration in an isolated state hospital to a private, urban practice in which psychotherapy would play an increasingly important function in the treatment of a growing array of human ills.

Because medicine made psychoanalysis "respectable," and assured it a serious hearing, this volume, like the first, will chart the changing relationship of psychoanalysis to American psychiatry. It will describe the popularization of psychoanalysis broadly defined, images of Freud and of therapy, and the early impact of psychoanalysis on mental hygiene, social work, and criminology. It also will be concerned with changing concepts of science within medicine and with shifting American attitudes toward sexual morality and behavior.

Part I examines the role of World War I in fostering Freud's influence on American psychiatry, the subsequent establishment of psychoanalysis as a profession, and the growth of its clientele from 1917 to 1940. During these years psychoanalysis functioned as an iconoclastic psychology of instinctual drives and was closely associated with the formation of "modern" views of sexuality, art, and literature. In highly diluted form psychoanalysis filtered into education, social work, and criminology. At the same time, developments within psychoanalysis as well as the experience of war and totalitarianism prepared the way for a psychoanalysis centering on the regulation of instinctual drives by agencies of the self. This view would flourish in a more conservative America after 1945. Both outlooks reflected ambiguities and tensions within the structure of psychoanalysis, and, often enough, they uneasily coexisted.

Part II takes up the role of psychoanalysis in World War II, its extraordinary expansion to the mid-1960s, and its transformation by a powerful, popularizing American culture. It then explores reasons for the apparent decline of psychoanalysis in psychiatry to the mid-1980s. These included the rise of a newly successful somatic psychiatry, the identification of psychoanalysis with medicine and evaluations of psychoanalysis based on medicine's changing norms of the scientific. The decline resulted as well from the proliferation of alternative modes of psychotherapy and from the growing criticism of psychoanalysis by behaviorist psychologists, somatic psychiatrists, as well as emerging militant movements of women and gays. All these developments led to the American psychoanalytic profession's current crisis. The study focuses chiefly on what has been called "mainstream" psychoanalysis, centering on the American Psychoanalytic Association, for many years the largest and dominant professional body within the psychoanalytic subculture. In 1917 the year America entered the First World War on the side of the Allies, the psychoanalytic subculture was still tiny, consisting of a few dozen psychiatrists and psychologists and a perhaps larger group of lay enthusiasts. Wartime experience persuaded segments of the medical community and the wider public, well beyond that nascent subculture, of the utility of Freud's message.

PART I

*Creating a Profession
and a Clientele:
1920–1940*

1

The Great War:
A Human Laboratory

In the colossal human laboratory of the Great War some of Freud's theories seemed strikingly confirmed. A few Freudian conceptions already current among an advance guard in American psychiatry—conflict, instincts, the conversion of emotions into symptoms, the importance of dreams and of early experience, repression, defense, catharsis—gained additional currency through their use in treating shell-shocked soldiers.[1]

The war gave psychiatrists a new sense of mission and an expanded social role. Some of them argued that only those who could treat the irrational elements of human nature that the war so abundantly revealed were fit to guide national destinies. The need for widespread psychiatric services for shell-shocked soldiers and veterans led to the founding of hospitals, clinics, and schools for social workers, many of whom were trained under psycho-analytic auspices.

The war brought Freud a new American reputation as a philosopher of the irrational and the brutal in human nature. This new emphasis in Freud's thought sharpened the difference between his European pessimism and the optimism of many of his American followers. Freud's "Reflections on War and Death," offered in the hope of furthering international understanding, angered many Americans. Freud argued that the war had stripped away the constraints of civilization, revealing the primal man, whose murderous impulses lurked in everyone's unconscious. Too many human beings in every nation lived beyond their ethical resources, the prey of instincts untamed by love and no longer subject to the rewards and punishments of culture. Elmer Southard, the head of the Boston Psychopathic Hospital, promptly classified Freud as a "subtle spokesman for Teutonic crimes," and an example of the "devil-worship" that constituted the "philosophy, the religion" of Germany: another reviewer denounced the essay as an "indictment of the whole German people."[2] Frenzied patriotism led some Americans to associate Freud and psychoanalysis with German decadence, atheistic pessimism, and sexual looseness. This was especially true of those who believed in the superiority of Anglo-Saxon culture and who, early, hoped for American intervention on the side of the Allies. A famous novelist, Marie Corelli, pleaded for "clean brains" and warned that Germany wallowed in "moral filth." Moreover, others observed, psychoanalysis spoiled and coddled patients, while the war clearly demonstrated the superiority of discipline and the need for self-sacrifice.[3]

Other Americans found Freud's analysis persuasive. Despite the fact that he was an enemy alien, popular and professional interest in psychoanalysis increased during the war years. One of the most expansive, favorable accounts appeared in the *Ladies' Home Journal* in 1917, eight months after Congress had declared war on Germany.[4] From 1917 to 1919, twelve new books on psychoanalysis appeared and were widely reviewed, eight more in 1920, and twenty-four in 1921. Moreover, the public was learning of startling "confirmation" of aspects of Freud's theories that emerged from the human laboratory.

When the Germans invaded Belgium in 1914 under cover of massive artillery bombardments, a baffling phenomenon occurred among Allied troops. Some stumbled out of the Belgian forts with "staring eyes, violent tremors, a look of terror, and blue, cold extremities." Others were deaf or dumb, blind or paralyzed. Some wept uncontrollably, or were jumpy and irritable, a prey to hallucinatory dreams. Still others suffered from heart palpitations or dizziness or amnesia.[5] When the French developed similar symptoms, the Germans at first assumed that like the Belgians they were a psychopathic, degenerate race. But as French artillery power matched that of the Germans, the same symptoms appeared among German soldiers.[6] Even for seasoned troops who had experienced hand-to-hand combat in the Boer or Russo-Japanese wars, the new conditions were uncanny. The Great War's techniques were terrifying: "liquid fire, high explosives, tanks, poison gas, bombing planes, the 'war of attrition' in the trenches."[7] Pluck, agility, cleverness, strength, or wit was of little avail.

Men who succumbed to this new illness were articulate about the war's horrors:

> The sights were awful, dead men all over the place, some half buried by shells . . . it was simply a case of looking death in the face and waiting to be hit. I never got into a worse hell.[8]

An American officer recalled the onset of his sickness:

> I heard the most terrifying thing I ever heard in my life—the loud, malicious scream of a big shell. . . . As I was falling, the whole world blew up. . . . I heard a man screaming, holding his body with both hands. . . . Then my eyes rested on the boy who had laughed . . . blood was pumping out of his body like red water . . . My head hurt, my face hurt, my ears and eyes . . . I hurt all over.[9]

An American physician who experimented with psychoanalytic techniques at St. Elizabeth's Hospital summed up the new kind of collective destruction:

> Streams have been choked with the dead and rivers have run red with the blood of the wounded. The terrible pictures of the war have been pictures of death en masse; death of men, women and children; death of trees and shrubs, even the grass; death of hope and everywhere the despair of death.[10]

Because many soldiers who exhibited the new symptoms had undergone terrifying bombardments, the syndrome was called "shell shock." Explosions had killed men who showed no visible wounds at all, while autopsies revealed micro hemorrhages in the brain and spinal cord. As a result of this observation, some British physicians at first concluded that the symptoms of shell shock might result from concussion which caused minute damage to nervous tissue. Yet, contradicting that hypothesis was the observation that symptoms seemed to bear no real relation to any actual physical disability. "Shell shock" was rare among prisoners or the wounded, including men with severe head injuries.[11] It appeared as well in men who had never been near battle. In the British army at first, some were diagnosed as insane by doctors who had never seen such symptoms in men during peacetime. Other doctors and many officers and men simply believed the shell-shocked soldier was "yellow," deliberately malingering to escape pain and death.[12]

The French (and many British) blamed constitutional instability, inherited or acquired. Prolonged strain, fatigue, and hardship reduced resistance, then the physical and emotional shock of an explosion or any other battle trauma could set off the illness.[13] The French and British learned early that without proper treatment the symptoms tended to become fixed and sometimes incurable. Men treated close to the front had the best chance of recovery. Although some never got well, a very high proportion of cases recovered quickly, sometimes under odd circumstances. One mute soldier spoke after seeing a Charlie Chaplin movie; another on hearing the news that Romania had entered the war on the side of the Allies. As experienced neurologists and psychiatrists saw more cases, some of them concluded that for the first time in history the functional neuroses seemed to be occurring on a mass scale because of the new conditions of war.[14] By the end of the war, there were an estimated 800,000 cases in the British forces, 800,000 in the French, 15,000 in the American.[15]

American neurologists and psychiatrists (the term neuro-psychiatrist was a wartime invention) followed closely the warring armies' experiences with shell shock.[16] Its puzzling nature stimulated debate over theories and therapies and reflected the eclectic variety of American psychiatric thought. A few, like Dr. Southard, believed that the French had won the war on the plane of theory. The suggestion theories of Charcot's pupil Babinski had been brilliantly confirmed. On the other hand, the psychoanalyst Smith Ely Jelliffe argued that Babinski's views were out of date and neither as explanatory nor as effective as the dynamic theories and therapies deriving from Janet and Freud.[17]

Some of those who were either tolerant of psychoanalysis or committed to a broadly eclectic version of its theories were active in the American war effort; a few held influential positions. Sidney I. Schwab, among the first Americans to appreciate Freud, directed the American Expeditionary Force's principal hospital for shell-shock cases in France. A. A. Brill, Freud's American translator and the leader of the orthodox group in New York, treated neurotics in the neuropsychiatric ward at the Plattsburg army camp. John T. MacCurdy, a Canadian from the New York Psychiatric Institute and the Cornell University Medical School, who had been trained at Johns Hopkins, studied British treatment of shell shock and wrote an account strongly influenced by psychoanalytic theory, that in turn affected American views.

The army's neuropsychiatric services were largely planned by the National Committee for Mental Hygiene, which Clifford Beers had founded in 1909. Before the war, the committee was still fighting for humane treatment of the insane in state hospitals, rather than in jails, poorhouses, or county asylums. Before America entered the war, the Surgeon General of the army asked the committee to examine mental health problems among troops stationed along the Mexican border. The rate of mental illness was seven times greater than among civilians in New York State, and facilities were nonexistent. The committee drew up comprehensive plans for the army, helped recruit and train personnel, many of them from state hospitals, and helped to organize psychological tests for newly inducted men. At training camps, the aim was to weed out as many potential shell-shock cases as possible through rapid psychiatric interviews and intelligence tests, used for the first time on a mass scale.[18]

The National Committee's medical director, Thomas W. Salmon, largely determined policy for treating nervous and mental illness for the AEF overseas. Six feet, four inches tall, with a warm sympathy for patients and the disadvantaged, Salmon suffered from migraines and had recovered from tuberculosis. When he was a child, his mother had suggested that they both drown themselves. As a young man, he had failed as a country practitioner in upstate New York, then had joined the Public Health Service at Ellis Island, organized the treatment of mentally ill immigrants in the New York hospital system, and then moved to the National Committee. He was a courageous fighter against red tape and an advocate of the expanding reformist role of psychiatry in schools and prisons. A good friend of the psychoanalysts William Alanson White and Smith Ely Jelliffe, he represented the newer dynamic psychiatry.[19]

In June 1917 the Rockefeller Foundation sent Salmon to England to study how the British dealt with shell shock; later he was made senior medical consultant in neuropsychiatry to the AEF. Partly because of lack of time, Salmon did not visit the French clinics.

Suffering more than any other nation from a shortage of men, the French distinguished sharply between what they considered cases of hysteria or emotional exaggeration and functional, nervous symptoms of a possibly physiological origin, a type they called "physiopathic."[20] Pearce Bailey, chief of neurology and psychiatry in the Surgeon General's office, visited France and sent Salmon a detailed report commending French treatment methods. The "physiopathic" cases were treated largely by sympathy and bed rest. The emotional, "hysterical" cases were treated harshly. Patients were told that such symptoms as trembling, paralyses, and deaf-mutism were failures of will and character, not symptoms of disease. They were treated by denial of leave, solitary confinement, persuasion, painful electric shocks. Bailey believed that with these methods the French had returned a large proportion of patients to active service.[21] He feared that the Americans would have a higher rate of shell-shock cases than even the British—one-seventh of all British medical discharges were from that cause. Americans were used to having their own way and were unaccustomed to obedience, and French psychiatrists had noticed their "excessive nervousness."[22] He enjoined, therefore, the use of strict French discipline.

Salmon rejected Bailey's recommendations as inappropriately punitive. "The whole idea of punishment seems out of place in the treatment of any kind of sickness, functional or organic," he wrote.[23] Possibly Salmon's own dislike of authority, his psychiatric convictions, and his very deep sympathy for patients inclined him to reject French methods. He was chiefly impressed by the practice of a few British physicians and psychologists whose approach seemed closer to the recent developments in American psychiatry. They were experimenting with an eclectic psychotherapy that included reeducation, suggestion, hypnosis, persuasion, and catharsis. And like most physicians they also employed physical theories about the somatic effects of shock and physical therapies such as rest and electricity.[24] A few of the British were heavily influenced by the dissociation theories of Pierre Janet and the psychoanalytic views of both Freud and Jung, as well as by aspects of the new American psychiatry of Adolf Meyer, which Salmon already had absorbed, with its rejection of theories of hereditary degeneracy and pessimistic psychiatric classification. Some British physicians and psychologists had concluded that shell shock, like the peacetime neuroses, represented failures in adaptation, as Jung had suggested. Unconscious mechanisms much like the conflicts in hysteria were the cause of symptoms. These were occurring in even the "hardiest"—a break with prevalent theories of constitutional predisposition.[25]

Dreams were conspicuous among the symptoms of shell shock. Soldiers often experienced frightful nightmares—that they were being bayoneted by the enemy or blown to pieces. William Brown, a British psychiatrist, found the dreams so terrifying to patients that they had to be dealt with. As Freud had once done, he would place his hand on the patient's forehead to help the recall of battle memories. The soldier would twist and turn and shout in a terror-stricken voice, reliving the forgotten experience; sometimes his memories went back to earliest childhood. Brown also developed a method which he called autognosis: explaining to the patient the psychological mechanism of his dreams and symptoms.[26] In 1916 G. Elliot Smith, dean of the medical faculty of the University of Manchester, and the psychologist T. H. Pear argued that very often shell-shock cases originated in childhood emotional disturbances, caused by the cruelty or nervous irritability of parents. Realizing that psychoanalysis was violently opposed by a number of British authorities, they urged physicians to distinguish between psychoanalysis as a set of techniques and as a set of specific theories. The very word "psychoanalysis," they cautioned, aroused so much "misunderstanding, so much criticism, flattering and hostile, well-informed and ill-informed . . . and so much enmity. . . . " Psychoanalysis meant, essentially, a set of useful methods, including the "valuable assistance" derived from studying dreams, "associations" free or "constrained," and "other mental phenomena." When traditional psychotherapeutic means such as suggestion, kindness, rest, persuasion, and hypnosis failed, psychological analysis and reeducation might prove effective. Their work was favorably reviewed in America because of its emphasis on psychological cause and treatment.[27] Some of these English advocates of psychotherapy were teaching at hospitals, such as Maghull near Liverpool, where American officers were being trained in English techniques to serve as division psychiatrists with the AEF.

Salmon, never a Freudian, nevertheless also was influenced by MacCurdy's study of English treatment methods which was favorable to psychoanalysis. W. H. R. Rivers, the English physician and anthropologist who introduced the work, in words reminiscent of earlier debates over psychotherapy, asserted that "materialistic" preconceptions inherited from the 19th century at first had made physicians emphasize physical causes. But more experience had demonstrated that fatigue, shell explosions, or other catastrophes of warfare had merely released "forces of a psychical kind."

These forces, however, were not Freud's sexual drives, but rather conflicts between the self-preservative and the herd instincts, which MacCurdy regarded as equally fundamental. The "herd instinct" had been introduced by the English surgeon Wilfrid Trotter as a kind of social instinct. It represented "the mind of the gregarious animal" conferring "upon herd opinion, the psychical energy of instinct" and functioned as the cause of repression.[28] Those who suffered from anxiety had wished for death during the period of strain and fatigue preceding the collapse, while sufferers from conversion hysteria had hoped for a disabling wound or illness. Those who broke down also had shown weakness in adapting to civilized sexual conventions. His mode of treatment was reeducation in which a patient was given insight into the processes that caused his symptoms. In a few talks it was possible to lead a soldier to see how his "sublimation" had broken down, how he had come to think of "self rather than of army and country" and so become a "prey to fear and horror." The soldier then became ashamed and quite speedily controlled his symptoms.[29]

Salmon came to believe that the war neuroses resulted from conflict between the "instinct of self-preservation" and the acquired "higher ethical considerations that are represented in honor and love of country." A soldier's symptoms represented "escape from an intolerable situation in real life to one made tolerable by neurosis."[30] Concrete experience and psychological factors intimately and directly determed symptoms:

> Thus a soldier who bayonets an enemy in the face develops an hysterical tic of his own facial muscles. Hysterical abdominal contractures occur in men who bayonet enemies in the abdomen, hysterical blindness follows witnessing particularly horrible sights, hysterical deafness appears in those who have found the cries of the wounded unbearable and men detailed to burial parties develop hysterical loss of the sense of smell.[31]

Salmon was proud of his psychiatrists and the American troops they treated. "Many a scared kid," he wrote, "is being saved (for future demolition) by a little rest and bucking up and good advice from these men."[32]

At La Fauche, in the Vosges Mountains close to the front, Base Hospital 117 was set up for treatment of 399 to 1200 cases of war neurosis. Sidney I. Schwab, La Fauche's commanding officer, gave what he considered a sympathetic test to Freud's theories under conditions of "actual service." He was especially indebted to the interpretations of Rivers, MacCurdy, and William McDougall and praised the conception of the herd instinct as full of "wisdom, insight and inspiration." He concluded that as a result of wartime experience with shell shock, some of the Freudian "mechanisms"—repression, conflict leading to symptom formation, neuroses as defense mechanisms—were "helpful and clarifying" and had been definitely proved. These "mechanisms" could be accepted by men who might not welcome "anything else coming from that school." Yet he also concluded that the war equally conclusively had negated Freud's theories and therapy based on sexual etiology. Self-preservation, not sex, was the instinctual basis of the war neuroses and probably of peacetime neuroses as well.[33]

Treatment methods at La Fauche were varied—rest, explanation, suggestion, persuasion, reeducation, work, hypnosis, electricity. Modified psychoanalytic techniques were used in treating the anxiety neuroses: explaining the meaning of dreams, ventilating and assimilating forgotten battle experiences rather than struggling to keep them "out of mind." Patients were encouraged to talk freely about their experiences and to face them squarely. "It was in a sense a modified psychoanalytic procedure adapted to a war-born condition, divorced from a good deal of the technical complications of the method used in peace time."[34]

Whatever the reservations of eclectic psychiatrists, orthodox Freudians were convinced their theories had been triumphantly proven, and Freud believed the cause of psychoanalysis had been materially advanced by the war. He wrote that when peace came the Central Powers were preparing to establish centers at which psychoanalytically trained physicians could study and treat war neuroses. The psychogenic origins of neurosis, the importance of mental conflicts and unconscious instinctual impulses, had been "accepted almost universally," he wrote in 1919. He acknowledged that opponents insisted his theories of sexual etiology had been disproven. But he argued that the war had done nothing to discredit them, because no one had carried out a thorough analysis of a single case of war neurosis.[35]

At the Fifth Psychoanalytic Congress in Budapest in 1918, to which the Central Powers sent observers, analysts defended a sexual etiology by suggesting that the war neuroses occurred in unusually "narcissistic" men, predisposed by unresolved, unconscious conflicts over sexuality or aggression. Ernest Jones cited MacCurdy's studies to show that they felt slighted and unappreciated, wounded in their self-love; they lacked sociability and affection for friends and relatives and often were sexually impotent.[36] Like Salmon and many British physicians, the assembled psychoanalysts expressed their dislike of harsh, disciplinary treatment, which Karl Abraham described as a "system of tortures" to force neurotics back to health—dark rooms, solitary confinement, hunger, painful electric currents. Often these treatments were speedily effective, but patients quickly relapsed. Psychoanalysis, by releasing a patient "from the fetters of his unconscious mind," might offer a more permanent cure.[37]

Chris Feudtner has argued from the British example, that psychological theories of shell shock met important social needs. The etiology of unconscious conflict absolved the soldier patient from military failure as well as from failure to fulfill the prescribed ideal of masculine behavior in "manly duty." It allowed physicians to avoid labeling, as malingerers or insane, patients who otherwise had led responsible lives and fought bravely. It allowed physicians to adjudicate the complex military problem of the physically healthy soldier who nevertheless could not fight.[38]

The war was creating in the American public an understanding of psychiatry that would otherwise have required years of peace, Pearce Bailey wrote Salmon in 1917.[39] Popular journalism reflected, sometimes accurately, sometimes ineptly, the medical developments and the variety of military viewpoints. It dealt mainly with attitudes toward the shell-shocked soldier, speculations about cause, and methods of treatment. In 1915, when "shell shock" was first being recognized, it was presented as the mysterious result of the new, unique horrors of the war. This impression was best exemplified in May Sinclair's postwar novel, *Anne Severn and the Fieldings,* about a shell-shocked British veteran who suffered from nightmares of battle. In 1915 Americans learned that an eminent German psychiatrist insisted that the war neuroses were the same as those seen in peacetime and were the result of predisposition. They also learned that British physicians were discovering that episodes of battle could cause "psychical" shocks that created a variety of symptoms—loss of memory, headache, temporary deaf-mutism and blindness.[40] Despite an immediate American interest in "shell shock" when America entered the war, more than three times more popular articles dealt with psychoanalysis than with the war neuroses from 1915 to 1921.

Attitudes toward the shell-shocked soldier and these soldiers' attitudes about their own illness were conflicted. Like some military men, a few journalists thought the shell-shock victim a cowardly malingerer. Others reported that ordinary soldiers overseas seemed both curious and tolerant of them. Some shell-shocked patients were hopeful about getting well; others were resigned and despondent. Some felt bewildered by their mysterious malady, cut off from sympathy and understanding. Sometimes they struggled to keep friends or relatives from learning that they were being treated in a "crazy" hospital. Some patients at St. Elizabeth's felt a terrifying sense of inferiority: they believed they might be incurable "sexual perverts" or might break down again at any moment.[41]

Psychiatrists in their public pronouncements usually tried to arouse sympathetic understanding for shell-shock victims, as they had for peacetime neurotics, defending them against what they believed was ignorant and unreasoning prejudice. Some were angered by false press reports that 2100 out of 2500 "shell shock" cases awaiting shipment home had been immediately cured when the armistice was announced.[42]

Some civilians took an active interest in helping the shell-shocked veteran. *Touchstone,* a magazine published in New York, hoped to make the rehabilitation of such veterans its major war work. Inspired by a psychoanalytic psychiatrist, L. Pierce Clark, *Touchstone*'s editors hoped to establish a convalescent club at Palm Beach, to be housed in a cluster of Venetian villas being designed by the fashionable New York architect Addison Mizner.[43] Mary Jarrett, who helped found and direct the Smith College School of Social Work in 1918, in an article on the "Home Treatment of Shell Shock" recommended that relatives of soldiers suffering from war neuroses read William Alanson White's *Principles of Mental Hygiene.* White offered a comprehensive explanation of the problems of nervous and mental disorder, which he argued were similar in peace and war.

Journalists described shell-shocked soldiers as ordinary people who fell ill in spite of themselves; conscious will or control had nothing to do with the matter.[44] Two months after America entered the war, French treatment of shell shock was criticized in the *New York Times* as inadequate in theory and practice.[45] After that, most popular stories reflected British and American, not French, attitudes. American journalists enthusiastically reported experiments with "color treatment" in rooms for neurotics at London's Maudsley Hospital: blue ceilings, yellow walls, a "purple room for nervous headaches."

In 1918 popular articles about shell shock contained more psychoanalytic conceptions, for the most part the simple model of theory and practice Freud had outlined in the Clark lectures, and that many psychiatrists had come to accept. This model included catharsis and trauma, conflict between instinctual wishes and social constraints, repression, dreams, unconscious mental processes. By 1918 these could be referred to without reference to Freud as "light" shed by the "newer psychology."[46]

One of the most ironic public tributes to Freud came from Moses Allen Starr, by then professor emeritus of neurology at Columbia, who had denounced him as immoral in 1912. In an article on shell shock in 1918 that failed to mention Freud, he noted that a "peculiar phenomenon has recently been described, called the conversion of emotion, in which bizarre physical conditions (tremors, convulsive spasms, twitching limbs, pain . . .) appear as relief of the emotional strain. Such states are called subconscious and are not under the control of the will and cannot be arrested by any voluntary effort." They could be cured by reaching the subconscious through hypnotism or persuasion.[47]

In 1918 Dr. William Brown's endorsement of Freud's theories of mental conflict and repression was carried in *Scientific American Supplement*. A year later W. H. R. Rivers added his qualified but more enthusiastic acceptance. The war, Rivers asserted, had proven that emotion and instinct were more important than intellectual or "mental" factors and operated by processes not "directly accessible to consciousness." By conflicting with social traditions they could create symptoms, which could best be cured by therapeutic "self-knowledge and self-reliance." The "uncompromising hostility" to psychoanalysis shown before the war had been overcome and the "chief Freudian" (presumably Ernest Jones) was addressing a "London medical society" without the slightest fuss. Rivers was gratified to note, however, that Freudians were recognizing the importance of the "self-preservative" instinct. This lukewarm endorsement of Freud angered the *New York Times*. In an article that may have been inspired by Brill, Rivers was accused of at once disparaging Freud and adopting his views. He was a Freudian without honestly admitting it, a superb specimen of Freudian "conflict and repression."[48]

By 1920 the simple psychoanalysis of the Clark lectures, shorn of its later complexities and refinements, had become popular and respectable. Emotion, readers could conclude, was more important than reason, and insight than virtue. The glories of "self-knowledge" were consecrated in *Current Opinion,* sounding a solemn "warning against the effort to forget painful experiences." Instead of pulling themselves together, exercising willpower, and forgetting all about whatever it was, the nervous were advised to face reality, no matter how painful.[49]

The war brought to psychiatrists an exhilarating sense of hope and the promise of an expanded social role; the war had given psychiatry a "large body of exact knowledge" and placed a hopeful psychotherapy at the disposal of the physician. Perhaps psychiatry, because of its special new knowledge, like preventive medicine, could cure the world's irrational aberrations by destroying the conditions that caused them. The American psychiatrist Stewart Paton announced that only psychiatrists, not diplomats or historians, could explain the war at all. Only psychiatry revealed the deep-seated, irrational, biological necessities that had led to the conflict. Old-fashioned academic psychology, rooted in philosophy and in the analysis of the intellectual faculties, was useless; only the new "dynamic psychology of fears and instincts" made sense.[50]

The new American psychiatry, an eclectic mix of Adolf Meyer's psycho-biology and the various psychoanalytic schools, found a powerful auxiliary force among psychiatric social workers, for whom new, important training institutions were established as a result of the war. Indeed, Freud would call social workers the "Salvation Army of Psychoanalysis," and they did much to spread psychoanalytic conceptions. The National Committee for Mental Hygiene helped recruit psychiatric nurses and saw the need for social workers to aid in hospital and rehabilitation work. The first college training course was inaugurated at Smith, with sixty-three students, in the summer of 1918. A year later mental hygiene and psychiatric social work were added to the curriculum of the New York School of Social Work. The Pennsylvania School of Social Work also introduced courses in psychiatry at about the same time.[51] At Smith, it was assumed that the rehabilitation of veterans required techniques derived from the new psychiatry, and a number of psychoanalysts lectured there, among them James Jackson Putnam, A. A. Brill, Horace W. Frink, and the new director of the National Committee for Mental Hygiene, Frankwood Williams. Smith's staid president, William Allan Neilson, recalled that the "kind of subject matter which was brought . . . to their notice was quite frequently the kind that is not supposed to be talked about in the presence of young girls, much less, said to them."[52]

In America and Europe, the war brought to some intellectuals a starker realism, a sense of disillusionment with received values and institutions. Psychoanalysis as a philosophy of sexuality and aggression fostered aspects of that general disillusionment. But it also offered to social workers in America and in Europe, to teachers, physicians, and psychiatrists a new path to hopeful social intervention.

Despite deep philosophical differences with many of his American and European followers, Freud shared some of their scientific utopianism. Even in "Reflections on War and Death," he assumed that although all men were murderers, at least in the unconscious, impartial science would survive the war. In America the psychoanalytic psychiatrist William Alanson White, finding Freud's "Reflections" too gloomy, wrote *Thoughts of a Psychiatrist on the War and After,* a perfect embodiment of the moralistic outlook of progressive America and of the new eclectic American psychiatry.[53] He argued that conflict, rightly interpreted as the overcoming of obstacles, was a positive influence in the development of character. Moreover, man's instincts were more varied than Freud supposed. They included the parental and the herd instincts, which automatically regulated the individual for the good of the whole. This essay, with its easy acceptance of Wilsonian idealism, typified the spirit of progressive reform that survived among zealous psychiatrists in the 1920s. It was characteristic of the new American dynamic psychiatry that, in the guise of mental hygiene, would extend the psychiatric domain to education, child-raising, and criminology in the years from 1919 to 1940.

White's idealism and a more disillusioned strain of psychoanalytic social criticism in America agreed on replacing received "tradition" with psychiatric knowledge. In the *Psychoanalytic Review* in 1919 one lay enthusiast who had gleefully debunked religion now called Americans to move beyond "conventional or unconventional moralities." This new psychoanalytic wisdom would banish the "social vengeance" of punishing criminals: "For jails we would substitute hospitals and schools. The hangman we would replace by psychoanalysts, psychiatrists and educators."[54]

Psychoanalysts and the new dynamic psychiatrists apparently had solved the mystery of the cause and treatment of "shell shock" in the war's human laboratory. In so doing, they convinced a growing number of psychiatrists and neurologists well outside the tiny psychoanalytic movement of the usefulness of a few key if highly generalized and diluted psychoanalytic conceptions. These included the role of environmental stress and trauma in creating symptoms; the specific mechanisms of symptom creation such as the conversion of unconscious instinctual conflict; the diagnostic importance of dreams; the usefulness of catharsis in exorcising repressed traumatic memories. No matter how drastically modified, psychoanalysis seemed to provide the basis for a more effective psychotherapy. In coping with the emotional and mental illnesses of returning soldiers, new psychiatric hospitals, clinics, and training programs were created, laying the basis for professional expansion in the postwar years. Then, the psychoanalysts themselves established modes of psychoanalytic training to advance their own professionalization and at the same time greatly expanded the scope of their theory and therapy.

2

A New Generation of Psychoanalysts: The Institutes, 1920–1940

A few years after the armistice, a novel *rite de passage,* training in a psychoanalytic institute, began to form a new generation of American and European analysts, endowing them with a militant sense of professional identity. Founded in Europe in the 1920s, established in America a decade later, the institutes transformed the inner life of the movement. They made possible the transition from a system of patriarchal patronage centering on Freud to a system of professionalization that codified theory and therapy. Nothing quite like this combination of moral seminary, art and trade school, and university graduate school exists in other professions. The institutes also created some of the movement's persistent problems, among them a curriculum that changed little over the next 70 years.[1]

From a sociological perspective, like other nascent professionals, the psychoanalysts attempted to ensure autonomy, and the control and monopoly of their specialized technique and theory.[2] This professional thrust was carried furthest in America, but the problems that gave rise to it were universal, common to both Europe and America, and psychoanalytic congresses, societies, and journals had failed to solve them. The first set of issues concerned the relation of the movement to the outside world of other professionals, governments, and the public; the second set concerned the internal problems of the movement.

The relation to the outside world was crucial. The psychoanalysts claimed to ply the only truly causal and fundamental psychotherapy and needed to ensure a clientele by convincing the public—laymen and physicians as well as government officials—of the utility of their new science. But how would this new science be defined and its practice regulated?

The psychoanalysts organized at first against "wild" analysts, those physicians who Freud believed misunderstood the application of his theories and might prescribe sexual intercourse as a cure for anxiety hysteria.[3] But the attempt to establish control foundered almost from the beginning on the issue of internal authority. This issue in turn encapsulated all the difficulties surrounding the status of psychoanalysis as a science.

What criteria would determine acceptable developments in psychoanalytic theory and therapy? In fact none was ever satisfactorily agreed on. What would determine the validity of supporting observations? Working within the existing tradition of clinical medicine rather than laboratory or experimental science, the accepted standards seemed to be whether or not a given hypothesis was confirmed by other analysts. But how was such confirmation to be determined and consensus to be assured? The problem already had come to a head over whether or not libido, for instance, was sexual in origin, or whether, as Jung claimed, it was a generalized neutral energy. Freud, as the founder, believed he retained the ultimate authority as to what was or was not psychoanalytic. His dissenting followers, beginning with Adler and Jung, left him to develop their own theories, therapies, journals, and organizations. Thus, each major disagreement over theory or therapy seemed to require a new validating social group, a psychoanalytic tradition that recent splits within Freudian institutes seem only to confirm.[4]

The early psychoanalysts turned their newfound weapons on each other, and, as each split occurred, neurosis and insanity became part of the rhetoric of anathema. Was not Adler narcissistic or Jung possibly schizophrenic? And the departing replied in kind: Freud was a sexually obsessed neurotic tyrant, his orthodox followers deluded sycophants.

The splits exacerbated a continuing conflict within orthodox psychoanalysis over the merits of assimilation and possible dilution as against isolation and purity. Should psychoanalysts remain apart to develop their science undisturbed? Should they try to make psychoanalysis part of the medical, educational, and governmental establishments? Freud's own views on the matter were conflicted. For example, he first welcomed, then later denounced, the American alliance of psychiatry and psychoanalysis. Yet, the assimilation and regularization of psychoanalysis was surely one of his hopes. He advocated the teaching of psychoanalysis to university and medical students. He proposed that governments and private charity make free psychotherapy available to treat neurotic suffering among the masses. He was pleased when Sandor Ferenczi became professor of psychoanalysis at the University of Budapest, an appointment as brief as the tenure of Bela Kun's revolutionary government that appointed him. He was delighted if skeptical in 1919 when it seemed possible that Karl Abraham might obtain a similar appointment in Berlin through a friendly social democratic regime.[5] It remained for a younger generation of psychoanalysts to carry medical assimilation to perhaps its greatest extreme in the United States, an assimilation Freud decried and that small groups of American psychoanalysts, chiefly refugee Europeans at first, would oppose.[6]

Strong isolationist currents also marked psychoanalysis. Freud wished his science to remain an independent discipline, and some of his followers were far more isolationist than he. Max Eitingon urged ceaseless vigilance in guarding psychoanalysis against premature fusion with other fields and methods. In 1930 Edward Glover, an English graduate of the Berlin Institute, argued that because of the opposition of conventional science and the need to make their own terms precise, analysts should ignore charges of being "too stiff necked and exclusive" and should "give first place to communication among themselves." That same year in Germany analysts were enjoined not to support the highly eclectic Medical Society for Psychotherapy in which prominent Berlin analysts, notably Georg Simmel and Karen Horney, had been participants. As late as 1960, a president of the American Psychoanalytic Association cautioned against any assimilation of psychoanalysis that might dilute its essential nature.[7]

Yet, immediately after World War I, relations with the medical profession, for instance, became important. The war had brought to prominence Freud's theories of trauma and catharsis in the psychotherapy of the war neuroses. Physicians who had treated shell-shocked soldiers wanted to learn more about psychoanalysis. Responding to requests for information from physicians in Berlin and other German medical centers, Karl Abraham began giving courses for them in 1919.[8]

Three issues complicated the relations between the psychoanalysts and the medical profession: lack of systematic training in psychoanalysis, eclecticism, and the popularity of psychoanalysis among laymen. In medicine, recognized training procedures were prerequisites to professional status, but psychoanalysts had not yet developed a comparable professional discipline.

Moreover, the "new" psychoanalytic psychology of the 1920s often was an eclectic mix of Adler, Jung, and Freud. To many outsiders Freud was merely the first among equals; he had not yet assumed the exalted status he later acquired, although the process was well under way, particularly among his followers.[9] The psychologies of Jung and Adler at first were powerful competitors. To eclectics, it came as a comforting revelation that each of the three major figures might possibly possess a kernel of psychological truth, and that anyone quite properly could choose the most congenial elements from each. Between 1918 and 1924 a spate of books about the "new psychology" by physicians and laymen displayed to the orthodox the dangers of syncretism. London's Tavistock Clinic is an example of its institutional embodiment. Inspired by wartime experience, Hugh Crichton-Miller, a neurologist with a fashionable practice at his own private hospital, established Tavistock to be resolutely eclectic in its psychotherapy.[10] In America the *Psychoanalytic Review* continued to publicize Jung, Adler, and Stekel as well as Freud. Finally in 1922 Ernest Jones founded the *International Journal of Psychoanalysis* to promote orthodoxy in English-speaking nations.

In addition to the dangers of eclecticism and the lack of established methods of training, another difficulty also threatened—the competition of untrained lay practitioners. Physicians in Europe as well as the United States were alarmed by the psychoanalytic enthusiasms of pastors, journalists, artists, and mind cure practitioners.

Some analysts, chiefly in America, but also in Europe, undertook to popularize psychoanalysis. Hanns Sachs and Karl Abraham in Berlin cooperated with the makers of the first psychoanalytic movie, *Secrets of a Soul,* starring Werner Kraus, who also played the lead in the *Cabinet of Dr. Caligari,* one of the first horror films. Paul Federn's *Psychoanalytische Volklsbuch* introduced psychoanalysis and its applications to the educated layman.[11] Because psychoanalysis operated outside the medical establishment, there was nothing to prevent its practice not only by trained laymen but by anyone who chose to try, and this sometimes embittered relations with physicians in Europe and America.

On several issues, including the scientific status of psychoanalysis and the practice of laymen, governments and professional medical organizations in Europe and America became directly involved. Did lay analysis violate laws governing medical practice? Some Viennese bureaucrats, and the California Attorney General, thought so. In Austria, doctors objected that lay competition would threaten their means of livelihood. In Switzerland lay analysts were admonished by the Swiss Psychoanalytic Society to treat only in conjunction with a licensed physician. Did psychoanalytic treatment cause insanity or immorality in patients? Were its theories and its therapeutic results the unscientific product of suggestion?

The British Medical Association launched a full-scale investigation that ended in 1929 by denying the charges and granting the Freudians "the exclusive right to the name psycho-analysis," on the basis of "Freud's priority in the field and the authority and professional organization of his school."[12] Ernest Jones, who sat on the investigating committee, made much of the rigor of psychoanalytic training to make the new calling respectable; it took "at least three years," with "centers" in Vienna, Berlin, Budapest, Frankfort, London, and New York.[13] Although the three existing institutes in Vienna, Berlin, and London were in fact fledglings, and the time it took some Americans to pass through them was well under three years, they nevertheless already had done much to instill orthodoxy and establish systematic training.

The training the institutes replaced had been casual, personal, and brief, including training analyses by Freud himself. The first analysts had chosen themselves, usually as the result of an intensely emotional conversion experience. After the requirement of analysis was instituted to purge the analyst of the neuroses that might blind him in treating patients, for some years training analysis remained an informal process. Usually a senior analyst would accept an aspirant on an apprenticeship basis; personal liking was an ingredient in the choice.

The first psychoanalytic institutes, because of their small size and informality, played a far less important role in the life of the first and some of the
second generation than the emotional ties among members. The nature and
intensity of these ties goes far to account for the bitterness of conflicts among
psychoanalysts in Europe and later, in America. Explanatory models for these
ties and for the inner dynamics of their movement have been supplied by the
analysts themselves.

Perennially anxious over the possibility of impending death, an anxiety
intensified by cancer of the jaw in 1923, Freud regarded the movement
unconsciously as his child, a product of his own body.[14] Assuring its future
was a major preoccupation. Freud sought to direct the movement's course in
detail. He read the literature from abroad, corresponded regularly with major figures and issued minute directions. Did René Laforgue and the first
French analysts propose a new definition of schizophrenic states or fail to
understand the precise implications of the latest development in Freud's
theories? At once Freud dispatched letters correcting these errors. Did the
Americans need a capable leader, one more skillful than most of their inferi-
or compatriots? Once Freud's wishes were known, the New York Society
unanimously elected Horace Frink, Freud's patient, as president. Did Franz
Alexander wish to emigrate to Chicago from Berlin? Freud argued that it was
an unsuitable move. Did the Americans wish to ensure that analysis be
practiced exclusively by physicians? Freud vehemently objected to this vulgar limitation. Whatever Freud's motives, he kept elaborate watch over the
development of his child.

Freud also regarded his closest followers as sons and daughters, sometimes interfering in their personal lives, in Frink's case with disastrous results.
Freud advised Frink, who went to him for analysis in 1921, to divorce his
wife and marry a former patient, an heiress married to an older rich man, on
grounds that it was "the good right of every human being to strive for sexual
gratification and tender love. . . ." The prospect set off a series of manic-
depressive episodes, and Frink returned twice to Freud for more analysis.
After Frink had recovered from a depressive episode, Freud pronounced his
analysis complete. Freud also suggested that Frink make a financial contribution to the psychoanalytic movement, presumably with his new wife's money.
As Frink's state deteriorated, he sought treatment with Adolf Meyer, was
divorced by his second wife, and bitterly recalled Freud's interference. And
Freud's experience with Frink, on whom he had pinned high hopes, deepened his distrust of Americans, who seemed to be useful only if they brought
money.[15]

As striking as Freud's minute direction of the movement were his followers' intense feelings for him as an authoritative father and, occasionally, as
a nurturing mother. Freud functioned not only as the primal father but as the
primal analyst, the first exemplar of a new profession. Some of his followers
unconsciously imitated his mannerisms, a sign of their identification. They
saw themselves as pioneers, defying a scornful world, defending the truths
Freud's genius had discovered.

Close personal association with Freud was not a requirement for seeing him as a father and imitating him as a model. Some followers, such as A. A. Brill, who saw him rarely, and others who never knew him, held similarly intense feelings, fantasies, transferences, identifications.

The intensity of the relationships, especially among the first generation, made difficult if not impossible the attainment of Freud's announced ideal of an organization of scientists, each committed to advancing the psychoanalytic model. He wished his followers to add their contributions to the young and incomplete science. Freud himself remained independent, never tying himself to routines in therapy, often experimenting, sometimes issuing certificates to those he had analyzed in defiance of increasingly stringent training rules.

Freud once wrote that were scientific opinions ever to attain the significance of religious ties, the same intolerance toward outsiders that flourished during the wars of religion would recur, an inadvertent commentary on psychoanalytic disagreement and apostasy. Indeed, Erik Erikson once likened the early movement to the first years of Pauline Christianity.[16]

To the first generation, bound as they were by filial ties, radical disagreement implied heresy and patricide. This was hardly an emotional atmosphere conducive to the resolution of differences. As primal authority Freud himself found it difficult at first to take seriously or to assimilate the new ideas of those who left the movement. Yet some of the later development of his own theories, as well as those of his followers, can be viewed as attempts to integrate elements of what Jung, Adler, and Rank independently emphasized.[17] For example, Rank's birth trauma and the relation to the mother are echoed in studies of the child's earliest tie. Adler's emphasis on aggression appeared in Freud's discussions of war and the death instinct.

The individualistic and paternal system which dominated the first generation would be drastically changed by the new psychoanalytic institutes and their regularized training procedures. Training was taken out of the hands of individual psychoanalysts by a decision of the International Psychoanalytic Congress in 1925 and became the responsibility of societies and institutes.[18] Educational committees became the overseers of training.

Berlin provided the model for the rest of Europe and America, but the development of training in Berlin was almost an accidental byproduct. The Berlin Policlinic was founded specifically to carry out Freud's hope that therapy be made available to the masses, the gold of classical analysis perhaps adulterated by suggestion or hypnosis. Because it was unlikely that governments could be persuaded to finance so unorthodox a venture, Freud appealed to private initiative.

The organizations that carried the psychoanalytic message depended on the philanthropy of wealthy converts who made possible the founding and development of psychoanalytic institutions. The psychoanalytic publishing house in Vienna resulted from the largesse of the Hungarian Ernst von Freund; the Berlin Institute was bankrolled by Max Eitingon, a physician from a family of prosperous fur merchants. Princess Marie Bonaparte,

Freud's patient and a wealthy aristocrat, supported the French Psychoanalytic Society in its difficult early years. In America, the New York Institute was partly financed by A. A. Brill's very successful practice; the Chicago Psychoanalytic Institute was funded in 1932 partly because the spouse of a local heiress had been successfully treated for stomach complaints by the analyst Franz Alexander.[19]

Outside the academic, medical, and bureaucratic establishments, the German psychoanalysts became identified with the intellectual, aesthetic and political radicalism of Weimar Berlin. Social service to the masses through the institute's clinic was an essential part of the Berlin psychoanalysts' mission. Excluded from the system of medical insurance, founded in a time of dizzying inflation, the clinic was financed by the Berlin psychoanalysts who pledged free time and 4 percent of their income. Swamped with patients from its opening, the clinic emphasized treating those who could not afford to pay, or could pay only nominal fees. There were experiments with the treatment of psychopaths, criminals, and delinquents, and the pattern seems to have been that of classical analysis, with treatment ranging from one to three years.[20]

The clinic provided patients for the training of analytic candidates. Hanns Sachs, the senior Berlin training analyst, likened the probationary period of psychoanalytic training to an empirical equivalent of the Church's novitiate.[21] By 1927 the pattern of training had become obligatory—a training analysis, treatment of clinic patients under supervision, case seminars, and lectures. The lectures were not only medical and psychoanalytic but also broadly humanistic, touching on sociology, law and criminology, philosophy, religion, education. Central to the curriculum were exegetical lectures and seminars on Freud's writings. This still provides a major core of psychoanalytic training, and has given the curriculum a markedly historical, conservative cast. Freud's writings, with all their intrinsic richness, charm, and insight, became quasi-scriptures.

The students, though mostly physicians, also included social workers, teachers, police officers, nurses; many were auditors hoping to apply psychoanalysis to their own professions.[22] It soon became obvious that not all those who presented themselves for full psychoanalytic training were suitable. As Karen Horney, one of the institute's founders, rather tartly noted, it was essential to eliminate elderly ladies no longer fulfilled by their family duties or men whose studies or careers had foundered and who believed that psychoanalysis offered an intellectual occupation that required no special preparation.[23] Such prospective candidates could be eliminated by a trial analysis, the method also used to weed out patients unsuitable for analytic treatment. By 1929, about 711 men and women were taking the courses, including training candidates and auditors.

The first didactic analyses in Berlin were deeply rooted in a fresh emotional experience and carried profound conviction, Therese Benedek, who later taught at the Chicago Institute, recalled. They were also briefer and far less complex than they became later. For analysts and patients alike, psychoanalysis was a profoundly innovative new experience, not yet a part of the common cultural or intellectual baggage, as was later the case in America.[24]

Benedek was able not only to analyze her training candidates but to meet with them for discussions of the analytic literature in her own home, behavior later discouraged in America. Analysands traipsed off to Menton or Dubrovnik following their analysts on vacation. The Viennese, who prided themselves on their relaxation and *schlamperei,* nevertheless issued their graduates diplomas in imitation of Berlin. Freud himself strongly supported the new institutes and wrote that they breathed a different spirit into a psychoanalytic society.

At the same time, partly because of illness, he became an increasingly remote and exalted figure: Gregory Zilboorg decided that Freud was too great, too mysterious for Zilboorg's generation fully to understand.

The Berlin Institute fostered a fierce enthusiasm among many of its trainees, especially the young Americans. Zilboorg unfavorably contrasted the material prosperity and slender contributions of American psychoanalysis with the crowded rooms, small means, and enormous creativity of Berlin.[25] However, Rudolph Loewenstein, who joined the movement in 1924 at the age of 26, found the Institute's approach a "very cold German way of teaching you A, B, C."[26]

The institute had momentous consequences for the psychoanalytic movement, some favorable, some limiting, above all a shift in inner authority and self-image. The intensely filial relationships to Freud of the first generation were gradually replaced by highly emotional relationships to a fantasied Freud, still the primal founder, but also to organizations, to peers, to superiors in the institute hierarchy—above all, perhaps, to the training analyst who took on new power and influence within the movement. Tracing one's analytic lineage through the training analyst, the training analyst's analyst, and, if possible, back to Freud and his circle became a determinant of psychoanalytic prestige.

Weeded out after more and more rigorous selection procedures, the institute trainees were in fact a new professional elite and so regarded themselves. They were more confident and less defensive than Freud's first followers.[27] Perhaps the most typical products of the institute were those who codified theory and therapy or, especially in America, worked to reconcile psychoanalysis with medicine and the universities. The young European-trained American analysts were responsible for the formalization and the incipient bureaucratization of the movement in America, as the increasingly complex organization of the New York Psychoanalytic Institute illustrates. New York copied and ultimately rigidified what Berlin had initiated.

The history of the New York Society also demonstrates the particular pressures under which psychoanalysis grew in the United States. Whereas in Europe laymen had been trained and become full-fledged analysts and training analysts on an equal footing with physicians, by the mid-twenties the New York Society had restricted membership and even attendance at meetings to physicians.

Psychoanalysis still was under attack by conservative neurologists and psychiatrists, and the position of psychoanalysis within medicine in America was sometimes precarious. For example, the New York State Board of Charities and the city's medical authorities refused to sanction the New York Society's proposal for a psychoanalytic clinic. Physicians were particularly sensitive to charges of quackery and to lay encroachment in any area of treatment regarded as a medical specialty, such as the treatment of nervous and mental disorders. American medicine was in some ways more open and less rigidly organized, with more independent centers than European medicine, but at the same time it was imbued with a particularly crusading sense of newly minted professionalism and scientism following the Flexner report on the deficiencies of American medical education. Morris Fishbein, the American Medical Association's chief publicist, particularly enjoyed tilting against quacks, and the American psychoanalysts were eager to distance themselves from lay practitioners.

The Europeans, including Freud, had complicated matters by training laymen, sometimes very briefly, and sending them back to the United States to practice. Freud's disciples Otto Rank and Sandor Ferenczi on their short, hectic visits to America, analyzed psychiatrists and social workers, and Rank became a guru for the Pennsylvania School of Social Work. A proposal for him to give a course of lectures at the New York School for Social Work in 1926 so angered Charles L. Dana, the influential professor of neurology at Cornell University Medical School, that he wrote to Frankwood Williams, medical director of the National Committee for Mental Hygiene, that he was resigning from the committee.[28]

In April 1926, the New York state legislature, after exposures of medical fraud, forbade the practice of medicine by anyone who was not a registered medical doctor and the unauthorized use of the title "doctor" by anyone involved in "public health" or the diagnosis and treatment of physical illness.[29] Williams informed Freud in November that he believed the local physicians and the medical analysts were behind moves to have the New York state legislature prevent the practice of lay analysis, and he asked for permission to translate Freud's essay on the subject as soon as possible. Freud replied that he already had given the translation rights to the American writer George Sylvester Viereck.[30]

In 1927 lay analyst Theodore Reik was accused of quackery and harmful treatment in Vienna by an American patient; Freud intervened on Reik's behalf and the charges were dropped.[31] Pursuing medical guildism, the New York Society insisted that laymen could be trained only to further their work in fields of nonmedical specialization, such as anthropology, criminology, theology, law. It warned the Europeans that it would cooperate with the state in enforcing medical licensing laws and deplored the training of laymen by visiting psychoanalysts or any practice in America by laymen trained in European Institutes. Candidates for psychoanalytic training must be physicians already trained in psychiatry, present evidence of good character, and not represent themselves as analysts until their training was completed.

Then, in 1929, after the psychoanalytic congress at Oxford, Brill engineered a compromise in which laymen were to be admitted to the New York Society. But he had to assure the Board of Regents that the institute was not training laymen to practice medicine. Ernest Jones earlier had informed an American analyst that the British society advised psychoanalytic candidates to acquire a medical qualification unless there were "special reasons to the contrary"; "moreover the layman had to possess a scientific background and special abilities. Without such restrictions Jones feared the profession would be "absolutely flooded by a host of uneducated and unsuitable lay people who would before long change the whole character of the psychoanalytical profession."[32]

Freud's persistent animus against America, partly inspired by the lay-analysis issue, surfaced in a chilly reply to Williams's invitation to Anna Freud to attend the International Mental Hygiene Congress in 1930. First he questioned Williams's right to consider himself a psychoanalyst. He had failed to dissuade Williams in a personal interview from his enthusiasm for Rank; moreover Rank had ceased to be an analyst, and Williams's "few months with Rank were not congruent with what we understand psychoanalysis to be." "Unless, therefore, you have undergone a radical change of opinion, I must question your considering yourself one of us." Freud noted that most mental hygiene workers in America were not ready for psychoanalysis and knew little about it: "As long as this condition exists, my interest in the dissemination of lay analysis in America is very slight indeed. What good can be expected from lay-analysts if they undergo analysis with Rank?" Moreover, the congress seemed "rather American . . . with its emphasis on quantity at the possible expense of quality. . . . I am inclined to believe, therefore, that the time is not yet ready for my daughter to come to America."[33]

In New York, the rules for full-fledged training candidates became stricter, approaching more closely the Berlin model. By 1929, if a candidate applied for training to a society member, the latter must notify the chairman of the education committee, who would refer the candidate to the original analyst only after consulting with the committee. As in Berlin, the control analyst who supervised the candidate's case work had to be different from the training analyst, and both would report to the Education Committee.[34]

Training, which the society had been attempting to regularize, finally was taken over by the institute, organized September 24, 1931, to "advance the science of psychoanalysis as developed by Freud and his pupils." Sandor Rado was brought from Berlin as director. He had moved from hero worship of Freud to growing criticism and an intense desire to make psychoanalysis acceptable to American medicine, science, and the universities. He had been attracted to psychoanalysis by desultory reading around 1910, joined Ferenczi's circle in Budapest, and was overwhelmed by hearing Freud deliver a flawless lecture at the University of Vienna in 1913. During World War I, he treated shell-shocked soldiers and in 1922 went to Abraham for analysis and became director of training in Berlin. Gradually, he came to detest what he regarded as the "Byzantine Court" that surrounded Freud and Freud's preoccupation with his own greatness.[35] Rado became a powerful force in the New York Institute at first, but as he became more critical of Freud's theories, he was increasingly hated by the orthodox, especially the refugees. He also became contemptuous of the Americans, who, he wryly observed, never read books and contributed nothing at all to theory.

By 1933 the Education Committee of the New York Society had established annual official lists of training analysts. They had to have been members at least five years, made scientific contributions, and devoted most of their time to psychoanalytic practice. Candidates in turn must meet committee standards of "maturity, integrity, and aptitude for psychological work."[36]

By 1935 training in the New York Institute had been elaborately codified, and the medical qualifications were further tightened. Physician candidates must receive their medical training at a school accredited by the American Medical Association, have completed an internship and an additional year working full-time in a mental hospital also approved by the AMA. A candidate's failure to complete a preparatory analysis of 300 hours to the satisfaction of the analyst would terminate candidacy. In 1936 fifty students already were in training.

The formal winnowing of candidates, the training analysis, the case seminars, and the new medical and psychiatric requirements profoundly altered the professional role of the analyst himself. He was once an outsider, attracted to a new idea, for which he was willing to brave disapproval. He became part of an organization in which tradition became more important than originality, orthodoxy than creativity. In this important transition, the 1920s marked a beginning that was carried to its most rigorous conclusion in the new American institutes. As training in psychoanalysis was combined in the United States with prior medical and psychiatric education, limitations of perspective inevitably occurred, sometimes including ignorance about parallel work in related disciplines such as psychology. The political radicalism, social service to the masses, broadly inclusive student body, and humanistic topics that characterized Berlin were diminished in importance in the American institutes in the thrust for professionalization. Now psychoanalytic clinics largely became training grounds for candidates, reversing the original Berlin emphasis. What was retained were the routine of training, the stress on Freud's writings, the classical technique. The aim of training was to ensure competence and psychological health, but training and selection also involved elements of tension and anxiety. Would the committee or the training analyst find the candidate too neurotic, perhaps suffering from difficulties he himself never had known or faced? Would he measure up in this intimate disclosure enforced by the primary rule of free association? Abram Kardiner observed that candidates might develop anxiety because of their powerlessness and dependency. During his training with Horace Frink, he had been terrified lest this or that trait be disapproved of. An unconscious wish to murder his own father appeared—a standard enough wish in the analytic repertoire—but Kardiner asked himself how Frink could be the patron of a man who entertained thoughts of patricide.[37]

Without the approval of the training analyst, there would be no profession—no certification, no referrals. And this terror Kardiner experienced had occurred long before the institute had codified and systematized psychoanalytic education. The institute reinforced the analyst's status as a "dreaded judge." Michael Balint observed that systematic training forced a strong identification with the training analyst, who was incorporated as an internal object. In the control analysis and in case seminars, the candidate's position was even weaker than with the training analyst, with whom close ties had been forged. This process, Balint argued, made for uncritical subservience and conformity.[38]

Hanns Sachs, Berlin's first training analyst, argued that all candidates were attracted to psychoanalysis to solve present or past neuroses. The real issue was the degree of their pathology, and Sachs considered undesirable those with egos severely restricted by obsessions, the weak and vacillating, those with psychotic tendencies, psychopathic or antisocial types, drug addicts, those in whom perversions replaced normal genitality.[39] The special virtues sought in candidates were psychological insight and intuition.

There were good reasons for the growing rigor of selection. Difficult and neurotic personalities were attracted to the movement, particularly in the early years. Some committed suicide, others became psychotic, and still others caused scandal. Their numbers may have been few, but they compromised the movement. Institutes, at the least, hoped to guarantee relative stability of personality and reasonable technical competence.

The increasing length of analyses began in the 1920s, as analytic goals became more ambitious: some wanted analysis to reach the earliest pregenital years or insisted on transformation of the total personality. By the 1930s Freud was arguing that the analytic process should be renewed for analysts every five years. And analyses stretched from the original few weeks or months to year after year.

The foundation of the institutes, the tightening and systematization of training, made the psychoanalytic movement more homogenized, and conservative. For instance, cultural and national differences between the American and European movements became less conspicuous than they were before 1917. One major result of this more close-knit uniformity was the relative containment of dissent. Those who left the movement during the 1920s and 1930s, such as Otto Rank or Wilhelm Reich, collected only small groups of personal disciples to validate their individual insights. In America when others, such as Karen Horney or the followers of Harry Stack Sullivan, left the orthodox movement, they set up institutes of their own, very much on the pattern of the Berlin prototype. For the most part, in America and Britain, dissenters such as Melanie Klein or Sandor Rado tended to remain within the movement. Perhaps only in France, where political splintering was an established social model, did a truly important split occur much later, that between Jacques Lacan and the orthodox Freudians. The institutes promoted not only a new homogeneity, they also created new grounds for internal disputes, particularly over which model for analytic practice was taught.

A truly systematic training was an important step in attaining respectability in the eyes of the medical profession, and, in America, in the eyes of the public. Its very length and rigor seemed to guarantee the special qualifications of those who were winnowed and, finally, had been chosen. Because of the new institute controls, regulations, and hierarchy of committees and training analysts, more than ever before it became possible to officially detach the trained from the untrained and the "wild" analysts.

The institutes and their new elites are intimately a part of an important, underlying development in the social and economic life of Europe and America in this period: increasing professionalization. The achievement of efficiency through esoteric, expert training also was an ideal of the professional classes psychoanalysts increasingly treated—the upper echelons of business, communications, the law, medicine, education, and that new adjunct chiefly to woman's professionalism, social work. The institutes set up a professional initiation of accumulating intensity. Those who successfully ran the gauntlet imposed it even more rigorously on those who followed. Finally, the institutes had a profound effect on theory and therapy, and, because of their clinics, an acquaintance with new varieties of patients.

3

Women, Character, and Anxiety:
Theory and Therapy, 1920–1940

Europe provided the models of theory and therapy that Americans absorbed in the new European institutes and that European analysts would bring to the United States. The elements of nearly all the later American developments were formulated in these years: theories of sex and gender, of classical and modified therapy, of character, anxiety, and ego psychology. Most of them were summed up in Otto Fenichel's massive, brilliant *The Psychoanalytic Theory of Neurosis,* begun in Europe and revised and published in the United States in 1945, the first comprehensive orthodox text of the American movement.

The new departures occurred partly as the result of institute clinics, where teachers and students saw a far wider gamut of patients and symptoms than Freud's practice had encompassed. New types of patients were added to the clinical roster. Instead of the failing clerk of Freud's obsessional Wolfman there appeared the businessman, failing because of his character flaws in the inflationary chaos of the postwar world. Instead of the Victorian woman with repressed sexual drives, a liberated woman appeared with different difficulties.

The role of clinical theory in psychoanalysis requires brief consideration. After therapy, creating theory is perhaps the main psychoanalytic enterprise and guides practice for several reasons. Theory makes sense of analytic observations, providing maps of the patient's myriad associations. The product of daily sessions over months or years, the verbatim record of an analysis is dauntingly extensive. This welter of observation requires organization if it is to become meaningful and coherent. Moreover, analytic therapy functions within a puzzle-solving framework: finding the specific origin, meaning, and pattern of the patient's symptoms and complex behavior, unknown at the outset. Theory not only organizes this quest but assuages the therapist's and the patient's anxieties in the face of these unknowns.[1]

However, the relation of clinical data to theory and to the case narrative is complex and problematic; often enough in Freud's cases it is obscured by strategies we no longer can reconstruct completely.[2] Moreover, case reporting and interpretation tend to respond to fashions in theory. Thus after Otto Rank decided that the trauma of birth was the Ur-experience of human anxiety and separation, cases were reported in which a dream of leaving an enclosing space would be interpreted as a dream of birth.[3] For this reason it is difficult to sift, in retrospect, a genuine "discovery" from an imposed "confirmation." That there were new observations seems clear; but there was also much scholastic drawing-out of the implications of existing theory. Some theoretical developments clearly resulted from working out the logical results of Freud's hypotheses. The psychosexual development of the child, with its orderly stages and accompanying traits, was logically carried through to a theory of adult character structure that encapsulated this childhood basis.

The years from 1920 to 1940 marked a shift in the emphasis of psychoanalytic theory. Many of the first theories of libidinal character and of gender were imprisoned in a mystique of the body that seems a direct heir of 19th-century theories of physiological determinism, rather like the cruder derivation of psychological traits such as intelligence from conformation of the skull. With the second generation of theorists the environmental and psychological causality implicit in the psychoanalytic model was carried further, partly through the Marxist convictions of theorists such as Wilhelm Reich and Otto Fenichel. The effect of a mother's personality and modes of training on her children were observed, and theories were constructed explaining the social determination of character.

Why did the first analysts find it plausible to construct typologies presumably derived from elementary biological functions and attributes such as sucking or defecation or absence of a penis? A long historical tradition may provide one answer. Classifications of character and personality from biological functions are venerable. Richard Burton in the *Anatomy of Melancholy* attempted to explain "Melancholy, cold and dry, thick, black and sour," as "begotten of the more feculent part of nourishment . . . etc." But there were closer precedents in the 19th century, some of which Freud surely had read. Herbart, the major early-19th-century psychologist who was studied in the Austrian school system, suggested that constant nutritive discomfort might cause "choleric bitterness" in "a few sad cases in children."[4] French theorists linked physical sensation with femininity, motor activity with masculinity.

Toward the century's close, the perspective broadened and there were innumerable theories linking character with heredity, with a mixture of "disposition and milieu," with childhood impressions, or, as with Freud's favorite French psychologist, Le Bon, with unconscious associations of feelings and ideas.

In the Berlin and Vienna institutes in the 1920s, clashes over psychoanalytic theories of gender and their relation to "biology" led directly to formulations of a cultural determinism that later were exploited in America. Women became problematical for psychoanalysis in a new way: How did they become sexual women? The psychoanalytic answer to this conundrum had far-reaching consequences. In the 1960s it drove proponents of women's liberation to excoriate Freud as a male chauvinist, blinded by Victorian stereotypes of femininity. It led to controversy over the nature of the female orgasm. In the 1920s it aroused bitter clashes among psychoanalysts themselves.

Freud determined that his first women patients suffered from neurotic symptoms caused by conflicts between their repressed sexual wishes and the repressing elements of their personality. As Freud developed his sexual theories, he noted that girls envied boys their penises, that the clitoris substituted for the penis, and that for girls to become sexually mature vaginal must replace clitoral sensitivity.[5] But these were, on the whole, passing observations.

The emergence of the problem of female sexuality coincided with a seemingly new female patient in the late teens and early 1920s in the psychoanalytic literature. She was not "repressed" as Freud's first patients had been. She insisted on orgasm as a right, and she was untroubled by extramarital sexuality. Her problems seem distinctly different. Her major symptoms—obsessions, frigidity, vaginismus—were interpreted by analysts as the consequence of the female castration complex and penis envy. One patient daydreamed of being a "female Napoleon," with all Europe at her feet.[6] Some women expressed marked hostility toward men, sometimes taking the form of a desire to castrate or maim them. Psychoanalytic feminine psychology, like character theory, exhibited a blend of model elaboration, biological determinism, and social convention.[7] Freud began by regarding all libido as essentially "masculine," then sharply modified that position. He argued later that he was not equating activity with masculinity and passivity with femininity, and pointed to the mix of active and passive in other species and in humans, regardless of gender.[8] Nevertheless, he continued to insist on the determining role which absence of a penis played for women's character development.

In addition to this biological element, a second strand of psychoanalytic gender theorizing was a rigid model of sequential psychological development taken from the male. The male child passed in orderly stages from his first love object, his mother, by overcoming his Oedipal ties, to similar objects, other women. Analogously his partial sexual sensations became subordinated to genital primacy. But this model immediately presented problems if one were to explain female development by it. In the first place, if the mother were the girl's first object, how did she learn to love men? The analytic answer was labyrinthine, and it was preceded by a full-scale discussion of the female castration complex that exemplifies at its most simplistic the early analytic reduction of social to biological data and the paradigmatic supremacy of male development.

The reason women believe that men have greater freedom in sexual life or the professions is because women universally see themselves as castrated; their vaginas are wounds from which a penis once had been removed. One typical and symptomatic expression of the normal female castration complex was the "great enjoyment many women obtain from using a hose for watering the garden." To become women, they must learn to love a child as a gift and a penis substitute. But some women could not adapt to this female sexual role and analysts observed that they were well represented in the woman's movement; their repressed homosexuality took the form of masculine interests of an intellectual and professional character, while they proclaimed that these essentially masculine pursuits are "as much feminine as masculine."[9]

Elaborations of the psychoanalytic theory of women involved a clash between two young analysts, Helene Deutsch in Vienna and Karen Horney in Berlin. Basing her observations on cases of sterility and frigidity, Deutsch's explanation rested on the development of the libido before genital maturity had been reached and preserved an enduring attachment to the male paradigm. She argued that at the oral stage the father's penis became the equivalent of the nurturing mother's breast, and was accompanied by fantasies of conception by oral copulation. Much later, the penis acted to focus libido on the vagina, thus overcoming fixation on the clitoris as a penis substitute. Finally, in coitus, in a return to the penis-breast equation, the vagina became the instrument for carrying out early fantasies of oral incorporation. In a startlingly direct analogy with male orgasm, she also argued that orgasm in women was accomplished in two stages, first by coitus, then by childbirth, an "extrusion" analogous to ejaculation. In a final bow to the male paradigm, she suggested that a mother who hastened to feed her child because her milk flowed between feedings behaved like a male with *ejaculatio praecox* who attempted, unsuccessfully, to hasten consummation of the sexual act.[10]

It was precisely the paradigmatic position of male sexuality that Horney attacked. She posited instead an innate femininity with its own "maturational processes," a position Ernest Jones and to some extent Otto Fenichel also would adopt.[11] Horney argued that the analytic scheme of female development followed all too closely that of the male, indicating not an unprejudiced view of female sexuality but the fact that psychoanalysis was the creation of a male genius and that civilization was male-dominated. The denigration of the positive pleasures of motherhood was still another indication of this skewed perspective. For in motherhood women held a true biological superiority and enjoyed a real satisfaction. Indeed, analysis showed plenty of men who envied this female function. But this envy could be successfully sublimated in cultural creativity. No equally acceptable cultural sublimation obtained for the girl's primary penis envy. Male-dominated culture entered to reinforce it in a powerful yet subtle way.

Horney argued that the central mechanism that activated a truly neurotic penis envy and sense of castration in women was the inevitable disappointment of the girl's intense love for the father and her desire to have a child by him. Guilt aroused by these feminine wishes impelled the girl to reject her feminine role, a rejection reinforced by all the actual disadvantages from which women suffered in social life. From birth onward women were exposed to suggestions of their inferiority. Thus male-dominated culture operated in two major ways—in the very construction of psychoanalytic theory itself and in reinforcing woman's flight from her own role. This was the beginning of Karen Horney's development of a theory of cultural determinism that would find its full expression after her emigration to America. In the 1920s she was still an orthodox Freudian, but a Freudian with a difference— one keenly aware of the power of culture, an insight she partly owed to the sociologist Georg Simmel.

In passing, Horney had observed that it was time the clitoris was regarded as a natural part of female genitalia, rather than as a substitute penis. Much of Helene Deutsch's views of feminine development had centered on the replacement of clitoral sensation by vaginal primacy. Indeed, generations of female analysands since the 1920s probably sought the "vaginal orgasm" that psychoanalysts in this period came to identify with true womanhood and feminine maturity.

Dissenters appeared quite early. One was a British psychotherapist, Paul Bousfield, outside orthodox circles, who argued that in French gynecological experience women lacking clitoral sensitivity were invariably frigid. All female orgasm, he insisted, depended in part on the clitoris.[12]

Still another attack on the equation that passive equals feminine and active equals masculine was leveled by the American Jungian analyst Beatrice Hinkle. She argued that the standard definitions of male and female were purely conventional. Her own work had indicated such a regular admixture of psychological attributes in most people that stereotypes were meaningless. Rather, she argued, the definition of woman as passive, receptive, docile had confused female sexuality with Jung's general introverted type. Analogously, the male as active, conquering, intrusive had been derived from what Jung had called the extroverted type.[13]

Despite orthodox resistance, the issues had been raised—the role of the clitoris in feminine sexuality and the role of convention in definitions of male and female. The American *Psychoanalytic Review* published both heretical views.

A third issue in the gender controversy was the presumably ubiquitous feelings in women of castration and resentment of men. Horney insisted these female attitudes were widespread: "I once had a penis; I am a man who has been castrated and mutilated. . . ." One cause, she argued, was society's obstruction of the sublimation of woman's masculinity in extrasexual and intellectual ways.[14] Another explanation may have been resentment provoked by male hostility toward women.

Although the early analysts often did not identify their patients by occupation and social class, some of the women treated by Deutsch and Horney seem to have been professionals like themselves. As therapists they may have been unusually sensitive to such problems in their female patients.

The psychoanalytic profession in Europe was unusually welcoming to women. But at the same time, in Germany, there may have been an increase of generalized male resentment against women, particularly in times of severe unemployment. Women had taken over men's jobs during the war; after the war, more of them attended universities, and the number of women doctors increased dramatically. The hostility toward men exhibited by some women may have been a response to a growing male resentment of women's competition.[15]

Finally, two opposing views of what kind of woman was emerging were taken by the analysts themselves. According to Deutsch, the number of masculine women who deprecated childbirth was increasing; Karen Horney argued that Helene Deutsch's generalizations about women's hostility to childbirth may have been based on the treatment of selected cases: upperclass women unusually troubled by castration anxiety. She suggested that Deutsch's theories could become fully comprehensible only if her clinical material were published in detail. According to Joan Riviere, a London analyst, the older manifestly masculine type of professional woman was disappearing. She was being replaced—perhaps at least in England—by women who were feminine and often were successful mothers, thus masking their castration anxiety. Despite these differences, the analysts agreed that a type of woman was emerging who was problematical in new ways.[16]

In the 1920s, the major vehicle for the expansion of psychoanalytic theory was the development of characterology.[17] Partly through character theory, psychoanalysis took under its purview a wide new list of ailments, ranging from vague inefficiency and unhappiness to delinquency and some kinds of criminality. The basis also was laid for what might be called an optimal character type, the genital, which resembled some of the ideals of secular ethical culture. The first generation of analysts primarily elaborated what could be called libidinal character types, based on constellations of traits rooted in the erogenous zones. The second generation expanded the concept of character to embrace a far more flexible interplay of instinctual demands and environmental pressures. It included self-defeating behavior, for example, the person who courts failure with consistent cleverness or the woman who invariably chooses a lover who deserts her. Several of the major second-generation analysts—Karen Horney, Helene Deutsch, Franz Alexander, Wilhelm Reich, Otto Fenichel—emigrated to the United States, bringing their theories with them.

Freud's cautious initial adumbration of types and their expansion into a score of subvarieties by Karl Abraham and Ernest Jones require brief examination. The Freudians thought they were developing a new genetic, biological explanation, rooted in modes of psychosexual development. Erik Erikson's stage theories derived in part from this early character theory.

The logic of character theory is best exemplified in Freud's first essay on the anal character in 1908. Freud argued that, without previous theoretical leads, he had been struck by patients characterized by a "certain set of characteristics"—notably orderliness, parsimoniousness, and obstinacy. They regularly had taken an unusual interest in defecation, partly because of an innately strong anal eroticism, and had resisted learning to control their bowels. Those who exhibited the adult traits had lost all conscious memory of their earlier anal interests because of disgust, morality, and shame. The adult traits represented either sublimations, prolongations, or reaction formations against the early anal drive. He also noted the connections in common speech between money and feces. Almost his only direct clinical material concerned the observation that such patients remembered that their siblings took unusual pleasure in holding their stools and playing with feces and that they had been hard to toilet-train. Thus, the early libidinal eroticism was assumed to give rise to the adult traits through a defensive environmental modification of the instincts. Finally Freud suggested that other erogenous zones might give rise to adult traits, as in the burning ambition of former bedwetters. How many patients Freud based his observation on is uncertain, as it is in most psychoanalytic generalizations.[18]

Perhaps the most remarkable expansion of the concept came from Ernest Jones, whose description of anally based traits leaned heavily on analogy with a minimum of clinical material, and ended in a maximum of derivations. Dust, dirt, writing letters, thought, the sense of duty, hate of injustice and taxes, food, sausages, soiled linen, money, children, mud pies, marbles, one's last will and testament—all could symbolize feces and thus could be seen as derivatives of anal eroticism. Postponement of defecation to enhance anal pleasure or willful withholding of the stool could give rise to myriad desirable or undesirable traits: individualism, determination, love of order, competency, reliability, generosity, and a bent toward art and good taste, or irritability, bad temper, hypochondria, miserliness, meanness, proneness to bore, dictating and tyrannizing, obstinacy, and so on.[19]

Jones and the Berlin analyst Karl Abraham stressed the environmental effects of the parental handling of anal impulses. Jones noted that the way parents treated their children could cause frustration and anger, hate and sadism. Abraham centered attention on the evil effects of too early and fearsome a demand for sphincter control and cleanliness. Habits prematurely forced on the child could create inner resistance, a fixation of libido at the anal level and a disturbed capacity to love. Thus, the determining balance was tipped away from innate tendencies and toward parental handling.[20]

An adult character type based on fixations at a still earlier stage of erogenous development than the anal was the next important addition to characterology. Analysts conceded that the "oral character" was more nebulous and less precisely delineated than the anal, partly because more oral erogenous elements were gratified in maturity—the pleasures of eating, smoking, speaking, and so on. Some of the clinical data came from new studies of alcoholics and drug addicts. Sucking and biting, incorporation and expulsion were the modalities from which oral traits were derived, just as anal traits were derived from attitudes toward the act of defecation and anal products.

Once more the observation of adult characteristics was correlated with fantasies in which patients recalled early oral material directly or symbolically. The speculative nature of the derived traits is unusually evident in a paper by Edward Glover in which he argued that because it is so easy to imagine the traits that follow from the oral stage, once its nature is described, the need for clinical corroboration was all the more urgent.

The relation of orality to adult traits was far less obvious than the derivation of stubbornness from an early refusal to evacuate on command. The oral phase, the earliest of psychosexual development, was literally the infant's first approach to object relations, notably by suckling at the nourishing mother's breast. Later the infant could bite the breast, and any object it could take into its mouth, in sadistic pleasure. These two acts, sucking and biting, were thus the primal experience of ambivalence—expressing love and sadism toward the same object. The oral phase also was characterized by easy gratification, absence of control, a sense of omnipotence, yet a need for constant emotional support. Fixation by too much oral gratification could result in corresponding adult traits—an undue optimism, a sense that the world, like the breast, would nourish and protect; oral optimists tended to undue verbosity. The orally disappointed, on the other hand, became unduly pessimistic, expressing their sadism in snappy, biting, hostile speech or extreme taciturnity. Oral characters tended to mood swings, from sanguine to bleak, and they also were unusually impatient, angry at delay, prone to insist on rapid mastery of objects, to be done with things in sexual as in other activities. Often they were envious, the result of seeing other children nursed. They reacted quickly and disproportionately to disappointment, and Glover noted that this characterized many of the drug addicts he had analyzed.[21]

It was inevitable that appropriate psychological virtues be assigned to the development of libido from primitive oral and anal pleasure to the primacy of the sexual organs. Despite Abraham's protest that psychoanalysis held up no norm of human attainment, he nevertheless posited a distinct and definite one. And the end product was remarkably close to what Alfred Adler had once called "social interest."

The human being who had attained genital primacy was able to adapt to the "interest of the community," although this allowed for great individual variation. Genital primacy assumed the overcoming of ambivalence, the simultaneous love and hate of the same object. It assumed the conquest of narcissism, of destructive and sadistic as well as avaricious and mistrustful impulses. It also assumed a harmony of character traits, none of which was pushed to excess. And at true maturity the interests of the individual and of the community coincided.

At each stage deleterious fixations would be conquered, and corresponding virtues retained. Thus from the early oral stage the mature man would retain his "forward-pushing energy; from the anal stage, endurance and perseverance; from sadistic sources, the necessary power to carry on the struggle for existence."[22] The traditional equation of "character" and virtue was swaddled in a new psychosexual costume.

The further expansion of the concept of character was almost entirely a contribution of second-generation analysts, although Freud had briefly foreshadowed this development. In one of his type descriptions the emphasis was no longer on traits but on behavior that brings about a particular kind of gratification. Thus some persons commit crimes because they already feel guilty, and the act satisfies this sense of guilt.

It was this arrangement of complex behavior unconsciously to gratify neurotic needs that became the key to Franz Alexander's concept of character as a life-style or a repetitive mode of behavior. The emphasis shifted from symptoms and relatively clear-cut neuroses in an otherwise integrated personality to a more generalized conception of human illness, as an habitual restriction of behavior. Often these patients did not feel subjectively ill but might feel ineffective or blocked. They had few circumscribed neurotic symptoms, except perhaps for mild forms of hypochondriasis, compulsive doubt, sexual inhibitions. Some, however, acted out vaguely antisocial behavior. Some complained of a recurring inability to adapt, enduring recurring crises of a stereotyped form.

A case of Franz Alexander's in a paper of 1923 best illustrates the new conception of character disorders, in this instance a personality shaped by a severe castration complex. The patient was a forty-year-old Jewish refugee whose business was lost in a social upheaval. Once wealthy and well known, he was struggling to regain his fortune. He had no children and rewarded his wife for sexual intercourse by buying her presents. The most unusual thing about him was that his reversals of fortune invariably occurred through friends whom he had helped in business. Alexander interpreted the frequent experience of ruin at the hands of friends as a reversal of primary active castration feelings directed toward his father. Now they were turned toward himself; and the damage inflicted by business associates was a derivative of his reversal of castration. By losing money, which he unconsciously equated with feces and his penis, he arranged for his own castration. He punished himself to assuage the guilt aroused by his own once active wish to castrate his father. Thus, Alexander interpreted the pattern of his life as a consistently arranged reflection of castration anxiety.[23]

Alexander later extended this approach to criminals from a sense of guilt and to tricksters who habitually conned society. Unlike neurotics, who developed symptoms, these people used the entire environment as a stage for acting out their neuroses. They developed a neurotic way of living, a stereotyped attitude "in the whole rhythm of their lives, at the most decisive moments and most important turning points."[24]

Alexander's generalized character theory would lead in America to the elaboration of a number of influential character typologies: the criminal and the psychopathic, the "accident-prone" and other psychosomatic personalities, and finally the narcissistic.

All later discussions of character were influenced by Freud's two most important essays of the 1920s, *The Ego and the Id* (1923) and *Inhibitions, Symptoms and Anxiety*, published three years later. Certain of their postulates are essential to later psychoanalytic characterology. In the first essay Freud divided the psychological apparatus into three interpenetrating components. The id represented the drives, unorganized and unconscious. The superego, or unconscious conscience, was formed when the child renounced the object of its libidinal tie and identified with the hated, rival parent, internalizing his commands and prohibitions. The primitive severity of the superego resulted from charges of inhibited aggressive and destructive drives. It remained for the Ego, the conscious self of perception and motility, to mediate between the inchoate drives of the Id and the harsh demands of the Superego.

The second essay marked a fundamental shift in psychoanalytic theory. Instead of holding that unsatisfied libido became changed into anxiety by repression, Freud argued that repression itself was caused by anxiety. The ego perceived the danger of a traumatic situation, either a flooding of unmanageable excitation from the id or the danger of punishment from the outer world. Particular experiences of anxiety were appropriate to specific stages of development. Thus for the baby the primary experience of anxiety is the loss of the loved and nurturing object, a loss that exposes it to the frustration of tension and need. In later childhood, fear of the rival father and the threat of punishment by castration for Oedipal strivings is the nuclear cause of anxiety; and still later it becomes social anxiety and the fear of punishment by the superego. At each stage, anxiety had to be "bound," or mastered by a number of defensive devices: sublimation, repression, reaction formation.

Two elements in these essays turned psychoanalysis from its preoccupation with the unconscious and toward a greater concern with the external world. The first was the conception of anxiety as ultimately the result of a fear of punishment for the expression of drives. The second was the concept of the superego as a precipitate of parental standards, in part socially determined. A relaxation in the severity of the superego toward the id led to hope for the treatment and perhaps the prophylaxis of neuroses, a hope Freud expressed in *Civilization and Its Discontents*. However, the existence of destructive impulses, derivatives of the death instinct, blocked this possible solution. Their existence, and not merely parental prohibitions reflecting social values, created the severity of the Superego. Only through the binding of such impulses by libidinal ties was social life possible, yet this very binding intensified internal punishment. Thus Freud's final scheme was highly enigmatic and rendered problematical the ultimate outcome of social change.

Many later theorists, including Wilhelm Reich and the American neo-Freudians, discarded the existence of innate destructive impulses, making them depend on environmental factors, frustration, insecurity, and so on, in order to offer substantial hope for social amelioration. By reformulating psychoanalysis in terms of the central experience of anxiety, Freud opened the way to all that was to come in fundamental alterations of analytic theory—the primal anxiety of the existentialists, the anxiety aroused by competitive capitalism of Karen Horney, the anxiety created by insufficient and inauthentic love of Eric Fromm, the ego psychology of Anna Freud and Heinz Hartmann.

Anna Freud's ego psychology, developed after her analysis with her father, led in two antithetical directions, a conservative insistence on innate conflicts that educational influences could not alter, and at the same time a novel emphasis on the social environment and on moral values.[25] She based her major conclusions primarily on her work with children and adolescents and published them in Europe in 1930 and 1936. Observing the treatment of delinquents carried out by August Aichorn in Vienna, she became particularly aware of the role of environment in the child's development, specifically the impact of parents in the formation of the child's "objective anxiety," his conscience, and his sibling rivalry. Because working-class mothers were able to pay less attention to their children, the latter exhibited less competition for her affection than did the children of the bourgeoisie. Parental prohibitions of instinctual activity created the "objective anxiety" or "dread of the outside world" experienced in childhood neuroses. Neglected children were unable to internalize control over their impulses or accept social restrictions, because no restraints had been imposed on their instinctual life and because they lacked the incentive provided by affection.[26]

This dependence of anxiety and infantile neurosis on parental prohibitions suggested to some educators an optimistic meliorism: by disciplining the child gently, without any threats of violence suggested by voice or manner, childhood anxieties could be minimized. But Anna Freud cautioned that psychoanalysis destroyed this happy prospect by observing that as the ego shifted from the pleasure to the reality principle, the ego itself became hostile to the instincts, particularly when the superego failed to protect it or the demands of instinctual impulses became excessive. Thus the child's "endopsychic" conflict was beyond the reach of education.[27] To the standard repertoire of psychoanalytic defenses against the instinctual drives— repression, projection, displacement, reaction formation, isolation, and undoing—she added an original contribution—identification with the aggressor. A child, just hurt by the dentist, was angry and cut up a rubber ball with a knife, then cut string into tiny pieces, and continually sharpened and broke off pencil points. He was identifying with the dentist's aggression. By "impersonating the aggressor, assuming his attributes, or imitating his aggression, the child transforms himself from the person threatened into the person who makes the threat."[28] This mechanism was a stage in the normal development of the superego. The child identified himself with the parents' threats of punishment and internalized their criticisms of him. But he could also project the forbidden impulses onto others and thus escape self-criticism with its accompanying pain and sense of guilt.

"True morality begins when the internalized criticism, now embodied in the standard exacted by the super-ego, coincides with the ego's perception of its own fault. From that moment, the severity of the super-ego is turned inward instead of outward and the subject becomes less intolerant of other people."[29] Many people never fully internalized this critical process but remained at an intermediate stage in the development of conscience.

What was also novel was the suggestion that the superego played a useful role in the creation of social morality and the break with the often routine psychoanalytic insistence in the 1920s on the superego's pathology, that it was the "root of all neurotic evil," even while its mitigation might remain therapeutically important.

Yet another defensive mechanism was the "restriction of the ego," also derived from Anna Freud's observations of children. Thus, a child might give up an activity such as drawing because he found that an adult or another child did it better than he. Even in the most kindly school setting, a child might behave as if intimidated: "the mere comparison of their achievements with that of the other children robs their work of all its value in their eyes."

In a reliance on psychoanalytic biologism, she argued that this restriction of activity, this neurotic inhibition, originally sprang from envy of other's "larger genitals" or the "hopeless rivalry of the Oedipal phase." Similarly she insisted that the little girl in giving up clitoral masturbation renounced her "masculine striving."[30]

The therapeutic implications of the new emphasis on the ego were serious and complex. Analysis of the ego was a delicate operation because in cases where the ego feared being submerged by instinctual drives, psychoanalytic therapy that rendered the defenses inoperative weakened the ego still further. Yet the major goal of psychoanalysis was precisely the opposite, the "restoration of the Ego to its integrity."

Wilhelm Reich, for some years an ardent Marxist, represented the meliorism Anna Freud regarded as impossible. He viewed Sigmund Freud's theory of innate aggression as disastrous to a sound psychoanalytic critique of society. By retaining Freud's concept of anxiety as the result of repressed libido, yet accepting the new tripartite division of the self, Reich could interpret character as a defensive armor, a protection of the ego against the demands of the id and the dangers of the outer world. This hardening of the ego restricted the range of its activities and its available energy. The character traits that created resistances in analysis resulted from the same factor that caused the character distortions in the first place. Essentially that factor was the fear of punishment embodied in parental behavior which in turn was determined by the prevailing social order. Civilization increasingly punished the gratification of impulses, and fear of punishment created the anxiety that led to the frustration of impulses.

In neurotics character became so rigid that both sublimation and genital gratification were impaired, constantly increasing the predominance of regressive pregenital gratifications and reaction formations. The genital character on the other hand achieved both sublimated and orgastic potency and thus, by adequate discharge of tension, a "regulated libido economy." The superego was "sexually affirmative," in harmony with the id. Because the genital character did not have quantities of dammed-up libido, it did not become aggressively sadistic.

Other characteristics of Reich's genital character moved far from Abraham's ideal of nonambivalent social adjustment. Reich's ideal type developed a Nietzschean quality, transcending received morals by the rational deployment of love and hate. The genital character could hate society and alter social institutions; thus, for instance, such a character could be free to accept or reject monogamy. If monogamy were satisfying, it would be maintained. But if polygamous urges became too clamorous the genital character would yield to them in a reasonable way. Wars between the id and the superego in Reich's ideal type were no longer possible. Without the cramping character armor of the neurotic, the genital man was open to experience without reserve. For Reich, as for the neo-Freudians, aggression resulted from frustration, sadism, from blocked libido.

Two of Reich's major conceptions, genital sexuality with orgasm as the regulator of libidinal economy and character armor, were incorporated into orthodox psychoanalysis, most notably in Otto Fenichel's *The Psychoanalytic Theory of Neurosis*. In Berlin, Sandor Rado had assigned Fenichel the task of systematizing the sprawling corpus of psychoanalytic theory. To read this work, begun in Europe, revised after Fenichel emigrated to Los Angeles, is to explore an apparently seamless web. Psychoanalytic theory is presented as monolithic; its major points have been indubitably confirmed; the unknown factors and points of dispute are minor. The great developmental scheme stands.

But in fact Fenichel adroitly reconciled clashing views and synthesized fundamental disagreements. The text is totally ahistorical, written as if psychoanalytic theory had grown all at once, without a complex and often tortuous development over time. The text itself forced into a single whole views that were beginning to diverge disruptively by the early 1930s—the cultural approach of Eric Fromm and Karen Horney, the sexual economy of the early Wilhelm Reich, the new ego psychology of Anna Freud, the monstrous wonders attributed to the preverbal child by Melanie Klein. Fenichel also attempted to balance the social determinism of the Marxists and the libidinal determinism of orthodox Freudians.[31] He markedly expanded the conception of character disorders and defined character as the adjustment the ego makes to the instincts and the external world. In Fenichel all is brilliantly smoothed together in a synthesis that codified the corpus of orthodox psychoanalytic theory for its greatest period of medical reception in America in the 1950s.

When he revised his text for publication in 1945, Fenichel placed defense against anxiety at the center of psychoanalytic theory and had accepted the growing emphasis on the perceiving and judging functions of the ego. There was less emphasis on instincts and the unconscious and more on the environment and the superego. Finally, and perhaps most significant, Fenichel argued that character was socially determined: changes in society had created changes in symptomatology. Ego psychology and character analysis had been discovered because of the harsh necessities of therapeutic disappointment in dealing with new kinds of patients. The disorders displayed by psychoanalytic patients had shifted from such isolated symptoms as compulsions or hysterical paralyses to problems involving the entire personality structure. Fenichel attributed this in part to changes in morality, reflected in indecisive and wavering patterns of child-raising. He completed the transition from the early biologism of psychoanalytic character theory to a far more socially determined system, one in which the environment played a key role. This very environmentalist emphasis would make psychoanalysis more congenial to the Americans.[32]

As the major vehicle for the expansion of the psychoanalytic model in the 1920s, psychoanalytic characterology is difficult to assess. That it contained shrewd observations seems clear, particularly in the suggestion that consistent patterns of behavior could occur in such seemingly disconnected areas as anal functioning, sexuality, and work. Some psychologists have argued that nonpsychoanalytic studies have confirmed the validity of the oral and anal character types while their developmental origin remains problematic.[33] Perhaps the weakest element in these theories is the lack of sampling or the lack of almost any attempt to make correlations systematic. Moreover, the distinction between a symptom and a trait, for instance, remained a matter of tortuous hair-splitting, even for Fenichel. Psychoanalytic characterology left unanswered the serious question of trait stability from infancy to adulthood. In America, libidinal character theory diminished in importance from the late 1930s on, as the new psychoanalytic ego psychology seemed to promise a more comprehensive theory of personality, one more readily reconcilable with academic psychology. But other derivatives of character theory, often based on the environmentalist factor of early mothering, were created and flourished.

The psychoanalytic emphasis on the ego was one way in which the psychoanalysts coped with an emerging problem: the waning of the early rapid "wonder cures" of psychoanalysis and the growing length of analyses. Psychoanalysts themselves offered several explanations for the difficulties. Perhaps the most famous was Otto Fenichel's suggestion, already discussed, that the hysterias and compulsions of an earlier period were changing to problems of character that were far harder to treat. A wide variety of symptoms were included in the new character disorders—inferiority feelings, chronic difficulties in work or relations with others, emotional coldness and unreliability, infantile fixations that prevented successful functioning, unstable, odd, impulsive, antisocial, or criminal behavior.

Contradictions created by the sexual revolution which the war had accelerated were giving rise to still another type of patient, Freud's rejected disciple Wilhelm Stekel observed. He was now treating the children of patients he had seen earlier who had joined the ranks of the sexual revolutionaries but who had brought up their children according to the old morality.

Among this clientele, compulsion neuroses had replaced hysteria, which had vanished with the freer expression of sexuality.[34] These new patients were pursued by compulsive ideas, by inner voices that urged them to perform illogical acts, whose omission would bring calamity or death; they were in constant conflict with the cultural environment and thus reflected the destruction of moral authority. Despite the new emphasis on character disorders, the statistics of the Berlin clinic suggest that the largest diagnostic categories were those psychoanalysts had been treating all along—hysteria, anxiety hysteria, neurotic inhibitions, and compulsion neuroses—and accounted for more than half the clinic's patients.[35]

Another reason advanced for the difficulties of therapy was the growth of intellectual resistances as psychoanalytic knowledge became more general. Psychoanalysts were confronted by informed and self-referred patients, who were inspired to seek treatment by growing public knowledge about psychoanalysis.[36] More and more patients, particularly school teachers, social workers, physicians, writers, and artists, knew a good deal about psychoanalytic theories. Most analysts agreed that the informed patients inhibited their own therapy by intellectualizing, that is by substituting theories for feelings. Because psychoanalysis still was largely an "unmasking" therapy, to have the mask already torn from the sphinx, as it were, was to compromise the effect of the analyst's major tool, interpretation.

Partly in response to these problems of therapy, partly because of the needs of institute training, therapy, like theory, became more systematic and ambitious. To teach therapeutic methods required agreement on diagnoses and techniques that could be transmitted. Freud's exposition of the classical technique remained the basis of institute training.

What, then, was the "classical technique"? Freud had explained it in a series of essays beginning in 1912. Briefly these concentrated on transference and resistance, repetition and working through. Patients were to be led to remember, rather than to act out, earlier pathogenic experiences in relation to the analyst, particularly Oedipal relations, and to resolve these anew in the light of a more mature ability to cope with instinctual demands once repressions were lifted. The analysis of resistances, that is, the unconscious factors that blocked free associations from becoming conscious and thus blocked a knowledge of instinctual drives, was the major avenue to understanding the repressing forces. The latter were essential elements of the unconscious conflict between drives and the socialized self. The positions of libido or instinctual energy through the stages of development, and particularly in relation to the Oedipus complex, were the major objects for investigation.

The analyst's role was to enforce the primary rule, that is, to insist that the patient say whatever came to mind, no matter what it was. Seated behind the patient, invisible to him, the analyst nevertheless could observe and follow, partly with his own intuitive unconscious, the threads of the patient's associations. The analyst was to adopt the emotional coldness of the skilled surgeon, eschewing intimacy. Like the surface of a well-polished mirror, he was to be opaque to his patients, showing them nothing but what was shown to him. He was not to "educate or instruct or exchange intimacies" but to uncover "what is unconscious." Nor was he to be overwhelmed with therapeutic zeal, which might cloud his vision.[37]

It was Freud's practice to see his patient every day, perhaps six days a week, for an hour. His interpretations were sparing with some patients, and he might call attention to unconscious infantile wishes when these easily could be inferred, or ask for associations to dream elements. It was a long, meandering, indirect process. Freud spoke little, but "clearly, concisely," with excellent timing.[38] But having made the rules Freud also could break them. Sometimes he chatted with patients, or argued with them, or saw them socially.

In Berlin analysis became more rigidly systematic, and for some of its graduates, such as Edward Glover, even the handshake might be eschewed as provoking unnecessary emotional contamination.[39] Therapeutic aims followed the development of theory closely. Thus as new libidinal positions were postulated, such as narcissism, or fixation on the self, or the death instinct, the task of analysis would include discovering this element in psychosexual development. Similarly, oral and anal stages, and the entire development of the infantile libido, were to be recovered systematically. The Berlin answer to new theoretical developments seemed to be single-minded: longer and more thorough analyses.

Freud's new structural theory was reflected primarily in a search for the pathological elements of the Superego. Recently psychoanalysts have projected into the 1920s some of their concern with ego psychology. But the first ego psychology as it was reflected in treatment and case discussion concerned not the Ego's mastery of conflict but the tyrannies of the childish conscience as it directed aggression toward the self. The strictures against harsh repression were replaced by therapeutic disapproval of the repressing, unreasonable Superego.

It is impossible not to regard Freud's analysis of conscience as part of the general attack on received moral authority that became more severe on many levels during the 1920s—in serious literature, philosophy, popular journalism. Gide's *The Counterfeiters* celebrated gratuitous crime and Thomas Mann glorified the trickster in *Felix Krull,* both examples of the literary denigration of moral authority.

Yet Freud's purpose was by no means the kind of truculent attack on convention he had propounded in "'Civilized' Morality and Modern Nervousness" in 1908, with its extolling of the strong, Nietzschean male who achieves sexual satisfaction despite convention. Freud's critique of the superego came from his discovery of the tendency to repeat traumatic events and his postulation of an instinct of death and aggression. The taming of the superego's immature, aggressive folly was to be in the interest of a more reasonable morality and a less destructive handling of aggression. By a gentler tolerance of drives and a more realistic rather than condemning attitude toward them, some of the force of the death instinct would be mitigated.

Structural theory and the new importance of the ego were reflected in still another way. From the beginning analytic therapy had depended on the patient's combined emotional and intellectual "insight," that is, his or her ability to perceive the historical roots of patterned present behavior. Freud always had stressed the importance of mature judgment. In the 1920s this function became allied with structural theory and assigned to the ego. This element of the personality, the link with the external real world, became split, as it were. A portion became concerned with observing, the other with experiencing. The observing portion could view experience more objectively in the light of its roots in the past, noticing patterns and connections without surrendering to them.[40]

It might be added that this very split between observation and insight on the one hand, and intuition and emotion on the other, reflected disagreements within orthodox psychoanalysis on what was important in therapy. Theodor Reik, who also emigrated to America, resisted the kind of schematic and systematic emphasis that characterized Berlin, arguing that intuition and "surprise" were essential. Otto Fenichel adroitly fashioned a compromise, warning against placing too much weight on either side. Intellectualizing was bad, but then so was too much wallowing in feeling and intuition.[41]

Despite all the elaborations of psychosexual theory, the role of trauma remained important. Indeed, many of the case histories used to support the new character theory depended upon traumatic events fixating particular modes of libidinal satisfaction. Instead of the single overwhelming traumatic event, such as adult seduction of children, that Freud first had postulated, a series of complex, interacting traumas were now regarded by many analysts as essential elements in the development of adult neuroses. Parental handling of oral, anal, and genital behavior could act as traumatizing elements.

But all this—the systematic reconstruction of libidinal cathexes, the gentling of the superego—was to be carried out by rigorous adherence to classical techniques. The Berliners and the Viennese failed to find an appropriate alloy to mix with the "pure gold" of Freud's classical psychoanalysis. Without real analysis, they felt, no success was possible. They did modify the method somewhat in dealing with borderline psychotics, delinquents, and criminals, but it is significant that the average duration of completed analyses in the Berlin clinic remained 17 months. The Berliners did experiment with breaking off analyses that seemed to be progressing well before they were formally completed, a tactic Franz Alexander later developed systematically in Chicago.[42]

The training analysis itself was a powerful mode of creating and cementing tradition. For as Edward Glover observed, analysts tended to ape the techniques of their trainers, sometimes too slavishly.[43] Therapy, theory, and technique tended to follow the style of the training analyst in a succession of apprenticeship generations. Sometimes authority backfired, and the trainer's method would be ostentatiously rejected. This powerful model of initiation, once established, remained an aspect of the analyst's own unresolved transference to his teacher.

It is important to recall that from early on, despite all the attempts at systematization, analysts, including Freud, were clearly aware of the importance of tact, of the timing of interpretations, of intuition in grasping the unconscious feelings and ideas that patients tried to verbalize. Moreover, they were aware that although, as Michael Balint has observed, they clearly agreed on psychoanalytic goals in therapy, there was no single method of attaining them. Each individual analyst had his own particular technique, based on his training and experience. Each tended to vary the technique in idiosyncratic, highly individualistic ways. Beneath the apparent uniformity of psychoanalytic theory and therapy, even among the orthodox, individual variety reigned.

The orthodox analysts held an important symposium on therapy in 1936 at Marienbad, where they attempted to explain the therapeutic action of psychoanalysis, arguing that it was uniquely able to create lasting cures. In addition to the basic techniques of interpreting transference and resistance there was a new emphasis on structural theory and the synthetic function of the ego as the key to recovery. This meant the ego's capacity to regulate, adjust, assimilate, and unify in relation to both the drives and the external world. At a moment of external danger, for instance, a strong ego could enhance such functions as perception, "reality testing, critical judgment etc." The essence of the method remained in facilitating, through transference interpretation, a conscious comparison by the patient between his or her "archaic imaginary objects" of childhood and his or her "actual and real ones" of the present. And showing the influence of Melanie Klein there was a new emphasis on "introjection," for instance, in the patient's absorption of the analyst as a more tolerant superego object.[44]

A few analysts in the early 1920s already had rejected classical methods. The major therapeutic experiments, notably those of Sandor Ferenczi and Otto Rank, were initiated outside institute settings. They argued in 1924 that theory had outstripped the development of treatment methods and they wanted a more emotionally charged therapy to overcome intellectualization. They opposed what may have been the Berlin emphasis on a too schematic recovery of pregenital stages of psychosexual development.

Their therapy centered on the reactivation of Oedipal impulses in all their intensity with the analyst as their object. It was the method of doing this that was novel. Taking advantage of Freud's recent insistence on the importance of the tendency to repeat traumatic and other situations, they argued that the analyst should actively encourage this repetition. Only then would the patient's defenses, created by guilt and anxiety, be broken through and the original feelings become clear. The analyst did this by abandoning his role as mirror, reflecting and interpreting. Instead he should subject the patient to careful doses of privation to reestablish those conditions under which the neuroses developed in the first place. He might prohibit what seemed to him neurotic modes of defecation or urination or other satisfying compulsive activities. These activities would mobilize anxiety and neurotic infantile libidinal cravings in the transference, and it was the analyst's task to interpret them continually. He was thus encouraged to regress to the period of the

Oedipus complex, then to endure his own unrequited Oedipal love. When the analyst as an object had replaced the original compulsion he would set a definite time for ending the treatment. The patient would learn to give up for good the satisfaction of his infantile libidinal cravings for new and more realistic satisfactions.

Freud, they emphasized, earlier had moved toward a more active role for the analyst by insisting that in certain cases a phobic patient, for instance, should be forced to experience whatever provoked his fears; and in some cases he too had set a limit for the termination of treatment. He also had insisted on "abstinence," that is, forbidding patients certain neurotic satisfactions that served as resistances to understanding unconscious drives. The aim of therapy was not plausibility and logical necessity but direct perception and experience.[45]

One element of the analyst's new activity was an expanded, even a utopian social role. This new social authority would apply psychoanalytic insight to the family and bring about a reunification of scientific knowledge. Society's morals and customs would be reformed and thus Freud's old dream be realized of a psychoanalytic prophylaxis of the neuroses.

These therapeutic innovations, at once simple and grandiose, aroused considerable opposition. Alexander attacked the prohibitions and the activity for ignoring Freud's insistence on memory rather than repetition as strengthening the neuroses of masochists, already too submissive. Yet in America he too would seek a more convincing therapy, one based on a "corrective emotional experience." Opposition to Rank and Ferenczi's innovations became more complicated by Rank's publication a year later of the *Trauma of Birth*, based in large part on the results of these therapeutic departures. Rank insisted that in every treatment the analyst became a mother substitute. And when he set a limit to the duration of therapy, a peculiarly severe reaction occurred, precisely analogous to the painful severance of the child's primal tie to the mother. It was from this data that he directly inferred the trauma of birth, his paradigm of all traumatic situations.

Toward the end of the 1920s, Rank moved away from a medical model of therapy and toward an existential one, with overtones of Martin Buber's I-Thou philosophy. He found a sympathetic audience in Jessie Taft and other American social workers, but it was nearly four decades too early for a wider American echo. In the early period it was the scientific and what Rank called the mechanistic appeal of psychoanalysis that beguiled the Americans.[46] Later developments in American psychoanalytic therapy such as a more active, interventionist role for the analyst, even some of the tendencies toward an anti-medical and existentialist orientation, resembled these earlier experiments, even if they may not derive directly from them.

Not the departures of Rank and Ferenczi but the systematic organization of Berlin and Vienna and their conservative view of therapy stamped the orthodox movement in America. But it was also America that would see the flowering of dissent, even among some of those who had taught in Berlin.

4

Culture and Rebellion,
1912–1930

While psychoanalyts in Europe were developing new theories and institutions, in America rebellious intellectuals supplied an important sustaining agent in the spread of psychoanalysis—an enthusiastic clientele. The writers among this group were the first to publicize psychoanalysis, interpreting it in their own idiosyncratic ways. The Great War provoked a disillusioned turn to their rebellion against traditional American culture, a rebellion in which psychoanalysis already had played a role in the prewar years. The war provoked as well a new, more hard-boiled interpretation of psychoanalysis.

Around 1912 idealistic young intellectuals had launched attacks on the entrenched American faith in morality and the superiority of Anglo-Saxon race and culture, a complex of values some historians have defined as "Victorian" and that the rebels themselves uniformly denounced as "Puritan." In this assault, psychoanalysis offered a sweeping criticism of traditional sexual mores and virtues. It supplied theory and rhetoric for the attack: the overwhelming importance of the sexual instinct and the evils of "repression." Psychoanalysis also supplied therapy for the internal conflicts rebellion engendered. Finally, it is not too much to see in the adoption of psychoanalysis an attempt to establish a new, universal, and iconoclastic image of man, one that became associated with varieties of "modern," "liberal," social, and cultural reform and that supplied a new faith for those who had repudiated traditional religious doctrines.[1]

The young men and women who launched this spirited assault on "Puritanism" and provincialism were among the first representatives of a new cosmopolitan, "liberal" American intellectual. By taste or background they felt themselves to be marginal outsiders to the standard prewar culture. Some, like the writers James Oppenheim and Waldo Frank, were from German or Eastern European Jewish families; others, Floyd Dell or Randolph Bourne, for example, were from older American groups. They came in surprising numbers from the Midwest, but also from the eastern seaboard via the universities of Harvard, Yale, or Columbia, where they found that some of their most interesting friends were representatives of other cultures. Walter Lippmann, John Reed, and Mabel Dodge were from wealthy families, but Dell had been exposed to real poverty; most were children of comfortable middle-class parents.

Young writers first proclaimed their vision of psychoanalysis in the bohemias of Chicago and New York. They popularized it in bowdlerized form in the mass-circulation magazines and wrote more frankly in the magazines on which some of them worked—*The Masses, The New Republic, The Little Review.*

Growing up in Davenport, Iowa, Chicago, or Boston they were rebelling against the ugly social "prison" and the literary tradition that New England Puritanism presumably had fostered. In 1908 a midwestern rebel, Floyd Dell, who would become a proselyte for psychoanalysis, explained to George Bernard Shaw that most New England literature was worthless. New England rebels, the critic Randolph Bourne remarked, made the most delightful bohemians. His friend Sophonisba had fled a New England town and family to write for little magazines in New York. "She has expelled the terrors of religion and the perils of thwarted sex," Bourne wrote, "but their nearness still thrills. . . . " "Her allegiance went, of course, quickly to Freud," and, testimony to the eclecticism of the Americans, she was analyzed by one of Jung's assistants in Zurich one summer.[2]

The young intellectuals and the medical psychoanalysts agreed on a similar agenda. Both shared a lofty vision of the artist's mission. The psychoanalysts attributed high importance to writers and artists as intuitive discoverers of truths they themselves unearthed with difficulty in the clinic. Artists revealed the unconscious in sympathetic, palatable form and by their art helped to purge themselves and their audience of neuroses. Both psychoanalysts and intellectuals stood for greater frankness in life and literature and opposed "rigid" moral judgments. Just as the patient should squarely face his repressed impulses, so writers should deal realistically with the whole range of human passion. Honesty would purge the soul of failure, longing, and conflict.[3] Physicians and artists considered themselves guides to a new and healthier society in which unconscious needs were more frankly met. Writers, Dell insisted, were the psychoanalysts of society itself.

But the two groups also diverged in significant ways. Although they shared an optimistic faith in progress, they disagreed about how it should be realized. The psychiatrists believed progress would come from a lifting of repressions to allow more conscious control over instincts. The intellectuals, on the other hand, tended to believe that progress would come from freer and franker self-expression. They also tended to ignore Freud's observations that feelings about sex were as determined by internalized moral standards as by bodily desires. This moral element in Freud had been emphasized by one of the first American psychoanalysts, the Harvard neurologist James Jackson Putnam, and in a more sophisticated way by Freud's favorite American disciple, the New York analyst Horace W. Frink. But novelist Theodore Dreiser read the psychoanalysts for a lesson in the horrors of repression, not the anxieties provoked by transgression of one's internalized ego ideals.

Some of the young intellectuals went beyond the analysts at their most sanguine in one crucial respect: they believed that instincts were neutral or positively good. If instincts were given freer rein people would be happier and more truly virtuous. This profound belief in the goodness of man—Dell cited Rousseau in its support—made them want to be "natural, fearless, unashamed, joy-loving" American pagans. Sexuality, they implied, was something sacred, to be enjoyed, not elaborately controlled. Repression, the intellectuals concluded, made people sick. This romanticization of instinct was not Freud's understanding of sexuality. Freud understood it in terms of tension and discharge, the precise determination of love objects and sexual aptitudes.[4]

Both doctors and intellectuals cited Forel, Havelock Ellis, and Ellen Key, other important liberating authorities on sexual matters. But the intellectuals tended to value them as justifying variety in sexual behavior, and they were fondest of the English writer Edward Carpenter, whose sexual romanticism was close to their own.

Few of the intellectuals gave heed to the social ideals of the American psychoanalysts, to William Alanson White's social adaptation or A. A. Brill's well-regulated libido and the normal life. The society to which analysts asked one to adjust, they thought, was itself in need of thoroughgoing change. While the analysts generally counseled conformity to conventional morals, the intellectuals experimented with free unions which they urged society to recognize. Nor were the physicians as enthusiastic about progressive education or feminism.[5]

The difference between the two groups is admirably symbolized by their appearance. Photographs display the doctors in stiff collars, looking for all the world like substantial businessmen. The intellectuals wore orange neckties, flannel shirts; the women bobbed their hair, favored batik skirts, and, like Emma Goldman, smoked cigarettes in public. They fancied themselves "disinterested devotees of art, revolution and psychoanalysis."[6]

Both groups shared a deep faith in science, freed from its "narrow" 19th-century limitations. They believed Freud had created a science of the emotions, close to the realities of daily life. Dell urged all intelligent people to learn about this "new and splendid and terrible knowledge."[7]

New York, with the largest number of psychoanalytic practitioners, became the center for contact between intellectuals and psychoanalysts. In 1912, Jung, on one of his forays across the Atlantic, gave a long interview to the *Times* on the menace of nerves in America, and on a later trip he spoke to the Liberal Club, which had become a center of Greenwich Village life. Brill's discussion of his own first book about psychoanalysis in the *Times* attracted the attention of a number of intellectuals because of its emphasis on dream interpretation.[8]

Despite growing publicity, the vocabulary of psychoanalysis still was esoteric. In 1921 after Margaret Anderson had published excerpts from Joyce's *Ulysses* in her *Little Review,* four issues were burned for obscenity and the staff was hauled into court. When a witness testified that an objectionable chapter "was merely an unveiling of the suconscious mind in the Freudian manner," one of the judges observed that the witness might just as well be talking Russian and asked that he speak English so the court could understand.[9]

Partly because they shared a common language and outlook, the intellectuals created a loosely knit but close network of personal associations; like the few Freudian physicians, nearly everybody knew everybody else. They worked on the same magazines, went to the same parties, met at Provincetown or the Liberal Club. The range of acquaintances who knew something about psychoanalysis included well-known literary figures of the prewar and interwar years—Van Wyck Brooks, Waldo Frank, John Reed, Eugene O'Neill, Louis Untermeyer, Sherwood Anderson, Edna St. Vincent Millay.

Floyd Dell's conversion to psychoanalysis began when he moved to New York from Chicago in 1913 and started to work at Max Eastman's magazine, *The Masses.* Despite five years as an editor of the distinguished *Friday Literary Review* of the Chicago *Evening Post,* he regarded himself as still an incorrigible ingenue. He had picked up some knowledge of Freud from reading Havelock Ellis, but his new friends in New York knew far more than he, so he decided to learn all he could. Ignorant of German, like most of the young intellectuals, he waded painfully through the available translations, chiefly Brill's.[10]

The magazines of the rebellion were the first to explore the social implications of Freud. The sober *New Republic,* dedicated to the rule of the intellectual, propounded the most conservative view. Freud promised the most advanced scientific method for the control of human instincts, sublimation. Walter Lippmann, one of the *New Republic*'s youngest and most brilliant staff members, offered an interpretation close to the vision of the medical popularizers. Lippmann had learned about Freud from Alfred Booth Kuttner, a Harvard friend with whom he shared a cabin in Maine in the summer of 1912. A patient of Brill's, Kuttner was translating *The Interpretation of Dreams* while Lippmann was writing his first book, *A Preface to Politics.* The *Preface* called for a major overhaul of human institutions, based not on "absurd" notions of moral reform, but on a knowledge of human nature. Character was motivated solely by the dynamisms of "rooted lusts" that were neither good nor bad in themselves. They could not be controlled by old-fashioned taboos, precedents, preposterous idealisms, or ghostly magic phrases. Freud offered a new and superior way, "the greatest advance ever made toward the understanding and control of human character." He had proved the existence of what Lippmann's teacher, William James, had called "moral equivalents." This doctrine assumed that instincts and desires could emerge with equal ease in "crime and civilization, art, vice, insanity, love, lust, and religion." Freud showed that every desire could be enlisted in the service of some civilized interest. What counted were training and opportunity."[11]

Five months after the *New Republic* began, Lippmann wrote an unabashed panegyric to Freud. No laymen could afford to ignore him, because, in an "intimate and drastic way," Freud revealed corners of the soul believed safe from everybody's knowledge. For illumination, steadiness, and "brilliancy of mind," Lippmann ranked him among the "greatest who have contributed to thought,"[12]

In March of 1915 Kuttner announced that "gross abuse" of Freud was no longer "good form" among neurologists and psychologists and a year later he reviewed D. H. Lawrence's *Sons and Lovers* at length for the *Psychoanalytic Review.* This passionate novel, obviously autobiographical, would have been incomprehensible without psychoanalysis, he argued. In dealing with the hero's intense relation with his mother, Lawrence was making a "priceless commentary on the love-life of today." Like every artist, Lawrence was sick with the "problems of his generation." But by his art he had cured himself, and by inducing catharsis in others, he was helping to heal them. His stature could be measured by the universality of the problem his art transfigured. Kuttner's devotion to psychoanalysis continued into the 1920s. He contributed a long chapter on "nerves" to the anthology *Civilization in the United States,* a manifesto of intellectual alienation published in 1922 and edited by Harold Stearns. The attention Kuttner's article devoted to psychoanalysis indicated how much Freud had become a part of the younger intellectual's equipment.[13]

In the first blush of enthusiasm Lippmann and Kuttner had visited Freud in Vienna and Freud had reviewed *Politics* in *Imago.* Lippmann, however, gradually lost interest. In *Politics* and later, he touched on one of the early limitations of psychoanalysis—its exclusive concern with unconscious sexuality. In 1916 Lippmann welcomed Wilfred Trotter's "herd instinct" for supplying the social motive for the repressing mechanism. He found Freud's postwar theory of the ego and the superego too metaphysical for his taste and had already dismissed Jung as an impossible mystic, the founder of a new religion. Nevertheless, he also believed that "in the breakdown of orthodox religion and moral philosophy . . . psychoanalysis supplied a way of interpreting the universe."[14]

If Lippmann and the *New Republic* construed Freud conservatively, *The Masses* stood for "fun, truth, beauty, realism, freedom, peace, feminism, revolution." It offered a more carefree vision that mixed Freud and Jung, as did several eclectic American psychoanalysts. According to Dell, Freud re-

vealed that "sexual emotions would not be repressed without morbid consequences. . . . " Moreover, psychoanalysis would transform education, morals,
the "very shape and color of our lives."[15] Like most writers on *The Masses,*
Dell preferred Jung and called him the "clearest, sanest and wisest" of all the
psychoanalysts. Dell's good friend Louis Untermeyer considered Jung's *Psychology of the Unconscious* "the greatest contribution to the history of thought"
of his generation. Perhaps Jung was more congenial because he was more
flattering to a writer's self-esteem. Where Freud regarded art as catharsis, the
transformed expression of the repressed, Jung considered the unconscious a
positive creative force. Dreams could dramatize a patient's state of mind and
suggest the correct solution to conflict. Artists directly portrayed the powerful archetypes of the unconscious. In effect, Jung was more cheerful, seemingly more respectful of impulse and emotion. *The Masses'* light-hearted
welcome to psychoanalysis is best symbolized by one of its cartoons in 1917:
a young woman tells her boyfriend, "I dreamt you were drafted!" He replies,
"Wish dream or nightmare?"[16]

The editor of *Seven Arts,* James Oppenheim, poet, journalist, and former
muckraker, also proclaimed the superiority of Jung's vision of the artist and
the human soul. Jung was broader and more creative than Freud, whose
emphasis on the sexual failed to take into account the nobler reaches of
human endeavor. After analysis with the Jungian Beatrice Hinkle, Oppenheim "found himself" and became a lay analyst for a time. Patients constantly asked him for a simple book on psychoanalysis. None was available
that did not deal chiefly with Freud's "narrow sexual theory." So he wrote a
series of articles and a book arguing that Jung's collective unconscious offered patients "wisdom and guiding power."[17]

The ineradicable primacy of sexuality that Freud had posited and the
absurdity of sublimation were enunciated by the older novelist Theodore
Dreiser, a good friend of A. A. Brill's, in a vein that was far more typical of
the 1920s. In the essay "Neurotic America and the Sex Impulse," Dreiser,
like many interpreters of Freud, discussed "sublimation" in terms solely of
adult, genital sexuality. Sublimation was nothing more than a pious fraud, a
sop to moralists. He quoted the analyst Horace W. Frink's *Morbid Fears and
Compulsions* to show that the sexual impulse in America was "consistently and
unremittingly warped, cramped and deformed in every conceivable and unnatural manner." Dreiser blamed religion—Quaker, Methodist, Puritan,
Catholic—for this severe repression. Americans considered the sex impulse
debased and degrading, yet fed themselves on oceans of cheap suggestive
literature and gratified their desires clandestinely. Despite campaigns against
vice and prostitution, the mistress and the prostitute flourished. Krafft-
Ebing, Havelock Ellis, and Freud had demonstrated the "pathos of sex-
repression." The brilliant, revealing researches of Freud alone had unlocked
"grisly prison doors," Sexuality was an inexorable, chemical drive, varying in
intensity from individual to individual, a great natural force that had to be
reckoned with. In every field men were moved by love or lust, the first
merely an "intellectual sublimation" of the second. But Dreiser offered no

easy solution. Sexuality never had been or could be controlled by "exact rule." The least one could do, he implied, was to acknowledge its power with sincerity and frankness.[18]

In addition to proclaiming Freud a cosmic psychologist or a medical apologist for more relaxed mores, some of the rebels turned to psychoanalysis for treatment. Usually these patients, some of whom wrote about their analyses, insisted they did not suffer from serious neuroses—morbid compulsions or hysterical paralyses. Rather they suffered from vaguer, more general disabilities—diffuse anxiety, loss of identity, inability to create, unhappiness. Some analysts have speculated that these complaints became general later when repressions and reticences about sexuality had been eased. Perhaps as members of the avant-garde, who endlessly talked of their impulses and expressed their sexuality more freely, the intellectuals were exhibiting early these presumably new varieties of neurosis.[19]

Cultural rebellion created its own conflicts. It was no simple process to repudiate the values of one's parents, especially of one's mother. For the American mother was the guardian of her children's moral purity. In their sexual emancipation the rebels were destroying standards which she had taught. They suffered from what the medical psychoanalyst Horace W. Frink called conflict between instincts and internalized, but consciously repudiated, ego ideals. Dell and Eastman, both troubled by sexual problems, were closely attached to their mothers; so, too, were the writers Hutchins Hapgood and Waldo Frank. Dell and Frank believed they would have to be freed of their profound involvement with their mothers to fulfill their creativity and sexuality. These intense Oedipal concerns and a very early awareness of their own sexuality in childhood made them unusually receptive to Freud's message. Hutchins Hapgood became aware of his sexuality at age 7 or 8, and Frank, at about the same age, would watch his own erect penis during his Friday night bath. For them, infantile sexuality seemed altogether plausible.[20]

It was possible that agonizing over sexuality occurred simply because intellectuals were specially constituted, tender-minded types. Dell insisted that American mores always had been relaxed, that only attitudes, but not behavior, changed after 1910. "They myth of the puritanical American is bunk," he told Joseph Freeman. "You will find very few Americans who go through the internal torments, the shame, the self-reproach typical of certain intellectuals."[21] Yet sexuality troubled Dell far more than this casual manifesto would suggest.

Joseph Freeman, younger than most of the prewar rebels, summed up the problem: "Sons and daughters of the puritans, the artists and writers and utopians who flocked to Greenwich Village to find a frank and free life for the emotions and the senses, felt at their backs the icy breath of the monster they were escaping."[22] Some also suffered from pangs of jealousy and insecurity to which their free unions freely exposed them. What was to prevent abandoning one attachment for another? Sometimes promiscuity or, more accurately, the procession from one serious affair to another seemed empty and sterile. Dell, for example, longed to stay in love, marry, and have children.[23] Many of the villagers reflected the moral system they were repudiating in their emphasis on fidelity in their free unions, which some formalized in marriage, others in stigmatizing casual sex.

Still others were troubled by problems of sexual identity. Probably, from the standpoint of Theodore Roosevelt and of most Americans, the rebels were blurring sexual roles. For the male they held up a new image of the artist instead of the frontiersman or the businessman; for the woman, the role of militant feminist, "Glorious Playfellow," instead of mother. The heroes in Dell's novels, always sensitive young rebels, are uncertain of how to act toward women and tended to play dreamy, passive roles. Their girl friends, like the heroine of *Moon Calf,* preferred conventional males who could provide stability and a home. Some rebels feared unconscious homosexual or narcissistic drives. The problem of identity, what one thought of oneself in relation to one's society, troubled some rebels who were never analyzed. Sherwood Anderson referred to himself as a "confused child in a confused world"; he remained skeptical about analysis because he believed that passion could not be turned into science. Margaret Anderson lamented, "I have no place in the world, no fixed position. I don't know just what kind of thing I am. Nobody else seems to know either."[24]

Those who sought help from the analyst sometimes were seriously disturbed and no one else seemed quite so fitted to deal with their disorders, or perhaps was so sympathetic to their point of view. They had largely rejected parental values and conventional social guides. Few of them had ever been deeply religious, or they had rejected what faith they once practiced. The analyst offered something quite new in American life: a casuistry of the soul, scientific, pragmatic, up-to-date—and associated with a new frankness. In free association, you could express yourself with complete, if sometimes painful, candor.[25] Where Christian Science and New Thought healers were "vague and emotional," the analysts were "sophisticated and precise." They combined the novelist's knowledge of motives, the poet's of symbols. Ministering to both mind and body, this priest of the future could preside at weddings, and with information gained through intimate confessions would contribute to a knowledge of women's psychology.[26]

Yet, for many of these intellectual patients, the analyst was not ringed with a supernatural aura and was not even an authoritative figure. Therapy was something of an untried scientific game; any intellectual worth his salt had every right to be critical. At least that was the attitude of Max Eastman and to some extent of Mabel Dodge. Despite such occasional skepticism, it became more and more usual for New York intellectuals to consult psychoanalysts. Walter Lippmann reported that by the late 1920s he was the only one of his circle of friends, chiefly writers, who had *not* been analyzed.[27]

The experiences of three patients—Dell, Mabel Dodge, and Max Eastman—illustrate some of the problems of sexual emancipation and the ways in which psychoanalysis met profound personal needs. Dell spent much of his life searching for harmony, order, reconciliation. His mother, a former school teacher, whom he adored, expected great things from him, and he was something of a prodigy. He grew up at a time when his father, once a prosperous butcher, had been reduced to odd jobs and glorious memories of the Civil War. One Christmas Dell, then six, realized that his family was pitifully poor, that his father was ineffectual and had failed in ways school texts and manuals united in condemning: he could not make a living. Socialism, to which Dell became converted in Davenport, Iowa, allowed him a reconciliation with his father, who was now not a failure but a brave man who had endured the ravages of an unjust society. Dell grew up something of a mamma's boy, an aesthete, a constant reader in the public libraries of mid-western towns. Dell's first shy and tentative relationships with girls changed into affairs. In Chicago he saw Isadora Duncan dance, lectured at Hull House, and married a school teacher. But there were other love affairs and the marriage broke up. In Greenwich Village, where Dell went at the age of 26 to become perhaps its best-known symbol and spokesman, the end of a long-standing liaison scandalized his older friends, who took free unions more seriously. Dell grew tired of falling in and out of love, and wanted to settle down.[28]

Dell was not living up to his own expectations, which had always been high. His realization of his family's poverty had crushed his ambition to go to college and become a Republican president. In both Chicago and New York he was considered an able, imaginative critic, but he aspired to more than journalism and dreamt of writing a novel.

Like other young intellectuals he cultivated the habit of self-expressive confession and left a long record of his psychoanalysis. Although he was unhappy and dissatisfied, he hesitated to be analyzed because like most laymen he believed a sharp line separated the sick and the well. You were either "all there" or should be locked up. The "miraculous results" of psycho-analysis were for people *in extremis,* on the point of suicide, for example. Besides, psychoanalysis was a new faction-ridden science, not yet a "recognized branch of the medical profession." He found its literature full of "strange and baffling technical terms not to be found in any dictionary," and full of "Teutonic heaviness and mugginess."

In 1917–18 Dell consulted Dr. Samuel Tannenbaum, who charged a pittance. Perhaps Dell, like Eastman, was too glib a patient. Dreams, associations, memories poured out apparently without resistance. The analysis was never completed, but Dell considered it a great success. It gave a "new emotional center" to his life, a sense of order and harmony and a world view as important, he believed, as the Darwinian or Marxian. He also gained self-knowledge: he was still a child who never wished to leave its mother's arms; he was afraid to settle down for fear he might be hurt.[29]

The analysis left Dell more productive than ever before. He was "freer and happier"; he could even read the "hidden secrets" of the many friends who consulted him as if he were a fortune teller. He finished his novel, *Moon Calf,* which went through eleven editions and sold 38,000 copies in 1921. It established his reputation, in the opinion of some critics, as a significant literary talent, the equal of Sinclair Lewis. He married and had two children.

For all his delight in nude swimming parties and uninhibited girls, beneath the surface of his bohemianism were longings for peace, quiet, and the desire to fulfill a responsible social role. Perhaps he hoped to succeed where his father had failed. In 1920 he moved to Croton-on-Hudson, a refuge for the more serious Greenwich Village inhabitants, who disliked the postwar invasion of eccentrics and rich people from uptown.[30]

Dell never felt at home in the disillusioned postwar world. He hated the new literature of violence, chaos, and despair, what he called the bloody and stinking "disjecta membra" of psychoanalysis. Ironically he was admired as a courageous apostle of Free Love after he had renounced that enthusiasm. It is ironic, also, that his novel *Janet March* was banned in New York and Massachusetts because it "reeked of sex." Like most Dell novels, it dealt with premarital relations that always ended in marriage because hero and heroine longed for home and children. But it also contained references to venereal disease, prostitution, abortion, Greenwich Village orgies, and psychoanalysis. As Dell's novels became more sentimental, critics who once thought him promising ignored him.[31]

Dell also hated the new lack of seriousness, the abandonment by many of the younger intellectuals of the old causes—feminism, progressive education, politics. Dell quite logically became an ardent mental hygienist and considered the movement "one of the most gigantic and romantic in human history." His study of sex, *Love in the Machine Age,* was puritanically devoted to monogamy, normalcy, homes, and children—"comfortable spawning," his old friend Max Eastman called it. The psychoanalytic psychiatrist, William Alanson White considered the book superb; the *Times of India* compared him to Malinowski and Havelock Ellis. Dell mixed Marxism and psychoanalysis to insist that patriarchal society, based on the inheritance of property, was inimical to emotional maturity, defined as the capacity to enjoy marriage and parenthood. A new system of education was needed that would bring both sexes together early so they could find the right mate and marry young. Monogamy was an innate human instinct, and child-raising the most important of all social functions. In fact, every individual psychic maladjustment not directly physiological in origin was "always found to be due to bad parental influences," Dell wrote. He denounced Ellis, the god of the rebellion, for not studying the family with sufficient zeal. Dell became something of a lay authority on psychoanalysis and mental hygiene, and spoke at the first International Congress on Mental Hygiene in 1930. By 1933 women's clubs, which he often addressed, were becoming more interested than the intellectuals in psychoanalysis. Like socialism, psychoanalysis and mental hygiene had brought Dell another kind of reconciliation. Beginning as an outsider, he became, in his own fashion, an authority and an expert. Malcolm Cowley recalled that his postwar generation of younger writers referred to him derisively as "Freud" Dell.[32]

Psychoanalysis did not domesticate Mabel Dodge as it domesticated Dell. Coming from the secure, upper reaches of Buffalo society, she found rebellion an enjoyable experience. It did not, as in the case of Dell, exacerbate already existing anxieties about one's family's alienation from approved patterns of American success. Mrs. Dodge was wealthy enough to do as she pleased. She epitomized the sexually emancipated woman pursuing serious love. Moreover, she was sustained by a faith in her own inner light. Her road from Buffalo to Italy to Greenwich Village, from Maurice Stern to John Reed to D. H. Lawrence, and marriage to the Taos Indian Tony Luhan was fairly straight. From childhood she had a thirst for excitement Buffalo did not slake. There, as Van Wyck Brooks remarked rather dramatically, she always knew "those privities that people 'didn't tell each other' until someone was discovered hanging from a hook in a closet." She rebelled against reticence by a life-long dedication to telling her own and other people's secrets.[33]

Her first approach to psychoanalysis sounded purely experimental. One day at lunch, probably in 1914, she told the writer Edward Arlington Robinson that she might try one of the new soul doctors. "Dangerous business, perhaps," he replied. "Maybe the cure is worse than the disease."

In fact, acute emotional pain and jealousy in an unhappy love affair drove her to analysis. Her friend—Maurice Stern, a sculptor and painter who had spent a year living in Bali—had tea one day with an attractive Russian woman. This gave Dodge a sleepless night and drove her to write to Dr. Smith Ely Jelliffe: "I want very much to see you to discuss the possibility of your analyzing me. I am obliged to admit to having a jealousy complex which has produced an anxiety neurosis with an increasing compulsory action on my behavior. . . . "[34] Jelliffe was bursting at the seams with knowledge, a Freudian with "Roman Catholic emotions" and a "religious love for Bergson's philosophy," Max Eastman recalled.

In his analysis of Dodge, he informed her that she should give up Stern, and talked endlessly about Phoebus Apollo and the psyche. She wrote to Jelliffe, "I am aghast at the mystery of psychoanalysis! No wonder it's called a major operation! *You* can hardly know more than your patients what will come out of an analysis!"[35] Jelliffe kept elaborate notes on her dreams. But while Jelliffe was away she had a crisis. "I went out of my head one night— then got hysteric pains—then chills and fever which they called malaria." In Jelliffe's absence, she consulted A. A. Brill. He was "brisk and business like" and wanted her to be active in "movements, Leagues, Unions." Normality was his goal for patients. "Well, my job is with the norm," he said. "The normal, average life—that is quite an achievement, you know. Do not call it subnormal until you can live it."[36]

Sometimes Brill's interpretations startled her, and she liked him because he was "so real and substantial":

> At times one could see his eyes alter in expression while he sat peering at one behind his specs. Something swam and fused and glowed in his gray pupils, and one was able to observe the act of ratiocination. . . . After a moment of this fireless cooking, he would generally announce something devastating but intense that would make one jump. . . .

Dodge found Brill's brand of psychoanalysis too coldly scientific, too antimystical, too dogmatically antireligious. "He consistently tried to remove every vestige of my belief in an inner power . . . and said scathing things about a Jehovah complex."[37]

She was poised between two incompatible viewpoints, the vestiges of Transcendentalism and the rigors of scientific materialism. Like some of the rebels, she accepted her intuitions as manifestations of the life force but Jelliffe's Bergsonian and Jungian idealism was unsatisfactory. On the other hand, Brill was too scientific. All the while she was seeing Brill, she was also consulting a mystical healer, Emma Curtis Hopkins, who had developed her own "spiritual lessons" after studying with Mary Baker Eddy.[38] But Dodge remained a friend of Brill and Jelliffe, and kept them informed of her reading and her enthusiasms. Brill replied with fatherly admonitions. He wished D. H. Lawrence, for instance, had used more delicate language in *Lady Chatterly:*

> I think it is a very good book and I really feel that it was an abreaction on his part, to make it so pornographic in spots. Of course, you will say that it is just a frank expression of things. I maintain that he could have expressed himself in the same way without having recourse to some of the expressions he uses. It would have made the book universally acceptable instead of limiting it to a small circle of readers.[39]

Of all the rebellious intellectuals, Max Eastman became perhaps the most disillusioned with psychoanalysis. Like Mrs. Dodge, he had tried other varieties of mind cures. He entered psychoanalytic therapy because he was afraid he might commit adultery.[40] He came from a long line of New Englanders and his father and mother were both Congregational ministers; being virtuous was a family calling. Like Dell, Eastman was deeply attached to his mother, something of a bluestocking who enjoyed prescribing panaceas for her family—raw food, walking barefoot in the dew, Fletcherism, deep breathing. Eastman attended Columbia, studied philosophy with John Dewey, and agitated for women's suffrage. When he took over *The Masses,* he gathered a brilliant group of contributors, including his associate editor John Reed.

Yet despite his literary success, his good looks, his ability to move in both academic and Bohemian circles, he was uncomfortable, worried, and anxious. Sex deeply troubled him. He began to be afraid he might be unfaithful to his wife, although, he said, lust did not distress him unless it was "cheap, flip, facetious and vulgar."[41]

Dr. Beatrice Hinkle, who became a Jungian analyst and whom he had met at a New Thought sanitarium, suggested he try Jelliffe, who charged him only a small fee. Like Dell, Eastman read every book he could about psychoanalysis and became a "kind of amateur specialist in mental healing." All the psychoanalytic explanations of his neurosis seemed plausible, but not very helpful: "homosexuality, mother fixation, Oedipus, Electra and inferiority complexes, narcissism, exhibitionism, autoeroticism, the 'masculine protest.'" Jelliffe failed to convince him. Eastman found that Brill, whom he also consulted, had an "intuitive sensitivity toward people . . . that made . . . him a master in the clinic." Eastman concluded, however that psychoanalysis with its "pseudo-scientific jargon" was for the really sick. All he needed was a little common sense about his own problems, and psychoanalysis got in the way of it. So he abandoned treatment without result.[42]

Like a number of other radical analysands, Eastman was bothered by the economic conservatism of the analysts. Psychoanalysis seemed to take the radical starch out of its patients. After therapy, rebels against bourgeois morality became conventional or lost their political radicalism. Joseph Freeman speculated that since troubled sexuality was one of the chief causes of rebellion, once sexual problems had been solved the way would be opened for a reconciliation with society.[43] Eastman finally decided that Freud was not a scientist, and neither liked nor practiced rigorous experiment. Instead, he resembled Paracelsus, who was interested in magic as well as science. Nor did he know the whole field of psychology well. Freud was a prude and Puritan who believed cocaine was a miracle. Nevertheless he had made psychology dynamic by discovering that repression led to neurosis and by incorporating the wish and the instinctive drive.[44]

Brill, Jelliffe, and Beatrice Hinkle remained the favorite analysts of the intellectuals. But the Village was the home of a few practitioners who operated well outside the circle of respectable physicians. Dell had consulted one of them, Samuel Tannenbaum. To the left of nearly every other Freudian, he had once caused scandal by suggesting that prostitutes were more healthful for young men than abstinence or masturbation. Later he repudiated psychoanalysis altogether. In the 1920s Samuel Schmalhausen, alias S. D. House, a layman, also practiced therapy. He collaborated closely with V. F. Calverton, the Marxist editor of *Modern Quarterly,* and edited a number of popular books such as *Why We Misbehave* and *Sex in Civilization.* Newspapers attributed the death of a favorite enemy of the rebels, John Roach Stratton, the fundamentalist preacher, to a debate in Boston with Calverton.[45]

The most notorious of the lay analysts, Andre Tridon, propounded a "hard boiled" and cynical interpretation of a hybrid psychoanalysis in the early 1920s. A French immigrant with a heavy accent, Tridon wore a lustrous black beard, dressed impeccably, and gilded his toenails for costume parties. His books probably sold better than those of any other psychoanalytic popularizer. An advertisement for one of them read: "Do you ever dream of your 'ideal' mate . . . why do lovers kiss? How do our glands affect us? Now science has revealed the cause of love. . . . " With some exaggeration Bernard de Voto remarked that Tridon was so popular in the early 1920s that he made "every sofa a consulting room." A number of intellectuals, among them H. L. Mencken and Joseph Freeman, found that Tridon made Freud intelligible. Tridon was "good propaganda," Freeman thought, for psychology's "war against the stale and desperate morality which we have inherited from the muddled ages preceding ours."

Tridon's version of psychoanalysis was close to that of Emma Goldman, with whom he worked at the anarchist Ferrer School. Born outside Paris, he had trained for the diplomatic service, emigrated to New York in 1903 at the age of 25, and worked for the *New York Tribune* and the *Sun.* He celebrated sexual passion in a play, *Ave Venus,* written for the Ferrer School, and in 1913 published *The New Unionism,* a study dealing mainly with syndicalism and the I. W. W. in which he dismissed Bergson as a dilettante and Sorel as a traditional Christian moralist who regrettably advocated chastity. To Tridon, prostitution and "platonic love" were equally morbid and unnatural.[46] The origins of his interest in psychoanalysis are not entirely clear, but he may have heard of it from Emma Goldman or from the Dodge circle. Possibly he translated Freud's essay "'Civilized' Sexual Morality and Modern Nervousness" for Dr. William J. Robinson, who campaigned for birth control and sex education. The young publisher B. W. Huebsch, who had brought out Tridon's study of unionism, sensed the need for a simple manual on psychoanalysis and asked Tridon to write one. *Psychoanalysis, Its History, Theory and Practice* was published in 1919 and sold some 10,000 copies. Tridon turned out still others.[47]

Tridon's books were almost caricatures of the eclecticism, optimism, and simplification of the American medical popularizers. His interpretation of psychoanalysis was probably the most extreme and libertarian then published in America. He repudiated the vitalism of Bergson, which had given a spiritual emphasis to White's and Putnam's discussion of libido theory. He repudiated romantic love and tenderness. He thought sublimation an absurdity. He was a thoroughgoing moral relativist, a materialist, and a behaviorist in the rawest sense. He became the "enfant terrible" of psychoanalysis and the bane of the serious medical analysts.[48]

Psychoanalysis and Love, published in 1923, was his most "shocking" book. Because men and women were "rutting animals," lasting love could only be a variety of fetishism and therefore "tainted with neurosis." The healthy animal was neither willing nor able to forgo sexual gratification. The "successful lover" enjoyed the best of health, the regular action of heart and glands. Depression, even to the point of suicide, awaited the "unsuccessful lover." Despite this apparent toughmindedness, Tridon was a utopian. "Free love," based on sexual and intellectual attraction, if practiced together with birth control, would rid the world of morons, neurotics, and the insane.[49]

Tridon refused to identify sexual libido with the "life force." Libido was entirely physiological, "one of the manifestations of the electric stream produced in the brain and seeking an outlet." Endocrinology made sublimation, that relic of old-fashioned ethics, ridiculously implausible. Tridon talked far more incautiously than the analyst Horace Frink about Pavlovian reflexes and gland secretions. The biological researches of Edward J. Kempf, a psychiatrist at St. Elizabeth's who was revising psychoanalysis, suggested that in a "few years" physicians could produce or remove by "chemical or physical means' heredity or instincts. Rejecting the pessimism of many conventional psychiatrists, Tridon used Kempf to suggest that 80 percent of all insane patients could be cured.[50]

Since love was physical, romantic love, or "sex romance," was a "poisonous element" in human life. "Tenderness," "admiration," and so on had been given "unique prominence for the purpose of drawing a veil over the gross physical phenomena of sex." Here was a full-scale repudiation of romantic love, and that repudiation, according to Joseph Wood Krutch, was the chief contribution of psychoanalysis to the modern temper. Always eager to shock the middle classes, Tridon announced that "the wife who never tires of singing her husband's praises is always somebody else's mistress."51

To Tridon the Puritan was a pervert, possibly with a homosexual tendency, who wished to destroy the attractiveness of women. Prudery was the "usual cloak for unbridled sexual craving," he remarked in a reference to purity crusaders.52

Yet he was not merely a joyous, amoral pagan come to lead New Yorkers to Cythera. He attempted to establish a "scientific" ethic. Since life was meant to be lived fully and joyfully, men would learn to ignore the Bible or the Talmud or Lao Tse, and would cite Pasteur or Edison instead. But he did insist that free lovers should agree to live together until their children reached the age of 15.53

Tridon's eclecticism exceeded White's; nobody was an orthodox Freudian any more, he insisted. He claimed to have joined Adler's Association for Individual Psychology after the discovery within himself of something more important than sex—a "positive, progressive egotistical impulse."54

Tridon may have been especially sensitive to the new styles of role behavior the intellectuals were setting and refused to draw any line between the typically masculine and the typically feminine. The new woman could seek men for gratification without "silly shame."

Psychoanalytic therapy, in Tridon's version, was a simple exercise. Unconscious troubles, he wrote, turned out to be as powerless and insignificant as a "small mouse." Without much apparent effort, the analyst "disintegrated" complex after complex. He even resuscitated the pre-Freudian tradition of self-help: "self-analysis" if made as common as the toothbrush miraculously would reduce conflict and strife.55

Tridon's first primers were well received by some reviewers. The *Nation* considered *Psychoanalysis, Its History, Theory and Practice* "useful"; Dell thought it a "satisfactory" introduction. Even more beginning texts were needed, Dell insisted, if psychoanalysis were to be widely understood. William J. Fielding, a journalist whom Tridon appreciatively quoted, welcomed the book in the *New York Call*. In the social workers' *Survey*, Bernard Glueck, a psychiatrist trained at St. Elizabeth's, announced that Tridon and other popularizers would be welcome as long as the academic psychologists kept up their attacks on psychoanalysis.56

Some found Tridon trivial and confused but his most indignant readers were the medical psychoanalysts who in 1922 were confronted with a mysterious new volume allegedly by Freud. Called *Dream Psychology for Beginners,* it purported to be a new work to which Tridon had been invited to write an introduction but was in fact excerpts pirated from previous English translations of Freud's studies of dreams. Tridon's American publishers refused to withdraw it despite protests, and Ernest Jones noted wryly that the *Psycho-analytic Review* had reviewed it at face value. Tridon, he informed Freud, was "an unscrupulous and ignorant exploiter of psychoanalysis."[57]

In an interview with an American correspondent in 1921 Freud expressed his anger at Andre Tridon's piracy: "That man is a thief. That man stole the text of two of my articles, combined them into a book and signed his own name to it. . . . Under American law that kind of stealing seems to be permitted."[58] It was neither the first nor the last of Freud's animadversions on the American scene.

In 1922 Tridon enjoyed another triumph in an address to four or five hundred members of the National Opera Club at a "psychic tea." The chairwoman hailed the spirit of the "unclad flapper" and urged members to throw off their corsets so they could "learn wonderful things." Tridon defended psychoanalysis from all the "horrid charges made against it." It was not a bath in sexual filth or a means of carrying on an obscene conversation with a decent woman. Rather, it was a scientific method of understanding and treating nervous disease. Tridon was followed on the Opera Club program by a speaker who believed it was possible to photograph spirits.[59]

Seven months later Tridon died of cancer at the age of 46. He had summoned the press to his deathbed and his entourage gave out laudatory but dubious information which became enshrined in the *Times* obituary. It called him the "foremost psychoanalyst in America," who had translated the works of Sigmund Freud and Alfred Adler. His six or eight books on psychoanalysis had been adopted at Dartmouth College and the University of Oklahoma. He had planned to give a paper before the Psychoanalytic Congress in Munich.[60]

The radical image of psychoanalysis initiated in America by Emma Goldman in 1910 was carried to its most extreme by Tridon in the 1920s. Tridon identified psychoanalysis with Greenwich Village, bohemia, free love, and socialism. Perhaps with the example of Tridon in mind, Freudian physicians soon took steps to see that no layman could become a psychoanalyst.

Because they believed that instincts were beneficent and conventional morals rather absurd and unhealthy relics of Puritanism, the intellectuals made the psychoanalytic process far easier than did the medical psychoanalysts. To Dell, Mabel Dodge, and Tridon, it was a glorified catharsis, not very difficult or demanding in itself. Once one's childish and primitive wishes were fully brought to the surface of consciousness they were easily tamed. Dell gave therapy an aura of magical self-improvement: somehow it led to greater happiness and creativity, to internal peace and social success.

The prewar rebels became more influential in the early 1920s. Floyd Dell, who before had been relatively obscure, became, for a time, a widely admired writer. O'Neill, Sherwood Anderson, and Theodore Dreiser were reaching a wider audience and achieving critical approval. Members of the younger generation, such as Joseph Freeman, who graduated from Columbia in 1919, had been admirers of Dell and his generation because of their courageous unconventionality. With books like *Janet March* and *Love in*

Greenwich Village, Dell continued to exploit that reputation. The war had accelerated changes in styles of behavior that the rebels had self-consciously adopted before it. The intellectuals themselves and the causes they advanced became associated with psychoanalysis by both admirers and opponents.[61]

However, a radical, liberationist vision was not the only way in which American intellectuals construed Freud, although it was the most conspicuous mode in the 1920s. By 1929 Walter Lippmann had become disenchanted with the "liberation" that flourished not only in novels but in life. He attempted to create a humanistic, nonreligious moral system based on some of Freud's theoretical departures of the 1920s. He believed that psychoanalysis fostered a conscious, mature adjustment to reality and a stoical detachment from passion. According to Lippmann, Freud taught that "the passage from infancy to maturity" was a "transition from the dominion of momentary pleasure and pain to the dominion of reality."[62] Following the argument of Freud's follower Sandor Ferenczi, Lippmann announced that the infant's and the child's sense of pleasure and omnipotence clashed rudely with external reality, including the wishes of other people. Gradually, in those who attained real maturity the pleasure principal was renounced for a "full appreciation of the force of circumstance." Psychoanalysis demonstrated that powerful passions of which people were unaware often swayed their lives, and analysts had developed an elaborate technique for helping a patient "thread his way back through a chain of associations to the buried passion and fetch it forth into consciousness." This essential principal of psychoanalysis had been "discovered and rediscovered" by shrewd observers of human nature over the past two thousand years: "that to become detached from one's passions and to understand them consciously is to render them disinterested." The rewards of such maturity were a "sustained and more even enjoyment, and serenity in the presence of inescapable evil." Judging from recent novels and from the lives he knew, Lippmann concluded that those who had exercised their new sexual privileges without external restraint or inhibition had found not happiness, but "the wasteland."[63]

5

Popular and Applied Psychoanalysis: Mental Hygiene, Criminology, and the Schools, 1917–1940

Before America entered the Great War, the popularization of psychoanalysis had reached far beyond literary circles and New York's Greenwich Village. Publicity in mass magazines and popular books had begun around 1915 and reached a peak in the early 1920s. The next forty years saw a widening public acquaintance with psychoanalysis, and the beginning of its influence on American criminology, child guidance, the schools, and attitudes toward sexual behavior. This chapter will take up that early influence, the popular images of Freud and psychoanalysis, and the growth of a psychoanalytic clientele.

Cultural and generational conflicts in the years between 1920 and 1940 exacerbated the anxieties that led a growing number of Americans to consult the new experts in personality—the psychologists, psychiatrists, and psychoanalysts. One major conflict that still persists occurred between the traditional religious values of Roman Catholics and fundamentalists on the one hand and "modern," "liberal" values on the other. An important aspect of this clash occurred over the accelerating breakdown of "civilized" morality after the Great War. The "scientific" experts dispensing advice about problems of sexuality, family, and child-raising came down on the side of the "liberal" and the "modern," in identifiable dogmas that still persist. Anxieties also were generated by the demands of an increasingly technological, bureaucratic, and consumer-oriented society, which required higher levels of education, technical expertise, social adroitness, and "adjustment." The Depression later added new anxieties.

These cultural cleavages and social demands exacerbated problems of sex and career, intensifying the old American preoccupation with the imperative of self-improvement, a task which was becoming increasingly complex in the new society. Appropriately, Alfred Adler's "inferiority complex," the forerunner of a lack of "self-esteem" became a frequent complaint in the interwar years. One of the rewards promised by a popularized psychoanalysis was increased vocational efficiency and personal satisfaction.

For many members of the educated middle and upper middle classes, the groups most deeply involved in the changes in cultural styles, the physician, rather than the clergyman, became the adjudicator of personal and social problems. As an authority versed in esoteric knowledge of both body and mind, the medical psychoanalyst became a uniquely qualified guide in a period of changing sexual mores and social styles. As religious laws and decrees were giving way to "scientific" ones among many of the well educated, psychoanalytic theory prescribed the softening of the too rigid conscience and accommodated new and untraditional modes of behavior.

The writers and intellectuals who favored these cultural departures and who first consulted a psychoanalyst about their troubles contributed the nucleus of what an American sociologist has called the "friends and supporters of psychotherapy," an unstructured urban coterie that provided a major source of patients. A psychoanalyst recalled that in the early days his referrals came primarily from laymen, not from physicians; the best recommendations for psychoanalysis were from the intimate friends of those who had been successfully treated.[1] The members of this coterie tended to come from particular occupational groups, young professionals in the arts, education, social work, entertainment, and communications, all professions that placed a premium on verbal skills, the very basis of psychoanalytic therapy. Patients also included businessmen, students, engineers, dentists, physicians, and middle-class housewives.

At first centered in New York, Washington, Baltimore and Boston, psychoanalysis gradually spread to large cities in the Midwest and on the West Coast, as physicians and laymen with or without training experimented with psychoanalytic methods and attracted new loose coteries of patients. Then in the 1930s the few trained practitioners outside the eastern seaboard were reinforced by the influx of European analysts who were encouraged to settle in the cities of the hinterlands. Psychoanalysis remained a phenomenon anchored in major urban centers.

From the beginning, psychoanalysis was expensive and required a well-to-do clientele, except for those patients analysts saw in clinics and public mental hospitals. Beginners and some Greenwich Village practitioners may have charged little, especially during the Depression. However, by 1936, established psychoanalysts were earning $5 to $10 or more an hour, and their patients were paying $5000 and up for a year's treatment.[2]

Members of the social elites and some college teachers and their families took up psychoanalysis, and by the 1930s supporters could be found among Boston Brahmins, wealthy New Yorkers, Philadelphia Main Line families, Chicago's merchant princes—Putnams, Tiffanys, Biddles, Fields, Warburgs —and among faculties at Harvard, Yale, and Smith, for instance. Some were patients, others were in training as psychoanalysts here or abroad, some were patrons of the new psychoanalytic institutes or interested intellectuals from a variety of university disciplines. The professional and upper-middle-class clientele of psychoanalysis was well established by 1940.

Psychoanalysis appealed to these patients because it promised an optimistic therapy for a wide variety of human ailments, from sexual disorders to some kinds of mental illness. Moreover, for many patients, the literary qualities of psychoanalysis, the fascination of its case histories, the drama of its therapy and the verbal skills it required held a special attraction. Psychoanalytic preoccupations pervaded the new literature of the 1920s and cut close to the bone of human experience: dreams and the unconscious, childhood and sexuality, family relationships, love, aggression, and death.

All these topics were reflected in the growing publicity about psychoanalysis which attracted new patients who in turn provided a market for yet more information. A stream of books of varying quality and seriousness dealt with psychoanalysis, ranging from popular tomes such as J. Arthur Thompson's *Outline of Science* or the Encyclopedia Britannica's *These Eventful Years* to the "Little Blue Books," tiny paperbacks published in Girard, Kansas, with provocative titles such as *Sex in Psychoanalysis, Freud on Sleep and Sexual Dreams,* and *How to Psychoanalyze Yourself.*[3] By 1940 newspapers in major cities including New York, Chicago, Washington, Baltimore, Boston, Kansas City, Topeka, San Francisco, and Los Angeles had dealt with Freud and his therapy. Journalists interviewed psychoanalysts for newspapers and magazines, recorded their testimony in criminal trials, and sought their opinions about social problems. New York's New School for Social Research, a center for avant-garde and radical views, sponsored popular lectures by European psychoanalysts, including Sandor Ferenczi, Fritz Wittels, Erich Fromm, and Karen Horney. After one of Ferenczi's lecture trips, the psychoanalyst Smith Ely Jelliffe wrote to Ernest Jones that the "Bolshevik, free love Feminists, Greenwich Village bunch" had enveloped Ferenczi like a cloud.[4]

Publicity fed an apparently insatiable hunger for more news about the new psychology, psychiatry, and "mental hygiene." "The demand for information is so great that we are simply swamped with inquiries and appeals," Frankwood Williams, a psychoanalytic psychiatrist and medical director of the National Committee for Mental Hygiene, observed in 1924. His medical school friend Harry Kerns, the newly appointed mental hygiene psychiatrist at West Point, asked for suitable reading because he was "besieged by people who want to read books on psychoanalysis."[5] In 1925 the *Occult Digest* advertised two Chicago "colleges" offering courses in psychoanalysis, "a dignified and remunerative profession," that would enable a student to become "a master of men."[6] By 1940, the newspaper- and magazine-reading public was familiar with a number of psychoanalytic conceptions defined in widely varied ways: the unconscious, the importance of early childhood and of sexuality, repression, psychological conflict, a continuum between normal and abnormal, dreams as expressions of repressed emotions.[7]

The 1920s began, friends and foes agreed, with a popular cult of psychoanalysis that envisioned it as a mode of sexual liberation and a debunking of romantic love by a new generation of writers.[8] The college student hero of Percy Marks's popular novel *The Plastic Age* "had heard plenty of fellows argue that love was nothing but sexual attraction anyway, and that all the stuff the poets wrote was pure bunk. Freud said something like that, he thought, and Freud knew a damn sight more about it than the poets."[9] A character in Eugene O'Neill's *Strange Interlude* considered himself "immune to love through his scientific understanding of its real sexual nature."[10] This popular vision of a hard-boiled and de-romanticizing psychoanalysis was closely associated with postwar disillusionment and with the celebration of sexuality in the novels of James Joyce, D. H. Lawrence, James Branch Cabell, and Ernest Hemingway, the very opposite of the "bloodless old maid's catalogue" of polite prewar fiction. "The Freudian novel, at times hell-bent on novelty and shock is in the ascendant," wrote an unsympathetic psychologist.[11] A hostile critic argued that "Hemingway did not write until after the latter-day psychologists had robbed man of his consciousness—and of all his impulses except those issuing from fear, hate and lust."[12]

Some psychoanalysts believed Freud had inspired much of the modern avant-garde literary output. Karl Menninger, the Kansas psychiatrist and psychoanalyst, observed that Joyce's *Ulysses* resembled the free associations of analytic patients, and that Eugene O'Neill had introduced more people to psychoanalysis "than all the scientific books put together." Psychoanalysis supplied material for the theater and the movies and treatment for actors and playwrights. Three years before O'Neill began *Mourning Becomes Electra,* with its theme of mother fixation, he had lain on the black leather couch of the psychoanalytic psychiatrist G. V. Hamilton in treatment for drinking and marital problems and learned that he suffered from an Oedipus complex. He may have provided data for Hamilton's survey of sexuality among professional New Yorkers, *A Research in Marriage.* Moss Hart's *Lady in the Dark* in 1941 was a highly successful musical comedy about the heroine's psychoanalytic treatment, written as a tribute to Hart's own analyst.[13] In the 1930s several other major playwrights, among them Lillian Hellman, were psychoanalyzed, and Thornton Wilder visited Freud in Vienna. Psychoanalysis burgeoned in Hollywood as well, and psychoanalysts Ernst Simmel and Ralph Greenson were treating movie people, some of whom had come from Germany where they first had become acquainted with Freud.[14]

A few conspicuous events marked the course of the popularization. At the Loeb-Leopold trial of 1924, psychoanalytic psychiatrists testified for the defense of two teenage Jewish boys who had murdered a younger boy. In 1930 the International Mental Hygiene Congress brought 3000 people, including a bevy of psychoanalysts, to Washington, D.C. In 1931 a banquet in

New York honoring Freud's birthday was attended by major liberal and "progressive" American cultural heroes, among them Theodore Dreiser; John Dewey, the educator; legal reformers such as Jerome Frank; social workers; psychiatrists A. A. Brill and Adolf Meyer; a sprinkling of the socially elect.[15]

The 1930s brought a new seriousness to some of the popularizations, reflecting a more accurate knowledge of Freud's theories. This partly resulted from the determined efforts of the new institute-trained psychoanalytic elite to purify psychoanalysis, linking it to science, medicine, psychiatry, and above all to new and systematic training, Freudian orthodoxy, and the elimination of quack analysts. Protagonists argued that psychoanalysis, like much of modern technology, was a triumph of inductive reasoning, "observation and experimentation," and was creating a "science of man." The new psychoanalytic institutes were establishing the most exacting professional standards, "a record of responsibilities and self-exactions of which the public is little aware."[16]

The image of Freud as well as of the profession grew steadily larger and more flattering in the years from 1920 to 1940. From an iconoclast, he had become, by 1939, a liberal sage, the victim of Nazi persecution, and even more than Albert Einstein, a creator of the outlook of 20th-century man. This achievement was attributed to him despite the fact that many, like Havelock Ellis, regarded him as more artist than scientist.

As a celebrity, Freud was interviewed by American foreign correspondents, including in 1923 Dorothy Thompson, a pundit briefly married to the novelist Sinclair Lewis. She found in Freud a sense of humor that contrasted with the solemn reticence of his Viennese pupils, who seemed like the secretive adherents of a religious sect in sharp contrast to their talkative American colleagues. "The professor is a stocky man with a pointed beard and keenly humorous eyes. He hates affectation and pose, and I wondered, listening to him, how he could stand his pupils. He joins them in hating dilettantism in a study which is a serious science, and speaks with exasperation of the American movement as a 'fad,' but he does not shut up all inquiry with a phrase." When Thompson asked Freud whether he would like to "psycho-analyze Europe in the hope of finding a cure for her ills," he replied, "I never take a patient to whom I can offer no hope."[17]

The foreign correspondent H. V. Kaltenborn reported that Freud was one of the few "supermen" who had remained balanced and detached during the war. Granted a five-minute interview, he discovered that his cab driver knew the way to Freud's apartment, where "30 or 40" patients improbably filled the tiny waiting room. Freud cautioned against psychoanalytic "fakers." "I am not responsible for the extent to which my teachings are being misused and misapplied," he told Kaltenborn. "One should have nothing to do with self-styled psychoanalysts who have not had direct contact with me."[18]

The assumption of Freud's powerful influence on modern culture was shared by those who believed in his mission and those who detested it. Particularly in the 1920s, the departures of Adler and Jung suggested to observers as sympathetic as Havelock Ellis that Freud was a cult leader who expelled dissenting followers.[19] Andre Tridon announced in 1920 that leadership had passed from Freud to Jung, Adler, and the American psychiatrist Edward J. Kempf, who was busy biologizing and behaviorizing psychoanalysis. Some found Freud's history of the psychoanalytic movement narrow and mean-spirited.[20] But for most psychoanalytic psychiatrists, the prestige of Jung and Adler steadily declined as the American psychoanalytic movement became more professionally organized, more self-consciously "scientific," strengthened by the new institutes and the arrival of Freud's followers among the European refugees from Hitler's Germany.

In 1938 the Modern Library published *The Basic Writings of Sigmund Freud,* his first collection to sell widely in America. The 1930s ended with Freud's exile from Nazi Austria to London and the tributes at his death in 1939 when he appeared on the cover of *Time.*[21] A sign of his growing influence and respectability came when the *American Journal of Sociology* devoted an entire memorial issue to him in November 1939, with tributes from sexologists, analysts, sociologists, literary critics.[22]

In 1939 the critic Bernard de Voto argued that Freud had provided nothing less than a new language to describe human nature. The "basic principles of his work" had become part of the common intellectual property of mankind. "They are now implicit in the way men habitually think about one another and the most casual traffic of human beings, an advertisement on a billboard, two minutes' conversation on a subway platform—have shapes and emphases that result from a changed way of looking at the world." Reflecting a growing orthodoxy and the decline in the American fortunes of Jung and Adler, he argued that devotion to "the facts of behavior" distinguished Freud's scientifically purified psychoanalysis from Jung's "uncontrolled mysticism." Finally, as the new literature steadily had moved to coincide with Freud's world of subjective exploration, his theories had directed "light into the dark places of the mind." Moreover, "basic Freudian ideas have worked into education, the law, economics, history, sociology, criminology, and all other studies of society and the individual. . . . " Rejecting 19th-century optimism and positivism, Freud had explored the irrational to create a more accurate vision of reality. The result was a noble, stern, exalted, and tragic vision. The First World War had shown man to be incapable of discharging the obligations civilization required. "The new war, breaking out at the moment of his death, has given that terrible judgment the dignity of an old Testament rhapsody."[23] Freud's genius had been to explain to his contemporaries the profound sources within themselves that were responsible for the malaise of their own time.

Whereas before the First World War, psychoanalysis had been debated largely among conservative and radical intellectuals, by the early 1920s it was denounced in conservative mass magazines, associated not only with the new literature but with the debunking of traditional virtues, with the "unclad flapper" and what seemed to be an immoral rebellion of the young. A sympathetic observer noted that "Freud, in spite of his self portrait in the disguise of a mournful master of disillusion, has really abolished fear and phobia and helped the age to jazz and freedom. Besides this, jazz and freedom seemed to be bringing us to a higher standard of morality. . . . " But for a critic in the *Ladies Home Journal,* psychoanalysis was "indecency cloaked in scientific phrases"; it should be thrown out as a part of the lewd "jazz path to degradation," the road to the "disgraceful art of shimmy and toddle."[24] Psychoanalysis was associated with rumored changes in sexual behavior, with the new frankness about sex and what seemed to be endless discussions of it. A hostile Adlerian observed, "Freud found sex an outcast in the outhouse and he left it in the living room, an honored guest."[25]

The cultural struggle over psychoanalysis pitted conservative psychiatrists, psychologists, and religious leaders against liberal to radical Freud sympathizers within the same professional groups. But more than clashes within professions were involved. Psychoanalysis became a player in the cultural wars that pitted those who continued to defend "civilized" sexual morality, which prescribed continence, intercourse only for procreation, monogamous, lifelong marriage, and reticence about sex, against those who advocated birth control, divorce by mutual consent, and frank sex education. In these wars the psychoanalysts, as "scientific" and "modern" authorities, advocated birth control and sex education and supported the defense of Mary Ware Dennett, who was tried in 1929 for distributing obscene literature—a frank pamphlet of sex information she had written for her own children that was widely distributed by some Protestant churches, YMCAs, and mental hygienists.[26]

The cultural clash over styles of sexual behavior were clearly exemplified at Mrs. Dennett's trial. For her, the old attitudes were based on shame and fear and New England Puritanism, which she herself had rejected. Sex was a joyful, vitalizing normal human function, and masturbation a harmless outlet. To her opponents, her views were suggestive, lurid, obscene, advocated by "male and female bawds," and might debauch the weaker members of the younger generation. John Roach Stratton, pastor of New York's Calvary Baptist Church, observed that "this breaking down of standards of modesty and reserve, has come just at the time when there is every opportunity for indulgence in forbidden things—the unchaperoned dance, midnight joyrides, stage lewdness, vice and crime, portrayed by the moving pictures, with the inevitable ending of each romance, a hugging match and a kissing bee."[27]

The *Reviews of Reviews* summed up the clashing opinions in 1927:

> Psychoanalysis is a cult, unimportant because transitory; it is a pernicious influence of decadent modern life, leading to broken homes, immorality, and violent death; it is an interesting phase of a developing science and it is the salvation of the human race.[28]

The worst strictures of the conservative critics were reserved for the tenets of the popular cult which they assumed were the true doctrines of Freud. Charles Burr, a Philadelphia neurologist and an old enemy, argued that the literature of "Freudism" had harmed "thousands of unbalanced youths" with its popular doctrine that "suppressed unconscious desire is the great cause of mental disorder and that libido is the only really controlling thing in man." Burr recommended that Freudian practitioners be examined by a psychiatrist before being allowed to practice.[29] The Columbia psychologist Robert S. Woodworth, angered by a psychoanalytic study of Abraham Lincoln, denounced psychoanalysis for putting "a smear on high and beautiful things, lowering the level of thought and feeling . . . and all this under a pretense of scientific authority to which it has no better claim than it has to ordinary right mindedness or plain common sense."[30] And a Catholic physician who had become a member of a religious order insisted that according to Freud, absolute continence was incompatible with bodily or mental health and that psychoanalysis, a real danger to society, was out to conquer the world. At the same time some Protestant ministers, such as the popular liberal preacher Harry Emerson Fosdick, were finding the "new psychology," that is, psychoanalysis, valuable in the "daily work of their pastoral confessionals."[31]

Psychoanalysis was invoked to debunk and to satirize. H. L. Mencken, tongue in cheek, suggested that Freud preached the evils of repression:

> We know by Dr. Freud's appalling evidence what the suppression of the common wickednesses can do to the individual—how they can shake his reason on its throne, and even give him such things as gastritis, migraine and angina pectoris. . . . A vice crusader is simply an unfortunate who goes about with a brothel in his cellar; a Prohibitionist is one who has buried rum, but would have been safer drinking it.[32]

The "staid and solemn church deacon bets on horses," echoed another journalist. Social workers were informed that the English professor "who chuckles too audibly at Restoration literature is, perhaps, finding relief from a repressed emotional or sexual life." Max Eastman was delighted by the historian Preserved Smith's psychoanalytic study of Martin Luther's violence and sexuality. Theodore Roosevelt, Woodrow Wilson, and Abraham Lincoln were all "psyched."[33]

The most vocal of the analysts, A. A. Brill, who liked to shock, diagnosed Abraham Lincoln as a manic depressive and observed that an actor who was unfaithful to his wife "has the courage to put into operation what the average person secretly desires."[34] The *Psychoanalytic Review* published a series of anti-religious tracts by psychoanalytic enthusiasts. Franz Alexander judged Buddhist training to be an "artificial catatonia." Lorine Pruette, a psychologist trained at Clark and Columbia universities, argued that "the marriage vows were underwritten by the inferiority complex." Theodore Schroeder informed fifty clergymen that "institutionalized religion is the great single force in our society to preclude the better mental hygiene. . . . " Traditional religious values were to be replaced by an ill-defined "higher morality," of "healthy and unified impulses and emotions."[35]

The Harvard philosopher William Ernest Hocking lumped psycho-analysis with the ever-present party of revolt against authority in the name of the natural that had become endemic in the West. It was "a revolt which has commonly been as dogmatic and intuitional as the authority itself."[36] Toward the end of the 1920s views of Freud began to change with his own shifts in theory.

A few journalists as well as some of the American analysts took pains to counteract what they saw as pernicious misinterpretations of Freud. Harvey O'Higgins, a popular writer, argued:

> A great deal that passes for Freudianism in the popular mind is a poisonous doctrine that was never taught by Freud and that an antidote to it is seriously needed. He did not mean by 'repression' that continence and self-discipline in sex which civilized life makes necessary. He never advocated such a license in sex expression as is now commonly accepted as the Freudian prescription for the repressed.[37]

Martin Peck, a Boston analyst, argued that psychoanalysis itself was partly to blame for its own sexual reputation because of its early over-emphasis on the "biological and more simple instinctive foundations of mental life." The psycho-analytic psychiatrist Frankwood Williams observed that the "Big Town philosophy, 'I am what I am and must be myself'" was merely "taking off the diapers before sphincter control has been gained."[38]

Perhaps the most optimistic conservative interpretation came from Karl Menninger, who indefatigably popularized in three influential books and an advice column begun in the *Ladies Home Journal* in 1930. Born in Kansas in 1893, raised by a devout Presbyterian mother and a physician father, Menninger had been a student at Harvard Medical School and had worked under the neurologist Elmer Southard at Boston Psychopathic Hospital before returning to his family's clinic in Topeka. Smith Ely Jelliffe, a psychoanalytic psychiatrist in New York, steered him toward psychoanalysis, and in the early 1930s he was trained at the Chicago Psychoanalytic Institute and analyzed by the immigrant analyst Franz Alexander.[39] Menninger had a gift for clear, popular exposition and for dramatic illustrations culled from case histories and the press.

Menninger's *The Human Mind,* published in 1930 and written before his psychoanalytic training, was close to the prewar American version of psycho-analysis in its optimism, environmentalism, and moralism. It was a general, eclectic account of the new psychiatry and the new psychology which Menninger identified with psychoanalysis. Both amused and disturbed by the popular cult, Menninger wrote, "I have heard a little girl implore her mother to throw away her inhibitions and take her to the circus." Psychoanalysis did not countenance "uninhibited self indulgence" or preach that

> continence, chastity, self-denial . . . are bad. . . . In fact, the whole Freudian thesis tends in the opposite direction; namely, that the neurotic patient is one

who is failing to maintain his inhibitions and needs help in the mastery of his escaping desires. Freud and Freudians recognize even better than the rest of the world how necessary it is to suppress primitive desires except in legitimate directions. Freud no more advocated promiscuous indulgences in sex than he did promiscuous indulgences in eating. Anita Loos got it right in *Gentlemen Prefer Blondes* when she has her heroine say, "Dr., Froyd said that all I needed was to cultivate a few inhibitions and get some sleep."[40]

Neurosis, according to Menninger, resulted from what resembled a traditional moral struggle. The neurotic's unconscious mind was "the scene of a terrific battle between unreconciled tendencies and opposing trends." He wanted to achieve the fruits of culture yet retain more primitive forms of satisfaction. For civilization and culture "owe their existence to the thwarting of primitive tendencies, particularly the sexual instinct, and in this sense civilization itself is a neurotic product."[41] The sexual instinct was the "unselfish race preservative instinct."[42]

Menninger did his best to make the psychoanalyst a sympathetic scientist. Not a sorcerer surrounded by clouds of incense and velvet hangings, the psychoanalyst rather was a careful investigator, a scientific listener. At the same time, in diagnosing and treating mental illness, he "must be first of all a diplomat, secondly a detective, thirdly a doctor of medicine, and finally, in the role of therapist, a magician, a scientist, and a priest."[43] He was, above all, a non-judgmental listener; Menninger described a counselor talking to a distraught college girl: "He did not tell her she was lazy, indifferent, failing, and disappointing everyone, nor that she ought to buck up and do better. He said simply, 'Tell me all about it.'"[44]

"Practically no intelligent and informed scientist today disputes the main thesis and findings of psychoanalysis," Menninger insisted. This bold claim provoked the Boston psychiatrist Abraham Myerson to conduct a survey of neurologists and psychiatrists in 1939 which came to more equivocal conclusions about the status of Freud and psychoanalysis.[45]

For Menninger, psychoanalysis, although not applicable to most patients, provided an important model of outpatient psychotherapy for psychiatrists with the requisite training. Arguing that heredity was less important than it had been thought to be, Menninger insisted psychotherapy could be astonishingly effective. Unlike the leopard, human beings could "change their spots." Psychotherapy could "strengthen a failing repression, or it may remove certain unnecessary repressions and lighten the load, or, finally, it may change the form of the disguised escapes from the harmful to the useful variety."[46] Perhaps his most inflated claim for psychiatric knowledge came in his *Ladies Home Journal* column in 1931. Commenting on the newspaper account of a man who had killed his children, his wife, and himself because he feared the poorhouse, despite several hundred thousand dollars in the bank, Menninger argued that "probably this man and his family could have been saved by a little knowledge of mental hygiene."[47] Just this optimism and the use of cases from the press were bitterly criticized by Abraham Myerson:

It is time to protest in the name of Freud against . . . the marvelous analyses of the quick and the dead who have never been examined at all. . . . If psychoanalysis is anything, it is a laborious, painstaking, technically correct, individual study, and when psychoanalyses are made in a few seconds on the basis of a newspaper account, a cheapening of Freud's technique and contributions takes place, which even the hardened non-Freudian reviewer resents.[48]

In Menninger's next popular book, *Man Against Himself,* published in 1938, he ingeniously expounded Freud's most pessimistic theory with an optimistic American twist. Like his psychoanalytic mentor, Franz Alexander, Menninger argued the case for Freud's death instinct but paired this with a faith that Thanatos could be tamed by judicious therapy. A year after Freud's disillusioned essay, "Analysis Terminable and Interminable," Menninger claimed that psychoanalysis was the "queen of the therapies." Persistent psychoneuroses often yielded to it in a "spectacularly successful manner," although one did not know why it worked and also knew that it was not always successful. The cures psychoanalysis could bring about in laboriously changing a single person suggested hope for the human race.

Reminiscent of older doctrines of original sin and salvation, he insisted that the ubiquity of innate aggression be squarely faced. The "extraordinary propensity of the human being to join hands with external forces in an attack upon his own existence is one of the most remarkable of biological phenomena."[49] And he elaborately catalogued modes of self-destruction: swallowing red hot pokers, ground glass, or poison; hugging red hot stoves; cutting one's throat on barbed wire; "diving into white-hot coke ovens"; piercing the heart with darning needles and corkscrews, self-crucifixion. Less obvious forms were alcoholism and antisocial behavior, and in his debunking mode, he added asceticism and martyrdom.

But aggression could be neutralized by intelligence and love, by diminishing the sense of guilt and the archaic superego through the prompt intervention of the psychiatrist. Countering the death instinct was the professional task of the "physician to whom the masses of the people, from peasant to president, look for salvation . . . from their own self-destructiveness."[50] Aggression could be directed away from the self by the choice of appropriate love objects, and by channeling aggression through work, sports, games, politics, business, hobbies. Aggression could be countered by overcoming narcissism and, despite disclaimers on Menninger's part, by what amounted to a prescription for Christian love. "Thus again psychoanalytic science comes to the support of a great religious leader who said, 'He who seeketh his own life shall lose it but whosoever loseth his life for my sake shall find it.'"[51]

The optimism exemplified by Menninger was carried to utopian extremes by the mental hygiene movement in which he was active. Its watchword was "Science," that is, the new "sciences" of psychiatry and psychology which would replace traditional religion. Mental hygiene would supplant theology as the foundation of the new order. Its priests would be the psychiatrists, the social workers, the psychologists, the experts of the new scientific psychology. They would replace the authority of the family in matters of health, child-rearing, and education. They became important clients of the psychoanalysts and devoted friends and supporters of psychotherapy.

Mental hygiene personnel represented one segment of the rapid growth of American professionals in the 1920s. College and university faculties also burgeoned and so did the philanthropic foundations that contributed vital funding to psychiatric and mental hygiene projects.[52]

Hygienists carried over the reform impulse of prewar progressivism to their crusades of the 1920s. These were directed at cultural rather than economic objectives or the social system: criminal justice, sex education, child guidance, mental health clinics, the school. The movement was led by the National Committee for Mental Hygiene, founded in 1910 to aid the mentally ill. This goal within a few years was replaced by one far more ambitious. Thomas Salmon, who had been the major organizer of Army psychiatry in the Great War, led the committee toward nothing less than the prevention of mental illness and delinquency by concentrating on childhood, "the golden period of mental hygiene." The intent was philanthropic and reformist, and it was implemented in part by generous grants from the Rockefeller Foundation and the Commonwealth Fund. The aim was to create through scientific child-rearing a personality adjusted to the demands of modern social life.[53]

In the 1920s the committee, under Salmon's successor, Frankwood Williams, became the major sponsor of an ideology that combined elements of Adolf Meyer's psychobiology, behaviorism, and, increasingly, psychoanalysis. It reduced these disparate elements to a set of highly generalized, vague propositions: the importance of the environment in determining character; the formative influence of parents on the young child and of early experience in setting adult patterns of behavior; and the psychological origin of problems previously thought to be physiological, genetic, or social, such as delinquency, crime or neurosis. Some of these theories reflected not only an eclectic psychoanalytic theory but educational theories as well. What was new was the insistence that delinquency, "dependency, domestic difficulties, and industrial and social unrest," instead of reflecting inherited taint, were a symptom of psychological troubles, maladaptation, or mental illness in the individual. Moreover, these ills could be prevented easily through the intervention of the social worker, the teacher, and the psychiatrist during childhood, and particularly in the school through a new understanding that would replace punishment.

A number of specifically psychoanalytic contributions filtered untidily into educational psychology and pedagogy. These included the bad effects of "too severe" repression; the search for "underlying" causes of behavior; the investigation of sexuality and the stages of sexual development, including tolerance for masturbation; the sublimation of infantile impulses for social ends; the "family romance," that is, the Oedipal attachment of the child to parents; the role of the teacher as a substitute parent; the continuum of normal and abnormal; and "mechanisms" such as the projection of unacceptable wishes onto others.[54]

Williams, a short, intense, amiable man, became interested in psychoanalysis through William Alanson White and was analyzed by Freud's pupil, the lay analyst Otto Rank, who gave some of his New York seminars in Williams's house. A psychiatrist, Williams was perhaps the only American member of the New York Psychoanalytic Society to support lay analysis. As editor of *Mental Hygiene,* he published articles by the psychoanalysts and favorable reviews of psychoanalytic books. An indefatigable worker, he was so much in demand for conferences, speeches, and reports that he had been unable to read his mail for several weeks in 1924.[55] He analyzed Harry Hopkins, Franklin D. Roosevelt's director of public works.[56]

Russian delegates to the International Mental Hygiene Congress in Washington, D.C., in 1932, asked Williams to visit the Soviet Union, and Williams grew increasingly sympathetic to the Russian "experiment." In Russia he discovered a psychiatric and sexual utopia. While the focus of mental hygiene on the individual had done nothing to stem the rising tide of mental illness in America, the incidence of nervous and mental disease in Russia was falling. An eminent Russian psychiatrist told Williams he had been unable in three months to find a new case of "manic depressive depression" in Moscow to demonstrate to his students. Learning about sex early and frankly, with premarital experience likely, the Russians, Williams found, were "potent" and unconflicted. Birth control and competent abortion were universally available. When Williams saw a crowd of tattered sleepers in a railway station he assumed not that they might be in need but that they were simply waiting for their trains. A number of Williams's psychiatric colleagues, among them Bernard Glueck, were skeptical of Williams's rosy impressions. Williams eventually resigned from the NCMH and died in 1936 while returning from a visit to the Soviet Union.[57]

Williams and others brought child guidance into the purview of the mental hygiene movement. Focusing primarily on individual development, hygienists paid special attention to the baneful psychological influence of parents. The 1920s here and in Europe were rife with anti-parent manifestos launched by educators, psychiatrists, and social workers. Miriam Van Waters, a referee with the Los Angeles Juvenile Court and in 1927 vice president of the National Conference of Social Work, published *Parents on Probation,* included a chapter listing "nineteen ways of being a bad parent." These included not being "orientated in the modern world," not having a "democratic home," being fatalistic or "repudiating a child in dire need." She claimed that "scientific research shows that not only temper tantrums and disobedience, but enuresis and convulsions are psychogenic and preventable." Jealousy, "hypocrisy, antagonism between parents may cause in their children mental retardation, physical disease or delinquency." The remedy was a therapeutic airing, derived from psychoanalysis. "Frank revealing of such emotional experience helps to restore the child physically, mentally, morally." Quoting Otto Rank, she insisted that detaching the "growing individual from the authority of the parents is one of the most necessary, but most painful achievements in evolution."[58]

The NCMH launched a crusade to take advantage of the golden, formative years of childhood. With a grant from the Commonwealth Fund, in 1922 it sponsored seven model child guidance clinics at strategic locations across the country staffed by a psychologist, a social worker, and directed by a psychiatrist.[59] By 1927 there were 16 guidance clinics; by 1933, some 35, although several closed during the depression. The fund also became a major source of grants for training in child psychiatry. Between 1922 and 1944 the fund provided fellowships to 800 psychiatric social workers and to 3000 psychiatrists, although the number of fellowships to Jews and women was minimal. Some of the Commonwealth Fund fellowships supported psychoanalytic training in Europe. Mental hygiene clinics also were established in major universities: Vassar, Yale, the University of California, Washburn College in Topeka, and, by 1930, at Harvard, Smith, Brown, Wellesley, Mt. Holyoke, and the universities of Chicago, Vermont, Colorado, Michigan, and Northwestern. Their aim was to foster the optimal adjustment of their late adolescent students through clinical services and mental hygiene courses.

When the psychiatrist Harry Kerns, a friend of Williams, inaugurated a mental hygiene service at West Point and later at Yale, he asked Williams's advice about people who had sought his help. The range of Kerns's patients was wide. He had been consulted about a sergeant's son who had stolen and had exhibited himself, a Princeton student who was failing academically, a depressive suicidal consular corps member, a stammerer, an early "dementia praecox" patient. Some mental hygienists saw academic or disciplinary problems as "symptoms" of emotional difficulties, and like the 19th-century psychiatrists, they tended to scorn too much intellectualism.[60] Deliberately eclectic, child guidance personnel tried to deal with children in a "revolutionary," "non-judgmental" way, avoiding "moral rigidity" and "traditional attitudes."

Worried middle-class mothers, anxious and bewildered by loss of authority over the sexual behavior and school performance of their children, sought help and advice at the new child guidance clinics. By 1930, 50 percent of the patients at the Judge Baker clinic in Boston were no longer youthful delinquents referred by the courts, but children brought voluntarily by middle-class mothers. This new category of clinic patients, who seemed to exist in appreciable numbers, were nervous, withdrawn children, "unhappy, troublesome non-delinquents."[61]

The clinics' methods at first reflected the highly eclectic "mental hygiene point of view," then became increasingly psychoanalytic; social causes of delinquency and children's problems gave way to psychological ones. The behaviorist influence was clear in the early emphasis on "habit training" reinforced by "star charts" and authoritative advice. Toward the end of the 1920s psychiatrists began to argue that behavioral methods failed because they did not deal with "underlying" emotional causes. After 1930 the clinics increasingly purveyed a one-to-one therapy that dealt with "deeper, instinctive drives" derived from psychoanalysis. Despite claims for this presumably more thorough treatment, the new therapy did not provide superior results.[62]

The clinics, like the popular guidance literature, avoided specifically Freudian concepts such as the oral, anal, or Oedipal stages of development. Nevertheless, Douglas Thom of the Boston Psychopathic Hospital, who had worked at the shell-shock treatment center at La Fauche in France during World War I and later founded a group of independent "habit clinics," incorporated a few eclectic psychoanalytic conceptions, and his views were influential. He argued that sexual development began in infancy and that children should be given full and frank sex instruction and not be punished for masturbation. Like both behaviorists and Freudians he argued that "too much petting and fondling" should be avoided lest it excite the child sexually. The "oversolicitous mother" and the tyrant father created "spineless, dependent individuals" as well as resentment against authority. Thom also incorporated Adler's "inferiority complex," insisting that the child depended on adults for his evaluation of himself and that parents should be careful not to instill feelings of inadequacy.

Equally important for the long run, the psychoanalyst David Levy developed a persistently popular theory of "maternal over protection" as a major cause of neurosis and delinquency. Mothers lavished too much care on their offspring and controlled them too rigidly, usually as a result of their own personal neuroses. The over-protection compensated for "affect hunger and thwarted ambitions." Both rebellious and overly submissive children were created by this faulty mothering. Levy's views became cornerstones of treatment in some guidance clinics and have persisted to the present. Faulty mothering became one psychiatric explanation for the large number of neuropsychiatric casualties in World War II. For the most part guidance personnel tended to reinforce the demands of the younger generation, arguing that children needed far greater independence. They required not so much "discipline" as "understanding," especially in matters of education and sexuality.[63]

"Psychodynamic" and psychoanalytic models of psychotherapy were adopted partly because they provided new status and specialized professional roles for social workers and psychologists, Margo Horn has argued. In the guidance clinics the psychiatrist remained at the apex of the hierarchy, presiding over psychologists and social workers. The psychiatric social worker took on the role of "treating" the mother, while the psychiatrist treated the child.

The second focus of NCMH, was the assignment to the public schools of a new therapeutic function, molding "the healthy personality" through a "mental hygiene attitude" disseminated by visiting teachers and guidance counselors. The progressive reformers condemned "old fashioned education," a stereotype they themselves had created: children sitting stiffly in "formal rows of rigid desks," the bare walls garnished with "gloomy prints of Washington, Lincoln, and the Coliseum of Rome," a setting effective in "putting the child in his place, and repressing spontaneous outbursts." Some were horrified by the sight of children doing homework beginning at the age of eight or ten "evening after evening from supper time to bed time bent over these atrocious text books."[64] The education historian Sol Cohen has argued that the schools' therapeutic goal led mental hygienists to seek to eliminate school failure and harsh disciplinary procedures and to water down a subject-matter-centered curriculum. Failure would be controlled by minimizing competitive pressures including examinations, as well as by "democratizing" discipline.

Mental hygienists, psychoanalysts, and progressive educators influenced each other, sometimes profoundly.[65] Some educators here and abroad combined ideas from psychoanalysis with those from John Dewey, Maria Montessori, and other educational reformers. Freud once told Max Eastman that he regarded Dewey as one of the few men in the world whom he regarded highly, while Dewey admired Freud's powers of observation although he thought the subconscious and the machinery of repression were "so much mythology."[66] Both Dewey and Freud were anti-traditionalists who opposed repressive modes of dealing with instinctual drives. Both emphasized the importance of emotion over intellect. Dewey's theory of eliciting the child's interest could be interpreted as sublimating libido in the service of learning. Both would have agreed on the value of the child's play. Both were against too rigid discipline. As Sol Cohen has argued, before World War I Freud decisively insisted that education not repress instincts with undue severity lest this cause neuroses and destroy efficiency and the capacity for enjoyment. If asocial and perverse instincts were not repressed but sublimated they would make "precious contributions to the formation of character."[67]

In the 1920s psychoanalysis inspired several European and American experiments in education that stressed liberation and permissiveness. A highly optimistic psychoanalytic pedagogy was developed by the European child analysts, most of them former school teachers. Fritz Wittels, a physician and one of Freud's early followers who settled in New York in the 1920s, summed up the most radical ideals of the new psychoanalytic education: "No set programme, no wearisome examinations, no note-taking, no punishments. The pupils must never be discouraged, and censoriousness must be avoided like the plague."[68]

Some of the Europeans applied psychoanalytic pedagogy with radical vigor, for example, at the Malting House School in Cambridge, England, directed by the psychoanalytic psychologist Susan Isaacs. No restrictions curbed the children's verbal expressions of sexuality or aggression, and as Dewey had suggested, learning was carried out as much as possible in the context of what students wanted to learn and of practical tasks.[69] Vienna also was a center of psychoanalytic pedagogy and the new education. In 1927, Anna Freud started an informal school for children who with their parents had come from America for analysis. Influenced by the currents of progressive education and the desire to elicit the young child's creative potential, the teachers Peter Blos and Erik Erikson, both of whom later became psychoanalysts, taught what most interested them. One year they concentrated on the Eskimos, their art, culture, and the scientific implications of living in a cold climate. Erikson recalled, however, that the atmosphere of the school was not "permissive," and there was a serious emphasis on subject matter.[70]

In New York, Margaret Naumberg, inspired perhaps more by Rousseau and Jung than by Freud or her teacher, John Dewey, established the Walden School to foster the child's creativity. Part of the Greenwich Village subculture, deeply interested in modern painting, married to the writer Waldo Frank, she had flirted briefly with socialism but decided that transforming the individual was the necessary first step to changing society. A more permissive environment would release the child's libidinal energy, to be directed into "positive forms of work and personal expression" and thus foster adjustment to reality. The school could correct the emotional problems of children (the fault of parents) through the efforts of carefully selected teachers who were not neurotic and who understood their own unconscious lives. Analyzed by the Jungian Beatrice Hinkle, she recommended psychoanalysis for her teaching staff.[71]

Other progressive educators also were strongly influenced by psychoanalysis. Caroline Zachry, who headed the Bureau of Child Guidance of the New York Board of Education, was a close friend of the analysts Frankwood Williams and Lawrence Kubie and with the pediatrician Benjamin Spock attended the New York Psychoanalytic Institute in the 1930s.[72] She argued that the principles of progressive education and Freud's theories of psychological development were consistent with each other and were widely accepted, although some educators explicitly rejected psychoanalysis and others were unfamiliar with its terminology. Principles common to progressive education and psychoanalysis included directing the child's impulses into "creative channels," a version of sublimation; the child's assimilation of his society's cultural demands, that is, the development of his superego; and the teacher's quasi-parental and therapeutic role, that is, the psychoanalytic conception of transference.[73]

By the end of the 1920s, after Freud had granted a primary role to aggression as well as to sexuality, the doctrine of extreme permissiveness was drastically revised by European psychoanalytic educators, Anna Freud and Susan Isaacs among them. They began to place less emphasis on the direct impact of environment than on the innate drives and dispositions of children. Influenced by Melanie Klein's theories about the importance of aggression and the formation of a harsh superego as early as the child's first year, Isaacs, although urging more freedom for children than most schools then granted, now insisted on the need for order, stability, and "adult support of the child's loving and constructive impulses against his own hate and aggression." An ordered environment fostered the child's belief in love and his sense of security. Children needed to feel that they could be made to do things and that the adults around them represented "the forces of ordered creation."[74] Taking aim probably at A. S. Neill's Summerhill School, she condemned the attempt of some educators to "do away with every type of restraint or limitation upon the children's impulses."[75]

The psychoanalyst Willi Hoffer, who observed the Viennese experiments, argued that psychoanalytic attempts at the sex education of children had created disturbing results. There had been no curbs on masturbation or expressions of jealousy; "the parents bodies' were not hidden from the children's sight." Informed parents and teachers had tried to minimize instinctual frustration, and replace "paternal authority" by explanations and appeals to the child's insight and affection. Yet children brought up under this regime displayed serious character and behavior disorders. They were less inhibited and perhaps brighter. But they were also less curious, had little perseverance, clung to infantile habits, and were unable to concentrate in school.[76] The tenor of the psychoanalytic approach changed markedly and would have profound effects in the development of psychoanalytic ego psychology.[77]

But the views of American educators did not seriously reflect these developments. The Americans were inspired more by Dewey's optimism and by a faith in infinite human malleability. Although Zachry, for example, deplored the "free and uninhibited expression of impulses" permitted in some early psychoanalytic experiments in education, she also insisted that the curriculum, for instance, be tailored to the needs of the individual child, not to the requirements of the university.[78] American educators institutionalized the permissive trend in the mental hygiene position by making the schools the molders of healthy, well-adjusted personalities partly through a softening of discipline.[79] American mental hygienists insisted there were no bad children, only children who had been mishandled by misguided parents. The teacher should replace authority and punishment with understanding and guidance. Failure and non-promotion should be minimized. Applying August Hoch's psychiatric concept of incipient schizophrenia, mental hygienists insisted that the aggressive child was healthier than the shy, "shut-in," and perhaps over-studious child. By the late 1920s such concepts were accepted by influential segments of the helping professions. The "mental hygiene" point of view pervaded the White House Conference on Child Health and Protection in 1930, and under the slogan "meeting the needs of adolescence," had a great impact on the Progressive Education Association's efforts to transform the American high school.[80]

Mental hygiene also pervaded the "new criminology," which insisted that crime, like insanity, as a medical problem and that delinquency was a disease to be treated. Accordingly, the psychiatrist, not the judge or the attorney, should determine policy for prisons, punishment, and rehabilitation. The psychiatrist's profound understanding of the causes of crime was rooted in his knowledge of the individual psychology of the criminal. Outmoded punishment should be replaced by therapy and rehabilitation. If psychiatrists were called in when minor crimes were committed, major crimes might be anticipated and prevented.[81]

The most spectacular identification of psychoanalysis with the new criminology occurred during the trial of the teenaged youths Nathan Loeb and Richard Leopold in Chicago in 1924, for murdering 13-year-old Bobby Franks and stuffing his body in a drain pipe, a crime that aroused public clamor for the death penalty. Leopold and Loeb had confessed and a court hearing would determine their sentence. Both were highly intelligent; Leopold had graduated Phi Beta Kappa at 19 from the University of Chicago.

Their wealthy families hired Clarence Darrow, the nation's most famous defense attorney, who decided on a psychiatric argument: The boys "are unbalanced mentally and do not live, think nor act in the way that rational beings, as the medical world knows them, do in their everyday life. Therefore from a psychological standpoint, the two boys are not guilty of the murder of Bobby Franks as the legal world looks upon killing." This argument required the expert testimony of the new criminologists.

Freud had declined separate invitations from the publishers William Randolph Hearst and Robert R. McCormick to come to the United States to psychoanalyze the boys. But three Freudian psychiatrists testified for the defense. At issue were traditional views of crime and punishment, that is, that only insanity could excuse murder; the new criminologist believed that influences in early childhood could diminish judgment and control in pathological but not insane personalities. A Chicago reporter wrestled with the problem: "If the search of the physicians for a physical insanity factor has been unavailing, the coming examinations by alienists will have to be based on the Freudian and neo-Freudian schools of insanity—on the theory that brains which are capable of functioning properly as far as the mechanics of thought are concerned, have become twisted and incapable of sane thought through some psychological influence in the past of the youths. Inhibitions, suppressed desires, frustrated ambitions, satiated wants. Was one of these psychological factors responsible?"[82] The Chicago *Tribune*'s special reporter, Genevieve Forbes, presented the issues:

> At five minutes past ten this morning, Dr. William A. White of Washington, D.C., psycho-analyst and professor, will take the stand . . . and try to explain just how insane a sane man can be without being so insane he needs a jury to determine just how insane he is. Not an easy job.[83]

At a fee of $250 per day, White, director of St. Elizabeth's, the federal government's hospital for the insane in Washington, D.C., and president of the American Psychiatric Association, argued that at the time of the crime the boys "were wandering in an infantile state of mind—a mind of the doll-playing age insofar as responsibility goes." The boys were "emotional infants, 6 or 7 years of age," living out a fantasy life playing king and slave. Their personalities [were] split by overdevelopment of intellect and retarded emotional growth."[84] A competent psychiatric examination of the mind, he insisted, was as reliable as an x-ray of the body. The skeptical prosecutor remarked, "You thought it was more important to inquire into what happened when they were five years old than it was to ascertain the details of this astounding crime, didn't you?"[85]

William Healy, a pioneer in the study of delinquency and the new criminology who became increasingly influenced by psychoanalysis, gave the boys a battery of psychological tests and a thorough examination. Healy had been a director of the new Chicago Juvenile Psychopathic Institute, which later became one of the major institutions for the recruitment of psychoanalysts, and in 1917 he became head of the Judge Baker Institute in Boston, which also became a psychoanalytic center. He testified that both Loeb and Leopold suffered from a "psychosis," and had a "most strange pathological relationship."[86] Leopold had told Healy that he reveled in the fact that he "had no ground for conscience," and Healy judged him unbalanced, paranoiac, and socially dangerous. Testimony about the homosexual aspect of the relationship was given in the judge's chambers, and the *Herald Tribune* delicately reported "a childish compact" involving "unmentionable privileges," while the International News Service reported simply that "Dickie Loeb was 'queer.'" Leopold did not endear himself to the press with his pronouncements from prison favoring atheism, Nietzsche, and Oscar Wilde. In an interview Leopold remarked, "If I am hanged I will arrange to have a good jazz band on hand and plenty of hard punch. I am planning the last supreme shock for the world in the form of my farewell speech. I may be overrating myself, but I really think I can make it worth anyone's while who is fortunate enough to obtain an invitation."[87]

The judge opted for life imprisonment on grounds of the boys' ages, 18 and 19. Although he regarded the "mass of data" about the "physical, mental and moral condition" of the defendants as a "valuable contribution to criminology," and had clearly shown them to be "abnormal," he would not take it into consideration, because the information was relevant to legislative not judicial action.[88]

In this trial, psychoanalysis became identified with a radical view of crime which seemed to suggest leniency for murder. Some congressmen were sufficiently angered by White's testimony and his fee that they launched an investigation of St. Elizabeth's Hospital. White, although stung by the criticism, survived the inquiry successfully and remained a remarkably able propagandist for his vision of mental hygiene and psychoanalysis, speaking eloquently to service clubs, congressmen, and the press.[89]

Sheldon Glueck, a criminologist at Harvard Law School, propounded the legal consequences of a psychoanalytic view of crime. If clinical evidence demonstrated that some crimes were committed to induce punishment for an unconscious sense of guilt or were the result of early childhood experience, in many cases punishment was useless and absurd. If the theory were sound, many criminals gained "neurotic satisfaction from the very social reaction that is supposed to deter and frighten them."[90] Ten years later, in 1940, Atwell Westwick, a superior-court judge in Santa Barbara, California, repeated similar arguments and set up a program for the examination of offenders by psychiatrists and psychoanalysts. "The way to reform is to educate, and the way to educate, is to psychoanalyze," he wrote. "Much criminal behavior is so utterly irrational and so deeply rooted in the unconscious, that without psychoanalysis its meaning and its causes and the corrective possibilities involved are entirely beyond the ken and reach of judges, probation officers, social workers, teachers, wardens, prison directors, psychologists. . . . "[91]

Recruits from the "Salvation Army of Psychoanalysis," the social workers, helped to staff the institutions created by mental hygiene and the new criminology. In their struggle for professional legitimation, social workers were increasingly receptive to versions of psychoanalysis. It provided them with explanatory theories and with a new social role as therapists. The profession developed a specialist in the psychiatric social worker, who reigned at the top of the social work hierarchy and whose approach became increasingly psychoanalytic.[92]

At first psychoanalysis suggested ways in which the social worker could conceptualize the client's problems and explain failures in case work. In providing fundamental knowledge, social workers argued that psychoanalysis played a role in their profession similar to that played by physiology in medicine. Grace Marcus, one of the orthodox Freudians, argued that the theory of the unconscious explained the frustrating, irrational behavior of clients. Such behavior, determined by forgotten early childhood experiences and repressed primitive impulses, "thwarted the most elementary practical aims for clients." Like some analysts in this period, she found a villain in the superego, whose "savage prohibitions" may sacrifice "man's creative capacities and cripple his social development." Social workers "came to see how much repression may lead to neurosis; how too little repression and integration of love and aggression may lead to acting out."[93]

Psychoanalysis provided not only theory but a new therapeutic role and technique. Gradually, then very quickly after World War II, growing numbers of social workers became therapists. Eager for personal analysis and for psychoanalytic training, they provided an important new cadre of patients for psychoanalysts and thus joined "the friends and supporters of psychotherapy." In the interwar years and beyond, the New York, the Smith College, and the Pennsylvania schools of social work all were directed by personnel strongly influenced by varieties of psychoanalysis. Everett Kimball, director at Smith, and his wife were analyzed by Otto Rank during his brief forays to America in the 1920s. Rank's disciples and analysands Jessie Taft and Virginia Robinson, who raised two adopted children together, developed a Rankian approach to case work at the Pennsylvania School.[94] They used non-directive techniques of "understanding and acceptance," whereby the social worker could release a spontaneous "growth process" in the individual client.[95] At the New York School of Social Work, Bernard Glueck, a psychoanalytic psychiatrist, had introduced courses in abnormal psychology in 1918. He was succeeded by Marion Kenworthy, who became professor of "mental hygiene and psychiatry" in 1924 and devised "ego libido" charts for the guidance of her social work pupils. She carried on an extensive psychoanalytic practice, played an important role in setting up programs for screening women for the armed services in World War II, and later was active in the postwar expansion of psychoanalytic psychiatry.[96]

Psychoanalysis may have strengthened a shift among social workers away from social reform and toward a focus on the psychology of individual clients, although such tendencies were evident in the early 1920s before psychoanalytic influence became important.[97] The suggestion that poverty might result from individual psychological problems could seem especially plausi-

ble in the boom years of the 1920s. It accorded with the relatively conservative economic views of some psychoanalysts, Brill and Karl Menninger, for
instance.[98] It is not implausible to regard this individual emphasis in social
work as a new version of earlier views that poverty was the result of a lack of
virtue, or of mental defect or a low I.Q., as sometimes was argued in the late
teens and early 1920s. However, during the Depression, while psychoanalysis became more influential in case work, social workers generally renewed their commitment to social reform, and a few, notably, Bertha Rey-
nolds, another analysand of Frankwood Williams, combined psychoanalysis
and Marxism. The image of the social worker was changing from the flat-
heeled dispenser of charity to that of counselor and therapist.

The popular stereotypes of the analyst and the analytic process had been
established before World War I: the uncanny analyst, who combined the
qualities of secular priest, uncondemning listener, and scientific soul surgeon; the magical power of catharsis to dispel neuroses. In the postwar years,
the analyst's role as a scientific priest grew more conspicuous. Partly because
psychiatry purported to be free of harsh moral judgments it was taking over
the jurisdiction of "personal problems."[99]

In the interwar years, the nature of a publication dictated its degree of
frankness about what brought people to psychoanalysis. In mass magazines,
the major complaints of patients were fears and anxieties, like the insomnia
and fear of death of a Los Angeles meter reader, or an inability to work,
especially the writer's block that plagued the journalists who publicized their
analyses. In novels the complaints were often frankly sexual—impotence or
frigidity, for instance. Margaret Mead recalled that it was not uncommon in
the 1920s to be analyzed in order to improve one's sex life; the frigid, it was
assumed, could be made to "quiver with delight."[100]

Impotence was a complaint that one fictional analyst was able to cure in a
brisk exhibition of the eclecticism and superficiality of the 1920s image of
analytic therapy. For the writer Ludwig Lewisohn, the psychoanalyst was the
priest for a non-religious age, and he cast him as the hero of *The Island
Within,* a novel which had a 25th printing in 1929. A fledgling Jewish psychoanalytic psychiatrist cured a writer's impotence in a single session by a
single interpretation. The analyst spoke "with firm yet gentle decision. . . . It
was his first important case. If he could use the Adler short-cut here and
avoid a long psycho-therapeutic process it might be the beginning of a practice." The psychiatrist informed the patient that his impotence was the result
of a "suppressed truth": that his girl friend resembled his first wife, who was a
"sloven." "You were afraid you were making a desperate mistake a second
time. You didn't want to admit it to yourself. So your body made the admission for you. You're probably cured now. If not, come back to me."
Lewisohn's hero was asked to treat more and more "members of the literary
or editorial set. His patients were nearly all Jews, "who suffered intense
feelings of alienation in the Puritan American world, Jews who did not want
to be Jews." At parties, "they railed and jeered at the neo-Puritan obsession,
at the Fundamentalists. They made common cause with . . . attacks on the

nation's brutal and massive attempts to draw its traditional forces together and extrude the people and the influences that seemed to threaten its fierce loyalties and ignorances and solidarities."[101] Lewisohn had visited Freud in Vienna, who pronounced his *Mr. Crump* an "incomparable masterpiece." It was a novel about a composer married to an older woman who would not divorce him, so he killed her accidentally.[102] Lewisohn believed that although he held a doctorate from Columbia University, he had been denied an academic post because of anti-Semitism. Later he taught at the Wisconsin and Ohio state universities before becoming an editor at the *Nation.* His second novel was confiscated by Anthony Comstock, the prewar purity crusader.[103]

Accounts of analytic therapy in popular magazines dealt with more publicly discussable complaints than impotence. Lucien Cary, a journalist friend of Floyd Dell, revealed in the *American Magazine* that psychoanalysis not only cured his writer's block but increased his enjoyment of life and led to a bigger income as well. His seven months' analysis revealed that he had wanted to fail, had been unwilling "to leave home and go out into the world" and stand on his own two feet. The origins of this disability lay in the analytically resurrected "situations of . . . childhood which were too painful to contemplate."[104]

Childhood trauma caused a man's obsessive fears that he would kill his wife, the subject of the German film *Secrets of the Soul,* shown in Cambridge, Massachusetts, under the auspices of the Massachusetts League of Women Voters and the Shady Hill Film Guild. A reviewer wrote that it was "based upon an actual case in the note-books of Dr. Sigmund Freud."[105] This movie featured a vivid nightmare in which the hero, a mild-mannered chemist, saw himself tried and condemned for murdering his wife. A psychoanalyst unraveled the cause of this obsession: he was jealous of a male cousin with whom he and his wife had played as children, and who was returning from Sumatra for a visit. With the recall of childhood trauma, his obsession vanished.

Reflecting some of the postwar conflicts over values, a writer, Virginia Terhune Van de Water, described her psychoanalysis in 1926 in the *Century* magazine as denigrating a parental upbringing that had taught such traditional virtues as self-control and obedience. She had decided to be "psyched" because she found work difficult and lay awake at night, obsessed by "absurd dreads and fancies." The analyst informed her that she had never escaped the domination of her parents and their "idea that I should be trained in self control, in obedience, in respect for their commands, in regard for the laws of decency." When she protested to her analyst that she was not really at heart a murderer, an adulterer, "thief, liar, or coveter of other men's goods," she was informed that this was simply resistance.[106]

By the mid-1930s the debunking and the crusades against Puritanism diminished, giving way to a new emphasis on the association of psychoanalysis with medicine. This new image was particularly stressed in *Fortune,* the magazine of big business and finance. In a 1935 series on the nervous breakdown and the nation's leading private mental hospitals, one learned that at the Menninger Sanitarium, Karl Menninger combined "medical efficiency" with an intense interest in psychoanalysis.[107]

Gradually, popular descriptions of psychoanalysis became more sophisticated. A novel by a New York psychiatrist conveyed some of the intricacy of the analytic process. Hailed as a sober and scientific account of psychoanalysis that reflected its new maturity and an end of its early days of "magic making and witch doctors," *Spectacle of a Man* was published anonymously in 1939.[108] It purported to be a fictional record of the year-long analysis of a 32-year-old engineer who stammered, was painfully shy and isolated. He had unsatisfying relations with women who always "let him down." Unlike the magazine popularizations, this account dealt with resistance, with the modification of a harsh and inappropriate superego, and with Oedipal jealousy and fear. In addition to these authentic Freudian themes there were also suggestions of compensation for Adler's inferiority complex, and of a very active analyst who interpreted frequently and with high authority.

The therapist's aim in the novel, typical of the psychoanalytic outlook in the 1920s and early 1930s, was greater spontaneity of the patient achieved partly through lessened defenses and the modification of an unduly harsh superego. Because of the patient's shyness, he had introduced himself by a long, careful, frank letter. Its very order "indicated how little influence your natural, spontaneous inclinations have had with you," the doctor observed. He hoped to modify the patient's superego by reassuring him that hostile feelings were universal. After a dream in which the hero had revealed a death wish by hesitating to call a doctor when his girl friend was dying of poison, the analyst remarked:

> It was your dream . . . without knowing it you accuse yourself in a secret court of justice for wishes of this sort and punish yourself with nervous habits of various kinds. Now it is no sin to have had a thought like that . . . because everyone at one time or another has had death dreams about people they love.

It was as natural as having two legs. The hero's inner conscience was formed by the opinions of others in early childhood, and tended to be strict, severe, and over-moral. The patient's adult conscience, more wise and tolerant, needed to take over the function of judgment.[109]

Far more than any previous popularization, this novel presented psychoanalysis as a painstaking, serious process with a successful outcome earned by hard analytic work and the slow overcoming of painful resistances. It was no longer as easy as "switching on a light," as it had been in some of the first magazine accounts. Rather it became an austere exercise in painful therapeutic self-discipline that ensured greater happiness and spontaneity. This would be the widespread image of analysis after World War II.

The popularization of psychoanalysis was one factor in a massive shift in the American moral system away from what Freud termed "civilized" sexual morality. Sexologists, psychoanalysts, rebellious writers, and intellectuals had been repudiating this system in the years before the First World War. Freud, for one, had done much to divorce the sexual instinct from the function of reproduction and to emphasize its pervasive power. He had also strongly insisted on the sexual nature of women and the importance of sexual satisfaction for women as well as men.

The first part of the repudiation of "civilized" morality was a slow and uneven "repeal of reticence" about sexuality, a gradually increasing frankness in public discussion. In the 1920s, there still was censorship, formal and informal. In newspapers and magazines, discussions of homosexuality, for instance, were often periphrastic, as in the Loeb-Leopold case, and in quasi-medical essays on sexuality, oral sex might be described in Latin.

Nevertheless, in 1930 A. A. Brill greeted the new frankness with satisfaction:

> Times have really changed, sexually speaking. . . . The hypocritical reserve so widely prevalent 30 or even 20 years ago may still be lingering in the remote mountain fastnesses in some of the less civilized nooks of our nation, but the scientific and more liberal-minded people of metropolitan regions are becoming distinctly more honest and outspoken in their attitude to sex.[110]

Before the war, the popularizations of psychoanalysis had been characterized by considerable delicacy in dealing with sexuality; they became franker in the 1920s and 1930s, and some of the "little blue books," for instance, were forthright. The earlier emphasis on sublimation, muted but still present, was paired with a new preoccupation with sexual enjoyment and fulfillment, as *Spectacle of a Man* clearly indicated.

Did psychoanalysis influence changes in sexual behavior in the interwar years? The question is perhaps impossible to answer because so little is known about the history of sexuality; what knowledge we do have, although growing, is fragmentary. By 1930 psychoanalysis had not penetrated the pulp magazines, and its influence is likely to have been confined first to patients, next, to the college-educated and those who read the new literature, finally, perhaps, to some readers of the mass magazines. The evidence for its reputation as an excuse for sexual liberation came chiefly from its opponents, but also from the observations of sympathetic men and women who lived through the 1920s. One of the first Smith College social workers recalled that although the members of her generation were controlled in their behavior, psychoanalysis reduced their sense of guilt and helped those with personal problems. "We came from very guilt ridden backgrounds. We couldn't make fudge or travel on Sunday." But gradually the old prohibitions broke down, particularly during World War I. There were also those who believed in *neurose oder ausleben,* that is, express your sexual impulses or suffer neurosis, the psychologist F. L. Wells recalled. Others had heard that Freud had warned that too much sexual repression was bad, although there was more talk than "acting out." Walter Lippman remembered that for some people psychoanalysis had seemed to license "free, promiscuous sex." Malcolm Cowley and Joseph Freeman remembered that men had used psychoanalysis to seduce girls on grounds that it would prevent neuroses. But then, Havelock Ellis and other sexologists had been similarly invoked. "Liberate the Libido," was indeed the watchword of the popular psychoanalytic cult.[111]

The range of opinion about desirable sexual morality and behavior was as great as the symposia on the subject were numerous.[112] Bertrand Russell, for instance, insisted that sexual intercourse should spring "from the free impulse of both parties, based upon mutual inclination and nothing else." It was evil for institutions to cramp love. There were those who insisted that sexual intercourse was a purely private matter as long as children were avoided and that love, not marriage, "was the only justification of sex relations." The insistence that the sex act be abstained from except under "carefully prescribed circumstances" was a primitive taboo and not a "rational moral principle." Society should prescribe no single line of sexual behavior for its members and girls should have as much freedom as boys. Judge Ben Lindsay and other sex reformers advocated early and companionate marriage with divorce by mutual consent. Some argued that a rise in illicit relations had been the result of more tolerant attitudes among women and some pointed to anthropological studies to show the vast variety of existing sexual customs, with the implication that no absolute standard of behavior was desirable. Margaret Mead's popular *Coming of Age in Samoa* was an important tract in this relativization of morality. The repudiation of traditional religious standards and the substitution of "scientific" sanctions for sexual behavior reached a peak between 1924 and 1926 and seemed to coincide roughly with the peak of interest in psychoanalysis. The most radical opinions appeared in intellectual magazines, the most conservative, in the most popular.[113]

Where the American analysts stood in the gamut of opinion is unclear. They certainly made no public display of sympathy for extreme radical views such as those of Bertrand Russell, nor did they advocate unrestricted sexuality. Recent scholarship has suggested that some analysts, perhaps primarily the Europeans, endorsed premarital relations, and Freud seems to have been neutral about the affairs, including adultery, of some of his analysands. Franz Alexander apparently encouraged the Menninger brothers to carry on extramarital relationships, and even urged William Menninger's wife to take a lover.[114] But the American analysts, including A. A. Brill, while not as conservative as many other American psychiatrists, had gone on record in a *Mental Hygiene* survey in 1920 as believing that sexual relations generally be confined to marriage.[115] Some psychoanalysts, notably Karl Menninger, made vague, reformist pronouncements that were notably lacking in specific recommendations. In 1938 he argued that moral, religious, and superstitious factors had combined to "place heavy restrictions on sexual expression" and that "intelligent discrimination" could now guide the "more enlightened and emancipated." But he added that the economic, physical and psychological "barriers" were "not inconsiderable" and that a need remained "for sublimation and for friendships."[116] Even so, he called for a "more biologically and psychologically sound sexual morality," but never clarified what this might entail. The American analysts certainly advocated birth control and sex education. They argued that the unconscious conscience was an element in sexual behavior that needed consideration, although in this period they also stood for its softening by "mature" judgment. In the case of Floyd Dell, psychoanalysis resulted in a more conventional life-style centering on the family. For some analysts and patients, psychoanalysis could lead to divorce and remarriage, as in the case of Karl Menninger.

Probably changes in sexual behavior were slow during the entire period from 1917 to 1940 and varied across social classes.[117] The age of marriage declined slightly from 1900 to 1940; the mean for women as 21.9 in 1900 and 21.5 in 1940, and for men, 25.9 and 24.3 respectively. Paula Fass has persuasively argued that college youth in the 1920s established dating and petting as their new modes of sexual behavior, but probably not premarital intercourse, except for the engaged. And high school youth in *Middletown* tended to follow a similar pattern. Alfred Kinsey's studies indicated that more of his sample of American women who came of age in the 1920s had experienced premarital intercourse than those born earlier, 18 percent before age 20 and 36 percent between 21 and 25, while half the women who had experienced premarital intercourse did so with a future spouse.[118] There are indications that males frequented prostitutes less and had more relations with women of their own social class. Knowledge of birth control and use of the diaphragm more than doubled among white married women between 1899 and 1929 and condoms became readily available. Marriage manuals toward the close of the 19th century began to emphasize the sexuality of women and to argue that it was equal in intensity to the male's. By the 1920s and increasingly in the 1930s what a sociologist has called the "cult of mutual orgasm" dominated the literature, with an emphasis on techniques of foreplay and coital positions.[119]

Some of the first surveys of American sexual behavior were undertaken in the interwar years by physicians and psychologists who had some acquaintance with psychoanalysis. Katherine B. Davis's *Factors in the Sex Life of Twenty-two Hundred Women* relied on psychoanalytic testimony to the universality of masturbation and the importance of early childhood impressions of sexuality, and cited psychoanalytic explanations of homosexuality as narcissistic fixation. Some 61.2 percent of the women surveyed said that intercourse was not necessary for physical or mental health, while 38.7 percent thought that it was. The average age of her sample was 38. Davis believed that only data "from the life experiences of sane, intelligent men and women" should determine "norms of sex behavior."[120] One of the first students of homosexual women, she argued that they were far more numerous than previously believed, especially in educational and penal institutions. Gilbert V. Hamilton's *A Research in Marriage* was more seriously psychoanalytic, although Hamilton was an eclectic psychiatrist who criticized Freud's methods of observation. He had established a colony for the study of primates in Santa Barbara and had treated Stanley McCormick, the schizophrenic scion of Chicago's International Harvester family. Hamilton used not only a questionnaire but in-depth interviews with his sample of 200 cultivated New Yorkers, most of them under 40. His subjects could have been chosen as likely friends and supporters of psychotherapy and included psychologists, psychiatrists, scientists, teachers, lawyers, architects, social workers, sociologists, and businessman in advertising, manufacturing, and imports. He was convinced that Freud's insights corresponded "in the main, to the realities of human psychodynamics." But he also judged Freud's metapsychology to be too metaphorical for "scientific realism" and preferred a behaviorist interpretation of psychoanalysis. At the same time he used Freud's developmental categories of oral, anal, and Oedipal stages of development and the relation of anal erotism to character traits such as sado-masochism. He discovered that questions about homosexuality and masturbation were far more upsetting to men than to women.[121] Lewis Terman, in a study of the psychological factors predicting marital happiness, found little correlation between the attractiveness of the opposite sex parent—his way of determining a possible Oedipal relationship—and happiness.[122]

One of the most important surveys of sexuality deliberately ignored Freud, but it testified to the survival of "civilized" morality among American married women, many of whom suffered from frigidity partly because of conventional ideals of coldness. "Even in maturity, innocence and virginity are highly rated and the classic behavior of women is formulated on frigid lines," wrote Robert L. Dickenson, a gynecologist and crusader for birth control and sex education, who encouraged Alfred Kinsey's early work. In contrast to some previous gynecologists who had celebrated the maintenance of "purity," Dickenson celebrated the sexuality of women, and the importance of mutual pleasure in intercourse.[123]

Thus psychoanalysis played a significant role in the breakdown of the older ideal of reticence, by encouraging an interest in sexuality and by legitimating sexual expression and public discussion of it. The psychoanalytic linkage of repression with neurosis was important, and for some people psychoanalysis probably provided an excuse for sexual freedom, at the same time that most of its practitioners took a relatively conventional stand on issues of sexual morals. By 1940 psychoanalysis was popularly associated with cultural "modernism": with more relaxed sexual mores, with a reformist, even radical revaluation of criminology, with progressive education, with a radical psychotherapeutic approach to the treatment of the psychoses, and a new psychological approach to social case work. The optimism associated with the mental hygiene movement, in which a few psychoanalysts played important roles, and its emphasis on prevention and community service carried over into the rapid expansion of psychiatry and psychoanalysis after World War II. Psychoanalysis thus was closely associated with currents of center and left-of-center cultural reform and, for a few, with radical politics. Pricked by ridicule, annoyed by the popular cult and by self-appointed psychoanalytic practitioners, the American psychoanalysts mounted intense efforts at professionalization and organizational discipline.

6

Psychoanalytic Training: Young Americans Abroad

A young generation of physicians created the American profession of psychoanalysis after seizing power from their elders in a covert and sometimes divisive struggle in the early 1930s. These Americans and their European mentors established training institutes and new journals, presided over the development of psychoanalysis as an elite specialty, and guided its rapid expansion in the years after World War II. This self-conscious phalanx, with few exceptions, had been trained in the European institutes and its members included Ives Hendrick, Ralph Kaufman, Bertram Lewin, Gregory Zilboorg, Karl Menninger, and Lawrence Kubie. Products of the first systematized psychoanalytic training, they burned with the gemlike flame of truth and discipline. Only those winnowed by similar training could become true psychoanalysts. Ernest Jones, sympathetic to exalted training standards, nevertheless deplored the personal consequences of generational strife. Informed by Ives Hendrick about the deficiencies of the older American analysts, Jones replied that such disputes signified a primitive level of character development that analysts should have overcome.[1]

European analysts, most of them fleeing the rise of fascism, both threatened and reinforced the new tough-minded American leaders. Immigrants helped to found institutes in New York, Boston, Chicago, Topeka, and

Philadelphia, functioned as training analysts, and competed for patients. Together with the Americans, some important immigrants worked to tighten and rigidify the institute system, to the chagrin of other Europeans—and a few of the older Americans. They also brought to America talents in which the American movement had been weakest—systematic theory, child analysis, and an emphasis on the humanities and social sciences. They represented the leaders of the Austrian and German movement, some of Freud's closest and older disciples, some of the energetic rising generation, such as Franz Alexander, and a few unknown young trainees, such as Erik Erikson. In the generational wars, many of them sided with the young Americans whom they had largely trained, and who in turn had rescued them from the menace of Hitler. Their relations were often warm and cordial, but on both sides there were undercurrents of suspicion and occasional hostility.

Both sides in what Ernest Jones called the American "psychoanalytical civil war," which lasted from about 1931 to about 1938, recognized that it was a fight of the young against the old over the issue of professionalization. What made a psychoanalyst? Could he be a layman, self-appointed and publicly eccentric? Both young and old agreed that he could not. Could he be a layman, sober and trained? Most of the native American analysts argued once more that he could not, partly because of the importance of the ties of psychoanalysis to psychiatry.

What if the psychoanalyst were a well-known eclectic psychiatrist, who proclaimed his own version of psychoanalytic theory and therapy, a man such as Harry Stack Sullivan, who specialized in the treatment of schizophrenics, or L. Pierce Clark, who ran a sanitarium for alcoholics, epileptics, and drug addicts? What if he were Paul Schilder, a famous Viennese neuropsychiatrist and a member of Freud's Vienna Psychoanalytic society? Here the American generations tended to divide. None of these men had been trained systematically, an explosive issue because none of the older leaders, including A. A. Brill, had been trained either. They had taken up psychoanalysis before systematic training had been institutionalized. William Alanson White, an eclectic, spent a few expensive hours with Otto Rank during one of the latter's dashes to New York in the mid-1920s. Brill had discussed some of his patients with Freud. Smith Ely Jelliffe had spent time in Vienna during summers. But as representatives of the first generation, they had chosen psychoanalysis. Psychoanalysis had not chosen them. They had represented psychoanalysis as a tiny avant-garde in American psychiatry. Brill, who supported the founding of an institute, nevertheless believed that too exclusive an emphasis on psychoanalytic training as a prerequisite would weaken ties with important eclectic psychiatrists. But it was the ambition of the young Americans to turn psychoanalysis into a recognized medical specialty based on its own rigorous qualifications.

This generational dispute had occasional overtones of snobbery and may have reflected the growing number of psychoanalytic recruits from well-to-do families, educated at the best medical schools—Harvard, Yale, Cornell, Columbia, Johns Hopkins. One American recalled that Freud, as an Anglophile, had looked down on the East European Jews who represented psychoanalysis in America. Ives Hendrick, who was mildly anti-Semitic, dismissed Brill's tactics in psychoanalytic politics as crude and naive, adjectives with clear social overtones.[2]

The self-image and ideal of the younger generation was the scientific expert, and for them the "scientization" of American psychoanalysis became an important enterprise. The young saw themselves as the "best trained," the most "uncompromising," the saving remnant of the movement in America. They had absorbed the "best modern educational policy" of European psychoanalysis. They were particularly galled by the "charlatans," medical and lay, who purported to practice psychoanalysis but who had no professional qualifications beyond their own claims.[3]

To the young, the older generation seemed incompetent, intellectually slack, undisciplined. They could be neither respected nor admired, and thus were inadequate professional father figures.[4] Lawrence Kubie blamed Freud himself for the very aspects of American psychoanalysis Freud deplored. "He has been content to give men inadequate training and to send them home as though they had been trained merely because they have worked with him for a few months. This has created a group of badly trained, and intellectual and emotionally inadequate people in the older group."[5]

To their elders, particularly to A. A. Brill, who had piloted the American movement without rival since the psychotic breakdown of Freud's approved nuncio, Horace W. Frink, the young were galling. They tried to pack committees and meetings to force the adoption of their policies. They were vituperative intriguers, disturbers of the peace, narcissistic, possibly in one instance psychotic. "I cannot stand for all this petty paranoid plotting," Brill wrote in disgust to Ernest Jones, "and I feel that left to themselves they will either cut each others' throats, which if it is going to happen may as well happen—or they will make mistakes and finally make good adjustments and learn some sense." Jones earlier had written that the new group was composed of "rather restless and ambitious new customers."[6]

The young possessed one inestimable advantage—energy. Brill observed that the older generation of the New York Psychoanalytic society were either inactive or indifferent.[7] Jelliffe lamented his growing physical infirmities, chiefly deafness. Few of the older men were diligent enough to "keep thoroughly abreast of what is going on." They were overburdened with "numerous cases of variable nature," he explained to one of the militant young. "It is probable that I shall soon be hardly more than an interested and appreciative spectator of the march of the newer young men now so busy in carrying the banners."[8]

Born in the 1890s or the early 1900s, the young Americans came from origins that differed from the group of young men Brill had first recruited in New York largely from hospital psychiatry. The new generation included upper-middle-class WASPs, upwardly mobile natives, a few Jewish immigrants, and, for the first time, a new element, sons of well-to-do Jewish merchant families. Among the leadership group, Jews slightly outnumbered gentiles. They tended to be fifteen to twenty-five years younger than the first American psychoanalysts.

How had the younger generation decided to become psychoanalysts in the first place, particularly in a period when it was not yet a recognized medical specialty? Presumably the Americans, like most psychoanalysts, were partly attracted by personal difficulties of their own. What these were is difficult to determine: in some instances, thwarted ambition; in others, complex, difficult marriages, psychosomatic illness, anxiety—a set of complaints not too different from those of their patients, if less intense. One aim of professional winnowing in psychoanalysis has been to exclude those whose difficulties might prevent them from functioning as effective therapists.

This generation of recruits first learned about psychoanalysis in highly diverse ways. Some must have first heard of Freud in the daily press, like the forensic psychoanalyst who, as an adolescent, was fascinated by the psychoanalytic testimony of William Alanson White in the Loeb-Leopold case. It was impossible to have been a literate American in the 1920s and not know something about Freud, no matter how distorted.

Like Freud's European followers, many of the young American leaders had strong literary or artistic interests, almost the hallmark of the psychoanalyst. Bertram Lewin, for instance, was an authentic prodigy who could read seven languages, wrote verse, and devoured books—forty-three, for example, during a vacation from medical school in 1918. His reading lists, kept into his years of training at the Berlin Institute, included most of the new literature of modernism: Proust, Schnitzler, H. G. Wells, Mann, Dreiser, Lawrence, Van Vechten, Spengler, Dos Passos, Wedekind, Weininger, Havelock Ellis, and Eleanor Glynn.[9]

Some of these younger psychoanalysts first learned about Freud in college: Lawrence Kubie from the Harvard professor Edwin Bissell Holt; Leo Bartemeier from Dom Thomas Vernor Moore, professor of psychology at Catholic University in Washington, D.C., the first Catholic American to espouse psychoanalysis. Drawn from a wide geographical area, 37 members of the psychoanalytic organizations in 1931 went to 27 different colleges, from the University of Texas to Harvard, and no single college contributed more than two or three. Medical school was more decisive. Of 81 members, 44 came from schools on the eastern seaboard, some 27 of them from schools in New York. About 30 of 81 came from Ivy League medical schools, and at nearly all of these some acquaintance with psychoanalysis was available in the 1920s, chiefly at Columbia, Cornell, and Johns Hopkins. Most of those who became psychoanalysts had chosen to become psychiatrists or neurologists, and internships and residencies at particular institutions were more decisive: the New York State Psychiatric Institute or other hospitals in the New York state mental hospital system, Bellevue or Cornell, Johns Hopkins, the Boston Psychopathic Hospital, or St. Elizabeth's in Washington, D.C.

Bertram Lewin and Lawrence Kubie both learned something about psychoanalysis at Johns Hopkins. During his residency Abraham Kardiner watched one of Freud's first American disciples, Horace W. Frink, demonstrate that a case of paralysis of the upper extremities was not organic, by causing it to disappear under hypnosis. Frink "cured" the patient in a month of therapy, having decided that he had become paralyzed and helpless because he hated his mother-in-law and didn't want to support her.[10] Still others, especially in the 1930s, became fascinated by the promise of psychosomatic medicine.[11]

Greater geographical dispersion occurred with the new institutes and analytic groups established in the 1930s in Chicago, Topeka, Los Angeles, Detroit, San Francisco. The largest concentration of analysts remained, as it began, in New York and the cities of the eastern seaboard, with the additions of Los Angeles and Chicago.

None of the second generation seems to have experienced the kind of conversion that typified the pioneers. Their approach was colder, more cautious. Often conviction occurred only in the course of systematic training and involved a new sense of the professional self, and a bond with those who shared the same initiation rite.

The experience of the young Americans in Europe illustrates the transition from the informality of apprenticeships, especially with "Freud himself," to the more systematic socialization of the institutes. It also illustrates the importance of Americans for the European movement. American fees helped to ensure the survival of a number of Central European analysts after World War I. The Viennese continued to treat large numbers of American patients, and Americans made up a considerable proportion of the trainees in Berlin and Vienna. By 1938, nearly half the candidates in Vienna were American, 12 out of some 23, because the Viennese themselves were too poor to afford analytic training. The American patients and some of the trainees in Vienna and Berlin were well-to-do, while other young analysts were in Europe on Commonwealth Fund fellowships; some scraped together money for the European pilgrimage from relatives or savings; some made periodic trips back home to earn enough money to return.

Usually they were referred by older American analysts. Smith Ely Jelliffe, whose European contacts were extensive, steered John Murray to Vienna and Lawrence Kubie to Edward Glover in London. Harry Stack Sullivan suggested Alexander in Berlin to Ives Hendrick.

The importance of the ties between patient and therapist, candidate and training analyst would prove crucial in the rescue of the European refugees from fascism because analytic pupils and patients were sometimes in positions of professional influence or had important social connections. Thus, when Helene Deutsch was looking for housing in Boston she was driven by Irmarita Putnam's chauffeur. Erik Erikson was befriended in New York by the Tiffanys. Freud himself, of course, was rescued by his former patients, the Princess Bonaparte and the American ambassador to Nazi Germany, the wealthy William Bullitt.

Whatever their personal motivations, the young American physicians primarily expected to learn a new psychiatric technique and sometimes were unsettled by what they discovered in themselves. Abraham Kardiner's five-months analysis with Freud in 1921 indicates how personal Freud's methods could be and how unsystematic. Kardiner was one of a number of young Americans who went to Freud in the immediate postwar years and returned, perhaps euphoric and arrogant, with a figurative diploma from the world's greatest living psychologist. Freud informally controlled some of the patronage of the growing profession and his good opinion was therefore important.

Freud's model of therapy and training included treatment in which problems were uncovered that were to be worked through later by self-analysis. Kardiner, aware only of a childhood fear of Indians and Italians, was unprepared for an anxiety attack experienced on Freud's couch at the end of an hour early in his treatment. Two repeated dreams, sexual and fearful, that his first American analyst, Horace Frink, had been unable to interpret, led back to Kardiner's relationship with his father. Freud's suggestion that Kardiner's account of it was too good to be true, "*un peu retouché*," precipitated the anxiety attack. Freud politely dismissed him, agitated and disturbed, to return the next day.

"Well, apparently we hit something very important there," Freud remarked at the next session. Beneath Kardiner's idealization of his father lay deep fear and a memory of brutal quarrels between his father and his mother. Later Freud suggested that a masked immobile face that appeared in a frightening dream might be Kardiner's dead mother. His sister later confirmed that she had returned home from school to find him in a state of shock and bewilderment in the room where his mother had died. Freud listened to Kardiner's account of his early life on the East Side and his struggles through medical school. "I think you have made much of yourself . . . you ought to be a very interesting subject for analysis." Freud had emphasized the Oedipus complex and the problem of dependency and passivity, but there had been little emphasis on looking at the survivals in Kardiner's present life of early neurotic remnants from childhood. Kardiner's experience of Freud remained positive, but not quite worshipful. He cherished a vision of him as charming, witty, erudite, the movement's only genius. Yet Freud demanded absolute loyalty. Once Kardiner asked him about his theory of primal parricide. "Oh, don't take that seriously. That's something I dreamed up on a rainy Sunday afternoon." But then, Kardiner observed, if you didn't take Freud seriously, your head would come off.[12] Kardiner later came to feel that his training had been old-fashioned by comparison with that of the graduates of the institutes.

Freud could be directly personal with patients and admonished another American not to vacillate about a recent marriage. "You have married now not under the influence of compulsion and not under the influence of friends. Truly by your own choice, and now you have to show us that you are right and that you are able to be happy."[13]

Smiley Blanton, who began as a child psychiatrist, and later collaborated with New York's most celebrated Protestant preacher, Norman Vincent Peale, author of the best-seller, *The Power of Positive Thinking,* found a far more tolerant, gracious Freud than had some other Americans. He saw Freud for short periods from 1929 to 1938 and was astonished by Freud's open-mindedness and relative lack of dogmatism. Freud insisted on hearing his patient's associations and Blanton found nothing formulaic in his interpretations. Freud also made no objections to Blanton's collaboration with clergymen, insisting that there was nothing in an analysis to detract from "human achievement and moral dignity." Once, Freud talked to Blanton through almost an entire hour's session. He was voluble about his contempt for America, with its poor education and culture, and was bitter about the stand against lay analysis and the cliques in the New York Psychoanalytic Society, where Blanton felt like an outsider. Blanton believed his treatment with Freud gave him a sense of increased power and radically transformed his self-understanding; Freud became for him a beloved father figure.[14]

Roy Grinker, who worked with Freud in 1933, was equally enthusiastic. He wrote to Smith Ely Jelliffe, who had steered him to Vienna: "Perhaps you may credit my feelings toward him [Freud] as transference during analysis, but from the very first day I felt his personality as being the most inspiring and confidence giving one I have ever met." Freud was the "one and only genius" and unlike his Viennese disciples who were busy creating new theories and expounding them, he "studies his material and waits until he has the evidence. The 11 volumes of the *Gesammelte Werke* are my bible right now."[15]

Institute training was far more systematized than Freud's but it remained informal, and the role of committees seems to have been less important in Vienna and Berlin than it later became in America. Training also was often brief. The Viennese remained the most orthodox in theory, with their close ties to Freud and his first disciples. Vienna also placed considerable emphasis on training teachers, on child analysis, and work with juvenile delinquents. Berlin, on the other hand, stressed the social sciences and perhaps above all the training of physicians. The institutes did not prohibit the Americans attending lectures or reading about psychoanalysis while they were undergoing their didactic analyses. They were allowed to take on patients after perhaps a year of training, sometimes much less. Gregory Zilboorg, for example, began control analyses with patients after the first six weeks of his analysis with Franz Alexander.[16] The social life of the institutes also mixed therapists and patients at parties, a practice that would have scandalized later American purists. Sandor Rado observed that the Americans were merely passing participants in the analytic ritual, seldom staying long enough for thorough indoctrination.[17]

Most of the young Americans had learned about psychoanalysis during their psychiatric education. Subsequent training at a psychoanalytic institute effectively achieved the conversion of the vacillating, particularly when they began working with patients, and forged a greater uniformity of outlook than analysts had shared before. Under the special conditions of the Depression and with the American faith in professional expertise, the young Americans would harden the institute into a more rigidly organized training machine.

Few of the Americans knew German, and the language barrier was formidable when combined with the esoteric nature of analytic theory. One candidate understood but a fraction of the lectures he attended. Nevertheless, his analysis in Vienna was "one of the best things" he had ever done.[18] Some never mastered German, others succeeded after dogged efforts. How well their European analysts understood the nuances of American speech remains an undiscussed topic.

The American analytic innocent abroad is most fully, if eccentrically, represented by Ives Hendrick, whose long letters to his journalist-historian father and, more important, to his mother, charted in detail his analytic acculturation. Snobbish about his old New England roots and values, Hendrick represented the upper-middle-class WASP, newly threatened by Jews and foreigners.

Shy, awkward, given to periods of hard, sustained work alternating with periods of slack, close to his mother, whose visits during his medical and psychiatric training invariably gave him renewed bursts of confidence, Hendrick approached psychoanalysis cautiously, even skeptically. He had learned about it at the Boston Psychopathic Hospital under C. Macfie Campbell and at Sheppard Pratt, where he worked with the prickly Harry Stack Sullivan in 1927 and 1928. In turn, Sullivan described Hendrick as a "perhaps amusing, certainly damned annoying young man," "well, DIFFICULT is as good a word as I could find."[19]

Hendrick had picked up the generalized "psychoanalytic psychiatry" of his generation before his European training. He wrote to his mother, who was seeking a rest cure in a sanitarium, that the "real root of imperfect adjustment" is "too deeply buried in the early years to be apparent." Many people found it difficult to adjust their wishes to demands of home and community. Yet imperfect adjustment and emotional restlessness energized creative work and the fulfillment of ambition. Hendrick displayed the generalized analytic formulae of the 1920s—the importance of early childhood, conflict between individual instinct and social demands, the creative role of neurosis.

Freud, he wrote to his parents just before starting his analysis with Alexander, had made the "greatest contribution" to psychology and to helping "normal and near-normal" people. "What Freud uncovered in the unconscious of the sane, was clearly seen in the everyday behavior and speech of the insane. . . . " "One cannot work with serious mental illness for two years, and fail to observe that these conditions (in which the 'unconscious' is 'naked') confirm Freud's early work in most startling manner." Freud had proven that much of behavior is determined by "emotional trends and habits of thought of which we are unaware"; much behavior was symbolic, "a medium of expression of unconscious desires"; dreams were purposeful; and the psychoanalytic method could help some individuals "who are less happy and productive than they might be."

Yet he insisted that he did not wish to belong to the psychoanalytic school, and he distrusted Freud's followers with their "bewildering galaxy of conflicting and controversial additions, abstruse and difficult of analysis." In much of psychoanalysis was "apparent a fanaticism, a bigotry, an intolerance,

a tendency to parallel religious doctrine even to use such phrases as 'orthodox Freudian,' 'convert,' 'faith,' which is most discouraging to the scientist."
Psychoanalysis would have to submit to a "methodology which can be harmo-
nized with the methodology of other sciences."

In a revealing passage that prefigured much of his later campaign against
lay analysis and indiscriminate popularization, Hendrick warned that

> more and more conspicuous becomes the number of people professing under-
> standing of psychoanalysis and even professing to treat patients by it, who are at
> best dilettantes, and at worst charlatans. The boundary between these and real
> analysts is very vague—the subject is too new to have a tradition and a legal
> sanction which exercises so powerful an ethical influence as we have in medicine.
> This fertile crop of pseudo analysts is the result of the popular appeal of the
> subject, and its peculiarity in that it appears quite simple and clearly understood
> by the dilettante. I am afraid of having my status confused with that of these
> enthusiasts, fanatics, and mercenary charlatans, who have neither the scientific
> attitude nor the practical experience to qualify them for the work.

He was not intending to confine his practice to psychoanalysis, and preferred
to see his present work as training in a "special field of psychology, as further
education in psychiatry . . . . "[20] He was undertaking it now because it was
the one field in which Europe was more advanced than America.

It was not necessary to be analyzed to understand it, but it would help
him to understand it better. Finally, he hoped to derive some personal benefit from it:

> All analyses are not successful, any more than all medical treatments are. But I
> know of none who has had a successful analysis who does not feel he has been
> helped by it in understanding himself, in meeting the demands of his environ-
> ment, and in making the most of his potentialities for happiness and success. It
> requires no special comment to prove that it is [*sic*] plenty of room for improve-
> ment in me in these matters.[21]

He had chosen the Berlin Institute because it was more cohesive, better
organized than the Viennese. Moreover, Franz Alexander was the best man
in Europe who understood English. The one Viennese he would consider
seeing, Paul Schilder, shortly would leave for America. His two months in
Vienna, he wrote regretfully, had not been spent in systematic study. But he
had avoided English-speaking people, had cultivated a Polish *freundin* in
order to learn German, had drunk his coffee with whipped cream in the
cafés, and had attended as much Wagner as the opera afforded. In Berlin he
saw Max Rinehardt's production of the American play *The Artists,* and decided the Berlin theater was the best in the world.

Berlin was to be all work and no tourism. Indeed in its dazzle, crowds,
preoccupations, and the loneliness of the stranger, it reminded him of New
York. He enrolled in a course in German for foreigners at the university and
grasped most if not every word of a lecture on Frederick the Great. At the

university psychiatric hospital he was given a locker, a gown, and the keys to the hospital and encouraged to talk to patients and take case histories. He described his weekly routine to his parents. His day stretched from 8:30 a.m. to 10 p.m. when the institute, largely a night school, resumed in the fall after summer recess. He worked at the hospital in the morning, had his analytic hour from 12:00 to 1:00 with Alexander, studied German at the university from 3:15 to 5 p.m. Then he was at the institute every night. Monday: seminar on Freudian technical theory began at 9:00, with Otto Fenichel, "the best most stimulating thing I have had at the Institute," preceded by a "series of lectures on Goethe's and Frederika's love [probably by Theodor Reik], which I take because it is interesting and my evening is spoiled anyway." Tuesday: meetings of the Psychoanalytic Society. Wednesday: seminar for discussion of cases. Thursday: seminar for review of books preceded by a "very good but rather elementary course by Dr. Rado which I might as well take as the evening is spoiled anyway. Friday: seminar on Freud case histories."[22]

Rado's course artfully condensed by rhetorical question and answer the psychoanalytic theory of the 1920s. Psychoanalysis was a set of arbitrary hypotheses that nevertheless could be systematically elaborated and confirmed by the psychoanalytic method. Rado placed special emphasis on the drive for self-preservation and on the fusion in normal life of Freud's erotic and destructive instincts, and he largely omitted the theory of character, which had undergone special elaboration in Berlin.[23]

Alexander pleased Hendrick from the outset. "I have begun my analysis, and am quite satisfied I could not have found a better man. The probabilities are that I shall get my money's worth." Alexander was "vigorous, energetic, virile, quite young." "He has a good deal of common sense, always maintains a sufficiently practical view of human fallibility. He has none of that fanatical fervor, that blatant self-satisfaction, that contempt for the unenlightened, that blindness to logic, which characterizes a large proportion of those little idiots who prance about the world calling themselves psycho-analysts." On Alexander's advice, Hendrick tried to delay a proposed visit from his mother because it might slow up his analysis, "as all the aspects of an adult personality and emotions are intimately connected by threads which lead directly back to the mother." Alexander had said there would be no objection to a visit later, while he was completing his analysis. Alexander also gave him permission to attend courses at the institute on grounds that learning more analytic theory than he already knew could do no harm. A critical attitude, Hendrick explained to his parents, was a hindrance to the analytic process, which dealt with "emotions, loves, hates, desires, frustrations, feelings, purposes which are more fundamental than intellectual processes."[24]

He wrote little about his analysis to his parents—except for one problem. He was lodging with Karl Abraham's sister and her husband, and was impressed by Abraham's daughter. "No freak, fanatical father of a family could ever turn out a daughter like this: she was as intelligent, cultivated, feminine, natural and unaffected a young woman as you will ever meet, reminding me of the Fletcher girls. So, after all, it is probably true of psycho-analysts as it is of doctors, teachers, ministers, parents and others, the method is not so important as the individual. The well-balanced, intelligent and sympathetic person always does a good job in the 'altruistic' professions. And such people are quite as necessary to the full utilization of the theories and techniques of psychoanalysis as to other procedures. The proof is in the results—in this case, a very splendid type of young woman."

However, Hendrick was shocked by a revelation about them. They were Jewish. "I have felt I was being stifled by a noxious, alien, all-pervading vapor." In retrospect he could find no characteristic stigmata; they were "physically, culturally and temperamentally" the finest type of German—Nordic in lineaments, yellow-haired. Even his analyst was a Hungarian Jew. Alexander's family was like the Castillian Jews in New York. They had enjoyed "long freedom from orthodox principles, and [were] long accepted as one of the leading and influential and socially eligible families of Budapest. But he completes the ring of Jews who have enmeshed me."[25]

Hendrick was forced to admit that the "attenuation" of his enthusiasm for Abraham's daughter and her parents could be explained only on grounds of "emotional complexes, race prejudice without (in these cases) any adequate reasons." In another case, he admired the talent and culture of an American Jew in Berlin, yet was repelled by his "radical ultra-modernism"; "the ultra modern is too marked a contrast to my New England standards that it tastes very bad." It was apparent in the man's painting, his "radical socialism," his "denial of everything worth while in Wagner (strangely, on that point finding a common ground with father)." These "racial prejudices" had become a conspicuous feature of his work with Alexander, and he was planning to spend two or three years studying the Jews and wanted to be "as free from unconscious emotional prejudice in regard to that as I can." Yet he deplored the conspicuousness of Jews in Alexander's entourage, although Alexander had been recommended to him by three non-Jews, Sullivan, S. B. Sniffen, and George Daniels.[26]

Probably Hendrick had absorbed his anti-Semitism from his father, who at the height of the Red Scare had written a book about New York's Jews and the dangers of Jewish socialism. It was typical of the anti-Semitism of some upper-middle-class Americans, who considered themselves part of the "New England" tradition. Like Madison Grant, the snobbish bachelor who directed the Bronx Zoo and who wrote *The Passing of the Great Race,* they deplored the foreign menace to American culture, particularly when it came from new immigrants and Jews. Hendrick retained tinges of his anti-Semitism, but he also usually got along well with his Jewish colleagues. At the tenth anniversary celebration of the Berlin clinic, at Eitingon's house, he thought the assembled analysts "the first gathering of professional colleagues for social purposes I have ever thoroughly enjoyed." They were "really a fine group of people, distinguished . . . not only by professional accomplishments but by general congeniality and character—no eccentrics at all."[27]

The clinic itself was impressive. Some 137 patients were then in treatment, one hour a day from three to six times a week for six months to several years. They were being treated by "doctors whose personal qualifications and training are perhaps not to be matched by 15 in America."

Indeed, it was only when Hendrick himself had been allowed to treat patients that his psychoanalytic conversion, till then quite gradual, had crystallized. He was eager to begin after a year of analysis, apparently had been turned down, and threatened to give up and go home if his expectations were not fulfilled. Although bookish, he found that books did not give the "constant impetus of problem and query and curiosity that always pushes one on to further work" that came from patients. A summer in Marburg at Westphal's clinic had convinced him that American psychiatry was vastly superior in its methods of treatment and its results, and particularly its application of psychoanalytic principles to a wide range of cases.[28]

Within a few months of conducting analyses, his interest in psychoanalysis suddenly had solidified, and he was unwilling to leave Berlin and his cases even for Christmas in Vienna.[29] His patients were showing

> results which no other means could have produced. That's more convincing than all the intellectual expostulation and queries and jokes and misunderstandings of people who only know psychoanalysis as a set of queer sounding books in which the word "sex" appears with seeming unmitigated frequency.[30]

In February, before he had begun treating patients, Alexander had told him that his analysis had approached the stage which "is fundamental in order to do really good work." He was the only one of the dozen or so candidates who had mastered the language and been declared ready to treat patients.

As Alexander began making plans to attend the International Mental Hygiene Congress in Washington in 1930, Hendrick felt "a bit depressed." He had been working on a paper but its progress was "very slow and tedious."[31] He had put Alexander and Rado up at the Yale Club, and asked his parents to put their anti-Semitism in their pockets. Both were "highly intelligent and cultivated men."[32]

The analyses of some of the young Americans who had trained in Europe had not been deep, and several undertook a second analysis later, a procedure that became increasingly common in the 1930s. Lawrence Kubie, for instance, who had undertaken his analysis for training as well as some alleviation of his own "compulsive tension," found that his work with Edward Glover in London in 1927 and 1928 had about it a "dream-like quality.":

> Foremost, perhaps, is my sense of having been almost as though I were deaf throughout it, deaf and perhaps dumb as well. I can remember so little of what I said myself, or what I heard. I have a sense of amazement at the rigidity of my own productions, feeling as though they must have been obstinately stereotyped.[33]

It was as if he had not achieved "any degree of superego relaxation" or won the "analytic struggle for free association." Part of this he blamed on Glover's technique of interpreting very early his hostile feelings about the analyst, his negative transference, which later prevented the emergence of his feelings of affection for Glover. The constraint of his London therapy contrasted with some recent violent dreams that had reached a curious sense of "stability and calmness."[34] He undertook a second analysis with the Viennese refugee Hermann Nunberg.

Whatever deficiencies some young analysts may have felt marred their didactic analyses, the training experience gave them a sense of professional expertise and status that set them apart from the uninitiated. From 1927 to 1930 perhaps forty American psychiatrists, most of them young, went abroad for psychoanalytic training.[35] Some were on the staffs of public mental hospitals, others worked part-time at clinics or taught at medical schools in the United States. Some continued to practice psychoanalysis part-time; other physicians, perhaps internists or urologists, also established part-time practices. Still others practiced analysis full-time. The earnings of physicians who worked part-time for salaries and devoted the rest to private practice often was higher than those in private practice alone.[36] In 1938, for instance, Ives Hendrick looked for a part-time or fully salaried position to improve his financial situation.

Hendrick had worried about his future prospects during his European training. Early in 1928 he had canvassed the possibilities: psychiatrist in a boys' school, a study of American Jews, a job at Boston Psychopathic Hospital. His psychoanalytic training, he informed his parents, would be a "better recommendation even than evidence of ability" to the "mental hygiene people, who have more to do with granting positions than any organization in the country . . . ."[37] If he set himself up in private practice, he needed a single reasonably well-to-do patient to cover his office rent and then would begin to earn income.

American prosperity and favorable exchange rates made Europe economically feasible for Americans during the 1920s. In 1928, for instance, a young American could live very well in Berlin, paying $35 a month for a room and breakfast, and other meals might run around 60 to 75 cents apiece. There were subsidized concerts for 50 cents, and even expensive performances were cheap by New York standards. Vienna was possibly cheaper.

Although a few Americans continued their training in Vienna into the late 1930s, the Depression and the rise of Adolf Hitler made European training less practical. Meanwhile, at home, the American psychoanalysts were developing their own institutes and consolidating their profession.

7.

The Depression, Schisms, Refugees, 1929–1942

When Hitler came to power in 1933, the diaspora of psychoanalysts from central Europe began, and by 1942 the analytic movement's center of gravity had shifted to the United States. The young American trainees and their European mentors completed the professionalization of psychoanalysis during the worst depression in the nation's history.

Hard times complicated the reception of the Europeans and exacerbated the American "analytical civil war" which broke out in 1931.[1] Ives Hendrick, one of the militant young, observed that the development of psychoanalysis was being crippled not only by conflicts of the young and the trained versus the older eclectics but by further divisions of "Jew against gentile, American against European, older against younger generations, city against city, personal rivalries of intensely narcissistic people (probably inevitable in most with analytic talent) . . . . "[2]

A dispute involving a split between generations and marking the introduction of orthodoxy as an issue occurred in the New York society in 1931 and 1932. It began when a new constitution reorganizing the American Psychoanalytic Association was proposed. Direct membership was abolished and the association became an umbrella for local societies which would directly control membership and training. The old eclectic association, whose standard of admission by the 1920s was a medical degree but not a "course in psychoanalysis," was dissolved. The aim of the new organization, Lawrence Kubie explained to a San Francisco psychiatrist who no longer found himself on the roster, was to raise the standards of training.[3] After a number of disagreements the association's new constitution was adopted in 1935. Smith Ely Jelliffe, an older analyst whom Brill had asked to serve on one of the many committees dealing with reorganization, refused. "We once had a society without any [constitutions]. It was glorious."[4]

The more orthodox faction in New York threatened to exclude from the new national organization the eclectic Baltimore-Washington society. The dispute was worsened by Sandor Rado's dislike of Karen Horney, who taught in Washington-Baltimore, even as Rado's own disagreements with Freud were beginning to polarize New York. "Both sides stink," the refugee analyst Herman Nunberg observed.[5] In addition, more stringent qualifications for the role of training analyst were being drafted, and the lay analysis issue was exacerbated by quarrels over the attempts of European-trained American laymen and of European lay analysts to set up practices.

The Depression's effects lasted well into the late 1930s and made private analytic practice precarious, particularly in 1932 and 1933. Some analysts complained of the difficulties of making a living, and in 1933, Jelliffe informed Karl Menninger that some New York analysts were shifting candidates to themselves for training analyses.[6] Jelliffe worried about a slackening patient load; patients had no money to spend on therapy. Harry Stack Sullivan observed in 1932 that he was having a hard time establishing himself in New York. John Millet, a recent trainee of the New York institute, wondered how he could finance his son's last two years of college.[7] Answering a request for help to a refugee, William Alanson White, director of St. Elizabeth's, the federal government's hospital for the insane, described the stringencies imposed on his hospital. Its budget had been slashed by $396,923 in 1933:

> Personally, I have nothing. The government is shutting down on the activities and throwing hundreds of thousands of people out of jobs and I am under absolute and strict orders not to employ anybody, nor to incur any additional obligations of any sort. I cannot even fill a vacancy. The great foundations are in similar shape. Their funds have shrunk tremendously in the past few years.

The Child Guidance Clinic in New York was to be closed because the Commonwealth Fund had had to retrench. "If there are jobs for anybody it might be rather poor diplomacy to employ an alien, and it might be expected that an American citizen would get the job."[8]

Brill warned Ernest Jones that many members of the New York society scarcely made a living. It is likely that eminent Europeans, who quickly became training analysts, competed with the younger Americans, particularly for analytic candidates. Ives Hendrick complained to William Healy in 1937 that perhaps he should have been content to foster the "natural growth of an extremely good practice, instead of starting the immigration of those for doing work I should have been qualified to do in a few years."[9] As the Americans left for the Armed Services after Pearl Harbor, the émigrés began to dominate and German could be heard at New York society meetings.[10]

The Depression in its worst years exacerbated some of the endemic problems of psychoanalytic practice: how to ensure an adequate living and how to reconcile making a living with research. Some were forced to crowd in a large number of patients, perhaps seven to nine or ten a day. Often when a particular standard of living had been reached, or when a reputation for unusual competence brought a flood of patients seeking help, it was hard to turn down the fees or the patients to save time for "scientific pursuits." This has been a persistent dilemma of psychoanalysts, for whom few if any research careers have been available.

The problems of Lawrence Kubie, who was just starting a practice in 1932, and the advice of his training analyst, Edward Glover, illustrate the difficulties. Glover suggested that he begin with "two hysterias, one sexual perversion, one obsessional, and if possible, a so-called normal individual. Your first vacancy thereafter should be a psychotic." Because his family's finances, once securely affluent, had become precarious, Kubie was forced to take on a heavy schedule, chiefly people of limited means, and some of the most promising cases had to be carried "for purely nominal payments." He took on nine patients.[11]

Glover reiterated his advice to Kubie about limiting his practice, arguing that in time the "heavy list will also become a good paying list. It is at this later point that your temptation will come. You may by then have got use [sic] to cutting down the time necessary for reflection and reading, and be tempted to carry on the heavy list when it is no longer economically necessary. I hope that when this time comes—and I have no doubt it will come sooner than you expect—you will take yourself very vigorously by the scruff of the neck and force yourself to allow time for scientific work."[12]

Kubie wrote to Glover that he had learned more in his year and a half of analytic practice than from "twice that time" at the Johns Hopkins University clinic. His cases were typical of the practice of the 1920s and 1930s. He was treating a painter suffering from a long-standing anxiety hysteria; a young bank clerk, a compulsion neurotic; a young lawyer who "had a phobia that he was homosexual" and who was recovering after being "on the verge of an intensely agitated suicidal depression, and we balanced for weeks on the edge of the precipice"; an obsessional, anxious young alcoholic, a neurotic character; a depressed middle-aged man; a young woman with "obsessional fears"; a male anxiety hysteric of 38; a young accountant with a "deeply narcissistic, homosexual problem"; a young physician "with a phobia about knives and heights"; a young music critic with neurasthenia; a fifteen-year-old boy, a transvestite since the age of four.

He had begun by imitating Glover's techniques and now was experimenting with his own. Above all, he was impressed by watching the "play of unconscious phantasies, their dynamic power, and their extraordinary persistence in the face of all reality considerations."[13] It had taken Kubie two years to dissociate himself from his earlier organic and neurological interest; he had been afraid that his neurological techniques and acumen might be blunted through neglect. His focus had slowly but decisively shifted to psychoanalysis.

Kubie became, in effect, like other analysts, a medical entrepreneur in the tradition of American private practice, in a new specialty which had, he insisted, the most lengthy apprenticeship in all of medicine.[14] He held out an austere but glittering promise of successful treatment: "transformation of energy," peace, pleasure in activity, freedom from disturbing states of depression, anxiety, guilt, fear, jealousy, or nervous symptoms. The goal of psychoanalysis was not a shifting, relativistic definition of health but a "strenuous, uncompromising ideal," that is, freedom from "masked" as well as obvious neurotic trends.[15]

Daily treatment, lasting about two years at an annual cost of $2,600 to $2,750, was the road to this result. This image of psychoanalytic practice blazoned an esoteric, costly science, practiced only by the carefully chosen and meticulously trained. It was difficult, called for sacrifice, but promised in effect almost superhuman benefits.

As a practical matter, if the analyst averaged six patients a year at Kubie's projected rate of average cost, his annual gross income would have been between $12,000 and $15,000. Fees ranged from nothing to $30 an hour, and the average in New York was well under $10. Indeed, the $20 to $25-an-hour patient was becoming rare and social workers were paying around $2.00.[16] How many analysts drew a clientele paying $2,750 a year is impossible to determine.

It is only by comparing these figures with the actual income of physicians that the elite status of psychoanalysis, and indeed the economic incentive to practice it, becomes apparent. The Menninger Clinic, for instance, announced four residencies available in 1937 at a salary of $120 per month, "without maintenance." But then residents were usually poorly paid. What is surprising is that the mean gross income for physicians in the United States was $7,020 in 1936, the year Kubie's book was published, up from a low of $5,368 in 1933. Gross earnings of physicians in New York were *below* the national mean and below the earnings of physicians in other cities of more than 500,000.[17] Thus an analyst who did establish a full practice could look forward to earning substantially more, perhaps double, the gross income of most physicians.

The incomes of precisely those groups that provided most of the patients of the psychoanalysts, the college-educated entrepreneurs, investors, and particularly professionals, dropped proportionately more sharply than those of any other group except the "moderately" low-income, grammar-school-educated workers.[18] Kubie argued in opposition to analysts at the Berlin psychoanalytic clinic that free treatment would be useless because patients would lack incentive, and that if they suffered severe financial reverses their analyses might have to be interrupted.

American analysts could combine this acceptance of capitalist medical economics with a strongly liberal cultural orientation. During World War II, Kubie would take a militant stand against segregation in the armed services. And there was also a very small radical wing within the American movement.[19] On the whole, the Europeans were further left: most were socialists or social democrats, and a few were dedicated Marxists. The radicalism and socialism of some became muted as they moved into closer ties with American medicine and psychiatry. Their interests focused on theory and technique, on social work, the systematization of psychoanalytic training, on psychiatry and psychosomatic medicine. Some of the refugees, including Siegfried Bernfeld, found the politics of the New Deal hopeful and congenial. Fritz Wittels, who had emigrated in the late 1920s, cautioned him that to become involved with political or economic issues would destroy the unique vision of psychoanalysis.[20] America has been accused of taming Otto Fenichel's radicalism. But his privately circulated *Rundbriefe* were primarily concerned with theoretical issues such as a lengthy critique of James Burnham's recent book, *The Managerial Revolution,* and developments in psychoanalytic theory. As time went on Fenichel became increasingly caught up in the organizational and doctrinal disputes within the psychoanalytic movement. His widow recalled that he had never been actively involved politically in Europe as had Wilhelm Reich.[21]

Despite the Depression the analytic movement steadily grew; one new journal and a bulletin were founded. By 1939 there were half as many candidates as there were already practicing members of the existing institutes. The psychiatric profession also grew. Between 1929 and 1936 the number of physicians employed in public mental hospitals rose moderately in California, New York, Illinois, and Massachusetts. Even St. Elizabeth's employed sixteen more physicians in 1936 than it had in 1930. This modest increase reflected an expansion of some mental hospital systems, notably New York's, and a long-term rise since 1924 in first admissions. One reason may have been greater demand for treatment.

Whether the Depression increased the amount of nervous and mental disorder in America is a matter of dispute. Suicides, particularly among males, rose in all areas in Chicago. Harvey Brenner has argued, on the basis of the experience of New York State, that there has been a close correlation between economic downturns and rising mental hospital admissions. Indeed, during the Depression precisely those groups most adversely affected by it, and particularly the males among them, had the highest rates of increase. Whether the hospitals were a kind of social refuge, as they were for the aged, or whether the incidence of mental disorder actually increased remains unknown. Because of their economic role as providers, males were particularly susceptible to the tensions brought on by unemployment and loss of income during the Depression. If the rate of mental illness in fact increased among those groups most adversely affected by the Depression, it is quite likely that the psychoneuroses—anxiety, mild depression—also increased with intensifying social stress.[22]

College-educated professionals were those most likely to seek the help of the private psychiatrist or the psychoanalyst. Despite a drop in income, perhaps the promise of greater energy, freedom from anxiety and fear may have seemed well worth the high cost of analytic treatment. Perhaps there was, as Franz Alexander thought, a real growth in the demand for it.

A major outlet for the energies of the younger analysts was the founding of the *Psychoanalytic Quarterly* in 1932, an act that, along with reorganization of the American Psychoanalytic Association, crystallized the split between generations. Although Frankwood Williams, who was sympathetic to Rank, was one of the founders, the other three editors—Dorian Feigenbaum, Bertram Lewin, and Gregory Zilboorg—represented the orthodox group within the New York Society. Franz Alexander wrote to Smith Ely Jelliffe that they might reject an article of his because one member of the editorial board found it "extremely revolutionary and in contradiction to certain 'sentences' in one of Freud's early writings."[23] Jelliffe, one of the two editors of the old and deliberately eclectic *Psychoanalytic Review,* observed that "if by any chance their 'high standards' or other nonsense should exclude" the paper, he would be delighted to publish it.[24] Jelliffe and William Alanson White, his co-editor, had pitched their journal deliberately at the level of the psychiatric social worker "with problems to solve."[25] They had rejected a paper by Melanie Klein, a German child analyst settled in London, because it was too abstruse. The *Review* had survived since 1913, they insisted, because its policies were flexible.

It was an odd time to launch a new journal, just as the Depression deepened, and existing psychoanalytic publications already were threatened, their finances marginal. Both the *Review* and Ernest Jones's *International Journal* depended on American support. Jones argued that with only a few hundred subscribers each, a new psychoanalytic publication in English posed a serious threat. The "boom in psychoanalysis" was long over and only one in ten psychoanalytic books paid for itself. Thus it was a matter of some importance which journal printed official transactions and had first rights to European translations.[26]

The editors of the new *Quarterly,* whose average age was 42, about fifteen years younger than Brill, tried to gain wide support, inviting selected members of the older generation to participate as advisory editors, particularly Brill, White, and Jelliffe. Brill, reluctant at first on grounds that a new journal was otiose and the editors "too young" to work with, shortly acquiesced.[27] Jelliffe agreed at once, but tried to get the editors to change the journal's proposed name because it would be indistinguishable from the *Review.* He suggested alternatives: "Psychoanalytic Reporter, Psychoanalytic Investigations, Psychoanalytic Clinic, Clinical and Theoretical Psychoanalysis, the Bulletin of Psychoanalysis, Studies in Psychoanalysis, Psychoanalytic Progress, Psychoanalysis and Conduct, Medical Psychoanalysis, Psychoanalysis and Medicine . . . . "[28] The editors were adamant and pointed to such common periodicals, none confused with the other, as the *New York Times,* the *New York Sun, Psychological Index, Psychological Bulletin,* and so on.

The title remained simply the *Psychoanalytic Quarterly,* with a distinctive format.[29]

The editors had had the "impudence," Brill observed, to try to enlist Freud's support, and two articles by him appeared in "authorized" translations in the first issues, and in anonymous translations in Jones's *International Journal.* Jones complained to Brill: "Are we both to tout about for original papers and translations; are the same things to be published in both journals and necessarily translated twice over, or haven't they thought about the matter at all?"[30] The *Quarterly* quickly became the vehicle for the younger militants, and the growing number of immigrant analysts, among them Helene Deutsch, Otto Fenichel, and Erik Erikson. It presented a translation of Geza Roheim's lengthy new anthropological studies, Fenichel's syntheses of theory, new work in child analysis. The *Quarterly* maintained a high level of both orthodoxy and sophistication, while the *Review* continued in its old ways, publishing the eclectics, articles for social workers, and occasional poetic effusions, such as ". . . let us wait without the Empyrean, where men and angels lie, intent upon the Mama-God. . . . "[31]

When White died in 1937, Jelliffe at once sought to add more psychoanalysts to the *Review*'s editorial board, a suggestion White earlier had rejected on grounds of preserving freedom from "entangling alliances" and preserving catholicity about not only published matter but about "internecine warfare and intrapsychic conflicts, et al."[32] Hendrick responded to an invitation to be a contributing editor by noting his delight in being asked to collaborate with the *Quarterly,* a slip of the pen Jelliffe taxed him with.[33] By 1937 Jelliffe had become reconciled to the *Quarterly*'s existence and its very real success. It had been kept afloat by financial contributions from the editors.

And the young tried to mollify their elders. After a particularly scathing review by Lawrence Kubie of one of Jelliffe's papers, Jelliffe wrote that "Even such an unanalyzed old fogey as myself feels that an analyzed person such as the reviewer . . . ought to recognize his own Oedipus remnants." Kubie replied that he could not pass over "with soothing words a bit of work that is not representative of our own best standards . . . . I think I can honestly say that my 'Oedipus remnants' are so far resolved that I can fight our elder leaders quite openly and vigorously and at the same time look upon them with much veneration and respect."[34]

The unrepentent *Review* continued to publish one of the most brilliant of all the eclectics, Paul Schilder, an immigrant Viennese psychiatrist and member of Freud's Vienna society, who had settled in New York in 1929. In 1935 Schilder was disqualified as a training analyst by the New York institute, on grounds he himself had not been trained.

Schilder's scalp represented a major trophy taken by the militants after tortured negotiations and a final personal appeal by Schilder to Freud himself. Even more than the *Quarterly,* the Schilder affair dramatized the new professionalism of the American movement, the split between the policies of Brill and the younger, European-trained analysts. It led Brill to withdraw from the New York society's activities for a time and to take up a largely ceremonial role. The imbroglio also indicated the fledgling status of the New York institute, whose educational committee's dictates could be defied by Schilder. Versed in neurology, psychiatry, philosophy, and psychoanalysis, Schilder had received an M.D. from the University of Vienna in 1909 and a Ph.D. in philosophy in 1922, for which he had begun to study during his military service in World War I. He had been assistant to Julius von Wagner-Jauregg, director of the Psychiatric Division of the Vienna General Hospital, who tolerated his psychoanalytic bent. Prolific, hoping to achieve a synthesis of psychoanalysis and psychiatry, he wrote several hundred papers and books. He was killed on November 7, 1940, by an automobile on a New York Street after a hospital visit to his wife and twelve-day-old daughter.

With a high, squeaky voice and an impenetrable German accent, Schilder was research professor of psychiatry at New York University from 1929 to 1940, clinical director of psychiatry at Bellevue, and had cultivated close relations with American neurologists and psychiatrists, Adolf Meyer among them. But he had never been psychoanalyzed or systematically trained, although he had trained some students in Vienna and New York.[35] Ives Hendrick thought so highly of his work in 1928 that he almost went to him for analysis instead of to Alexander.

Brill informed Ernest Jones that Schilder's ouster resulted from the machinations of a clique within the New York society, chiefly the editors of the *Quarterly* and a few others, notably Lawrence Kubie, a member of the education committee, and Ruth Mack Brunswick, an American disciple of Freud's who had returned from Vienna with the news that Schilder was not recognized there as a training analyst. Meanwhile three of Schilder's students had been accepted by the New York society (for work with controls), and Schilder had become "very popular in neurological and psychiatric organizations" and had contributed "considerably to psychoanalysis." A query to Anna Freud about Schilder's status elicited a cable "so ambiguous that it lent itself for any kind of translation," Brill noted.[36] Then, the education committee learned that a physician, tentatively rejected for training until after his therapeutic analysis, had been taken on by Schilder for training. The committee rejected Schilder's credentials, and Schilder threatened to sue. Brill, who was president of the New York society, appointed a committee headed by Jelliffe which concluded that he should remain as a training analyst. The younger analysts believed that the committee was deliberately packed by Brill with his supporters in an effort to curry favor with American psychiatrists. At a stormy meeting, the younger members, reinforced by the vote of Ives Hendrick, who had come down from Boston for the occasion, rejected the committee's report, eighteen to eight. Schilder resigned from the New York society in April 1935, then was asked to return.[37]

Before doing so, he appealed to Freud as the "highest tribunal in psychoanalysis." He asked two questions: "Do you want me to stay in the psychoanalytic movement? Do you consider it as justified that I do training analysis?" Schilder noted that his opinions differed from Freud's, but scarcely much more than Ernest Jones's, and that every movement needed freedom of expression. He recalled that Freud had told him that the early American analyst James Jackson Putnam also had held opinions of his own but that had not disturbed his relations with Freud or the psychoanalytic movement. Then he turned to the issue of training. "As you remember, I am not analyzed. I share this with rather important members of the Viennese group and especially with yourself. Some might be inclined to consider this fact as detrimental, for one's psycho-analytic activities. I must confess I do not share this opinion." Despite standardization of the technique, "there are known differences in the opinions of training analysts and beyond that personality factors are not completely eliminated by the technic." He closed with the reiteration of his admiration and esteem.

Freud came down hard on the side of the new regulations. In a long and revealing letter, he wrote that Schilder had never placed any value "on a closer personal relationship with me." Their differences in theory could be fruitful and his membership in the psychoanalytic association was valuable and desirable. "Hence if you leave the IPV you cannot place the blame on my intolerance or that of the Association. . . . "

But he completely disagreed with Schilder's views of the training regulations. Schilder had refused to be analyzed himself and had justified his stand by noting that several other analysts of the first generation had not been analyzed either.

Freud countered by arguing that despite difficulties many of the first generation in fact had been analyzed, including Jones and Ferenczi, whose analyses had been lengthy. "You belong to the second generation and are not an exception. Your defect is of your own choosing."

Moreover, Schilder's analyses of his patients were superficial:

> An analysis of three or four months is generally not sufficient to clear up infantile amnesias, to reconstruct the psychic development, and to have the patient live through whatever of the repressed is capable of expression. Such a short analysis can hardly be more than a purely intellectual instruction. . . . "
>
> If the Association makes rules for the training of analysts, it must insist on their compliance without exception. . . . You could have accepted this refusal as the inevitable consequence of your exceptional position, without feeling wronged.

If the New York society acted inconsistently, "that is beyond my understanding. However, I do not know the conditions in New York and have no influence upon them."[38]

On January 28, 1936, Schilder announced that he did not intend to reenter the New York Psychoanalytic Society; already he had founded a society of his own, the New York Society of Psychology. Brill felt bypassed during the affair, his authority questioned, the peace of the New York society destroyed. He wrote to Jones: "Instead of referring matters to me, and following my suggestions when I am supposed to be an authority, you people in Europe listen to every Tom, Dick and Harry and allow yourselves to be influenced by them. I would never have had any difficulty in managing the local groups if there had not been all kinds of subterranean and other influences from Vienna and other places to individual members who then came and gave it out as authoritative. Now I am going to withdraw from active work, but I feel that for the future of the psychoanalytic movement there should be rules and regulations which should be implicitly enforced regardless of whether it will be considered tyrannical or not."[39]

From 1936 to 1938 Brill stayed away. He explained to Jones that he needed a "good vacation," not from psychoanalysis, but from the crowd:

> I am very happy that I have stuck to my resolution. There is so much over-compensation for infantilism on the part of some of the leading members that I could not possibly sit down there and say nothing.[40]

> It is hard to grasp that we have been in the movement over three decades and that we (I mean you and I) are still heart and soul in it, and still have to contend with a lot of G-damned fools for whom we have done so much, but *c'est la vie!*[41]

Earlier Jones had urged Brill and the older members not to leave the New York society: "It would discredit our work too seriously to contemplate."[42]

In the generational wars, the orthodox European analysts tended to side with the young Americans whom they had largely trained. However, some Europeans, such as Hanns Sachs, Otto Fenichel, Siegfried Bernfeld, and Theodor Reik, viewed the increasing bureaucratization of the institutes, and particularly the American attitude toward lay analysis, with profound misgivings. Franz Alexander, who tended to side with the young, nevertheless remained aloof from strife in Boston between orthodox and eclectics, to the chagrin of his former pupil, Ives Hendrick, who believed Alexander was letting down the very standards he had inculcated.

The Europeans transformed the American movement. They brought long experience, the cachet of European "profundity" and of working with Freud himself, as well as formidable talent. They predominated as training analysts and their publications surpassed those of their native American colleagues in both quality and quantity. They played a powerful role in the American psychoanalytic movement especially after World War II.[43]

Their attitudes toward America were as diverse as their attitudes toward psychoanalysis. Some, like Sandor Rado, were contemptuous of what they regarded as the lack of learning and originality of most American psychoanalysts. Others, like Franz Alexander, welcomed the American experience as an opportunity to regularize psychoanalysis and foster its assimilation by psychiatry, medicine, and the universities. Those who had been closest to Freud himself and had been long-standing members of his Vienna circle tended to be the most orthodox in theory. The Berlin analysts, on the other hand, notably Karen Horney, and to a lesser extent the two Hungarians, Rado and Alexander, were eager to develop views that inevitably departed from what protagonists called the "mainstream" of psychoanalytic theory, that is, the views of the orthodox members of the American Psychoanalytic Association.

The Europeans came in three distinct groups. The first were those such as Schilder, Fritz Wittels, and Dorian Feigenbaum, who settled in the late 1920s because opportunities seemed brighter than at home. The second group began with the arrival of Rado, who was invited to organize the New York Psychoanalytic Institute on the model of Berlin's in 1931, and of Franz Alexander, who came for a year as professor of psychoanalysis at the University of Chicago, then worked with William Healy at the Judge Baker Institute in Boston, and founded the Chicago institute a year later. At the outset neither had thought of settling permanently, leaving homes, friends, and practices.

Hitler's assumption of power in January 1933 convinced Alexander and Rado to remain, and the number of emigrating analysts rapidly increased. Many of those leaving Germany settled at first in other more congenial European countries. Only a few came to the U.S. directly. Erik Erikson, who had been trained by Anna Freud in child analysis, arrived in 1934 and was astonished to be offered a job by Stanley Cobb at Harvard Medical School, an unthinkable position for a lay analyst in Europe whose only formal degree was a diploma from the Montessori Teacher's School in Vienna.[44]

Certain aspects of the immigration require emphasis: the factors that fostered an unusually favorable welcome to psychoanalysts; the problems of concentration in East Coast cities; the issue of medicalization and professionalism; and the shocked reactions of Europeans and Americans to the appalling demonstration of systematic barbarism in post-World War I Europe.

In April, 1933, Ernest Jones described the first wave of flight: "We are having a hectic time over here with political refugees." "Some seventy thousand Jews got away from Germany as the blow was falling. Among them are most of the German Psycho-analytical Society; I only know of four or five members still left in Berlin. The persecution has been much worse than you seem to think and has really quite lived up to the Middle Ages in reputation. It is a very Hunnish affair."[45] By September, Jones was appealing to Brill for funds. Young, promising, but unknown analysts with families were suffering the most. Payment of their passage and a sum sufficient to live a few months "just might save the situation." Theodor Reik, a lay analyst at the Berlin Institute, Jones wrote, had fled to Holland, "was on his beam ends," and was being supported by Freud out of his meager earnings. "Did you ever see such a crazy world."[46] Ernst Simmel, one of the major Berlin analysts, had been arrested, then released, and had waited for months in Brussels for a visa to the United States. He, too, was partly supported by Freud. He had been asked to teach a study group headed by the lay analyst David Brunswick in Los Angeles, but Brill did not believe the group could receive formal recognition from the American Psychoanalytic Association and thus qualify as a legitimate sponsoring organization.[47] In 1935 another German analyst, Edith Jacobson, who had stayed behind, was held by the Gestapo for two and a half years before finally being allowed to emigrate. Her patients had been arrested earlier, and one had been murdered. During her incarceration a friend had issued this appeal to "all international psychoanalysts":

> Let every analyst realize for half an hour how it is to live in a cage, seven to ten feet, without light, without sun, damp, dark, lonely, without communications with others, without chance of freedom, without life, and let him realize that E.J. is suffering already for eight months. A few months more will suffice to take away her vitality, health and freshness.[48]

With Hitler's march into Austria, March 11, 1938, the final diaspora of Central European analysts began. Individual analysts had been helping the émigrés for some years, and an informal committee of the New York Society had been doing so since 1933. The American Psychoanalytic Association formed a Committee on Relief and Immigration in June 1938 to cope with the flood of refugees after the *Anschluss*. From 1938 to 1948 the Committee raised a total of $47,695 from American analysts. Refugees were expected to repay assistance whenever possible, and some $6000 was ultimately returned to the committee by 1948 when it went out of existence. Laura Fermi has described the committee's successes and occasional tragic failures. The family of the German psychoanalyst Karl Landauer was stranded in Amsterdam, unable to obtain an exit visa. Although the committee had paid $1,680 for a transit visa, the family was interned in a concentration camp, where Landauer died.[49] Between 1938 and 1943, some 149 refugees entered the United States, with the help of the Emergency Committee on Immigration of the American Psychoanalytic Association: 41 medical analysts, 13 lay analysts, 14 physicians in analytic training, 50 psychiatrists, two neuropathologist, two medical students, four psychoanalytically trained psychologists, 12 teachers and psychiatric social workers with some psychoanalytic training, and 11 persons in allied fields.[50] Some of those the committee helped—Bruno Bettelheim, Leopold Bellak, Rudolph Ekstein, Heinz Hartmann, David Rapaport—became major figures in the American movement. Some of the lay analysts or analyzed teachers and psychologists were absorbed with little trace.

The committee was beset by difficulties. It needed to raise funds to help with emigration and to support those who already had left. To extricate people from Germany and Austria required affidavits and guarantees of jobs if they were to enter under the Austrian and German quotas, which were only two-thirds filled. Those entering outside the quota system needed not only guarantees of their character and skills but jobs when they arrived. For teachers this meant having taught for two years in their country of origin. But in 1938 the State Department did not recognize psychoanalytic institutes in Europe or the United States (except the London institute) as qualified teaching institutions, and thus they could not sponsor teachers.

The refugees faced formidable problems: a foreign language in which to listen and interpret nuances of the most complex and intimate matters, and the difficulty of finding patients, hard enough for medical analysts but a particularly dangerous issue for lay analysts. Most of the émigrés hoped to settle in New York or some other big city, where they could find congenial colleagues and other Europeans and thus lessen their sense of loneliness and isolation. The Europeans often helped each other, exchanging information about visas and positions and occasionally recommending patients to needy colleagues.

The prospect of leaving New York aroused anxiety and depression in those who already had been tragically uprooted. Some had relatives in concentration camps or prisons, others had family stranded in Europe, hoping to emigrate. When Paul Federn, then 67, arrived in New York in 1938, he wrote to Jelliffe that his wife would have a lonesome time, except in Boston, Chicago, or New York. His youngest son was in a German concentration camp, his daughter detained in Vienna.[51] Jelliffe suggested that if Federn could wait until a remunerative practice developed, and he received the privilege of practicing, he should stay in the city "where at least there is some money to be made and where intellectual contacts are possible."[52]

Another reason for the concentration of refugee physicians in New York was the relative ease of getting a medical license. Only a passing grade was required on the qualifying examination. But one had to become a member of the New York County Medical Society before becoming a member of the New York Psychoanalytic Society.[53] In twenty-one states it was virtually impossible for a foreigner to get a license; in the others requirements varied, but usually included citizenship or an internship of a year or more.

The Emergency Committee on Immigration of the American Psychoanalytic Association deliberately encouraged refugees to settle in cities where the competition and concentration of analysts were less than in New York. At least twenty-six of the immigrants did so, in Detroit, Chicago, Topeka, San Francisco, and Los Angeles. The Menninger Clinic was particularly welcoming to analysts.[54] The committee placed a few psychoanalysts with public psychiatric hospitals. Geza Roheim, the psychoanalytic anthropologist, for instance, went to Worcester State Hospital in Massachusetts. One analyst was sent to teach foreign languages at a western agricultural college. Most, however, remained on the eastern seaboard.

A number of factors contributed to concentration. The analysts needed a private clientele, hardly possible in remote areas where psychoanalysis was unknown. Psychoanalytic training was highly centralized at the few institutes and societies. A training analysis and treating cases under supervision might require as much as five or more hours each week, making long commuting difficult.

Economic difficulties continued to face most American analysts during the ongoing depression. In 1933 A. A. Brill informed Ernest Jones that the Depression had alerted the medical profession to the activities of psychologists and lay analysts and the New York County Medical Society was investigating psychoanalytic practice.[55] A year later, the New York Board of Regents, which controlled medical licensing, prosecuted Mrs. May Benzenberg Mayer for practicing psychoanalysis without a medical license. Apparently an untrained and self-proclaimed lay analyst and the director of Pojodag House at 118 East 76th Street, Mrs. Mayer was fined $500 after a client complained that she had paid $3,185 for "lessons," a course of dream work, and unsuccessful treatment for a leg paralyzed since childhood. Mrs. Mayer's lawyer argued that psychoanalysis did not come within the meaning of the law against practicing medicine without a license. She also had received support from "persons 'high in social and political life,'" who testified to her integrity, intelligence, and sincerity, among them John Haynes Holmes, pastor of the Community Church, who once had debated atheism with Max Eastman.[56] American analysts insisted that the hostility of the medical authorities to lay analysis was so great that the agreement with the Europeans whereby the New York Society had accepted some lay analysts as members was rescinded at the Psychoanalytic Congress at Lucerne in 1935.[57]

The American medical analysts argued that only they could diagnose whether a patient's symptoms might result from a neurosis or an organic illness, such as a brain tumor. Moreover, only those with psychiatric training could distinguish neurotics from psychotics. The latter could be made worse by the process of free association, which might weaken a psychotic patient's already tenuous hold on reality and impulse.

In 1938 the American Psychoanalytic Association set up new rules which stated that only physicians who had completed a psychiatric residency at an approved institution could become members. The Americans and the Committee on Relief and Immigration, dominated by the young militants, attempted to enforce their new professional policies, including the requirement of a medical degree, on the European immigrants. In addition to warning incoming analysts that practicing psychoanalysis without a medical license was illegal, they tried to steer lay analysts or laymen with aspirations to practice into other professions, such as social work or teaching. They also insisted that no European analyst, no matter how exalted his status, train others without authorization of an existing institute. All refugees were asked to join local societies, and thus meet the new American professional requirements. The International Training Commission on the other hand tried to ensure that the Europeans could resume practice wherever they settled, and the Americans for a time withdrew from the International Association over the issue.[58] The Americans did agree in 1938 that already trained lay analysts who were members of the International Association could continue to practice but that thenceforth no other laymen would be trained to do therapy. At the insistence of the Boston institute, laymen could be trained but only to apply psychoanalysis to their own fields. However, in most cities, lay analysts, particularly those who treated children, were quietly allowed to practice, and it was assumed that teaching psychoanalysis, even conducting training analyses, did not come within the prohibition.

But the issue of lay analysis was disruptive, and it crystallized some of the conflicts between native Americans and the incoming Europeans. "What in the world would we do with all these additional analysts?" the president of the New York society said to the lay analyst Walter C. Langer, an American who had been in Vienna during the *Anschluss*.[59] In Boston, Hanns Sachs resigned over the issue. In Topeka, where the Menningers had an unusually liberal policy of cooperation with both clinical psychologists and lay analysts, the issue was raised by some members of the American Psychoanalytic Association. And a local medical society objected to the psychologist David Rapaport working in a Kansas state hospital for the insane.

As a group, the refugee physician psychoanalysts, caught up in the need for psychiatrists during and just after World War II, probably did better than many of the 4,408 physicians who emigrated to America. A survey of refugee physicians in New York in 1945 indicated that 51 percent were failing or likely to fail if competition increased.[60]

Many of the refugee psychoanalysts were helped by a network of physicians, social workers, professionals, and intellectuals, some of them wealthy, and some of whom had been their patients or trainees in Europe. Analytically trained teachers were placed at Smith College, Bryn Mawr, or Holyoke. Jewish hospitals and organizations were particularly helpful in providing residences, internships, and jobs.

The social ties of the analysts, some of the institutions that welcomed them, indeed the neighborhoods in which they settled, testified to the increasingly elite status of the profession. Those who remained in New York, perhaps a third, clustered around Central Park West, on Park Avenue, around Columbia University. In Boston, they lived in Brookline, Back Bay, or Cambridge.

Yet the esoteric status of psychoanalysis as a profession in 1939 is signified by the fact that no refugee analyst was mentioned in a dazzling list of those for whose presence America could "thank Hitler." The *Reader's Digest* listed musicians, scientists, actresses, writers, painters—Einstein, Otto Klemperer, Vicki Baum, Thomas Mann, George Grosz—but no analysts.[61]

Theodor Reik and Franz Alexander represented two extreme poles of the European movement, one a lay analyst and literary intellectual, the other a physician and psychiatrist, and they pursued quite different but successful careers in America. They projected diametrically opposed visions of psychoanalysis, one a pliantly adaptive response to the American environment, the other a nostalgic throwback to prewar Vienna. The lay analysis issue dogged Theodor Reik, whom Freud consoled on his chilly New York reception by issuing him a certificate as "one of the few masters of applied psychoanalysis" and by once more expressing his final contempt for the United States. "What ill wind has blown you, just you, to America?" he wrote in 1938. "You must have known how amiably lay analysts would be received there by our colleagues for whom psychoanalysis is nothing more than one of the handmaidens of psychiatry."[62]

"Where else should I have gone?" Reik wrote to Siegfried Bernfeld's wife. "To Palestine where I was some little while ago (and where it is considerably cooler than it is here) and where I am also not wanted?"[63]

Reik's American career at first was bedeviled by the lay analysis issue. He wrote to Bernfeld, who had settled in San Francisco, that he was making very little money and that his savings were slowly dwindling. He was also trying to support his sister and brother in Vienna, who he thought otherwise would die of hunger. "The American analysts with the exception of Sachs and Nunberg have behaved down right abominably."[64] "I have resolved to take revenge on our American colleagues who thought they could humble me without being punished for it."[65]

He asked Bernfeld whether he might be able to get a college position in California or San Francisco or whether he might find enough patients there to earn a living. ". . . I have outstanding letters of recommendation from Freud, Einstein, T. H. Mann and a few American institutions . . . three of my books have appeared in English. . . . " Reik recalled that "most members of the New York Psychoanalytic Society treated me condescendingly, and I was strongly admonished against practicing, or rather forbidden to practice."[66] Reik did gradually establish himself, despite the New York Society, and founded his own society and institute of lay analysts, the National Psychological Association for Psychoanalysis. New York was too large, too various, too chaotic, and the demand for analysis was too great for stringent control by the New York society. Robert Lindner, who wrote a postwar best-seller, *The 50-Minute Hour,* was a Reik trainee, and Reik's own books were as popular as many novels. In the years of mounting postwar demand for therapy, like Reik, increasing numbers of laymen established successful practices.

Corpulent, aging, given to reverie, detesting the heat of American summers, Reik also detested the brisk American vision of psychoanalysis as a hard medical science with its own lingo, "psychoanalyze," as well as its overtones of moral uplife in the promise of "sexual maturity." It was *not* a science that could be inculcated by seminars, lectures, systematic study, and even more systematic training analyses, he insisted. On the contrary, psychoanalysts were born, not made, and their chief gift must be delicate and free psychological intuition, and the capacity for self-analysis. Freud had discovered psychoanalysis as a result of the attempt to understand not only his patients' neuroses but his own, through an act of self-discovery, "self-observation, and self-recognition, directed by an extraordinarily fine ear for his inner voices."[67]

At the heart of Reik's psychoanalysis was the process of association, freely floating from one thought to another, richly unexpected, full of allusions, personal, literary, musical. Reik's books bristled with references to Mahler, Schnitzler, and Mozart, the gods of Vienna.

In cultivation and erudition, Reik's associations resemble perhaps more those of Proust than they do the usual analytic case. Even more than Freud, Reik presented his cases and his own self-discoveries as if they were detective stories, suspenseful, fantastic, unexpected. Psychoanalysis was a kind of "white magic." "Here in broad daylight magic penetrates a scene that is utterly matter-of-fact and prosaic. A room, like any other, with a couch, a chair, and ash trays, becomes the place for passionate emotions, for deeply felt reminiscences, for good and evil deeds in thought."[68]

Reik distilled for the American popular mind the image of the silent, uncanny analyst:

> It is the task of the analyst to transform the unconscious magical views of the patient into conscious psychological insight. . . . The analytic situation offers evidence to convince even the hard-bitten skeptic that magic works even in this age of modern technical achievements. It takes only a few moments to make the transition from the realm of the telephone, telegraph, tractor, and radar to the domain where psychical reality alone is valid. Here time and space are unimportant, contradictions may coexist, the rigidity of logical thinking disappears. We are in the land of fantasy, in Prospero's kingdom. Facts lose their force, truth and fancy emerge.[69]

For Reik the unconscious had a distinct existence of its own, a reified reality, with its own "inaccessible potentialities." It had its own rhythms, revealed in psychological circumstantial evidence and in fleeting impressions. It was an unknown territory, through which there were no royal or systematic roads. The blind urge within the psychoanalyst, not systematic campaigns, would "teach him the right way."[70]

"In the beginning is silence." "The analyst hears not only what is in the words; he hears also what the words do not say. He listens with the 'third ear,' hearing not only what the patient speaks but also his own inner voices, what emerges from his own unconscious depths."[71] Opposing the American tendency to "help" patients at once, he proposed first understanding their unconscious symptoms.

Reik's intuitive approach, his consideration of telepathy, brought him, he wrote, the contumely of his young New York colleagues. But he was proud to be a pupil of Freud, which long implied the status of a minority outsider.

He consoled himself with a daydream, his revenge. He daydreamed that on the left side of a pair of scales were handbills bearing the names of members of the New York society, Dr. J. E. (Jules Eisenbud), G. Z. (Gregory Zilboorg), Dr. L. K. (Lawrence Kubie). On the other were three other bills: Albert Einstein, Sigmund Freud, Thomas Mann. The more names that were piled on the left or New York side of the scales, the closer the right side touched the ground. The meaning was obvious. What the three men thought of his work outweighed the opinion of all the members of the New York Psychoanalytic Society.[72]

Reik represented the quintessence of psychoanalysis as a romantic science, in which literature and discovery were united. Helene Deutsch, a physician, once observed that Reik and Hanns Sachs were fonder of literature than of treatment. Reik's sense of discipleship also summed up the spirit of the Viennese. They were Freud's closest followers, his primal sons and daughters.

In 1948, after four books, Reik had become a literary celebrity. Lunching at the Algonquin, he announced that love and work were the basic aims of

Freud's therapy.[73] To a *New Yorker* interviewer, he likened the American analysts' high expectations of human nature to those of Robespierre or Hitler, who respectively wished men to be godlike and heroic. "Freud thought of man as a difficult to domesticate animal, and I agree with him. American analysts who are sometimes rather stuffy and Buddha-like, by the way, don't make enough allowance for such weaknesses as greediness, cruelty and avarice. No one should ever have a guilt feeling about his thoughts"; an impulse to steal in front of Tiffany's windows was inevitable.[74] To the literary critic Diana Trilling, who made higher moral demands on the "physician of the mind" than on other human beings, Reik was "undignified," "wearisomely pessimistic," full of grievances and self-justifications."[75]

Equally confident, but in an entirely different style, was one of the most popular training analysts at the Berlin institute, its first graduate, the Hungarian Franz Alexander—built, Ives Hendrick observed, "like a football man." He arrived in America in 1930 with the ambition of putting "psychoanalysis on the map."[76] Then, Alexander recalled, there was as yet no "bandwagon of psychoanalysis"; no one could have foreseen the "future victory march of Freud's views." Wishing never to be a member of a persecuted minority, Alexander hoped to make psychoanalysis an integral part of medicine and psychiatry. He believed the Americans chiefly were interested in practice, not theory, and when they had come to Europe for training they had been amazed at the intensity of the European theoretical wars.

Alexander had been invited by Frankwood Williams to present his views on criminology to the International Mental Hygiene Congress in Washington, D.C., in 1932. Alexander made the pilgrimage to Vienna to discuss his American prospects with Freud. Freud argued against moving to America, because the American interest in psychoanalysis threatened the Central European psychoanalytic societies by draining away talented members. Freud knew psychoanalysis only as a revolutionary force, Alexander recalled, and could not well visualize its development after it had become an "integral part of contemporary culture."

Invited by Maynard Hutchings, Alexander spent a year as the first professor of psychoanalysis at the University of Chicago, where he found the social scientists, among them William F. Ogburn and Lloyd Warner, more sympathetic than the medical faculty. One physician walked out on Alexander's first lecture after he had remarked that psychoanalysis was a clinical science based on verbal communication, not an experimental one. Outside the university, he found the community at large ready to be sympathetic. As in Europe, psychoanalysis had penetrated literature, influenced the thinking of social philosophers and the general public. Regression, psychoneuroses, dreams, slips of the tongue, unacceptable unconscious tendencies—all were familiar.

After his year at the university, Alexander left Chicago for a year in Boston to work on a study of juvenile delinquency at the Judge Baker Institute with William Healy, who had been analyzed by Helene Deutsch during several summers in Vienna.[77] Then he was asked to return to Chicago to organize an institute by a "group of leading private citizens—businessmen, a physician, a lawyer, a university professor of social science." From the outset, Alexander hoped to make it an integral part of Chicago's medical community. He cultivated connections with members of the Rosenwald family and others of Chicago's social elite, the Fields and the Swifts.

By 1960 Alexander had come to believe that American psychoanalysis was overly conservative, slavishly upholding everything for which Freud stood in theory and practice, a conservatism he attributed to the influence of Freud's European disciples, who knew "too well" Freud's reservations about dilution in America. There were legitimate fears of psychoanalysis becoming a "free for all" for self-trained or poorly trained physicians, even quacks. Yet Alexander feared the field was in danger of being frozen, and that organizational fervor was taking the upper hand. The trend was toward standardization and uniformity. A split was growing between what analysts practiced and what the institutes taught—which was chiefly classical technique.[78]

His first book, *The Medical Value of Psychoanalysis,* written during his year in Boston, was a reaction to the sometimes skeptical response of the physicians at the University of Chicago. To make psychoanalysis acceptable to physicians, he argued that psychoanalysis was empirical and represented the same revolution in scientific methods that Mach represented in physics, that is, an overcoming of 19th-century rigidity. For years on the borderline of respectability, insofar as it was a therapeutic method, psychoanalysis belonged to medicine. Accordingly Alexander sketched its usefulness in psychiatry and, perhaps most important, in understanding the role of the emotions in physical illness, the field of psychosomatic medicine. He insisted that no matter how sophisticated the "cell physiology of the brain" became, it was improbable that physiological or pharmacological methods would be used to influence people's minds, "for example to persuade someone or to explain a mathematical thesis." Probably the best method of influencing psychological disturbances would always be psychological methods. Pointing to the well-known influence of emotion on such physiological phenomena as blushing, weeping, and so on, he argued that mental processes belonged to the biological system, to what Adolf Meyer for years had been calling "psychobiology." With typical hubris, Alexander argued that Freud had provided not only a method of therapy but a universal "dynamic theory of personality, with a bearing on "all psychological sciences which deal with products of the mind." He did not question the validity "but the exclusiveness of the somatic analysis of biological phenomena."[79]

Finally, in the midst of a depression, and at a time when psychiatric training in medical schools was infrequent and spotty, Alexander proposed nothing less than the training of the entire medical and psychiatric profession in psychoanalytic psychology, a marriage of the Berlin institute curriculum with the psychiatric residency, including didactic analyses, theory, and controlled cases. In the first year of medical school, all students would learn about psychoanalytic normal psychology. And the psychiatric intern also would learn about art and psychoanalytic approaches to literature and sociology on the grounds that the humanistically trained physician developed a more sympathetic understanding of the mentally ill.

It was a dogmatic and provocative program. By 1938, as president of the American Psychoanalytic Association, Alexander was prescribing the disappearance of the psychoanalytic movement, and the rejection of its old romantic attitude of a militant, embattled, and isolated minority, a reflection, he thought, of Freud's reception by Viennese physicians. America had provided congenial soil for psychoanalysis, and its more open-minded scientists and physicians were asking for quantified, hard, scientific data rather than the mere reiteration of theory. In fact there was more research in psychoanalysis in the United States than there had been in Europe. Rather than "disseminators of a gospel," analysts should become "self-critical scientists."[80] Alexander attempted to carry out this ideal in the postwar years, through experiments in therapy and in the critical analysis of the therapeutic experience. He remained, however, a primary exponent of the psychodynamic, arguing that no matter what the advances in physiological knowledge, irreducible psychological data remained. Among the medical analysts, he also was one of those who defended Reik's intuitive approach against the self-appointed hardheaded proponents of psychoanalysis as a biological medicine.

8

The Second Psychoanalytical
Civil War and the
California Case, 1939–1942

A new "analytical civil war" began in 1939 and culminated in a split between orthodox, or "classical," psychoanalysts and revisionists who founded their own psychoanalytic training organizations. This was no longer a generational dispute but one involving conflicting groups of Europeans and their American trainees. The schisms and the problems they created led finally to a postwar revamping of the American Psychoanalytic Association which drastically centralized power and control. Although European psychoanalysts were on both sides of this dispute, the Europeans, particularly Freud's Viennese followers, helped to cement the orthodoxy of both the local societies and the American Psychoanalytic Association. And more Americans than Europeans joined the "dissident" groups.

These battles were fought out principally in New York, the American capital of psychoanalysis, for a number of reasons. Its society was the largest and represented increasingly divergent points of view. In 1939–40 it had 20 members and about 106 students.[1] It encompassed a small, able, and vocal group of "dissident" analysts. It also had a solid majority of orthodox analysts whose ranks were now augmented by growing numbers of refugees, several of them—such as Paul Federn, hailing from Vienna—with close ties to "Freud himself."

Two other factors made the schisms possible. First, the demand for psychoanalysis and the number of trainees grew steadily in New York, and as American psychiatrists were drawn into the armed forces after Pearl Harbor, in December 1941, those analysts who remained were assured of a clientele. Moreover, a change in professional affiliations did not effect an analyst's practice because patients tended to be loyal to their analyst, regardless of the analyst's institutional affiliation. Thus it was possible to leave one psychoanalytic organization and join another without losing patients and endangering one's livelihood.[2]

The intensity of the struggles in New York reflected in part the vulnerability of Freud's position in America and the defensive ardor this aroused, as Susan Quinn has observed in her insightful biography of Karen Horney. Freud's popular reputation had outdistanced his professional esteem among neurologists and psychiatrists, many of whom remained hostile or skeptical.[3] He had not yet attained the heroic, mythological stature, both popular and professional, that would come with the postwar years and would culminate in Ernest Jones's worshipful, if sometimes critical, biography. Freud's ill health and his exile made his disciples especially sensitive to criticism of his theories in 1938 and 1939. The questions of who would wear Freud's mantle after his death and how his heritage would be preserved were crucial ones.

Psychoanalytic explanations for dissent came all too easily. Robert Waelder wrote to Otto Fenichel that dissidents such as Rado and Rank had used Freud's ideas in order to attack him. They had "borrowed the father's penis" in their castrative assault on the "the hated father" and thus unconsciously kept their tie with Freud intact.[4] Nine months before Freud's death, Fenichel observed that in Europe Freud was a nearby living presence and analysts had developed libidinal ties to him which sometimes had hampered the development of psychoanalysis. But in America Freud was perceived as very far away and so near death that he held no magical significance for the American analysts.[5] Three years after Freud died on September 23, 1939, Karl Menninger observed to his old friend, Smith Ely Jelliffe, "Freud's death seems to have released a lot of hostility and narcissism in some of the brothers just as he predicted."[6] Such psychoanalytic rhetoric flung by the protagonists at each other only exacerbated the disputes. Finally, the psychoanalytic world was a small and incestuous one. People knew each other, sometimes all too well, and this intimate knowledge characterized the relationship of analysts and their trainees.

In America, "classical" psychoanalysis was unusually threatened by a powerful and traditional eclecticism. It was represented by important psychoanalytic psychiatrists such as Harry Stack Sullivan, who was contemptuous of the orthodox. A few major analysts in New York, some of them sympathetic to Sullivan, were moving away from classical theory and therapy. The protagonists coined language to describe their disputes. The traditionalists pitted "classical," "orthodox," "Freudian," psychoanalysis against "deviant," "advanced," "dissident" views. The neo-Freudians contrasted their "liberal," "progressive" psychoanalysis with the "autocratic," "Viennese Talmudic" tradition.

The disputes were all the more threatening because the psychoanalytic training organizations in America were so new; the New York institute was a mere eight years old. Moreover, the national organization, although venerable, was weakened by its recent reorganization as a federation of local societies, each pledged to enforce the new training standards. Reflecting exactly the position of his young and militant professional generation, Lawrence Kubie described the old American Psychoanalytic Association founded in 1911: "For the larger part of its history [it] represented a conglomeration of highly diversified technical methods and aims, in no true sense psychoanalytic in its fundamental point of view."[7]

The American psychoanalytic professional organizations were being established at a time when Freud's reputation was still equivocal and his personal fate uncertain. "Freud himself" had set the terms of doctrinal disagreement in psychoanalysis. In the quarrels with Jung, the "sexual theory" became the hallmark of orthodoxy and its repudiation the test of heresy. New York followed this pattern.

The issues of orthodoxy and dissidence were played out in a vulnerable student culture. The vulnerability came partly from economic competition, partly from the dependency that analytic training created. In 1939 the concentration of analysts in New York was so great that Sandor Rado wished to limit the number of psychoanalytic students in each institute, and Bertram Lewin observed that competition in New York was exceptionally hard on them. These students were all adult psychiatrists and physicians "primarily interested in earning a living."[8] Yet they were dependent on their teachers for certification as analysts and as members in good standing of the New York society. It is no wonder that the student body was rife with discontent, rumors, fear, adoration, and defiance, and students played an important role in the ensuing schisms, as actors and as pawns.

The contending forces were generaled by powerful and imperious personalities. Lawrence Kubie, president of the New York Society in 1938, had been trained by Edward Glover, who had codified the "classical" technique for English-speaking analysts in an unusually formal manner. Kubie was brilliant, gracious, and had mastered a raging temper, sparked by boyhood fights with his brother who was a year older. This early pugnacity later was "sublimated very largely in intellectual combat," according to Glover. In 1938 Kubie had helped establish the new professional standards for the American Psychoanalytic Association.[9] What he regarded as his own contumaciousness was matched by a "compulsive benevolence." He was also remarkably productive, and was particularly concerned with evidence and scientific method. Like several earlier American psychoanalysts, he attempted to reconcile psychoanalytic theories of anxiety with the conditioned reflex theories of Ivan Pavlov.[10]

Kubie was not only interested in providing a scientific basis for psychoanalysis, he also was a proponent of meticulous classical methods and had argued that any student's personal analysis be "scrupulously orthodox in technique."[11] Later he rejected many of the new developments in Anna Freud's and Heinz Hartmann's ego psychologies because they seemed too abstract yet also too anthropomorphic and less explanatory than a theory of conflicting drives. And it is ironic that as a result, Kubie came to feel alienated from the New York education committee where ego psychology by then held sway.[12]

Also in the "orthodox" camp were Gregory Zilboorg and Fritz Wittels. Zilboorg, a flamboyant and explosive personality who, according to Brill, had created endless trouble in the New York society and whom Jelliffe described as of the "rule or ruin variety," served with Kubie on the education committee. Wittels, a Viennese physician, was an unusually militant champion of Freud, perhaps because he had once been asked to leave the Freudian circle and had returned after modifying a biography of Freud that had offended its hero. His original break with Freud had occurred in 1910 when he published a thinly veiled autobiographical novel in which he described his affair with a girl who also was involved with Karl Kraus, the Viennese editor and enemy of psychoanalysis. In an autobiographical sketch Wittels recalled, "We knew from Freud that repressed sex instincts made men neurotic to such an extent that an entire era was poisoned. What we did not know then was that former puritans running wild will not help either." At the time, Freud had warned that the novel's publication would only damage psychoanalysis, but Wittels published it anyway. After a reconciliation with Freud in 1927, he had come to America in 1928 because economic prospects were brighter there. He had firmly established himself as an analyst in New York and a popularizer of psychoanalysis, lecturing at the *New School for Social Research*. All America, Wittels believed, echoed his praise of Freud's greatness.[13]

Wittels disliked what he regarded as Kubie's neurotic compulsivity, exemplified in a symposium Kubie organized in 1941: "We had a panel discussion about drives," he wrote to Siegfried Bernfeld, "which unfortunately are called instincts here, a term which has always meant something entirely different from our drives in psychoanalysis. . . . We listened to biologists, experimenters of all sorts, with many drawings and moving pictures. For hours and days definitions were sought until they decided to adjourn in order to reconvene in two months to make more definitions. The sterility of the undertaking was total."[14]

The dissidents included personalities as strong as Wittels and Kubie— Abraham Kardiner, Sandor Rado, and, most important, Karen Horney. Rado, who hoped to strengthen the ties of psychoanalysis with medicine and psychiatry, had been flirting with Adolf Meyer, Brill wrote, and had come to be increasingly skeptical of Freud's sexual theories, particularly innate bisexuality.[15] Rado was a clear and brilliant lecturer who had impressed the Americans who had heard him in Berlin. He was also contentious and touchy. With Abram Kardiner he was one of the most popular teachers in the New York institute.[16] Kardiner had become increasingly absorbed in sociology, anthropology, and field theory and had just published *The Individual and His*

Society, one of the founding texts of the American school of culture and personality. He too was skeptical of classical sexual theory.

Horney also was profoundly influenced by sociology. She had had a long personal relationship with Eric Fromm, whom the orthodox viewed with deep distrust. In addition she had close ties with Harry Stack Sullivan and Clara Thompson, an analysand of Ferenczi, whose later views on therapy Freud had repudiated, because, according to Rado, he didn't want to turn the psychoanalytic technique into a "whorehouse." All three were living in New York, and with William Silverberg, who had succeeded Sullivan at Sheppard Pratt, formed a small informal "Zodiac Club" which met Monday nights for dinner and conversation. All of these connections would have made her suspect to the more orthodox in the New York institute.

Energetic and with a remarkable gift for clearly written criticism and popular exposition, Horney had been disagreeing with Freud since the 1920s, particularly over the sexual development of women. This tendency toward independence had intensified since her arrival in America and a brief and rather stormy period at the Chicago institute with Alexander. Like Alexander, she was not one to accept a subordinate role—nor indeed were any of the major protagonists in the New York dispute. Opinions about her differed sharply. Those who were orthodox and male tended to regard her as a virago and one analyst referred to her as "Mr. Horney"; Freud had thought of her as able but malicious. Those who were sympathetic regarded her as warm, motherly, and generous, particularly to her students.[17]

In two books written since her arrival in America, *The Neurotic Personality of Our Time* and *New Ways in Psychoanalysis,* published respectively in 1937 and 1939, Horney had increasingly rejected standard psychoanalytic theories. She argued that social and cultural factors, not the presumably uniform "biological" experiences of infancy and early childhood, such as the Oedipus complex and the other "stages" of psychosexual development, were crucial to the formation of neuroses. They were caused by a basic insecurity created by the conflict between hostile impulses and the need for affection. She was rejecting precisely the grounds on which Freud had established the criteria of heresy: the primary importance of his sexual theories. And in some passages she seemed to be founding a new school. The orthodox codifier of clinical theory, Otto Fenichel, pronounced her views to be psychoanalysis no longer.

Discussions of Horney's and Rado's theories became increasingly acrimonious in the New York society, partly because of the arrival of more Europeans. Phyllis Greenacre, who briefly left the New York society, speculated that Freud's death and the bitter experience of exile fostered among some of the European refugees a compensatory insistence on orthodoxy and the finality of Freud's vision. And the Europeans, especially the Viennese, found enthusiastic, if sometimes ambivalent allies among their former American analysands in the fight for orthodoxy. Paul Federn, for instance, then struggling to win recognition in New York, attacked Rado's views, and Kubie, while disagreeing with Federn, nevertheless tried to minimize the attack, arguing that Rado could not bear criticism.[18]

In Boston the growing atmosphere of orthodoxy inspired the Harvard psychologist Henry Murray to write to Franz Alexander, "I have a certain amount of unspoken aggression against the Boston Psychoanalytical Society because of their total lack of interest in experimental methods and any innovations in theory." Although he had great respect for some of the analysts among them and found analytic views more congenial than any others, he claimed,

> I cannot participate in meetings while any divergence from the accepted dogma is treated as heresy. . . . I have more to learn from them than from any other group, but I simply cannot stand being perpetually preached and dictated to, even if the preaching happens to be true. The main point is that the Society is organized around a theory or doctrine, rather than around a subject matter. Thus it is essentially a political or religious body, not a scientific body.[19]

As an example of the growing passions in New York, shortly after Horney discussed her views at a meeting of the New York society, Karl Menninger wrote to Otto Fenichel that he had asked her why the opinions in her book were in such contrast with her "gracious and reasonable manner in everyday life." She had replied that "perhaps she envied Freud's penis, and perhaps did not quite understand the English language, and she was obliged to tell the truth." She began to shout, her voice broke, and she "hurried off the platform. It looked as if she were crying."[20] Menninger's first analyst, Franz Alexander, charged him with "emotional orthodoxy" because of his irritation with Horney. Menninger had just finished a second analysis with Ruth Mack Brunswick, one of Freud's favorite Americans, who had returned from Vienna. He had also been pleased when Freud had commended his loyalty to the death instinct. And he had developed an ambivalent reverence for the superior insights and rigors of European psychoanalytic culture.[21]

In 1939 Kubie had taken charge of educational matters at the New York institute. He consulted the students about educational reform, after they had presented a series of demands for more flexible courses and additional teachers. Then apparently without consulting them further he had promulgated a new and more systematic educational program that met few of their wishes.[22]

Three years before, in a popular guide for prospective patients, he had staked out precisely the ground he would take in the controversy—the high ground of the thoroughness of orthodox psychoanalytic training, longer than any other apprenticeship "in all of medicine and surgery."[23] Its quality was guaranteed by psychoanalytic organizations and it entailed first a thorough foundation in the "fundamental Freudian discipline." The authority of these organizations was moral and depended on the recognition and support of physicians and the public, whose duty it was to check whether anyone who claimed to be a psychoanalyst was a member. Thus, Kubie identified legitimate psychoanalysis with formal membership in a professional guild. Training and membership distinguished real analysts from the abundant charlatans, medical and lay. Such careful training was limited to orthodox Freudians. He argued that "none of the conflicting schools of psychological therapy" that had grown out of Freudian psychoanalysis had "developed organized methods or standards of training which approach even remotely this severe discipline."[24]

> Under these circumstances it does not seem unreasonable to demand that those who are drawn towards the "unorthodox" experiments should first perfect their understanding of the more fundamental Freudian discipline. Upon this as a basis, anyone is free thereafter to make whatever new departures his own scientific ingenuity and skill make possible.[25]

Kubie justified the need for educational reform in the institute on grounds that the development of cliques threatened "to wreck the New York Society completely." "Each group," he wrote to Edward Glover in 1939, is "more or less hermetically sealed from the other, and you can imagine how much confusion, lopsided and inadequate training, and mutual distrust and hostility all of this generated." He reverted to the ad hominem defense that classically characterized psychoanalytic controversies, that is, that one's opponents were neurotic, an assertion that often enough may have been partly true. "Out of it all," he continued, "however, comes one very firm conviction, namely, that something must be done to draw into psychiatry and into analysis a less frantically neurotic and anxiety-ridden type of human being. Just how we can do that, however, isn't so easy to see."[26]

Kubie pointed out to David Levy, a well-known psychoanalytic child psychiatrist and president of the American Psychiatric Association, that instruction in the institute after his reforms still represented quite diverse points of view. An introductory course in theory combined a "fairly simple classicist, Van Ophuijsen, yoked with a quite original independent and unorthodox fellow like Spitz." "We have literature taught by Clara Thompson, who is by no means a rigid conservative but rather close to the Horney view. . . . " In the course of their three years' training, students would be forced "to accept exposure to at least three or four, and in some cases five, quite different clinical points of view." "Nor is this any lip service on my part to the principle of diversification of influences. You must have realized from my own recent paper and from my discussions that I am no rigid classicist in my own point of view." But the hermetically sealed groups meant that each received "only one exclusive kind of influence and that invested with extraordinary bitterness and virulence and denunciation of all the others."

Kubie conceded that the "old timers," as Rado contended, were sterile and fixed in their thinking. But Rado's hostility made them "naturally react in a highly defensive way, defending the ancient doctrines" and the superiority of European over American ways. "It is partly their loyalty to Freud in this case, and partly the temporary state of mind of the refugee who doesn't want to feel that everything that he has had and everything he knows has been swept away and superseded by something better." If tactfully handled, the younger refugees would, after a short period of adjustment, react to our American attitude of criticism with great eagerness—provided only that the criticism is couched in friendly terms. The Zilboorg-Rado technique of sticking a dagger into a topic and then turning it in order to cause as much pain as possible, is the one thing that we ought to try and eliminate from our scientific discussions. If we can eliminate it from our criticisms of the old holy writ, I think you will be surprised to find how these Europeans will come more than half-way to meet us.[27]

Till then, Kubie seems to have been relatively neutral in the dispute. His hand may have been forced by a tirade against Horney circulated through the society by Fritz Wittels in March of 1940 and addressed to Kubie. The society faced, Wittels warned, "impending disintegration." Quite classically, again, the ruckus was over Freud's sexual theory, with Wittels's indignation fanned by acclaim for Horney in the lay press. Defining the terms of heresy, he wrote: "She denied the existence of instincts, the influence of libido development on neuroses and character formation, Freud's Oedipus complex, Freud's concepts of transference, his superego and his technique of therapeutic analysis. Forty years of patient scientific work were thrown to the dogs." He suggested Horney may not have been sincere in the "acquiescent" tone of her presentation of her views to the society. "Did she perhaps feel that the time had not yet come to smash Freud's psychoanalysis in his own stronghold? The issue is Freud or no Freud." He accused her of surrounding herself with a group of the "younger and youngest" society members some of whose blooming transferences to her led them to confess openly their "deep gratitude" for her help. Her group was trying to "scare into submission the majority of our society." At business meetings, they "elaborate amendments, sit together, vote together, a regular shock-troop and make fools of us by insisting on what they call democratic methods in a scientific body." He accused Kubie of falling for "this slogan of democracy." Indeed, in a scientific body, democracy "if not restricted by scientific fundamentals must necessarily wreck any successful work." Finally the educational committee's policy of having students analyzed by Horney, then supervised by more orthodox Freudians, had compounded the students' confusion. Wittels suggested Horney either "recant," that is, "come back to Freud's principles," or teach her principles under a new name "with an educational staff of her own." In short he suggested she create a separate training school under a new name.[28]

Kubie's response was measured. He was glad to have Wittels's frank opinions but he also defended Horney's sincerity. Moreover, "not because of anyone's malice, but from a series of natural causes," a group of young students had been given a "one-sided" and disastrously warped training. He hoped the proposals for reform by the educational committee would ensure "adequately rounded training." If so, then "we need not fear . . . contact with any teacher, no matter how divergent that particular teacher may be." Such a rounded training would "insure true academic freedom."

Finally, he brought up his serious disagreement. "I am basically opposed to any form of purge in a scientific organization. I feel completely with

Voltaire in this matter, and would defend the right to teach of those with whom I disagree profoundly, provided only that they are experienced and gifted teachers, able to inspire students to thinking for themselves, and able to move students to enthusiasm. In my opinion no such drastic steps as you describe are necessary, or desirable, "so long as members accepted the committee's insistence on "prescribing a balanced diet for every student." He ended, however, on an ominous note. If a teacher under the "slogan of democracy" claimed to "limit a group of students to any one set of ideas" and refused to abide by the decision of the education committee then "such a teacher would certainly have to be deprived of teaching functions. I am hopeful, however, that no such situation will arise."[29]

Five days later, the society granted the committee power to choose the training analyst for each student. And the character of the committee changed, becoming even more strongly dominated by the orthodox. Clara Thompson and Abram Kardiner, who ran for election, were defeated. Wittels was elected a member, and Zilboorg, chairman. Kubie, whose term as president of the society ended, remained on the committee while the term of David Levy, who had been a disinterested supporter of Horney, was over.[30]

After investigating students' charges of intimidation by orthodox analysts, Levy concluded that indeed an appalling, "unhealthy atmosphere" of intimidation existed, the result of rivalries and dissension.[31] Before Levy announced the results of his investigation on April 14, the education committee had decided that Horney should be stripped of her functions as a training and supervising analyst, but remain a "lecturer." Kubie later defended the reasons for the New York society's position. Apparently forgetting the defensive zeal of the orthodox, he made a serious accusation: that the dissident teachers had used their preparatory and training analyses of students to "win converts to an unproven cause." Students had been given

> no opportunity to work out their unconscious hostilities in their own analyses, with the result that all of this unanalyzed hostility was displaced onto their relationship to all subsequent instructors, to the Institute, and to psychoanalysis itself, so that from these students one could hear a bitterness and a venom about analysis which would be hard to equal from some of its most implacable opponents. . . .

While still in their preparatory analyses students were "behaving in a controversial and heckling spirit . . . long before they could have the opportunity to form mature and independent judgments about the matters at issue." Kubie noted that those trained by instructors of "divergent convictions" "almost never" went to 'classical' instructors in order to balance their diet," while classical instructors "regularly" sent their students to "work also with instructors of divergent and radical points of view."[32]

On April 29, 1941, the society voted to relegate Horney to the status of lecturer. She, Clara Thompson, a student of Ferenczi and a friend of Harry Stack Sullivan, and three young analysts walked out of the meeting and resigned. In 1941 Horney and her group founded the American Association for the Advancement of Psychoanalysis, whose very title further infuriated the New York institute. Horney and those who left charged that academic freedom had been violated, students intimidated, and scientific sessions had degenerated into "political machinations." The institute countered with the arguments that hardened the position Kubie had been defending. Its job was to teach "basic Freudian psychoanalysis and not what any individual may consider his interpretation or his deviation from Freudian analysis to be." Such views should be reserved for special graduate courses. An acrimonious and complex dispute ensued, the New York Society defending its claims to academic objectivity, its opponents accusing it of intolerance and coercion.

Almost a year later, on March 20, 1942, David Levy resigned from the society probably for several reasons. He felt "insulted" that a course in child psychiatry had been set up and a European refugee instructor chosen without consulting him. For several years Levy's own course on child psychiatry had been attended by a large number of physicians and educators, among them the young pediatrician Benjamin Spock, who became the nation's most popular postwar adviser in child-rearing and the first unabashed Freudian nanny. Levy believed that European child analysts, medical or lay, lacked the "type of training we consider essential in this country," notably a background in "child guidance, psychopathology, clinical psychology, and medicine." Then Levy had been asked to "disavow" any support for Horney and her group, as well as the implications they had drawn from his earlier investigation of student charges of intimidation. The first of these implications was that the society had become a "hotbed of political intrigue"; the second, that "religious fervor" had replaced free inquiry and dogma thus had "firmly established itself under the guise of science." Levy argued that although the first conclusion could not be drawn from his work, it was obvious enough. The second charge was "rather too sweeping to be true," but "some members of the faculty could be recognized quite readily by the implications made." Finally, Levy could not "stomach" the society's refusal to accept recommendations that Zilboorg be disciplined after a former patient accused him of fleecing him for money and favors, charges Levy and Franz Alexander both believed to be true.[33]

A year earlier, Rado's job as educational director had been abolished, probably because of his increasingly unorthodox views, and he was appointed director of research. In 1942 Rado and a group of other analysts, including David Levy, George Daniels, Abraham Kardiner, and Carl Binger, departed to found the Association for Psychoanalytic and Psychosomatic Medicine. They hoped to establish an institute affiliated with the Department of Psychiatry at Columbia University, in partial fulfillment of Rado's dream of creating close ties between psychoanalysis and medicine. Nolan D. C. Lewis, then chairman of the Columbia Department of Psychiatry, recalled that by having the medical school administer the institute, he hoped to do away with "all that politics."[34]

The new organizations of Horney and Rado posed serious problems for the American Psychoanalytic Association. Franz Alexander believed that the "organizational" aspects of psychoanalysis were only important "for the little psychoanalytic universe. Neither the outside world nor the good type of student pays any attention." The best students came to "learn something useful for their therapeutic or research work and not to get official recognition." Most planned to be accredited by the national board in psychiatry. "In my eyes," he wrote Levy, the correct policy for you in New York should be to found a good teaching institution and not even bother whether or not the American will recognize it." A few weeks later he wrote that the leaders of the New York institute might be willing to accept "other groups in New York," including a new institute and possibly a new society. He hoped all three New York groups would participate in preliminary discussions.[35] This sanguine prospect never materialized, partly because of developments in the most remote outpost of psychoanalysis, California.

The psychoanalytic movement in California became a successful example of professionalization through national insistence on the new standards of a medical degree, systematic training, and doctrinal orthodoxy, at the same time allowing informal recognition of lay analysts. By the late 1950s California and especially Beverly Hills had the largest and best-paid concentration of organized psychoanalysts outside New York. Moreover, psychoanalysis in California slowly gained considerable influence within psychiatry by an alliance with the medical profession, after difficulties in the late 1930s and early 1940s. The appointment of psychoanalysts to teaching positions in medical schools began just before World War II and increased rapidly after it. At the same time, the role of laymen was crucial. The first major enthusiasts had been laymen from a variety of disciplines, some already were well known and distinguished in their own fields, and their interest is a sign of the growing inroads of psychoanalysis in academic and popular culture. The issue of lay analysis was excerbated by stringent medical licensing laws and by the leadership role of a few prominent refugees who were either laymen or physicians who never acquired a California medical license and who functioned as training analysts. Finally, California lacked an official psychoanalytic organization. All these issues—lay analysis, orthodoxy, organizational structure—were complicated by the fact that California psychoanalysts were under the tutelage of the Topeka Psychoanalytic Society, whose opinions sometimes were decisive.

Three of the refugees were unusually able men who had been leaders in the European movement, and all three were technically laymen in California: Otto Fenichel, a physician who had taught in Berlin and wrote the first comprehensive psychoanalytic text; Ernest Simmel, another physician and a founder of the Berlin institute; and Siegfried Bernfeld, a lay analyst who also taught in Berlin and had been a pioneer in the application of psychoanalysis to education. Simmel and Fenichel settled in Los Angeles, and Bernfeld, in San Francisco, and they played important roles in their respective areas. All three were from the political left wing of the European movement. All three were profoundly committed to orthodoxy and to systematic training.

These refugees helped to give psychoanalysis a militant, liberal cast by holding out the promise of a new and scientific solution to problems of violence and oppression. They also gave psychoanalysis the role of a beatific St. George fighting the very real Nazi dragon. Many of them had been victims of Hitler's oppression. Simmel had been imprisoned before he was allowed to leave for America. Concern about family and friends still left in Central Europe was a constant source of anxiety.[36]

The refugees in California acted as stout defenders of orthodoxy as Karen Horney and Sandor Rado pressed their "deviant" views. Karl Menninger, leader of the Topeka society, wrote that the influential Franz Alexander seemed to condone, if not accept the new departures. "I think Doctor Alexander may underestimate the pernicious influence of the sort of rebellion that Rado and Horney have encouraged, because he sometimes has a tendency to minimize such aggressive acts because of his own generous and amiable disposition."[37] In 1940 the American Psychoanalytic Association's committee on certification had insisted that candidates in training be taught "what is accepted as basic Freudian psychoanalysis and not what any individual analyst may consider his interpretation of or his deviation from Freudian psychoanalysis to be."[38] The official hardening of orthodoxy had some direct consequences. In the Topeka group, a European analyst and his wife were carefully screened for Jungian tendencies in dream interpretation and for ignoring the transference in their patients. Ralph Greenson, because of his initial work with the anathematized Wilhelm Stekel, had difficulty at first in joining the Los Angeles study group and becoming a candidate for training. He had found that Stekel's brief methods had failed to cure his patients and he wanted a more thorough, painstaking technique. He recalled that Simmel told him: "We can't have people coming to our meetings who at least don't agree with certain basic principles, because we don't want someone to have to give a paper and then somebody like you get up and argue "Is there an Oedipus complex? I don't believe in it."[39] Those who, like Greenson, had had some training under unapproved auspices particularly needed to demonstrate their seriousness and their loyalty to the Freudian cause.

Psychoanalysis demanded not only orthodoxy, but signal "sacrifices" and proofs of devotion from its prospective candidates in these years. Those who already had flourishing psychiatric practices were asked to give up any claim to being analysts until they had finished their training. Greenson modified a comfortable practice to undergo a personal analysis, with no guarantee that he would successfully complete the requirements. In Boston, a prospective candidate was rejected by the Boston institute because it judged that he would not sacrifice a thriving practice or attempt to resolve what were thought to be his personality problems and pursue his analysis seriously.

In California the impact of the refugee analysts made the lay issue unusually acute, partly because there were no well-known medical analysts to play a leadership role, men such as A. A. Brill, who championed psychoanalysis in New York, or the Menninger brothers, who brought psychoanalysis to Topeka. California's first trained analyst was a laymen, David

Brunswick, who held a doctorate in psychology from Johns Hopkins, had been analyzed by Freud in Vienna, began practice in 1931. He later organized a Los Angeles study group.

In Depression-era California, physicians jealously guarded their monopoly of medical treatment. Against the fear of an invasion of foreign competitors, in 1937 they insisted that all foreign physicians who might aspire to practice in the state should complete not only an examination but a year's internship. Few of the European medical analysts, with some exceptions, were able to comply. Yet for the refugee lay or medical analysts, often highly qualified and experienced, the ability to practice was crucial if they were to make a living. To fulfill the requirement of an internship meant a substantial loss in income at a time when they were just getting started. Otto Fenichel had four patients in analysis after his arrival in Los Angeles, "a city in which nothing that we are used to in Europe seems to have validity." He described his dilemma about a medical license to his friend Edward Bibring. "I came here with the best intentions of studying medicine again. However it has become impossible for me; I can only take the examination if I first complete a entire year's unpaid internship which I cannot afford. I shall therefore not do it and shall work without a license as I did in Oslo and Prague."[40]

To complicate the issue, the lay and some of the medical analysts regarded lay analysis as one of the hallmark's of Freud's movement and deplored the close ties of psychoanalysis and psychiatry in America. Robert Waelder, a lay analyst from Vienna, wrote to Otto Fenichel that in the eastern United States, analysis was a variety of psychiatric therapy and that a man's standing in psychiatry was more important for his prestige in a psychoanalytic organization than were his contributions to the psychoanalytic literature. Waelder had difficulties obtaining patients in Boston, while his wife, a physician analyst, had been quite successful.[41] In Los Angeles and San Francisco, psychoanalysis remained close to the European model with an important contingent of lay analysts, and in 1950 Los Angeles split into two institutes, over precisely the issues of lay analysis and orthodoxy. In 1939 there had been suggestions for creating a separate national organization around some of the lay and unlicensed medical analysts. Fenichel, despite his belief in lay analysis, argued against the possibility on grounds that, consisting almost entirely of relatively powerless Europeans, it would have increased the anti-immigrant mood and made life miserable for the émigrés.[42]

From the moment of his entry into the United States, Bernfeld had been plagued by the lay analysis issue, which became troublesome in San Francisco. Bernfeld, an eloquent lecturer, unusually tall, with piercing eyes and a commanding voice, had asked Franz Alexander for a letter of recommendation in 1936 before his immigration to the United States. Alexander had stuck to generalities about his "scientific eminence" and refused to give the slightest hint that he might earn money to support himself from analytic fees.[43] Karl Menninger later declined to recognize a physician candidate of Bernfeld's because Bernfeld did not have official "training analyst standing."[44]

Joseph W. Thompson, a friend of Kroeber's and a physician who detested the medical profession, had taught a small coterie of lay analysts in San Francisco. An eccentric, he had sent odd little communications to the *Psychoanalytic Review* from the South Seas and lined the hall of his home with cages of Siamese cats. Earlier he had been in the Washington-Baltimore area and may have been Clara Thompson's first analyst. He and his group saw most of their patients at night and charged $5 an hour. The few interested social workers in clinics and hospitals would have nothing to do with Thompson. In a long letter describing the San Francisco scene to Anna Freud, Bernfeld saw those interested in psychoanalysis unflatteringly as "ambitious and busy people of all ages," most of them "obviously neurotic and depressive." The well educated and the immigrants were among the few who realized that psychoanalysis played a role in medicine. Bernfeld also noted that psychoanalysis and Freud had achieved enough notoriety to be the topic of books and articles in the drugstores. He even thought he detected a special California flavor in such titles as "How to Psychoanalyze Yourself" or "Personality Concentration, Food Therapy and Psychoanalysis by the World's Greatest Living Psychologist."[45]

A serious interest began among university faculty when Alfred Kroeber, an anthropologist at the University of California, Berkeley, reviewed Freud's *Totem and Taboo* in 1920 and discussed psychoanalysis in his seminars. A friend of Joseph Thompson's, he began a psychoanalytic practice, which he broke off after three years because he said he could not pursue careers in both anthropology and psychoanalysis at the same time. By the late 1930s and early 1940s in the San Francisco area, interested faculty at both Berkeley and Stanford included Harold Jones, the child development expert; the psychologists Edward Tolman and Nevitt Sanford; Lewis Terman, the educational psychologist; and Robert Oppenheimer, the physicist. Several of them had been attending Bernfeld's seminars.

Bernfeld had thought of addressing the joint session of the American Psychiatric Association and the American Psychoanalytic Association when they met in San Francisco in the early summer of 1938, but Karl Menninger had cautioned him that the American Psychiatric Association was a medical organization and his status as a laymen as well as his limited command of English made that inadvisable.[46]

Clearly, psychoanalysis was a matter of popular interest in San Francisco, and during the meetings, the San Francisco press publicized Freud's exile from Vienna to London. The *Chronicle* presented Freud's new image as a Jewish victim of Nazi persecution. His picture dominated the title page of the *Chronicle*'s Sunday magazine section, *This World*. Austria's "foremost scientist, frail and ailing, left Vienna surrounded by a "sorrowful little group of women." "Nazi Austria had rid itself of a pornographic Jewish specialist. Two days later London welcomed a neurologist of world reputation—the man who had put into the common language such words as 'inferiority complex' and 'repression.'"

Freud taught that "all the nervous ills and worries that beset human beings are directly attributable to sexual impulses and the restraints that civilized man has been compelled to put upon himself." Dreams were the "royal road to the subconscious mind," "the attempted outlet for ideas and impulses that are imprisoned in the subconscious by inhibitions. By getting patients to confess their dreams to him . . . he has not only been able to relieve their troubled minds but also to prove many of his theories." Psychoanalysis had derived its greatest impetus from the fact that conventional medical science had "gone a long way in curing sick bodies" but not sick minds and as a result psychoanalysis had become very popular in America.

Here were the elements of the liberationist image of psychoanalysis: the version of catharsis Freud had presented at Clark University in 1909 allied with his new status as a Nazi victim.[47] The psychoanalytic meetings added one more element to this popular conception, the notion of crime as sickness. Simmel, according to the *Chronicle,* had argued that "murderers and thieves may not know it, but they are victims of love sickness." The "criminal neurotic . . . is one which is constantly searching for love objects whom he wishes either completely or partially to possess. He wants to love. His love is hate. That is his crime."

While Freud was highly publicized, the attention given psychoanalysis in the professional psychiatric meetings was definite but minor. A. A. Brill and Karl Menninger addressed the section on psychoanalysis, and Dexter Bullard, superintendent of Chestnut Lodge, a psychoanalytic sanitarium near Washington, D.C., described the uses of psychoanalysis in a psychiatric hospital. Franz Alexander and his student Leon Saul expounded the new psychosomatic medicine, arguing for the role of stress in high blood pressure.

The major psychiatric interest at the meetings concerned two new somatic treatments for schizophrenia, insulin and metrazol shock, explained by their respective inventors, Manfred Sakel and Ladislaus von Meduna. A skeptical Stanford medical statistician argued that neither method had been shown to be of value.[48]

In Los Angeles, Ernst Simmel, then 52, and technically a layman, at Brunswick's request, had organized a new Los Angeles study group in 1934. Short, energetic, friendly, and expansive, he hoped to duplicate his European successes in California. Simmel had helped to organize the Berlin institute's program of supervised analyses and clinical case seminars for training candidates. Interested in addicts and mild psychotics, he had established a psychoanalytic sanitarium outside Berlin where Freud had stayed when he came to the city to be treated for his cancer of the jaw. A pioneer in the application of psychoanalysis to the war neuroses, Simmel was fascinated by Freud's death instinct and its applications in psychosomatic medicine.

Like Freud, Simmel was not an astute judge of men or finances, and he had a rather zany sense of humor. At the Los Angeles Institute's tenth anniversary he jokingly noted the application of relativity to psychoanalysis: "libidinal energy can turn into matter. Example: Erection."[49] In Los Angeles, the increasing number of German refugee intellectuals and artists, particularly actors and directors in the cinema, already familiar with psychoanalysis, strengthened the pool of supporters and analysands.

The San Francisco and Los Angeles groups were highly informal during the early years. Wives and interested laymen attended, and perhaps fifteen to thirty people would meet in each other's homes; often discussions lasted long into the night. The child of one analyst remembered listening over the bannister to the heated talk in the living room below.[50]

Simmel attracted not only physicians but people from other disciplines, and he held seminars for teachers and social workers. He developed a flourishing practice that included a number of celebrities, among them, the composer George Gershwin. By 1939 he had collected a sizable group of community leaders to sponsor his most ambitious project, a Los Angeles Psychoanalytic Institute, which would include a clinic, a sanitarium, a nursery school, and a training institute. His patrons included John Atwell Westwick, of the Santa Barbara Superior Court; Pryns Hopkins, a wealthy heir, also from Santa Barbara; King Vidor, a director from MGM; Walter Hilborn, a trustee of the Federation of Jewish Welfare Organizations of Los Angeles; faculty from Cal Tech and the University of Southern California; and Elizabeth Woods, supervisor of educational research from the Los Angeles Board of Education.

Freud gave his blessing, but balked at lending the sanitarium his name. On January 9, 1939, shortly before his death, he wrote to Simmel:

> If at the time of its opening I am no longer alive you may anyway do as you please. If contrary to expectations, I am still here, a cable from you will make possible a quick decision. In any case it is pleasant to hear that after the cruel mutilations of recent years our hydra is growing new heads in California.[51]

Simmel pinned high hopes on the conquests achieved by psychoanalytic insight, which the new institute represented—nothing less, in fact, than the understanding and ultimate control of man's "primitive forces of hatred and destruction." Psychoanalysis had demonstrated this possibility "repeatedly" in individual cases and could reach those plagued by broken marriages, family estrangements, suicidal impulses and some serious illness, "the origin of which is hidden in their unconscious . . . the residue of childhood conflicts." Further research might aid the solution of "political and social problems."[52] But Simmel's expansive plans were defeated by procedural difficulties, opposition from Topeka, and the lay analysis issue.

Between 1938 and 1941 the analytic groups were having their own difficulties with a few lay analysts. In Los Angeles one lay analyst suggested that a candidate hide in a closet to learn technique while the analyst conducted a session. The analyst was expelled from the group.[53] Simmel was even more unlucky with a lay analyst in an attempt to foster a "socialization" institute for the study and treatment of criminals and delinquents in Santa Barbara. It was founded June 18, 1940, by Judge Atwell Westwick, an enthusiast of psychoanalysis, who had been sending young men on probation to the

psychiatrist G. V. Hamilton for psychiatric and what he thought was psychoanalytic treatment. Hamilton was an eclectic psychiatrist who had done important research at his primate colony in Santa Barbara and had written a
pioneering study of sexuality, *Modern Marriage,* Westwick hoped that Hamilton would train probation officers to do psychoanalytic psychotherapy, and
he also hoped to recruit Karl Menninger for the board of trustees. Menninger at first refused, on grounds that no physician should train laymen to
do psychoanalytic treatment, and that Hamilton was not a trained psychoanalyst himself, although he might subscribe to some of its theories and use
some of its methods. Menninger argued that Judge Westwick seemed to
confuse all psychiatry with psychoanalysis and that he needed to found a
psychiatric clinic, "not an organization of psychoanalysts or pseudo-
psychoanalyzed laymen, ambitious to do clinical work." "No American psychoanalyst, Menninger argued, "can under any circumstances, condone the
training of lay people to do psychoanalysis."[54] He suggested that Westwick
consult Simmel, which he already had done.

Simmel had just the right man for the job, a refugee lay analyst from
Berlin, Hugo Staub, who had written a book on criminology with Franz
Alexander and had worked at the London Institute for Criminal Psychology,
headed by the British analyst Edward Glover. Staub had escaped from Vichy
France to Spain by walking over the Pyrenees. In December 1940 Staub
informed Menninger that he had taken Hamilton's place as director and
insisted that he would not break the rules of the American Psychoanalytic
Association regarding laymen. He would lecture social workers, probation
officers, and judges, analyze some of them as well as treat criminals, all under
the supervision of local physicians. But he would not train any of them to
psychoanalyze. On January 23, 1941, Menninger joined the institute's advisory board.

By August, 1941, the institute and its prospects had evaporated. "I am
sorry to say that psychoanalytic criminology in Santa Barbara, which seemed
so hopeful, had ceased to exist," Simmel wrote to Menninger. Staub left
Santa Barbara for New York, "under circumstances clouded by strife and
scandal."[55]

In 1941 the state board of medical examiners, after inquiries from "various" physicians "throughout the state," asked for an opinion as to the legal
status of the practice of psychoanalysis by laymen. Earl Warren, the future
Chief Justice of the U.S. Supreme Court and then the state's attorney general, ruled in May that lay analysis violated the California Business and Professions Code.[56]

By 1943 wartime needs had mitigated the issue. Simmel reported that
physician analysts like himself, without medical licenses, were being asked to
help in the war effort and that the attorney general's office seemed to have an
"excellent understanding of psychoanalysis."[57] Nevertheless, he urged every
new psychoanalyst settling in California to obtain medical credentials. As late
as 1946, a year before he died, Simmel was questioned by the board, which
was investigating the practice of psychiatry without a medical license.[58]

Psychoanalysis in California already was taking on a medical cast. In San Francisco, Jacob Kasanin, a physician analyst, opened a psychiatric department at Mt. Zion Hospital in 1939, and its child guidance clinic was headed by a sympathetic pediatrician, Ernst Wolff, who was analyzed by Bernfeld. The influence of physician analysts grew stronger because of a group of young neurologists and psychiatrists who began training in both Los Angeles and San Francisco.

In 1941 Simmel hoped to found a California society formally affiliated with the American Psychoanalytic Association. There would be a special category of accredited membership for qualified lay analysts in training before 1938. Three physician analysts, May Romm, Charles Tidd, and Joachim Haenel, refused to join any California society which included lay members, because they feared the board of medical examiners and the county medical societies might disapprove. Simmel then added the proviso that every lay member should have completed training and be subject to medical supervision, provisions to which the major lay analysts had agreed. But this failed to convince the three.[59] Moreover, Bernfeld was reluctant to subject himself to any medical psychoanalytic organization because he feared that if patients became scarce, the medical analysts could jeopardize the practice of the lay analysts. He suggested that as charter members their participation in scientific activities and in education and training and non-medical activities be formally recognized.[60]

On March 8, 1942, ten other physicians, chiefly in San Francisco and Los Angeles, founded a San Francisco Psychoanalytic Society after adopting a provision that lay analysts could not vote, hold office, or serve on committees, but could be listed as accredited members. It was hoped that this dual position would forestall conflicts with the medical profession as well as the American Psychoanalytic Association.[61] Fenichel and Simmel were both among the ten founders, and Simmel was elected president.[62]

Simmel's very modest proposal for lay membership was defeated at the national level. When the issue came up at the annual meeting of the American Psychoanalytic Association in Boston in May, 1942, partly on the insistence of Tidd and Romm, the San Francisco Society was accepted without Simmel's special category for lay members, a defeat which the Californians reluctantly accepted. Fenichel believed that the "progressive suppression" of trained and qualified lay analysts was a "symptom of the . . . progressive degeneration of psychoanalysis into a psychiatric method."[63] For a time Bernfeld threatened to refuse any collaboration with the new society and contemplated creating a separate local organization for the lay analysts. But a saving compromise was suggested by Kasanin. In mollification, Kasanin wrote to Bernfeld on June 19 that he had been unanimously elected as honorary member, training analyst, and permanent advisory member of the education committee. Moreover, the society would maintain a special list of lay analysts who would enjoy complete scientific participation in the society. Bernfeld replied with heavy irony: "I feel somewhat bewildered by the various honors, titles, and duties which you Doctor—as you informed me—kindly bestowed upon me."[64]

One consequence of the controversy over lay analysis was Fenichel's decision to begin a year's internship in 1945. He had become convinced that only a physician could carry reasonable weight in the politics of the American Psychoanalytic Association.[65] Internships normally were undertaken by young men, and were physically punishing even for them. Fenichel died of a stroke at the age of 49 after six months of his internship.

By 1942 California had a recognized branch of the American Psychoanalytic Association, with ten members, all physicians, and the days of tutelage from Topeka were ended. A number of able Europeans, with or without medical licenses, functioned as training analysts. There were interested and influential laymen in social work, child guidance, the law, and the universities in both the San Francisco and Los Angeles areas. The dominant role of physicians was assured, as was systematic training and orthodox theory, summed up in Fenichel's massive *Psychoanalytic Theory of Neurosis,* revised and published in 1945. Fenichel had become convinced as he began his internship that more important than the correct application of psychoanalysis to sociology was the fight for "the very existence of Freudian psychoanalysis" against the new "advanced" views of the neo-Freudians.[66]

The California group almost immediately played a key role in the issue of orthodoxy versus neo-Freudianism. This time orthodoxy was entwined with the issue of whether or not one or more institutes could exist in the same locality. Those who at first favored this departure included the neo-Freudians; those opposed, the orthodox and particularly the Europeans.

The issue was broached by Sandor Rado's request for recognition by the American Psychoanalytic Association for his proposed institute at Columbia University and by threats of resignation from the American by Rado and some of his colleagues who also had left the New York society.[67] Rado's proposals were debated at highly emotional sessions of the American Psychoanalytic Association's May meetings in Boston. Eleven members of the New York society, which was smarting under allegations of ideological intolerance, proposed that before any members be allowed to secede to found a new psychoanalytic organization they await a formal investigation by analysts from other areas as well as non-analytic physicians and "friendly laymen." The New Yorkers argued, probably in words supplied by Lawrence Kubie, that multiple institutes would create "self perpetuating educational autocracies, training candidates in a single point of view," dominated by "stormy and headstrong factions . . . jockeying for votes . . . log-rolling with disaffected factions in other communities, converting our annual sessions into a maelstrom of political manoeuvering." The New York analyst Philip Lehrman argued that because the number of students had not increased there was no need for a new institute. The Boston society agreed with the New Yorkers, called for an impartial investigation, and urged the American Psychoanalytic Association never to recognize Karen Horney's group. One of its oldest members, Isador Coriat, argued that "the fundamental data is the same wherever psychoanalysis is taught" and that therefore multiple institutes "would be for personal advantage." Helene Deutsch questioned the proponents' motives and argued that the separation of dissident groups into separate institutes would lose "for teaching purposes the exchange of ideas and opinions, mutual corrections, etc." Surprisingly, William Silverberg, Horney's friend, agreed with Deutsch, observed that "none of the dissidence has been on purely scientific grounds," and backed an investigation.

Franz Alexander, who had hoped that Horney's and Rado's groups might be accepted, likened "previous teaching . . . in psychoanalysis to the church in that there was one doctrine, one concept and nothing but that was taught. If someone disagreed he had to leave the Association and found his own Association." He emphasized that "we are working in a new field in which nothing is settled; that we can agree on some principles and not on others; that we should encourage free thinking and free inquiry."[68] The Chicago and Philadelphia society representatives argued that the personal animosities of both sides made it impossible to resolve the issues, and so regardless of the merits of the controversy they should separate.

On a national level, the schisms, undertaken in the name of academic freedom, led ultimately to a tightening of centralized control by the American Psychoanalytic Association. The first proposal came after Austin Davies, the executive secretary of the American Psychiatric Association, called in as a consultant, had reported in December 1941 that the national organization was weak, loosely organized, with little authority. Karl Menninger, then the president, appointed a committee on reorganization, chaired by Thomas French of the Chicago institute. He proposed that responsibility for setting standards of training and membership be taken over by the American Psychoanalytic Association. It would prescribe minimal standards, evaluate institutes, and admit institute graduates to membership in the national organization after an examination. This would solve the problem of schisms by divorcing institutes from control by local societies and by authorizing more than one institute in a given area.

Meanwhile, the Topeka society had been formally accepted. That made eight official psychoanalytic societies in America—New York, Boston, Washington-Baltimore, Chicago, Detroit, Philadelphia, Topeka, and San Francisco. Boston, New York, and San Francisco were by far the most orthodox, while Philadelphia, Chicago, and Baltimore-Washington were the more favorable to the neo-Freudians.

The Horney affair and the proposal to authorize more than one institute in a given area had aroused severe conflict. "Controversy is a miracle of understatement," Lionel Blitzsten wrote to Fenichel, "raging battle, mud slinging and destruction would be more adequate terms."[69] The issue of multiple institutes quickly became tangled in a procedural dispute. Karl Menninger, who at first had opposed the proposal, changed his mind and successfully urged the Topeka society to vote for it. Menninger and Bartemeier, the association's secretary, assumed that a simple majority vote of the constituent societies sufficed for passage.

That opinion inspired Lawrence Kubie and others to consult the association's attorney, who declared that a constitutional amendment required a vote of two-thirds or more of the local societies, so that at least six of the societies would have to vote in favor of the proposals. To his New York colleague, Leonard Blumgart, Kubie wrote:

> If those weak devils [presumably Menninger and Bartemeier] are willing to buckle under to five willful men [presumably Rado and the other founders of the Columbia Institute], then by God the three soundest societies in the Association have a right to stand on their specific constitutional rights. Now let's watch the fur fly.[70]

The proposal was defeated because of the opposition of New York, Boston, and, above all, the new San Francisco society, led by Fenichel and Simmel, both strong opponents of the neo-Freudians.[71] Simmel argued that multiple institutes with "different teachings" would create an "intramural battleground" that would destroy the association, which he regarded as the "last organized bulwark against all adversaries of psychoanalysis."[72] Simmel invoked a Freudian explanation of the strife at the American Psychoanalytic Association meetings in Boston. The long anticipated effects of the death of Freud, the archetypal father, had been felt among the analysts after the outbreak of World War II:

> The surviving generals in the psychoanalytic movement seem to me to have just concluded that stage in which the murdered father is killed once again. (In that some of us write books against him and against the unconscious.) We are now entering the phase in which the sons begin to kill each other. For the time being we are doing that under the pretense of improving the constitution, for instance by proposing that there should be more than one society or institute in a given location. I believe this proposal does nothing more than prepare the field of battle on which Freudian psychoanalysis will be "scientifically" shot down by the "others."[73]

Menninger urged Simmel to reconsider his attitude toward the proposed institute and wrote ruefully, "Trying to keep in line an Association made up of eight Societies composed of hostile, mutually jealous members (as well as some who are generous spirited and open-minded) is a difficult job."[74] To Rado he observed,

> If you have any respect for the mental health of your president and secretary you will bear with us in great patience, as we are about to become distracted, owing to the ebb and flow of procedures, decisions and emotions regarding the new Institute. . . . anyway one figures it, the amendment has failed to receive the endorsement of two-thirds of the constituent member societies of our Association.[75]

But Menninger remained conflicted over the problem of orthodoxy. He urged on Fenichel the logic of a compromise that would retain control of the new Institute within the American and would thus avoid a split:

> By very careful steering we can keep psychoanalysis from becoming a cult with orthodox tenets on the one hand, or a loose all-embracing psychological medi-

cine on the other, the conflicting concepts and theories of which will dissipate and destroy it.[76]

Yet to Rado he wrote: "I am assuming that you and your colleagues are acting in good faith in your project of forming a new Institute strictly devoted to Freudian psychoanalysis. . . . "[77]

Menninger and Bertram Lewin, as successive presidents of the American Psychoanalytic Association, were both in favor of the new institute, but formal acceptance hung fire until the reorganization of the American Psychoanalytic Association in 1946. John Millet, one of Rado's colleagues, believed that the dogmatism of the orthodox psychoanalysts was creating a scientific vacuum that prevented the creation of new knowledge.[78] However, some of the Europeans found the new departures intellectually unconvincing. Grete and Edward Bibring, members of the Vienna society who had settled in Boston, observed that psychoanalysis had entered a necessary "phase of critical self-evaluation." But like any other science, it could only develop "organically." The tendency to "replace Freud" was decidedly stronger than the tendency to work out the existing problems in psychoanalysis "steadily and persistently." Psychoanalysis, like other psychological sciences, was inexact, but it was also a pioneering science with no established tradition. The new theories were weak and were bolstered by distorted clinical observations.[79]

These organizational and theoretical skirmishes were fought out in the growing shadow of World War II.[80] The May meetings of the American Psychoanalytic Association had included symposia on the war neuroses, and Franz Alexander was organizing a committee to develop an appropriate short-term psychotherapy. Fifteen members and forty students of the New York society already were in the service. Kubie, who long had believed the war was America's struggle as well as England's, had been working with the National Research Council studying the war neuroses of torpedoed merchant seamen. Ralph Kaufman, the Boston psychoanalyst, had become aide to the director of the Army's new "indoctrination school for psychiatrists," whose aim was to give hospital psychiatrists "an opportunity to learn something about the neuroses before undertaking the care of troops."[81] That appointment and others like it would lay the foundation for the rapid penetration of psychiatry by psychoanalysis in the postwar years.

Issues of orthodoxy and the control of training would remain to plague psychoanalytic organizations although with somewhat less consuming intensity. On November 17, 1942, Kubie wrote to Edward Glover that the many petty intramural squabbles among the analysts were "too lugubrious a commentary on analytical human nature to read."[82]

9

The Psychoanalytic Impact on American Psychiatry, 1917–1940

While psychoanalysis was becoming a medical sub-specialty with its own training institutes, increasingly high qualifications, and an emerging standardization of orthodox theory, its impact on psychiatry slowly grew. Given impetus by the psychological interpretations of shell shock in World War I, psychoanalysis drew American psychiatry toward a psychodynamic model of sickness in which emotional factors caused disturbances from ulcers to schizophrenia. This chapter will describe the slow growth of the psychoanalytic impact, the experimental use of psychoanalytic psychotherapy in the treatment of the psychoses, and the role of psychoanalysis as an explanatory medical psychology, taught to an increasing extent in the psychiatric programs of medical schools. The following chapter will deal with major teachers who fostered the psychoanalytic impact: Adolf Meyer, Harry Stack Sullivan, and the psychosomaticists Flanders Dunbar and Franz Alexander.

The psychodynamic style that psychoanalysis fostered can be defined best by contrast with its predecessor, the somatic style of the late nineteenth century. Then, heredity and neurological functioning, often interpreted in a highly speculative manner, were seen as independent variables in nervous and mental disorder. By contrast, the psychodynamic style emphasized psychological and social factors as causes of strain or anxiety which in turn resulted in neuroses and psychoses. The strain or anxiety itself came either from conflict within the personality or, in many American interpretations, from environmental influences within the family, chiefly the way parents dealt with their children in infancy and early childhood. Increasingly the European analysts themselves had been moving toward a more environmentalist position. Harry Stack Sullivan, one of most optimistic of the Americans, although allowing for innate differences, focused on "the difficulties of living which arise far more from misfortunes in developmental history."[1]

The growing influence of psychoanalysis and the psychodynamic style resulted from several factors. One of the most important was the prestige of the scientific expert and, especially, the psychological and the medical expert. As Gerald Grob has argued, psychiatry between the two world wars was drawing closer to medicine in its search for social legitimation and authority.[2] Psychoanalysts, although viewed by many rival professionals as mystical soothsayers, claimed above all to be scientists with a unique knowledge of unconscious motivation and irrational behavior derived from their special method. As psychoanalytic training became more rigorous and systematic, closely linked to medical and psychiatric expertise, these claims to scientific status were advanced more boldly.

Within psychiatry the success of psychoanalysis resulted in part from the failure of somaticism to offer unquestionably effective treatments and convincing theories of cause. In the 1920s a minor fad for curing mental illness by removing focal infections, such as diseased teeth, collapsed on the psychoanalyst Phyllis Greenacre's objective analysis of the results. In the 1930s a number of somatic methods, including insulin and metrazol shock and lobotomy, were energetically pushed, but some psychiatrists remained skeptical of their results and their theoretical justification. Finally, the inconclusive outcome of dogged, ongoing attempts to find a somatic pathology for the psychoses strengthened the proponents of a psychodynamic style, of whom the psychoanalysts were then the most militant. In 1931 Bernard Sachs, a neurologist who denounced the psychoanalysts as agents of moral decay, conceded that the results of anatomical and pathological studies had been disappointing.[3]

Alternative academic psychological theories to psychoanalysis such as behaviorism, learning theory, or gestalt had not yet developed persuasive clinical applications, despite a few early attempts. So in the crucial years while psychoanalysis was being transformed into a disciplined specialty, the disappointments of somaticism and the absence of developed psychological alternatives made psychoanalysis seem unusually useful and promising. Psychoanalysis gradually became the major American medical psychology, and there were increasing claims for the effectiveness of psychoanalytic treatment, even in the psychoses.

Through the years from 1917 to 1940 there was an apparently rising demand for psychiatric services. Its sources are obscure, but psychiatrists consistently remarked on it. The sociologist Andrew Abbot has argued that the psychiatrists effectively took over from the clergy the realm of "personal problems."[4] Even during the Depression the demand for psychiatric services was greater than the supply of trained personnel. How much of this demand reflected an increased incidence of nervous and mental disorder, possibly resulting from the Depression? How much resulted from a growing aware-ness of these disorders and an eagerness to use the services of psychiatrists, created by intensive popularization and "mental hygiene" campaigns spon-sored by psychiatrists themselves? How much came from the highly pub-licized claims of psychotherapists and, above all, of psychoanalysts? None of these questions can be easily resolved. But the extent of the demand seems incontrovertible. Physicians estimated that 35 to 50 percent of the patients seen in ordinary private medical practice were suffering from psycho-neuroses. In New York City alone, in 1929, some 30,000 patients sought psychiatric treatment in 67 clinics, while some 7,500 of these were diagnosed as psychoneurotics.[5]

Growing demand after the nadir of the Depression fostered not only the modest expansion of the psychiatric profession but also its ancillary profes-sions such as mental hygiene, child guidance, and psychiatric social work; and these disciplines, in particular, reflected the impact of psychoanalysis.

Social conditions may have contributed to the growth of private psychi-atric practice. American prosperity especially during the 1920s had fostered the rapid growth of the middle and upper middle classes and the college-educated, precisely the groups most likely to have voluntary recourse to the psychiatrist or the psychiatric psychotherapist. By the late 1930s the number of analysts and candidates nationally was growing. Harry Stack Sullivan, after initial difficulties, claimed that he quickly became one of the best-paid psy-chiatrists in New York.

The modern office practice of psychiatry emerged during the period from about 1920 to 1940, and psychoanalysis and psychoanalytic psycho-therapy provided important models of office treatment. Psychiatrists increas-ingly took over the domain neurologists had staked out for themselves since the 1880s—the private treatment of the nervous and mental disorders of the well-to-do. Neurology, meanwhile, was becoming a more narrow somatic specialty. Many psychiatrists exchanged the low salaries of public hospitals for more lucrative urban, private practice, while some psychoanalysts were treating not only neurotics but some psychotic patients as well.

Public hospitals, which cared for the vast majority of the nation's mental-ly ill, treated chiefly psychotics, but also a very few patients classified as neurotic.[6] However, the role of psychoanalytic psychotherapy was slight, and it was tried on a largely experimental basis in only a few public hospitals. Practice there was difficult for many reasons—the overwhelming number of patients, the lack of personnel, and the length and cost of psychoanalytic psychotherapy. Some psychiatrists argued that only a small proportion of mental hospital patients were suitable for intensive psychotherapy. St. Eliz-abeth's, which had set up a special psychotherapeutic department in 1918, employed three psychoanalytic psychotherapists. Gregory Zilboorg for a time worked at Bloomingdale, in White Plains.

Psychoanalysis was applied more intensively at a few private hospitals. From Chestnut Lodge, Dexter Bullard described the sometimes tempestuous and intense transference relationships between therapist and psychotic patient.[7] The Menningers in Topeka for some years had been adapting psychoanalytic techniques to the treatment of hospitalized neurotic and psychotic patients.

However, psychoanalysis did provide an important medical psychology which many psychiatrists believed fostered a new and deeper understanding of their patients. It helped to fill a notorious void left by academic psychology which had contributed "practically nothing" to a knowledge of "human nature," according to Henry Murray, Harvard's distinguished and impulsive psychologist.[8]

Freudian psychoanalysis was one strand in a highly eclectic American medical psychology, described in this period as "dynamic psychiatry." An equally or more important strand was the "psychobiology" of Adolf Meyer. A survey of psychiatric training showed that the latter supplied a knowledge of the "normal" while psychoanalysis largely supplied knowledge of the "abnormal," or psychopathology.[9] And this eclectic, complex mix also included minor threads of Jung, Adler, Pierre Janet, and Morton Prince.

Three groups of physicians contributed to the impact of psychoanalysis. The first was the tiny group of psychoanalysts themselves, a surprising number of them, at first, recruited from institutional psychiatry. Some of them continued to work in public hospitals and clinics, often on a part-time basis. A few were nationally prominent—William Alanson White, director of St. Elizabeth's Hospital; A. A. Brill, who taught at New York University and often publicized his specialty; or Frankwood Williams, the paladin of mental hygiene.

A second group was made up of eclectic psychiatrists who absorbed aspects of psychoanalysis, but who remained outside the movement, men such as C. Macfie Campbell, director of the Boston Psychopathic Hospital, or Adolf Meyer himself, chief of psychiatry at Johns Hopkins University Medical School. Making up still a third group were interested physicians who had picked up a smattering of psychoanalysis from a variety of sources.

The assimilation of psychoanalysis seldom was systematic. Often its theories were translated into a set of practical "saws," for instance the generalization that frigidity might result from a deep-seated fear of fulfilling the female role.

Medical publications give a rough indication of the growing interest. The major psychiatric journals, the *American Journal of Psychiatry* and the *Journal of Nervous and Mental Disease,* the latter edited by two psychoanalytic psychiatrists, became increasingly receptive to the psychodynamic style and to psychoanalysis.[10]

Even critics could find advantages in the psychoanalytic viewpoint: it had "removed the fig leaf in psychiatry" and permitted a more open approach to sexuality. It had led psychiatry to concentrate on the "life history" of the individual patient and had given meaning to the psychological events in his or her life.[11]

Outside the specialized journals, psychoanalysis was appearing in articles by physicians with few if any ties to the movement. These were usually anachronistic, bearing little relation to recent psychoanalytic theory. In 1921 in Topeka, for instance, a physician defended psychoanalysis as a "radical" cure which discovered the real causes of nervous disorders in conflicts between selfish motives and the moral and ethical forces of the personality. It was the model James Jackson Putnam had offered shortly after the Clark conference in 1909.[12]

Psychoanalysts increasingly dominated the medical literature of psychotherapy, and for several years in the mid-1920s the amount written about psychoanalysis, most of it by psychoanalysts themselves, was almost double the amount on psychotherapy.[13] Nevertheless, many physicians continued to use hypnosis, suggestion, and the general educational therapies of Morton Prince and Pierre Janet. Even most psychoanalytic psychiatrists were resolutely eclectic, combining somatic and psychological treatment.[14]

Because of their focus on the complexities of the individual life, psychodynamic psychiatrists and psychoanalysts were far slower than academic psychologists to attempt to apply quantitative, statistical methods. The case history approach, without statistical controls, tended to remain characteristic of both psychodynamic psychiatrists and psychoanalysts into the period after World War II.[15]

The status of psychoanalysis and its attempted use in treating the psychoses were debated in 1934 after the establishment of a special section on psychoanalysis within the American Psychiatric Association. The geographical limitation of psychoanalytic influence was clear: only three psychiatrists from outside New York State played prominent roles in establishing the section: Franz Alexander, director of the Chicago Institute; Karl Menninger, representing both his family's psychiatric clinic in Topeka and the rising generation of trained American analysts; and Ross McClure Chapman, director of Sheppard Pratt, a private mental hospital near Baltimore.

A psychiatric unit without psychoanalysis was incomplete, according to Leland E. Hinsie, assistant director of the New York State Psychiatric Institute. Psychoanalysis provided understanding of a patient's otherwise baffling symptoms as well as a promising experimental treatment. The results of psychoanalytic psychotherapy in manic-depressive psychosis were favorable although still suggestive, while the results of drug treatment, the most widely used method, were often doubtful.[16] Psychoanalysis also gave the "most comprehensive understanding of the structure and function of the psyche." By knowing the meaning of the patient's "symptoms or signs and symbols," the psychoanalyst could trace these "back to their original source." Moreover, "impulses from the psychic sphere" were constantly expressing themselves through behavior. "Compulsive acts, phobias, anxieties and their many symbolic representatives are often experienced by the patient as either vicarious or direct activities of a dysfunctional organ or set of organs. . . . "[17]

For Karl Menninger, glad to represent the West at this symposium, psychoanalysis facilitated not only research in "borderline cases and mild psychoses" but also patient management. The psychoanalyst could arrange for "occupational treatment" to give an "outlet" to constructive tendencies, while recreation and athletics could give an outlet to "destructive" tendencies. Patients who "don't bring out memories easily but act out . . . as we say in psychoanalysis" could be moderately controlled in an institution and thus afforded opportunities of treatment, while depressed patients could be more safely analyzed.

A few older institutional psychiatrists also testified to the merits of psychoanalysis. Dr. Richard Hutchings, superintendent of New York's sprawling Utica asylum, had been increasingly convinced of its usefulness for understanding the "inner lives" of patients since reading a paper of Brill's in 1909. Earl Bond, superintendent of the Pennsylvania Hospital for the Insane, had come to Brill on critical occasions for advice. The section on psychoanalysis within the American Psychiatric Association was itself a tribute to Brill's long, persistent career as a psychoanalyst and his insistence that Freud's method was, above all, part of psychiatry. But difficulties, some already noted, marred the rosy outlook.

The first was the case load. Even at Sheppard Pratt a single physician had charge of thirty patients. Moreover, in a hospital such as St. Elizabeth's, with seven or eight thousand patients, what could three psychoanalysts do? Systematic group psychotherapy had not yet been developed, although there had been some experimentation with it outside orthodox circles. Moreover, budgets were usually too small to attract the psychoanalytically trained psychiatrist, while hospital psychiatrists warned against the untrained physician who could do real harm by trying to interpret a patient's dreams or behavior.[18]

One crucial issue never was fully resolved by the psychoanalysts. Those who favored the use of psychoanalytic psychotherapy in the psychoses realized that there was a shortage of trained analysts for work in mental hospitals. Yet once trained, psychoanalytic psychiatrists usually moved into private practice where they could earn more and where their methods were more applicable. Moreover, the call for trained analysts occurred precisely in the years when requirements and consequently the cost of training were being raised, increasing the pressure for higher earnings. Thus a permanent dearth of psychoanalytic personnel in the hospitals was likely to remain.

One skeptical psychiatrist, then the head of Bloomingdale, where Zilborg had worked, noted at the symposium that he had yet to see "any very striking results" from psychoanalysis, but he had seen extreme views in psychoanalytic treatment that were destructive to sound institutional methods. Franz Alexander agreed with him, expounding what he called Freud's latest position that although psychoanalysis contributed to an understanding of psychotics, the technique could not be transferred uncritically and had not yet proven its worth in the psychoses. He foresaw a combination of psychological with somatic therapy and the working out of a specific technique for psychotics.

Bernard Sachs, a New York neurologist who had badgered Brill for years and who blamed psychoanalysis for undermining the sense of responsibility and a "healthy social order," brandished a telegram from the neurologist Frederick Peterson, who had advised Brill to study with Jung. "It is possible," Peterson wired, "I may be accused of having introduced psychoanalysis into this country. If I did, I apologize."[19]

Despite opposition, by the 1930s most first-rank medical schools on the eastern seaboard from Virginia to Massachusetts included some teaching in psychoanalysis. But psychiatric instruction itself still was limited and was complete in only 13 of 67 medical schools; an additional 30 were upgrading their programs. In 1932, there was considerable opposition to psychiatry and especially to psychoanalysis, while professors of pediatrics objected to mental hygiene and child guidance as well.[20]

In a major survey of psychiatric education published in 1942, Franklin Ebaugh, a student of Adolf Meyer's and chairman of the Department of Psychiatry at the University of Colorado, argued that it was difficult to see how a course in psychopathology could be taught without including some of the "basic psychoanalytical concepts." Many of the "mental mechanisms . . . and many workable hypotheses in psychopathology" owed their origin to "psychoanalytical research."[21] A few departments of psychiatry— notably, New York University's—were "frankly psychoanalytical." Although some schools ignored psychoanalysis, most of them steered a course between acceptance and rejection. Of 114 hospitals with psychiatric residencies, psychoanalysis was available on some basis in about 38.[22]

Equally significant, some of the Meyerians already recognized the training programs of psychoanalytic institutes as conferring an important expertise. Ebaugh warned against the superficial teaching of psychoanalytic techniques to medical students:

> The acquisition of this refined method requires long periods of intensive training and to encourage the medical student in the idea that he has mastered the subject sufficiently to use even part of the method is to do him and the science itself a grave injustice.[23]

Psychoanalysis also may have appealed not only because of its complexity and the rigor of its training, but because of the relatively systematic nature of its hypotheses. By contrast, Ebaugh noted a lack of clarity, direction, cohesion, and purpose in the courses on Meyer's psychobiology. This disorganization contrasted markedly with the far more clearly delineated conceptions of psychoanalysis. This definiteness, which Meyer himself considered to be premature dogmatism, probably provided one of the greatest attractions of psychoanalysis. Leland Hinsie concluded that psychoanalysis supplied a "far more comprehensive and intelligent understanding" of psychiatric patients than had been possible "before the advent of Freud."[24]

A seductive medical analogy also provided part of the rhetorical appeal of psychoanalysis, an analogy elaborated by analysts and nonanalysts alike. The apparent precision of psychoanalysis in describing the "structure and function" of the psyche was like a knowledge of anatomy and physiology in medicine, and underpinned the new art of psychotherapy. Psychoanalysis was a "radical dissection of the whole mind of the patient." In a study of psychotherapy, Leland Hinsie argued that the psychoanalyst proceeded much as might the physician faced with a patient who complained of sudden, severe pain in the left side and frequent urination, for example. Using all the available investigative techniques he would arrive at a diagnosis of kidney stone. Yet even the symptoms and stone were not themselves the disease process, but were its results. Similarly, the phobias, hallucinations, and compulsions of the psychoneurotic patient were the "pains of the mind," but not the disorder itself. Merely to remove them would be as unethical as merely removing the pain caused by kidney stone. Rather, the psychoanalyst, using the same "general principle of tracing back to original sources" as the physician, explored the disorder that lay beneath.[25]

Often the symptoms were inimical to the conscious self, as in the case of the minister compelled to blaspheme, the young man who joined the police force to keep his own "offensive impulses in abeyance" but who finally succumbed to his irresistible impulse to "club innocent citizens," or the wealthy benefactor of a children's charity who hit the children he presumed to love or the young man so afraid he might cause his ailing father's death that he constantly tested the gas jets to be sure they were closed. In such cases as these, psychoanalytic knowledge of the unconscious was invaluable.

This focus on the unconscious provided the greatest contrast between Freud's system and Meyer's psychobiology, which dealt with known environmental factors. Hinsie noted that the two movements were coming closer together and that the analytic movement, with some exceptions, fortunately had been led by psychiatrists.[26]

In a thoughtful evaluation of the merits and defects of psychoanalysis published in 1937, Hinsie argued that the effectiveness of psychoanalysis as a therapy did not yet equal its contributions to psychopathology, for it had serious limitations. Perhaps the most important—and a recurring problem—was the limitation of practice. Time and expense placed it beyond the reach of most patients. It was available to a "mere fraction," perhaps 4 percent, of the psychoneurotics who sought treatment in New York City. The sixty members of the New York Psychoanalytic Society in 1929 carried on about 300 classical analyses in one year. Thus the tremendous demand for hopeful psychotherapies could be met only fractionally by psychoanalysis.

Hinsie also deplored the lack of extensive well-defined facts about psychoanalytic therapy. Yet the analysts had available in the training analyses of future analysts useful control material for a comparison of apparently normal and neurotic patients. But the analysts had not gathered such information, and he urged them to be more informative about their private practice.

In one of the first comparative studies of therapeutic results, based on the only unit of measure then available, the physician's considered judgment of outcome, Carney Landis concluded that most methods of psychotherapy achieved roughly the same benefits. Thus 87 percent of neurotic patients were treated successfully by psychobiological methods at the New York Psychiatric Institute. A rate of 70 percent was achieved by eclectic methods at the Cassel Hospital in London, while the Berlin Psychoanalytic Institute had an overall recovery rate of 58 percent, but a rate of 91 percent for completed cases. The unresolved difficulties of these statistics were also emphasized: a lack of controls, no agreement on the causes of nervous disorders or on the nature of improvement or recovery.[27]

In 1941 Robert Knight, then a psychoanalyst at the Menninger Clinic, published a survey of all the existing literature on the results of psychoanalysis, indicating more favorable results than Hinsie had suggested. Psychoanalysis was effective for psychoneuroses and sexual and psychosomatic disorders, with some promise for addictions and psychoses. Cases of psychoneuroses treated between 1932 and 1941 at the Menninger Clinic for at least six months were 80 percent successful. Combining all the psychoanalytic statistics, the highest percentage of success was 78.1 percent for organ neuroses and organic conditions; 63.2 percent for psychoneuroses; 56.6 percent for character disorders; 48.5 percent for sexual disorders; and 25 percent for the psychoses. Knight's standards for recovery were the disappearance of symptoms, real improvement in "mental functioning," and improved "reality adjustment.[28]

The mode of practice of the psychobiological psychiatrists and the psychoanalyst differed in these years. The psychoanalyst was more likely to be in private practice. You might find him, for instance, in an apartment on Central Park West, with paintings on the wall. The psychobiologist, however, attired in a white coat, would be found more likely in the aseptic clinic of a teaching hospital.

When Karl Menninger announced in his best-seller *The Human Mind* that practically all informed scientists accepted psychoanalysis, Abraham Myerson, a Boston pioneer in the practice of office psychiatry, in 1937 decided to "squelch" him by a survey of opinion among 428 psychiatrists, neurologists, psychologists, and psychoanalysts, of whom 307 replied.[29]

Myerson set up four crude categories: (1) complete acceptance; (2) a favorable attitude but a certain skepticism; (3) rejection in the main, but a belief that Freud contributed "indirectly" to human understanding; (4) total rejection. Only 5 percent of Myerson's psychiatrists rejected psychoanalysis; 53 percent expressed a positive attitude and 44 percent a negative one. The largest number of psychiatrists fell in groups (2) and (3). Nolan D. C. Lewis, who had succeeded William Alanson White as director of St. Elizabeth's Hospital, argued that it was a "research method . . . for the deeper dissection of mental content" and was the most valuable therapy in certain types of cases.

Yet some of those who viewed psychoanalysis favorably believed that it ignored the patient's "living and adjusting to the community" and concentrated too exclusively on the "psyche of the patient." Others argued that it sometimes led physicians to neglect physical factors and physical treatment and to concentrate instead on a theoretical psychoanalytic formulation of the patient's problems. The neurologists were less accepting than the psychiatrists; indeed they divided 48 percent to 48 percent among those favorable and unfavorable. One "well-known neurologist" noted that psychiatrists in mental hospitals in the United States were "so saturated with the Freudian concept that real investigation of mental diseases was almost entirely excluded." The psychologists were the least favorable.

Some psychoanalysts objected to the näiveté of the questionnaire's categories, and Lawrence Kubie found the first category "too blindly sectarian." Smith Ely Jelliffe observed, "Questionnaires of this type do not mean much to me. I think they are usually very stupid. But 'chacun à son gout,' as the old lady said when she kissed the cow." Of those identified in the questionnaire, the oldest physicians were those least favorable to psychoanalysis. Myerson then placed himself in group (3) with leanings toward (2) and (4). He accepted Freud's greatness, the importance of sexuality and conflict, but rejected the unconscious, infantile sexuality, symbolism, the decisiveness of the earliest years of life, and argued that although by then an old therapy, psychoanalysis had not yet "conquered the field" by its effectiveness.[30]

The survey demonstrated that since 1917 psychoanalysis had made solid inroads among American physicians and neurologists, but was still highly controversial and was rejected by an important, vocal minority, including Myerson himself. Most significant, it suggested that it was identified with a younger generation in both fields.[31] This generation had felt the impact of a few gifted teachers who acquainted their students with psychoanalysis. By 1939 psychoanalysis had won a growing place as an explanation of nervous and mental disorder in psychiatric education; it was being tried as a therapeutic approach at a few public and private hospitals; and it was winning an increasing role in medical texts.

10

Teachers of Psychiatry, Psychoanalysis, and Psychosomatic Medicine: Adolf Meyer, Harry Stack Sullivan, Flanders Dunbar, Franz Alexander

The impact of psychoanalysis in psychiatry was far greater than the tiny enrollment of American psychoanalytic organizations would indicate—79 members and 213 students in 1939. The disparity between numbers and influence reflected the work of a few charismatic teachers in hospitals and medical schools, the creation of psychosomatic medicine, and the support of private foundations.

Adolf Meyer shaped much of the medical reception of Freud and psychoanalysis. By 1940, his students occupied chairs in psychiatry at most of the leading medical schools. Apart from his prestige and influence, he is important for several reasons. He welcomed the introduction of psychoanalysis as an ally in the fight against a narrowly somatic, hereditarian psychiatry, which he hoped to supplant with his own system of psychobiology. His successes and failures prepared the way for the rapid rise of psychoanalytic psychiatry after World War II. Although he successfully transmitted his general outlook he failed to make his personal psychiatric formulas persuasive. Finally, his differences with the psychoanalysts have left, through his students, important traces on the eclectic psychiatry of the present.

Meyer himself despaired of his own mission toward the end of his life. "What was it that failed to go across? Did I pussyfoot too much? *Wherein did I*

fail? Did I?"[1] These depressed ruminations were written in the early morning hours of November 2, 1947, three years before his death at eighty-four in
1950. He was upset because his disciples, not he, had published the major
formulations of his own system of psychobiology. His psychiatric vocabulary
never had taken hold, and he had seen psychoanalytic psychiatry become
popular without a "single outspoken reply on my part."

A number of Meyer's personal failings are exemplified in this soliloquy,
notably his ambivalence and paralyzing caution. The most complete statement of his system, delivered in 1931, finally was edited and published
posthumously by his assistants in 1957. He once attributed a piece of student
research he declared to be brilliant to the researcher's roommate, then repeatedly changed his mind about its suitability for publication. An immigrant
from German Switzerland in 1892, he never mastered English prose, and he
sometimes failed to communicate his ideas to his students because he often
meandered and qualified. Some students feared him because he was often
highly critical of them. Others found him warm and approachable, helpful
and even humble. Above all he was brilliantly erudite, and had an unusual gift
for communicating with deeply disturbed patients. After he left for America
his mother suffered from a severe depression pronounced hopeless by the
great Swiss psychiatrist August Forel. But she mysteriously recovered, and
this seemed to Meyer to contradict the then prevalent notion of mental
illness as a hopeless disease process.

His hopefulness was shared with the first American psychoanalysts, several of whom Meyer trained, at Worcester State Hospital, the New York
Psychiatric Institute, and later at Johns Hopkins. Welcoming at first, then
increasingly skeptical, Meyer introduced two generations of American physicians to Freud. Some of them shared Meyer's skepticism. Others turned from
Meyer's psychobiology to psychoanalysis. They included members of the
first generation of the psychoanalytic movement—A. A. Brill, Isador Coriat,
and Horace Frink—as well as representatives of the second generation—
Bertram Lewin, Phyllis Greenacre, and Lawrence Kubie. The latter were
among those who established psychoanalysis as an institutionalized profession in the 1930s and shaped it through the 1960s.

Meyer's increasingly influential psychobiology and a psychoanalytic psychiatry intersected, particularly in the Washington-Baltimore area, from
1910 to 1940. Both systems shared a common view of scientific method, as
well as elements of therapy and of etiological theory.

The psychoanalysts and the Meyerians were reacting against the excesses
of the somatic style of the late nineteenth century. Meyer's students claimed
that he liberated psychiatry from the "pathology of dead tissue" and an undue
emphasis on classification. Both welcomed a psychological approach, while
rejecting schools of academic psychology that required experimentation or
introspection, or that, like behaviorism, rejected consciousness.[2]

They shared a messianic sense of the psychiatric mission. The new wisdom born of the clinic would shed light on every facet of individual and social
lie, replacing encrusted and outmoded tradition. They accepted a medical

model of nervous and mental disorder and regarded the individual case study, the patient's "life history," as a "natural experiment," more revealing than the manipulations of the psychological laboratory. Both relied on the accuracy and sufficiency of the trained physician's observations of his patient, without worrying overmuch about problems of refined scientific method or epistemology. Regarding psychoanalysis as too private a transaction, Meyer preferred the same case to be studied by several physicians, while the psychoanalysts, at least those in training, insisted on supervisory discussion of a candidate's cases. Both also shared a general distrust of statistics, and regarded their psychiatric material as too intricate for quantification. Both were heavily influenced by English evolutionary Darwinism.

Not only were their outlook and methods similar, but so, too, were their modes of therapy. Both groups placed less emphasis on the immediate symptom than on the "total personality" and its historical development or "underlying" patterns. Both also held up adaptation to the environment, or what Meyer termed "harmonious self-regulation," as the goal of therapy. For Meyerian psychiatrists, psychoanalytic techniques were among those "special methods" which might be used to uncover "less accessible material." Such methods included free association, word association tests, the study of dreams. Both gave special importance to the relationship of patient to therapist, the Meyerians emphasizing positive rapport, the analysts insisting on the importance of transference, that is, the repetition in relation to the analyst of earlier attitudes of love and hate developed toward early caretakers, usually parents.

Finally, both groups overlapped in etiological theory. By 1930 Meyer gave increasing attention to family interaction and to early experience. Etiological theories involving intimate family experience, such as the Oedipus complex, were at the heart of psychoanalysis. Meyer also gave considerable importance to sexuality and to greater frankness about it.

These broad similarities, often overlooked, have been emphasized because without them the rapid transition to a psychoanalytic psychiatry after World War II appears too unnatural and sudden a mutation. It was easy to make the transition from Meyerian psychiatry to psychoanalysis, and many did so. Anyone trained by Meyer would have been exposed to some aspects of psychoanalysis, if not always to an accurate or favorable view. It could be argued that the Meyerians borrowed much from Freud, and psychoanalytic hypotheses acted as radical propositions that the Meyerians had to take into account. They either had to accept or reject the Oedipus complex or soften it into a theory of family interaction. In some instances they accepted psychoanalytic theories of cause, such as the homosexual etiology of paranoia, or the insistence that factors outside awareness played crucial roles in hysteria or compulsion neuroses.

Yet, without understanding how the systems differed, and what Meyer detested about psychoanalysis, the slow development of psychoanalytic psychiatry in the 1920s and 1930s and its overshadowing by Meyerian psychobiology is less comprehensible. Meyer's differences with the psychoanalysts were elaborated during the 1920s and 1930s before the spread of psychoanalytic ego psychology and during the most reductionist period of analytic theory. For example, it was a period in which the surgeon's skill could be interpreted not as a cognitive and tactile discipline but as a sublimation of early sadism. Meyer's differences with psychoanalysis have surfaced in the themes that have been given new prominence in the eclectic post-Freudian psychiatry of the 1970s and 1980s, some of them advanced by Meyer's pupils. For example, although Meyer came to regard early childhood as laying the foundation for the human personality which took "relatively final form in early adult life," he also regarded the human's "experiential resources" as cumulative "throughout life to the last breath."[3]

This theme of plasticity and the importance of later experience has been elaborated by some analytic ego psychologists as well as developmental psychologists. Meyer also denied that unconscious factors and sexuality were as determinative as psychoanalysts then claimed. He stressed cognitive skills, such as language and attention, as ego psychologists and others have increasingly done. He also stressed the importance of rapport between patient and therapist, a matter which became of importance in psychotherapy research. Meyer's stress on the role of the community anticipated an important direction within psychiatry that would flourish in the 1960s.

Meyer's native Swiss commonsensibility was heavily reinforced by the American pragmatists William James, Charles Peirce, and particularly John Dewey, whom he knew in Chicago and later in New York. Meyer insisted that his students look for "the facts" patients presented for open observation, without relying on what he obviously considered to be the esoteric procedures of psychoanalytic investigation.

Rooted in the "common sense" observation of the "normal human being," never rigorously defined, Meyer consciously strove for balance and comprehensiveness, taking into account a wide measure of social and psychological forces. He consciously avoided "imaginative interpretation" and "prejudgment" of the "facts," and rejected commitment to any single, delimiting theory. He eschewed "analogical dogma and simplification," or any system that relied on a single aspect of human behavior, such as sexuality or aggression, as an overarching explanation. He could borrow from psychoanalysis without being committed to it as a coherent theory.

The flavor of Meyer's teaching was recorded by a future psychoanalyst during his student days at Johns Hopkins. "[Meyer] . . . seldom speaks of symptoms. . . . He looks on man as an organism with a wide range of adjustment and activity, some perfect, some imperfect, some entirely unsuited to the situation." Meyer could be frank about sexuality. Thus he presented a schizophrenic patient who believed "the Devil was inside her, had gnawed out her G.I. tract and her uterus. The Devil had "opened his pants on the street-car and disappeared in the ground." But the relation of all this to her psychosis remained undescribed.[4]

Later, associating psychoanalysis with sexual liberation and a false overemphasis on sexuality in general, the Meyerians took a relatively conservative view of sexual morality. In 1924, Meyer argued that Freudians, despite Freud's disclaimers, referred everything to sexuality, and that psychoanalysis tended to preach that repression was unhealthy. He was judging partly from his treatment of Horace Frink, Freud's American disciple who had become psychotic after analysis with Freud in Vienna.[5] His student Wendell Muncie, who wrote a comprehensive Meyerian psychiatric text, noted that "It may be difficult for youth to recognize that many people past middle life lead, even in the married state, celibate lives for years on end without any apparent detriment to the affection and mutual pooling of interests in the home and without any need for philandering." Continence "in youth and mature" life could cause no "possible damage," the only difficulty being the "development of inferiority feelings by comparison with others."[6] Like physicians of the period before him, he argued also that women's sexual desires were less than the male's and that "a fair proportion of married women assert that sex relations offer little gratification, and they comply with their husband's demands only because of the conventions of marriage."

Meyer regarded many of the formulations of psychoanalysis as premature generalizations based on inadequate facts, and he rejected what he considered to be its oversystematization. He remained insistently eclectic, strengthening this already strong current in American psychiatry.

Meyer was more skeptical in his prognoses than some of the American psychoanalysts, and he particularly hated their sometimes enthusiastic claims to cure. This skepticism touched a number of his students. Bertram Lewin wrote to his friend Lawrence Kubie before his conversion to psychoanalysis that although he "balked" at many of the assumptions and concepts of the psychoanalysts, he wondered whether their claims to cure compulsion neuroses were true, because such cases practically never had been cured at Meyer's Phipps clinic. If they were true, "has not good old Freud something no one else has?"[7]

Instead of interpreting by what he regarded as preconceived notions, Meyer, like Carl Rogers later, repeated back to patients what they had said to him. This, he thought, was a way of solving their problems in terms acceptable to them.[8] Unlike the psychoanalysts, he placed considerable faith in conscious introspection, and required of each student and some patients a frank, comprehensive autobiography.

Meyer's therapy was far more overtly directive than that of the psychoanalysts, and some of these differences probably emerged from his focus on hospitalized psychotics and neurotics. Thus he gathered information not only from the patient but from relatives, friends, and teachers. He manipulated the hospital environment and attempted to educate relatives so that family attitudes as well might be changed for the patient's benefit. His directive therapy included a deliberate focus on the patient's skills and assets. Some of his pupils insisted on new material at each session or, like Meyer, would plan the patient's day, including his rest, activity, and diet. Meyerians used the standard drugs of the period, including insulin and metrazol, but with caution because of their complications. They also gave their patients a physical examination, which analysts had come not to do because of its possible "contamination" of transference reactions.

Yet Meyer's very virtues of comprehensiveness, openness, and "common sense" also contained liabilities, as his students, particularly those who turned to psychoanalysis, suggested. His "openness" and refusal to commit himself also meant that he offered few organizing constructs. His conceptualization remained highly general, and he provided few illustrative detailed case histories in his published papers. Some of this reticence may have been partly personal in origin. Thus he frankly acknowledged his mother's depression after he left for America and later when his brother became engaged, but failed to explore the family relationships that might have made those events significant.[9] These were the limitations of his particular outlook.

His etiological theory emphasized conscious thought and placed too little weight on affect and emotion, according to his own students. Moreover, his etiological speculations included little developmental theory. How an early experience related to a later one was seldom clearly established.

His therapy, like his theory, remained far too rational, his critics believed. Thus his investigations of sexuality, although often very frank and a standard part of his system of examining patients, seldom if ever dealt with fantasies, except as these were frank psychotic productions. There was a way in which Meyer knew too much in terms of observable facts, yet too little about the subjective lives of his patients, particularly relations among family members.

Nevertheless, Meyer's insistence on open-mindedness, on public observation, on verification of hypotheses, even on eclecticism recently has received renewed emphasis. And his argument that patients were suffering not from disease entities but from syndromes developed during specific life experiences has remained fundamental to important segments of American psychiatry; so, too, has his emphasis on the positive aspects of the patient's personality.

The ambivalent absorption of psychoanalysis by the Meyerians can be traced in the successive editions of one of the most popular and widely used texts in America in the years from 1925 to 1940. It was written by Edward A. Strecker, professor of psychiatry at the University of Pennsylvania, and Meyer's student, Franklin G. Ebaugh, head of psychiatry at the University of Colorado. The first edition, published in 1925, remained heavily somatic, with guarded prognoses for schizophrenia and manic-depressive insanity paired with an overall optimism. The authors took from the psychoanalysts not only the specific concept that defense against homosexuality might be a factor in paranoia but also that in schizophrenia (dementia praecox) regression to early childhood behavior occurred in such matters as smearing feces. They agreed that psychotherapy was the most important mode of treatment for the psychoneuroses, and included along with more general directions for reeducation a brief description of psychoanalytic "catharsis." They routinely investigated each patient's sexual behavior, dreams, relations to parents. Ventilation, rapport between patient and therapist, "reeducation" were general methods of psychotherapy shared with the less orthodox psychoanalysts. From the behaviorists they picked up the conception of the "desensitization" of traumatic material.[10]

In the 1931 edition, they noted that psychiatry was moving out of the hospital and into the community and would become largely extramural and they included more psychoanalytic material, for example, a chapter on the psychological concepts of mental disease, based on Bernard Hart's pre-World War I *The Psychology of Insanity,* and a chapter on child guidance that incorporated a few elements of psychoanalysis.

The normalization of masturbation remained an important theme because of existing widespread worries among parents that it might cause insanity in their children, a warning some churches still were issuing. For instance, the development of schizophrenia had been prevented by the psychiatric treatment of a fifteen-year-old boy who had given up all his former interest in school and athletics because of guilt over masturbation. In psychotherapy he was told that masturbation of itself did no harm, but brooding about it did. The authors congratulated themselves that without early treatment he undoubtedly would have developed into a "definite case of dementia praecox."[11] Drawing evidence from recent studies of sexual behavior, psychiatrists were to reassure parents that two-thirds of college women masturbated, and that even sexual contact between children was not to be judged by adult standards.

In this model of the child, habit shaped by environment controlled the formation of character, a conservative reflection of the more radical behaviorism of the 1920s. Behavior was viewed as symptomatic of underlying causes, and instincts were subsumed in needs such as hunger, thirst, sleep, elimination, play, and sex. The hope clearly was that simple information and the manipulation of habits would heal illness and elicit desired behavior. Meyerian methods also included an investigation of the child's environment, his school and neighborhood, and his family relationships, a broader focus than the psychoanalytic concentration on the individual child.

One of the most radical formulations of an eclectic psychodynamic style was created in the interwar years by Harry Stack Sullivan. He developed his self-consciously "American" theories of schizophrenia as a repudiation of European and early 20th-century American psychiatric pessimism. He rejected all theories that posited a gulf between the normal and the schizophrenic. Thus he condemned organic theories as implausible without the "aid of carelessness, overlooking of negative instances, and lively pathological imagination."[12] Nor could he accept Eugen Bleuler's view that the associative processes of schizophrenics differed essentially from those of other people. Bleuler's conclusions, Sullivan argued, came from working with large groups of patients whose symptoms had become rigidly fixed in the institutional setting of the mental hospital.

He also rejected two psychoanalytic views of the period, Freud's suggestion that schizophrenics, because of their intense narcissism, were incapable of transference relationships, and Gregory Zilboorg's that schizophrenics preferred their state to normality. On the contrary, Sullivan insisted, they could and did form relationships, and they were in a painful, personal hell.[13] Like Jung, Sullivan regarded schizophrenia as a possibly creative travail in which, through quite primitive processes, chunks of previously unintegrated experience were reorganized within the personality.

Sullivan's general outlook is best approached through his personality and experience and his earliest papers. These displayed a remarkable, self-taught erudition, ranging from the semanticists Count Korzybski and Ogden and Richards through the American sociologists and anthropologists. What is conspicuously lacking in Sullivan is a large element of the literary culture that formed the awareness of many analysts. His early papers are highly charged with emotion, sometimes displaying a sensitive empathic linking of personal problems with those of his patients. They chart the painful construction of a highly individualistic viewpoint that began with Adolf Meyer's psychobiology and moved through ambivalent adoptions from psychoanalysis to a unique theory of interpersonal relations and social causation.

Some of Sullivan's formulations clearly mirrored his own experience. Growing up as an only child in a Roman Catholic farming family—the only such family in his upstate New York community—Sullivan had lived a seriously isolated childhood. His only friend was a neighbor, a boy five years older, who also became a psychiatrist and also never married. His bookish mother was a close friend of his high school principal. Sullivan was a brilliant, gifted student, won a scholarship to Cornell, and left after a year with poor grades under unknown circumstances. There have been rumors of scandal and psychosis, but few facts. He put himself through what he called a "diploma mill" medical school in Chicago, and in 1922, became liaison officer for the Veterans Administration to St. Elizabeth's Hospital. Fascinated by the schizophrenic patients he encountered, he became a psychiatrist and displayed an extraordinary ability to communicate with patients. A colleague recalled that a patient he had tried in vain to reach was talking to Sullivan within five minutes.

Yet for all his empathy and charm, Sullivan could be a devastating critic, brutal and cutting. William Alanson White described him to a hospital superintendent to whom he had applied for a job as a "keen, alert Irishman, who has a facade of facetiousness which it is a bit difficult to penetrate." But he obviously liked Sullivan and they became friends. Sullivan absorbed White's practical, eclectic psychoanalytic psychiatry, which included a strong interest in demographic and socioeconomic factors. When Sullivan left to set up private practice in New York in 1930, White helped him obtain medical accreditation there.[14] In a revealing passage, Sullivan wrote that his mother, whose family had been professional people until her marriage to his father, a skilled workman, had "no use for me except as a clothes-horse on which to hang an elaborate pattern of illusions." He settled in Bethesda, Maryland, in 1939, where he cultivated day lilies, and lived with his adopted son Jimmie.[15]

From Adolf Meyer, Sullivan derived the view that a psychosis was a total "psychobiological" reaction to a life situation, as well as Meyer's insistence that psychological processes were expressed through symbols, of which language was the most developed. The rudiments of a self-system, that is, conceptualization of the self as "good me," "bad me," and "not me," as well as a rejection of Freud's libido theory, Sullivan owed to Edward J. Kempf, who had been on the staff of St. Elizabeth's.[16]

From the psychoanalysts Sullivan adopted Freud's insistence that dreams linked the psychotic and the normal. He also took over the importance of symbols, whose meanings were often unconscious, and the familiar Freudian "mechanisms" of condensation, compensation, projection, transference, regression. The psychoanalytic emphasis on psychosexual phases and zones, particularly the oral, Sullivan also adopted from the theorists of the 1920s, notably Ferenczi. He placed anxiety (which Freud came to regard in the mid-1920s as the central issue of the neuroses) at the heart of his system. But he dealt with it early in his career as an aspect of self-esteem.

Sullivan from the outset made no effort to place his system within orthodox psychoanalytic theory and indeed sharply criticized the psychoanalysts: their tendency to overgeneralize, the dogmatism of some who were filled with the "holy light" of their own personal analyses; the theory that mental disorder resulted from fixations at past stages; and what he regarded as the projection into infancy and childhood of sexual elements taken from the genital developments of adolescence. Thus he could not regard the Oedipus complex as an early wish for sexual possession of the mother. Sullivan clashed particularly with the younger, trained, orthodox analysts, such as Zilboorg, who also were interested in the treatment of the psychoses.

Sullivan's infant, in contrast to the psychoanalytic infant, was emptied of drives, particularly destructive ones. The child had "needs," but these were not instincts or drives in the analytic sense but physical tension states. Again, the central concept of anxiety did not come from the child's own impulses and their fantastic dimension; rather, anxiety was inculcated directly by the anxiety of the mother. Here the child became a more passive, plastic agent than in psychoanalytic formulations. Difficulty in maturation came then not from the child's impulses but from parental behavior and attitudes, particularly moral attitudes.

Sullivan emphasized a purely psychosocial factor in the creation of mental disorder—America's religious sexual morality. For Sullivan, a major cause of dissociation, which was fundamental to psychopathological processes, was parental disapproval of sexuality, a disapproval bound up with "spook morality," as Sullivan characterized traditional religious ethics. Not sexual cravings or fantasies in themselves but the "foreshadowed loss of esteem in the eyes of others." Self-esteem received its most lasting wounds from the subjective sense of social, moral, and religious condemnation.

Sullivan was critical not only of the moral system but of morality's most important enforcer, the mother. One of the first opponents of "momism," Sullivan argued that the Oedipus complex itself was not a normal development in the male child but the result of feelings of sexual sin in both mother and father. Mothers inculcated Oedipus complexes in their sons by fostering hatred of fathers and by fierce prohibitions against masturbation. "A hand on the penis is a hand against God," was the sentiment his patients were taught.

Sullivan's early papers are filled with the cases of young men whose attitudes of fear and rejection of their sexual experiences or cravings precipitated psychoses. His patients felt a sense of rejection in interpersonal relations from all the significant figures in their early lives. Repeatedly Sullivan referred to the "black wickedness of all things sexual" and the "diabolical moral 'virtue'" associated with Puritanism.[17]

Sullivan argued that satisfactory sexual experience, either heterosexual or homosexual, was a positive good, a prophylaxis against schizophrenia, for the adolescent.[18] Like others interested in psychoanalysis in this period, Sullivan began to collect data on sexual behavior. On October 6, 1928, he wrote to White, "I am plodding along assembling data on the impure excitements of adolescents. I do not know what the outcome will be, and I am far from certain that anything much will result."[19] Indeed, he placed as much or more emphasis on adolescence, because of the importance of sexual maturity, as had the pre-Freudian French psychiatrists, for instance.

In outlining his technique of treating schizophrenics, Sullivan defined psychotherapy as an educational process occurring within an interpersonal relationship. First, the patient was removed to a special ward. There trained personnel of the same sex were placed because of their self-awareness, and because of their lack of unconscious sadism, commonplace ethical superstitions, or morbid expectation of results.

Sullivan then conducted a searching initial interview, and with unresponsive patients he used ethyl alcohol to induce three to ten days of "continuous mild intoxication," which "usually results in considerable readjustment." Then, possibly with an assistant present, Sullivan would help the patient construct an "actual chronology of the psychosis." At intervals "free associational technique" would fill in "failures of memory." The aim was to make the patient understand that no matter how mysterious his illness seemed, it involved relations with a few significant people "in a relatively simple course of events."[20] Above all, no interpretations were forced on the patient, and none were offered except "as statistical findings." If the patient made progress, he might be discharged to a suitable psychoanalyst, one "not too rigid in devotion to technique." Or if the chronology of the illness was accompanied by the growth of insight, the sessions themselves might approximate a "liberal variant of the orthodox technique." Sullivan's claims to a 75 percent rate of success were endorsed by his successor at Sheppard Pratt, William V. Silverberg, in a period when combined recovery and improvement rates were running around 40 percent.

But his entire method was denounced as superficial, a mere preliminary, by Gregory Zilboorg. A social recovery, such as Sullivan might achieve, was not enough; what was required was a "thorough reconstruction of the entire personality." Sullivan replied, "It seems beyond argument that there is an improvement in personality if one changes from obvious psychoses to a considerable measure of ability to live in one's environment. . . . It seems a century or two too early for enforcing perfection in this one field of human welfare work."[21]

Sullivan claimed to use what he regarded as the fundamentals of psychoanalysis: interpretation, free association, and transference. He frankly confessed that his failures with women patients had led him to seek 300 hours of psychoanalysis, probably with Clara Thompson.

By stressing the social factor of morality, the lack of self-esteem caused by the application of that morality by significant people in the environment, Sullivan adopted a cultural view of the causation of mental disorder. By 1931, after contact with anthropologists (he had met Sapir and Malinowski in 1926), he suggested that schizophrenia itself might be defined by relation to the common culture of a group.[22] A person who might be considered normal in one group could be schizophrenic in another; schizophrenia might be one way to describe the degree of deviation from common group norms. Here was a whole new direction in American social psychiatry that placed social factors at the heart of the causation of mental disorder and linked social science and psychiatry.[23] The ensuing years saw a more sophisticated working through of these insights and the development of Sullivan's special vocabulary. These early years also brought clashes with some of the younger generation of psychoanalysts, who distrusted Sullivan because of his unorthodox views and career and who denied that he was a psychoanalyst at all. Sullivan returned the distrust with acerbity and vehemence.

In the 1930s he fostered two institutions to develop his views. In 1934 he suggested to William Alanson White the possibility of a new journal or a section of the *Psychoanalytic Review* devoted to "our American variance from Freud." The *Quarterly,* he complained, was a "private organ of the group here with which I am most completely lacking in sympathy." The *American Journal of Psychiatry* was unfriendly to analysis. A new forum would allow "quite a number" of people to get out "more of what we say at this or that meeting."[24] Four years later the journal *Psychiatry* was founded as an organ of the William Alanson White Psychiatric Foundation, which launched the Washington School of Psychiatry in 1936 for training physicians, anthropologists, and psychologists. It placed a strong emphasis on the social sciences, and founders of the American school of culture and personality were listed among its faculty: Karen Horney, Erich Fromm, Ruth Benedict.[25]

In Sullivan's view, *Psychiatry* would take a breathtakingly inclusive view of the discipline: it concerned "the doings of each and every person, and with more or less personified entities, from birth to death, in waking and in sleep, in work and in play, in love and in hate, in peace and in war—in short, universally."[26]

Until the rapid expansion of the immediate post-World War II period, the Washington School remained small, and at the outset had financial difficulties. William Alanson White died in 1937 and A. A. Brill had resigned as a trustee of the foundation after the name was changed from Psychoanalytic to Psychiatric Foundation in 1937.[27]

The number of subscribers to *Psychiatry* rose from 515 in 1938 to 775 in

1945, a larger number than had subscribed by that date to either the *Psycho-analytic Review* or the *Journal of Nervous and Mental Disease*.[28] A course given in 1940–41 by psychoanalyst Robert Waelder, who commuted from Boston, barely paid for itself. By 1947 the foundation still was without an endowment.

Sullivan himself was a frequent lecturer and publicist, particularly during his years as consultant to the head of Selective Service, General Hershey, and he displayed the messianism that characterized a number of important American psychiatrists and psychoanalysts. "New Type of Psychiatry Seeks Cause, to Cure Society's Ills," the *Washington Star* reported in 1939. Sullivan's psychiatry would in effect extend the medical model to an entire society. It was "strikingly different" in point of view from the outlook of the clergyman or the lawyer, because it did not "involve, per se, any concepts of right or wrong. Tuberculosis is neither moral nor immoral . . . legal nor illegal. Sermons or laws never cured a single case of involution melancholia. The physician's problem is to find out what is causing the trouble and set it right." Sullivan had diagnosed a "weird hate-disease," race hatred, that motivated the anti-Semitism of the Nazis and aroused a disturbing responsiveness in democratic countries. Stumbling over the concept of displacement, the *Star*'s reporter suggested that possibly Hitler and some of his followers "hate their Jewish neighbors so intensely . . . because they really hated their mothers and fathers, gagged on this kind of hatred, and had to find some convenient place to put it."[29]

By 1940 Sullivan was warning the nation against "mass paranoia," which he considered a natural reaction to panic. Instead of hysteria, Americans were "developing . . . a multitude of mild panics—chaotic, purposeless mass reactions of terror which accomplish no purpose to the advantage of the individual." The stage for it had been set by the economic insecurity of the Depression, yet even then there was faith that bad times would pass. But now, panic was creating hate of the German Empire [*sic*] and fear of fifth columns at home, and, according to Sullivan, in case of a German victory, "We will have to cope with an ever-accumulating confusion of illogical hatreds."[30]

An influential vehicle for the spread of psychoanalysis was the psychosomatic movement in medicine. It had begun in the early years of this century was a reaction against what some physicians saw as the excesses and the cold impersonality of the somatic style. Ambitious doctors would humanize medicine by stressing the role of emotions in disease. For Flanders Dunbar, one of the pioneers in the field, psychoanalysis appealed because it treated the "whole person," not merely a symptom.

Psychosomatic medicine was important in these years for two major reasons. It dealt with widespread, chronic disease whose precise causes were unknown—hypertension, ulcers, arthritis, ulcerative colitis, hyperthyroidism, and asthma. Psychosomatic medicine also provided one foundation for that distinctive mark of psychoanalysis in America, its absorption by medicine and psychiatry on a scale unknown elsewhere. Psychoanalytic psychosomatic medicine, systematically developed in the 1930s, was applied to the understanding of the war neuroses during World War II.

From about 1910 to 1943 psychoanalysts developed theories about the psychological meaning of symptoms, and to a lesser extent about how emotions altered physical functions. They offered fresh, detailed observations and highly speculative hypotheses as well as optimistic claims for their modes of explanation and treatment. Through the ventilation of the patient's hopes and fears in the therapeutic relationship, they would rechannel his or her energies. They argued that the prevailing somatic models, which had produced such triumphs as the extirpation of diphtheria, had failed in many widespread chronic diseases. Somatic treatments for arthritis, for instance, ranging from the use of gold salts to vitamins, nitrates, radium, vaccines, the removal of tonsils and teeth, had been random and useless. Somatic models could not explain why in some diseases patients grew better or worse for no ascertainable reason, nor could they explain the authenticated cures of faith healers.

The psychosomatic movement grew out of five developments in the years from about 1910 to 1943, the medical historian Robert Powell has observed. Four, briefly enumerated, were Walter Cannon's studies of the effect of emotions on the central nervous system, Pavlov's work on conditioning, gestalt psychology, and the psychobiology of Adolf Meyer. Their complex interrelations need not detain us. American and European psychoanalysts provided the fifth element, their own radical version of the psychodynamic style, including theories and techniques for the interpretation of symptoms and a method of treatment.[31]

Understanding of the apparent persuasiveness of the psychoanalytic contribution requires a brief note on the state of psychosomatic medicine around 1930. Two approaches had been developed, the situational and the characterological. Medical observers long had established the relation of certain symptoms to shocks and strong emotions. The most diverse events had been known to precipitate asthma attacks: a chandelier falling, a fire alarm sounding, news of a parent's death, quarrels, defloration, anger at pregnancy, the capture of Paris in 1870.

A more systematic approach dealt with typologies, and by the 1920s character theory and its relation to disease were well developed. The somatotypes of the German psychiatrist Ernst Kretschmer paired given body configurations with a tendency not only to specific mental illnesses, but to particular somatic diseases as well. Thus the rounded pyknik was more subject to manic depressive insanity and to arteriosclerosis than the thin asthenic, who inclined toward tuberculosis and schizophrenia. In America the Mayo gastroenterologist Walter Alvarez observed that ulcers tended to occur in active, keen, hard-living men. At Columbia Presbyterian Hospital the internist George Draper stressed the relation of physical morphology to specific illnesses. His ulcer type was thin and fearful. He also argued that for ulcers, psychotherapy or psychoanalysis was as important as somatic treatment.[32]

By 1930 psychoanalysis already had given a major impetus to the psychosomatic movement and inspired a growing number of clinical studies of the effect of emotions on disease. Into the existing welter of precipitating events and personality types, the psychoanalysts introduced technical ingenuity, frequent speculation, dogmatic parsimony, and a remarkable optimism based in part on theories of energy and of the power of unconscious factors. They began with Freud's view of hysteria in which the undischarged energy of emotion repressed by conflict was converted into such physical symptoms as functional paralyses. The earliest psychoanalytic theories assumed that symptoms were the direct, symbolic expression of psychological conflict. Thus Smith Ely Jelliffe, the American psychoanalyst, could interpret psoriasis as an "hysterical conversion symbolization."[33]

Although the psychoanalysts insisted on the unity of mind and body, repudiating the narrowness of the somatic past, they concentrated enthusiastically on exclusively psychological factors. Although most granted a role to constitution or to the occurrence of disease at crucial phases of early development, some of them took up extreme, incautious positions. Freud himself rebuked Georg Groddek, the most extravagant of the European psychosomaticists, for arguing that psychological factors alone caused disease.

The first American psychosomaticists were touched by a native optimism. Flanders Dunbar, a psychoanalyst with doctorates in divinity, philosophy, and medicine, had close ties with religious healers, among them Elwood Worcester, who had founded the Emmanuel Movement in Boston. An engaging and energetic hunchback, Dunbar construed the healing implications of libido theory: Freud's therapy "reversed the flow of energy from the symptom back to the original but repressed emotional impulse which when made conscious, could then be given a less injurious outlet." "Vital energy," she speculated, operated according to the laws of thermodynamics, and ultimately, she hoped, its effects could be measured and traced.[34]

Through the technique of free association, a "microscopic instrument of precision," analysts sought the emotional origin and meaning of symptoms. Felix Deutsch, a Viennese analyst, first refined these techniques after he had been intrigued by the case of a woman whose cardiac symptoms cleared up whenever her son returned safely from the front in World War I. Deutsch asked patients to disclose their uncensored associations, and the bodily sensations that accompanied them—heart flutters, a dry mouth, tensed muscles, and so on. Dunbar brought back this method from Deutsch in Vienna to apply to research supported by the Macy Foundation at New York's Presbyterian Hospital. She compiled the first comprehensive survey of the field in 1935, *Emotions and Bodily Changes,* a monumental summary of the existing literature. She also founded and edited the *Journal of Psychosomatic Medicine,* and indefatigably popularized the field in magazines and books.[35]

Dunbar and Franz Alexander, the Berlin psychoanalyst who founded the Chicago Psychoanalytic Institute in 1932, created psychoanalytic versions of the characterological approach. Dunbar's psychosomatic profiles were broadly physical, psychological, and social. She based them on a study of all the patients aged 15 to 55 admitted to Presbyterian Hospital between 1935 and 1938 who suffered from cardiovascular disease, diabetes, fractures, gastrointestinal disorders, or allergy—some 1600 people.

A particular personality type for each disease seemed to emerge from the data. Her cardiac type, the ambitious man, often highly placed, who drove himself relentlessly, anticipated Friedman and Rosenman's Type A personality. Even accident victims, whom physicians regarded as the most "normal" of hospital patients, turned out to share a common typology. Most of them were "egalitarian good fellows" who deeply resented authority and who hurled themselves into "some form of ill considered activity in situations of particular emotional stress," usually outbreaks of aggression that led to accidents.[36] Dunbar was aware of the limitations of her findings—an absence of control groups and the difficulties of generalization. One could not conclude, she wrote, that everyone with a "given personality structure . . . is predisposed to certain syndromes," without discovering whether there are persons subject to this same constellation who do not develop the syndrome." But her popularizations sometimes belied this sense of caution.[37]

Alexander hoped to correct what he regarded as the greatest weakness in Dunbar's work—the embarrassing fact that quite different personalities could develop the same disease affecting the same organ functions. Not surface personality traits but a specific "underlying conflict" was the determining factor in each distinct psychosomatic disorder.[38] The ulcer-prone, for example, suffered from conflicts over dependency needs and tended to hypersecrete in situations of real or threatened loss.

Alexander distinguished sharply between a conversion symptom and a symptom, such as an ulcer, which was a response of the autonomic nervous system and the vegetative organs, such as the stomach, to emotional states. A conversion symptom symbolically expressed unconscious psychological content through the voluntary neuromuscular or sensory-perceptive systems, for example, hysterical paralysis or hysterical blindness. A vegetative symptom did not "express" anything, but was the physiological response of the organ to "constant or periodically returning" emotions. Thus the peptic ulcer had no psychological significance in itself but reflected a reactivated and chronic conflict over dependency.

Psychoanalytic therapy provided a way of observing over a long period of time the relation between psychological factors and organic symptoms. Instead of the undisciplined "psychologism" current in some medical schools, Alexander argued that psychoanalysis offered concrete, highly specific, detailed empirical observations. He cited two cases to demonstrate that many organic disturbances occurred in this sequence: a chronic psychic stimulus, a functional disturbance, an organic change.[39]

One of his illustrative cases was a middle-aged married man with chronic gastritis and incipient peptic ulcer. When his repressed wish to be "loved and treated by his wife as an infant" became manifest in the transference to his therapist, the stomach symptoms disappeared. But then when the analyst attempted to make his patient face the fact that the transference gratified his

infantile dependence, the symptoms reappeared and his wish to be dependent was again repressed. Alexander argued that the first form of being cared
for and loved is nursing, and that nutrition first gratified the passive receptive
tendencies. Thus the "permanent unconscious longing for dependence and
being loved in an infantile way can exert a chronic stimulation of the stomach
secretions, the result of which may be chronic hyper-acidity." What remained
for investigation was under what conditions nervous hyperacidity led to organic changes such as peptic ulcer. Psychoanalysis as a therapy attacked the
first of the chain of causal factors, "the chronic psychic stimulus," in this case
the wish for dependence.[40]

Another case, that of a young married woman, demonstrated the psychological etiology of constipation as an unconscious protest against an inat-
tentive, self-centered husband. Alexander worked from the psychoanalytic
theory that in toilet training the child could express its first spite and stubbornness when the "early coprophilic tendencies were broken by training in
cleanliness." By withholding its feces, the child could show its independence
and stubbornness. As soon as his patient's husband became attentive, her
constipation was relieved. That the longing to be loved like an infant occasionally produced stomach symptoms or that repressed spite may cause constipation was "no more mystical than laughter, i.e. convulsive contraction of
diaphragm and laryngeal muscles as a result of seeing a comic situation or
hearing a good anecdote."[41] Later Alexander placed a new emphasis on
multicausal explanations, including somatic and genetic factors, concomitant
somatic and psychological treatment, and on predictive studies.[42] But on the
investigative level his emphasis continued to be primarily psychological. Alexander and Dunbar both incorporated the research on stress of Walter B.
Cannon, Hans Selye, and Harold Wolff as the somatic basis for their psychological theories. Both psychoanalysts also developed brief methods of active
psychotherapy, for which they claimed highly beneficial results.

The rhetoric of psychoanalytic psychosomatic medicine moved from
diffidence to dogmatism. The first papers of the 1930s were cautious; the
first psychosomatic medical texts were far more confident; the popularizations attained certainty. For example, a study of asthma by one of Alexander's
students offered at first "only hints" as to the "possible biographical experiences" that might lead to later psychosomatic symptoms. In medical texts,
modesty gave way to systematization and greater certainty. Thus *Psychosomatic Medicine* (1943), the first text for medical schools, by Edward Weiss and
O. Spurgeon English, summarized the Chicago institute's work on asthma
and added a striking case history in which a lifelong sufferer was freed of
asthmatic symptoms by psychoanalysis. Possibly the necessities of teaching
helped to harden formulations. Directors of a program in psychiatry for
medical residents noted that the more authoritative they were in presenting
material, the more pupil "resistance" weakened.[43]

The Weiss and English text offered a simplified compendium of psychosomatic diagnosis and treatment set forth with axiomatic authority and illustrated by graphic cases. They extended the psychosomatic approach to an

impressive list of symptoms and diseases—constipation, diabetes, impotence, frigidity, insomnia, migraine, vertigo, and puritis ani. Whenever an
enthusiastic psychiatrist looked at yet another disorder, he seemed to find
evidence of emotional factors and, more impressive still, of recovery, even
cure, through psychotherapy. Take the common cold: fifteen patients of
Leon Saul were entirely freed of colds, he claimed, after psychoanalytic
treatment for other complaints.[44]

Weiss and English argued, as had Dunbar, that psychological and environmental factors were more easily modified than somatic factors. Preventive
psychotherapy might forestall a host of diseases at minimal social cost. One
result was to redefine the ordinary physician's role and to expand the role of
the psychiatrist.

Every physician should be "trained to use the psychologic microscope as
he had been trained to use the optical microscope." Psychoanalytic psychotherapy would lead to real insight and to the resolution of conflicts so that
"the necessity for symptom formation is abolished." The physician should
become a psychological diagnostician, with an ability to empathize with his
patients and identify with their emotional pain.[45]

Much of the early psychosomatic research had been funded by the Macy
Foundation, the Rosenwald Fund, and the Rockefeller Foundation, which
also had helped fund psychoanalysis in America. Alan Gregg, medical director of the Rockefeller Foundation, who had seen Freud "in the flesh" at James
Jackson Putnam's camp in the Adirondacks in 1909 and had become fascinated by psychoanalysis while at Harvard, secured Rockefeller grants for the
Chicago Psychoanalytic Institute—a three-year grant of $100,000 in 1935
and a five-year grant of $120,000 in 1938. Gregg, whose approach to psychi-
atry and psychoanalysis was strongly biological, had urged Alexander to emphasize the somatic aspects of his research, and Alexander had in fact shifted
the institute's focus in that direction. But Alexander also by the late 1930s
had begun to emphasize social issues in an attempt to gain more public
attention for psychoanalysis. And Gregg gradually became disillusioned with
the quality of Alexander's physiological research, his high salary of $21,000 a
year, and what he took to be psychoanalytic causal theories. He told Alexander that "it seemed characteristic of Freudian explanations as well as some
other [sic] to endeavor to ascribe things to causes which operate so early in
lie that no one can deny that they may have been operative, e.g. you stutter
because you were frightened as a child—no, not as a child, as an infant, and
then some one comes along, and says that the real difficulty occurred before
birth, leaving the heavy burden of proof (other than presumptive) to those
who say it did not."[46]

The Macy Foundation, headed by Frank Fremont Smith, a close friend
of Gregg's and also sympathetic to psychoanalysis, argued in 1940 that the
psychosomatic movement would permit medicine to "regain its historic role
as the mediator of science to human welfare."[47] In 1943 the 14th edition of
Sir William Osler's magisterial text *The Principles and Practice of Medicine*
opened with a brief note on psychosomatic medicine.[48] On the eve of World

War II, while psychoanalysis in America still was a controversial medical psychology, psychosomatic medicine was becoming established, with a theory, a brief therapy, and, in institute-trained psychoanalysts, a cadre of skilled personnel. By 1940, the infrastructure of psychoanalysis as a profession had been completed and it had established an influential clientele. Its impact on psychiatry was growing. World War II seemed to confirm the claims of psychoanalysis and psychosomatic medicine. Their golden period, accompanied by extensive popularization, grew directly out of wartime experience.

PART II

Rise and Crisis:
1942–1985

11

World War II:
Psychoanalytic Warriors
and Theories

The Second World War brought psychoanalysis to a position of precarious prominence in American psychiatry. Precisely the types of illness in which psychoanalysts specialized—the neuroses and psychosomatic disorders— took an unexpectedly heavy toll among American servicemen. For these illnesses which seriously impeded the war effort, the traditional hospital psychiatrist was ill prepared. The psychoanalysts seized this unique opportunity to apply their theory and therapy. Many of them rapidly rose to positions of leadership in the Army, the Navy, and the Air Force and taught the green young physicians who filled the ranks of service psychiatry. Wartime experience, partly by chance, seemed to demonstrate the success of psychiatry and especially of psychotherapy, with which psychoanalysis became identified. As a consequence, the war accelerated vital shifts in American psychiatry from a hospital specialty relying primarily on somatic treatment to an eclectic psychodynamic model in which psychotherapy and preventive treatment in a community setting played an important role.[1]

The scale of the war and the complexity of its far-flung battlefields were without parallel. More Americans than ever before were fighting on fronts widely scattered over the world, and the number of neuro-psychiatric casualties at home and abroad was equally unprecedented. Between 1942 and

1945 psychiatrists rejected 1,875,000 men for military service, 12 percent of the fifteen million men examined.

There were 1,100,000 admissions for neuropsychiatric disorders.[2] Only 6 to 7 percent were victims of mental illness, or psychosis, about the same percentage as in World War I. The vast majority were diagnosed as suffering from psychoneuroses, chiefly the result of combat.

Nothing of this magnitude had been anticipated, neither the high percentage of men rejected for service nor the large number of neuropsychiatric cases. All the lessons of World War I, from providing adequate psychiatric care to treating victims close to the battlefield, had to be painfully relearned.

At the time of Pearl Harbor the Army had just 35 psychiatrists, many of them not fully trained in their specialty. Of the approximately 3000 psychiatrists in the nation, perhaps 70 to 80 percent worked in state and private hospitals for the mentally ill. The training and experience of these institutional psychiatrists in the treatment of neuroses and psychosomatic disorders was slight, and that of most other physicians slighter still. Knowledge of the war neuroses was confined to an even smaller number of physicians; among them were psychoanalysts who had contributed some of the existing studies from the First World War and after.[3]

American psychiatrists hoped to weed out potential cases of nervous and mental illness at induction. The psychoanalytic psychiatrist Harry Stack Sullivan, a major figure in setting up screening for the draft, believed that the "science" of psychiatry could predict those likely to become neuropsychiatric casualties. Unlike the First World War, when grounds for rejection were confined to largely palpable neurological symptoms, or gross psychiatric ones, the grounds Sullivan and other psychiatrists devised were based on a very wide net of presumably neurotic psychological characteristics, including instability, seclusiveness, and "psychopathic" traits such as impulsivity, delinquency, and homosexuality, as well as any history of psychiatric or nervous disorder. The psychiatric interviews to detect this myriad symptomatology usually lasted two minutes, often conducted by physicians with no psychiatric training.

The psychiatrists based their faith in prediction on theories then current. Some placed major importance on the shaping of adult traits by very early experience, a proposition accepted most fervently by the psychoanalysts and to a lesser extent by the students of Adolf Meyer.[4] For many psychiatrists, not environment and early experience but heredity and constitution provided the basis for prediction. And some psychiatrists, including some psychoanalysts, rejected the assumption that prediction was even possible.[5]

Actual experience would disprove cherished predictive assumptions. Some presumably risky cases, those with past histories of neuroses, homosexuality, or psychopathy sometimes fought well, while some seemingly normal, well-adjusted individuals cracked under the strain. Ultimately one lesson became clear: environmental stress was far more significant than presumed predisposition.

At first psychiatrists were treating men who broke down during training before they were shipped overseas.[6] In 1942 more pressing demands for psychiatric help came as American troops moved into battle in the South Pacific and North Africa. Line officers and physicians alike were unprepared for what occurred.

The only psychiatrist on Guadalcanal, Martin Berezin, a future psychoanalyst then acting as a division surgeon, faced an unexpected flood of neuropsychiatric combat cases, a third of all his casualties. Two years of experience in a mental hospital had taught him "next to nothing" about how to treat these patients:

> My own training had led me only to understand descriptively the schizophrenias, the manic depressive, and the organic psychoses—but this was different. What I saw were men in varying degrees of "startle" states. I recall seeing one man who remained half conscious, sometimes talking gibberish, who practically had convulsive seizures whenever a bomb dropped. Fortunately, such a reaction was rare.[7]

Berezin's commanding general insisted that neuropsychiatric casualties be court-martialed. Most of his officers believed that such men were a disgrace and should be returned to duty immediately. Berezin could save them only by diagnosing them as victims of "blast concussion."

In the North African campaigns that began in late 1942, neuropsychiatric casualties made up 20 to 34 percent of all patients. A psychiatrist in the Tunisian campaign recalled that the commanding officer of a combat unit, who had been a tough law enforcement officer in civilian life, developed severe neurotic symptoms. During heavy shelling, he refused to leave his dugout. As he became more isolated and remote, morale deteriorated and more of his men fell victim to combat neuroses; matters improved only after he was removed from his command.[8]

In the dearth of appropriately trained physicians and mounting neuropsychiatric casualties, psychoanalysis had much to offer: a well-developed theory of war neuroses and psychosomatic disorders, methods of therapy, texts, and, above all, trained personnel, many of them energetic and able.

Psychoanalysts could provide psychiatric leadership partly because of the recent internal development of their specialty. The status of psychoanalysis differed markedly from what it had been in America at the outset of World War I. Then, it was still the property of a tiny advance guard in neurology and psychiatry. By 1941 there were more than one hundred psychoanalysts, nearly all of whom had been trained in psychiatry and formed by the new psychoanalytic institutes. This dual training gave them an unusually flexible background that allowed them to combine drugs and other somatic treatments with psychotherapy. The institutes also fostered zeal and dedication. Although the role of psychoanalysis in psychiatry was by no means central, it was a growing influence to be reckoned with, especially among the younger generation.

Both professional and theoretical developments within psychoanalysis made it a more plausible body of theory and practice to the young doctors who became acquainted with it in diluted and sometimes disguised form under wartime conditions. The First World War had demonstrated the psychogenesis of the war neuroses and the usefulness of such very general psychoanalytic concepts as conflict and the recall of forgotten traumatic memories. That war also had marked the beginning of a major reorientation of psychoanalytic theory; the early emphasis on drive theory had given way to anxiety as the central problem of the neuroses. Psychosomatic medicine, to an important degree the creation of psychoanalysts, had caught the attention of a growing number of general physicians. Some of the military's newly inducted medical officers already had been exposed to psychoanalysis and to psychosomatic medicine, possibly in medical school. They were prepared to accept particularly the conception of defense against anxiety, the connection of symptoms with fantasies and feelings, and, sometimes, when patients themselves expressed the link, the relation of symptoms to very early experience.[9]

The first wartime appointments in the Army reflected the state of American psychiatry. They represented, first, personnel from the public hospital system; next, the men trained by Adolf Meyer who dominated the departments of psychiatry in medical schools; and, with the appointment of William Menninger to the post of chief psychiatrist for the Army in December 1943, a rising group of young psychoanalysts. Menninger, who had directed his family's clinic in Topeka, Kansas, was personable and convivial, and had a remarkable capacity to inspire confidence among military officers.

As the war went on, psychoanalysts came to occupy additional strategic posts and there is some evidence that they tended to appoint men who they knew had psychoanalytic training. For instance, of five civilian psychiatrists chosen by William Menninger to report on policy and practice in the European theater in the spring of 1945, four were psychoanalysts, including Menninger's brother Karl.[10] John Murray, a psychoanalyst from the Boston institute, was made chief of Air Force psychiatry. His Boston colleague Ralph Kaufman became psychiatric consultant in the South Pacific and later for the Tenth Army during the Okinawa campaign. Psychoanalysts also served as instructors in psychiatric training programs, in basic training camps, and as chiefs of hospital services.

The men already trained in psychoanalysis were in their early forties. A younger group, in their late twenties or early thirties, whose interest in psychoanalysis was piqued by the war, began their training immediately after it. Among them were John Appel, head of the Army's Mental Hygiene branch, which produced the film series "Why We Fight." Two others were Herbert Gaskell and Norman Brill, who had worked with Menninger in the Army and later became deans of psychiatry in medical schools.

A profile of seventeen psychoanalysts who either served in the armed forces or acted as consultants indicates the changing state of psychoanalysis. No longer confined to major centers on the eastern seaboard, an equal number came from the Midwest and the East Coast and a few were from

California. They had graduated from a variety of medical schools, in almost equal numbers from Ivy League schools and major state universities. The new importance of the Midwest was a direct result of the Chicago Psychoanalytic Institute; of this sample, more were trained there than at any other single center. There was only one immigrant among them, indicating that in this crucial mission as interpreters of psychoanalysis to the military, the refugee analysts played a minor role.

The psychoanalysts not only supplied key personnel, whose influence far outweighed their numbers. They also developed theories, classification systems, and methods of treatment for the war neuroses. They contributed significantly to the training of the young physicians who made up the majority of the Army's psychiatrists. They also undertook special studies, such as Lawrence Kubie's report calling for a "radical and aggressive fight" within the services for true racial equality.[11] All these efforts were marked by a liberal political stance, sympathy for the victims of the war neuroses, and a hopeful environmentalism that contrasted with the emphasis of traditional psychiatry on constitutional predisposition.

The American psychoanalysts stressed the universality of fear and the ease with which anyone could develop neurotic symptoms under the severe conditions of modern battle.[12] Their explanations focused on the problem of anxiety and how the ego, never very clearly defined, failed to cope with the terror combat could induce.

One of Freud's American analysands, Roy Grinker, 43, chief of neuropsychiatry at Michael Reese Hospital in Chicago, and one of Grinker's residents, John Spiegel, 32, who had just begun training at the Chicago institute, provided one of the earliest and most widely acclaimed contributions to treatment, based on their experiences in the Tunisian campaign.

Grinker wrote to his Chicago colleague Max Gitelson, July 15, 1943:

> Our psychotherapy is all "brief" and I believe we have learned a great deal that is applicable to peace time psychiatry especially concerning the ego's capacity for enduring anxiety and dealing with it in its healing processes. There are many dreary moments here—plenty of nostalgia and at times it seems as if it will be endless.[13]

In the New York *Times,* the psychoanalyst Carl Binger ranked their work as second only to such wartime triumphs as the use of "penicillin and the sulfa drugs . . . and life-saving transfusions with blood plasma."[14] The slender text entitled *War Neuroses* was printed by the Josiah Macy Foundation at the urging of the psychoanalyst John Murray, then chief of Air Force Psychiatry. Some 45,000 copies were distributed to service personnel, introducing them to Grinker and Spiegel's psychoanalytic psychiatry.[15]

Their treatment combined the barbiturate sodium pentothal with brief, highly directive cathartic psychotherapy. The method was used overseas in treating some combat neuroses and in hospitals at home for severe cases of "residual symptoms" of combat neuroses and conversion hysteria. For a time it enjoyed a considerable vogue.[16] Based on the treatment of 1200 cases, *War Neuroses* gave a gripping account of soldiers' symptoms. In both world wars these symptoms remained remarkably constant: startle reactions to sudden noises, amnesia, disturbed sleep, restlessness, fear, marked tremors, jerking limbs, incontinence of urine or feces, dejection, depression, confusion, occasional hysterical paralyses, recurrent nightmares, sudden fits of laughing or crying, muteness, feelings of weakness and dizziness, and functional gastric and heart disturbances. It was the clear lesson of World War I that the sooner and the closer to the battlefield such symptoms were treated the greater were the chances of recovery.

However, the Army at first made no provision for psychiatric treatment in forward echelons during the North African campaigns. Because Grinker and Spiegel saw their patients at base hospitals several hundred miles behind the front, symptoms tended to be more florid and fully developed than would have been the case in men treated immediately, close to the battlefield.

The symptoms of some patients were so severe that they had been misdiagnosed as schizophrenic. One 26-year-old infantry officer could not remember his name, trembled constantly, and was almost mute. Like many other patients he had forgotten the emotions and experiences of battle. Grinker and Spiegel believed that the recall of battle experiences and the immediate relief of anxiety were crucial for recovery. Pentothal, which the British were the first to use with combat casualties, achieved both results in an almost miraculous way and came to be known as the "truth serum." It dramatically reduced anxiety and fostered a "startling renaissance" of the inhibiting and unifying functions of the personality before the very eyes of the therapist. At the same time it broke down defenses and stimulated recall of the original experience, a total procedure they called narcosynthesis.

Clearly a method unsuited to battle conditions, narcosynthesis represented an eclectic mix of psychoanalytic techniques and theories with pre-Freudian methods of reeducation and exhortation. Patients were interviewed in private for fifteen minutes to half an hour every day or every other day for days or weeks, depending on the severity of the case.

The first part of the process was recall and catharsis. The patient was isolated in a darkened room; soon after the pentothal was injected, he became sleepy. In this twilight state, some patients began to talk spontaneously. Other had to be induced to do so. If the patient could not remember, the therapist might enact the role of a comrade in battle or bring up some piece of information known about the patient's experience.

The vividness of recall astonished them:

> The terror exhibited in the moments of supreme danger, such as the imminent explosion of shells, the death of a friend before the patient's eyes, the absence of cover under a heavy dive-bombing attack, is electrifying to watch. The body becomes increasingly tense and rigid; the eyes widen and the pupils dilate, while the skin becomes covered with fine perspiration. The hands move about con-

vulsively, seeking a weapon, or a friend to share the danger. The breathing becomes incredibly rapid and shallow. The intensity of the emotion sometimes becomes unbearable; and frequently, at the height of the reaction, there is a collapse and the patient falls back in bed and remains quiet for a few minutes, usually to resume the story at a more neutral point.[17]

In severe cases, the results of pentothal were dramatic: the mute could talk; the deaf, hear; the paralyzed, move; the terror-stricken, become calm.

In this process, the therapist deliberately played the role of a "reliable, but firm father figure," because under pentothal, soldiers often expressed terror at being left alone on the battlefield, in a rain of fire, "with no protective human figure to help and no physical cover to provide even the flimsiest security." In such conditions, even the strongest man was in the position of a helpless child. If the patient became convulsed with terror while remembering, the therapist would step in "as a protective and supporting figure, comforting and reassuring the patient, and encouraging him to proceed." As the soldier emerged from the memory of combat, he needed to be assured that he was truly safe from that menacing environment, and would not have to fight again. The mere recall of traumatic experiences under pentothal was not enough. Without psychotherapy and the conscious integration of forgotten memories and emotions, some patients failed to recover.

Of all the emotions, hostility was the most difficult to release and yet one of the most pervasive: rage at being abandoned to death and destruction by father figures, anger at the death of friends, resentment of inefficient officers and leaders. Some men repressed hostility because of fear of their own aggression and of retaliation, yet combat demanded an aggressive, hostile response. At times, under the drug, hostility would emerge with the "intensity of a convulsive seizure."

The therapist also attempted to utilize the soldier's conscience, first by mitigating its self-punishing aspects. The soldier saw himself as "yellow, a coward, an impotent useless failure," the weak link in his unit. He was assured that everyone had a breaking point and that he had stuck it out as long as he could. The therapist attempted to break down one source of the punishing conscience, the soldier's identification with the ideals and the friends, living and dead, of his former combat outfit. The therapist also exploited the positive aspects of conscience that pushed toward a return to strength and mastery. Finally, the patient would identify with the therapist and come to "see himself as the medical officer sees him—as a man who is fit to take care of himself, who has nothing to fear from the world, except possibly a return to combat; and who has a useful job to do for the army and for his country in non-combatant work."[18]

Two cases will illustrate the unusual severity of the symptoms seen early in the North African campaign and the pervasive problem of guilt. The first patient, the 26-year-old infantry officer who had been misdiagnosed on his emergency medical tag as schizophrenic and who could not remember his own name, was judged by Grinker and Spiegel to be suffering from acute anxiety. His behavior seemed to be the wordless reenactment of an actual event on the battlefield. He "would start violently with fear, tremble all over, and then hold his hands to his face, covering his eyes as if to shut out some horrible sight."

During his second pentothal session he was able to recall what had happened. His unit had been pinned down by mortar fire, and a shell exploded in a foxhole near him:

> Two men were in there, our First Sergeant and a Staff Sergeant. I could hardly look at them. The First Sergeant was on top. He was dead with his head blown open. There wasn't any top to his head. The other man was underneath. He was still alive, but the side of his chest was open, and I could see part of the lung. He was crying; God, I can still hear him crying.

Suddenly he remembered his name and said,

> I remember where I live. God, what a miracle that I can talk. I thought I would never be able to, but I tried. They must think I'm an awful baby . . . to be like this . . . What will they do with me. I can't go back there.[19]

His depression finally lifted, but he was sent home because of what seemed to be his strong dependency needs. Grinker and Spiegel attempted to relate his breakdown to early experience. He had been an anxious child and his quarreling parents finally were divorced. He was a hunter and excellent marksman but made sure he killed on the first shot, because he hated to see an animal suffer. His anxiety had disappeared when he got a job in college and was able to pay for his education. He and his wife were unusually dependent on each other.

The second case combined anxiety, nightmares, depression, and a somatic symptom. This 24-year-old co-pilot repeatedly dreamed that he was falling from his plane and crashing on the ground. Once he had to bail out, but because he had been slow to do so through no fault of his own, the pilot was unable to jump. The co-pilot just had had time to open his parachute, and as he had fallen, injuring his back, he saw the pilot crash in a "tremendous flash of flame." The patient blamed himself for the man's death. In time, his anxiety and depression were replaced by severe back pain, but it too disappeared, and he returned to duty. Then, on a mission he saw his best friend shot down. His anxiety dreams recurred as well as an obsession that his plane was falling off to the right, precisely the direction in which his friend's plane had crashed. When he was transferred to ground duty, his symptoms largely disappeared.[20]

Both these patients had suffered from real and severe trauma, but sometimes men would develop symptoms without ever having seen combat, from the most trivial occurrence. Why did some men succumb only after tremendous stress, others, after little or none? The problem of cause and effect remained puzzling.

In explaining why some men fell ill while others did not, Grinker and Spiegel invoked most of the major developments in psychoanalytic theory since the First World War: the central role of anxiety and of defenses against it; the punishing and cruel, as well as the positively motivating, aspects of the internalized conscience, or superego; the role of the ego in ordering and regulating experience; and psychosomatic research. The ego, they argued, echoing Freud, was threatened by "anxieties from the dangerous forces of reality, from its own powerful instinctual drives, and from the reaction of its own conscience."[21]

The liability to break down depended on the degree of tolerance for anxiety and the amount of ego strength, never clearly defined. "Anxiety on going into battle" was "an almost universal experience for normal soldiers."[22] Battle created for the ego the severest actual peril. A soldier had to fight or die; he could not run away without punishment from his own officers. The outbreak of neurosis resulted from a feeling of helplessness in a hostile environment and from the release of hitherto repressed aggressive and destructive energies.[23] What distinguished the neurotic was the excessive amount of anxiety, and its persistence after real danger had passed.

Relying on recent work in psychosomatic medicine, Grinker and Spiegel argued that battle mobilized protective, automatic, and purely biological reflexes, such as those of fight or flight, reminiscent of the self-preservation instincts psychiatrists had invoked in World War I. These emergency reflexes became associated with the "subjective sensation of anxiety," and this sensation in turn could lead to further emergency biological mobilization, thus heightening the anxiety in a vicious circle. Pentothal worked initially to break this physiological and psychological pattern.

Extrapolating from Freud's views on group psychology, Grinker and Spiegel emphasized the importance of morale, of identification with the military unit as vital to preserving the strength and intactness of the soldier's ego. They stressed relationships to buddies and to officers as father or brother figures. Bad leadership, deteriorating faith in officers, enforced inactivity, the death of comrades, and a series of defeats and retreats, as well as lack of sleep and rest, hunger, thirst, noise, and blast—all these served to weaken resistance.

Grinker and Spiegel were cautious about their results: they returned 72 percent of their patients to some form of duty, but a "pitifully small number" to combat. Even so, they thought their methods were worthwhile. "For the soldier, return to work is the best therapy—counteracting his dependent trends, bolstering his ego-ideal and permitting him to return home with the army, and not as a crippled failure."[24]

Their findings aroused controversy and disagreement, sometimes from psychoanalysts, sometimes from psychiatrists who believed the method impractical and inappropriate. Some questioned the prevalence of the florid symptoms they described, arguing that these characterized mainly fresh, green troops new to combat before group cohesiveness had been established.[25] They doubted the usefulness and the need for sodium pentothal treatment. It took an hour or more to administer the drug and additional psychotherapy to assimilate the remembered battle experience, luxuries hardly possible close to a combat zone. Moreover, Grinker and Spiegel had omitted any discussion of what proportion of their cases qualified for the treatment. Critics argued that it was appropriate in only 5 to 10 percent of cases found in forward areas.[26]

Accepting the fundamental usefulness of recall and catharsis, the psychoanalyst Ralph Kaufman devised a method of hypnosis that could be used close to the battlefield. Described by a *New York Times* correspondent on Okinawa as a "greying, chunky, dynamo of a man," Kaufman was in charge of psychiatry during the 10th Army's campaign against the Japanese. He had arrived in the South Pacific carrying Grinker and Spiegel's text and brought as much sodium pentothal as he could to Guadalcanal, the staging area for the Bougainville campaign.

Once while preparing a pentothal injection he found that his suggestible patient already was reacting as if he had been given the drug, so Kaufman began using hypnosis instead.[27] He argued that sedation could intensify amnesia and increase confusion, obstructing the recovery of forgotten memories. Hypnosis produced the same effects as pentothal, without its disadvantages.

Kaufman's hypnotic treatment was simple and direct. He would tell a soldier that he would relax and go to sleep, and the patient usually did within one or two minutes. Before treatment, patients blocked any associations that suggested explosions or bloodshed; after hypnosis, these associations arose spontaneously, indicating that the lost combat experiences had been successfully integrated. Rorschach tests seemed to confirm the results.[28]

Kaufman insisted on treatment by neuropsychiatric teams as close to the front as possible, preferably within the sound of artillery fire. During the first phases of the Okinawa campaign, some 83 percent of the psychiatric casualties were returned to duty. During the second phase, when Japanese artillery and *kamikaze* pilots operated in force, the percentage dropped to 57 percent; and in the final phase, as troops became increasingly exhausted in the face of stubborn resistance, the rate dropped to 38 percent.[29]

The *New York Times* correspondent enthusiastically endorsed Kaufman's methods:

> I saw the hypnotic treatment used. It looks ridiculously simple. The doctor softly reassures the patient that all is well, that he is safe. It is done in low tones, in constant repetition, until the patient just goes to sleep. And it works. . . . Hypnosis . . . helps the patient talk out his case. When he talks about it enough instead of burying it inside himself, the battle is won. . . .

Every soldier treated by these methods who was "mentally whole when he went into the Army" was cured and went back to active duty.[30]

Kaufman was unusually skillful in maintaining contact with line officers and in getting them to take a sympathetic attitude toward neuropsychiatric patients. He argued that the soldier who breaks is not a coward, but rather that his symptoms were caused by conflict between his desire to fight and not to run away and his biological instinct of self-preservation. Okinawa, the last campaign of the war, represented perhaps the high point of the direct influence of a psychoanalyst on combat psychiatry on a large scale.

Some psychiatrists rejected the psychoanalytic approach because methods based on insight had little value in combat situations. Moreover, they argued that any psychotherapy was self-defeating and destructive to morale because it allowed the soldier to identify with the psychiatrist, and this identification weakened his ties to his unit, his major source of "ego protection" in combat. Moreover, the listening psychiatrist was likely to empathize with his patient, confirming his belief that he was unfit for battle.[31] Others argued that the vivid memories of combat were "fictional" or "highly distorted." Finally, in initial interviews, recall of battle experience was not always desirable. Sometimes, traumatic memories were best left alone; amnesia was a kind of protective device. When facts became intolerable, the soldier forgot them or refused to discuss them, and it was wise to respect this. Only if amnesia were disabling or associated with marked anxiety would treatment designed to evoke recall be appropriate.[32]

Frederick Hanson, a consultant in the Mediterranean theater, developed treatment methods that relied heavily on simple exhortation and reassurance, rest, and sedation. Casualties in the Italian campaign were heavy and combat neuroses frequent. Hanson treated men close to the lines for two to four days under military discipline in a common ward, with the aim of reestablishing identification "with the all powerful group." Patients were told that everyone felt fear but that they should still be able to fight, and that relief from combat was dishonorable—family, friends, comrades, and country expected them to return and finish the job.

The crucial moment came just after the initial break. Then, any influence that suppressed fear and helped rapid recovery "was the psychotherapeutic method of choice . . . a wisecrack, an insult, an appeal to group need, an arm around his back, a diversion of interest away from his panic, or the ultimate concession," permission to rest with the kitchen crew.[33] Hanson claimed a 60 percent success rate with these techniques.

He argued that physical exhaustion and emotional stress acted together to create the combat neuroses. Soldiers brought to forward medical units usually were "fatigued to the point of exhaustion." They were "unshaven, dirty. . . . They had obviously undergone a period of severe physical strain. . . . Their faces were expressionless, their eyes blank and unseeing, and they tended to go to sleep wherever they were. . . . Lack of sleep, continuous shelling, strange night noises, flares, sentry and patrol duties, rain, snow, cold, heat, insects, the ever present threat of the enemy, made sleep at best intermittent and scanty." Moreover, fear increased in proportion to time spent in combat. The soldier became increasingly tired and less well nourished, and with this decrease in physical well-being, there was a corresponding decrease in his ability to cope with emotional stress. Although fatigue was not the only cause—casualties usually were light among troops advancing victoriously—the psychiatrist had to understand its role. The most effective treatment was its alleviation along with brief psychotherapy.

The psychoanalysts criticized Hanson's methods and theories. Grinker and Spiegel argued that for serious cases his treatment was a "covering up" therapy; they questioned his recovery rate and wondered how many of his patients relapsed. However, they were unable to supply firm recovery figures for their own methods, noting simply that in their experience they had proven effective. Ralph Kaufman claimed that Hanson's emphasis on exhaustion played a misleading role in both diagnosis and treatment. The diagnosis of "operational fatigue" usually led to treatment of the fatigue alone, and bypassed any "rational treatment of the underlying psychological problems," thereby minimizing the "most valuable adjunct" of treatment, the patient's insight into the origins of his problem.[34]

Hanson's exhaustion and intensity hypotheses were contradicted by still other psychiatrists who noted that there were very few neuropsychiatric cases among those troops who had endured extremely adverse conditions at Corregidor or Bataan in the first Philippine campaign. Moreover, units which saw a great deal of combat, such as the Japanese-American 100th infantry battalion, had very few neuropsychiatric casualties, although those that did occur tended to be severe and hard to treat.[35]

These different approaches to the war neuroses often reflected the physician's background and training. Thus, Hanson, whose residency had been in neurology, emphasized the cumulative effects of exhaustion; those already trained in psychoanalysis emphasized the therapeutic role of abreaction and insight. Others, associated with Sullivan's interpersonal psychiatry, tended to emphasize social factors and environmental pressures.[36] Karl Menninger came to believe that "combat exhaustion" was a "more accurate as well as less . . . stigmatizing" term for these patients than "neurosis" or "psychoneurosis."[37]

Psychoanalysts played important roles in the Army's programs for training psychiatrists. Kaufman had been among the first instructors at the Army's School of Military Psychiatry, established at Lawson General Hospital in Atlanta in December 1942 and then moved to Mason General Hospital, New York, in October 1943.[38] Still other training programs were undertaken at Columbia and New York universities, and Norman Reider, a psychoanalyst and trainee of Otto Fenichel's, was in charge of coordinating them. John Murray and Roy Grinker ran still others.

These programs were begun not only because of the shortage of psychiatrists, but because medical schools did not give adequate instruction in psychiatry, psychosomatic medicine, or the war neuroses. Physicians left medical school "without any clear understanding of the anatomy, the physiology, and the pathology of the psyche," wrote William Menninger, in a classical use of the medical analogy.[39] Military physicians and surgeons were confronted with the role of emotional factors in illness. Somatic symptoms sometimes bore little relation to actual physiological findings, and emotional factors clearly were involved. At many military hospitals, psychiatrists and psycho-analysts were working overtime consulting about such cases.[40]

The Boston psychoanalyst John Murray established a treatment and training center for the Air Force at Fort Logan, Colorado. Among the instructors was Ralph Greenson, who had been in psychoanalytic training with Otto Fenichel. Greenson, because of his skill with patients, often was asked for advice about how to treat war neuroses, and he began giving informal seminars in his house, where sometimes up to forty people crowded into his living room.[41] His most original contribution was to explain the severe state of dependency of patients who had been through intense, usually prolonged deprivation in prisoner-of-war camps or lonely outposts. These apathetic, passive, submissive, resigned patients broke down because they could not tolerate deprivation, that is, "loss of love in all its many equivalents." The loss created feelings of aggression which turned inward, causing severe depression. Often, such men had been orphaned or had come from broken homes. Like the other psychoanalysts, Greenson found that a "warm, kindly, paternalistic role" was therapeutic.[42]

The psychoanalyst instructors in the military courses usually did not present psychoanalysis as a system or a treatment method or use psychoanalytic jargon. Psychoanalytic theories chiefly were included in discussions of the "psychodynamics" of personality or childhood development. More than 1000 psychiatrists graduated from the Army's training programs. Many were not yet fixed in their careers and so stayed in psychiatry; significant numbers sought psychoanalytic training after the war.

Group psychotherapy was given an important impetus by the wartime demands of the military for mass treatment, and psychoanalysts, especially the British, played a major role in its creation. Although widely used, it was less systematically developed than individual therapy. At St. Elizabeth's Hospital in Washington, D.C., the psychiatrist E. W. Lazell had delivered "Freudian" lectures to schizophrenics on the sexual origin of their symptoms, while Paul Schilder, a psychoanalytic psychiatrist who had emigrated from Vienna to New York, tried group therapy using free association and dream analysis. Toward the end of the war, group therapy was increasingly used by psychiatrists, psychologists, aides, nurses, and social workers.

Extrapolating from Freud, some psychiatrists argued that if identification were established between a group and a paternalistic, permissive group leader, patients would increase their control over anxiety. One anxiety-provoking problem that group discussion made easier was the ventilation of hostility, particularly resentment toward officers and the military. The group leader might play an active part, asking questions, trying to hold hostilities in check, giving little talks on anger, rationalization, and fear. In a successful group a high degree of morale was attained, and usually this led to more efficient performance of duties and increased self-esteem. The overall results were not always encouraging, however. In one carefully chosen group, 66 percent were returned to duty, but only a fifth of these to full duty and the remainder to limited service. Some types of patients did not profit from group therapy, especially the paranoid or the very dependent, or those with psychosomatic complaints. One patient with a somatic symptom argued that "all this talk is a lot of crap"; what he wanted was medicine.[43]

In 1944 Menninger issued a bulletin about psychiatry for the use of the ordinary Army physician that strongly reflected psychoanalytic theory. "Neuropsychiatry for the General Medical Officer" explained the importance of unconscious conflict as a cause of symptoms, the determination of adult traits and attitudes in infancy and childhood, the role of insight in treatment and recovery, and the specificity theories of Franz Alexander's psychosomatic medicine. Psychoanalytic psychotherapy was recommended along with a highly eclectic mix including all the pre-Freudian treatments such as suggestion and education.[44]

The bulletin's rhetoric was as revealing as its orientation. It was obviously intended to combat a common medical prejudice against psychiatry and the neuropsychiatric casualty. Medical analogies abounded. Terms such as "drainage," "encystment," and "proud flesh" were used to suggest the medical and scientific status of psychiatric diagnosis and treatment. Psychiatric and psychological "findings" were as "real and valid as those in any other field of medicine," but required "intellectual" rather than "sensory" perception. Psychiatric syndromes were as specific and as distinct from each other as measles from pneumonia. Treatment methods such as cathartic therapy under sedation, hypnosis, or electro-shock produced results as "spectacular, immediate and satisfying" as drug therapy and surgery. The emphasis was placed on environmental influences, not only in infancy and childhood but in the immediate stresses of Army life and, above all, of combat. Thus, the general medical officer was presented with an authoritative manual that had its origins in psychoanalytic theory and, to a lesser extent, psychoanalytic practice.

The Army's new psychiatric terminology adopted August 19, 1945, a year after the bulletin for general physicians was published, represented a high point in the influence of Freud and psychoanalysis. William Menninger had worked on the project for eight months and had gathered suggestions from leaders in American psychiatry.[45] He justified this new departure by arguing that the cases seen most often, the acute combat states, the minor personality disorders, and the reactions to special situations, "defied any classification under the standard nomenclature." The old terminology had been worked out in detail only for the psychoses, which represented about one-seventh of the Army's neuropsychiatric patients.[46]

Battle experience was directly reflected in the most innovative new category, "transient personality reactions to acute or special stress." These included "combat exhaustion" and "acute situational maladjustment" to a new environment or an "especially trying and difficult" situation. Reactions caused by poverty or racial discrimination also were included in this category.

The section on the standard psychoneuroses was entirely psychoanalytic, emphasizing the central role Freud gave to anxiety, aggression, and defenses such as repression, conversion, and displacement. Psychosomatic disorders were explained much the way Franz Alexander, Menninger's analyst, had explained them and included an array of functional disorders: "cardiac neuroses, peptic ulcer, constipation, mucous colitis, some types of hypertension, psychogenic genito-urinary reactions, impotence, frigidity, dysuria, . . . hives and . . . psychogenic allergic reactions, and general fatigue."[47]

The old grab-bag, "psychopathic personality," was discarded for three new categories that nevertheless reflected the moralism of the older term. First was the "anti-social personality" who had a "normal moral background" but was always in trouble. The second, the "asocial" personality, included those who became "gangsters, vagabonds, racketeers, prostitutes," often as the result of a "lifelong abnormal environment." The third, the "sexual deviate," was reserved for homosexuality, transvestism, pedophilia, fetishism, and sexual sadism. To make disposition easier, physicians were asked to record not only the type of case, but the degree of incapacity, predisposition, and precipitating stress. After the war, this new nomenclature became the basis for the first Diagnostic Manual of the American Psychiatric Association.

Throughout the war, treatment of the war neuroses had provoked debate over a number of vital issues. The psychiatrist and particularly the psychoanalyst, with his view of the unconscious and involuntary origin of symptoms, was caught in a role conflict. As a physician he must protect the interests of his patient; as an officer he needed to satisfy the military's demand for fighting soldiers. Ernst Simmel once expressed the dilemma neatly: on the one hand the psychiatrist was a "good father" who protected the patient from the holocaust, on the other, he was the "bad father" who was expected to "drive men back into the fire."[48]

In 1942 William Menninger and General George Marshall clashed over whether or not war neurotics were yellow cowards and malingerers or involuntary sufferers from a real disorder. Concerned about the loss of manpower from neuropsychiatric casualties, Marshall drafted a statement about the war neuroses that was leaked to a *Washington* newspaper. Putting his finger on a major problem of psychiatry, Marshall argued that psychiatric disorders were for the most part invisible and depended for their detection on the diagnosis of psychiatrists. Such disorders could not be "measured" or confirmed by laboratory tests or "objective findings." To the specialist, the psychoneurotic was a "hospital patient," but to the line officer he was a malingerer. His imaginary ailment became so fixed in his mind that it caused his "mental pain and sickness." No patient had been convicted of malingering because "no doctor was willing to testify that the pain was "nonexistent." Thus laymen or uninitiated line officers "incline to the belief that a medical officer's diagnosis of psychoneurosis is either wrong or else that the doctor is influenced by a hyperconsiderate professional attitude."

Incensed by the newspaper story, Menninger argued that the great majority of patients were combat veterans and had been "normally adjusted men" before their battle experience. Hundreds of them had been cited for bravery. Not only psychiatrists but all physicians recognized the reality of functional nervous disorders. It was a "generally established scientific fact" that the origins of the symptoms were "unconscious." Translating the conception of infantile narcissism into crude terms, Menninger noted:

> The problem is not so much any parental coddling as it is the exaggeration of individual freedom. Psychiatrically, it is a modification of the infantile, the immature stage of development, characterized by "I want what I want when I want it and to hell with the rest of the world."[49]

Thus Menninger invoked several psychoanalytic conceptions: the unconscious and involuntary nature of neurotic symptoms, and the role of narcissism, filtered through an old American gloss, that is, the insistence that the conflict between individual and society represented a clash between infantile selfishness and the presumably higher demands of society. Above all, Menninger insisted on the scientific status of the ideas he had invoked.

Some psychiatrists and psychoanalysts lost their confidence in predisposition and prediction during the course of the war yet still clung to vestiges of this belief. Grinker and Spiegel were among the first to conclude that undue importance had been given to constitution, life history, and genetic background. The conditions of war created the potential for neurosis in every soldier. Some with a history of neurotic anxiety did well, while others, with no apparent predisposition, broke down. On the whole, these physicians placed far greater emphasis on morale and the quality of military leadership than on existing character defects.

Nevertheless, they did ascribe a role to several types of predisposition. Some men were born with a lower threshold for tolerating anxiety. Those with a history of psychosomatic illness were likely to develop more malignant symptoms in battle; passive-dependent characters, the "overcompensated" tough guy, and schizoid and compulsive characters also were vulnerable.[50]

John W. Appel, head of the Army's mental hygiene branch, took a more radically environmentalist stand. Even in a "significant percent" of apparently predisposed cases, "the stress of the situation, rather than the weaknesses of the personality, was of more importance in having caused the . . . disorder."[51]

William Menninger argued it both ways. A "history of maladjustment in the family or in the individual, contributed to many of the casualties that occurred." On the other hand, environmental factors that "supported or disrupted" the individual were far more important.[52] Combat casualties could be divided into two groups "with no sharp dividing line" between them: the grossly predisposed and those with little or no apparent predisposition. But even those who seemed to be "normal personalities reacting to abnormal stress" must have had some predisposition, and this determined their reaction to combat.

The group of psychiatrists and psychoanalysts Menninger dispatched to Europe in 1945 to report on the combat neuroses also argued it both ways. It was impossible to determine who would make the most effective fighters, although severe intellectual and emotional limitations could be screened out at induction stations. They reported that the "previous personality structure" and the combat situation determined the "form" of the breakdown. At the same time, they emphasized situational factors, such as leadership and morale, and recommended a firm policy of rotating troops.

In retrospective studies, some psychoanalysts insisted that the outbreak of combat neurosis was directly related to previous unresolved problems. At the traumatic moment of battle, the connection was made unconsciously in fantasy with earlier neurotic difficulties. For example, a 21-year-old Marine had successfully participated in a "thunderous assault-landing," then developed gross tremors and terrifying nightmares. He had been deserted by two men assigned to protect him during a dangerous surveying mission. Armed with only a knife, after they left him he remained hidden, under fire, for an entire night before being able to make his way back to his battalion. Emerging from pentothal treatment, he recalled that the moment of desertion reminded him of the times when as a child, his mother had forced him to stay in a closet while she had sexual intercourse. At those times he had felt as if "the walls were closing in." The desertion by his fellow Marines and a letter from his mother that he had just received had precipitated his breakdown.[53] Martin Berezin, the Guadalcanal psychiatrist, argued that combat or merely the "enforcement of regimentation under masculine domination" reactivated unresolved, repressed conflicts.[54]

The psychoanalysts seem to have been caught in a logical bind whatever their wartime clinical experiences may have been. Psychoanalysis depended heavily on a deterministic theory, that is, the determinism of adult symptoms by early experience. Yet the analysts tended to oppose another kind of determinism, one resting on genetic or constitutional factors. What is significant is that by the end of the war, despite the postulate of childhood determinism, many psychoanalysts had come to stress the importance of immediate social and environmental factors.

More puzzling than the problem of predisposition and prediction was the fact that Americans had a considerably higher proportion of neuropsychiatric casualties than any other nation. Further, the number of men rejected for the service was 11 percent higher in World War II than in World War I, and the percentage of those discharged from the service was double the earlier rate. Yet the rates of psychoses and of strictly neurological disorders remained the same as during World War I.

The difference in these statistics was provided by the large increase in the category of psychoneuroses and character disorders. This in turn was an artifact of psychiatric definition and classification, much of it psychoanalytic in origin. The psychoneuroses were a broad category ranging from hysterical paralyses to acute anxiety. The high percentage of rejections by draft boards may have been partly the result of the comprehensive yet vague criteria established. But this high percentage of rejections did not substantially lessen the number of neuropsychiatric casualties, although psychiatrists argued that such casualties would have been even higher without the screening program.

Some 50 percent of all medical discharges from the American forces were for neuropsychiatric reasons. The Russian figure was about 17 percent, the British, about 30 percent. Not only psychiatric definitions and policies were involved; part of the reason for the difference was morale. Unlike the British or the Russians, the Americans had been neither bombed nor invaded. They had no direct motives for revenge. Neither their national existence nor their families were threatened. Far from the battle lines, most Americans regarded the war as remote and abstract, especially the war in Europe.

Then, too, the American Army, unlike the British, had no policy of systematic rotation, with the result that soldiers stayed in combat for long periods without relief. This may well have increased the percentage of psychiatric casualties. John Appel, after touring the Italian front, led a campaign in 1944 to ensure more food and rest for combat troops as well as a policy of rotation, but rotation was implemented only to a limited extent toward the end of the war.[55]

There is no way of knowing which of the different treatment methods returned the most men to combat or to some form of duty. Definitive statistical studies linking methods to outcome are not available. John Whitehorn, who had been a student of Adolf Meyer's and headed the Johns Hopkins Department of Psychiatry, concluded that rest, support, and psychiatric reassurance without total disruption of ties to the soldier's outfit were more important than specific treatment methods. A former president of the American Psychiatric Association, Edward A. Strecker, argued that recovery rates and methods of treatment in World War I and World War II were roughly similar except for the more extensive use of drugs and group therapy in World War II. He implied that the earlier simple methods were as effective as the more elaborate later ones. Strecker insisted that the therapeutic process needed further study to determine which of the many methods worked best: insight, identification with the therapist, authoritative direction, inspiration, reassurance, sugestion, relief from exhaustion, emotional release, friendly talks, and so on.[56]

The most careful retrospective study, published in 1955 by Norman Q. Brill and Gilbert Beebe, indicated that the simple removal of a man from combat could be a powerful therapeutic tool in itself, regardless of any other factor. Some 56 percent of combat and non-combat casualties were returned to duty after their first breakdown with essentially no treatment. Of those treated by rest and sedation, 68 percent were returned to duty, while of the cases who usually were given individual psychotherapy, 62 percent were returned to duty. The success rate for routine hospitalization alone was much lower, 48 percent. Combat neuroses, probably because they occurred in men who were more resilient to begin with, recovered the most readily; for example, 78 percent of those who broke down in combat recovered as compared with 49 percent of those who broke down in other situations. Some 42 percent of all the combat cases, usually the more severely ill, were treated by psychotherapy. For combat cases of moderate severity, 53 percent responded favorably to psychotherapy, but only 33 percent to hospital care alone. William Menninger estimated that with prompt treatment, 60 percent of combat casualties were returned to fight or serve in the forward area and an additional 30 percent were salvaged for non-combat duty.[57]

It is difficult to judge how widely the various methods were used— Grinker and Spiegel's narcosynthesis, Kaufman's hypnotic abreaction, Hanson's rest and exhortation, simple rest, food, and sedation. Treatment methods varied from command to command and area to area. Brill and Beebe indicated on the basis of admittedly scanty evidence that 6 percent of a representative sample of patients from all the services had "one or more interviews under sedation." Another 20 percent received some kind of individual treatment, usually psychotherapy.[58]

They concluded that, overall, there was little difference in the long run in the outcome of treatment, if patients were matched for type of stress, preservice personality, and severity of breakdown. This retrospective study was concluded a decade after the war partly on the basis of a follow-up study of a representative sample of servicemen. Although the results of psychotherapy were relatively modest, it nevertheless acquired the patina of overwhelming success, particularly in the popular press.

A number of psychiatrists came to feel, on the basis of their wartime experience, that psychoanalysis possessed superior explanatory power. Norman Brill, a psychiatrist who worked with William Menninger, believed that the psychoanalysts had more fundamental, thorough-going, and subtle explanations for the clinical phenomena of war than did, for example, the Meyerians, although the latter were quite sophisticated. Judd Marmor, who already had completed his psychoanalytic training, recalled that narcosynthesis provided dramatic confirmation of the existence of the unconscious. "You didn't have to go into profound theory to demonstrate such things as symptom substitution or repression. No one else had explanations for these things except the analysts, and they could mobilize them for treatment."[59]

Several examples may illustrate this psychoanalytic thrust. In World War I, for instance, war neuroses were sometimes explained as the result of a conflict between the instinct of self-preservation and the soldiers' conscience and sense of duty. But this could hardly explain a clinical phenomenon frequent among combat neurotics: survivor guilt and guilt about aggression. If the motive were self-preservation, what explained this sense of guilt? Ambivalence provided a logical answer. The coexistence of hostile as well as affectionate feelings toward the same person could explain the guilt felt by men who had survived the death of a comrade in battle. Such a patient unconsciously had experienced hostility toward his dead friend, and could scarcely acknowledge his relief that it was his friend, not he, who had died.

The theory that one's own unleashed aggression could create acute anxiety by arousing a guilty fear of punishment provided a logical explanation for other kinds of puzzling behavior. For example, an overtly belligerent soldier who had demonstrated little anxiety during combat frequently had spells of rage during which he acted violently—once he had killed prisoners trying to escape. He enjoyed killing Germans, and a few days before his breakdown, he had stabbed two in close combat. Then during an artillery barrage he became incapacitated by anxiety: his stomach felt like jelly; he began to sleep poorly and to have recurrent nightmares and thought continually of the Germans he had killed. At the same time he was not aware of feeling depressed or guilty. The psychiatrist argued that he had been overcome by "fear of punishment for his own acts of aggression."[60] The war neuroses also seemed to confirm once more the importance psychoanalysis attributed to dreams and the recovery of traumatic memories and to the "underlying" or "unconscious" conflicts that apparently provided the basis for symptoms.

Finally, the psychoanalytic emphasis on anxiety as the central phenomenon, caused either by external or internal stimuli, seemed to give a coherent account of the war neuroses. Rival explanations were seldom cited, and were not as well developed and elaborated.[61]

An example of the increasing influence and prestige of psychoanalysis was its growing impact on the former president of the American Psychiatric Association, Edward A. Strecker, professor at the University of Pennsylvania, which for many years had been a bastion of conservative eclectic views. He was senior author of *Practical Clinical Psychiatry,* perhaps the leading textbook from the 1920s well into the postwar period. Despite his insistence that further study of treatment methods was essential, in a postwar symposium on the war neuroses he cited psychoanalytic theories and authorities sometimes explicitly, sometimes without identifying them. He praised William Menninger's foresight, skill, and efficiency in supervising services for the mental health of seven million men.[62] He included Grinker and Spiegel's findings on the need to recall battle experience, the importance of ambivalence, and deeply buried conflicts over aggressive and sadistic impulses. He seemed, without mentioning Franz Alexander, to accept his theory that psychosomatic gastric symptoms were "an expression of the repressed helplessness-dependency needs (passive-love)." Psychosomatic symptoms were "functional disturbances" energized by repressed, unacceptable emotions and impulses and were thus an "elaboration . . . of the mechanism of conversion." He concluded that the "frontal, Adlerian, moral approach" of the British psychiatrist William Gillespie ran counter to the "nonintellectual methods of therapy which emphasize the importance of abreaction and analysis, which are so much in vogue today."[63]

Strecker concluded that a major contribution of psychoanalysis had been its attack on a psychiatry that failed to take into account the patient's subjective feelings. Before psychoanalysis, the patient had listened while the neuropsychiatrist talked. But psychoanalysis had loosened the patient's tongue and encouraged him to express his emotions. Even more important, psychoanalysis had accomplished the absolutely necessary task of illuminating "the dark and hidden places of sex." All psychiatrists used some psychoanalytic contributions in their daily work. Nevertheless, psychoanalysts were dogmatic and tended to over-generalize and to pile up unproven hypotheses. Their rigid reliance on a system seemed to Strecker a "surrogate for earlier emotional authorities." And their opponents could well base their arguments on "honest intellectual agnosticism" rather than, as the analysts insisted in their customary tactic, on "unresolved resistances."[64]

Despite such objections, the absorption of psychoanalysis by psychiatrists during the war had been remarkable. A reviewer in the *Nation* exaggerated only slightly when he noted that the surprising thing about psychiatrists in World War II was their "ready acceptance" of Freudian dynamic psychiatry.[65]

The favorable reception of psychoanalysis was part of a major reorientation of psychiatry the war had fostered. The war had demonstrated the importance of environmental stress over predisposition as well as the apparent effectiveness of prompt treatment outside the hospital in the context of the soldier's unit and his immediate experience of battle. The fact that early treatment could prevent more serious psychiatric illness from developing seemed convincing evidence for the dynamic theory of a continuity from the neuroses to the psychoses. And the emphasis on environmental pressures suggested that psychiatry might identify those stresses in civilian social life that were conducive to nervous and mental disorder.[66] Thus wartime experience placed a new importance on the environment, on preventive treatment in a community setting, on psychotherapy. These developments became united with two important additional elements, first the messianic and optimistic mental hygiene message of the educational and child guidance reformers of the 1920s and 1930s with their own emphasis on early prevention; second, the liberal-to-left idealism of the psychoanalytic movement, reinforced by European recruits from its broadly social democratic and socialist base. The psychoanalysts, of all the psychiatric groups, tended to be far more "liberal" in social attitudes than the nation's psychiatrists, if somewhat less radical than clinical psychologists and psychiatric social workers.[67] This general outlook inspired the psychoanalytic psychiatrists in their crusades for psychiatric reform.

The psychoanalysts played an important role in the postwar expansion of psychiatry, and many of them were drawn from the "mental hygiene" wing of the specialty. William Menninger was an indefatigable evangelist for psychiatry, often arguing for its utility on the basis of wartime successes. Attacking what he perceived as widespread pessimism about recovery from mental illness, he insisted that seven out of ten psychotic patients in the military were sufficiently recovered to return to their homes rather than be sent to a veterans' hospital. These results occurred not only because of the favorable age of military patients and the fact that their cases often were treated far earlier than they would have been in civilian life. These favorable outcomes also were the product of uniquely intensive treatment efforts—group psychotherapy, psychotherapy under sedation, and elaborately organized activities.[68]

After the war, veterans with neuropsychiatric discharges and rejected 4-Fs had difficulties finding employment. Others attributed to veterans what seemed to be a wave of postwar crime among males aged 18 to 24. Albert Deutsch, a columnist for PM, who had written the influential study *The Mentally Ill in America,* noted that the courts were receiving cases of untreated veterans who had gotten into trouble with the law. A few spectacular crimes by men with neuropsychiatric discharges made the matter seem more alarming still. The psychoanalyst Felix Deutsch, director of the Boston Psychiatry Clinic, suggested that "psychiatric veteranology" constituted a whole new field of social psychiatry.[69]

Menninger and other advocates believed that psychiatry, on the basis of its success in treating neuroses and psychoses in the military, should meet the problems of returning veterans and what was perceived as a staggering public need for mental health services. If the healthy young male population had so high an incidence of neuropsychiatric problems, how much greater must be the incidence among the general population who had not been so carefully selected? The needs of servicemen were but the tip of the iceberg.[70] Patients with mental illness would continue to fill one in ten of the nation's hospital beds; "mental and emotional illness" caused "health problems of vast and serious proportions with disabling and crippling results that are no less tragic because they cannot be measured by calipers and stethoscopes."[71] Thomas Parran, the nation's director of public health services, estimated that perhaps 6 percent of all civilians, that is, about eight million Americans, would require hospitalization for psychiatric reasons during their lifetime.[72] The nationally famous Mayo clinic internist Walter Alvarez urged all physicians to learn something about psychotherapy and psychosomatic medicine because "about one person in 13 in this country is insane or in need of psychiatric help and one in 19 will eventually be committed to a state asylum."[73]

At the same time investigations by Albert Deutsch and others drew attention to appalling conditions in public mental hospitals, many of which were no better than "snake pits." The often diminished budgets of the long depression and war years, deferred maintenance, and the growing influx of patients had created spectacular overcrowding and occasional abuse. The crusade for better conditions was taken up by magazines, newspapers, and the movies.

With adequate outpatient treatment, psychiatrists argued, they could prevent hospitalization on a mass scale, thus saving millions of dollars and helping thousands of Americans to lead productive lives. However, more comprehensive and better psychiatric services, including psychotherapy, required the training of more personnel. "We need literally additional thousands of psychiatrists, psychologists, psychiatric social workers, psychiatric nurses . . . to prevent the flood of mental illness from rising year in and year out," the chief of training and standards for the National Institute of Mental Health warned in 1948.[74] Sometimes psychiatrists used scare tactics to drive home the need for more psychiatrists. Lawrence Kubie, for instance, argued that if two or three thousand new psychiatrists were not trained, at a cost of $100 million, the public would pay well over $6 billion because neurotic veterans inadequately treated would become lifelong hospital patients. The only way to break what he termed the "rehabilitation bottleneck" was to train the medical doctors just being discharged from the armed services. If psychiatrists saved only 1.5 percent of the hospitalized neurotic veterans, they would save the public more than the entire cost of training the required number of psychiatrists.[75]

A small group of psychiatrists, crusading laymen, and federal officials exerted pressure that culminated in the Mental Health Act of 1946, which set up the National Institute of Mental Health. Its goals were to conduct research in neuropsychiatric disorders, fund the training of psychiatric personnel, and make grants to the states for clinics and treatment centers. As Gerald Grob has written, NIMH under its director Robert Felix promoted "a social model of mental diseases and an emphasis on community rather than institutional treatment."[76] It had an initial budget of $18 million, a sum that grew to $315 million by 1967. NIMH would play an important role in financing training in both psychiatry and psychoanalysis.

The prestige of psychoanalysis and of psychiatry never had been higher, and the war gave psychiatry a new psychodynamic direction. The sudden wartime needs of the larger society could be met partly because of developments within psychoanalysis. The psychoanalytic institutes created a professional infrastructure within American psychiatry and medicine that nurtured a group of zealous, talented native American physicians, many of them from well-to-do families and prestigious medical schools.

Between the wars, psychoanalysts had created a body of theory, derived in part from experience in World War I, that asigned a new role to aggression and anxiety, to guilt and the coping mechanisms of the personality. Psychoanalysts also developed much of the psychosomatic medicine that explained the appearance of physical symptoms on the basis of interrelated somatic and psychological causes. Psychosomatic complaints were ubiquitous in the military, and psychosomatic medicine took on far greater importance as the result of wartime experience. Psychosomatic medicine overtook psychoanalysis as a topic in medical publications by about 1947 and this trend continued until about 1965.[77]

Thus, the psychoanalysts filled a sudden and unforeseen vacuum in psychiatric leadership. The war gave psychiatry an aura of success and scientific status, which also accrued to psychoanalysis as these specialties became more closely identified. The medical rhetoric of the psychiatrists and psychoanalysts as well as the rhetoric of journalistic popularizers reinforced this appearance of scientific consecration.

The war trained large numbers of physicians in psychoanalytically based theory in official manuals, films, and courses—often without identifying the material as derived from psychoanalysis. William Menninger's new nomenclature for the Army and his psychiatric bulletin for Army physicians were signal examples. Thus a particular psychiatric point of view was inculcated in an authoritative, military setting in personnel who very likely had not built up strong alternative views. The attitudes of some psychoanalysts changed as a result of wartime experience. Lawrence Kubie became more alert to situational and environmental factors. William Menninger deplored the tendency for psychoanalysts to concentrate on a very few patients and realized, as had Freud, the need for mass treatment. The war and its aftermath made glaringly apparent the need for a shortened therapy of wide application.

How would the psychoanalytic profession respond to these needs? Would it accommodate the young medical officers seeking training? How would it relate to the other professions, such as psychology and social work, which also had been treating patients during the war? Could it contain and integrate the divergent tendencies in psychoanalytic theory—the social and cultural emphasis of Horney and Fromm, the new ego psychology of Anna Freud and Heinz Hartmann, and the attempts to make psychoanalytic theory more systematic? Would it become a highly divergent group of practitioners held together by a single professional organization or would it fission into several? These issues, which already had surfaced, required resolution.

12

The Subculture
of the Psychoanalysts

In 1947 psychoanalysts across the nation began to experience what one of them described as "something of a gold rush" for psychoanalytic training. The demand for psychoanalysis seemed insatiable and the shortage of analysts had grown serious. In Los Angeles the psychoanalytic scene took on "the aspect of a three ring circus." Waiting lists were long, and it was difficult to explain to patients and referring physicians why they couldn't get an appointment.[1]

There were still only about 400 psychoanalysts to cope with a postwar demand that resulted from a growing acceptance of psychoanalysis in psychiatry and a dramatic surge of popularization, topics to be explored later. The structure of relationships among the psychoanalysts and the issues they faced would determine the subsequent professional history of American psychoanalysis.

The general postwar prosperity and the seemingly unlimited demand for therapy eased the economic competition that had exacerbated the conflicts of the 1930s and early 1940s. The occasional distrust between immigrants and Americans was muted by the common war effort and the postwar expansion. Nevertheless, under the new postwar pressures old conflicts reemerged and new ones developed, although all of them were less intense than in the prewar years. Preserving a psychoanalytic identity in the face of growing popularity became a major concern, and so did older issues of orthodoxy, control over training, and medical monopoly. There was renewed friction between those who wished psychoanalysis to remain a separate and exclusive discipline and those who wished to foster its assimilation by medical schools and universities; between those who wanted more stringent standards of training and those who wanted less; between the newly hardened orthodoxy of the American Psychoanalytic Association and smaller independent training organizations, such as those set up by Karen Horney or Clara Thompson in New York.

All these issues crystallized in debates over the structure of psychoanalytic organizations, which had remained unresolved during the war. The decisions made between 1946 and 1957 by the American Psychoanalytic Association held momentous consequences for psychoanalysis, many of them unintended, some of them damaging in retrospect.

A proposal for drastic change in membership policies came from William Menninger when he became president of the American Psychoanalytic Association in 1946. Wishing to preserve it as an elite organization but also to expand membership, he proposed to enlist the rapidly growing number of interested physicians and social scientists. Physicians who had not been analyzed were to be admitted to non-voting affiliate membership, while psychologists and other scientists could join in a research capacity. Menninger argued that many psychiatrists already were applying psychoanalytic principles, although they made no pretense of treating patients with "orthodox psychoanalytic therapy." They were interested in the development of the field and were carrying out some of its most effective research. Moreover, many social scientists used psychoanalytic conceptions in their work and enough clinical psychologists already had been psychoanalytically trained to set up a section on psychoanalysis in the American Psychological Association.[2]

The proposal was part of Menninger's program to meet the burgeoning demand for mental health services. As an avid assimilationist, his greatest hope for satisfying current needs lay not with the "psychoanalyst per se" but with the "psychoanalytically oriented psychiatrist." Menninger argued that wartime experience had demonstrated that all psychiatrists needed a "dynamic orientation that can be provided only through indoctrination by those familiar with psychoanalytic theory and practice." To this end, psychoanalytic institutes should strive for "eventual integration" with medical centers.

He protested against using some of "our best analytic teaching power" for the "intensive training analyses of a handful of candidates, when those same brains could give a helpful working dynamic orientation to ten times the number of men."[3] His proposals, despite the fund of good will he commanded, were defeated, largely because of fears about "dilution" of the psychoanalytic enterprise.[4] One result was to exclude from the American Psychoanalytic Association competent social scientists familiar with research design and technique, with a few exceptions later.

Menninger's ecumenical vision was opposed by those who identified elite professionalism with science and orthodox Freudian theory and therapy, a combination that had become influential in the late 1930s and early 1940s. They felt that only the most highly qualified psychoanalysts with their unquestioned mastery of the psychoanalytic technique could contribute to psychoanalysis as a basic science.

One of Menninger's most vehement opponents was Ives Hendrick of the Boston Psychoanalytic Society, who argued that psychoanalysis already was threatened by scientific stagnation because of its rapid growth in membership.[5] Menninger's friend Bertram Lewin also was opposed on grounds that too much was still unknown in psychoanalysis for it to be applied indiscriminately. He had no patience with those who believed that Freud had "taught us everything, no use to reexamine all those 'truths,' just apply them. No need for chemistry, just improve the hypo needles for injecting the dope. . . . the tacit assumption that we know enough about the neuroses, that psychoanalysis stopped as a research approximately when Anna Freud's book on the defenses was published, is something I can't accept."[6]

Menninger also had proposed a committee to deal with integrating new psychoanalytic concepts. "It is no secret that there are important disagreements among us," he wrote. The committee could "reexamine older concepts, scrutinize new concepts objectively and thus clarify teaching and communication." Probably he hoped that this would prevent the kinds of disputes that had occurred in 1941 and 1942 over Karen Horney's resignation from the New York Psychoanalytic Society and Sandor Rado's proposal for a new institute at Columbia University.

Such a committee would exaggerate psychoanalytic dogmatism by attempting to legislate theories, Hendrick objected. And Menninger's former colleague from Topeka, Robert Knight, wrote that it smacked of "setting up dogmas and denouncing heresies. It could only result in making rigid a body of theory and a technical method which should by all means remain flexible."[7]

This proposal also was defeated, although increasingly stringent training and membership requirements passed. These represented a fusion of the desire of some of the Europeans to ensure orthodoxy and the medical and professionalizing thrust of their American pupils.[8] The new requirements were enforced by those psychoanalysts who had begun to assume leadership in the late 1930s, men such as Lawrence Kubie, Karl Menninger, and Ives Hendrick.

These leaders were surprised, gratified, and at the same time apprehensive to find that what was once an aggressive young movement within psychiatry was fast becoming a major subspecialty. The Americans often had made considerable personal sacrifices for their training in a period when psychoanalysis was still suspect, and they were determined to maintain what they believed were the highest standards of analytic competence and professional respectability.

High standards, it was argued, were particularly necessary in a period when demand for psychiatric services was so great that even a mediocre practitioner could make a comfortable living.[9] The flood of applicants for training included some who were brilliant, some mediocre, and some with personal difficulties. And now psychoanalysts were often representing their discipline before medical specialists and social scientists; only those who were truly well trained could be competent at these new ambassadorial tasks.[10]

The ideal of most members of the American Psychoanalytic Association, never so explicitly stated, seems to have been the creation and guarding of an elite profession, which because of its special knowledge and meticulous training would transform American psychiatry. The psychoanalysts would provide leaders for the medical schools, revivify the mental hospitals, and supervise the subordinate, ancillary personnel such as psychologists and social workers.

Because of its stringent requirements and the stature of its leaders, such as William Menninger, the American Psychoanalytic Association gained far greater prestige and influence than its small numbers would suggest. It remained small, although its growth was rapid. By 1951 there were 500 members and 700 students in its authorized psychoanalytic training programs. Four years later there were more than 600 members, with 925 students being trained in fourteen institutes and three training centers.[11]

The issue of whether or not laymen should be trained to practice became acute because of the apparently unlimited postwar demand for treatment. As early as 1932 Stanley Cobb had warned Lawrence Kubie that if psychoanalytic organizations failed to train lay therapists, they would be swamped and lose their leadership.[12]

However, prominent American-born analysts frankly wished to preserve the requirement of medical training because they believed it conferred unquestioned superiority on the American movement. In 1944 Leo Bartemeier, the president of the American Psychoanalytic Association and one of the few Catholic psychoanalysts, argued that psychoanalysis in America was more "wholesome" and "extensive" than in Europe precisely because American psychiatrists had diminished its isolation and exclusiveness and had established it as a "medical discipline." Psychoanalysis could no more be detached from psychiatry than histology or pathology from medicine, and the relationship between psychiatry and psychoanalysis was rather like that between the physician and the surgeon, that is, a specialty within a discipline.[13] Ives Hendrick, who was president of the American Psychoanalytic Association from 1953 to 1955, suggested that American psychoanalysis was in fact superior because a medical background conferred on American analysts, as it had on Freud, a better understanding of patients, particularly of the emotional components of medical problems.[14]

In pursuit of this alliance with medicine, psychoanalysts stressed the medically appealing "biological" nature of psychoanalysis which posited "instinctual forces of bodily origin" as the prime movers of the "mental apparatus" and a "genetic," that is, developmental, outlook. Such medical rhetoric was characteristic of the Americans as it had been of Freud. American analysts argued that only physicians could properly diagnose which symptoms were the result of emotional factors and which were organic. David Levy, a prominent New York psychoanalyst and child psychiatrist, had argued that the analysis of children as well as adults should be restricted to physicians, and even physicians could make mistakes. In 1938, when the issue of refugee lay analysts was debated, he had written to Franz Alexander, "just recently a child was sent to me, diagnosed by a physician, a pediatrist of high standing, as having hysterical seizures. It turned out to be Jacksonian epilepsy." Such critical dignostic distinctions were "completely outside the realm of the lay analyst."[15]

By the mid-1950s the proliferation of a variety of lay psychotherapists provoked opposition among medical psychoanalysts. The Veterans Administration and the National Institute for Mental Health had funded training programs in clinical psychology, and by 1960 there were 18,215 members of the American Psychological Association, many of them in clinical practice.[16] Psychologists and social workers were offering psychotherapy in increasing numbers, probably at lower fees, and in several states bills were introduced to license them as psychotherapists. This rapid growth of lay psychotherapists provoked a strong reassertion of medical guildism.

In 1954, the American Medical Association, the American Psychiatric Association, and the American Psychoanalytic Association issued a joint declaration against lay practitioners. The application of psychological methods to the treatment of illness was a medical function and should take place under medical supervision. Only physicians were qualified to distinguish between physical and mental illness and to prescribe a course of treatment. So strong was the position of the American Psychoanalytic Association that Max Gitelson, who was president in 1956, wrote to Hendrick that he was "committed to the ultimate liquidation of lay therapy in the United States," although he insisted there were transitional situations in which laymen made important contributions to training.[17] At the time "liquidation" was a formal possibility at least for the American Psychoanalytic Association because there were only six laymen out of the 590 members.

In 1955 Ives Hendrick stated the argument against lay analysts and inadequate training standards with indignant finality. He had lived through the days when critics "sometimes thought of us as crackpots, or emotional converts, or merely victims of perverted imagination." The psychoanalytic emphasis on medicine and on high training standards had resulted from a proliferation of "wild" analysts, both medical and lay, "fomented" by the "deviationists" Jung, Adler, and Rank in the 1920s. Then Hendrick outlined meticulously the growth of committees and sub-committees and on-site visits to institutes to enforce the minimal training standards and, thus, the membership requirements of the American Psychoanalytic Association. To violate these standards, especially by "unauthorized bootleg training" of either physicians or laymen, was to violate professional trust and organizational commitment. The association had voted overwhelmingly time and again to restrict training to physicians and psychiatrists, and only a vociferous minority had opposed these standards with "tantrum like" protests.

In the short space of 25 years, the American Psychoanalytic Association had grown from 65 members when Hendrick had joined in 1930 to more than 600 in 1955. Nearly 6000 patients were being psychoanalyzed by members of the association, most of whom were also applying "our science" to psychotherapy, mental hospital care, patients in general hospitals and child psychiatry clinics, the training of medical students, psychiatrists, and students in social case work and a dozen other ancillary professions. Psychoanalysis had become a "basic science of Psychiatry." "What specialty in medicine has a higher responsibility?"

That responsibility rested on the fact that "our profession derives from technical methods with which only analysts are equipped" and which were secured by standards that the American Psychoanalytic Association was pledged to enforce.[18] This was a lofty linkage of technical and membership requirements.

The very expansion Hendrick praised and the debates over psychologists in 1954–56 reopened the issue of assimilation versus exclusivity. "Classicists" such as Max Gitelson, Hendrick, and Lewin stressed Freud's view that psychoanalysis was a separate, independent science, primarily a research method based on clinical treatment. The "assimilationists" wanted psychoanalysis to play a broad role in mental health, medicine, and psychiatry.[19]

Gitelson, an influential "classicist," came to America from Russia with his parents in 1907 at the age of five. He had worked his way through forestry school and Syracuse University Medical School, supporting himself as an extern in a local hospital and as manager of a fraternity dining room. His interest in psychoanalysis had been aroused during an internship at the New York Psychiatric Institute when he took an introductory course at the New York Psychoanalytic institute. In 1933 he moved to Chicago where he became chief of staff of the Institute for Juvenile Research and head of the outpatient clinic of the Michael Reese Hospital, where he gained extensive experience treating children and adolescents. During his analytic training at the Chicago institute, he was one of those on whom Alexander experimented with shortened hours, canceled appointments, and other manipulations of the transference, which Gitelson believed were harmful. At a public presentation, he had challenged Alexander's report of therapeutic success with an ulcer patient.[20]

Gitelson argued that psychoanalysis could not be a therapy for the masses because it was concerned primarily with investigating the "function and operation of the individual psyche." It was an instrument of research on the frontiers of "knowledge of the mind, just as mathematical physics resides on the frontier of experimental physics and applied physics."

Not all members of the American Psychoanalytic Association agreed with Gitelson in rejecting the concept of lay therapists. As early as 1948 Lawrence Kubie had proposed an entirely new doctorate in medical psychology that would prepare laymen for the practice of psychotherapy.[21] Gitelson was challenged on the issue of lay analysis by Spurgeon English, a Canadian by birth, who had co-authored an important early text on psychosomatic medicine and, like Gitelson, had been interested in child psychiatry.[22] English argued that the demand for mental health services was too great to limit psychoanalytic training to physicians and psychiatrists. Psychotherapy had become a lucrative field and people were likely to seek treatment from quacks. Another analyst, G. Henry Katz, argued that the requirement of medical training particularly hampered child psychoanalysis. Women were unusually suited for it, Katz insisted, but there were few women physicians, and many women without medical degrees already had entered the field. High standards should be based on training and competence, not on attempts to corner the market by a medical monopoly.[23]

By 1964 Gitelson's position had changed, and he proposed that lay scientists be trained for full-time research careers in psychoanalysis to remedy what he perceived as a serious crisis of identity in American psychoanalysis. Psychiatrists who had become psychoanalysts, in their therapeutic zeal, as Freud had predicted, were diluting psychoanalysis, exchanging it for intensive psychotherapy and "psychodynamics." He doubted the ability of physician analysts to make theoretical contributions; moreover, psychoanalysis was becoming stodgy and was losing the kind of ferment that laymen often had brought to it.[24]

Anna Freud wrote to Gitelson in 1964, praising his altered position. "What you say . . . is so identical with my father's attitude to psychoanalysis, his fears for its fate in America, his warnings about the restrictions to therapy as the main issue and his ultimate hope for a different outcome that it is quite striking. This is exactly as I heard it expressed by him."[25]

To seal the standards of psychoanalysis as a new elite profession, Hendrick had argued that it was urgent to obtain formal recognition "by some senior medical authority," perhaps an agency of the American Medical Association.[26] The attempt to seek certification by official medicine failed largely because of the internal divisions within psychoanalysis.

Training and education remained the major bones of contention among psychoanalytic groups; whoever controlled training controlled entry into the profession. And training was inextricably linked with an ideology and subculture apparently unable to tolerate or resolve fundamental disputes without creating separate organizations. The splits in 1941 and 1942 had involved strong personalities, harsh passions, and, sometimes, moderation and compromise. These clashes of opinion could be likened to the disputes of religious sects, to the dismay or amusement of some analysts and the delight of their opponents. Later disputes were handled more amicably, but lines drawn between the orthodox and the less traditional led to additional splits in Los Angeles, Boston, Philadelphia, and Washington-Baltimore.

In 1945, the issue of the Columbia institute still was unresolved. Robert Knight wrote from Topeka to Bertram Lewin, the president of the Association, urging acceptance of the new institute:

> We are in the position of viewing with horror the founding of a new institute and a new scientific society in a city just because one Holy Society is already

there. . . . We are laughed at by the profession because of our intramural squabbles and split-offs and our prestige is not enhanced thereby.

The American Psychoanalytic Association's rigid setup enlisted no sympathy from psychiatrists or other physicians. "This might sound like heresy to some of the Europeans who hold to the original tradition, but we have outgrown that tradition, I believe."

Knight argued that the American Psychoanalytic Association should take over "centralized control" of training. Its power and prestige would be greatly enhanced, and it "could embrace all approved psychoanalytic teaching. . . . now, . . . new non-official institutes gain status just because we are so rigid. They readily enlist sympathy from other psychiatrists and medical men, as well as from many within the Association. . . ."

Lewin replied with a New York flourish that he did not believe that in the big cities psychiatrists and the medical profession

> stand for public opinion and the norm as perhaps they do out there among the Harvey houses. Au contraire, in New York at least these look to the analysts for guidance, and except for overt opponents of psychoanalysis, are content to let us go our own way without interference, indeed without malice. . . .
>
> It has not escaped your attention surely that for some reason so far as the affairs of our societies are concerned, analysts consider themselves incomparable business men, financiers, constitutional lawyers, etc., though in practice they do not always produce the goods, and indeed often make a hell of a mess.[27]

As a result of astute negotiations between the Columbia group and Lewin and Karl Menninger, successive presidents of the American Psychoanalytic Association, the institute was authorized as a training center in 1946. But the controversy left hard feelings. At Columbia's tenth anniversary David Levy, who had withdrawn from the New York Psychoanalytic Institute, viewed the Columbia institute as born from a "protest against authoritarianism in science . . . against a pollution of the atmosphere of free inquiry with the smog of doctrine, of dogmatism and of personal vituperation." And the institute for some years remained suspect to the more orthodox members of the American Psychoanalytic Association.[28]

Earlier yet more splits had developed, this time among the neo-Freudians. In 1943, Erich Fromm and Clara Thompson left the Horney group and with Harry Stack Sullivan founded a New York branch of the William Alanson White Psychiatric Foundation of Washington, D.C. The ostensible cause had been Fromm's status as a lay training analyst, which it was thought would compromise relations with the New York Medical College which had sponsored courses by the group at its Flower Fifth Avenue Hospital. Then the group closest to the New York Medical College, headed by William Silverberg, broke with the Horney group to found their own institute for the psychoanalytic training of physicians at the medical school. In 1946 Clara Thompson renamed her institute the William Alanson White Institute of Psychiatry and applied for recognition by the American Psychoanalytic Association. This was denied, presumably because of an announced intention to train lay analysts.

The splits and schisms and the founding of new training centers had led to formal reorganization of the American Psychoanalytic Association in 1946. Members of the new association would first be members of local societies, but local membership would not automatically qualify them for membership in the Association.

That affiliation was tantamount to certification as a nationally recognized psychoanalyst, the equivalent of certification by the national boards in neurology and psychiatry. Membership was conferred on recommendation of a committee and it became a final hurdle after completing the process of psychoanalytic training in an authorized institute, which might have taken as long as ten years after college, medical school, and psychiatric residency.

If training at a given institute was thought to be inadequate, the graduate could be advised to secure yet more training, and thus additional control was exercised over the educational policies of local institutes. To tighten control over training still more, in 1953 the APA passed a code of ethics that threatened with suspension or expulsion any member who carried out unauthorized training. There were allegations that well-known European analysts were preparing laymen for child analysis because that sub-specialty was not really a part of medicine. Such analysts, fumed Ralph Kaufman, chairman of the APA's committee on unauthorized training, "reserve the narcissistic right to do whatever they want regardless of rules, regulations or fair play."[29] Moreover, some members of the APA, such as Clara Thompson, were training in "unauthorized" institutes.

The activities of the association in ferreting out "unauthorized training" struck Robert Waelder, a senior European lay analyst in Philadelphia, as a "sort of vigilantism." Gitelson wrote to Kaufman: "There is a strong feeling developing that we have structuralized our training too rigidly out of the entirely laudable desire to avoid the cluttering up of the field in therapeutic psychoanalysis by unqualified people. . . ."[30] Anna Freud, worried about her American students, confidentially expressed her puzzlement over the policies of the APA concerning lay analysis to her close friend, Greta Bibring. "I can understand that, in the past, the American analysts had a desperate wish to be "recognized" by psychiatry; it was probably a question of professional standing, career, hospital positions, etc. But today, when analysts have all the professional prestige they can possibly want and are needed and sought after by psychiatry? It just makes no sense." Although she did not wish to become involved in the APA's politics, she suggested that the Bibrings might unite with others against the medical requirements identified with Hendrick and Kaufman.[31]

In 1955 Thompson and Silverberg, whose institutes remained "unauthorized" and who were threatened with possible expulsion from the APA, employed the Washington attorney Abe Fortas, who later served on the Supreme Court, to sue the American Psychoanalytic Association for restraint of trade. Fortas argued that the association was acting against the legitimate interests of the William Alanson White Institute and the New York Medical College and had no power to divide institutes into those authorized or unauthorized for training. The APA replied that it was not violating any antitrust laws by simply specifying requirements for membership.[32] Ives Hendrick, typically uncompromising, argued that the only possible policy was to avoid any "bending over backwards or any show of weakness to Mr. Fortas." Moreover, Fortas felt it his mission to "slay the gigantic ogre, the American Psychoanalytic Association," because of his ties with Harry Stack Sullivan and the William Alanson White Foundation.[33]

The analyst Robert Morse tried to persuade Hendrick that no matter who won the suit, the publicity would do "inestimable damage to the whole field of psychoanalysis." Fortas, he thought, would be clever enough to review in elaborate detail the history of "all the strife and turmoil" and what could be made to appear as the "many paradoxes, inconsistencies and reversals in attitude" within the association during past years concerning the "training of lay therapists, and unauthorized training generally."[34] An out-of-court compromise was reached and the APA did not expel Silverberg or Thompson.[35]

But the suit embittered relations and united the dissenters: the less orthodox members of the American Psychoanalytic Association, such as Abram Kardiner, John Millet, Sandor Rado, and others of the Columbia institute; Jules Masserman, Franz Alexander, and Roy Grinker from Chicago; the William Alanson White and New York Medical College groups; as well as Horney's Association for the Advancement of Psychoanalysis.

The result was the founding of the American Academy of Psychoanalysis in 1956. Full membership would be restricted to physicians, but other scientists also could join—and the new organization eschewed any control over institutes and training, the major bones of contention.[36] In 1943, Franz Alexander had argued for the autonomy of teaching institutes on grounds of academic freedom and unfettered scientific inquiry. "What we need is not conformity, but free development of divergent points of view and emphases. We must avoid suppressive attempts to standardize our new field by enforcing conformity of opinion."[37] Founders of the academy believed they were upholding liberal, scientific values against what they perceived as a narrow orthodoxy. But they did not believe they were establishing a rival to the American Psychoanalytic Association. The academy was to be a purely scientific, broadly interdisciplinary forum.[38]

One major result of the splits and the founding of the American Academy of Psychoanalysis was the failure of the attempt by Hendrick and others to establish formal certification. The academy protested that the American Psychoanalytic Association could not be regarded as the exclusive arbiter of theory or training.[39] The APA then voted against certification because the certifying board would be under control of the American Psychiatric Association. As a result the board might be unwilling to preserve "our own rigorous standards" and might become subject to "antithetical influences."[40]

By 1957, after acrimonious arguments, the American Psychoanalytic

Association had set a minimum of 300 hours with four analytic sessions a week for the training analysis, and 150 hours of supervised analysis of patients, two of which had to be carried to a successful conclusion.[41] In fact, between 1946 and 1957 the average training analysis lasted 609 hours, or about three years at four hours a week plus supervision.

In the face of the new expanding demand for psychoanalysis, the American Psychoanalytic Association thus enforced its increasingly rigorous membership policies. Enforcement was placed in the hands of a Board on Professional Standards and its approval was required for the establishment of new institutes.

The new requirements were intended to guard against what many psychoanalysts, especially the Europeans, perceived as unprecedented threats of dilution. They feared the abandonment of the psychoanalytic technique which they regarded as their fundamental mode of scientific research and discovery. Exclusivity also guarded doctrinal purity and the unquestioned truth of Freud's theories and ensured an absence of fundamentally dissenting voices. It also strengthened claims to superior prestige, a prestige particularly dear to those who had smarted under the ridicule and fun poked at psychoanalysts in the years when their professional status still was shaky and when practitioners on its fringe sometimes had been less than respectable. Restricting membership increased control over all these troublesome issues. And restriction also may have helped to guarantee greater financial rewards. Those who believed in the mission of psychoanalysis hoped to ensure that it would never become what Freud predicted as its American fate, the lowly status of a mere handmaiden of psychiatry.

The American Psychoanalytic Association's exclusive policies had a number of consequences, not all of them intended. It created advantages—and serious disaffection. It effectively restricted the supply of psychoanalysts. In a relatively brief time, it also had led to a new national organization totally divorced from training, at first largely made up of the less orthodox psychoanalysts and the "unauthorized" institutes.

The medical and psychiatric requirements determined the gender of American psychoanalysts. In Europe, a larger proportion of women, medical and lay, had joined the movement, and it had provided them with a new, if marginal, profession. More European than American women entered medicine, and there were a number of prominent refugee women analysts who were physicians: Helene Deutsch, Karen Horney, Therese Benedek, Grete Bibring. In 1958, women made up only 9 percent of the analytic students in training in America but 18 percent of the members of the American Psychoanalytic Association and 27 percent of its training analysts. The lower figures for those in training and the higher figure for members and training analysts reflected the fact that the number of American women entering medicine and psychiatry actually declined in the postwar period from a high in the 1920s.[42] These figures also reflected the larger proportion of women among the European refugee analysts. The contribution of women to American psychoanalysis was rich and diverse—from the psychology of women, children, and infants to psychosomatic medicine, theory and training, and the treatment of the psychoses. Some thought that a woman's nurturing, maternal characteristics peculiarly fitted her to be a psychotherapist.

In time, the new rules that required increasingly lengthy periods for compliance ensured that psychoanalytic organizations would be made up to a considerable extent of the middle-aged and the aging. Centralization and order, as well as the highly historical perspective of psychoanalysis with its constant harking back to Freud, the founding father, ensured a remarkable organizational conservatism. Proposals for change—for instance, for more rigorous research or for a wider membership—took decades to implement. Although psychoanalytic practice increasingly involved psychotherapy, which some analysts regarded as a more difficult art than psychoanalysis proper, many institutes for years failed to teach it on grounds that the ultimate and only model of therapy was classical psychoanalysis itself. Prodigious energy was channeled into issues of controlling training, maintaining the medical status of the profession, and ensuring orthodoxy. The new and tighter organization created among those who successfully passed the hurdles a cohesive loyalty and identification, based on a very real personal sacrifice of time, money, and effort.

By the mid-1950s many psychiatrists felt that without psychoanalytic training they would be "second-class" specialists. Between 1948 and 1951 the resources of existing institutes were strained as they received more than 4,096 applications for training from young psychiatrists. One major issue was how to pay for psychoanalytic training; the standard requirements had made it a costly apprenticeship.

Public funding was a major resource. The GI bill for the education of veterans and the National Institute of Mental Health (NIMH), some of whose staff members were psychoanalysts, paid for training in both psychiatry and psychoanalysis. Government funding probably increased the proportion of upwardly mobile analysts, which always had been considerable.

NIMH helped to organize the nation's largest single training center for psychiatrists, the psychoanalytically oriented program in Topeka, Kansas, run by the Menningers, which fed some of its most promising trainees to psychoanalytic institutes. Between 1948 and 1961 psychoanalytic institutes received $1,121,030, almost 0.1 percent of the NIMH budget for training. The Menninger Foundation alone received some $881,584. Two of the largest recipients of NIMH funding were Yale and UCLA, where psychoanalysts headed departments of psychiatry. Psychoanalysts often taught in medical schools and schools of social work and nursing, which together received 79 percent of the NIMH training budget.

The American psychoanalytic institutes aspired to impart the esoteric knowledge of theory and technique that made psychoanalysis unique and that undergirded its claims to be a profession. So zealous was one institute in this mission that it insisted on prolonged analyses and reanalyses for its trainees; it was "almost like a religious order."[43]

The institutes of the American Psychoanalytic Association were established on the professional model of the medical school; yet, unlike medical schools, the institutes for the most part were run by busy analysts in their spare time, and most remained night schools, with the major exceptions of Columbia, Chicago, and a few others.

Psychiatric residents provided the major pool of students for psycho-analytic training, and a revealing profile of them emerged from a study of the Menninger School of Psychiatry in 1958. About one-third of the psychiatric residents were Jewish, half were Protestant, and less than one-tenth Catholic, while the population at large was 20 percent Catholic and 3 percent Jewish. Born in large cities, they came from remarkably stable families—85 percent had parents who had never been divorced or separated. Most of their families were well-off. Only 2 percent came from families whose incomes had been $2000 or less during the mid-1930s, a time when 80 percent of the nation's families had incomes below that figure. The fathers of 59 percent held pro-fessional or managerial jobs, and 13 percent were physicians; only 12 percent were skilled or semiskilled workers. Some had become interested in psychia-try through literature and the social sciences; others, because of the inade-quacy of medical knowledge in dealing with patients suffering from neuroses or from disorders of psychological origin for which drugs did nothing; still others, from a desire for self-understanding and a realization of their own neurotic difficulties. The mental health of the residents was comparable to that of people starting out in medicine and other professions, and many were notable for a "high degree of healthy maturity." Some of the Menninger residents did not live up to their apparent promise; some were plodders with little or no talent. Those who showed outstanding psychiatric acumen and who were exceptionally brilliant, hard workers were the most likely to take up psychotherapy or psychoanalysis.[44]

As a group the analysts tended to be high academic achievers. Those selected for psychoanalytic training at the Topeka institute came from the top quarter of the Menninger program's psychiatric residents. Two surveys by William E. Henry from the early 1970s of 4000 psychotherapists and analysts confirmed the impression of academic distinction.[45] In a 1960 survey of some 888 students in psychoanalytic training, about 18 percent were from Ivy League schools (of these 50 were from Harvard) and about 11 percent from outstanding state universities—Illinois, Michigan, Wisconsin.[46] By the early 1970s far more psychoanalysts than psychiatrists had attended private colleges and Ivy League medical schools, suggesting the consolidation of an elite psychoanalytic profession.[47]

The analysts in the Henry survey were more upwardly mobile than the psychiatrists in the Menninger sample. Some 67 percent came from middle-class families or below, and Jewish psychoanalysts were more likely to be upwardly mobile than their non-Jewish colleagues.[48] About one-third of all the analysts were children of professionals—physicians, psychiatrists, minis-ters, managers, administrators, teachers; a surprising number of foreign-born analysts came from upper-class families, some 44 percent compared with 7.2 percent in the total sample of American analysts. The Protestant analysts tended to come from old native families. By the 1970s non-Jews outnumbered Jews, 48 percent to 42 percent.[49]

Of the 888 students in training in 1960 nearly half had decided to become analysts before medical school. One candidate had been inspired to become an analyst at age 13 by reading A. A. Brill's *Basic Writings of Sigmund Freud*. Popular books, such as Karl Menninger's *The Human Mind*, had intrigued other future analysts. Some 60 percent of this group had become interested while in the Armed Forces, where they had met psychoanalytic specialists whom they wished to emulate.[50] In their choice of a profession, about 25 percent of the psychoanalysts were influenced by psychiatrist relatives. Already interested in Freudian theory, intellectual development was an important reason why some chose psychoanalysis. A far more powerful motive than self-understanding was helping others; psychoanalytic training was sought in order to acquire an effective therapeutic technique.[51]

The American institutes may have been more restrictive in their policies than the Europeans had been. Of the 4,096 applications for psychoanalytic training between 1944 and 1957, some 43 percent were rejected, and in one institute rejections reached 66 percent.[52] Candidates were chosen after lengthy interviews, sometimes held by entire committees, and in some places after standardized psychological tests such as the Rorschach or the Thematic Apperception test. One of the pitfalls of the tests and sometimes of the interview process was that they overemphasized pathology and overlooked less obvious strengths, and thus lost desirable candidates.

What talents were institutes looking for and what did they regard as unsuitable? The last is more obvious than the first. A mild "analyzable" neurosis in an otherwise normal personality was considered acceptable, even useful in providing material for the training analysis. But homosexuals or psychopaths, the latter never clearly defined but presumably people who were dishonest or who consistently "acted out" unacceptable impulses, were rejected by the New York institute and presumably by other institutes as well. Neither homosexuals nor psychopaths, it was argued, would be sufficiently stable to endure the demands of psychoanalytic practice. Henry Abelove has argued that Freud defended the possibility of homosexual analysts who might be otherwise qualified, but that Freud was opposed particularly by the Berlin analysts. Smiley Blanton, however, remembered that during his analysis, Freud expressed disapproval of homosexual analysts.[53] Whatever Freud's precise views, American institutes followed the German policy.

Institutes also were wary of a "facade of normality" which might hide severe pathology, such as depression or schizophrenic reactions. The Boston institute rejected applicants for a cornucopia of tendencies: being rigid, compulsive, constricted, grandiose, borderline, impulsive, narcissistic, depressed, ambivalent, dogmatic, controlling, isolated, detached, and withdrawn. In retrospect, these restrictive policies may have been unduly successful: the first recruits after the war were seen by some as too ordinary and less creative than their predecessors.[54]

Some Europeans, among them Anna Freud and Rudolph Ekstein, believed that training in psychiatry and non-analytic types of psychotherapy made it harder to teach candidates the art of psychoanalysis. On the other hand some American analysts believed that too little training in psychiatry resulted in a lack of interest in even the simplest relevant facts of the patient's history, as if these were detrimental to "real analysis."[55]

The institutes placed special emphasis on personalities that would be suitable for plying the psychoanalytic technique. Because a candidate already had been selected for medical school and psychiatric residency, a certain degree of intelligence was presumed. He or she needed, above all, "psychological understanding," a capacity for introspection, an appreciation of his or her own motives, and the empathy that would lead to understanding his or her patients. Warmth and verbal skills were also needed to elicit the patient's understanding and to convey the therapist's. He or she had to be aware of the complexities of human nature and to be sensitive to the smallest clues of language and gesture. These qualities would be desirable in any psychiatrist.

But the requirements for the psychoanalyst were yet more demanding. For example, a brilliant, active, intuitive psychotherapist might be rejected for psychoanalytic training because he or she did not have the requisite *Sitzfleisch*.[56] Because an analyst's job was primarily one of listening and interpreting and because analytic treatment usually took years, he or she needed to be able to tolerate an extraordinary degree of passivity. The analyst would sit for 50-minute hours in an office with his or her patients, who each might be in treatment for as many as ten years or even more. Because results were often slow, the analyst needed to tolerate frustration. He or she also needed sympathetic detachment, assurance, and control in the face of the patient's inevitable anger and hostility or overvaluation and attachment. Such passivity has been seen as "feminine," and one study indicated that male psychiatric residents tended to identify with their mothers and have a stronger feminine component than men in general.

> Perhaps the core of analytic aptitude in the male resides in his psychologically accessible latent femininity and his correlated passivity. It is this component of his personality that contributes to his capacity to perceive his own unconscious and that of others. It permits him to wait and listen while the unconscious of the patient is striving to be born to consciousness. The aggressive masculine tendency to be "doing" must be subordinated to this passive capacity to listen and understand.[57]

However, too much passivity might create problems: latent or overt homosexuality, paranoid trends, or even a "hypermasculine protest" might interfere with sensitivity and empathy.

Fulfilling all these requirements would be a tall order for any given group of men and women, and the training analysis was considered the major instrument for preparing expertise in this delicate art. Lawrence Kubie observed that the life of the analyst imposed exceptional strains and that the

therapeutic goal of the training analysis is a degree of equanimity, a predominance of conscious purposes, a degree of freedom from unconscious conflict,
and hence a degree of emotional invulnerability which is far greater than that
"normality" with which ordinary men are content.

In addition to advancing this almost sacerdotal perfection, Kubie also advised
that the training analysis be used ruthlessly for screening out unacceptable
candidates. The Menninger study indicated that a training analysis improved
self-confidence, mood, clinical ability, maturity, control of emotions, and
warmth.[58]

Candidates were required to behave in the training analysis like any
other patient, giving their free associations no matter how intimate, embarrassing, sexual, or hostile they might be. Yet in many institutes the training
analyst sat on committees which evaluated the very candidate he was analyzing. This created obvious problems, and those candidates who believed they
were on the periphery of the institute's network of professional contacts
sometimes felt threatened. Analysts conducted endless debates over whether
or not the training analyst and the supervising analyst should discuss the
candidate's difficulties, whether candidates themselves should join in such an
evaluation, whether the training analyst's role should be passive, or whether
he should report at all.[59] It is thus not unexpected that candidates who were
apprehensive about revealing their difficulties were "inclined to cover up and
hide" problems.

In the hierarchy of the institutes, the education committee and the
training analyst became endowed with unusual power. They were the masters
of the apprentice-candidates. The European émigrés, among them many
women, quickly became training analysts because of their prestige and experience and the very great postwar demand.

Sometimes training analysts disagreed on the qualifications of a particular candidate. One candidate seemed to be in an "acting out" phase. He was
insolent and disorganized, and brought coffee with him to his seminar. Some
felt he was "too sick because of his depressions and anger and difficulty with
authorities." Others felt that despite these problems he had high potential,
and "some kind of organizing and integrating capacity." Still another candidate became "severely involved" with his patients and lost his boundaries.
Gitelson warned that training analysts were in danger of saying one was a
good boy and another, bad, on the basis of compliance or rebellion toward
the faculty and the training analyst, which had nothing to do with his "internal
dynamic."[60]

Language was the major tool of the insight therapist, the mode through
which problems were understood and solutions developed. The institutes
provided candidates with a special language, the common psychotherapeutic
tongue of psychoanalytic theory. Theory and technique were conveyed by
courses and seminars which changed little over time. They dealt primarily
with Freud and later orthodox psychoanalysts, though an occasional institute
might include information about Lacan or Melanie Klein, sometimes presented by protagonists of such "deviant" views.[61]

The expense of psychoanalytic training quickly became burdensome. By 1960, the cost from the beginning to graduation totaled $19,200, covering training analysis and supervision, a total considerably higher than the cost of training for other medical specialties. Most students, some of whom were practicing psychiatrists, used their current earnings and savings with minor assistance from their families.[62] Just how burdensome such training had become was clear from a 1957 study of 349 psychoanalytic institute trainees. One-fourth were more than 40 years old and about two-thirds were over 35. Many were psychiatric residents and their median salary was $3000 a year; living expenses ran around $4000 a year. They were paying $15 to $20 an hour for analysis, and $880 to $900 a year for tuition. Although most residency programs forbade private practice, a large number of analytic candidates were forced to take on private patients, involving long hours of overtime. Two-thirds expected to be in debt by the end of their residency by about $5000. Since three out of four residents were married, to help make ends meet in childless marriages both spouses tended to work, as did 30 percent of the wives who had children. One resident observed, "I don't think these figures convey any notion of the degree of hardships and privations imposed on a family by this training."[63]

Why were psychiatric residents willing to make such sacrifices? Psychoanalytic training had "caught fire," those who conducted the survey observed:

The analytically trained psychiatrist is the one who is sought by many university teaching centers, community mental health agencies, and the sophisticated public. This the psychiatric resident knows. There is a degree of factual basis in these realities since psychoanalytic theory is concerned with the *how* of mental functioning which provides the spring board for psychotherapy—the psychiatrist's major claim as a specialist.[64]

In institutes which required candidates to treat a certain number of low-fee patients, financial burdens were increased. The high costs and sacrifices required a profound commitment to psychoanalysis. Few dropped out during training, and few changed their profession after it. Then they were likely to be close to 40 years old and could do little else. Their geographical mobility was limited, and their professional ties to the analytic world already were established. Their professional indoctrination was complete. If training fees were burdensome to candidates, they were a major source of financing for institutes, and a number of them received from 40 to 80 percent of their income from them.[65]

How effective were the American institutes? A report in 1960 suggested a high degree of satisfaction with the overall effort. Well-qualified, carefully trained psychoanalysts had been produced in record numbers. Screening procedures had eliminated candidates with unsuitable personalities. The institutes were as meticulous as the best graduate schools. Indeed, one outside observer, a theologian, argued that psychoanalytic education represented an extraordinary achievement of the highest quality. However, there were also dissenters.

Siegfried Bernfeld, an eminent Viennese lay analyst, gave a mixed assessment in a speech announcing his resignation from the San Francisco institute's training committee after years of participation. Bernfeld agreed that the institutes turned out "a remarkable percentage of competent analysts." But he also deplored the increasing bureaucratization and "teacher centered" orientation. Because institutes were night schools run by "busy analysts" in their "spare time," they were not innovative and hewed to the teaching methods "of the past." European analysts "eager to establish a solid dam against heterodoxy" were determined to select newcomers by the most rigid methods, after a coercive, long-drawn-out period of authoritarian training. But they did so to the real detriment of psychoanalysis. To be effective, psychoanalytic treatment had to be voluntary; but the training analysis was required. Moreover, in violation of the classical stipulation of the neutrality and anonymity of the analyst, the training analyst became a powerful, "even decisive" figure in the trainee's reality, rather than a "mere transference figure." He judged every step of the candidate's career: his readiness for seminars, for treating patients under supervision, for completing the training analysis. Nor did the training analysis protect against "heterodoxy"; Alexander, Rado, Horney, and Frieda Fromm-Reichmann were all former trainees of the Berlin institute. Rigid training rules proliferated because the very process of conducting an analysis frustrated the ego and power drives, the moral, sadistic, and law-giving components of the analyst, Bernfeld argued.

> And, so, in consolation, we are burdened . . . with committees over committees; . . . we have the whole rigmarole of big business, the army, and any bureaucracy in order to govern a little band of a few hundred generally civilized and pleasant individuals, most of whom are seriously interested in helping themselves and their patients, and in doing some research in their spare hours.[66]

The continuous scrutiny and the uncertain ending of the training analysis, the difficulty of completing an analytic case, the dependence on the analytic milieu all served to "infantilize" candidates and increase their dependency. This was the conclusion of the sociologist Marcia Nunes, after a study of one psychoanalytic institute published in 1984. Moreover, the candidates' growing specialization in psychoanalysis increased their loyalty to "talk therapy" in general, and isolated them from the medical knowledge that would have given them expertise in prescribing the most recent medications for psychiatric disorders.[67]

In 1987 Otto Kernberg decried the "paranoid" atmosphere of psychoanalytic institutes, particularly those where the training analyst also reports on his analysands. Although ideally institutes should be modeled on university colleges and art schools, they more closely resembled technical schools and theological seminaries. Freud and the training analyst were idealized; recent technical departures were insufficiently taught. Candidates, naturally ambivalent, split off their negative feelings toward their training analyst or institute and deployed them against other analysts with different points of view, or other institutes or theories. The final symptom of sick psychoanalytic institutes was "diminished creative thinking and scientific productivity on the part of faculty, students, and graduates."[68]

In 1960 a comprehensive survey of psychoanalytic education noted 21 institute research projects, nine of them at the Columbia University institute, and eight at Chicago. Organized psychoanalytic research in America had begun with the founding of the Chicago institute in 1932, and its subsequent studies in psychosomatic illness. Other projects included the results of psychoanalytic therapy; factors in ego strength and the predictive value of admissions procedures; the selection of candidates; the extent of consensus in psychoanalytic interpretations; the effect of parent loss in childhood; studies of the gifted adolescent and of infant experiences and adult behavior in animal subjects; and critical examinations of Freudian theory.

Charges that institute research was inadequate and that more high-quality research was needed have been persistent self-criticisms of analysts for decades. Clearly research in treatment outcomes was easier to carry on in institutes that maintained clinics. For the most part, the most successful psychoanalytic research has been conducted in connection with medical schools, teaching hospitals, and universities. Perhaps one reason for the relative paucity of research is that institutes, as Nunes observed, are primarily training institutions and clearing-houses for private practitioners. The advanced age of institute graduates, according to some theorists, ensured that they were past their period of greatest creativity. Finally, psychoanalytic institutes, because they were primarily training centers for practitioners, had no established ways of financing research careers. Unless a psychoanalyst received a grant or worked for an institution that financed research, time spent on research and away from practice inevitably decreased income. This dilemma was posed for the New York analyst Lawrence Kubie by his training analyst Edward Glover as early as 1932, and it surfaced whenever the issue of research arose. Thus, the very sociology of the independent institute, unless it were endowed and not dependent on student fees for a high proportion of income, militated against organized research. To cope with this problem, the American Psychoanalytic Association sponsored research fellowships beginning in 1987, and there has been a new emphasis on replicability and standardized procedures.

Some of the unintended consequences of organized training left the institutes vulnerable. The insistence on medical and psychiatric training meant that recruitment depended on the number of medical students choosing psychiatry as well as the number of psychiatrists choosing psychoanalysis. Dependence on student fees meant a drop in available funds if their numbers decreased. Later, as the number of psychoanalytic candidates declined, a reflection in part of the decline in psychiatric residencies, a larger percentage of candidates were accepted, and consequently more with "pathologic" personalities. By 1972 acceptances had risen from 40 to 80 percent of those applying in some institutes.[69] Even so there was some evidence of decline in absolute numbers of candidates. The full acceptance of laymen for psychoanalytic training in the late 1980s, however, changed this pattern, and a growing percentage of lay candidates included women, many of them older, experienced psychotherapists.

The psychoanalytic organizations offered the prize of esoteric knowledge and greater control of unconscious processes in themselves and in their patients. This, analysts believed, was their distinguishing mark of expertise. The professional organization of psychoanalysis and a favorable popular climate made possible its growing influence in American psychiatry.

13

Psychoanalysis and Science: American Ego Psychology

The American-born analysts and the European refugees together created in the immediate postwar years an American ego psychology rooted in the attempt to make psychoanalysis "scientific." It reflected a more conservative psychoanalytic vision, partly the result of the social experiences of the interwar years, the rise of Nazism, and a repudiation of the facile, iconoclastic liberationism of the 1920s. It coincided with a more conservative social and political temper in America, although psychoanalysis retained its general liberal stance. "Scientization" fitted the pragmatic and professional temperament of the first and especially the second generation of American medical psychoanalysts. And it matched the temper of such different European émigrés as Franz Alexander, who represented a strong medicalizing trend; Heinz Hartmann, who was steeped in the rigors of Viennese logical positivism; and David Rapaport, a Talmudic neo-Kantian trained in psychology. This trend had begun in Europe before the war from the needs of institute teaching and as a response to criticism.

A persistent scientific stance was Freud's unique distinction in contrast to the outlook of the dissenting analysts, Jung, Adler, or Otto Rank, Heinz Hartmann claimed. Perhaps reflecting the influence of the Vienna philosophers, Hartmann insisted against the European phenomenologists that psychoanalysis was a science of causes, and not merely a psychology of the "understanding" and description of patients' subjective states. The goal of psychoanalysis was the "explanation of causal relationships," that is, the study of the "laws regulating mental activity."[1] Mere description of subjective understanding was not enough because the actual connections between phenomena might not be in the subject's experience. For instance, in behavior induced by posthypnotic suggestion the subject would not know the reasons for his actions. Or the subject might only partially understand the actual connections between mental phenomena such as emotional relationships, the "direction and strength of instinctual impulses," or "moods or feelings induced by somatic intrusions, such as drugs or narcotic intoxication."[2] The implication was clear that the elucidation of such relationships required a skilled observer, that is, the psychoanalyst.

As a guide to scientific research, both Hartmann and Rapaport granted a major role to systematic theory, which in their hands often became denser and more abstruse than in Freud's. Theory, they argued, because it could tease out the implications of observation, could suggest decisive steps for further exploration.

The determined attempts of American psychoanalysts to make their discipline "scientific" were led within the psychoanalytic community by psychologists with psychoanalytic training and those analysts who have had, on the whole, the closest ties to universities and medical schools, a small but important minority. Perhaps the majority of practicing analysts paid little attention to these abstruse theoretical issues, and "never put much stock in that abstract stuff," as the psychoanalytic psychologist Robert Holt wryly observed.[3]

Some of the responses to criticism have illustrated contradictions and strains inherent in psychoanalysis from its beginnings. Freud's psychoanalysis was, after all, a unique blend of medical tradition and humanist preoccupations, framed in a psychological theory that preserved many of the assumptions and the rhetoric of 19th-century biological and evolutionary thought, of which Freud's instincts, or "drives," is the best example.

Some of the first American attempts from the 1920s to the 1940s to make psychoanalysis scientific involved a rapprochement with both neurology and Pavlov's behaviorism. The postwar attempts, launched by refugee scholar-analysts and their American disciples, attempted to systematize psychoanalytic theory. This effort accompanied the major expansion and period of highest prestige of psychoanalysis in the United States, roughly from the late 1940s into the late 1960s, and came to be known as "American ego psychology."

The ego psychologists attempted to realize one of Freud's major ambitions, to make psychoanalysis a "general psychology," applicable alike to normality and pathology. The first thrust was to tidy up psychoanalytic theory, with the ultimate aim of creating testable propositions. A second goal was to encompass normal development and functions, such as perception and intellect, which would make easier a rapprochement with academic psychology. A third ambition was to incorporate systematically the role of the social environment and to meet the criticism energetically pressed by "dissident" analysts such as Karen Horney, Harry Stack Sullivan, and Abram Kardiner, and within "mainstream" psychoanalysis by Erik Erikson.[4] One reason, seldom discussed, for development of the new ego psychology was a reappraisal of the nature of the drives, particularly of aggression, inspired in part by the social experience of the First World War and by the rise of the Nazis and World War II. In the light of aggression, psychoanalytic ego psychologists reviewed the liberation of instinct and the concomitant "permissiveness" of the first decades of psychoanalytic history. David Rapaport observed that because of Freud's early emphasis on the drives, many of his followers assumed the individual's "absolute autonomy from the environment. From this vantage point, society appeared as a factor interfering with nature, man was looked upon as a born individualist, and therefore the therapeutic aim was often regarded as the liberation of human nature from societal bonds."[5] But unlike sexual drives, aggressive drives were dangerous because they could involve the destruction of their object.[6] Anna Freud observed that readiness for fighting was the internal consequence of mass violence and violence within families in those who failed to develop "true morality."[7] Heinz Hartmann, one of the founders of ego psychology, made the lesson from historical experience even clearer. For him the combination of the worship of instinct and irrationality was particularly noxious. Psychoanalysis mistakenly had been expected to be a "powerful ally in the fight to free humanity altogether from the heavy load" of an imposed and malignant morality. In a clear reference to Nazism, he argued that when "biological values" were acknowledged to be supreme, "one has approached dangerously near to that malady of the times, whose nature it is to worship instinct and pour scorn on reason."[8]

At the same time, aggression could be deployed in the service of self-preservation and moral values, as in the case of a young Viennese Jew who lost his anxious symptoms while fighting an anti-Semitic street gang. Moreover, in a reaction against the reductionism of analysis, the ego psychologists observed that although altruism, for example, might be a reaction formation to unusually strong anal sadistic impulses, it could become, like other such qualities, independent of the conflict that had given rise to it and thus relatively autonomous.[9]

In addition to the obvious dangers of uncontrolled aggression, the denigration of rationality and of positive qualities derived from instinctual conflict, another factor in the development of ego psychology may have been the partial failure of some kinds of earlier permissiveness, particularly prescriptions for child-raising. In the early years of psychoanalysis, probably into the 1930s, parents had been urged to allow expressions of infantile, pregenital sexuality. Indeed, more openness about sexuality, less harsh bowel training, more satisfaction of oral needs, and more tolerance of masturbation had yielded positive results in the view of some analysts. But when aggression was accorded the status of a basic drive, and when permission was given for the expression of "early and violent hostilities," such as death wishes against parents and siblings, neurotic insecurities increased. As a result of attempts to diminish the severity of the superego, or internalized conscience, Anna Freud observed, "children produced the deepest of all anxieties, i.e., the fear of human beings who feel unprotected against the pressure of their drives."[10] The necessity for a renewed investigation of controls and values seemed obvious. Still another reason for a new orientation came from those who, like Anna Freud, were concerned with the prevention of neuroses in children because prevention could not be undertaken without a clearer notion of normal development, a subject to which psychoanalysts had devoted little attention.[11]

Begun in the 1920s and 1930s as an investigation of unconscious defenses against instinctual drives, ego psychology developed, especially after World War II, a new emphasis on mechanisms of control, on fostering "ego forces strong enough to hold their own against the pressure of the drives."[12] This direction had been anticipated by some of the American analysts, notably Ives Hendrick, who argued that the ego was the instrument not only of perception but of moral choice, of sublimation, of "what chiefly distinguished man from animal, adult from child."[13]

Some of the refugee analysts were sympathetic to these American developments.[14] In his discussions of morality in America, Heinz Hartmann softpedaled the Nietzschean commonality of good and evil on which he had insisted in the 1920s. Morality, he now argued, was an ineradicable, functional aspect of personality. The "ego strength" of the new psychoanalytic psychologists closely resembled the enlightened will of traditional American psychology. Its essence, as William James and the new psychoanalysts defined it, lay in the capacity for postponement.[15]

One of the restraining "ego forces" was intelligence, an example of an ego function that was presumed to develop at least in part outside the battleground of conflicting drives. The role of intelligence was examined by Hartmann, dean of the refugee analysts. A descendant of two distinguished generations of the European professoriat, a polymath who had been privately tutored until his university years, he attended Max Weber's last seminar in Vienna, earned a medical degree, and worked in Wagner Jauregg's psychiatric clinic with Paul Schilder, whose ability to communicate with schizophrenics and remarkable case descriptions impressed him deeply.[16] Hartmann also had been immersed in academic psychology and in the work of the Vienna circle of logical positivist philosophers. He completed important experimental studies of twins and of the psychoanalytic theory of symbolism.[17] Invited by Freud to be his last trainee, Hartmann spoke with all the authority of closeness to the master and, for the Americans, the prestige of exalted European culture.[18] He had a firm grasp of the need for clear, coherent psychoanalytic propositions and of the incomplete, often inconsistent nature of Freud's successive developments of theory. The Rockefeller Foundation partly subsidized the publication in 1927 of Hartmann's *Fundamentals of Psychoanalysis,* an attempt at theoretical systematization.

Leaving Austria when the Germans invaded, Hartmann arrived in America in 1941 after three years in Paris, Geneva, and Lausanne, and later headed the New York institute's outpatient department. He was a scholar with a wide knowledge of contemporary psychology and sociology, but his style was highly abstract, and his psychoanalytic papers were seldom illustrated with case histories.

Hartmann and his immediate colleagues, two other refugee analysts, Ernst Kris and Rudolph Loewenstein, vastly expanded the role of the ego, which in Freud's writing had remained sketchy. The ego did not develop from the id, as Freud had suggested, but rather both emerged from an undifferentiated phase governed by inborn givens.[19] Two of Hartmann's key modifications were, first, to insist on the importance of what he called the "conflict free" sphere of ego development, and, second—closely related—to elaborate the "neutralization" of sexual and aggressive drive energy. Both served adaptation, which had become increasingly important as psychoanalysis devoted more attention to the total personality. Indeed the goal of psychoanalytic therapy was "to help men achieve a better functioning synthesis and relation to the environment."[20] And in a reach toward a secular ethic, he wrote that a human being was well adapted "if his productivity, his ability to enjoy life, and his mental equilibrium are undisturbed."[21]

Hartmann argued for the adaptive function of several capacities that psychoanalysts had interpreted chiefly as defenses against the drives. For instance, the development of intellect could be hampered by conflicts and taboos, but intellect also could act as a defense against instinctual danger, especially at puberty. This defense could be regarded as a mode of adaptation to reality, because "ordered thinking is always directly or indirectly reality-oriented." The choice of this method of instinctual mastery depended partly on "an autonomous intelligence factor," which like other given capacities had a constitutional basis:

> Learning to think and learning in general are independent biological functions which exist alongside, and in part independent of, instinctual drives and defenses. . . . The attempt to lay hold on the instinctual processes by connecting them with ideas which can be dealt with in consciousness, is one of the most general, earliest and most necessary acquirements of the human ego.[22]

Moreover this defense against instinctual drives could result in heightened intellectual achievements.

Hartmann also noted the adaptive possibilities of other defenses. Fantasy, for instance, could be used as a preparation for the mastery of reality, and played a role even in the presumably super-rational realm of science. Denial and avoidance could serve to get away from difficult environments and prompt the search for more benign ones. Hartmann cited other learning and maturation processes that could develop outside conflict. These included "perception, intention, object comprehension, thinking, language, recall-phenomena, productivity, the well-known phases of motor development, grasping, crawling, walking, and the maturation and learning processes implicit in all these and many others."[23]

This list encompassed many of the concerns of academic psychology and child development.[24] Hartmann argued for the equally traditional aim of an objective knowledge of "ability, character and will" that would make possible a more adequate definition of "ego strength."[25] Hartmann also hoped that the psychoanalytically informed direct observation of children would fill the gaps in psychoanalytic knowledge derived from the analysis of adults, and he had a wide acquaintance with the research in childhood development of Jean Piaget and Arnold Gesell.

If the conflict-free sphere opened psychoanalysis to the possibility of a rapprochement with the concerns of academic psychology, Hartmann's concept of "neutralization" reflected the new importance given to the control of aggression. Hartmann detached aggression from Freud's theory of the "death instinct," arguing instead for a "primary aggressive propensity in man."[26] Just as Freud had posited the sublimation of libido, so aggression also could be detached from its instinctual aims. "Neutralization" was the neologism Hartmann coined for the detachment of the energy of drives from their instinctual origins.

Neutralization played an especially important role in the more potentially "dangerous" of the two drives of psychoanalytic theory, aggression and sexuality. The capacity to form permanent object relations depended not only on the ability to bear frustration but on the ability to sublimate aggression. Moreover, de-aggressivized, neutralized energy played a decisive part in the mastery of reality.[27] It "supplies ego and superego with motor power and equips particularly the ego for its function in action."[28] Indeed, the capacity to neutralize aggression was one of the major criteria of "ego strength."[29]

Hartmann also mounted a spirited defense of the role of theory in creating a scientific psychoanalysis. Concept formation in psychoanalysis or any other science did not differ in principle. Psychoanalytic hypotheses served three major functions. First, they ordered the phenomena of observation. Second, by spelling out, often on a high level of abstraction, the implications of observation, they made it possible to test hypotheses by "further research."[30] Third, these hypotheses also guided observation in the first place.[31] Like Robert Waelder, Hartmann argued that theory in psychoanalysis was more complex than in any other psychology, because the phenomena it dealt with were themselves complex and encompassed a large number of variables.[32] While some psychoanalytic hypotheses were close to observation, others were at considerable remove from it.

However, a possible flaw could compromise this method of using hypotheses to guide observations. The interpenetration of theory and observation was apparent in the simplest psychoanalytic assumption about unconscious processes. Highly abstract hypotheses, such as "libidinal cathexis," were reported as data of observation, to the confusion of both theory and clinical practice. Here Hartmann was giving a potent weapon to those philosophers of science who regarded psychoanalytic data as an artifact of psychoanalytic theorizing.

Hartmann had argued that psychoanalysis was a coherent theory whose propositions could not be selectively detached from one another without damage to the whole. Here he had in mind the selective choices of the neo-Freudians, none of whom indicated how his or her revisions affected the totality of the theory, thus creating what the orthodox considered an "incoherent patchwork."[33] Moreover, many psychologists who tried experimentally to prove or disprove the relationships posited by psychoanalysis were unaware of the variables involved in what they set out to test.[34] They often betrayed a conspicuous ignorance of psychoanalysis as a systematic theory. For all these reasons, it seemed increasingly important to determine what was essential in Freud's legacy and what could be modified or discarded. But to do so required the melding of psychoanalysis into a coherent whole, which Freud never had attempted.

A new attempt to systematize Freud's general theory of the mind into a tightly woven set of linked propositions was undertaken by a "stiff, prickly, immigrant Jew," David Rapaport, who had suffered since childhood from a rheumatic heart condition.[35] A refuge psychologist from Budapest, he possessed a strong Kantian philosophical bent, extravagant erudition, and a driven capacity for work. He was a passionate polemicist, discussing "abstract metapsychology with the thunder of a Hebrew prophet," and had little of the cool, magisterial detachment of the aristocratic Hartmann.[36] Rapaport and Lawrence Kubie, each equally imperious in their respective ways, accused each other of being "High Priests" for their clashing interpretations of Freud.[37] Rapaport was something of an evangelist for Kubie's *bete noire,* ego psychology, lecturing at psychoanalytic institutes across the country. And Rapaport attributed a real role to dissident analysts in the creation of ego psychology—Adler, Rank, and Horney (particularly the latter's emphasis on the integration of ego defenses).[38] He also accepted the cultural and historical relativism of the "cultural school," arguing that what might be normal in Bali would be considered pathological in America. The passivity and quiet of the early analysts, for example, was rooted in a bygone "Victorian" culture, sure of its values:

> . . . I want to make the point that only in a civilization which had as clearcut norms as the Victorian had, could you draw such sharp lines between character structure and symptom, and ego structure. The analyst could afford to be in general quiet without showing specific values excepting permissiveness, because his general value system was taken for granted—it was the society's. No such thing exists now.[39]

After studying physics and mathematics, Rapaport had written a doctoral dissertation on association theory from Bacon to Kant at the Royal Hungarian University in Budapest and had been analyzed. He was also an early and ardent Zionist, living for a few years as a very young man in a kibbutz.

Established in the United States with the help of Lawrence Kubie, Rapaport worked briefly as a psychologist at Mt. Sinai Hospital in New York, at a mental hospital in Kansas, then at the Menninger Clinic in Topeka from 1940 until 1948, when he moved to the Austen Riggs Center at Stockbridge, Massachusetts, where he remained until his death in 1960. At Menninger's and Stockbridge he attracted a group of gifted researchers, psychologists, and medical psychoanalysts including Merton Gill, George Klein, Roy Schafer, Philip Holzman, and Paul Bergman.[40]

Rapaport's brilliance and erudition early had impressed Frank Fremont-Smith at the Macy Foundation, and he had made an exception of the foundation's policy of funding only medical research to support some of Rapaport's first work. *Emotions and Memory,* published in 1942, was an exhaustive survey of the experimental, theoretical, and psychopathological literature.[41] During World War II, he devised clinical personality tests, wrote the widely used *Diagnostic Psychological Testing,* and was a founder of the Division of Clinical and Abnormal Psychology of the American Psychological Association. He translated several of Hartmann's writings, notably *Ego Psychology and the Problem of Adaptation,* and collaborated in editing a two-volume collection of the papers of Otto Fenichel. He also was an exhaustive and exhausting critic of his many friends' and students' books and papers. Rapaport felt the effects of the battles over lay analysis in the early 1950s; Ives Hendrick, among others, opposed his membership in the International Psychoanalytic Association because he was a layman.[42]

Hartmann and Rapaport both shared the ideal of "shouldering tradition and responsibility, not throwing the old away but taking on the new nevertheless."[43] Their program of ego psychology appealed to young psychologists "trained in academic experimental psychology and the social sciences." Robert Holt, one of Rapaport's students, recalled its promise: it "presented psychoanalysis as a reasonable, intelligible discipline, by no means exclusively focused on intrapsychic conflict and unconscious infantile wishes, but with much concern for a person's real setting, especially his social, cultural, and historical milieu, the groups and traditions that shaped his identity, and the mis-en-scene of interpersonal relations in which his life was played out."[44]

Although Rapaport had had psychoanalytic training and treated patients, he did not consider himself a psychoanalyst. The goal of his systematization was to make possible the severest test of psychoanalytic theory. He once wrote to Lawrence Kubie:

> . . . I am interested in tracing a consistent theory in all the confusion of psycho-analytic writing, not for the purpose of creating a canon, but rather for the purpose of seeing whether or not once it is clearly systematized it will fall under its own weight or will open possibilities to verification.[45]

Rapaport believed that psychoanalysis possessed a more powerful and comprehensive explanatory theory than academic and experimental psychology for several reasons. First, psychoanalysis dealt systematically with the multiple determinants of complex phenomena while academic psychology deliberately had narrowed the variables with which it dealt. Second, psychoanalysis drew connections among phenomena not previously linked. For example, Freud had made the first consistent attempt to coordinate within one theory the irrational—peremptory obsessions, delusions, dreams, anxiety—and rational, practical, logical thought.[46] Third, it was a valid "postdictive" scientific theory like the theory of evolution because it explained an existing state, in this case, "already present neurotic symptoms." Postdiction was as valid a mode of confirmation as prediction—if one carefully distinguished between what was given in the data and what could only be inferred by postdiction.[47]

Freud's enterprise of coordination, Rapaport argued, was contained in his general theory of the mind, enshrined in his most abstract writing—the seventh chapter of the *Interpretation of Dreams* (1900), the papers on metapsychology (1915), *The Ego and the Id* (1923), the *Problem of Anxiety* (1926), and the *New Introductory Lectures on Psychoanalysis* (1933).

The explanation of how Freud's general theory encompassed the development of rational thought from a matrix of instinctual drives became the focus of Rapaport's intricate, sometimes forced, exposition. This complex process involved two major concepts: delay and structure. The absence of an object that would satisfy a drive, thus creating postponement of satisfaction, could lead in two directions: to gratification through dreams, hallucinations, fantasies, or emotional discharge, or to rational thought and realistic calculation, to experimental operation with small quantities of energy. In the latter case, the pleasure principle was superseded by the reality principle. The original drive which had aimed at lowering tension at all costs was modified by new organizations of energy that became structures.[48]

By structures, Rapaport meant psychological functions which changed slowly, as opposed to drives, which by definition operated rapidly for immediate discharge. Rapaport taught that individual behavior was far-reachingly determined by relatively stable, slowly changing internal configurations that set limits on what behavioral opinions were open to a person and gave an individual a distinctive, persistent, and thus recognizable style. The closely interrelated pattern of defenses and abilities Rapaport called a person's ego structure.[49]

It was precisely the positing of these mental structures operating between stimulus and response that differentiated psychoanalysis from other psychological systems, especially from a conditioned reflex theory. Structures played for psychoanalysis the role "prior learning" played for behaviorism.

Rapaport's ambitious synthesis of Freud was fully developed in *The Structure of Psychoanalytic Theory*, published in 1960. It was a complex but lucid, compact analysis of his vision of Freud's theory. Rapaport defended the scientific status of psychoanalysis and recounted its problems and modifications, particularly Hartmann and Erik Erikson's attempts to integrate social factors into general psychoanalytic theory. All this was shoe-horned into 183 pages and included in a series of monographs edited by Sigmund Koch dealing with psychological systems.[50] Rapaport had to follow a prescribed and rigidly detailed format and carrying it off was a tour de force.[51]

Rapaport's highly schematic and abstract summary of Freud's "general theory of the mind" was heavily weighted toward the assumptions of later ego psychology, particularly in its emphasis on delay and the development of "structures."[52] In contrast to Rapaport's presentation, Freud in fact had emphasized the persistence of the primary, unconscious processes, and, despite the abstractions of his various formal theoretical expositions, Freud's arguments were illustrated by clinical examples.

Rapaport presented four major models Freud used but never entirely integrated to construct his theory of the mind: reflexive, Darwinian, Jacksonian, and, most important, economic. The economic model assumed that tension reduction was the basis of "all motivated behavior," and laid the conceptual foundation for the pleasure principle and wish fulfillment. The exemplar of this model was a sequence of infant behavior: "restlessness $\rightarrow$ sucking on the breast $\rightarrow$ subsidence of restlessness." In this model, restlessness was the equivalent of tension, of an accumulation of "cathexis," of a drive reaching threshold intensity. Sucking on the breast was the equivalent of drive action and led to subsidence of restlessness, that is, to drive gratification. Most actions, however, were not this simple. As already suggested, they were modified by an elaborate set of "psychic structures."[53]

The Harvard psychologist Henry Murray praised Rapaport's synthesis—with notable reservations—as by far

> the most sophisticated representation of Freud's theories that ever has been or will be published. I am sure SF's ghost is viewing you with special favor and delight in the realization that you have done what SF could not have done himself—made his theories fit, so far as possible, the super-exacting standards of the New Fashion." . . . You write as defense attorney arguing for your client before the Supreme Court of Logical Positivism, etc., leaving to others the duty of pointing out conspicuous defeats, contradictions, and omissions. Is all the religiosity necessary? Would you be expelled from the psychoanalytical society if you talked naturally, that is, discussed Freud's ideas as you would those of any other great scientist?[54]

Rapaport's text elevated Freud's theory of drives to the primary theory of psychoanalysis and paired it with the ego psychologist's new emphasis on control, exemplified by the "delay" of drive discharge. It was just this central position of the drives and of structural theory that some of Rapaport's ablest students would reject.

Rapaport also was clearly aware of the unsolved problems of psychoanalytic theory. The first major difficulty was the fact that clinical observation often was at "a great distance" from psychoanalytic generalizations. Only "a tightly built theory (with clearly stated definitions and implicative rules)" could "support confirming tests."[55] In many ways, this argument granted theorizing and metapsychological explanation a role which Freud had not accorded them, and they had remained for Freud a clarifying but modifiable, even discardable, element of his system.

The second major problem of psychoanalysis was the difficulty of quantifying major psychoanalytic constructs. Neither intrapsychic drives nor their modifying structures could be measured. Nor could the drives be equated with any measurable "known kind of biochemical energy," although they might become so in the future.[56]

Third, in addition to the difficulties of quantification, psychoanalysis lacked a clear notion of what constituted "valid clinical research" or confirming clinical material.[57] Rapaport was fascinated by the clinical process of therapy and defended radical experimentation. The successful clinical therapy of the American psychologist Carl Rogers and the evidence for "spontaneous cures" suggested how little was known about treatment.[58] But Rapaport defended the general validity of psychoanalytic technique and its search for the unknown in each individual case. To his friend, the psychologist Paul Bergman, he wrote, "If you think I, who am reasonably convinced that psychoanalysis contains fundamental truths about human nature, go at a patient knowing what I will uncover, you are wrong." Each patient "is such an entirely new combination of everything."[59]

Writing in 1959 when psychoanalysis was a powerful force in psychiatry, Rapaport foresaw rosy possibilities for its future, regardless of the fate of the therapy. Psychoanalysis was one of the most exciting research methods of the last 65 years and the "only sensible theory of the complexities of the human mind."[60] Some of its basic methods and concepts had entered the public domain, for example, an interview method which found the past relevant to understanding the present; the repetition of patterns first learned in relation to significant others such as parents, siblings, and nurses, which formed the basis for the conception of transference; and the insistence that human behavior was neither learned nor innate, but a combination of the two.[61] He even envisaged that if psychoanalysis developed a valid theory of learning, and thus of psychological structures, it might become "the core of psychology proper." But if the problem of learning were solved elsewhere, psychoanalysis still would remain the core of psychology's clinical and motivational theories, but its concepts would be "reducible to more fundamental ones."[62] At the time of his death at the age of 59, Rapaport was working on just such a psychoanalytic theory of learning.

Rapaport sometimes experienced "conflicting strains of feeling" about psychoanalysis. He was deeply admiring of the "Freudian achievement," yet he was also critical of it, and he despised "the sycophants who dance a can-can around it, in a fashion that one does not always know whether it is the science or Mammon they are worshiping."[63]

Profoundly loyal to what he considered to be a European emphasis on theory and careful textual exegesis, he deplored the general pragmatism and anti-theoretical attitude of American analytic trainees. He blamed this on general cultural attitudes, the length of training, the wish to maintain a family, and to "live up to the Jones's (who usually live on Park avenue)."

However, recent developments in psychoanalytic theory were not always appreciated even by transplanted Europeans. Bruno Bettelheim once wrote to Rapaport:

> Sometimes one gets the feeling that the theory has become so rarefied that it exists for itself and then leads to the attitudes you rightly criticize . . . namely that the beauty of the operation (this time the operation of the intellect) takes precedence of the problem of whether it really still benefits the patient.[64]

Piqued, Rapaport replied, "If a European does not care about theory, who the hell will? Does he not know that without consistent and substantial theory he can fume against [Franz] Alexander but cannot demonstrate where Alexander is actually wrong?" Theory gave the background and justification for the approaches taken in therapy. "We are living amidst a crew of pragmatic simplifiers, and it is not simple to point out why we find the job more complicated than they seem to consider it."[65]

Rapaport and Hartmann were central figures in the American synthesis of ego psychology, and for a time their theoretical density and their attempts to create a consistent theory dominated American psychoanalytic thought. The impressiveness of this theoretical achievement and its beginnings of rapprochement with general psychology reinforced the image of psychoanalysis as a weighty and worthwhile scientific and philosophical enterprise. Erik Erikson's attempts to widen the dimensions of psychoanalysis to include the entire lifespan and the reciprocal interaction of the individual and his social environment further broadened the psychoanalytic appeal.

Perhaps the most popular version of American ego psychology among orthodox analysts and institutes has been the often elegant theories of the New York analyst Charles Brenner, who adroitly defended psychoanalysis as a "specialized method of scientific investigation" for "observing the sequences of a person's conscious mental life." He also defended metapsychology against the criticism of Rapaport's students and defined it as the total of psychoanalytic theory based solely on clinical data from the psychoanalytic encounter.[66] Hartmann's conflict-free sphere and Rapaport's systematic synthesis of Freud's theory of the mind were conspicuous by their absence, replaced by a renewed emphasis on the ubiquity of conflict and the primacy of childhood determinism.

Brenner based his approach on the supreme scientific value of psychoanalytic clinical observations. Indeed, there was no other basis for psychoanalytic conclusions, which followed the same laws of cause and effect and a determinism as strict as those of the physical world.[67] No direct psychoanalytic observations of pre-verbal children, no evidence not derived primarily from transactions on the psychoanalytic couch were relevant to such specifically psychoanalytic findings.

These rested on the patient's saying whatever came to mind without reservation, revealing his "wishes, fears, fantasies, dreams, physical sensations expressed in words and gestures." Such were the fundamental data of psychoanalysis. It was, Brenner argued, "the only method as yet available for the study of human psychology which . . . provides access on a large scale to the truly important aspects of man's mental life . . . i.e., to his uniquely personal motives, memories, and current experiences." The observation of these by the analyst made possible an independent, objective appraisal of the human psyche, an appraisal more valuable than anything available to introspection.

Brenner reduced most psychological operations to psychic conflict among five components: drives and "drive derivatives, anxiety and depressive affect, defense, and various manifestations of superego functioning."[68] The conflicts thus created resulted in compromise formations. The key to Brenner's theoretical parsimony, these were defined as "the data of observation when one applies the psychoanalytic method and observes and/or infers a patient's wishes, fantasies, moods, plans, dreams, and symptoms."[69]

Drives, an aspect of cerebral functioning, were defined as "generalizations drawn from the psychoanalytic study of wishes," the wellsprings of human motivation. The drives were two, libidinal and aggressive, and their derivatives were quite specific: "the wish of a particular patient for a particular kind of gratification from or at the hands of a particular person under particular circumstances."[70]

Affects, the second component of conflict, were ideas and sensations of pleasure or displeasure generated by drive derivatives. The two primary affects were anxiety and depressive affect. Anxiety involved an idea of impending calamity, depressive affect, an idea of past calamity. The typical calamities of childhood were object loss, loss of love, and castration, the latter becoming important during the critical Oedipal phase of development.

Defenses could further gratification of a drive derivative or ward off the unpleasure of anxiety or depressive affect or both. Brenner argued against Anna Freud and other analysts that there were no specific mechanisms of defense; he subsumed them all under "compromise formations" and included the superego or internalized conscience in the same category. The superego was formed during the Oedipal period, when morality for the child consisted in avoiding the "calamity of being punished" and always depended not only on objective parental behavior but on the child's fantasies.[71] Moreover, masochism was an important element in superego formation, that is, self-imposed unpleasure was the child's way of avoiding childhood calamities or winning parental love. The conflicts formed in the Oedipal period and the compromise formations that resulted remained pervasive models for later behavior.

Thus, Brenner presented an ingeniously argued classical psychoanalysis strongly emphasizing conflict and the decisive influence of childhood on all subsequent behavior. He cut through much of the complexity and ambiguity of psychoanalytic theory, reducing it to a comprehensible and eminently teachable order. And in insisting on the uniqueness of each individual development, he preserved a close link with clinical evidence. By severing the connection of psychoanalysis to a presumed somatic energy, he countered some of the criticism of metapsychology from Rapaport's students.[72] Unlike Freud, who sometimes believed that a somatic basis for the drives and for their intensity ultimately could be discovered, Brenner argued that they were a purely psychological concept, based on data from the analytic situation and might not even have as their source the traditional psychoanalytic erogenous zones—mouth, anus, genitals. By arguing that there were no specific defenses associated with the ego, he stripped the ego of its possible status as a homunculus with special attributes. Finally, by focusing on psychoanalysis as a science of the data of conscious life, observable in the clinical exchange, he disarmed the suggestion that psychoanalysis dealt with an impalpable, undemonstrable psychological realm. But his eminently clear and logical approach was limited.

For Brenner, evidence for theories was often described as "clear and indisputable." Yet there was a certain circularity in some of his arguments, as the important role of inference suggested. Warded-off drive derivatives could influence a patient's thought "enough so that they can be inferred w. some certainty by the listening analyst."[73] In his illustrative examples it is occasionally difficult to separate inference from observation. He also accentuated the traditional psychoanalytic view of women, insisting on their ubiquitous penis envy and castration anxiety.[74] Reminiscent of the expansive reductionism of the 1920s, Brenner ground out applications of conflict and compromise formation as "the chief stuff of all psychic life," normal as well as pathological.[75] He applied his formula to dreams, daydreams, folk tales, myths, legends, Greek drama, novels, and, of course, religion. All were products of compromise formations from the same basic conflicts. With dogmatic thoroughness, he argued that "every later object is psychologically a substitute for the original objects of early childhood." Thus, religion does not make people moral; rather, morality is the outcome of Oedipal conflict, and moral and religious codes reflect this.[76] The Christian communicant in identifying with Christ "welcomes . . . physical torture and mutilation as the necessary condition for libidinal gratification."[77] The legend of Moses was a disguised legend of parricide. The legend of Jesus also was a compromise legend of parricide, because Jesus, who was also God the Father, was crucified, and so on.

The strength of ego psychology lay in its attempt at orderly propositions, more comprehensive systematic theory, and the reappraisal of instinctual drives. But at the hands of Rapaport and Hartmann it also was highly abstract and complex. It represented a response to changes in the social world in which psychoanalysts practiced and an attempt to escape the sometimes crude reductionism of much of what passed for psychoanalysis in the 1920s. It coincided with a period of postwar conservative optimism in American political life, with functionalism in American sociology, and with the unprecedented growth of psychoanalysis.

14

The Rise of a Psychoanalytic Psychiatry, 1945–1965

While American psychiatry was undergoing the most rapid growth in its history, a younger generation of psychiatrists, many of whom had served in the military during World War II, established a new pattern of practice and theory heavily influenced by psychoanalysis. Many of them were trained in psychoanalytic institutes and they played an increasingly important role in hospitals, clinics, and university departments of psychiatry. During World War II they believed they had seen Freud's theories translated into effective procedures that could be applied to the mental health of large populations. An estimated 9 percent of psychiatrists who had completed the Navy's Psychiatric Training program had entered psychoanalytic practice by 1951. About 78 percent of those who took up psychiatry after graduating from the Army's neuropsychiatric training program were psychoanalyzed or planned to be psychoanalyzed.[1]

This generation of young psychiatrists was convinced that the major causes of nervous and possibly of mental illness were psychological and interpersonal. Psychotherapy, because it dealt with such underlying factors, was their treatment of choice; and psychoanalysis, presumed to be the optimal treatment for the neuroses, provided the model for psychotherapy. Psychoanalytic research offered the exciting possibility of shedding new light on the psychological processes that might underlie the psychoses, psychosomatic diseases, neuroses, and what seemed to be a remarkable increase of character disorders. These hopes and claims and the prestige of wartime successes as well as the apparent shortcomings of existing psychiatric approaches inspired the increasing influence of psychoanalysis in medical schools and texts. The impact on psychiatry grew steadily until the mid-1960s.

Psychoanalytic psychiatrists, such as Karl and William Menninger, led campaigns to reform the nation's mental hospitals and to provide adequate treatment, including psychotherapy. Some psychoanalysts encouraged the application of psychotherapy and psychoanalytic theory to the psychoses; and perhaps one-fifth of the psychoanalysts' patients suffered from symptoms that could be classified as psychotic. However, in providing a model for psychotherapy and fostering the development of private office practice, psychoanalysis intensified the already growing trend away from the mental hospital and the hospitalized patient as the primary focus of the psychiatrist's energies. In 1947 more than half of all American psychiatrists were in private practice or worked in out-patient clinics, a 20 to 30 percent increase over 1940. By 1958 only 16 percent of the members of the American Psychiatric Association worked full-time in mental hospitals. By 1958 a third of the nation's psychiatrists emphasized psychoanalysis, and by 1973 half of all psychiatrists in general psychiatry specialized in psychoanalysis. This trend away from the mental hospital was reinforced by those who placed increasing emphasis on broad mental health services within a community setting.[2]

Largely because of National Institute of Mental Health subsidies of psychiatric education, the number of psychiatrists increased more than six fold, from 4700 to 27,000 in the 28 years from 1948 to 1976. In 1948 some $2,766,776, 70 percent of the NIMH budget, went for training. In the single decade from 1963 to 1973, the number of psychiatrists increased about 20 percent more rapidly than the total number of physicians.[3]

This cohort of younger psychodynamic psychiatrists established a new pattern of psychiatric practice which emerged in America by 1959 and continued to dominate until about the mid-1960s. Surveying a small sample of the profession in 1959, Frederick C. Redlich, chairman of the Yale Department of Psychiatry, noticed the emerging differences between the younger psychoanalytically oriented cohort and the older psychiatrists whom he saw as more directive and organic.

The new elite cohort had completed psychiatric residencies, were trained by psychoanalysts, and had an "analytic orientation." They were younger than the men who had institutionalized psychoanalysis as a specialty in the 1930s, and both groups filled the university positions in psychiatry. Their methods were "almost entirely psychological and non-directive." They saw about seven patients a day for 45 or 50 minutes each, an average of three times a week, for about 18 months.[4]

They were skeptical of organic therapies, and some knew little about them. They blamed treatment failures chiefly on the personal problems of the psychiatrist and believed that their choice of psychiatry as a vocation was related to their own personal lives and needs.

In contrast, the "directive organic" psychiatrists, many of them older, staffed the state hospitals, although some were in private practice. They used "suggestion, reassurance, advice and reproof," and prescribed drugs and shock treatments. They saw 12 patients a day for 15 to 40 minutes for an average of six months. One-half had "incomplete psychiatric residencies or none at all." The split between the psychodynamic and the "directive organic psychiatrists" was reflected in sometimes bitter political struggles within the American Psychiatric Association, particularly over issues of broad social and psychiatric reform.[5]

Most psychiatrists trained as psychoanalysts continued to choose private practice over full-time work in mental hospitals, just as they had in the prewar period. Nevertheless, psychoanalysts played a large and sometimes a dominant role as directors or consultants and, above all, as teachers, in public and private psychiatric clinics and hospitals, social work schools and agencies, and universities. Some 70 percent of the 340 members of the American Psychoanalytic Association in 1949 held teaching positions. In the Boston area, by 1961 psychoanalysts and candidates from the Boston institute held 70 percent of the psychiatric teaching positions in schools of social work, and 32 of the 44 professorial positions in the psychiatric departments of medical schools. They held 56 percent of the psychiatric positions in Boston's general hospitals and clinics, 54 percent in the V.A. psychiatric services, and 52 percent of staff of the largest private psychiatric hospital. In most of these institutions the senior positions were held by training analysts. Psychoanalysts also were offering psychotherapy to the larger community more directly than ever before through psychoanalytic clinics organized in the immediate postwar period by a number of psychoanalytic institutes.[6] The new generation of analysts was a talented group, and by the 1960s they had assumed leadership of the American psychoanalytic movement and partially dominated American psychiatry.[7]

To the end of the 1960s, one motive for psychoanalytic training may have been the lure of a more attractive private practice and higher earnings. In market economies incomes from private practice usually are larger than those from public service.[8] And the nature of psychoanalytic psychotherapy, with its one-to-one relationship and its frequent sessions, as often as five a week, traditionally has been more compatible with private practice, at least in the United States. So, too, has a general commitment to psychotherapy.[9] In 1954 the median income of the new group of analytic psychiatrists, among whom psychoanalysts must be included, was $22,000 for private practitioners and $15,000 for university psychiatrists. The median income of all psychiatrists was $18,000 and that of state hospital psychiatrists was only $9,000. The largest incomes went to psychiatrists in private practice who used somatic and directive therapies; their median income was $25,000. These organic psychiatrists could charge more for each treatment and could treat more than one patient each hour, thus they could earn more than the average psychoanalyst. Psychoanalytic incomes were limited by the psychoanalytic model of psychotherapeutic practice—an hourly fee and only one patient each hour. Although psychiatrists as a group earned near the bottom level of the medical specialties, next to pediatrics and internal medicine, this figure probably reflected the large number of psychiatrists working in public institutions where salaries were much lower.

Probably psychoanalysts earned more than the average income of physicians in these years. In 1949 physicians earned an average of $11,744 per year, while 70 percent of a sample of psychoanalysts earned more than $15,000. These figures included analysts in training, who were treating patients under supervision and who charged lower fees. Analytic fees ranged from less than $5 to $50 an hour, with a median of $14.50 an hour. In a different set of statistics, 14 percent of analysts earned up to $10,000; 37 percent from $11,000 to $20,000; 48 percent earned from $21,000 to $50,000. The highest fees were charged in New York and Los Angeles. Some 20 percent of analysts in Los Angeles and 4 percent in New York earned from $41,000 to $50,000. By the late 1960s psychoanalysts averaged an income of $37,000 while psychiatrists were earning $28,000, clinical psychologists $17,000, and psychiatric social workers $11,000.[10]

Most analytic psychiatrists in 1959 were satisfied with their incomes, and major sources of personal reward for them were intellectual and social— "learning how people think," "working with patients I like."[11] To some young physicians just specializing in psychiatry, private practice with an educated upper-class and upper-middle-class clientele may have seemed more attractive than earning the minimal salaries and dealing with the mass of severely ill, chronic, and elderly patients that had become the stock-in-trade of the state mental hospitals.[12] Moreover, most of these hospitals still were located in rural areas, far from universities or psychoanalytic institutes, and the treatment they dispensed was regarded as second- or third-rate.

There were many motives other than financial and social that underlay the attraction of psychiatrists to psychoanalysis. Psychoanalysis influenced psychiatry partly because it filled a conceptual and therapeutic need, much as it had done during World War II. In the long interval between 1890 and 1950 somatic psychiatry had made relatively few important advances. Classification systems were much what they had been 50 years before.

Ways of judging among psychiatric theories and therapies were poorly developed, and controlled research in medicine was relatively rare in the 1930s and 1940s. The quality and quantity of research in psychiatry, whether somatic or psychological, was below that in other fields of medicine, and psychoanalysis shared these research disabilities, although its theories were becoming increasingly systematized. Few psychiatrists were trained in research design, and the quality of most research dealing with the outcome of treatment was questionable. Sophisticated studies with control groups were few, the technical obstacles formidable, and often those who administered a given treatment also judged its results. Clearly defining clinical phenomena such as symptoms and degrees of recovery remained unsolved for the somaticists as well as for the psychotherapists. Proponents of lobotomy had as much difficulty setting up criteria as did psychoanalysts. "Recovery" or "improvement" remained vague. Finally, somatic therapies bore little logical relation to somatic theory or knowledge.[13]

As before the war, alternative psychological theories and methods of treatment, such as the behavioral, had not yet been fully developed in American psychiatry. Psychoanalysis thus had no serious rivals, except for the followers of Adolf Meyer, and in many ways their views converged. Indeed, both together inspired the burgeoning interest in "psychosocial explanations" of psychiatric problems that grew rapidly beginning around 1910 and reached a peak in the 1940s. Such explanations had been fostered by the discrediting of hereditarian views which had become identified with the racism of Nazi Germany. Psychosocial explanations formed part of a long trend of liberal environmentalism.[14]

In this complex situation, psychoanalysts offered attractive possibilities of definitive explanation and promising treatment. One psychoanalyst chairman of a department of psychiatry argued somewhat sardonically that psychoanalytic theory and therapy gave psychiatric students, often disillusioned with existing methods and bewildered by their patients, a "new light." A "coherent, logical and authoritative approach to the vexing problem of therapy for mental illness begins to take shape before the resident's eager eyes . . . discouragement and frustration are replaced by hope and enthusiasm." Moreover, psychotherapy required unique skills in a "private, highly variable situation that is, by its very nature, fraught with uncertainty for the psychotherapist." In these anxiety-provoking circumstances psychoanalysis provided a reasonably complete, systematic body of theory and practice.[15] Armed with Otto Fenichel's *Psychoanalytic Theory of Neurosis,* young residents went forth with more confidence to battle nervous and mental illness.

In Boston, one result of the psychoanalytic emphasis was what the sociologists Daniel Levinson and Myron Sharaf called the "quest for omnipotence in professional training." Given the importance of training in psychotherapy and the dominance of psychoanalysis in Boston psychiatry, the analysts functioned as supervisors and role models for young psychiatrists. Usually medical training had failed to prepare residents for the subtleties and difficulties of learning psychotherapy, in which the student had to accept the often intense emotions of his sometimes deeply disturbed patients, understand their motives and fantasies, and become aware of his own feelings as well. Professional training would make the novice skilled in the "right ways" of dealing with psychiatric problems, of belonging to a "recondite and special" guild, distinguished from social workers and nurses by their medical responsibility, the depth of their experience, and the fact that only they, the medical psychiatrists, could become psychoanalysts. And they were informed by their analytic teachers that one "can learn things about patients from psychoanalyzing them that one cannot learn from psychotherapy." Finally, psychoanalytic training was imagined "as a key not only to psychodynamic omniscience, but also—through the resident's experience as an analytic patient—to omnisentience and a liberation of the self." For those seeking analytic training, acceptance by the Boston Psychoanalytic Institute was the seal of personal worth and refusal "an almost catastrophic failure." Even the most qualified resident approached the institute fearful that his secrets would be "discerned by the all-seeing eye of the Institute's interviewing analysts.[16]

There also may have been more personal reasons for the fascination with psychoanalysis. Surveys of young medical students and psychiatric residents indicated that many of them, troubled by precisely the problems psychoanalysis dealt with—sexuality and emotional conflict—wished for personal psychotherapy. However, one large-scale survey of psychotherapists insisted that they resembled most other educated persons and were not a special, singularly traumatized group.[17]

Some psychoanalysts aggressively pushed impressive claims for their psychodynamic style in the immediate postwar period. These sometimes contradictory assertions were theoretical and explanatory as well as therapeutic. On the one hand, psychoanalysis claimed to be rooted in the biological instincts of the body, and thus was close to medicine and the biological sciences. On the other hand, it claimed to be operating on a purely psychological level, which was assumed by some psychoanalysts to be determining.

"Neurophysiology cannot explain human behavior. Psychoanalysis can," Sandor Rado, who organized both the New York and the Columbia psychoanalytic institutes, wrote in 1946. He argued that psychoanalysis investigated the inner life of the individual in telling detail on the decisive psychological level, which he described vaguely as the "inward self-expression of the cortex." Rado argued equally vaguely and grandly that psychodynamics included "all social sciences and services concerned with human relationships." The systematized findings of psychoanalysis constituted "psychodynamics," that is, knowledge of the forces controlling human personality.[18] Psychoanalysis claimed to be a basic "science of human behavior," providing a theory of both the "normal and abnormal," including the early stages of the child's development and their relation to adult pathology.[19]

The psychoanalysts were largely successful in appropriating the term "psychodynamics," which earlier had been applied to the psychiatry of Adolf Meyer, or to a mix of Meyer and Freud. Despite objections, psychodynamics increasingly became a synonym, and to some a euphemism, for psychoanalytic theory.

An understanding of psychodynamics was crucial for general medicine, it was argued, because there was an emotional or psychological component in numerous physical illnesses. One-third to one-half of the patients treated by general physicians were suffering from emotionally caused disorders, according to some estimates. Yet many physicians failed to recognize the emotional problems of their patients, ignoring them, denigrating them, or perhaps mistakenly treating them with drugs as organic diseases.[20]

Dynamic psychiatrists argued that psychotherapy was the optimal instrument for dealing with emotional factors in both somatic and psychiatric illness. Psychoanalysis provided the scientific basis for psychotherapy, and was its "central science and technology."

Psychoanalysts tended to assume that in a successful analysis a patient gained emotional insight and successfully worked out, through analysis of the transference, the complex, multi-determined origins of his illness, thus changing his personality in fundamental ways. A true understanding of cause would lead to a correspondingly symmetrical recovery. This might include the disappearance of presenting symptoms, but certainly it encompassed real improvement in mental functioning and reality adjustment. These goals in turn subsumed insight, acceptance of self, freedom from "enervating tensions"; release of aggressive energies for self-preservation; consistent loyal, interpersonal relations; free functioning abilities; improved sublimation; full heterosexual functioning.[21] This "thoroughgoing reorganization of the personality" would be proof against the substitution of new symptoms for old. Thus, psychoanalysis aimed for "structural," that is, "permanent" changes. Karl Menninger put it uncompromisingly: "Psychoanalysis remains . . . the supreme paradigm of psychotherapy . . . the most thoroughgoing, the most penetrative, the most intensive and persistent.[22] These were impressive claims and they influenced psychiatric educators and government administrators.

Psychoanalysts argued that because of the crucial importance of psychodynamics and of self-knowledge for psychotherapy, ideally every medical student should be psychoanalyzed. And psychoanalysis was a necessity for the future psychiatrist.

Through personal analysis, the medical student was "expected to explore resolutely and thoroughly the unconscious reaches of his mind, trace his development back to the formative experiences of his childhood, and arrive at a better knowledge and a realistic appraisal of himself as an individual and as a product of a given period and culture."[23] But for those who had not received this initiation, instruction in psychodynamics "should go only to the boundaries within which the unanalyzed mind feels at home.[24]

These arguments, if carried out for all medical students, would have led to an enormous new demand for psychoanalysis and psychoanalytic instruction. Although the American Psychiatric Association failed to endorse the psychoanalysts' insistence on the necessity for psychoanalytic training of the psychiatrist, psychoanalysis began to play a far larger role in psychiatry and psychiatric education.[25]

The increased visibility of psychoanalysis was partly the result of the Group for the Advancement of Psychiatry, which William Menninger organized in 1946 as an instrument of psychiatric reform. GAP was concerned as well with broad social and cultural issues, including racism, national aggressiveness, "education, industry, recreation.[26] In 1948, 66 of GAP's 148 members also were members of the American Psychoanalytic Association, including the chairman, William Menninger, and the secretary, Henry W. Brosin. In the first of a series of influential reports, GAP argued against the indiscriminate use of electroshock therapy. Soon it implied that psychotherapy and group therapy were primary treatments, while other methods including electric and insulin shock treatment and narcotherapy were "auxiliary."[27] Although insisting that personal analysis and thorough psychoanalytic training should remain optional, GAP insisted that psychoanalytic training conform to the "requirements of the American Psychoanalytic Association.[28] GAP was a powerful instrument in the expansion of a psychoanalytic psychiatry.

Under Robert Felix, NIMH pursued an eclectic mix that included biological, psychodynamic and social science approaches to mental health.[29] Psychiatry, Felix believed, needed to treat in a community setting the "ambulatory ill" and those with a high likelihood of breakdown in order to prevent the development of serious mental illness and subsequent hospitalization.[30]

Felix heavily emphasized the social sciences and NIMH supported a wide range of research projects, sociological and anthropological as well as somatic, genetic, and psychological. Of some $156,000,000 in research grants awarded between 1948 and 1963, NIMH gave a modest $3,966,376 to psychoanalysts, psychoanalytic projects, or institutions, including $446,716 to the Chicago Psychoanalytic Institute. Most of these projects were not directly for research in psychoanalysis; most were for psychoanalysts working in related fields, such as studies of family relationships in schizophrenia, autism, mental hospitals, psychosomatic studies of adults and children, and early infant development.[31] Between 1947 and 1973 NIMH gave $2,964,156 of its funds for research in psychotherapy to psychoanalysis, some 7 percent out of a total of $30,306,159. In the same period nearly 50 percent or $13,920,770, went to behavior therapy.[32]

Psychoanalytic research was privately funded also. The psychoanalyst Lawrence Kubie had treated Charles Murphy, a very wealthy patient, who for years had suffered from recurrent mood swings of depression and mania. A Yale graduate, he had been treated by two other psychoanalysts before Kubie. Kubie introduced him to Frederick C. Redlich, who emphasized the poor quality of psychiatric research and the tantalizing unknowns in the field. Together, Kubie and Redlich persuaded Murphy to set up the Foundations' Fund for Research in Psychiatry, over which Redlich would preside. "It was a time of enormous optimism about psychoanalysis, both as a research instrument and as a therapy," the secretary of the foundation recalled. "Through analysis, it was hoped, psychiatrists would understand the unconscious of the human mind and thus find ways to raise healthier children, prevent the development of mental illness, cure the mentally ill and even produce a saner society.[33] The foundation hoped to develop a stronger scientific basis for psychoanalytic hypotheses about sexual or aggressive motivation, for example, or sibling rivalry and generational conflict. Many of its first research projects were psychoanalytic. Beginning in 1953 grants were made to the psychoanalysts George Engel, Sybille Escalona, Anna Freud, Marianne Kris, John Bowlby, Franz Alexander, Merton Gill, and Erich Fromm. Erik Erikson's *Young Man Luther* was written on a foundation grant. Of 76 fellowships awarded, 15 supported psychoanalytic training for research. Thus psychoanalysts received a substantial, but comparatively modest share of both public and private research money. Considering the small number of psychoanalysts, some 850 in 1961, this funding attested to high faith in the psychoanalytic mission.

The promise of psychoanalytic psychiatry—its claim to be a fundamental tool of research, and a mode of equally fundamental explanation and treatment—attracted the enthusiasm of a growing number of psychiatric educators. From 1947 to 1963 psychoanalysis became a major presence in the psychiatric departments of medical schools and their texts.[34] It played a new role in the psychiatric training of medical students and psychiatric residents. By 1965, it seemed clear that "psychoanalytically oriented teaching in a medical school" increased the number of medical students choosing psychiatry as a career and that the presence of a psychoanalytic institute attracted residents "to training centers within commuting distance."[35] Gradually, disciples of Freud replaced the disciples of Adolf Meyer as chairmen of departments of psychiatry. By 1962, 52 of the 89 heads of psychiatric departments in America were members of psychoanalytic organizations.[36] Henry Brosin was appointed successively to the universities of Chicago and Pittsburgh, John Romano to Rochester, Normal Brill to UCLA, Lawrence Kolb to Columbia.

By 1954 a large majority of psychiatric residents described their orientation as Freudian or neo-Freudian, and desired psychoanalytic training.[37] Some 90 percent wanted to establish themselves in practice with a mix of part-time teaching and research, a reflection of the routine of many psychoanalysts. By 1962, 90 of 91 medical schools were teaching psychoanalytic theory to medical students, and many had psychoanalysts on their staffs.[38] In 1963, 1,009 of the 3,617 residents in psychiatric training across the nation were students in psychoanalytic institutes.[39]

Student attitudes coincided with the books they were reading or were assigned. Of the 17 books most often recommended to psychiatric residents, 13 were psychoanalytic, including Erik Erikson's *Childhood and Society,* Franz Alexander and Helen Ross's *Dynamic Psychiatry,* Charles Brenner's *An Elementary Textbook of Psychoanalysis,* Otto Fenichel's *Psychoanalytic Theory of Neurosis,* Anna Freud's *Ego and the Mechanisms of Defense,* and Stanton and Schwartz's *The Mental Hospital,* a study of the psychoanalytic sanitarium Chestnut Lodge. The most frequently recommended article was Freud's "Mourning and Melancholia," an essay on the psychological origins of depression.[40]

In addition to the Columbia institute, psychoanalytic training programs were established in the Downstate Medical Center in Brooklyn of the State University of New York, at the Flower Fifth Avenue Hospital of the New York Medical School, and at Tulane, in New Orleans, founded by psychoanalytic psychiatrists from Columbia.[41] By 1960, of 108 graduates of the Columbia program four were professors and chairmen of departments of psychiatry, 85 held academic appointments in medical schools, and 72 taught psychodynamics and psychoanalytic theories in universities, state mental hospitals, or federal institutions.[42]

Major psychiatric textbooks, which had been heavily influenced by Adolf Meyer into the 1940s, became increasingly Freudian. One of these, Arthur P. Noyes and Lawrence Kolb's *Modern Clinical Psychiatry,* by 1967 was the first choice for assigned reading. Noyes was trained at Boston Psychopathic Hospital and later at St. Elizabeth's under William Alanson White and had been attracted to psychoanalytic psychiatry in the 1920s. Kolb, a later co-author, was trained first at Johns Hopkins, and during wartime service with the Navy was impressed by the psychoanalytic explanations of patients' symptoms by his colleague Robert Cohen, who later became research director at NIMH. Kolb was analyzed by Frieda Fromm-Reichmann at the Washington Psychoanalytic Institute; under his authorship, the text became more insistently Freudian. Dedicated to Adolf Meyer, Strecker and Ebaugh's *Practical Clinical Psychiatry for Students and Practitioners* by 1957 was using a medical psychology that was almost entirely psychoanalytic. Again the shift in emphasis was associated with a new author, Jack Ewalt, appointed Massachusetts Commissioner for Mental Health in 1951.

These new texts differed from previous ones in major ways. They emphasized more strongly than ever the importance of early childhood, including Freudian stages of psychosexual development, presented psychoanalytic theories of the neuroses and of psychosomatic disorders more fully than ever before, and granted them more authoritative status. They suggested that psychoanalytic treatment was most successful for certain types of neuroses. New techniques of psychoanalytic psychotherapy were being applied with hopeful results to psychosomatic disorders and to psychoses such as schizophrenia, as auxiliary or primary treatment.

Nevertheless, as John Burnham and Gerald Grob have argued, American psychiatry has remained insistently eclectic, even during these years of greatest psychoanalytic impact. This was not as clear in medical psychology, which seeks to explain the origins of nervous and mental disorders, as it was in treatment. For example, the limitations of psychotherapeutic treatment, particularly in the psychoses, were emphasized. Noyes and Kolb neatly combined Meyerian and psychoanalytic psychotherapy by classifying both as "genetic-dynamic," the former dealing largely with conscious, the latter with unconscious factors. Moreover, in most texts, psychotherapy, particularly in the treatment of the psychoses, was combined with somatic treatment, which was dominated after 1952 by the new phenothiazine drugs which had largely replaced insulin and the more popular electroshock.[43]

Sylvano Arieti's *American Handbook of Psychiatry,* published in 1959, marked perhaps the high point of the psychoanalytic style in psychiatry, but it too was insistently eclectic. It included information not only on psychoanalysis and psychoanalytic psychiatry; there were chapters on genetic factors in the psychoses, with which the editor disagreed, on the newer drug treatments, on recent behavioral approaches, and on some of the newer neurological and biological research, which was just beginning to emerge. It was followed in 1967 by another even more insistently eclectic compendium, *The Comprehensive Textbook of Psychiatry,* edited by Alfred M. Freedman, which gave a larger place to behavior therapies.

The first postwar diagnostic manuals of the American Psychiatric Association, partly influenced by the psychoanalyst William Menninger's classification system for the Army, reflected psychoanalysis chiefly in descriptions of the neuroses. Thus hysterical symptoms were "symbolic of the underlying conflicts," while the symptoms of anxiety could be "controlled unconsciously and automatically by conversion, displacement and various other psychological mechanisms."[44]

One major tendency among influential psychoanalytic psychiatrists was to erase distinctions between the neuroses and the psychoses and to emphasize their existence along a continuum. The unitary concept of all nervous and mental disorder also had been advanced by Adolf Meyer, and it was reinforced by experiences in World War II. Because those with predisposition presumably had been screened out at induction, stress, such as length of exposure to battle conditions, seemed the decisive variable. In the postwar period, epidemiologists ignored conventional psychiatric diagnoses and the possibility of predisposition and assumed that social factors such as poverty, class, and rapid social change were the "civilian stress equivalents of combat and threat of death in the military."[45]

Karl Menninger's *The Vital Balance,* published in 1964, was an extreme example of continuity theory. His first tactic was to argue that "most people have some degree of mental illness at some time," just as "most of us have some physical illness some of the time."[46] With a suggestion of threat, Menninger then implied that those who did not accept this dictum and who scoffed at psychiatry could fall prey to more serious psychiatric illness than other people.[47] Diagnoses were useful only for treatment. Tilting at attempts to classify by course and outcome, such as Emil Kraepelin's classical nosology, he argued that mental illness was not like a physical illness caused by an agent such as a bacterium. Rather, it was a "defensive reaction" and therefore had no course of development predetermined by its category. The vast majority of patients improved or recovered, but a small number did not, and a still smaller number got worse.

Menninger's book represented a high point of the psychoanalytic psychological style, and it was profoundly optimistic:

> The old point of view assumed that most mental illness was progressive and refractory. The new point of view is that most mental illness serves its purpose and disappears, and does so more rapidly and completely when skillfully understood and dealt with.[48]

By 1965 a younger generation of psychiatrists had established a new style of psychodynamic practice in American psychiatry, based to a considerable extent on psychoanalysis. The new view argued for a continuum between the psychoses and the neuroses and advanced highly optimistic claims for explanation and treatment. Associated with the reform of psychiatric hospitals, the new style nevertheless fostered the growth of private practice. Zeal, hope, and intellectual curiosity motivated its proponents as well as financial rewards above those of many other psychiatrists, particularly those in public institutions. Psychoanalytic training and research were funded to a modest extent by the National Institute for Mental Health in its mission to increase the personnel and scope of psychiatry. Psychoanalysts began to dominate psychiatry at the most prestigious medical schools. Nevertheless, the practice of perhaps most psychiatrists remained eclectic, combining somatic methods with the new psychotherapy. At the same time, psychoanalysts energetically expanded their domain in psychosomatic medicine, the treatment of schizophrenia, and the "character disorders," and they launched experiments with shorter forms of psychoanalytic psychotherapy, developments to which we will now turn.

15

Expanding Applications: Psychosomatic Medicine, Schizophrenia, the "Borderline" Personality

The new institutional base in the medical schools, influential organizations such as the Group for the Advancement of Psychiatry, as well as high claims and optimistic nosologies, laid the basis for further expansion of the psychoanalytic domain. Some psychoanalysts applied their psychotherapeutic techniques on a larger scale than ever before to illnesses ranging from asthma to schizophrenia and to the "borderline" patient whose symptoms fell somewhere between the neuroses and the psychoses. All these were now within the "widening scope of psychoanalysis." A few cautious psychoanalysts emphasized the often intractable nature even of the neuroses, but in the immediate postwar years, it was the message of hopeful promise that was heard most often.

By 1954, Leo Stone, a circumspect New York analyst who had worked at Menninger's, noted the excessive applications. "In the last decade or two, at least in the United States, any illness or problem which has a significant emotional component in its etiology has become at least a possible indication for psychoanalysis."[1] Outside the psychoanalytic community, physicians were prematurely misapplying the concepts in diagnosis. For example, after an initial physical examination of a patient with a bowel complaint, which showed nothing abnormal, a resident might call for a psychiatric consultation, only to learn later than an x-ray showed cancer of the colon.

For many budding psychiatrists the rapid recovery of military patients from psychosomatic symptoms and war neuroses created a hopeful interest in psychosomatic medicine. The bulk of research in psychosomatic medicine from 1939 to 1959 was North American and much of it was psychoanalytic.[2] The field became dominated by psychiatrists and psychoanalysts, while other medical specialists contributed less and less. There was also a greater interest in conceptualization and experiment, and psychologists entered the field in growing numbers with consequences that will become apparent later.[3]

The high point of the psychodynamic emphasis in psychosomatic medicine coincided with the peak of psychoanalytic influence, from about 1945 to 1963. One of the most extreme statements of the psychological style in psychosomatic medicine was formulated by a Montreal psychiatrist in 1948:

> The fact that the mind rules over the body, no matter how much it was neglected by biology and medicine, is the most fundamental fact which we observe continuously during all our life. Our body carries out the most complicated and refined motor activity under the influence of such psychologic phenomena as ideas and wishes.

Medical analogies made Alexander's specificity theories plausible. Just as specific "pathologic micro-organisms" targeted specific organs, so different emotional conflicts also targeted specific organs. "Inhibited rage" involved the cardiovascular system; "dependent, help seeking tendencies" were related to "the function of nutrition"; while a conflict between sexual and dependent wishes influenced the respiratory system.[4]

Faith in the promise of psychosomatic medicine grew rapidly. The *Journal of the American Medical Association* accepted the plausibility of the general psychosomatic approach, as did a growing number of medical texts.[5] By 1948 medical interest in psychosomatic medicine was almost twice that in psychoanalysis.[6]

In the postwar years, one of the disorders most often studied by psychosomaticists was asthma, a serious, sometimes fatal illness in which the bronchioles constrict, causing patients to wheeze, cough, and have difficulty breathing. Psychoanalytic asthma research exemplified an increasing refinement of observations finally made partly irrelevant, whether accurate or not, by the development of more effective somatic treatment. It also exemplified the role medical specialists and psychologists played as critics of psychoanalytic hypotheses.

As with other psychosomatic disorders, the systematic study of psychological factors emerged from failures of the somatic style—ineffective therapies and contradictory theories. A variety of somatic theories had been developed to account for asthma, and by 1910 it increasingly was attributed to allergic sensitivity. Yet many asthma patients were not demonstrably allergic, while in other patients psychological factors seemed to play an obvious role. Since Hippocrates, some physicians had associated asthma attacks with strong emotions, and even at the high point of somaticism in the late 19th century, cases were reported in which emotional factors clearly precipitated attacks, and psychological treatment, such as suggestion or hypnosis, had relieved them.

In the face of these uncertainties, psychoanalysts hoped to explain and to treat this enigmatic disease. Early psychosomatic researchers hoped for clear answers to these questions. What sorts of personalities develop the disease? What kinds of parents raise asthmatic children? Does psychotherapy relieve or prevent asthma? To each of these questions answers were forthcoming that appeared to be an orderly elaboration of the psychoanalytic model.

The psychoanalysts' strategy for verifying hypotheses and demonstrating the success of treatment was the accumulation of clinical cases, often backed by psychological tests, chiefly the Rorschach. As one of Alexander's students, Leon Saul, phrased it, "the correctness of certain psychosomatic formulations is repeatedly confirmed by clinical experience."[7] The progression of psycho-analytic cases built upon each other and seldom alluded to the strictures of outside critics. Moreover, as with other analytic data, the distinction between theory and empirical case material was difficult to establish; in fact, the two were inseparable, psychoanalytic theory giving cues regarding what to investigate in the individual case, and in turn the case sometimes leading to emendations of theory. Analysts often modified previous findings on the basis of their own clinical experience when it did not fit existing formulations. Such was the fate of many of Alexander's hypotheses.

Repeated findings that asthma improved dramatically when a child left home for a period of time and worsened when he returned suggested that the relationship of the child to the parents was crucial. This observation apparently was confirmed and an exclusively allergic factor discounted in one group of children by a dramatic experiment in which those who had recovered in the hospital had their rooms sprayed with dust from their homes, yet they continued to remain symptom-free.[8]

As early as 1935, two English investigators had suggested that an over-protective mother might be involved.[9] By 1941 Alexander believed asthmatics suffered from "excessive, unresolved dependence" upon the mother, a deep-seated conflict between independent and dependent impulses. The asthma attacks represented a cry for her help and a substitute for feelings of intense anxiety. In confirmation of this hypothesis, it was observed that attacks often ceased when patients could cry or when they confessed something for which they felt guilty and expected rejection.[10] Asthma patients dreamed far more frequently than other neurotics of maternal, intrauterine symbols such as water, caves, and enclosed spaces.

The situation preceding onset was important. Asthma attacks occurred during situations of actual or threatened loss, particularly during periods of separation from the mother. A fourteen-year-old girl developed asthma when she had to leave home for boarding school for the first time, again when she graduated, and again, years later, when her mother to whom she had been deeply attached became dangerously ill.[11] Asthma might begin in a child with the birth of a sibling or symptoms might grow worse with the departure of a parent on a trip.

The statistical apparatus of most early clinical studies was simple. Alexander and French used other neurotic patients for comparison when they wished to demonstrate, for instance, that asthmatics dreamed far more often of intrauterine symbols. Simple percentages indicated recoveries.

The analysts' early attitude toward experimentation was summed up by Alexander in 1941. Psychology, he argued, had been rendered sterile for decades by the pursuit of precise laboratory correlations and by "uncritical and aimless experiments." Some modern scientists were blindly fascinated by quantitative, if irrelevant, data, and by a "peculiar depreciation of careful comparative observations" of phenomena "as they occur in nature."[12] However, because of the great complexity of the variables involved in a field such as psychosomatic medicine, only clinical observation could suggest meaningful hypotheses for significant experiment and correlation. Moreover, life situations could not be reproduced in the laboratory, making meaningful experiments unusually difficult.

Alexander reiterated his belief that a specific organ vulnerability, an "x factor," was requisite if asthma were to occur. Emergence of the disease required not only this "x factor" but also a psychodynamic constellation and an onset situation that elicited the constellation. In the 15 years after these theories were advanced in 1941, some psychosomaticists transformed his formulations about asthma, which had granted a considerable role to constitutional factors, into a more narrowly psychological model. They seemed to be constructing from the intricate material of psychoanalytic treatment simple typologies and clusters of traits that defined the conflicts of psychosomatic patients and the personalities of their mothers. Although they continued to insist on a strong distinction between personality type and underlying conflict, in practice this distinction became blurred. There was the promise, a psychologist critic observed, of "types neatly stacked in appropriate bundles: the ulcer type, the ulcerative colitis type, the characteristic 'pattern' of the hypertensive personality, the migraine character, the pruritic self-excoriator. . . . "[13]

In many American psychoanalytic explanations of disorders ranging from schizophrenia to psychosomatic symptoms, blame lay with the parents, especially the mother. In asthma, a crucial role was played by the mother's behavior toward her asthmatic child. The "asthmatogenic" mother was pathologically overprotective, yet in some cases she was also ambivalent, guilty, and unconsciously hostile and rejecting. The child responded to the rejection by increased clinging, especially when the mother tried to push the child toward premature independence.[14]

The role of the asthmatogenic mother seemed to be confirmed on an impressive scale by research using normal children as a control group. In a sample of 63 allergic and non-allergic school children, 98 percent of the mothers of allergic children, but only 20 percent of the other mothers, rejected their offspring, sometimes grossly. One mother of a three-year-old girl felt as if she could bash her child's brains out, while another remarked that her seven-year-old son made her physically ill. Some mothers lavished unusual care on their children to mask from themselves their own disapproving attitudes.[15]

In 1950 Alexander argued that both allergic and psychological factors together usually brought on asthma attacks; removing either sufficed to relieve the patient. He speculated that both were "parallel manifestations" of the same basic constitutional factor.[16] Demonstrating the efficacy of psychotherapy, one of Alexander's students reported that after analytic treatment four of five asthmatic children remained free of asthma although their skin tests still showed a positive allergic reaction.[17] In a case treated by another analyst, a young boy's asthma disappeared and he lost a long-standing sensitivity to animal hair so completely that he was able to have a hamster as a pet and to ride horseback.

In the psychoanalytic cases, the course of therapy was often lengthy, symptoms fluctuated, and the therapist's interpretations were regarded as crucial factors in successful treatment. Venting unexpressed feelings such as hostility to the therapist could create decisive improvement. Occasionally, less harmful symptoms were substituted for the asthma attacks: nightmares or crying spells or soiling in situations when attacks could have been expected to occur.[18] Sometimes the asthma might get temporarily worse, just before a final, complete remission. The clinical literature is full of illustrative, often successful cases, notably those by the psychoanalysts Lucy Jessner and Melitta Sperling.

The conception of a uniform underlying conflict in asthma and of equally uniform profiles for the asthma patient and the "asthmatogenic mother" were challenged, characteristically, by a number of psychoanalysts. The first concept to be attacked was Alexander's specificity theory. Sperling and a number of other analysts disputed Alexander's views of the character of the child and the maternal relationship. She argued that asthma occurred in children who had not been rejected, did not repress crying and did not have conflicts over wishes to separate or to cling. Rather many asthmatic children were indulged; they were crybabies and had temper tantrums. The asthmatogenic mother rejected the child when he was healthy and wanted to be independent. But she rewarded him when he was sick with a "high premium of exclusive attention and preoccupation with his illness."[19] Like Otto Fenichel, she argued that asthma represented a pregenital fixation with a large mix of oral and anal sadistic impulses.

Peter Knapp, psychoanalyst and professor of psychiatry at Boston University and a student of Felix Deutsch, in some of the most careful psychoanalytic studies of asthma, concluded that asthma patients displayed no single personality type and no single conflict, but rather a multiplicity of traits and conflicts. Attempts at "global" characterizations of mothers as rejecting or engulfing had outrun the evidence; clearly such traits appeared in the mothers of children who did not have asthma at all.[20] Knapp and other analysts questioned what they regarded as simplistic psychosomatic formulae on theoretical and methodological grounds. Too many investigators, they argued, had attempted to imitate germ theory by finding a "bacillus asthmaticus psychosomaticus," but asthma was far too complex to be accounted for by such a model. Lawrence Kubie questioned the entire specificity concept on grounds that medicine had moved toward increasingly complex explanations in which all biochemical and biophysical processes were involved in a single disease. The same neurotic symptom might have many different determinants, and patients with clinically identical disorders showed dissimilarities "as impressive as the similarities." Although the central neurotic process was "remarkably constant," the neurotic symptom was as "variable in its meaning as the dream symbol." A series of psychosomatic symptoms might replace each other: ulcerative colitis might be followed by severe dermatitis, to be replaced in turn by migraine, and finally perhaps by a psychotic break.[21]

Roy Grinker argued that there had been a lack of "critical challenge" to the few existing theories, that psychosomatic formulations had become stereotypes into which each patient's life history is molded by "special focusing, selective interpretation and omission, or neglect of the incongruent."[22] He called for the incorporation of field and systems theories to make the conceptual framework truer to the complexities of the problems involved.

Responding to criticism, Knapp and a few other analysts began to use prediction as a method of checking their own hypotheses. He presented a careful predictive study of a male patient who had been in psychoanalysis for six years. From notes taken during the treatment, 81 events that might or might not precipitate asthma attacks were chosen for review by two psychoanalysts and two internists. They were to select those events that they believed would precede episodes of asthma, and the case notes were edited to remove any medical clues that might suggest an attack. The psychoanalysts, with a success rate ranging from 69 to 82 percent were better at prediction than the internists, who had a success rate of 64 percent. The psychoanalysts had looked for precipitating events such as "stress, emotional arousal and the disruption of defenses."

Such precipitating factors activated an emotional core of conflicting, regressive, primitive fantasies of destruction that were inhibited by guilt and fear. At the same time primitive longings and urges to "take in, retain and eliminate through the respiratory apparatus" also were accentuated by the precipitating events. No single variable "predicted asthma or its absence with conspicuous success." Rather "complex and specific patterns, changes in repetitive configurations in the patient's life and the material he brought to psychoanalysis" gave rise to the fluctuations.

Where a knowledge of crucial variables or ways to test them experimentally were lacking, the clinical longitudinal study provided information obtainable in no other way, Knapp insisted. The "ebb and flow of material" revealed the structure of underlying dynamic patterns. By mobilizing "central conflicts" psychoanalytic treatment generated "unique data, relevant to a major disorder like asthma."[23] Knapp believed his evidence supported the central role of psychological factors. These alone, or in combination with biological determinants, could "initiate, sustain, or relieve" asthma.

Thus, by 1970, some psychoanalytic studies had included statistical evaluation of predictions, as well as correlations of psychological with physiological changes. But on the whole, these investigations remained primarily clinical studies, without formal controls, such as other matched subjects. They tended to assume the possibility that psychotherapy could alter physical symptoms by alleviating the "underlying" causes. At their best they represented careful attempts to observe the fluctuations of disease in relation to emotional experience over long periods of time and in the context of interpersonal relationships.

A renewed emphasis on biological factors and a marked expansion of the role of psychological factors in all disease were initiated in 1967 by George Engel, a psychoanalyst and psychosomatic researcher at the University of Rochester. He argued that in the traditional psychosomatic diseases, predisposing biological factors, present at birth or in early infancy, modified the "development of the psychic apparatus."[24] Patients with involvement of the same organ or organ system, the thyroid, for instance, resembled each other psychologically. He termed this formulation "somatopsychic-psychosomatic."

More important, for "literally the whole range of organic disease" an onset syndrome, the "Giving Up–Given Up" Complex, preceded the emergence of disease. It was not a necessary or sufficient condition, but it was a contributing one. The syndrome included despair, depression, grief, feelings of "irresolvable loss," or "deprivation." "It's no use," "I can't take it anymore," "I give up" were typical feelings.

The general effect of psychoanalytic psychosomatic studies was to extend the range of disorders in which psychological factors played an important role. And in some cases, psychological treatment was advanced as the therapy of choice. But such studies remained vulnerable to new somatic interventions and the criticism of specialists.[25]

In addition to their explorations in psychosomatic medicine, psychoanalytically trained psychiatrists began to work as therapists in the outpatient clinics that grew rapidly in the postwar period, some established by government agencies such as the Veterans' Administration, others by state hospital systems. The Los Angeles V.A. clinic applied a compendium of successive psychoanalytic therapeutic theories. The clinic claimed that none of them helped every patient, though most helped some of them. At first, therapists assumed that if veterans could express their feelings about their wartime experiences, particularly their hostility and aggression, they would recover. However, patients learned to express hostility but not to channel it effectively and appropriately. Next, when therapists tried doses of love and affection, patients became dependent and had greater difficulty expressing their anger. Then, therapists tried interpretation of emotions aroused by the family—"hostility, dependency, hate, rejection, and frustration"—as well as tender positive feelings. After that, the therapists became interested in ego strength as exemplified in previous adjustments to crucial situations. Finally, they began to emphasize integrative ego functions.[26] All these concepts had some utility, none was universally successful, but the last seemed unusually promising.

A few psychoanalytic psychiatrists energetically applied psychoanalytic principles to the psychoses and borderline conditions. Psychoanalysts had been among the conspicuous pioneers in the treatment of schizophrenia and other psychoses by psychotherapy. These attempts had begun with Jung, Karl Abraham, Paul Federn, and Ernst Simmel among Freud's early followers and had been developed partly independently in America by psychiatrists strongly influenced by the optimistic views of Adolf Meyer, Harry Stack Sullivan, and William Alanson White.[27] Washington-Baltimore, New York, Boston, and Topeka were the primary centers for these efforts. By 1944 psychoanalysts were consultants or staff members of at least nine private and four public hospitals, the latter including St. Elizabeth's in Washington, D.C., and Bloomingdale and the Utica State Hospital in the New York state hospital system.

The importance and excitement—and the unknowns—surrounding the psychoanalytic research and treatment of schizophrenia pervaded a 1950 conference at Yale. It was attended by major psychoanalytic and psychiatric workers, among them Frieda Fromm-Reichmann, Robert Knight, Kurt Eissler, Jerome Frank, and Frederick Redlich. The conference agreed that schizophrenia remained psychiatry's "number one riddle"; schizophrenics occupied one-fourth of the nation's hospital beds.[28] At that moment it was an open question whether schizophrenia had a somatic or psychological origin. In some cases it was possible to explain how schizophrenia developed after gathering all the constitutional, "physical, psychological, and historical data" about a given patient. Yet people with similar histories did not develop the illness. In other cases, the breakdown was far more serious than the difficulties of the patient's life would suggest. The champions of a psychological interpretation often clashed in an "antagonistic, emotional manner" with those who favored a biological approach, Redlich observed. The psychoanalyst Robert Knight suggested a soothing compromise, a division into "process" schizophrenia, the result of psychosocial catalysts, and "nuclear schizophrenia," caused by obscure constitutional factors.

Although psychotherapeutic treatment was prolonged and difficult, there were "a number of detailed case reports" on successfully treated patients. Each patient had needed hundreds of hours of therapy, extending over months or years. Although only a few patients could be reached by this method, it had tremendous research value in elucidating how symptoms developed. Moreover, the war had demonstrated that patients with "mild schizophrenic syndromes" induced by the stress of combat had recovered rapidly; Redlich urged the careful study of such recuperative processes.

How the somatic therapies in use—insulin, electroshock— actually worked remained unknown, and their results were equivocal. There were only a few good studies of the outcome of shock therapy and hardly any comparative evaluations of psychotherapy. But psychotherapy helped patients receiving shock treatment because it was directed against their outstanding symptoms and would always have a place in the rehabilitation of schizophrenics. The bulk of the psychological knowledge about schizophrenia had been obtained through psychotherapy, and new research might lead to more effective therapy in the future.

Redlich declared that if he himself developed a psychosis he would prefer "to obtain prolonged intensive dynamic psychotherapy by an experienced psychoanalyst who likes schizophrenics, carried out in a specially equipped hospital. I hope I would be able to find and afford such a therapist and hospital for they are extremely rare. If such procedure failed, I would consent to shock treatment, and later to a lobotomy."[29]

A few years after the Yale conference, Sylvano Arieti argued that psychoanalytic psychotherapy was superior to somatic treatment in schizophrenia because the latter produced only "symptomatic improvement, whereas psychotherapy tends to: (1) remove the basic conflicts which led to the disorder, (2) correct the psychopathologic patterns, and (3) permit the regenerative psychological powers of the organism to regain the lost ground."[30]

Psychotherapy with psychotics was a slow, painstaking, sometimes even dangerous procedure, and those who believed in it were in a distinct minority among both psychiatrists and psychoanalysts. A daring, sometimes bizarre psychoanalytic approach that gained considerable attention was developed by John Rosen, a psychoanalytic psychiatrist who believed it possible to enter the schizophrenic's world and communicate with the patient's unconscious through direct interpretation. The symptoms of a psychosis could be decoded just as could the symbols of a dream. Schizophrenia, he believed, began in the earliest oral stage of life when a perverse mother failed to meet her child's needs. Rosen believed so strongly in continuity theory that he also argued that if environmental pressures were severe enough, anyone could become schizophrenic, regardless of how healthy their development might have been. Like several other psychoanalytic psychiatrists, he believed that diagnostic categories meant little and that the illness rarely had an organic basis. He also argued that the deterioration so often perceived in patients resulted from institutionalization.

Rosen hoped to convince patients that they were understood on their own terms. He also believed that unmasking a symptom tended to dispel the need for it. "In its manifest content, what is the psychosis but an interminable nightmare in which the wishes are so well disguised that the psychotic does not awaken?" he wrote. "Why not then awaken the psychotic by unmasking the real content of his psychosis?"[31]

Rosen's technique was blunt. For example, a young man imagined himself flying over the Atlantic, sighted his mother floating in the water and dive-bombed her. Rosen recalled, "After this beautiful symbolic expression of incest, he screamed, 'Don't cut off my balls, Papa.' . . . Impulsively I screamed back, 'All right, I won't cut off your balls. I am your papa and I won't cut off your balls.'" In still another example of direct interpretation, when a patient said to Rosen, "You are a son of a bitch. Cock-sucker. Your father put his cock in your mother's mouth, and that is how you were born. I had a feeling stronger than ever to throw myself under an elevated train."

Rosen replied: "Father will fuck you in the ass. The train is a big powerful penis and you wish to lay under it."[32] Rosen claimed impressive results in bringing patients out of acute psychotic episodes.

Mothering acute schizophrenic patients was a technique tried by Rosen and other psychoanalytic psychiatrists. Careful doses of "loving affection" seemed to make contact on a primary, fundamental level and served to bring patients out of an acute phase of their illness.[33]

As with asthma, so now with schizophrenia, some perceived the patient's mother as the principal cause of the illness.[34] The schizophrenogenic mother, the "perverse mother," as Rosen called her, took her place alongside the asthmatogenic mom.[35] The schizophrenogenic mom was "aggressive," "subtly or overtly rejecting," domineering, and insecure, married to an inadequate, passive, indifferent father. Other schizophrenogenic mothers were fussy and overprotective, anxious to preserve "the symbiotic union." Similar characterizations have depicted the parents of children with bronchial asthma, ulcerative colitis, and rheumatoid arthritis.[36] In a thoughtful and perceptive review of Rosen's views, the psychoanalyst Leo Stone argued that contact could be established with schizophrenics simply by an attitude of "motherly gentleness" without making interpretations or assuming authoritative roles as Rosen had done. It was a mistake to cultivate the fantasy that the nurse's or physician's role was identical with that of the devoted parent. Real analytic work could be accomplished only by making the least possible concession to fantasy in thought or emotion that would permit "working contact with the psychotic patient."[37]

One of the most thorough-going attempts at psychotherapy with schizophrenic patients that also used a principle of judicious mothering was undertaken at Chestnut Lodge, a private hospital near Washington, D.C., where Frieda Fromm-Reichmann, one of the leaders in the field, was on the staff. A tiny 4'10", she was one of the few German women to earn a medical degree before World War I and during the war treated soldiers with brain injuries. She later worked with J. H. Schultz, the originator of the relaxation therapy autogenic training, who suggested she read Freud. She was trained at the Berlin institute, was married to Erich Fromm for a time, and with him rejected orthodox Judaism. After Hitler's rise to power she emigrated to France, then to Palestine, and finally, in 1935, to the United States. Her approach to therapy was low-key, supportive, and modest. Her *Principles of Intensive Psychotherapy* (1950) made no grandiose claims for the cure of schizophrenia. But she included case histories in which schizophrenics clearly recovered as a result of therapy, one catatonic patient, for example, after eight years of hospitalization and four years of intensive psychotherapy.[38] The autobiographical novel *I Never Promised You a Rose Garden* was written by a former patient, partly as a testimony to the success of her methods. She condemned "deep interpretations" such as Rosen's, even if they were effective, as "arbitrary, if not incorrect."[39]

Fromm-Reichmann's therapy was the natural outcome of her etiological theories. Schizophrenics developed a severe, anxiety-provoking conflict between dependency and hostility as the result of failed early mothering. They were desperately afraid of their own hostile and destructive impulses. The conflict arose because of the patient's neglect "by the 'bad mother' at a time when her attention was indispensable for the infant's and the child's survival."[40]

This neglect caused "resentment, anger, hostility, fury, or violence" in the patient, who responded with "regression into an early state of ego-development and of autistic self-concern and self-preoccupation." By focusing on the patient's defenses against anxiety in relation to the psychoanalyst, she hoped to clarify the "unknown causes" of his or her anxieties in general.[41] "Eventually, patients should learn to spot their anxieties," recognize their irrationality, and relinquish them as much as possible.[42]

She tempered her "maternal" approach with the recognition that too effusive mothering might "enhance fear of intimacy and dependence on the therapist." It might put into motion the "psychopathological chain of dependent attachment, resentment, anxiety, symptom formation." The therapist simply could not "make up" to the patient the lack of love in early life. "Patients have to learn to integrate the early loss and to understand their own part in their interpersonal difficulties with the significant people of their childhood." Ultimately, patients came to interpret the love and consideration given them by the therapist as "proof that they are not so bad, so hostile . . . as they feel themselves to be."[43]

The goal of her therapy was change in the "dynamic structure" of the patient's personality and the resolution of symptoms through insight into the unconscious roots of problems. This was only possible with long-term intensive psychoanalytic psychotherapy and differed from brief therapy which limited the role of insight and aimed only at social recovery.

She modified a number of traditional psychoanalytic views. Like Sullivan, with whom she had worked, she argued that the search for historical material, such as early Oedipal strivings, could blind therapist and patient to present problems including the patient's relation to the therapist. Moreover, the patient's transference was not merely a repetition of unresolved Oedipal constellations but also reflected relations with other significant people besides the parents. Dissolution of the patient's intense and often distorted transference by searching for its early roots was a prerequisite for successfully ending treatment. She also placed particular emphasis on the therapist's counter-transference to the patient at a time when the concept of the detached, "mirror" analyst was in vogue. Free association did not need to be a central part of intensive therapy because it was unnecessarily time-consuming and, as analysts had warned before, could increase "disintegrated thinking" in borderlines and psychotics. Nevertheless, it was useful if, for instance, the flow of thought ran dry. She saw patients 4 to 6 times a week usually for lengthy sessions.[44]

Fromm-Reichmann believed in an innate drive toward "growth and maturation." For schizophrenics this did not imply a "conventional adjustment" but self-realization, which had been given too little attention in the classic psychoanalytic literature. The insecure psychiatrist's own "virtuous adjustment to the conventionalities of his time" could "interfere with his ability to listen in a valid fashion" and understand the patient's real needs.[45] Genital maturity would come from reasonable freedom from "anxiety, greed, envy, jealousy," rather than the other way around. For a time her work was regarded with a jaundiced eye by the more orthodox psychoanalysts because of her theoretical and technical departures.[46]

The institutional setting in which Fromm-Reichmann worked represented one of the most ambitious attempts to realize the psychodynamic style in psychiatry. Chestnut Lodge, with 45 to 58 patients, was run primarily by psychoanalysts, several of them, like Fromm-Reichmann, with national reputations. Psychiatric residents on the staff were often in training at psychoanalytic institutes in Washington and Baltimore. The hospital was studied intensively by the psychiatrist Alfred H. Stanton and the sociologist Morris S. Schwartz, who published their findings in the classic *The Mental Hospital* in 1954.

The goal of treatment at Chestnut Lodge was no less than radical recovery, an adjustment so secure that the patient was less likely to break down than he had been before he first became ill. This was a stringent criterion and represented psychoanalytic ambition at its most impressive. The goal was to be achieved by intensive psychotherapy alone, with only the minimal use of drugs or physical restraints.

At Chestnut Lodge, patients and therapists alike agreed that psychotherapy was the treatment of choice, and the patient's hospital life revolved around the therapeutic hour three or four times a week. "Therapeutic" attitudes pervaded hospital discourse, and a kind of psychoanalytic subculture developed among the staff that parodied therapy and theory. There was a "fantasy of life as one great psychotherapeutic hour," and the belief that "everyone is mentally ill blunted the sharp reality of the handicap of mental illness." The staff was often hostile to relatives, particularly parents. Mothers usually were blamed indirectly for their children's illness, and patients accepted this; relatives often insisted on their own guilt. Among the staff, apology was frowned upon and a premium placed upon "straight talk," "frankness," "expressiveness." Conflict was interpreted as evidence of transference difficulties. The hospital aimed to keep the level of anxiety as low as possible because it was every patient's central problem and because gaining insight in psychotherapy always provoked some anxiety.

Sometimes reality was ignored in handling patients. One woman who in fact needed to make a will found that her announcement that she must do so was read by her therapist as a sign she might commit suicide and needed to be on the disturbed ward. At this, she became incoherent, which the therapist took to be confirmation of his diagnosis.[47]

The generalized therapeutic attitude of listening carefully to patients, based on the model of psychotherapy, could have highly beneficial effects. For example, a young woman of 23, who was in a state of acute catatonic excitement for two months talking incoherently, impressed a ward administrator by her use of the word clothing. She was asked whether she was worried about her clothes. She nodded and immediately became calmer. When she was told that she had torn up some of her clothing after she was admitted, her excitement disappeared almost completely. She had been anxious about the clothes she had destroyed because she was worried about the high cost of her hospitalization which she realized was out of all proportion to her family's income. Because of the concentration on formal psychoanalytic psychotherapy, the kind of practical understanding that this successful episode represented was widely known but little studied, and was of "relatively low prestige."[48]

How effective was the hospital? Stanton and Schwartz concluded that patients made real gains. Using the therapist's stringent criteria, over a five-year period, of a group of 77 paranoid schizophrenic patients who were treated by psychotherapy, 17 percent were well or much improved. This was a striking result because about 75 percent of all the patients had been ill for more than a year before being admitted to the hospital and therefore could be considered chronic. Their lives and their mental health were more satisfying to themselves and to those around them than before their breakdown. They also were less likely to fall ill than they had been before their first attack because they had developed insight into their illness, including partial understanding of *all* their symptoms, and had sustained lasting symptomatic improvement. Those "much improved" were less likely to break down and had insight into "almost all" their handicapping symptoms. Of the rest, 49 percent were improved and 13 percent were unchanged, were worse, or had died.[49]

However, these gains were achieved at high cost, against constant shortages of therapists, a fairly rapid turnover of personnel, and often considerable waiting before a therapist could be assigned to a patient. Typically, the staff psychotherapist had been a psychiatrist for only three years and had started out as a clinical administrator. As his psychoanalytic training advanced, he would begin to withdraw to see a few private patients, would continue this mixed practice for two or three years, and finally leave the hospital within eight years.[50] This pattern indicates clearly the contrary pull of private practice in even this outstanding hospital.

A total of about 165 people were employed to care for 45 to 58 patients—physicians, nurses, aides, occupational therapists, student nurses, a psychologist, a dietitian. The average monthly cost per patient in 1950 was $850, about three times the national median family income of $276. It was chiefly the patient's relatives, treated with "ambivalence and outright antagonism," who mostly paid the bills.[51] The hospital returned a profit.

The kind of psychoanalytic psychotherapy practiced at Chestnut Lodge was available chiefly to a small number of well-to-do patients in a very few private hospitals. The Menninger Hospital in Topeka, which also used psychotherapy extensively, had developed a method of studying the individual patient's "unconscious emotional needs". Then an appropriate treatment program involving psychotherapy as well as occupational, recreational, and bibliotherapy would be set up.[52]

There were growing attempts to apply psychoanalytic psychotherapy to psychotics, more often in group rather than individual therapy, in some public hospital systems, notably in New York, Massachusetts, California, and Kansas, where the Menningers strongly influenced psychiatric policy. By 1957-58, some 29 percent of hospitalized schizophrenic patients were receiving some kind of psychotherapy, largely as an adjunct to other methods. Some 23 percent of the patients in state hospitals and 43 percent of those in V.A. hospitals were in either individual or group psychotherapy. At private psychiatric hospitals almost all of the patients were receiving psychotherapy, and of these 10 percent were receiving psychoanalytic psychotherapy.

A majority of hospitals, about 57 percent, including most V.A. and state hospitals, were either noncommittal or unfavorably disposed to the use of psychotherapy with schizophrenics, while about 43 percent believed psychotherapy was beneficial. Many of those who favored psychotherapy believed patients also should receive somatic treatment.[53]

As psychoanalytic psychiatry grew in extent and application, psychoanalysts devoted considerable energy to defining the nature of psychoanalysis as opposed to psychoanalytic psychotherapy and to designating which disorders were optimally treated by each. American versions of classical psychoanalysis in the postwar period emphasized austerity and an absence of "transference gratifications," that is, an absence of suggestion in the form of reassurance or direct advice from the therapist.

In 1954 Leo Stone suggested that essential classical techniques could be applied to the continuing treatment of psychotics who had recovered, to patients with addictions and perversions, if these were experienced as illness, and to narcissistic, borderline patients. But there was a proviso. Such patients had to have what amounted to certain old-fashioned virtues: "courage, patience, deliberate purpose, tolerance for unavoidable suffering," a capacity for self-observation, and "self-appraisal." The "transference neuroses" and "character disorders" remained the disorders with which the classical method worked best:

> While the difficulties increase and the expectations of success diminish in a general way as the nosological periphery is approached, there is no absolute barrier; and it is to be borne in mind that both extranosological factors and the therapist's personal tendencies may profoundly influence the indications and prognosis.[54]

Roy Grinker took a broadly opposing view, arguing that borderline patients, because incapable of transference, were unanalyzable. He insisted that there were real nosological differences between schizophrenia, the neuroses, and borderline patients.[55]

The borderline patient requires further elucidation because psychoanalysts have claimed that they treat growing numbers of them. Originally the term "borderline" described patients whose disorder lay between the psychotic and the neurotic. Borderlines had a pattern of intense, unstable relationships. They lacked empathy and control, especially over angry and aggressive feelings, and experienced a "pervasive sense of aloneness" as well as chronic feelings of boredom and emptiness. They were convinced their difficulties came from outside themselves. They were subject to angry explosions and depression, and they lacked a consistent sense of identity. They could not synthesize positive and negative feelings and had a low tolerance for anxiety.

As with asthma and schizophrenia, the borderline syndrome was attributed to unresponsive mothering. A mother who could not meet the child's early need for autonomy or who withdrew prematurely confirmed the child's fear of his or her own aggressive fantasies. She needed to react to the child's aggression by non-anxious, firm limit setting while still providing love and understanding. At adolescence, when the borderline personality often first became manifest, the early themes of separation and individuation reappeared. Families sometimes withdrew from the adolescent's dependent needs, while others retaliated for the adolescent's strivings for autonomy, seeing them as a "hateful abandonment of the family."[56]

Otto Kernberg, a psychoanalyst trained in Latin America, where Melanie Klein's influence was strong, stressed the pathological internal object relations of borderline and narcissistic characters. His work fostered a marked interest in these conditions, and the borderline concept was included in the American Psychiatric Association's 1980 *Diagnostic and Statistical Manual III*.[57] Kernberg had worked at the Menninger Foundation with severely disturbed patients who often treated him with an indifference that masked devaluation and denigration, and he drew conclusions from their transference reactions to him.

Kernberg emphasized the crucial role of early "oral" rage in the formation of the borderline character. This excessive rage could, of course, be innate, Kernberg argued. But it also could be induced by a frustrating parent, often a mother who was rejecting, aggressive, chronically cold, and who failed to provide consolation and understanding. Such a mother might function well on the surface but was callous and indifferent and harbored "nonverbalized, spiteful aggression." As a result the child internalized a frightening image of the mother, sometimes of the father, an image freighted with the child's own intense anger. Without explicitly discussing the origin of positive feelings, Kernberg implied that the parents must have evoked libidinal hopes and ties, thus also creating positive internal objects. To protect themselves from the severe conflict engendered by these opposing positive and negative internal objects, borderlines resorted to "splitting," that is, to divorcing the libidinal and aggressive images, and to dividing external objects into all-good and all-bad, with abrupt shifts from one to the other. This resulted in "sudden and complete reversals of all feelings and conceptualizations about a particular person," with "extreme and repetitive oscillation between contradictory self concepts as well." Kernberg also emphasized the borderline's chronic diffuse anxiety; obsessive-compulsive symptoms, dissociations, hypochondria, paranoid and polymorphous perverse sexual trends, impulse neuroses, and addictions to alcohol and drugs.

Borderlines required a special psychoanalytic psychotherapy. This involved an active, as opposed to a classical "mirror" therapist, and frequent interpretation, primarily of the "manifest and latent negative transference." It required the confrontation of defenses, and the control of acting-out in the transference. The therapist could prescribe a structured environment, including possible hospitalization.

A particular narcissistic character, Kernberg argued, was a subspecies of the borderline. These patients greatly needed to be loved, and yet they displayed an unusual degree of self-reference in their interactions with others. They disparaged themselves yet also cherished an inflated self-image and needed inordinate "tribute from others." Deeply distrustful, they had little empathy with others' feelings; sometimes they were brilliant and functioned very successfully in the business or academic world. Their "haughty, grandiose and controlling behavior," was a defense "against paranoid traits," resulting from the projection of oral rage and against "primitive internalized object relationships of a frightening kind." Narcissistic patients identified themselves with their own ideal self-images in order to deny normal dependency on external objects and on the "internalized representatives of the external objects." For narcissistic patients, except for those with severe borderline characteristics, psychoanalysis was the treatment of choice. In both groups of patients, antisocial tendencies carried a negative prognosis.[58]

The results of therapy with narcissistic patients had important ethical consequences, reminiscent of Karl Abraham's genital character with its emphasis on social integration. Successful treatment resulted in a "growing identification with other people's happiness and achievements" that could benefit the patient over his entire lifespan, particularly as he grew old:

> The capacity to work through mourning processes, to be in love, to feel empathy and deep gratification in identifying with loved people and values, a sense of transcendence with nature, of continuation within the historical process, and of oneness with a social or cultural group, are all intimately linked to the normal activation of internalized object relationships at the time of loss, failure and loneliness.

Such progress gratified the analyst.

> To see a patient come alive during treatment, and begin to feel for the first time real concern for and interest in others as well as in an internal life of his own . . . compensates for the many months and years of emptiness and meaninglessness with which these patients try to drown the analytic situation.[59]

As the psychoanalytic domain came to include a wider gamut of patients, the need for briefer therapy became acute and led to renewed criticism of the classical technique: the mirror analyst, the parsimonious interpretation, prolonged treatment, the serendipitous coincidence of treatment and research. Franz Alexander, who organized symposia about brief therapy just after the beginning of World War II, argued that the effective element in psychoanalytic therapy came less from insight into the origin of the neuroses and more from a "corrective emotional experience." This occurred when the patient repeated old "interpersonal reaction patterns" in relation to the therapist, who then behaved differently from the original people in the patient's experience. Rank and Ferenczi had been the first to point out that re-experiencing previous dynamic patterns without necessarily remembering the original events that gave rise to them was sufficient to allow the patient to develop "attitudes appropriate to the present."[60] Originally, the aims of psychoanalytic therapy and psychoanalytic research had been united in the search for the origins of neurosis. For Alexander, intellectual insight tended to follow rather than to precede the corrective experience. The analyst was not a "blank screen," because his own reactions to his patient were "a significant factor in the therapeutic process." How the specific personality features of the therapist were perceived by the patient and how they influenced the course of treatment remained unknown. Alexander and others inspired a number of short-term psychoanalytic psychotherapies in the postwar period. As wider experience limited the types of patients for whom classical psychoanalysis was appropriate, psychoanalytic or "dynamic" psychotherapy was applied ever more widely and has remained perhaps the major American psychotherapeutic tradition.

By the late 1960s psychodynamic psychotherapy had become what the sociologist William Henry has called "the fifth profession." a common therapy plied alike by psychiatrists, clinical psychologists, social workers, and psychoanalysts of all the different schools, Freudian, Adlerian, neo-Freudian and so on. At the apex of this new profession were the psychoanalysts, the highest academic achievers, the best-paid, the most introspective—an appropriate personality profile perhaps for a passive therapist with heavy theoretical baggage.

Psychodynamics provided an entire language and a conceptual universe by which therapists explained their own and their patients' experience. In an analysis of the relation of religious backgrounds to therapy, Henry argued that Judaism placed fewer obstacles in the way of accepting a faith in psychological determinism but also provided less personal support than more "dogmatic faiths, and this left a vacuum psychotherapy could fill.[61]

The new therapies varied in degrees of eclecticism and departure from the "standard" analytic model and in the incorporation of other methods such as hypnotism, conditioning techniques, or drugs. In most of them the patient, instead of lying on a couch, sat up facing the therapist, who usually played an active role in treatment. Some of the new psychoanalytic therapies were informed by learning theory and the new behaviorism. They tended to focus on specific problems and were limited to a number of sessions, perhaps 30 or 40 for not more than a year. Many of these departures, like Alexander's views of the "corrective experience," were met at first with marked hostility by orthodox analysts.

Louis Wolberg, a New York therapist, built his system in part on Alexander's theories. He encouraged patients to verbalize their difficulties and gave them explanations for their troubles. He did not use free association or extensive dream interpretation and did not allow a transference neurosis to develop. Nevertheless, the therapist worked from psychodynamic principles, gaining some knowledge of the patient's relationship with his parents and siblings, his dreams, symptoms, and behavior. Wolberg might invite the patient to challenge his fears and try more rewarding behavior. He also used drugs or auto-hypnosis and relaxation to reduce anxiety so that the patient could master a feared situation. He encouraged patients to accept certain philosophical principles, such as responsibility. A patient should not make a "career out of blaming his parents and crediting to past unfortunate episodes all of his current problems, justifying his neurotic carryings-on by the terrible things done to him as a child over which he had no control."[62]

In a summary of modified psychoanalytic psychotherapy, Judd Marmor observed that in addition to Alexander's variations, the therapist might interview "significant others," modify "noxious environmental factors where possible," function as a "more active participant observer in therapeutic transactions," use crisis intervention, or apply psychodynamic principles to marital, family, and group therapy. In part this reflected a return to the more active therapeutic tradition of Adolf Meyer.[63]

In Boston, Peter Sifneos developed "Short Term Anxiety Provoking Psychotherapy," in which he would interpret conflicts before dealing with defenses, a technique that would give rise to anxiety and resistance, but which he believed could be overcome by the patient's strong motivation for improvement. A common technique in this and other psychoanalytic psychotherapies was the therapist's early interpretation of transference, pointing out similarities between the patient's reaction to the therapist and his reactions to his parents. Sifneos encouraged his patients to learn to deal with conflicts and solve problems after the therapy ended by having an imaginary dialogue with the therapist, imitating his questions and providing their own associations as answers. It succeeded best with a particular type of patient: one whose neurotic difficulties were circumscribed, who suffered from "unresolved Oedipal conflicts, loss and separation, morbid grief reactions."[64] Such patients also had good interpersonal relations, psychological sophistication, and motivation to change. Videotapes made it possible to study the therapeutic process in new and useful ways. Sifneos noted that few centers taught brief therapy, despite its obvious usefulness.

Nor was psychoanalytic psychotherapy necessarily always brief. For some patients, whom Robert Wallerstein has called "lifers," it could be as protracted as psychoanalysis, and indeed could last a lifetime on an occasional basis.[65] For these patients an ability to function was sustained by this lifelong contact with a therapist. There even have been cases in which therapy was carried on by telephone for bedridden elderly patients.

The expansion of psychoanalytic territory—into the psychoses, psychosomatic medicine, and the borderline personality—can be judged in several ways. From an economic point of view, it represented an imperialistic extension of psychoanalytic practice, in a period when that practice was becoming increasingly well paid and in wide demand and while official psychoanalytic training programs were restricting the supply of trained analysts. Expansion also represented a natural, almost inevitable thrust of the psychoanalytic model, of "our science" into areas where psychoanalysts firmly believed they could treat successfully new categories of patients. They thus brought, as one popularizer suggested, renewed "hope for the troubled." Expansion represented as well an exuberance of intellectual curiosity and an increasing agility in adapting psychoanalysis to perceived social needs. The golden years of psychoanalytic popularization were a natural accompaniment to these energetic efforts.

16

The "Golden Age" of
Popularization, 1945–1965

Wartime success and the postwar impact on psychiatry gave a new impetus to the popularization of psychoanalysis. The smart tongue-in-cheek skepticism of much of the 1920s publicity was replaced by a new seriousness in keeping with the rising status of the specialty. As psychoanalysis took hold in psychiatry, the journalistic accounts became notably more expert and favorable, ranging from easy, artful presentations in mass magazines such as *Life* to the careful exegeses of *Scientific American*. Again journalists often simplified, smoothed, and exaggerated the versions psychoanalysts and psychiatrists already had created. And probably many more journalists than ever before were in psychoanalytic therapy, thus bringing to bear first-hand experience, favorable or unfavorable.

In the accounts for mass magazines, stereotypes of the analyst, the patient, and the analytic process proliferated. First, writers, like the psychoanalysts themselves, tended to inflate the influence and achievements of Freud and to let them stand for an entire, complex cultural development, such as "modern psychiatry." Second, the popularizers devised a double image of the psychoanalyst: he was a regular, ordinary, successful American and at the same time, a highly trained scientific expert. Troubled patients were invariably people with whom the reader could identify. Third, they tended to mute Freud's sexual emphasis and, with reservations, made therapy more hopeful than Freud had believed it to be. At the same time, it became a severe personal discipline, corresponding to the "pure" American version of psychoanalysis, whose ultimate outcome was normalcy and happiness. Fourth, they needed to make even the most complex theory—and psychoanalysis in the hands of American ego psychologists did become unusually convoluted—seem natural and understandable through simplification. Finally, journalists tended to present both sides of any given issue, so that even in the period of greatest enthusiasm their popularizations were often ambivalent.

The confessional literature as well as the expository burgeoned. Celebrities, great and small, among them movie stars and journalists, recounted their experiences on the couch as more and more Americans joined the "friends and supporters of psychotherapy." But experience could be a two-edged sword, and a distinct if minority note of disillusion sounded as early as the 1950s, when stories surfaced about "how psychoanalysis broke up my marriage."[1]

During and after World War II, the wedding of psychoanalysis and psychiatry was celebrated in the cure of the war neuroses and the triumphs of early psychosomatic medicine. The euphoria reached a peak during the celebrations of Freud's 100th anniversary in 1956 and the appearance of Ernest Jones's three-volume study of Freud which was widely reviewed as one of the world's great biographies. Gradually, psychoanalysis became identified with the "establishment" in psychiatry and society, reconciled with conventional moral and religious values and sexual conventions. This basic conservatism was exemplified in psychoanalytic stereotypes of male and female roles, as well as analytic responses to the Kinsey reports and to the issue of homosexuality.

During and immediately after the Second World War the rhetoric of the psychoanalysts in both their medical and popular writings, and the missionary efforts of some of them, notably William Menninger and Franz Alexander, created a strong impression of the efficacy of psychotherapy and the scientific status of psychoanalytic theory and practice. This impression, based on apparent clinical experience, was particularly strong in popular writing about the war neuroses. There, the healing effects of the recall and catharsis of traumatic experiences, the importance and relevance of dreams, the benign and powerful role of the therapist, and above all the unshakably scientific standing of psychoanalytic conclusions were repeated time and again.

Until the spring of 1943, military censorship hampered journalistic coverage of the war neuroses, a censorship imposed because of the very magnitude of the problem. But the difficulty was not only censorship but the unappealing nature of the subject. The typical war story celebrated the heroic—the risks and horrors bravely borne, the lucky escapes, the rescue of buddies under fire, the selfless death and sacrifice of courageous men. Such stories made it difficult to write sympathetically about those who could not fight because of combat neuroses.

Popularizers, medical and journalistic, established saving stereotypes to deal with the unappealing psychoneurotic, and these crystallized at the high point of popularization of the war neuroses in 1944.[2] Psychoneurotic patients were heroes—big, apparently tough men, with long weeks of continuous fighting against the Japanese on Guadacanal or months of combat against the Germans in Europe or North Africa. Tom with a Silver Star, or Joe with a Purple Heart had risked his life to bring out a wounded buddy. One autobiographical account in the *Woman's Home Companion* began, "I fought the Jerry on more than a dozen missions. I fought until most of my outfit was killed, until I lost the ability to sleep, until hollows deepened under my eyes and my weight melted away."[3] Anyone might become a psychoneurotic patient, and everyone, even the strongest, had his breaking point. Because of the special horrors of modern warfare, that breaking point could be reached more quickly than ever before.

No other war had subjected men to such intense bombings, to such fiendish levels of noise, to such new and unpredictable tactics. In these circumstances, fear was inevitable and universal. "You've been up against dangers you'd never have to face in civilian life," a psychiatrist told his pilot patient. "If you hadn't, you'd probably have gone all through your life a normal person. So would most of the other chaps in here. But everybody has a breaking point. It's just a matter of degree. Once you're back home, you'll be all right."[4] William Menninger once had to explain that he had not argued that *everyone* in the service "would sooner or later become mentally or emotionally disabled," but rather that every soldier "may find himself in such a stressful set of circumstances that, great though his endurance may be, it may not be great enough."[5]

Not only were these patients heroes and the conditions of war worse than ever before, but the war's neuropsychiatric casualties were not crazy, like the mental hospital patient of peacetime. Rather, as *Time* informed its readers, they were "high strung, nervous people . . . who cannot face certain difficulties without developing bothersome symptoms such as headaches, tiredness, weakness, tremors, fears, insomnia, depression, obsessions, feelings of guilt."[6] If the patient was invariably heroic and not crazy, the psychiatrist was warmly sympathetic, understanding, charismatic, and possessed of uncanny insight.

The stereotypes of popularization bolstered certain conceptions that were derived from psychoanalysis but seldom were openly identified with it. The first of these, *Newsweek* reported, was the importance of catharsis. "Once they get it off their chests, half their battle is won," was a commonplace. "I used to hate to talk about it—what happened—but they told me it would do me good to talk," a patient observed. "They explained things to me, clear. At first I thought it was the bunk. But after a couple of days when I had these sessions with the doctors and when I talked with my buddies—it was a funny thing; my head stopped hurting."[7] One motive for soldiers' reticence was the simple wish to conceal symptoms so as not to be thought a coward. Frequently, men would continue to fight and attempt to ward off anxiety, keeping their terror to themselves.[8]

It was important that the experience of battle be recaptured in all its intensity and detail, for symptoms were determined in precise ways. "Now," one story in *Life* went,

> the colonel knew he was getting at the extraordinary, apparently coincidental reminiscence that almost always is the matrix of the specific symptoms of an hysterical conversion case. It is the thing which is remembered, sometimes dimly, sometimes surprisingly, right on the surface of the mind—and is copied as if by stencil for the service of the patient's neurosis.[9]

For example, a Marine became mute when his gun jammed while he was trying to protect his buddy from being killed by a Japanese sniper.

The role of dreams, a second element from psychoanalysis, assumed a new importance because recurring nightmares of battle were commonplace. Both dreams and symptoms originated in the "subconscious," and narcosynthesis or narcoanalysis provided a new and dramatic method for exploring it. This invention of the psychoanalytic psychiatrists Roy Grinker and John Spiegel became one of the most widely publicized treatments of the war neuroses. It was a "mental x-ray," a probe created by a drug-induced dream state, the *New York Times* observed, and it revealed the "hidden anxieties deeply buried in the . . . subconscious and . . . the causes that have brought about . . . neurosis."[10]

One of the most "amazing revelations" of the method, the *Times* reported, quoting Lt. Col. Grinker, was the "universality of guilt reactions, not only in men who have been removed from combat because of anxiety states but also in those who have successfully and honorably completed their tour of duty."[11] Such reactions arose because of the death of comrades and from guilt at ending a tour of duty that left still others facing battle. Men who felt this way could not slough off their "group superego," developed through identification with their unit, which received, through transference and identification, a considerable portion of the soldier's own self-love.

Perhaps the most widely circulated full-scale description of psychoanalytic narcosynthesis was John Hersey's fictionalized account in *Life* magazine. His soldier patient suffered from an hysterical paralysis, a relative rarity in the medical literature, but a symptom for which narcosynthesis was considered to be unusually successful, providing a dramatic illustration of the method. Striking photos recorded the soldier's facial expressions during the administration of pentothal as "he shows and speaks of shadowy memories, deep calm, worry, repressed desires, anger, guilt, hostility fear and finally, pleasure and peace."

He had become paralyzed after a mortar shell had killed his best friend during a night patrol. The friend often had helped him, and in this instance had undertaken a hazardous sortie in his place. As the drug took effect, "an electrifying change" occurred. "His eyes closed. Some gear shifted in his mind, and he began speaking in the present tense. He was evidently transported back to the very situation and had heard in his skull, the echo of a shot." His friend was screaming, and he had tried to pull him back, but the hand came along with a piece of the arm up to the elbow. "He gave a full minute's exhibition of unashamed, uninhibited terror; exactly what he had felt inwardly that night by the stone wall in Germany. He was, for a time, a man in the sharply recollected presence of death."

The case then unraveled like a simplified early psychoanalytic text, with illustrations of Oedipal hatred, feelings of inadequacy and ambivalence, transference, identification, and finally the development of a paralysis of the leg. This big, hulking soldier always had been picked on; his mother had wanted a girl, not another boy; and his father had been lazy, just like the friend who had been killed on the patrol. The soldier hated his father for having made him work unnecessarily hard as a child and a young man, while his father had always gotten out of chores by complaining of pain in his leg.

"Was it his right leg?" the psychiatrist asked. "Yes." "Just like yours." The psychiatrist reassured him, rather implausibly. "You don't have to be afraid of dying, any more, the way you think your father was afraid of working." At the end of the session, the patient walked, making a full recovery.[12]

In popular accounts, with monotonous regularity, treatment was followed by success. "Any doubts about the efficacy of psychiatric treatments have been dissipated in the heat of war. Thousands of men have been returned to normal life and even to combat life by uses [sic] of the new therapy."[13] William Menninger remarked modestly in the *New York Times* that "great strides" had been made during the war in the "prevention and cure of mental illnesses."[14]

Not only did the popularizations give the impression of remarkable success, they inevitably included little or no discussions of theory. They were dramatic stories, designed to entertain and to boost morale. Little of the psychoanalytic ego psychology that informed some of the psychiatric discussions surfaced in these popularizations. The psychoanalytic model seemed much like the one Freud described at Clark University 35 years earlier: the effectiveness of catharsis, the determination of symptoms by traumatic experience, the importance of dreams and the unconscious. The sense of often inappropriate guilt from a punishing conscience was perhaps the one new element.

Other methods functioned like narcosynthesis to recapture unconscious material, and thus underlined a fundamental tenet of psychoanalysis. According to *Science Digest,* hypnosis, for instance, provided a "quick method of uncovering recent conflicts and integrating them into the conscious personality." Combined with modern psychoanalytic insight, hypnosis had achieved "even cures of deep-seated childhood conflicts."[15]

John Huston, the great film director, witnessed hypnosis, narcosynthesis, and shock treatment in the course of making a film for the Army, *Let There Be Light,* about the treatment and recovery of soldiers from nervous and mental illness at Mason General Hospital, Long Island. For reasons Huston never understood the film was never shown, but at the time he gave himself a personal crash course in reading Freud and already knew that one day he would make a film about him.[16]

Psychodrama, the *Saturday Evening Post* reported, was almost as spectacular a way of unblocking traumatic memories as hypnosis and narcosynthesis. Joseph Moreno, a Viennese who had devised the method partly inspired by Freud's discoveries, had been using psychodrama at St. Elizabeth's Hospital, which treated servicemen as well as civilians. Moreno would induce a patient to act a scene from his past, perhaps from childhood, and urge him to "express himself, always spontaneously, by enacting the real-life episodes that irritate him." He had to use not only words, but gestures and movements. A veteran seaman with 20 years of experience who had tried to commit suicide, trembled frequently and kept repeating, "I'm guilty. Can't you see I'm guilty? Why don't you let me die? . . . It was my fault you died so horribly." Gradually the facts of his past emerged. Seven years before, his ship had been wrecked in the Indian Ocean, and he had barely escaped with his life. "Helplessly, he watched his closest companion slip from the life raft and fall a prey to man eating sharks. He was forced to listen to the screams of his friend as he was eaten alive." The audience insisted that the patient was not to blame, and he began to improve. Some 60 percent of the Navy men treated by the method at St. Elizabeth's had recovered within 90 days. Other methods were popularized as well; rest, occupational therapy, morale building. But none had quite the dramatic impact of catharsis, with or without drugs. Popularization made the principles of psychoanalytic cathartic treatment common coin, and seemed to demonstrate their unusual effectiveness.[17]

By emphasizing the important role of psychoanalysis in the war effort, William Menninger furthered the identification of psychoanalysis and psychiatry. In 1947, at the beginning of a new wave of psychoanalytic popularization, Menninger argued in the *New York Times* that military psychiatry had been enriched by the use of psychoanalytic methods. "Some of the skeptics became staunch supporters of psychoanalysis and hundreds of young military physicians became interested in this new, effective psychiatry."[18]

Menninger attempted to dispel what he perceived as a lingering suspicion of psychoanalysis as mysterious, immoral, "concerned primarily with sex," and unconcerned with the social environment. Indeed, a year before Menninger's article appeared, a popular and sympathetic discussion of the problems of "psychiatry at the foxhole level" by an Army general referred to the psychoanalysts as "couchers" who believed that the psychoneuroses were caused by unconscious sexual repression. "You mean a guy gets sick because of some sex urge he doesn't know he has, but if a doctor can help him realize what the urge is, he may be cured?"[19] Menninger argued that psychoanalysis was not obsessed with sex and that it was no more immoral than were surgery and medicine. Sex was itself an "all-pervasive motive in life" and American taboos about it contributed to a "high incidence of neurosis." This was the traditional "anti-Puritanism" the psychoanalysts usually coupled, as did Menninger, with the argument that Freud used the word sex to include "much more than genital activity." Then he struck what became an important note of postwar psychoanalytic conservatism, the view that patients often were obsessed with sexuality, and this preoccupation could interfere with "mature relationships . . . and constructive work." It was true that psychoanalytic treatment might lead to divorce or to lessened dependence on religion, but it could also lead to more satisfaction from marital relationships and a more "rational basis" for religious beliefs. The argument that psychoanalysis was unconcerned with the social environment and with everyday problems was a false generality, and "was not the practice of many in the analytic group." Rather, an "evaluation of the sociological, economic, cultural and other aspects" of both past and present was essential for treatment.

Menninger concluded by staking unusually high claims. Psychoanalysis provided the only basis for a "valid mental hygiene" and for a preventive psychiatry. It had contributed not only to the understanding of neuroses and psychoses, the deviate, the criminal, and the normal, but had gone beyond psychiatry to all of medicine. It provided an appreciation of the emotional factors in physical disease, knowledge which would constitute the medicine of the future. Already psychoanalysis was vouchsafing enlightenment about different cultures, art, and literature and soon could be expected to throw light on social relationships and group behavior. He ended with a curiously prophetic American note: that the future of psychoanalysis would be determined "exactly like that of any other commodity . . . by the need for it and by its utility."

Crucial to Menninger's argument was an insistence on psychoanalysis as a veridical, causative, scientific therapy, an argument enhanced by medical rhetoric and analogy. It is a technique, he wrote, which, "through evolution and refinement, has become a scientific therapy—a process of clearing away, stratum by stratum, diseased psychological material."[20] The management of unconscious conflict might be likened to the "treatment of a boil. The physician has to know how deep the boil is, its particular nature, when and how it should be lanced and whether lancing is a good idea." In some circumstances it was inadvisable; then conflict should not be "opened up" but rather, the patient should be helped by "reassurance, encouragement and the introduction to new interests." The ideal goal of psychotherapy was "insight," aiding "the patient to gain an understanding of himself, why he is sick, how he became sick, and how he can best modify his life to regain and retain his health."[21] Medical terminology sometimes reinforced the discourse of other military psychoanalytic psychiatrists. Grinker and Spiegel had written of the "dosed release of intense emotions" under sodium pentothal.[22]

The first full-dress popularizations of psychosomatic medicine in *Life* magazine began with Grinker and Spiegel's wartime triumphs with narcosynthesis; many of the war neuroses which had yielded to psychotherapy had involved psychosomatic symptoms. Moreover, these wartime triumphs pointed toward the easier conquest of a multitude of puzzling civilian illnesses.[23] Popularizations of psychosomatic medicine and of psychiatry in general vulgarized existing medical rhetoric. They displayed the scientist's formulaic view of himself and his past: the unsolved problem, the shortcomings of earlier approaches, the promise of present breakthroughs and future triumphs. Major medical authorities in psychosomatic medicine wrote popular tracts. In *Vogue,* Hans Selye, a major researcher on stress, propounded a close approximation of 19th-century bank-account theories of energy. In *Psychology Today,* George Engel, a major psychoanalytic psychosomatic researcher, culling newspaper stories, suggested that the emotions can kill. Engel and the proponent of the type A personality, Meyer Friedman, both disclosed in popularizations that they suffered heart attacks for reasons they regarded as partly psychological—in Engel's case one day before the first anniversary of his identical twin brother's death from a heart attack.[24]

Popularizations stressed the psychological origins of disease in early childhood emotions, the specific psychological profile or conflict that provided the basis for disease, and, above all, reiterated claims for the solid scientific basis of all these conclusions. The vogue for psychosomatic medicine had begun by 1947, and *Science Digest* noted that the comment, "He's psychosomatic" is becoming as frequent . . . as 'he's neurotic' was in the 1920s—and still is."[25] A few years later psychogenesis received its most extreme application: "possibly the most startling medical discovery of this generation is the fact that your personality can literally kill you." More mildly, *House and Garden* warned, "Your emotions can make you sick." According to *Time,* Flanders Dunbar believed that "80% of all accidents have a neurotic basis." "Illnesses caused or intensified by nervous and mental tensions—worry, fear, guilt, hate, frustration, aggression, anxiety—are on the march." In *Parents'* magazine one learned that "psychosomatic medicine states frankly that emotional factors are the CHIEF cause of gastrointestinal complaints."[26]

Vulgarizations of specificity and profile theory were even more astonishing. Thus, *Time* noted that "girls who do not get along with their fathers are likely to grow up sexually frigid and when they marry are candidates for indigestion and gallstones."[27] Or "hyperthyroid personalities are touchy and temperamental, shy, moody, perhaps artistic, sexually maladjusted, apt to be thin." Those with stomach ulcers were "aggressive, ruthless, with strong dislikes and likes which are subject to change." They were also apt to be "hard faced and sullen eyed."[28] *Science Digest* reported that according to Lucy Freeman, one of the popularizing analysands of the 1950s, Franz Alexander taught that the "overactive businessman and the slow-moving farmer" had different personalities yet both could develop ulcers, the result of "frustration of the individual's wish to seek help and love." Those with high blood pressure rebelled internally; "constant turmoil inside" kept their blood pressure high.[29]

The roots of psychosomatic disorders were laid down in early childhood, largely by parents. Thus, Flanders Dunbar, like most psychiatrists, looked "for the roots of psychosomatic illness in an unhappy childhood," according to *Time* magazine. Parents must take a more active role in preventing the psychosomatic diseases which insidiously had taken the place of the killers already conquered by medical science.[30]

If parents held the keys to prevention, psychotherapy offered cure. After psychoanalysis, one patient lost an allergy to horsehair and became an equestrian. *Newsweek* reported that after brief therapy, a wide variety of psychosomatic symptoms improved.[31]

One result of such efficacious treatment was expansion of the medical role. People must "learn to depend on doctors for analysis and treatment of emotional and social problems." "Open your heart to your doctor," became the watchword; the family doctor in mild cases, the wonder-working psychiatrist or psychoanalyst in more serious cases. Beyond conventional medicine, the psychoanalyst Smiley Blanton, a colleague of the New York clergyman Norman Vincent Peale, urged what in effect was a return to William James's theory of the energizing subliminal self. Blanton argued that the best prescription for psychosomatic patients was to use the limitless reservoir of energy and wisdom in the unconscious, which like a dynamo furnished the "power and drive of our minds." In Blanton, an older American tradition of self-help and self-healing was combined with the up-to-date vision of the newest scientific expert, the psychoanalytic psychiatrist.[32]

The "mushroom growth" of psychoanalysis in America, the emergence of a conservative psychoanalysis "more Freudian than Freud," as well as Freud's status as a modern Socrates, the "most famous psychiatrist of all time," were clear by 1947. Much of the attention came from reissues and new translations of Freud's writings. Then, a spate of widely popularized books about Freud and psychoanalysis began around 1950. Freud was viewed as either a philosopher-artist, as Havelock Ellis had characterized him, or as a scientist, his own self-image and that of most of his followers. The characterization largely depended on the allegiance of the judge. The American psychoanalysts viewed him above all as a scientist: he had conceived of psychological processes with the "logic of science" through his concept of the unconscious and his method of investigating it, according to *Scientific American*.[33] Americans also learned from the *Saturday Review* that Freud was a heroic healer who "labored tirelessly to cure men and women who were suffering horribly."[34]

Literary intellectuals tended to think of Freud as scientist, philosopher, and literary artist as well. Some of them saw psychoanalysis as at best an historical discipline, plying a trade with a cast of mythological dramatis personae. The poet W. H. Auden wrote of Freud: "To us he is no more a person/ Now but a whole climate of opinion," and also observed that, "Whatever we may think of that famous trio Ego, Super-Ego and Id, we can see that they are like Prince Tamino, Zorastro and the Queen of the Night and not like mathematical equations."[35]

The scientific validity of psychoanalysis was defended in *Scientific American* in a review of the New York University symposium which had pitted psychoanalysts against the philosophers of science. Robert S. White observed that the logical positivists who were particularly conspicuous at the symposium held unusually stringent standards of scientific proof, but that some other philosophers at the symposium had believed it was not sensible to "deny a promising branch of inquiry the title of science, especially in a time when this term carries so many overtones of goodness and righteousness."

Was it helpful to ask for "crucial experiments" in a "realm where crucial experiments are just about impossible"? Many of the laws of physics could not be demonstrated generally, and "surely we should not require that psychoanalysis surpass the rigor of physics." Moreover, many people had found the evidence from free associations convincing.[36]

Regardless of Freud's disputed scientific status, psychoanalysis, it was widely believed, had profoundly affected both professional and popular culture, including people who had never heard of Freud. In 1947 *Life* argued that because millions of servicemen had some contact with psychiatry, the war had created a new acceptance of psychiatry and psychoanalysis as "cures."[37] Five years later Auden observed:

> If an Isolde worries all day lest her absent Tristan should be run over by a bus, the dumbest Brangaene could warn her that her love includes a hope that he will never return. As for parents, not only the few who have read up on the Oedipus Complex and Erogenous Zones, but also the newspaper-reading mass, the poor things, are today scared out of their wits that they will make some terrible mistake. . . . [38]

The historian Crane Brinton announced in the *Saturday Review* that the larger families of America's intelligent younger postwar generation also were due to Freud's influence. And Lawrence Kubie argued in the same magazine that for the first time in human history, Freud's "scientific investigation and scientific therapy," as well as optimal modes of child-raising, offered mankind a way out of the "morass" of its enslavement to infantile hopes, lusts, and fears.[39]

Freud had supplied a new language, a new way of "thinking about ourselves." More important than patients in therapy, *Time* argued, were the millions whose lives were affected by the "penetration of Freudian theory. A social worker visiting a family with health and welfare problems looks for unhealthy father-son or mother-daughter relationships. The probation officer reporting on a juvenile delinquent discusses the family background with the court in terms of aggression and compensation. So does a truant officer." The murder of a younger boy by a fourteen-year-old was explained by his "romantic attachment to his mother and a desire to kill his father (straight Oedipus complex) that exploded on the young victim instead."[40] Juvenile delinquents in the Boston area became adept at "diagnosing" their problems in the Freudian lingo of the social workers.

The prescriptions of Benjamin Spock's *Common Sense Book of Baby and Child Care* for feeding and toilet training and "play with peers" were "solidly rooted in Freud's concepts."[41] Spock sold 19,076,822 copies of his book by 1965. For perhaps the first time a popular advice book for parents broke with the emphasis on habit training of 1920s behaviorism and was frankly psychoanalytic, couching in the most ordinary language Freud's concepts— childhood sexuality and the Oedipus complex, avoidance of sexual stimulation of children and primal scene trauma. For instance, Spock advised,

A boy loves his mother much more than he loves any little girl. He feels much more rivalrous with his father and more in awe of him than he feels towards any boy. So the sight of his mother [nude] may be a little too stimulating and the chance to compare himself so unfavorably with his father every day may make him feel like doing something violent to his old man.[42]

Spock's later editions reflected the new importance of internalized limits that the ego psychologists had come to see as crucial for child development.

A columnist in the *Chicago Sun Times* intoned:

Do we have a new concept of individual dignity? Do more employers recognize the psychological as well as economic needs of their employees? Are we more self-expressive in our clothes, in the blither colors of our homes and cars?

Do we merely lock up our criminals and juvenile delinquents as hopeless defectives beyond redemption? Or do we try to cure them by seeking out causes in their homes and childhood? Do we generally give our children more understanding, more room to grow emotionally, more sensitive treatment at home and in school?

Where the answer is yes, there are many authorities who trace this indirectly to Freud and those who followed him.

Finally, in a *Sun Times* story entitled "Seek to Take Sex Stigma from Freud," it was revealed that Freud had not even used the word sex, but rather the word "libido," and that this had a "much broader meaning—the stream of life forces . . . almost all the facets of human energy, not just sex."[43] Here, then, was the popularized American Freud, sanitized and made the author of most of the gifts of liberal culture—progressive education, psychiatric social work, permissive child-raising, modern psychiatry, and criminology.

Ernest Jones's three-volume biography, appearing between 1953 and 1957, was widely reviewed and consecrated Freud's image as the equal of Copernicus or Galileo. For Jones, Freud was an untiring and painstaking observer. Paradoxically, this biography which disclosed Freud's scientific training in neurology in some detail also reinforced the image of him as more philosopher than scientist, with a plethora of quirks, passions, ambitions, and neuroses. *Time* noted that Jones belonged to the "warts and all" school of biography, and, in fact, he launched Freud's personality and intimate experience, about which little had been known, on a career of their own. Jones disclosed Freud's speculative and literary inclinations, his impatience with precise definition, his dabbling in telepathy and occasional superstitions, and his sympathy with his friend Wilhelm Fliess's elaborate speculations about periodicity. Drawing on Freud's letters to his fiancée, Jones also pictured him as a family man, doting on his wife. Of the first volume, Brendan Gill noted that at forty, Freud had "won neither fame nor fortune." Yet, "If his discoveries prevail, he will have reached out to touch and perhaps in some measure to save every other life on earth."[44]

Even before the third volume, the *New Yorker* noted that some critics considered it "the greatest biography of our time." The third volume described Freud's exile from Nazi persecution and his very real stoicism, despite an unspeakably painful cancer of the jaw.[45]

But Jones's third volume as well as the second also dealt with the psychoanalytic movement from a constrictedly "orthodox" point of view. Erich Fromm, for one, criticized Jones's "grotesque attacks" on men who disagreed with Freud—Sandor Ferenczi and Otto Rank, for instance, whom Jones dismissed as psychotic heretics. Moreover, according to Fromm, Freud had created an essentially missionary cultural movement, a substitute for radical philosophical and political interests which demanded "little from its adherents except learning the nomenclature." The New York analyst Jacob Arlow rose to Freud's defense and implied that Fromm had been using the discredited smear tactics of Senator McCarthy by denouncing psychoanalysis as "an unpopular, subversive political movement, a movement which promulgates a rigid policy line, which re-writes history to suit its purposes, and which assassinates defectors and their reputations. . . ." Ferenczi, Arlow alleged, "sat . . . (patients) in his lap, spoke to them in baby talk, kissed and caressed them. This may be effective therapy—but it is not psychoanalysis."[46]

The popular celebratory and heroic image of Freud was summed up by Leonard Engel in *Science Digest*. Freud, creator of a revolutionary theory about the "strange, hidden part of the mind," was a "towering figure of the twentieth century, and one of the most hotly disputed." He had created modern psychiatry and turned its attention to a larger group of sufferers than the psychotic—the neurotics who "are so unhappy . . . that they are a burden to themselves and the people around them." Engel used the story of Anna O., which Freud himself had exploited in his Clark University lectures to demonstrate the effectiveness of analytic catharsis. But his view of Freud's influence on psychiatry also was qualified. He argued that "most psychiatrists" accepted Freud's view of dreams as the expression of unconscious desires and also his theories of the id, ego, and superego. He then conceded that "most psychiatrists" also believed that drives for power, the "urge to create," and "other psychological forces" were as important as sexual drives. Moreover, psychoanalysis was of little help in treating psychotics. Only "selected patients" received the "full couch treatment." "Most psychiatrists" used much briefer forms of therapy. Yet, the couch "remained a remarkable microscope for peering into the recesses of the human mind."[47]

The 100th anniversary of Freud's birth was celebrated in 1956 with university lectures, public addresses, congratulations from President Eisenhower, and a visit from Ernest Jones, the last of Freud's direct disciples, who, still in pain, was just recovering from cancer surgery. To the *New Yorker* Jones was a "small, hawk-faced, indomitable-looking man . . . of prodigious energy" who had introduced psychoanalysis to America and England and who was upset because he could no longer do the work of three men. He was also an authority on figure skating.[48] Jones's public image was one of enormous talent, courageous stoicism, devotion to a cause. "Our Attitude toward Greatness" was the title of his address to the American Psychoanalytic Association, whose meetings just preceded those of the American Psychiatric Association.

However, when the American Psychiatric Association met to do Freud honor, *Newsweek* recorded the psychiatrist Percival Bailey's heated denunciation in the association's annual academic lecture. Freud was an unscientific disdainer of women, and Jones's biography "one long paean of hero worship." Freud's inner "committee" to steer the movement, to which Jones had belonged, was a band of disciples like the followers of Jesus.[49] The religious role of psychoanalysis was important to Alfred Kazin, the literary critic, as well. In one of the few popular analyses of *why* Freud and psychoanalysis had achieved such a vogue in America, Kazin argued in 1956 in the *New York Times* that it was because of Freudianism's "insistence on individual fulfillment, satisfaction and happiness." Harking back to the popular Freudianism of the 1920s, Kazin insisted that psychoanalysis emphasized the "truths of human nature" against "the hypocrisies and cruelties of conventional morality," and stressed the role sex played in the imagination. "No one can count the number of people who now think of any crisis as a *personal* failure, and who turn to a psychoanalyst or to psychoanalytic literature for an explanation of their suffering where once they would have turned to a minister or to the Bible for consolation." Thus, for Kazin, psychoanalysis was a substitute for religion and an enhancer of sexual fulfillment. Psychoanalysts in America plied a "big business and a very smooth one." They were more interested in making cures than new discoveries, and complacently used the theory to explain everything. They provided a rather sad contrast to Freud himself, a "tough old humanist" who, like Darwin, had become "a part of nature."[50]

For the editors of the *Saturday Review,* Freud's popularity came not only because he had stood for frankness in a prudish Victorian world in which faith was crumbling, but for something like William James's conception of psychological energy. Freud was the exponent of "a paramount nervous force, of which recognizable disguises and distortions are responsible for mental disease." Freud's therapeutic aim was to "detach the unhealthy growths from the basic energy." He was a great scientist and a great therapist who labored until his death to relieve human suffering—a "pioneer on a frontier of nearly total darkness."[51] Geoffrey Gorer, the anthropologist, explained in the *New York Times* that Freud's American vogue resulted from the American faith in the innate goodness of the newborn child. If this goodness was not realized in later life, Americans believed that it was the fault of "circumstances"—"accident, a broken home, the wrong sort of parental care, the unkindness of others." Freudianism explained what had gone wrong and how this could be corrected. It gave American parents "scientific approbation for gentleness and indulgence of all the children's wishes and whims." Americans had made "good health a moral imperative," in contrast to Europeans, who had largely rejected psychoanalysis, because they accepted ill health as a part of destiny. "It is a curious quirk of fate," Gorer wrote, "that the ideas of an austere pessimist, as Freud was, should have had their greatest acceptance in a country predominately optimistic and hedonistic."[52] But

Robert White argued in *Scientific American* that Freud had become a hero for "many thoughtful people because he had dared look steadily at the dark forces within us and . . . held out hope, however cautiously, that they might be better governed." Freud had helped to explain why in a world of high scientific achievement, modern political history contained "mires of passion, hate and murder." He had used the scientific method to "investigate our worst selves," and had "told us, in the cool disillusioned spirit of the scientist, what chances we might have of happiness."[53]

Popular images of Freud revealed him as a painstaking observer, a tenacious worker, a great healer, a truly original explorer, a paragon of domestic virtue, the discoverer of a source of personal energy and a genius. All these attributes reflected American cultural values. It was perhaps inevitable that so idealized an image could not withstand the sharper scrutiny that shortly began. Meanwhile, Freud was the patron saint of a rapidly growing therapeutic establishment.

At its center was a tiny core of psychoanalysts and patients. There were not more than 1400 practicing analysts in the world in 1957, perhaps 14,000 people in analysis, and no more than 100,000 who had completed treatment.[54] About 942 analysts of Freudian-derived persuasion were practicing in the United States, including 702 members of the American Psychoanalytic Association, about 140 of the William Alanson White Institute and about 100 in Karen Horney's American Institute for Psychoanalysis. But their ranks were swollen by a far more rapidly growing number of psychologists and social workers who administered some variety of psychoanalytic psychotherapy.

Popular accounts firmly united psychoanalysis and psychiatry. *Time,* for example, attributed the reform of mental hospitals in "progressive states" to the leadership of psychiatrists who "owe most of their orientation to Freud."[55] The terms psychiatrist and psychoanalyst became almost interchangeable.[56] If, as most accounts agreed, "pure" psychoanalysis was rarely if ever used in the actual treatment of psychotics, its insights were nonetheless essential in understanding them and in guiding their treatment. Although some psychoanalysts and psychiatrists insisted that to use drugs would be to contaminate the "transference" of their patients, perhaps most psychiatrists were eclectics who used not only psychotherapy but drugs as well. Thus the image of the "pure" psychoanalyst was matched by the more "practical" image of the eclectic practitioner whose treatment method was briefer psychoanalytic psychotherapy with an admixture of drugs.

The "golden age" of Hollywood films about psychiatry and psychoanalysis followed the Freud centennial. After years of showing psychiatrists as absurd or sinister, for a short period, from the late 1950s to the mid-1960s, coinciding precisely with the high point of psychoanalytic influence, psychiatrists were presented as humane and effective. The number of Hollywood stars, directors, and producers who were "in analysis" was legion. Twenty movie stars who had been treated at the Menninger Foundation gave a party for Karl Menninger when he visited Los Angeles in 1953.[57] John

Huston's movie about Freud was a manifestation of the newly favorable climate, although the Freud children were opposed to any film about their father, and Anna Freud, fearing an inaccurate pastiche, had tried unsuccessfully to block production.[58] Another example was *Captain Newman, M.D.*, a 1963 film starring Gregory Peck. It was based on a book about the wartime career of Ralph Greenson, the Los Angeles psychoanalyst who later treated Marilyn Monroe. Newman was shown as an entirely human, singularly gifted therapist. Beneath his brusque and offhand manner, his patients saw "their confessor, their life-line to sanity . . . their hope of salvation: that miracle of insight and intercession which could heal them."[59]

Whatever the attitudes of stars and directors, the exigencies of popular drama dictated their own formulae. Unlike the journalistic accounts, the movies were intended to entertain, not primarily to inform. Often psychiatrists were used as mere plot devices, and psychoanalysis and psychiatry were confounded. Psychoanalysis was often a magical cathartic cure.

In journalistic accounts, most of the miraculous qualities of the analyst that characterized the first American popularizations were muted. In 1957, in *Life* magazine, Ernest Havemann took pains to make the psychoanalyst not only a sober scientist but a respectable square, which, indeed, he was becoming in reality. For example, he was no longer an exotic foreigner: about half of analysts were American-born. As they had from the beginning, psychoanalysts looked just like businessmen, bankers, teachers, dentists. Philip Wylie, the journalist scourge of "Momism," described his analyst in Hearst's *American Weekly* as about forty-five, good-looking and well-dressed. Another resembled the "junior vice president of a bank." Despite Freud's "startling theories," analysts were devoted to their families and their dogs. They had completed arduous training and had met lengthy qualifications. The spice of feminist glamour and a fascinating hobby characterized a young analyst in *Mademoiselle*. She was a mother of three and piloted her own plane: "There is something about those cool, azure eyes, the abbreviated nose, the short, blondish haircut . . . you can imagine her waving as she steps into the cockpit. . . ."

She was also the quintessence of the "mirror" analyst. She had "no 'personality': (no mannerisms, no like-me love-me smile) but a clean blank wall—the kind you might dash yourself against, now angrily, now hopefully, over and over again in search of some revealing clue." Psychoanalytic work, this analyst said, was like being a mother, who also wants her children to be independent.[60]

The male equivalent, and a sharp contrast, was the very talkative analyst described by the *New York Times* reporter Lucy Freeman. Where the female analyst in *Mademoiselle* was chic, daring, and reticent, Freeman's analyst was plain as an old shoe, and kept a cat, a dog, and a grand piano in the consulting room of his tiny New York brownstone apartment:

> He seemed able to strip the sheen off civilization and watch people naked and afraid, trying their best to live in spite of terror. . . . He derived satisfaction not from power or prestige but from watching sick persons grow healthier.[61]

Some popularizations emphasized the arduous preparation of the analyst, his medical background, his long waiting list of patients, and the fact that his own analytic ordeal, "the fire of personal analysis," had burned away whatever would make it hard for him to listen to the problems of others, especially if these problems resembled his own. Moreover, he did not make the large income that rumor suggested, although most analysts lived well enough.[62]

The obverse of this idealized analyst, perhaps a result of the inevitable human tendency to cut authority down to size, were novels and cartoons in which the analyst was ridiculous, calculating and sinister, as mixed-up and ineffectual as his patient, or dumber. From the analyst's point of view, these rather vengeful images represented either the patient's thwarted search for affection or else narcissistic resentment of the analytic probing that necessarily punctured illusions.[63]

For some patients, psychoanalysis in the postwar years was a therapy of last resort—expensive, protracted, but promising where more conventional treatment had failed. Lucy Freeman, the *New York Times* reporter, sought relief from an inflamed sinus no physician had been able to cure. Patients displayed other physical symptoms—a rapid heartbeat, difficulty breathing, headaches, severe colitis. Sexual issues plagued others—impotence, marital problems, frigidity, homosexuality, guilt for sexual transgressions. There were patients with phobias who could not ride subways, planes, or elevators or drive a car, or who feared being alone in open spaces. Still others suffered from alcoholism or were depressed, perhaps by a divorce or a career failure.

To make these patients attractive enough to be read about, perhaps identified with, journalists emphasized the seriousness of their symptoms, and that, like the analysts, they were ordinary people. Psychoanalysis was not a preserve merely of middle-aged wealthy women; its patients included professionals, students, working people of all kinds. The emphasis on the number and variety of patients distinguished the postwar from the earlier popularizations.

It is thus not surprising that those who wrote popular accounts of their analyses tended to be journalists, unwittingly carrying on a tradition that had begun with Max Eastman in 1915. Many were eager to convert others by the story of their own cure. And they were finding a wide audience.

The new postwar recruits to psychotherapy represented a particular generation that came of age shortly after World War II when Freud was replacing Karl Marx as a social guru for many American intellectuals. The sociologist Charles Kadushin, in his remarkable study of psychotherapy in New York, described them as only slightly younger than their therapists. They attended plays and cocktail parties, visited museums, and were sophisticated about psychiatry through reading and conversation. They probably constituted part of the market for psychiatric information—the books and articles of the mass media and the more specialized presses. About 75 percent of all applicants to New York psychotherapy clinics read about mental health, and, astonishingly, 70 percent of patients with an eighth-grade education could name a book in the mental hygiene field. The less sophisticated applicants to analytic clinics read popular psychology articles of the type found in the *Ladies Home Journal* and self-help literature. Some 60 percent of the applicants to psychoanalytic clinics were Jews, the rest, white Protestants.

The analytic clinic patients presented particular problems that distinguished them from patients at other clinics. They were dissatisfied with themselves, their interpersonal relations, or their careers, or they suffered from emotional problems such as depression. One-third complained of general anxiety. The analytic clinics attracted twice as many applicants with sexual problems, particularly among the young and single—frigidity, impotence, masturbation, insufficient or too much sexual activity; general feelings of sexual inadequacy; inability to relate to the opposite sex; homosexuality. In short the analytic clinics received patients with precisely the symptoms their theories declared were important, that is, anxiety and problems with sexuality and interpersonal relations. For example, a girl with a serious weight problem, after discussing therapy with a friend attending a psychoanalytic clinic, emphasized her own psychological and interpersonal problems at the same clinic, although weight remained her primary difficulty.[64]

There was little relation between presenting symptoms and diagnosis. In this period the most common tag at the New York analytic clinics was neurosis with "underlying schizophrenia." Clinics also universally classified homosexuals as sociopaths in accordance with the American Psychiatric Association's diagnostic manual. On the whole, the analytic clinics took the fewest patients because they wanted them for the training of psychoanalytic candidates and so required people who could articulate their problems and successfully complete psychotherapy or psychoanalysis.

One eclectic analyst's private patients illustrate the range of troubled people. There was a young widow, apathetic to people, places, and her life in general; a stockbroker with severe colitis; an architect worried about impotence; a 50-year-old bachelor still living with his parents; a "respected businessman" guilty because of an affair with a very young woman; a successful woman real estate broker who drank too much; a lawyer's wife who was afraid to leave her house; a beautiful and brilliant 23-year-old girl who was tormented by fears she could not describe and who had flunked out of school.[65] Surprising numbers of people discussed their analyses in print: the author Philip Wylie, the sociologist John Dollard, the publishers Marshall Field and Ralph Ingersoll, and numerous television, movie, and stage personalities.

The wartime image of therapy was of a fast and simple catharsis. The new, postwar popularizations made it a difficult, lengthy, painful process, lasting not weeks but months or years—seven for the television personality Wally Cox, five for the reporter Lucy Freeman. It was also limited to a very few people, who were not too old and who, it was assumed, were intelligent and worthwhile. Clearly, the rhetoric was designed to make psychoanalysis all the more attractive—a scarce, expensive, painful, but eminently desirable commodity.

The descriptions were seldom uniform and in fact reflected the available varieties of psychoanalytic therapy. Some, such as the comedian Sid Caesar, lay on the couch five days a week, baring his "inmost soul." Others went perhaps three times a week. Free association, "free floating attention," or "talking freely about whatever comes to mind" had an almost magical quality for Lucy Freeman:

> I came to know that my thought would steer, true as an arrow, to the heart of my troubles, tracing the torments of my life. Not the first or second thought but sometimes the fourth or fifth or sixth held real meaning.[66]

Dreams and early memories poured from the analysand's unconscious "the storehouse of the brain." Philip Wylie recalled his circumcision at age two; Sid Caesar, a fear of going to the barber because of the Biblical story of Samson.[67] Little time was spent on describing resistances or blocks to memory or "working through."

The aim of psychoanalysis was "fundamental change in the personality," a "slow, deep cure" releasing the patient from his neurotic fears and the "tyranny" of his unconscious. He would then be able to lead a fulfilling, normal life. But the results even in the neuroses were spotty, and the therapeutic promise was qualified by an analyst in *Life* in 1957: "If what's troubling you isn't too serious, and if you're lucky enough to go to one of the analysts who seems to be good at what they're doing, and IF you're a good patient and work hard then MAYBE analysis can help you."[68] For one successful analysand in *Good Housekeeping* psychoanalysis conferred inner freedom, self-acceptance, real love, and manhood, as well as an ability to sell staggering quantities of insurance.[69]

A principal agent of personal reconstruction was "transference." An analyst in *Mademoiselle* described it as the discharge onto the analyst of "feelings of powerful hate, of love, of dependency that they once had (and perhaps still have) for their parents." For Lucy Freeman, transference revealed an Oedipal attachment. She "ardently" desired her analyst. "I wanted to be his slave, mistress, friend—anything to be with him." To which her analyst dryly replied: "What you feel for me, you realize, is what you really feel for your father. . . . It's your father you've wanted all these years. . . . I fought the idea with every defense in my body. It was repulsive, repugnant, indecent."[70]

Although the popular accounts purported to be about psychoanalyses, the garrulousness of the analysts and the elaborateness of their explanations suggest psychoanalytic psychotherapy rather than strict analysis. The confounding of the two was common, and suggests a blurring of lines that probably could occur in reality. Moreover, it also reflects the important fact that a widespread popular interest in psychoanalysis preceded the very general vogue for psychotherapy which grew rapidly in the 1960s from the interest in psychoanalysis. Analysts were undeniably individualistic and, as their basic inability to agree on a definition suggested, probably within fairly definite parameters, practiced in quite varied ways. Some clearly "gratified" their patients by supportive measures; some remained fixedly minimalist, with few and sparse interpretations. The Freudian who was more Freudian than Freud and who would not utter a word of sympathy if a patient's parent died probably was in the minority, at least in the journalistic accounts. Certainly such minimalism could arouse hostility; when Lucy Freeman asked a friend how he felt about his silent analyst, he replied, "I want to kill him."[71] As journalists insisted time and again, most patients received briefer forms of psychotherapy, which also were effective.

Lucy Freeman, who published a popular account of her analysis, *Fight Against Fears,* in 1951, was a model recruit for the "friends and supporters of psychotherapy." A Jewish resident of an upper-middle-class New York suburb, a Bennington graduate, she was introduced to her future analyst in a New York bowling alley by a *Times* colleague. Her physician had suggested she try psychoanalysis because he could do nothing more for her beleaguered sinuses. Her therapy combined elements of catharsis (her sinus became unplugged when she cried in the analyst's office) with explorations of the standard psychoanalytic repertoire: her aggressive impulses and hatred, her childhood sexuality, her penis envy, her female castration anxiety, and her Oedipus complex.[72] At the bottom of it all was her feeling that her parents had not truly loved her. Reminiscent of the curious prose style then recommended by Rudolph Flesch (that is, few articles, lots of punchy verbs), *Fight* also was studded with clichés uttered by the analyst:

> [Neurosis] is the result of many moments of fear and terror, of feeling unloved and unwanted . . . to a child, no love is death. . . . For some, their parents unconsciously wish them dead so intensely they must die. . . . You feel sex belongs in the bathroom. You don't see it as a natural feeling belonging in every room of a house. . . . Men rape and murder because they are filled with hate, not love. . . . Our criminals are often those who, underneath, have the strongest consciences. . . . The happy person settles for one mate. . . . The doctor who is not a friend is not a very good doctor. . . . Feelings of unhappiness may have something to do with the way a child develops physically as well as psychologically. . . . People are intolerant because they are afraid. . . . We all possess in moderation the qualities of the manic-depressive and the schizophrenic. . . . You forgive your parents only as you forgive yourself.[73]

Published 13 years later, in 1964, disguised as a novel, *I Never Promised You a Rose Garden* became a best-seller and a movie. It was a sensitive, chilling, yet hopeful autobiographical account of a 16-year-old girl's overcoming of schizophrenia during several years of treatment at one of the nation's most prestigious private mental hospitals, Chestnut Lodge, with Frieda Fromm-Reichmann as the author's therapist.[74] Written with elegance and restraint by Hannah Green (Joanne Greenberg), *Rose Garden* was raw and truthful about the violence and squalor, the uncanny perspicacity, the bouts of literal self-laceration, the intuitive comradeship of seriously ill patients. Deborah, the heroine, lived much of the time in an imaginary world, at once beautiful and terrifying. Fromm-Reichmann in her fictional embodiment was a realistic yet eminently sensitive therapist, who although much in demand took the girl on because of her age and because of an intuitive faith in her capabilities: "Somewhere in that precocity and bitterness and somewhere in the illness, whose limits she could not yet define, lay a hidden strength. It was there and working; it had sounded in the glimmer of relief when the fact of the sickness was made known. . . ." [75] "The only reality I offer," she told the patient, "is challenge and being well is being free to accept it or not at whatever level you are capable. I never promise lilies, and the rose-garden world of perfection is a lie . . . and a bore, too!"[76]

The doctor explained the need for psychotherapy:

> The symptoms and the sickness and the secrets have many reasons for being. The parts and facets sustain one another, locking in and strengthening one another. If it were not so, we could give you a nice shot of this or that drug or quick hypnosis and say, "Craziness, begone!" . . . But these symptoms are built of many needs and serve many purposes, and that is why getting them away makes so much suffering.[77]

In both *Fight* and *Rose Garden* and in other accounts as well, estrangement from parents, slight or intense, ended in reconciliation, as patients came to understand their own impulses and their parents' problems. Popularization often provided reconciliation with other traditional social values, and some toning-down of the sexual elements of psychoanalysis. For instance, while psychoanalysis once had been regarded as a mode of liberation, some analysts now cautioned that it enhanced a sense of restraint and social responsibility. In *Life* magazine, Ernest Havemann informed readers that the ego was the "essentially conscious, sensible part of the mind," one that defended against conflicts, chiefly by repression, while the superego or unconscious conscience often was "rigid and unrelenting, fierce and vengeful." The psychoanalyst Arnold Cooper, according to *Newsweek*, argued that Freud's method was concerned not just with sex drives but with how the personality adapted to its "total environment," a reflection of Hartmann and American postwar ego psychology.[78]

As psychoanalysis became more firmly entrenched within psychiatry, some analysts suggested that its truths echoed those of the "great religions." Lucy Freeman's analyst talked about the displacement of fear by love, and quoted St. Paul: "Perfect love casteth out fear."[79] Within both liberal Protestant and Roman Catholic churches, acceptance of psychoanalysis, often carefully circumscribed, was under way and in some instances had been for several decades. Bishop Fulton J. Sheen, who once had denounced psychoanalysis, slightly modified his views after attacks from energetic analysts such as Lawrence Kubie, and the Pope indicated that his flock could be treated by some varieties of psychoanalysis. On the whole, however neo-Freudianism as well as Jung's ambiguous embrace of religion were more congenial than orthodox Freudian psychoanalysis to many church groups.[80]

Although analysts differed in their attitudes, there were those who admonished their women patients to fulfill traditional expectations of society.[81]

Lucy Freeman's male analyst wanted to know why at twenty-nine she was not married; when she asked him why a woman would choose a career, he replied, "Maybe unconsciously she doesn't like playing a woman's role." She herself wondered: "Did it not occur to me there might be something wrong with a woman who was not content to assume a passive role, who must try to be like the men she envies. . . . Why was I competing with men, holding a job that obviously scared me. . . . Deep inside I feared marriage, as my failure at it showed."[82] Another analyst advised his patient to give up her literary ambitions for home and motherhood.

Some psychoanalysts publicly deplored what they regarded as a blurring of sexual roles in America—with men doing housework and women pursuing careers. One psychoanalyst argued that men who were impotent or doubted their masculinity usually had a "dominant mother and a passive father."[83] At a conference in 1957, participants wondered how "a boy can learn what it means to be a man . . . when mother and father in so many homes carry out identical tasks . . . ." Dr. Irene Josselyn of the Chicago Institute for Psychoanalysis warned that we were "drifting toward a social structure made up of he-women and she-men." However, another psychoanalytic psychiatrist, Janet MacKenzie Rioch, countered that experts should not fan the dispute by "issuing pronouncements" on "who should do what."[84] Ralph Greenson argued in *Look* that women were more likely to be jealous than men and linked this to early penis envy as well as the real advantages society granted males. "Clinical evidence indicates that in the early years, little girls believe that boys have certain anatomical advantages over them. Little girls at play frequently imitate little boys, rarely do boys imitate little girls." As women became more liberated and powerful, men envied them and became increasingly sexually apathetic. Indeed, growing numbers of men, it was reported, wanted sex-change operations.[85] A Menninger physician urged that those who trained psychoanalysts should be free of "unconscious conflicts associated with aggressivity in women and passivity in men. I can think of no branch of the healing art in which it is more important for men to be men and women to be women than psychoanalysis."[86]

Prominent psychoanalysts and psychiatrists reacted with ambivalence and often with disfavor to Alfred Kinsey's studies of sexuality, although their views were by no means uniform.[87] Basing his conclusions on interviews, Kinsey argued that laws governing sexual behavior as well as sexual ethics should be based on what people in fact did. And what they did then seemed startling. Masturbation was almost universal; premarital intercourse and marital infidelity relatively prevalent. But his most surprising conclusion was that almost a third of American males had had a homosexual experience involving orgasm at some point in their lives.

A review of Kinsey's *Sexual Behavior in the Human Male* in the *American Journal of Psychiatry* by a traditional psychiatrist noted that it was "apt to serve the function of a burlesque show, giving people a somewhat socially acceptable excuse for sliding down to a little lower social level. . . ." Social scientists in the same issue insisted that Kinsey's statistics were fatally flawed because of his skewed sampling.[88]

Psychoanalytic objections went far beyond a criticism of Kinsey's statistics, and revealed much about American analytic attitudes toward sexuality in general; they involved norms of behavior and an insistence on the psychological meaning of a given act. Kinsey in fact had offered a highly ambivalent opinion of some psychoanalytic conceptions. While supporting Freud's view that human sexuality was present from "earliest infancy" and affected adult patterns of sexual behavior and personality, Kinsey believed his findings did not support a "pre-genital stage of generalized erotic response," and he concluded that Freud's theory of sublimation was merely an unscientific restatement of older religious concepts. He also denied the psychoanalytic notion that only a "vaginal orgasm" could provide a satisfactory response in the psychologically "mature" woman.[89]

Psychoanalysis had evolved its own concepts of normal development from infancy to adult sexuality in which partial sexual drives ideally came together in affectionate heterosexual intercourse. Karl Menninger and Lawrence Kubie agreed that Kinsey's studies of sexuality contained valuable information, and in part corroborated Freud's views of infantile sexuality and the ubiquity of polymorphous impulses. Menninger defended the first report and noted that Kinsey had "crashed the iron curtain of social hypocrisy" and demonstrated the serious but inevitable problems social morality imposed. And Kubie was sufficiently a representative of the earlier psychoanalytic protest against "civilized" morality to note dryly that "monogamous fidelity" or "extramarital sexual activity" could each result from normal "free choice" or from "profound neurotic guilt and fear."

But both Kubie and Menninger insisted on what they regarded as the decisive psychological element in human sexual behavior, and its often unconscious motivations. It was impossible to separate sexual acts from the feelings and fantasies, conscious and unconscious, that accompanied and had given rise to them. And this consideration made Kinsey's invocation of animal behavior irrelevant.

Prevalence or high relative incidence was no criterion for the normality of a given act. Kinsey's missionary approach was almost entirely quantitative, that is, concerned with the number of orgasms and the variety of "outlets" and their implications for legal reform. Kinsey seemed to argue that what people did in itself was normative, regardless of the possible causes of their behavior. Kubie charged that Kinsey had omitted both a social and a psychological dimension. Thus, the normality of a sexual deviation could be determined only from the painstaking investigation of representative samples of individuals practicing it and their "general life adjustments," that is, income and educational level as compared with background, "social productivity," and "general community achievements, family adjustments," and so on. Menninger insisted that Kinsey had a compulsion to force human sexuality "into a zoological frame of reference . . . to see normality as that which is natural in the sense that it is practiced by animals." For Kinsey sex was something "to be let out," and the orgasm was the "total goal and ultimate criterion of sexual satisfaction." But, Menninger argued, "The orgasm of a terrified soldier in battle, that of a loving husband in the arms of his wife, that of a desperate homosexual trying to prove his masculinity, and that of a violent and sadistic brute raping a child are not the same phenomena."[90]

Psychiatrists, he argued, believed that the separation of sex from love was abnormal. "Sexual promiscuity or experimentation or athleticizing . . . without feelings of tenderness and affection—is . . . destructive." And Menninger added an invocation of religion. Most psychiatrists and psychoanalysts agreed with religion that there were "other principles" more important than "sexual freedom" and that more abundant life is not necessarily implied by more abundant sex.[91] Other psychoanalysts insisted that Kinsey's divorce of sexuality from reproduction or the biological differences between the sexes was profoundly mistaken. In 1954, according to one of Kinsey's colleagues, Franz Alexander rushed to the platform at a conference where Kinsey spoke and "urged all psychiatrists to reject every one of his conclusions."[92]

Analytic opposition centered on the issue of homosexuality. Freud had regarded it as the outcome of an underlying bisexuality, and as a stage in psychosexual development on the way to heterosexuality. Those who persisted in homosexual object choice did so because of a failure in normal development that could result from a variety of factors—overvaluation of the penis during the autoerotic phase, frustration and identification with the mother, fear of the father during the Oedipal phase, constitutional givens, and so on. Freud differed from those contemporaries who regarded homosexuality as the result of heredity, either degenerate or normal, and saw it as an admixture of constitutional and environmental factors. Unusually tolerant for his time, Freud also was skeptical about transforming a homosexual to a heterosexual.[93]

It remained for Freud's American followers and some of the émigré analysts to insist that homosexuality was inherently pathological, a deep disturbance of personality, and to display a therapeutic zeal for its "cure." Ronald Bayer has lucidly set forth the position of those analysts beginning with Sandor Rado who explicitly rejected Freud's theory of bisexuality. They substituted for it the view that heterosexual object choice was the innate norm. Environmental factors, notably family pathology and a particular family constellation—a dominant, close-binding mother and a weak or absent father, or a pre-Oedipal inability to separate from the mother—had skewed this natural inclination. They paired this view with a therapeutic optimism about changing sexual preferences for those who were, "in agony over their condition."[94]

The émigré psychoanalyst Edmund Bergler argued that homosexuality was a serious regression to the oral stage of psychosexual development, and he warned that older homosexuals were using Kinsey's report to recruit young men. Kubie argued that homosexuals, more than heterosexuals, tended to be compulsively promiscuous because they were pursuing unconscious and unattainable aims. Thus the homosexual was "always on the prowl" and it was rare for him to establish "enduring relationships." Similar dynamics underlay heterosexual promiscuity and athleticism.[95] When the American Psychiatric Association removed homosexuality from its list of mental disorders in 1973, the American Psychoanalytic Association and Karen Horney's group opposed the change, although some psychoanalysts, notably Judd Marmor and Robert Stoller, supported it. Those who favored the change argued that psychiatrists saw in their practices homosexuals who were disturbed and not a sample of the general homosexual population. Since then other psychoanalysts have argued for a far more complex view, encompassing homosexuals who function optimally and those who do not.[96] The general effect of the psychoanalytic view, particularly in the response to the Kinsey report and the issue of gender, was to identify psychoanalysis with conventional attitudes toward sexual roles and behavior.

Popularization further inflated the already optimistic claims of some psychoanalysts. It probably won new recruits to the friends and supporters of psychotherapy. It certainly identified psychoanalysis and psychiatry, psychoanalysis and psychotherapy and tended to confound them in a single, confused amalgam. It also identified psychoanalysis with the established social authorities, and tended to exaggerate certain American tendencies already present among the nation's psychoanalysts: a downplaying of the iconoclastic, rebellious aspects of psychoanalysis which had so appealed to the intelligentsia of the 1920s. It tended to reconcile psychoanalysis with morality, religion, and received social values, particularly in its treatment of sexual roles and the issue of homosexuality. Strong continuities with the first American popularizations seem clear, with their more naive emphasis on therapeutic optimism, on moralism and simplification. Popularization crystallized a socially conservative image of psychoanalysis—from its identification of practitioners with dentists and businessmen to its vision of therapy as a tough, painful exercise that resulted as a rule in marital happiness, personal equilibrium, and vocational success.

That the hopes and claims of a popularized psychoanalysis were dangerously overextended soon became abundantly clear. Psychoanalysis was left vulnerable to the turbulent currents of the counter-culture of the 1960s, with its pursuit of utopian sexual liberation and its radical questioning of the wisdom of received establishments. Psychoanalysis also was vulnerable to the ardent publicity that accompanied the renewal of somatic psychiatry, which often made claims more rosy and sweeping than those of some incautious psychoanalysts and their publicists, and psychoanalysis was vulnerable as well to the claims of the newer, proliferating popular psychotherapies.

17

The Decline of Psychoanalysis in Psychiatry, 1965–1985

Between 1960 and 1985 nearly all the factors that had contributed to the rise of psychoanalytic psychiatry were in part reversed: doubts grew about the scientific validity and effectiveness of psychoanalysis; alternatives to the psychoanalytic psychodynamic style arose; psychoanalysis lost its identification with psychiatric reform; social conditions for psychoanalytic practice changed; partly because of a lack of demonstrable results, government and private funding for psychoanalytic training and research dwindled; some psychoanalysts retreated from the new therapeutic fields they had staked out, among them, psychosomatic medicine and the treatment of schizophrenia. This chapter will deal chiefly with the issue of psychoanalytic effectiveness and the complex problem of judging the results of psychotherapy, issues broached in the 1940s and 1950s. The next chapter will take up the retreat from psychosomatic medicine and the treatment of the psychoses as well as new problems of psychiatric practice.

These developments accompanied a major shift in psychiatric style away from the psychoanalytic psychodynamic emphasis of the postwar years. Psychoanalysis then had seemed to offer a promising departure from the apparently sterile somatic and classifying approach of traditional psychiatry. The new developments resembled the crisis of the somatic style that had inaugurated psychoanalysis in the first place. Originally, Freud's psychology had arisen in part from the limitations, contradictions, and failures of the somatic style of the late 19th century. Now, psychiatrists, psychoanalysts, and psychologists began to point out what seemed to be the limitations, overdrawn promises, and contradictions of the psychoanalytic psychodynamic style that had achieved partial dominance after the end of World War II.

This stylistic shift within psychiatry renewed a militantly hopeful emphasis on somatic treatment and genetic causes. Interest shifted away from the traditional case history to an insistence on experiment, quantification, and replication, made easier and more plausible by new modes of data processing and by the increasing use of an ever-broadening pharmacopia of psychotropic drugs. These and other developments fostered an explosion of knowledge about the brain and nervous system and sharpened criticism about methods that seemed to be neither experimental nor quantifiable. The origins of nervous and mental disorder would be found less in interpersonal and individual psychological factors than in somatic functioning. A renewed emphasis on biology began somewhat earlier in the social sciences.[1] Following the model of medical and laboratory research, it was presumed that the validity of therapeutic claims would be determined by controlled outcome assessments. The proliferation of drug therapies that accompanied and fostered this change in style drastically altered the treatment of psychoses beginning in the mid-1950s.

Psychoanalysts failed to demonstrate to their critics the superior effectiveness of psychoanalysis, not only in its applications to a widening array of disorders but also in those fundamental neuroses for which it had been devised.[2]

Psychoanalysis became the primary focus of a general attack on the efficacy of insight or "talk" therapies, leveled by behaviorists and somatic psychiatrists. Critics called for new and stringent standards for demonstrating effectiveness such as those used to test the efficacy of drugs: quantitative and comparative studies based on matched samples of patients uniformly diagnosed, randomly assigned, and treated with standardized procedures, with outcomes judged not only by therapists but by impartial observers not involved in the therapy. The psychoanalyst's and the psychotherapist's case histories, the basis for claims of therapeutic success and the source of data for theory were dismissed as merely subjective anecdotes, tainted by preconceptions and inadmissible in the courts of "true science."[3] The psychoanalysts, by identifying themselves with medicine and psychiatry thus were judged by changes in medical styles of "scientific" confirmation and psychiatric practice.

In addition to criticism of therapeutic outcomes and the rise of a neosomatic style, new alternative psychological and social approaches were created, notably the behavior therapies and the elaboration of the role of social rather than individual factors in nervous and mental disorder. Conditions such as poverty and disorganization, "life events" such as bereavement or sudden change, and the pressure of social roles were all examined as possible pathogens.

By 1975, five or six million Americans were paying one billion dollars a year for contact with mental health professionals. Much of this money went for psychotherapy, whose vogue psychoanalysis largely had stimulated. But psychotherapy had become an industry as large as the pharmacotherapy industry, manned not only by psychiatrists but by an army of non-medical counselors and therapists of every persuasion. The social investment in psychotherapy was enormous.

The development of alternative therapies and personnel had the most wide-ranging consequences for psychoanalysis. Beginning in the early 1960s, the proportion of psychiatrists entering psychoanalytic training began to drop. At UCLA, for example, the percentage of psychiatric residents in training at psychoanalytic institutes declined from 50 percent in 1966 to 27 percent by 1975, although those in personal analysis or psychotherapy remained constant at 69 percent.[4] The pattern of appointments to leading medical schools slowly changed, and fewer analysts became heads of psychiatric departments. By 1990 at ten top medical schools only three chairmen were psychoanalysts or members of psychoanalytic organizations.[5] The orientation of clinical psychologists, most of whom were therapists, also changed; where 41 percent saw themselves as "psychodynamic" in 1961, by 1976 this had dropped to 19 percent with over half describing themselves as "eclectic." By 1982, some 91 percent thought the future lay with eclecticism.[6] Conditions of psychiatric practice changed, with the decline of mental hospitals, the growth of community psychiatry, and, at first, gradually increasing insurance coverage for therapy. Then in the late 1970s and 1980s insurance funding for psychotherapy also declined in view of apparently inconclusive results and the possibility of uneconomic overuse, both highly controversial issues. Accordingly, the pool of private patients diminished.

Although these developments will be dealt with topically, a brief description of the tangled chronology of events will be helpful. In the 1940s and 1950s while psychoanalysis was rapidly gaining ground, outside critics as well as psychoanalysts themselves, reopening the debates of the 1920s, had begun to question the efficacy of psychoanalytic treatment. At the same time other critics were objecting to the presumed narrowness of psychoanalytic psychiatry. The debate was dramatically intensified in the mid-1950s by behaviorists, who condemned psychoanalysis as an "unscientific" and useless therapy and theory. Then, from the late 1950s to the present the somatic emphasis, including the use of drugs as well as research in brain and neurological functions and in genetics, became a major trend in psychiatry and provided fresh grounds for criticism. By the mid-1960s, however, a movement began within psychiatry calling for the mass delivery of community mental health services, and in some quarters questioning the entire medical model of psychiatry, with which American psychoanalysis had become identified. These developments, rooted in the social history of the 1960s, exacerbated the attacks on psychoanalysis. For such critics psychoanalysis was an unproven luxury, limited to the minor distresses of the well-to-do. Psychiatry and psychoanalysis were conformist, anti-feminist and relentlessly middle-class; they were also authoritarian and subtlety inhumane. Radical interpretations of Freud in this period were largely confined to intellectuals, well outside the psychiatric wing of psychoanalysis. As a result of these pressures, some psychiatrists felt they were losing their medical identity, and in the next decade, the 1970s, they strongly reasserted it, partly on grounds of the rapid progress of somatic treatment and research.

Although previous momentum kept psychoanalysis expanding, in the 1970s and certainly by the 1980s the expansion within psychiatry had ceased and retrenchment was under way. The culmination of psychoanalytic decline was emphasized in 1980 by the American Psychiatric Association's adoption of its *Diagnostic and Statistical Manual III* in which psychoanalytic explanations of the neuroses were conspicuous by their absence.

Criticism of psychoanalysis, always persistent, became better informed and sometimes more fundamental.[7] Critics represented not only psychiatrists but psychologists trained in academic standards of testing and research who had entered the psychiatric and psychotherapeutic fields. They brought a preoccupation with experimental research design which in turn created serious problems for psychotherapy research. The psychologists could not receive psychoanalytic training to perform therapy, according to the rules of the American Psychoanalytic Association, and this provided additional motives for criticism.

Objects of criticism ranged from the psychoanalytic model of psychiatric practice to the outcomes of psychoanalytic therapy, psychosomatic medicine, the treatment of psychoses, and a dialogue with Freud's ghost, as it were, over the validity of propositions derived from psychoanalysis, such as the significance of infantile sexuality or the role of parents in causing schizophrenia.

One variety of the postwar attacks, particularly in the 1950s, came from proponents of traditional models of psychiatric practice and from those who continued to espouse a primarily somatic psychiatry during the heyday of the psychodynamic style. They charged that psychoanalysts unduly narrowed the range of causes and the methods of treatment of nervous and mental disorder. Although psychoanalysts were trained as physicians, they were in effect practicing an exclusively psychological treatment and were thus no different from psychologists. By 1956 perhaps a fourth of American psychiatrists in private practice were "pure psychotherapists." Psychoanalysis was drawing psychiatry away from medicine and psychiatrists were in danger of losing their medical identity.[8]

One kind of criticism that largely vanished by the late 1950s came from those who found psychoanalysis repulsive. One state hospital physician argued that Freudians "bespattered" their patients' symptoms with "incest horror, emasculation phantasies, faeces-smearing, etc., until such symptom or character trait is broken up." "Is it possible," he asked, "that we are developing the equivalent of a secular church, supported by government monies, staffed by a genital-level apostolate unwittingly dispensing a broth of existential atheism, hedonism, and other dubious religio-philosophical ingredients?"[9]

The neurosurgeon Percival Bailey, in his vitriolic attack on Freud and psychoanalysis before the American Psychiatric Association in 1957, repeating old arguments, deplored the entire psychoanalytic "psychological revolution in psychiatry." It had solved none of psychiatry's major problems such as schizophrenia. Psychoanalysis was only a fad, like discredited lobotomy. Freud had displayed none of the scientist's patience with "cautious, laborious verification, step by step of one's hypotheses, establishing each one solidly before passing on to the next." Like a religion, psychoanalysis was a closed, self-confirming system. Bailey deplored psychoanalysts in positions of power in psychiatry and their slanting of its history which gave Freud a central position of honor, to the detriment of Bailey's own hero, the French medical psychologist Pierre Janet. "They have made the younger generation believe that, if you have not been analyzed, you belong to a lesser breed," and that without deploying orthodox Freudian language, you "are apt to have trouble with some of the associate examiners of the Board of Psychiatry." Finally, psychoanalysis was a pessimistic, value-less ideology that ignored the "social nature of mankind." "Must we bow before *dem goldenen Sigi?*" he asked, and prophesied that the problem of schizophrenia would be solved by the biochemist.[10] Bailey failed to note that Freud proposed a similar approach to the psychoses.

General physicians tended to see the new "dynamic psychiatrist" as one who might not administer electroshock treatment or sign commitment papers. He would not make house calls and would see patients only in his office, after crises had been handled by other physicians. The family doctor might be willing to retrieve a young drunk from a scrape, while the new psychiatrist waited immaculate to receive the patient, cleaned up and sober, in his office for insight psychotherapy.

Psychoanalytic psychiatrists observed that some young novices failed to make contact with relatives or spouses, or to give or receive information about a patient outside the therapeutic hour, perhaps fearing to contaminate the transference. Some lost sight of their patients in the "fog and snow" of technical psychoanalytic terms. They might know their Fenichel, but not their patients. The psychoanalytic model of treatment was rarely possible or appropriate for many kinds of psychiatric patients—drug addicts, delinquents, criminals, and many common psychiatric emergencies such as homicidal violence, suicide attempts, or psychosomatic crises.[11] Medical educators in the universities noted that, with a few exceptions, psychoanalytic institutes existed outside the control of departments of psychiatry, and thus were ruled by a group of private practitioners.[12]

More important than these criticisms were attacks on the presumed effectiveness of psychoanalysis as a therapy. Such criticism had been a persistent, if muted, issue among psychoanalysts themselves since the 1920s. Indeed, psychoanalysts have been among the unsparing critics of their own profession.[13]

The issue of therapeutic results had been reopened in 1942 in the midst of the schisms in the New York Institute. Clarence Oberndorf, a pioneer American psychoanalyst who had been briefly analyzed by Freud, warned his colleagues that the "numerous and violent controversies in psychoanalytic groups . . . and the frequent attempts to introduce new systems" were the result of "discomfiture and incertitude" about "theory, methodology and results."[14]

Some of the "high hopes regarding the wide scope and certainty of results with psychoanalytic therapy . . . have not been sustained." The statistical outcomes of psychoanalytic treatment, Oberndorf wrote, were no better than those of treatment by other methods—about 60 percent recovered or improved, and rigorous psychoanalytic training seemed to make no appreciable difference in results.

Oberndorf noted that especially in his early practice, he had treated patients successfully in very brief psychoanalysis. But deeper and lengthier analyses had come into fashion without any investigation as to whether the results were better or more permanent. Now, analyses were lasting from two to seven years, the latter "occurring, it is whispered, more often than is acknowledged." Psychoanalysts were treating more borderline and psychotic patients, and many of these were kept out of hospitals and at productive work. Nevertheless, outcomes were disappointing.

He proposed that after a patient had been in analysis for two or three years the case be reviewed by one or two consultants chosen by the analyst. Unless such an assessment became a standard procedure, vanity usually would preclude it. Five years later, Oberndorf offered a prize of $1000 for studies of the results of psychoanalytic therapy, and symposia on outcomes were held in Boston and Philadelphia.[15]

In 1947 Lawrence Kubie also was deeply concerned over the problems of psychoanalytic technique. He wrote to Edward Glover, his first analyst, that after seeing enough of the work of even his best colleagues, "it was no longer possible to believe that a bad therapeutic result could be explained away as due either to inadequate training or to inferior analytic ability. I had been forced to accept the fact that it was often the result of certain basic inadequacies in the therapeutic leverage of even the best and most skillful analysts. . . . Nowhere is this more evident than in the therapeutic results of our training analyses, where for many obvious reasons our therapeutic leverage is even less than with our patients. All of this bothered me deeply, both about the progress of psychoanalysis as an art and a science, and even more because of the tendency of mature colleagues to develop overt neurotic character disorders with the passing years. . . . Perhaps the time has come for a frank facing of the problem within our own analytic circles."[16] He urged Glover to republish his studies of technique, which had surveyed 24 members of the British Psychoanalytic Society and had concluded that despite agreement on a few fundamentals such as analysis of the transference, it would be difficult to argue that a standardized technique existed.[17] A later American study argued that no two psychoanalysts operated alike, despite their common assumptions. Each pursued, as already noted, an essentially individualized method.[18]

Kubie's concern may have been provoked by an attempt in 1946 to cast doubt on the claims of psychotherapy and psychoanalysis by Peter G. Denker, a neuropsychiatrist from Bellevue Hospital in New York.[19] In the midst of campaigns for more psychiatrists and expanded facilities for psychotherapy, Denker argued that in 500 cases of neurosis treated by general practitioners with "sedatives, tonics, suggestion and reassurance," 72 percent recovered within two years. These neurotic patients had been unable to work for at least three months prior to filing their claims for disability, which were paid until their recovery, and which were a disincentive to get well. Denker argued that these results compared favorably with those obtained by psychoanalytic clinics and hospitals in Berlin, London, Chicago, and Topeka. He concluded that the psychoneuroses ran "a self-limited course," and that therefore there was no reason for alarm over the national shortage of psychiatrists.

In an acrimonious discussion of Denker's results, the analysts and their opponents failed to agree on a major issue: how sick were the patients in Denker's series and how sick were those treated by analysts? The psychoanalysts argued that patients came to them not after three months of illness, but after years of being treated unsuccessfully by all other available methods. Denker countered that the patients in his sample had been ill enough to be unable to work at all, while many psychoanalytic patients were able to function.

Angered by Denker's claims, Kubie insisted that compensation cases were not representative of the psychoneuorses. The specialist saw "the severe, chronic, and often neglected and underrated conditions which may reach him too late for help, and only after the patient has been knocked around far too long, It is even more shocking and disturbing to hear this audience [of physicians] presumably of critically minded and thoughtful persons, taken in and rocking with laughter at this 'proof' that there is no need for more psychiatrists." The "curing of a symptom by the general practitioner all too often obscures a malignant process, which then goes on unchecked," he warned.[20]

Kubie later called for greater rigor in outcome research in psychotherapy and in psychoanalysis as well. He insisted that too little was known about the neuroses in general, about therapy or spontaneous recovery or about the influence of the patient's life situation to make valid judgments about comparative effectiveness.[21] He urged objective studies of free association, the fundamental tool of psychoanalysis, and wanted "all analytic data to be cross-checked, corrected and confirmed by precise investigations of the family background, early history and social situation." Analytic failures were too often explained by such verbal formulae as "excessive narcissism . . . weak egos overwhelmed by massive anxiety . . . negative therapeutic reactions . . . pseudo-neurotic schizophrenia." These "subtly put the blame on the patient for not having been gracious enough to get well."[22]

At a symposium in Boston in 1948 on therapeutic results, marked by candor and even humility, Kubie urged that because psychiatry lacked the correction of errors that the autopsy provided for medicine, therapists needed to study their failures systematically as well as their successes. Psychoanalyses could be recorded to create a degree of objectivity in clinical research.

Phyllis Greenacre, a New York analyst, explored the complexities of evaluating psychoanalytic treatment. The psychoanalyst dealt not with a circumscribed, specific disease process but with "interweaving disturbed functions embedded in . . . the very fabric of the patient's existence." Moreover, psychoanalytic treatment involved a "complicated set of techniques applied over a long period of time." There was the added variable of the individual administration of the techniques as well as the peculiarly important role of the transference, itself an interaction between patient and analyst. All these made analysts aware and "frightened of the enormous intricacies of the job." One needed to see not only whether symptoms disappeared but, more important, whether the patient sustained an improved "total functioning in life." She cautioned that she had become aware of the distorting effects of partisanship for a given method when she had investigated a New Jersey state hospital where remarkably successful results were claimed for the surgical treatment of the psychoses by removing sources of focal infection, such as diseased teeth or tonsils, with recovery rates of 85 percent. Despite the vast enthusiasm of the staff, her investigation showed that patients experienced fewer recoveries than an untreated control group and were worse off five years after treatment than at their first admissions to the hospital.[23]

Participants in the symposium raised most of the issues that would plague psychoanalytic, indeed psychotherapeutic, outcome research. The first was the problem of definition. Could there be common definitions of the patient's illness and of the precise nature of the therapy and of its outcome? If the data were not uniform and comparable, the statistics would mean little. There was difficulty getting agreement on data among therapists of the same school, not to speak of those from different schools. Therapists holding different analytic theories, such as those of Melanie Klein or Anna Freud, got equally good results. Was improvement due to the treatment or to some outside factor in the patient's life? How to judge the effect of the analyst's personality or variant of the method? Were the medical and the experimental laboratory models appropriate in judging psychotherapy? Who would evaluate the results? Would the judges be free of bias? Up to that time, psychoanalysis in America had been largely private practice, and problems of confidentiality and follow-up made research unusually difficult.

In December, 1947 a committee was appointed by the American Psychoanalytic Association to evaluate the therapeutic results of psychoanalysis. But soon the committee decided its effort might "come to grief" because of the great differences in defining psychoanalytic therapy and successful treatment. Definitions had plagued previous discussions of outcome, and the committee decided it needed to study psychoanalytic practice in detail.[24] Begun in 1952, the report was finally published in 1967 after three committees had worked on it. Over the years, the code identifying the 800 psychoanalysts who made initial reports on 10,000 patients was lost, so it was impossible to determine whether experienced analysts achieved better results than novices or men than women. There were, however, initial and final reports on about 3000 patients.

Psychosomatic patients made up 17 percent of the sample, the largest group; hysterical and compulsive patients, 12 percent each; depressed patients, 10 percent; schizophrenics, 8.9 percent; patients with anxiety, 8.7 percent; depression and anxiety, 5.9 percent; "sexual deviates," 4.6 percent; and paranoid patients, 2.3 percent. It had been hoped that a pooling of information would be helpful because the number of patients an individual analyst could treat was limited. Despite its drawbacks the report contained some highly significant information.

About 43 percent of the patients were in psychoanalysis and 47 percent in psychotherapy, and the analysts judged that psychoanalysis in general produced superior results. However, those in psychoanalysis probably had been pre-selected as most likely to benefit from it.

Analysts repeatedly had emphasized the profound "structural" changes in personality that psychoanalysis could achieve and placed less emphasis on cure of symptoms. In this sample, from the mid-1950s, there was a large discrepancy between symptom cure and overall "improvement." About 97 percent of the analysts and their patients believed they had improved in "total functioning." However, presenting symptoms were "cured" in only about 27 percent. Schizophrenic symptoms were cured in 9 percent of males, but a higher percentage of females, while more men than women were cured of depressive symptoms. More than half of all patients (54%) failed to complete treatment, but the more highly educated patients tended to finish.

The analysts' clientele was a well-to-do, well-educated, professional and managerial group. Professionals made up 43 percent of all patients. Some 22 percent had completed high school; almost half were college-educated while 35 percent had done graduate work. Of the professionals, those in science constituted 9.2 percent and in the social sciences 9 percent; the law, 3.7 percent; the arts 5.7 percent. Some 7.3 percent were psychiatrists. Managers and housewives constituted 18 percent each, and 1.2 percent were in business. In a period when the average annual income was $5,010, some 57 percent earned $10,000 or less; one-quarter $10,000 to $20,000, and 15 percent more than $20,000.

This study included no control groups, no judgments of outcome by anyone other than the therapist and the patient, no comparisons with other methods. Psychoanalysts insisted that with so lengthy a therapy, it would be unfair if not impossible to find a comparable sample of patients who might either be treated by other methods or placed on a waiting list to see whether they improved as much as the patients treated by psychoanalysis. No comparable outcome studies have since been undertaken by the America Psycho-analytic Association.

In 1952, at a time of growing psychoanalytic influence, the behaviorist H. J. Eysenck, a psychologist at the Maudsley psychiatric hospital in England, launched a major attack on psychoanalysis and psychoanalytic psychotherapy, indeed on all insight therapies: they were no more effective than no treat-ment at all, no better than "spontaneous recovery."[25] He insisted that rough-ly two-thirds of neurotic patients would recover or markedly improve within two years whether or not they were treated by psychotherapy. He raised these arguments initially against proposals of the American Psychological Association to train clinical psychologists in psychotherapy to meet a growing social demand.[26]

Eysenck cautioned that his data did not *disprove* the possibility of thera-peutic effectiveness, but failed to demonstrate it. He called for carefully designed studies that included patients randomly assigned to treatment and control groups. In 1965 he concluded that, in the few studies using control groups, the untreated patients did as well as those in treatment, except for the superior results of behavior therapy. He cited a review of the war neuro-ses which had found that soldiers who were untreated or who were treated by psychotherapy returned to duty in approximately equal numbers. He con-cluded that psychotherapies had not lived up to the hopes that had greeted them fifty years before. Like Denker, he believed that neurotic disorders were self-limiting.

Psychoanalysis was no more successful than any other method, Ensenck concluded, and, in fact, all methods of psychotherapy failed to improve on recovery rates "obtained through ordinary life experiences and non-specific treatment." Finally, he advised discarding the psychoanalytic model, because it failed to generate verifiable predictions, in favor of a learning theory model which seemed more promising in both theory and application.[27]

Eysenck's polemics stimulated the elaboration of behavior therapy and new research in psychotherapy and inaugurated more than a decade of disil-lusionment with psychoanalytic psychotherapy, at least among some aca-demic psychologists.[28] Clinicians tended to ignore the criticism, regarding their therapeutic enterprise as more valuable than what the researchers were doing. The controversy is richly detailed and still lively, and only a few of its most important elements can be dealt with here.

Psychoanalysts accused Eysenck of manipulating his data and of clinical naivete. Lester Luborsky, a psychologist then at the Menninger Foundation, argued that the patients in the studies Eysenck cited were not comparable. An adequate control group needed to be matched "on level of mental health, symptoms and duration of illness." Moreover, standards of improvement varied with the judges.[29] Elizabeth Zetzel, a psychoanalyst and an assistant clinical professor of psychiatry at Harvard Medical School, charged Eysenck with internal inconsistencies and with "shifting criteria in favor of his major assumptions." For example, in one very careful study the subjects were not neurotics motivated to seek treatment but youths in a delinquency prevention program. More serious, the controls, she suggested, probably had "transient or negligible" symptoms, while the patients suffered from more serious disorders, thus prejudicing results against the treatment. For example, patients seen at the first psychoanalytic institute clinics in fact were seriously ill, and more recent and sophisticated views of the applicability of psychoanalysis would have excluded many of them. Moreover, therapists in such clinics were inexperienced students in training. Finally, it was important to distinguish between symptom relief and over-all improvement. A man might recover from depression only to beat his wife. The aims of psychoanalytic therapy were "psychic growth and the liberation of maximal energy for adaptive purposes." The procedures were "detailed and microscopic" and appropriate techniques had to be created to do justice to them. But the statistical methods of social science were largely new, and had been developed as recently as the late 1930s.[30] Essentially, she was arguing that psychoanalysis did not meet the medical criteria of symptom relief, but was, in effect, a different enterprise.

Lawrence Kubie accused Eysenck of not facing up to the technical problems involved in assessing therapies. Relying heavily on analogies with medicine, Kubie, like Franz Alexander, argued for the usefulness of the case history. Medicine had advanced not by statistical surveys of "ill defined variables," but by intensive study of individual patients, "seeking to identify consistent and unitary processes among the many variable phenomena of illness."

Kubie raised fundamental issues in outcome research that still remain unsolved. He argued that Eysenck's work showed no "realization that a cluster of similar or even identical symptoms can arise out of many different psychopathological soils and that symptom clusters do not constitute unitary processes of disease in psychiatry, any more than they do in somatic medicine." Outcome studies had to deal with the same illness, the same method of treatment, and the similar skills of those carrying it out.[31]

Like Oberndorf earlier, Eysenck relied partly on statistics presumably establishing rates of "spontaneous recovery" in one of the first comparative studies of psychotherapy by Leland Hinsie published in 1937. These were figures for patients suffering from neuroses who, without formal treatment, were discharged from the New York state hospital system as recovered or improved. The other statistics came from Denker's 1946 series of insurance patients diagnosed as neurotic and treated by general physicians.[32] Eysenck had concluded with Denker that for untreated patients the recovery rate was around 72 percent, while the recovery rate for analytic patients was about 66 percent. Even that lower rate of psychoanalytic success was due, he argued, to the fact that they chose patients who were most likely to recover spontaneously.[33]

Examinations of Eysenck's evidence indicated that he had ignored studies with positive results and had favored behavior therapy in his statistical summaries. Thus, he had quoted a 90 percent improvement rate for behavior therapy that *excluded* patients who broke off treatment while lumping those who broke off psychoanalytic treatment with the treatment failures. Moreover, one examination of the statistics for spontaneous recovery indicated that it might be as low as 30 percent instead of two-thirds, with a median of 45 percent.[34] This argument was later disputed by the behaviorists, who, citing additional studies, supported Eysenck's original estimate of 65 percent and argued that the spontaneous recovery rate for obsessional disorders was lower than that for anxiety conditions, for instance, and that about one-third of neurotic patients did not recover.[35]

The high rate of 90 percent for those cured or much improved by behavior therapy was reported by a disillusioned former Freudian therapist from South Africa, Joseph Wolpe.[36] In the 1950s he pioneered behavioral desensitization techniques, and at first claimed overwhelming success by "reciprocal inhibition." Therapy usually began with a close inspection of the events that preceded and followed a particular behavior, such as phobic avoidance. A response that inhibited or suppressed anxiety would be evoked "in the presence of the anxiety-producing stimuli."[37] Anxiety-inhibiting responses might include relaxation or the expression of aggressive or sexual feelings. Other techniques were flooding, in which a patient was confronted with his most anxiety-provoking stimuli; modeling, in which the patient witnessed successful coping behavior; and assertiveness training. In aversion therapy, a stimulus would be paired with a painful consequence, such as a shock; this was tried in sexual perversions, for instance. In operant conditioning, control of the environment and reward for a given behavior was the major lever; for example, psychotic patients would be rewarded for socialized behavior by privileges or treats. Other methods tried with psychotic patients included desensitization with relaxation or satiation in which, for example, a woman who hoarded towels was given so many towels they became an "aversive stimulus" and the patient proceeded to get rid of them; she stopped hoarding and no other symptom was substituted for it. Behaviorists claimed that their therapies were swift and sure; taking weeks or months where psychoanalyses took years. Curse of 85 to 90 percent were claimed by behaviorists along with no evidence of symptom substitution.[38]

Controlled studies of the outcomes of behavior therapy suggested far more modest success rates than Wolpe originally claimed, but the effectiveness of behavioral methods has been substantiated, at first for phobias and later for more generalized neurotic conditions. Behavior therapies became highly developed and varied, usually targeting a particular symptom or a specific behavior. In one careful comparison using highly skilled behavior and dynamic therapists, including Wolpe, behavior therapy was slightly more effective in a wide variety of neurotic disorders than short-term psychoanalytic psychotherapy. But the difference was by no means great.[39]

The behaviorist attack sharpened important, still controversial issues surrounding the nature of psychotherapy and of neurotic disorder and how therapy was to be judged. It may be recalled that psychoanalytic psychotherapy was being applied to a wider and wider gamut of patients, from the neurotic to the borderline and psychotic. It was axiomatic that patients were suffering and, above all, anxious. Some of them might have crippling symptoms such as phobias about open spaces or flying in airplanes. Some had psychosomatic diseases such as ulcerative colitis or more general physical symptoms such as persistent, severe headaches. Others might have work blocks, perform badly at jobs, or fail to complete reasonable goals. Some patients were haunted by terrifying dreams; others had lost the ability to concentrate. Still others lived a pattern of transitory unsatisfying relationships, broken marriages, or compulsive sexuality. Many patients experienced low self-esteem, extreme irritability, or feelings of hopelessness and despair.[40] People with some of these symptoms could be classified as neurotic, others had had a history of treatment in a mental hospital and merged toward the psychoses, distinguished perhaps by behavior dangerous to the self or others, bizarre disorientation, hallucinations, or delusions.[41] Defining and classifying these disabilities was difficult enough. More perplexing was how to judge the results of treatment.

Improvement in a clear-cut phobic symptom such as a fear of snakes was relatively easy to assess. D. H. Malan, a British psychotherapy researcher at the Tavistock clinic, remarked ironically that you could quantify "the distance at which a phobic patient is able to approach a snake."[42] The elimination of physical symptoms also was clear-cut, and some of the best outcomes for psychoanalytic therapy were claimed in psychosomatic cases, such as peptic ulcer or ulcerative colitis.[43]

But psychoanalysts and many dynamic psychiatrists regarded symptom change alone as inadequate.[44] Some therapists insisted on generalized goals, such as insight or better overall functioning, "greater comfort and efficiency." Yet basic improvement and character change were difficult to define. There was obvious difficulty in measuring happier interpersonal relations, greater social skills, "improved functioning," or a greater sense of mastery and contentment, all subjectively real enough and all involving complex value judgments. To make matters more complicated, what if a patient were reconciled to a symptom such as masturbation or occasional outbursts of anger and yet his overall functioning greatly improved? Often patients reported that they still were subject to symptoms such as anxiety but nevertheless felt better and functioned better.[45]

Outcome criteria at least had to do justice to the "complexity of human personality," Malan argued.[46] He suggested listing all the "known signs of disturbance"; a parsimonious explanation of them; an individualized set of desirable outcomes for each patient, because every patient differed; and, finally, the comparison of findings with these criteria and their rating by a simple scale. Evidence from clinical findings had to be supported by changes in the patient's life.

More complex still was the issue of how psychoanalytic therapy could be tested. Was it possible to measure such psychoanalytic objectives as "alterations in personality structure, patterns of defense mechanisms and compromise formations," views of the world and the self, or changes in the super-ego or ego functions?[47] Could brief therapy, for instance, do justice to the psychoanalytic insistence on the necessity for the slow and careful "working through," especially in the transference of the details of patterns from the past? Could brief therapy effectively treat serious and long-standing disabilities that began in early childhood?[48]

Standards of judgment varied with psychotherapeutic goals, scientific attitudes, and values. The psychologist Paul Meehl neatly caught the rhetoric of the contending views in 1954. Statistical methods were "communicable, verifiable, public, objective, reliable, behavioral, testable, rigorous, scientific, precise, careful, trustworthy, experimental, quantitative, down to earth, hard headed, empirical, mathematical and sound." Clinical methods were "dynamic, global, meaningful, holistic, subtle, sympathetic, patterned, organized, rich, deep, genuine, sensitive, sophisticated, real, living, concrete, natural, true to life and understanding."[49]

At first the superiority of "experimental" approaches to the clinical case study was assumed by some proponents of psychotherapy research, but accumulating experience suggested that there were serious differences between the experimental model and the realities of psychotherapy. For instance, unlike a drug, psychotherapy was a "complex strategy" that varied from therapist to therapist and patient to patient; it was undertaken in complex social and environmental conditions that vitally affected it. The chief goal of research was to discover which psychotherapeutic method was most effective with a particular individual with a specific problem in a particular set of circumstances and, recently, "at what cost in dollars, manpower and institutional resources can it be most effective." Neither question has yet been answered. On the whole the tendency has been toward the increasing use of cognitive and behavioral therapies in psychotherapy research, although interpersonal therapy fared well in the National Institute of Mental Health's recent and impressive comparative study of treatment for depression.[50]

Controlled comparative studies began in the 1950s partly as a result of research of the client-centered therapist Carl Rogers, partly because of the behavioral and learning orientation of American psychologists.[51] Rating scales were one method of judging results in psychotherapy research, and psychologists and psychiatrists devised a number of them. Most dealt with obvious psychopathology such as mood, memory, and disturbances in the sense of reality, others with personality and social adjustment. In addition to rating scales, some sought the impressions of therapist, patient, and relatives, and evaluations by psychiatrists who were blind to the type of therapy used. Psychotherapy researchers still are seeking more sensitive outcome measures that might do justice to insight, possible moral issues, and the effects of therapy on the patient's relationships and environment.[52]

A number of studies came to contradictory conclusions. Some argued that inexperienced therapists did as well as experienced ones, but other studies indicated that the more experienced were more successful, particularly in difficult cases. The longer the treatment, the better the results, some concluded, while others found no difference between the results of therapy with a fixed number of sessions and therapy with no time limit.

One of the few consistent conclusions was that some therapists were more skillful than others, possibly because of the therapist's personality. An important impetus for considering this factor came from Carl Rogers's argument that the therapist's warmth, genuineness, and empathy were essential for effective therapy. A long-term psychotherapy research project at the Phipps Clinic at Johns Hopkins also suggested that the therapist's personality played an important role and confirmed that some therapists were distinctly more successful. The latter conclusion was strongly supported by still another recent study.[53]

The quality of psychotherapy research was sharply criticized by both practicing psychotherapists and psychologists. Clinicians argued that it was "banal and tangential" to clinical practice. In trying to be exact, they charged, the researchers lost sight of what was significant. Many of them had studied very short-term therapy and for this reason their findings could have only the most "diluted applicability" to lengthier treatments such as psychoanalytic psychotherapy.[54] Psychologists argued that research often did not take into account the fact that patients were more different than they were alike and that therapists varied not only in personality but in the way they carried out supposedly standard techniques such as psychoanalysis. Moreover, what the patient brought to treatment also was important, and some argued that different theoretical perspectives, such as those of Freud, Jung, Adler, or Sullivan, might have been derived from the different kinds of patients they observed. More recent outcome studies, such as those conducted by NIMH, used standardized therapeutic methods codified in manuals, uniform diagnostic criteria, and therapists who received uniform training.[55]

Studies from as early as the 1930s indicated that different methods of psychotherapy achieved similar results. In 1949 a Los Angeles psychiatrist argued that patients recovered or improved with different therapies— Adlerian, Jungian, Freudian—and that the burden of proving superiority lay with the system that claimed it.[56]

By the mid-1970s most of the controlled comparative studies involved short-term therapy only and arrived at the Dodo bird's verdict in *Alice in Wonderland*—"everybody has won and all must have prizes." This was true for comparisons between group and individual psychotherapy, client-centered versus other traditional psychotherapies, behavior therapy versus other therapies. However, a combination of medical treatment and psychotherapy was superior in psychosomatic illness. Patients treated by psychotherapy did significantly better than patients in untreated control groups, although in a third of these studies there was no difference between the two groups. In most of the comparative studies the insight therapies were poorly represented, indeed, psychoanalysis was not represented at all. Most of the therapies took a year or much less and the follow-ups were insufficiently long to catch "the assumed long-term benefits of the insight-oriented psychotherapies."[57] The thrust of these outcome studies was to weaken claims that therapeutic results came from the application of any specific theory or method. The argument that all psychotherapy operated according to the same general principles further challenged both psychoanalytic and behaviorist claims to uniqueness and special efficacy.

The most influential argument for the fundamental similarities underlying the different methods of psychotherapy was made by Jerome Frank, a psychiatrist at the Johns Hopkins University Medical School who conducted a long-term study of the therapeutic process.[58] The fairly uniform success rate of different methods suggested to Frank that common factors must be operating. *Persuasion and Healing,* published in 1961, implicitly attacked major therapeutic claims of psychoanalysis as well as its methods of training and marked a return to a pre-Freudian view of the neuroses and their treatment. Despite their apparent diversity, Frank argued, all methods attempted to heal by persuasion, specifically, by arousing hope in a demoralized patient, restoring the sense of mastery, and decreasing the sense of isolation. The elements of successful psychotherapy were: a trained healer, accepted by the patient and his social group; a sufferer seeking relief; and a structured series of contacts between healer and sufferer.

The patient's demoralization resulted from failure to cope "with internally or externally induced stresses that the person and those close to him expected him to handle." It was accompanied by damaged self-esteem, by "feelings of impotence, isolation, and despair, and rejection from others because of failure to meet their expectations."

Therapy offered consistent *explanations* for the causes of demoralization, a partially cognitive view of treatment. By labeling the "inner and outer forces" assailing a patient and fitting them into a conceptual scheme, therapy heightened the patient's "sense of mastery" over them. It helped a patient "correct errors and resolve conflicts in his assumptions concerning himself and others." The assumptions were organized into systems at varying levels of consciousness, and as they became expectations, others would respond to him in a way that would confirm them. Healthy systems were internally consistent and corresponded to actual conditions. Through conquering symptoms or gaining insight, therapy supplied an experience of success.[59] Therapy, in its attempt to persuade, shared common ground with religion, communist thought-reform, or placebo effects.

Judd Marmor, one of the founders of the American Academy of Psychoanalysis, in 1980 combined the behaviorist and analytic strains in another assessment of the factors that were common to all psychotherapies: first, a good doctor-patient relationship that gave "consistent emotional support"; the "release of emotional tension in the context of hope;" learning about the basis for the patient's difficulties; "operant conditioning toward more adaptive patterns of behavior"; "suggestion and persuasion, overt or covert"; "identification with the therapist or the group"; and "repeated reality-testing or rehearsal of the new adaptive techniques." Finally, Marmor also argued that many of the factors that were important in neurosis were not within the patient's knowledge, conscious or unconscious, and thus no amount of psychoanalytic probing could unearth them.[60]

Countering the argument that psychotherapy was ineffective, systematic outcome studies of "dynamic" psychotherapy began to show positive results beginning in the 1960s. D. H. Malan's research at London's Tavistock Clinic, published in 1963, indicated that brief dynamic psychotherapy could, in fact, produce "quite far-reaching and lasting improvements . . . in relatively severe and long standing illnesses."[61] Although Malan did not use a control group and the therapists evaluated outcomes, he carried out careful follow-up studies, defined the problems clearly at the outset, and used a scale for rating results. His study was an example of exceptional clarity in a field where lucid presentation was a rarity. His major criteria for successful brief therapy were the patient's motivation, the therapist's ability to formulate and focus on a central conflict, and his or her skill in linking the patient's reactions to him or her with those the patient had experienced in relation to his parents.

Begun in 1954, two years after Eysenck's major attack, the 18-year-long Menninger Foundation study of therapy attempted to determine what changes occurred in psychoanalysis and psychoanalytic psychotherapy and how they did so. Its overall conclusions were guarded and in some ways revolutionary about the results of psychoanalysis and the nature of change in psychotherapy, overturning some cherished assumptions.

In method, it was a "naturalistic study," that is, it took a group of 42 non-psychotic patients at the Menninger Foundation and assigned them to what seemed the optimal therapy for each case. Each patient was given extensive psychological tests, and detailed predictions were made to be confirmed or disproven during the course of treatment. There was extensive, prolonged follow-up. However, there were no control groups and patients were not randomly assigned, so there was no comparison across therapies.

The patients were a highly intelligent group, with a median I.Q. of 124. Some 19 of the 42 were from working-class, petit-bourgeois, or farming families, 18 from well-to-do, and 5 from very wealthy families.

If they were unusually intelligent they also were unusually sick. In the tradition of Ernst Simmel's first psychoanalytic sanitarium at Schloss Tegel, near Berlin, the Menninger Foundation since the 1930s had offered psychoanalytic therapy to patients who were far sicker than those in the usual private psychoanalytic practice. These neurotic patients had "serious, long-standing character pathology." Of the 42 patients, 15 suffered from severe alcoholism, the men tending also to use barbiturates and tranquilizers. Major symptoms were anxiety and depression. Some were dangerously impulsive, given to attacks of rage and aggression, verbal and physical assaults, tantrums. Sexual problems were even more widespread: impotence; homosexuality; frigidity; casual, sometimes vicious promiscuity; psychosomatic disorders of all sorts; paranoid symptoms; hysterical and narcissistic traits.[62]

In treating this group of "sicker than usual" patients, the study achieved new insights into the therapeutic process. Three of the conclusions in the summary of Otto Kernberg were striking. The first did not have particularly reassuring implications about the efficacy of therapy: it seemed to argue that those patients who already had the strongest personality resources did best. Thus, patients with severe symptoms but with the highest amount of "ego strength," particularly in the quality of their interpersonal relationships, showed the most improvement with either of the treatment methods used—psychoanalysis or psychotherapy. Patients with high ego strength who were treated by psychoanalysis improved the most. A second finding was that borderline patients with ego weakness did best when the therapist was supportive and focused on interpreting the defenses, especially the negative transference. Finally the more experienced and skilled the therapist, the better the results, particularly in supportive therapy with sicker patients. All the therapists were skilled in psychoanalytic techniques, but varied markedly in their ability to carry out supportive techniques, which required more activity from the therapist.[63]

The most recent, comprehensive review of the Menninger project by Robert S. Wallerstein, published in 1986, drew far-ranging and important conclusions, some of which seemed to question cherished therapeutic claims of psychoanalysis. First, the insistence that psychoanalysis was the *only* therapy creating long-lasting structural changes—because these were based on insight and interpretation—was not borne out. Equally long-lasting change occurred in supportive psychotherapy. Moreover, long-lasting "structural" change bore no necessary relation to insight, although both structural change and insight were more likely to occur in psychoanalysis than in psychotherapy. The project's results refuted the charge that long-term therapy at such high cost had only insubstantial results and that patients were prone to relapse after the analyst's support was withdrawn. The successful treatments remained successful.

However, using psychoanalysis to treat very sick patients on grounds that it was the only therapy likely to create fundamental change was not borne out, either. In fact the study suggested that "heroic indications" for the psychoanalysis of such patients was not justified. Rather, they required supportive hospitalization and a structured life. The overall success rate was about 60 percent for the psychotherapy cases and 55 percent for those in psychoanalysis. Many of the psychoanalytic cases were modified toward increased support and direct intervention by the therapist. Of the 17 cases that remained in standard psychoanalysis, 10 showed "really good" or "moderate" success, 6 "equivocal" improvement, and 1 failure. Of 26 patients in psychotherapy, 15 showed "really good" or "moderate" improvement, 5 equivocal improvement, and 6 failure.[64] Some of these findings, notably those regarding long-term structural change occurring without insight, suggest that therapy achieved its results through means that are not accounted for by standard psychoanalytic theories.

Significant but still controversial research confirming the overall success of psychotherapy was published in 1980 by three psychologists, Mary Lee Smith, Gene V. Glass, and Thomas I. Miller. They confirmed the Dodo bird verdict that found no significant difference in the effectiveness of the various therapies and concluded enthusiastically:

> Psychotherapy is beneficial, consistently so and in many different ways. Its benefits are on a par with other expensive and ambitious interventions, such as schooling and medicine. The benefits of psychotherapy are not permanent but

then little is. . . . [It] benefits people of all ages as reliably as school educates them, medicine cures them, or business turns a profit. . . .

It "reaches a part of life that nothing else touches so well"—the "inner experiences of emotion, feeling and satisfaction." Psychotherapy was almost as effective as drugs in the treatment of the psychoses, apparently including schizophrenia, and combining drugs and psychotherapy produced only somewhat better results than using one or the other exclusively.[65] There was scant evidence of negative effects or deterioration, and each therapy was sufficiently distinctive to make outcome comparisons possible.

The conclusion that startled them most was the scant difference among the "demonstrable benefits" of quite different types of psychotherapy. They agreed with Jerome Frank that the common elements of the different therapies probably were more important than what distinguished each of them. "Researchers who claim superior efficacy of their approach to others without having actually demonstrated it in controlled comparative studies are guilty of chicanery or arrogance."[66]

Their conclusions were based on the "meta-analysis" of 475 studies which had included a roughly equivalent untreated control group.[67] They argued that previous surveys often had chosen what to include in order to support the authors' prejudices, and so they did not exclude studies on the basis of research design; the differences in research methods, they argued, became negligible in the overall statistical comparisons.[68] In fact, the more rigorous the research the more positive was the outcome for psychotherapy, so that favorable effects were not simply the product of sloppy design.

Controlled comparisons indicated no difference between the effectiveness of behavioral and verbal therapies.[69] Symptom substitution, that is, the old psychoanalytic argument that therapy that concentrated on eliminating a specific symptom would not attack the "underlying" problems and thus would result in new symptoms, was not borne out. Length of therapy, whether individual or group, and the training and experience of the therapist apparently counted for little. Fear or anxiety were most affected by therapy, while personality traits, social adjustment, and work or school achievement were the least changed.

They insisted that their findings did not prove that factors specific for each therapy did not exist. They argued not for eclecticism, but for each therapist to pursue training and expertise in a single method. Moreover, much remained unknown and needed further research, especially what the client contributed to therapy, which might be more important than other factors. It still was impossible to match patients with a treatment method that might be best for them.

The reception of these findings revealed the acrimonious disagreements and the difficulties surrounding psychotherapy research in the 1980s, as well as the complications provided by a vast psychotherapy industry with a huge and distressed clientele faced with issues of cost containment and private and government insurance. Major problems of social policy were at stake in outcome research. Should patient's insurance carriers or government pay for a therapy whose efficacy was unproven?

Conclusions about the merits of psychotherapy so warmly described by Smith, Glass, and Miller were by no means uniformly welcomed. Their study suggested that "design and measurement practices" needed "substantial improvement" before the benefits of individual psychotherapy could be confirmed, according to a summary of psychotherapy research in the *American Journal of Psychiatry*. It also concluded that "the volume of satisfactory outcome research . . . is among the lowest and the proven effectiveness of the psychotherapy is minimal."[70]

By 1983 the Smith, Glass, and Miller study had been confirmed by two additional reanalyses of their data. But a third concluded that psychotherapy was no better than a placebo. It was possible that placebo pills given by general practitioners might be cheaper and simpler than than "long and relatively expensive treatment by trained psychotherapists." A placebo was defined as a patient's belief that a given treatment was efficacious.[71] Delighted with these results, Eysenck remarked that no theory of psychotherapy would have predicted the success of placebo treatment. "Do we have the right to impose a lengthy training on medical doctors and psychologists in order to enable them to practice a skill which has no practical relevance to the curing of neurotic disorders? Do we have the right to charge patients fees, or get the state to pay us for a treatment which is no better than a placebo?"[72] Still others countered that the use of a placebo was inappropriate in psychotherapy research because, unlike an inert medical pill, for instance, placebos in fact had real effects in altering behavior and that the issue was to find out how these were produced.[73] The fact that different conclusions were drawn from the same data suggested to one major researcher that each reviewer was governed by a different set of values.[74]

The specific issues involved in this controversy illuminate some of the serious problems of data analysis and method in psychotherapy research. Some argued that the meta-analysis Smith et al. had carried out was flawed largely because their database was poor. Eysenck called the entire enterprise "megasilliness," arguing that conclusions based on poor research were simply invalid. Other critics questioned whether meta-analysis should be applied to research "using grossly different patient populations, being subject to grossly different methods of therapy where the outcomes are assessed using different dependent variables."[75]

The old problems of definition and fairness emerged again. Did psychotherapy research bear any relation to psychotherapy as it was generally practiced? Were the methods used truly representative and uniformly defined? Did it compare the most thorough examples? Were the therapists competent and experienced? Were the conclusions reasonable?

Those who criticized the placebo study argued that its authors had grossly overgeneralized to all of psychotherapy from a tiny and unrepresentative sample. Reviewing studies that had compared the results of "psychotherapy" with a placebo control, they found that only four of 32 were of dynamic psychotherapy, while half were behavioral. The rest used a variety of techniques—counseling, problem solving, social learning. Treatment lasted 10 sessions or fewer in 69 percent of the entire sample, and more than 20 sessions in only 9 percent; one lasted three-fourths of a session; none lasted more than 36 sessions. Some researchers had argued that for comparative purposes at least six months of treatment was the minimum requirement.[76] Most of the patients were students whose average age was 23, and only 3 percent suffered from depression, whereas about 60 percent of patients in the "real world" suffered from depression and anxiety. Moreover, 81 percent of the studies used inexperienced or relatively untrained therapists—psychology graduate students in 12 of the studies, school counselors in five, elementary school teachers, psychiatric residents, psychiatrists, psychologists, and psychiatric social workers in the others. "Would one ever want to test the efficacy of an intervention when its practitioners represent this "kind of conglomeration"?[77]

Others argued that the placebo category had been misused and included treatments such as relaxation, which had been found to be clinically helpful, thus boosting the effectiveness of the placebo theory. The lack of relation between duration of treatment and therapeutic outcome in the original Smith, Glass, and Miller study could be accounted for by differences in the severity of the illness from which the patients suffered. Finally, usually in private psychotherapy, patient and therapist exercised some mutual choices, and research had shown that outcome improved where there was choice at least on the part of the therapist.[78] Hans Strupp, a major psychotherapy research, argued that the placebo issue was simply misleading, arising from a false analogy between psychotherapy and medical treatment. Outcome measures were still too "crude and wobbly" to assess the results of therapy. The therapist's skill, training, and theories were essential elements of the therapeutic process, while the dyad of patient and therapist should be the focus of research. Moreover, some therapeutic goals were modest while others were highly ambitious, for example, overcoming the "crippling effects of early childhood trauma." Such differing goals require different lengths of treatment. His position amounted to a strong reassertion of the claims of the psychodynamic model. Strupp also argued that people were sufficiently different and the setting of their lives sufficiently complex to suggest that no single technique would be likely to be effective across a wide variety of cases. Still another authority has argued that Frank's non-specific factors were important for the initial stages of therapy, while interpretive and cognitive elements became important later. Different established and successful therapies should be compared in matched groups of patients. Such a research strategy would be made more rewarding by the recent development of more sensitive outcome measures and standardized treatment manuals for the different forms of psychotherapy. One major researcher concluded in 1990 that in effect the Dodo bird verdict still was valid: the success rate of different varieties of therapy were about the same, despite attempts to link outcome to theoretical orientation.[79]

Varying attitudes about neurotic patients also surfaced in the assessments of Smith, Glass, and Miller. An Australian psychiatrist who had confirmed their findings and had found behavior therapy especially effective noted that "in some depressions, if the drugs haven't worked, psychotherapy or behavior therapy may be life saving. . . . People seeking therapy are trying to save their own lives, to stop the continual self-defeat in work and love that constitutes neurosis."[80] A British psychologist, however, argued that the interest in psychotherapy was not due to its efficacy but rather because of the existence of a pathetic population at risk: they were "the weak, the insecure, the nervous, the lonely, the inadequate and the depressed whose desperation so often is such that they are willing to do and pay anything for some improvement of their condition."[81]

In 1988, as Lawrence Kubie had suggested 30 years earlier, psychoanalysts were urged by the president of the American Psychoanalytic Association to "do more outcome studies, collect scientific evidence, and put forward the case for psychoanalysis."[82] This was surely testimony to the glacial slowness with which institutional psychoanalysis responded to challenges. For by the mid-1980s, while the efficacy of psychotherapy, including psychoanalytic psychotherapy, and the fact that some therapists are more skilled than others seemed reasonably established, the status of psychoanalysis as such remained equivocal in terms of comparison with any alternatives. There has been an accumulation of hundreds, perhaps thousands, of clinical reports of psychoanalyses and a few controlled outcome studies of successful single cases.[83] Even allowing for observer bias, it is hard to claim that these are all simply tendentious fairy tales. Nevertheless, there still have been no studies comparing psychoanalysis on a controlled basis with any other therapy, except perhaps in the Menninger study where the comparison was psychoanalytic psychotherapy.

Thus psychoanalysts failed to demonstrate the superior effectiveness of their therapy in the context of new standards derived largely from somatic medical practice—and the appropriateness of those standards as a model for judging psychotherapy also was seriously questioned. At the same time a militantly somatic style began to dominate psychiatry and claimed unprecedented success. Finally a multiplicity of rival psychotherapies developed as alternatives to psychoanalysis. All these factors resulted in a contraction of the psychoanalytic domain.

18

A Diminishing Psychoanalytic Realm

Criticism impugned not only the therapeutic claims of psychoanalysis to special effectiveness but also the quality of psychoanalytic research and extrapolations from psychoanalytic theory. Partly as a result of criticism, psychoanalysts began to withdraw from the fields they had staked out in the early postwar years—psychosomatic medicine and the psychotherapeutic treatment of the psychoses. Finally, drastic changes in the social context of treatment profoundly affected psychoanalytic practice.

The psychoanalytic model in psychosomatic medicine was scrutinized by both psychologists and medical specialists and faulted largely on grounds of methodology. More important, in a growing number of instances, new somatic research and treatment made psychological considerations less pertinent. Some suggested that psychosomatic disease might have a decisive genetic or constitutional basis. Others insisted that many of the chronic diseases, such as hypertension, were not homogeneous, but represented complex subgroups which differed in mechanism and origin. If so, how could a common "personality type" or "underlying conflict" or mode of mothering fit such complex somatic data? The most vehement critics dismissed psychoanalytic case material as merely anecdotal. Some required of psychosomatics and of psychoanalysis a scientific nicety that hardly prevailed in clinical medicine.[1] Only one-tenth of the procedures used in clinical medicine have been validated by controlled studies, according to some estimates.

One set of questions was posed repeatedly. How widely did the psychoanalytic findings apply? How representative were the patients who had been studied? Were they typical of all patients with the disease? Many had been chosen for the simple reason that they were in psychoanalytic or psychiatric treatment. Too few studies included appropriate control groups such as matched well people or patients with other chronic diseases. Could one accept findings in which psychoanalysts themselves shaped not only all the questions but supplied the final answers as well? These kinds of objections were voiced in 1958 by Fred Brown, a psychologist who had worked for ten years in the field. How, he asked, could one accept unverified clinical reports of such traits as "dependency," "aggressiveness," "rejection"? Would independent observers agree on definitions and criteria? He criticized attempts to establish a general profile for women with cancer, for example. They had presumably expressed more "negative feelings toward pregnancy and birth . . . and specific disturbances in feminine identification." Would this generalization from a tiny group "be valid for cancer patients in general, would it have any bearing upon factors involving the etiology of cancer? Does it differentiate this group sharply from women with the same orientation who have no cancer or who suffer from asthma?" He concluded that much had been promised with small results. The Rorschach test used so often to verify clinical findings was itself heavily dependent upon subjective clinical judgment. There was need for more longitudinal studies, cross-validation, closer cooperation with biologists. Psychoanalytic theory itself was too often regarded as if it were a set of "established principles and laws" rather than a set of shrewdly conceived hypotheses. The old questions remained unanswered: "Why this symptom and not another? Why this organ system and not another? Why this patient and not another?"[2]

In asthma research there were reiterated pleas for greater rigor from the 1950s into the 1980s and a growing number of contradictory findings.[3] Allergists argued that the great differences among the psychiatrists' hypotheses justified skepticism.

Illness itself might create such psychological reactions in patients and their families as overprotection, dependency, anxiety, or rejection. Like other chronically ill children, asthmatics often were anxious, insecure, and dependent. Moreover, living with a chronically ill child could have created special reactions in parents that resulted in the finding that they were more neurotic than the parents of well children or accident victims.[4]

A comprehensive attack on psychosomatic asthma research, launched in 1964 by a group of San Francisco allergists and psychologists, was followed by fewer American psychoanalytic studies. Five years later, yet another study called for more careful research and noted that in view of contradictory claims no conclusions could be drawn about the role of the family in asthma.[5] Epidemiological data indicated that asthma was twice as likely to occur in boys than in girls, and in half of all patients began around the age of three.

Could "mothering" be so different for each sex or was a somatic factor likely to be accountable? More puzzling still, estimates of the importance of emotional factors in asthma varied from 1 to 21 percent or more while estimates of asthmatics who needed psychotherapy varied from "hardly any" to "almost all."[6] Finally, new discoveries about the physiological basis of asthma attacks created new and more effective medical interventions and made psychological interpretation and treatment seem less crucial.

In 1977, a magisterial survey of the whole psychosomatic field, Herbert Weiner's *Psychobiology and Human Disease,* raised important questions about all the psychosomatic disorders and summed up a powerful trend toward a renewed somatic emphasis and rigorous standards of comparison. The fluctuations in course and outcome of these diseases indicated that none was a single, uniform disease entity but a variety of subgroups.[7] In asthma, for instance, allergic, infectious, and psychological factors all were important. Some cases seemed to be primarily allergic, others did not. Children with asthma differed in their psychological behavior, their capacity to express feelings, their conflicts. The attitudes of their mothers also varied from outright rejection to sensible supportiveness to overprotection. These parental attitudes often, but not invariably preceded the illness. Possibly each subgroup, those with either allergic or non-allergic asthma, had different predisposing factors, both psychological and somatic. Possibly similar parental attitudes or other psychological factors might play a role in different psychosomatic diseases. For all these reasons in studying any disease, patients had to be carefully chosen to ensure their comparability. Above all, Weiner insisted, studies needed to be predictive and prospective. Because treatment for a child often was sought long after the symptoms had become stabilized, it was impossible to determine in retrospect how important a role parental attitudes or, indeed, any psychological factor, might play. Only prospective studies could assess the relative importance of various factors leading to the onset of asthma or any other psychosomatic disorder.

Despite these methodological objections, Weiner regarded a considerable number of the psychoanalytic findings that described asthma patients as reasonably confirmed. Alexander's specific conflict over dependency applied to perhaps half of asthma patients, while other conflicts, notably over elimination, aggression, rebellion, and sexuality dominated in others. Many of the attitudes attributed to asthmatogenic parents also characterized the parents of children with other psychosomatic illnesses and with psychiatric illness, and thus could not be specific for asthma. It was conceivable that the same parental attitudes were factors in different disorders. But the fact that the very same attitudes occurred widely in families with healthy children suggested that determinants other than parental influence must be operating. Clearly, the observed conflicts and parental attitudes were relevant for some asthmatics, but not for others. Moreover if dependency was the major conflict, why did 30 to 45 percent of asthmatic children outgrow the disease? Had they also resolved their dependency conflicts? Weiner argued that asthma was not a "psychogenic" disease; that is, purely psychological factors alone could not induce it. Such factors could operate only in those biologically predisposed to broncho-constriction. He noted that Franz Alexander always had insisted on a somatic predisposition as fundamental to the emergence of psychosomatic disorders.[8]

A number of alternatives to the psychoanalytic approach to psychosomatic medicine were developed. Not the individual psychological predisposition or conflict, but the more general factors of stress and the social environment, as well as quite specific patterns of behavior, became the focus of a number of researchers. For Hans Selye the causes of stress were general and wide-ranging and included any adverse condition such as extreme heat or cold, surgery, strong emotion, occupational tension. He elaborated a theory of a generalized physiological response to stress which he called the "General Adaptation Syndrome." It occurred in stages in response to adverse stimuli: first, alarm, then resistance, and, finally, exhaustion. As a medical student he had been struck by the similarities in the state of illness that cut across diagnostic lines, notably the appearance of pain, loss of appetite, fever. He concluded that a variety of stressors could elicit this non-specific generalized response. The sudden development of gastric ulcers among people in heavily bombed areas of England during World War II seemed to confirm his observations. He concluded that chronic, consciously perceived anxiety rather than any specific psychological constellation such as unconscious dependency needs led to peptic ulcers. Harold Wolff, a neurologist, placed the emphasis on more broadly cultural and sociological factors, such as unstable social conditions, and combined them with a number of psychoanalytic hypotheses.[9]

In the mid-1960s two psychologists undertook studies of life changes that large numbers of people experienced as stressful: the death of a spouse, divorce, loss of a job, moves, even favorable changes. Major illnesses tended to occur within two years after such events and the more frequent the stressful changes, the more likely for illness to occur. But why one person fell ill and others did not remained unexplored in these studies.

David Hamburg, a psychoanalytic psychiatrist, and others investigated "coping" behavior, and concluded that it was how individuals reacted to stressful situations, rather than the situations themselves, that governed the outcome. Here, the emphasis focused once again on the individual. For example, severely burned military personnel, polio sufferers, or parents whose children developed leukemia who were able to seek appropriate information, talk out their feelings, and devise strategies for dealing with trauma suffered few or no harmful results. Later research suggested that the ability to cope depended on both "body chemistry and personality. . . "[10]

The conception of a personality type, or profile, as predisposing to some kinds of illness remained important. A new global theory, advanced by the Boston psychoanalytic psychiatrist John C. Nemiah in 1975, held that, unlike neurotics, psychosomatic patients were unable to communicate their emotions effectively. Reflecting the new somatic emphasis, Nemiah speculated that the condition might result from an underlying somatic state, perhaps a "discontinuity between the functions of the cortex and the limbic system . . . resulting in a failure to integrate the affective and intellectual components of mental functioning." But this syndrome, which Nemiah called alexithymia, was criticized as too general and as possibly arising from selecting patients by education and social class (the more educated, the more verbally expressive). Others suggested that an inability to express feelings was not a distinguishing feature of psychosomatic patients. Rather their common personality structure involved difficulties in maintaining physiological homeostasis, in regulating the intensity of intimacy and emotion, and vulnerability to loss.[11]

A major attempt to link personality and disease was Meyer Friedman's and Ray Rosenman's studies of the "Type A" personality—anxious, tense, hard-driving, competitive, time-obsessed—as a major predisposing factor in heart disease. Their approach both to description and treatment was behavioral rather than psychoanalytic, defining and modifying specific pieces of action and attitude. An eclectic psychiatry, plied by psychoanalysts and psychiatrists and combining many of these approaches, flourished in a number of general hospitals and focused on the emotional concomitants of physical illness.[12] Behavioral methods were successful in treating some psychosomatic conditions, and biofeedback, relaxation, and meditation techniques also were used with some degree of success.

What remained of the psychoanalytic component of psychosomatic medicine? This writer's sample of 23 texts current in 1980 in internal medicine, psychiatry, allergy and immunology, gastroenterology, and cardiology presented a complex picture. The status of psychoanalytic and psychological conceptions in psychosomatic medicine depended very much on who was talking—a medical specialist, a psychiatrist, a psychologist. Not unexpectedly, psychiatrists were the most sympathetic. Many medical authors still seemed to be fighting psychogenesis, which few if any psychosomaticists ever nakedly held, and some, like the allergists, insisted on defending the psychological normality of their patients. Most texts tended to subscribe to multicausality, emphasizing both somatic and psychological factors. They insisted on the impact of disease itself as having special psychological importance, and they accepted a role for emotional factors in the exacerbation of disease and, possibly, in its genesis. But they were uncertain about how important such factors were in comparison with others. The most widely accepted psychoanalytic theories seemed to be those for the causation of peptic ulcer and ulcerative colitis, and a few texts chiefly in internal medicine accepted modified psychoanalytic theories of psychosomatic disease in general. But within each speciality, many authors emphasized the theoretical and methodological difficulties of psychosomatic hypotheses. In gastroenterology the role of chronic emotional stress in the genesis of peptic ulcer was considered likely but unproven. One physician derided Alexander's formulations: "in this view, milk is love and the mother; a peptic ulcer makes it possible to be taken care of and mothered in a respectable fashion!"[13] One internist advised physicians to satisfy the ulcer patient's dependent needs. With ulcers, as with asthma, new and successful medical treatment made psychological consider-ations, whether accurate or not, less relevant.

It is not surprising that the allergists and immunologists were nearly unanimous in rejecting a psychological origin for asthma. Emotions alone could not in themselves produce allergic symptoms but could bring on at-tacks and even affect allergic susceptibility. But asthmatics were not more neurotic than other people.

One result of psychosomatic and psychoanalytic influence remained: a renewed insistence that the physician understand and deal with the emotional components of illness. Thus the physician was urged to become a common-sense psychotherapist. He should listen and bolster self-confidence by ex-plaining the symptoms and the disease simply and clearly; but an allergist cautioned against delving too deeply or giving complicated and "far-fetched" explanations.[14] In unusual cases the physician should refer the patient to a psychiatric professional.

It is important to recall that in the history of psychosomatic medicine a large number of quite specific hypotheses had been advanced by psycho-analysts and modified by means of psychoanalytic case observation alone, for example, the dependent personality and the rejecting mother in asthma, the reaction formations against dependency in ulcers. Psychoanalytic data soon clearly indicated that not a single conflict but several core conflicts were associated with different psychosomatic syndromes. Moreover, the best psy-choanalytic work emphasized the complexities of the emotional field and, when possible, careful correlations with somatic states. Thus, psychoanalysis gave rise to a series of hypotheses that could be accepted or refuted, some of them by the psychoanalytic method itself.[15]

The major unsolved problem remained how widely the psychoanalytic findings applied. But this could be said of other psychological findings in the field, and of many somatic findings as well. The importance of "psychosocial" factors in the development of disease, including the functioning of the im-mune system, were reasonably well established. The concept of a genetic element came to mean a "genetic potential," whose activation depends on the "history of the organism and its transactions with the environment." Increas-ing physiological knowledge showed more direct interaction than had previ-ously been supposed. But precisely how these factors operated, and the old problem of the relation of "mind and body," remained unsolved.[16]

The neo-somatic style that began in the late 1950s affected psychoanaly-tic approaches to the psychoses as well as psychosomatic medicine. A re-newed emphasis on somatic causes and treatments and the new insistence on stringent outcome criteria prejudiced the apparent applicability of psycho-analytic psychotherapy and the relevance of psychoanalytic theories.[17] A second important influence was the development of behavioristic psychoso-cial treatments, teaching coping and social skills.

Partly as a reaction to the earlier attempts to discard classifications in psychiatry, there were renewed efforts to make classification more precise. The aim was to solve one of the fundamental problems of psychiatry: finding comparable patients for outcome research.[18] It was hoped that more careful nosologies might facilitate attempts to find somatic and genetic as well as environmental explanations. Psychiatrists at Washington University in St. Louis and others urged the use of standardized psychiatric interviews, statistical techniques, and psychometric rating scales. These made it possible to obtain fairly uniform results in diagnoses whenever the criteria were carefully defined.[19]

The most influential tendency in redefining schizophrenia, for example, was to restrict the term. The World Health Organization found that among the most frequently reported specific symptoms were auditory hallucinations, flatness of affect, voices speaking to the patient, and delusions of being controlled.[20] Loose classification systems, it was argued, had hampered attempts to discover the real nature of schizophrenia and had inflated prevalence rates. For example, under the earlier, expansive definitions, 40 percent of American mental patients were diagnosed as schizophrenic, a much higher incidence than in Britain, where the rate was calculated at 24 percent; the incidence of affective disorder, the bipolar, or old manic-depressive insanity, was correspondingly higher in Britain. The differing statistics had resulted solely from different methods of diagnosis. Using the more restricted criteria, the prevalence of schizophrenia ranged from about 0.6 to 6.7 percent in the United States. This suggested correspondingly higher rates for affective disorder. In another careful study of an American hospital, not diagnosis but methods of treatment seemed to be the controlling factor. The amount of schizophrenia and affective disorder both increased over a 20-year period, while the diagnosis of psychoneurosis markedly declined, probably reflecting the increased use of drugs, briefer hospital stays, and less use of intensive psychotherapy.[21] The narrower definition of schizophrenia was included in 1980 in the American Psychiatric Association's *Diagnostic and Statistical Manual III.*

This new manual, adopted after a bitter fight, represented the growing influence of those who desired "diagnostic precision" and a somatic approach. The manual dispensed with theories of cause in describing disorders whose etiology was unproven, and this included all the psychodynamic or psychoanalytic formulations that had been used in DSM II. For instance, neuroses were no longer defined as "defenses" against underlying anxiety. The manual, partly inspired by the influence of the St. Louis neo-somaticists, represented a return to the tradition of sharply defined classification that Emil Kraepelin had begun in the late nineteenth and early 20th century.[22]

The struggle over DSM III "reflected a deep and important division within American psychiatry," according to Robert Spitzer, chairman of the Department of Psychiatry at Columbia University, who led the committee that produced the manual. On one side were those who believed that a classification system should be based on standardized, reliable criteria that "could provide the basis for testable hypotheses." On the other were "those who argued that decades of experience with the clinically complex issues" of psychotherapy had established the validity of the psychodynamic perspective. "Psychoanalysts who had, until recently, provided the dominating professional scientific paradigm of psychiatry were confronted by those who challenged the scientific value and clinical utility of their etiologically rooted approach to diagnosis."[23]

The reception of the new manual echoed these divisions. It was praised as a renewed commitment to "medicine and scientific method," representing wrote Gerald Klerman, professor of psychiatry at Harvard,

> a strategic mode of dealing with the frustrating reality that, for most of the disorders we currently treat, there is only limited evidence for their etiologies. There are competing hypotheses and theories that involve various mixtures of biological, social, developmental, and intrapsychic causation, but for most disorders the evidence is insufficient and inconclusive.

DSM III was soundly based on "descriptive psychopathology"; moreover, only if diagnoses were precise could etiology be soundly established. Finally, the manual had been successfully tested in the field for reliability.

Psychodynamic advocates disdained it as "anti-analytic," as "an unnecessary and ideologically mistaken handicap," and as parochial and reductionistic. The psychoanalyst Otto Kernberg remarked that the text was a "disaster. It is a straitjacket and a powerful weapon in the hands of people whose ideas are very clear, very publicly known, and the guns are pointed at us."[24] George Vaillant, professor of psychiatry at Dartmouth, wrote that the manual paid too little attention to the "longitudinal course" of illness. It gave insufficient heed to "pathogenesis; it is as if cough were not distinguished from pneumonia." "Like it or not psychiatry IS dynamic. It has more in common with the inevitable ambiguity of great drama than with DSM-III's quest for algorithms compatible with the cold binary logic of computer science."[25]

Psychiatrists also reassessed the role of genetics in schizophrenia and in bipolar disorder. Although earlier twin studies of schizophrenics had been criticized for not taking sufficient account of the effects of environment, new studies of the relatives of schizophrenics and of adopted twins indicated a significant genetic component.[26] Its extent and importance and what exactly is transmitted remained controversial. Even if the incidence of schizophrenia in both identical twins ranged from 25 to 40 percent, that would leave 75 to 60 percent of identical twins who did *not* develop the disorder, although the other twin did. For manic-depressive psychosis some believed the incidence to be 50 to 100 percent in identical twins and 40 percent in fraternal twins.[27] The figures for schizophrenia and the estimate for bipolar disorder suggested that factors other than heredity played an important role. These included birth traumas and defects and very early role imprinting in children perceived as defective, weak, or vulnerable as well as ongoing family interaction. There were also those who believed heredity played no role at all.[28]

The role of the family environment in schizophrenia was fundamentally reassessed, along with downplaying the purported role of the schizo-phrenogenic mother. Sylvano Arieti argued in 1974 that only one-fourth of the mothers of schizophrenics fit the "schizophrenogenic" stereotype. The earlier impression came from taking at face value the way patients described their mothers.[29] Some studies of the families of schizophrenics suggested peculiar patterns of communication and behavior, such as the "double bind" theory of Gregory Bateson and his collaborators.

Despite arguments that psychotherapy with psychotics was being out-dated or not cost-effective, a number of psychoanalytic psychiatrists contin-ued to treat schizophrenics, believing psychotherapy to be the treatment of choice; in one controlled study of inner-city black patients, schizophrenics treated by experienced psychotherapists did far better than patients treated by drugs alone.[30] Some psychiatrists combined dynamic psychotherapy with drugs, behavior modification, psychosocial retraining, or family therapy.

Dynamic psychotherapists and the newer therapists, such as those who advocated behavioral methods or the teaching of social skills, found new common ground, that is, an insistence on social and psychological factors and treatments. The best results with schizophrenics required psychosocial treat-ment and rehabilitation, they argued. "Most importantly, drugs cannot teach life and coping skills, nor can they improve the quality of a person's life, except indirectly through suppression of symptoms."[31] Moreover, the nega-tive side effects of drugs remained disturbing, including possible addiction and, especially, tardive dyskinesia from phenothiazine. This irreversible ner-vous system disorder produced "rhythmical, involuntary movements . . . protrusion of the tongue, puffing of the cheeks, puckering of the mouth, chewing movements."[32]

The outcome criteria, such as the necessity for randomized control groups advocated by psychotherapy researchers, would have ruled out the earlier case reports from the 1930s to the 1960s that suggested the effective-ness of psychoanalytic psychotherapy in the treatment of psychoses: those of Sullivan, Frieda Fromm-Reichmann, John Rosen, and Chestnut Lodge.[33] De-spite the more stringent outcome criteria, some of the results of genetic studies and of psychotherapy research, such as Smith, Glass, and Miller's, would justify psychoanalytic investigation and psychotherapeutic treatment of schizophrenia. However, there also were studies suggesting that highly stimulating treatments, such as the uncovering and interpretive methods of psychoanalysis or the intensive use of group therapy, were harmful to chronic schizophrenics. The result of one major study indicated that "reality adaptive, supportive" psychotherapy and family therapy were more effective. Enthusi-asm waned for intensive methods, such as the shocks and insights John Rosen once delivered and which many psychoanalysts at the time opposed. One follow-up study of Rosen's patients indicated that an untreated control group did as well as the patients he had treated. A low-key supportive educational method was seen to be more helpful. Such an approach, with interpretation, was a hallmark of Frieda Fromm-Reichmann's techniques.[34]

Psychoanalytic psychotherapy was used less often in those private hospitals which had been centers of the psychoanalytic approach. For instance, at Chestnut Lodge by 1989 psychotherapy was "no longer considered the ulti-mate treatment." At the Menninger Foundation, a major center of psycho-analytic psychiatry, there was a marked decline in the use of both psycho-analysis and psychotherapy. Where psychoanalysis might have been used with schizophrenic patients, at least on a trial basis, in the 1940s, a regime of four to six weekly sessions on the couch "had virtually disappeared from the hospital scene in 1965." More patients at Menninger's were receiving somatic therapy, while the percentage receiving psychotherapy fell dramatically from 62 percent in 1945 to 23 percent in 1965.[35]

In a 1985 symposium on schizophrenia, psychoanalysis was conspicuous by its absence. Major roles, rather, were played by biological models, includ-ing biological speculation about brain function, by batteries of new psycho-logical tests that defined patient status and family attitudes. A successful program of family therapy that reduced relapses relied on a behaviorist mod-el emphasizing communication and problem-solving. It carefully avoided "uncovering" techniques and any implication that the family might have caused the illness. It was directed mainly at modifying, directly or indirectly, a family's emotional involvement or its criticism of the patient, which was found to be particularly noxious with young males.[36]

By the mid-1980s the etiology and pathology of schizophrenia remained unknown. Probably, like the affective disorders, it was a "syndrome" of "heterogeneous etiology and pathology." Its causes were many, partly genet-ic, partly environmental. One recent model assumed biological vulnerability interacting with additional somatic and social stress, including stressful family relations, a weakening of social support networks, and a diminution of coping skills.[37] Where psychoanalysis once held out the promise of unraveling the psychological components of schizophrenia, it was being overshadowed by new somatic, genetic, social, and behavioral approaches to theory and therapy.

As early as the mid-1960s, some psychoanalysts noted a general decline in the prestige of their specialty. O. Van Buren Hammett, director of the Department of Psychiatry of Hahnemann Medical College in Philadelphia, found that fewer patients could be convinced of the usefulness of psycho-analytic treatment. Psychoanalytic training focused on theory to the exclu-sion of genetic and biological knowledge and lacked interest in operant conditioning and other new approaches. Psychoanalysis was highly successful in resolving some kinds of psychopathology, but it was ineffectual with many types of patients, even with the symptom neuroses for which it had been devised. Moreover, some analysts and patients held a fantasy of the "Holy Grail of Total Cure," that could not but create disillusionment."[38]

In 1968, George Engel, a major psychosomatic researcher, warned that because of the "failure of psychoanalysis to mount productive research pro-grams, the National Institute of Mental Health and private foundations were reappraising their policies after 15 years of generous, sympathetic support: The bulk of psychoanalytic literature consisted of poorly documented clinical reports and theoretical papers. In 75 years psychoanalysis had not progressed beyond the stage of "observation, data collection and theory building," partly because of the limitations of the method itself. It was applicable to only a "very circumscribed group of patients." The analyst's free-floating attention made it difficult to record what he was observing, and he too often made inferences without reporting the data on which they were based. Non-medical researchers, such as psychologists, some of whom were doing the most interesting work in the field, usually were excluded from institute faculties and thus were cut off from physician analysts.[39]

In the 1960s both NIMH and the Foundation's fund for Psychiatry devoted less money to psychoanalytic projects and more to somatic research. Like Engel, some investigators at NIMH believed that the results of psycho-analytic research had been disappointing. Myra Pines, who had worked for the Foundations' Fund, recalled the earlier high hopes:

> Through analysis . . . psychiatrists would understand the unconscious of the human mind and thus find ways to raise healthier children, prevent the develop-ment of mental illness, cure the mentally ill, and even produce a saner soci-ety. . . . There were exciting hypotheses to test about personality development and adaptive or maladaptive behavior—for instance, generational conflict, sib-ling rivalry, and sexual or aggressive motivation.

The fund's directors had hoped that social scientists more readily than psy-choanalysts might be able to devise techniques for testing psychoanalytic hypotheses and accordingly supported their psychoanalytic training. But dis-appointment set in when "we got only glimpses and hunches, not really convincing facts," observed Frederick Redlich, who had helped to found the organization. Moreover, the "creative work of the social scientists was not enhanced, because the institutes were created primarily to train practitioners rather than researchers." The fund made 28 research grants to psychoanalytic projects out of 205 between 1953 and 1962, then from 1962 to 1973 only 9 out of 194, and from 1973 to 1978, none.[40]

Additional criticism centered on hypotheses derived from psycho-analysis—childhood determinism, infantile sexuality, the nature of dreams, and, in particular, women's sexual development. A few examples from this very large literature will indicate the nature of these strictures. The sugges-tion that all neuroses began in childhood and that there were distinct neurotic continuities from the earliest years were questioned.[41] Some studies sug-gested that there was no evidence to support notions central to Freud's theory of dreams, that is, that they were caused by repressed instinctual wishes, or that they protected sleep, or that there were distinctions between latent and manifest dream content. Rather, dreams seemed to be the result of autonomous biological rhythms, although there was evidence that they did fulfill a venting function or reflected current problems.[42]

Some psychiatrists and psychoanalysts argued that Freud's theories of infantile psychosexuality had never been adequately proven. The facts of sexual behavior in childhood to which Freud drew attention seemed clear enough, but the psychosexual implications of that behavior remained highly problematical. Again, the objections were partly methodological. Reconstruction from adult analyses as well as the observation of children could be too easily contaminated by the analyst's presuppositions, and this was especially so in compliant and informed adult patients and in the analyst's interpretations of childhood behavior. Children themselves did not communicate their feelings and experiences easily and their memory processes differed from those of adults. Adult observers, then, had ample opportunity to interpolate their own assumptions. Moreover, there were serious problems of defining childhood sexuality. Did infantile sucking of the thumb or the breast or the experience of expelling stool really relate to adult sexual pleasure in fellatio or anal intercourse?[43] Another psychiatrist questioned the attainment of "genital maturity" as a prerequisite to adequate sexual functioning. He argued that "there is . . . no exact relationship between sexual dysfunction and emotional illness, and . . . that the presently held psychoanalytic explanations must in some way be modified in order to allow for an adequate sexual life in an otherwise troubled person." The presumed implication of psychoanalytic theory had been that only those "who have reached the genital stage of psychosexual development are capable of genuine, adequate sexual response. . . ." But there were too many clinical examples of disturbed people who performed "in a sexually satisfactory way."[44] The problem here, of course, was how "adequate sexual response" was defined, that is, what psychological behavior was involved.

The most notorious example of a dispute over analytic findings concerned the challenge to Freud's views of women and their early development. Both direct observation of girls and evidence from analytic treatment led to profound revision of Freud's argument that a girl turns to her father and renounces masturbation when she discovers her "castration," her lack of a penis. While some have continued to uphold the letter of Freud's views, others have modified or replaced them on the basis of observations of the early sense of femininity in girls, of their awareness of the vagina, and an absence of a "negative Oedipal phase," in which a girl presumably wishes to get rid of her mother in order to possess her father. There were, of course, some analysts like Lacan who argued that no amount of empirical observation could negate doctrines established in the clinical interview with its data based on subjective meaning. And, indeed, different analysts deduced different theories from very similar observations.[45]

The psychoanalytic emphasis on early family relationships as the cause of nervous and mental disorder resulted in blaming parents, and especially mothers, for such illnesses in their offspring. On a semi-popular level it provided one more example of the dramatic over-extension of psychoanalytic hypotheses by non-analysts. For example, an angry psychiatrist described how he and his wife were held responsible for what was diagnosed by school consultants as the functional childhood schizophrenia of their six-year-old son; the consultants ignored a previous diagnosis of autism with brain damage by a child psychiatrist. A school social worker suggested that the disorder was functional and reversible and that the parents were to blame for it. When his mother became depressed, this was taken as additional evidence that the parents were schizophrenogenic. The parents finally founded their own day school and after several years their son had lost nearly all his hyperactivity and autistic characteristics, but remained retarded, as the neurologist originally predicted. In another instance, a social worker suggested to a woman, without any evidence whatever, that she might have contributed to her husband's illness, perhaps by infidelity or by lack of sympathetic support; the illness turned out to be a fatal, unsuspected brain tumor.[46]

Other psychiatrists, some sympathetic, criticized psychoanalysis for the vagueness of its language, its lack of conformity to the standards of the exact sciences, and for elitism and alienation from the pressing problems of mental health. Roy Grinker, who had been analyzed by Freud in the 1930s, complained in 1965 that psychoanalysis, a once brave outpost, with notable exceptions had become "a crumbling stockade of proprietary dogmatism . . . , by maintaining itself aloof from the progress of behavioral science and looking askance at conceptions of rigor." Because the sciences of psychiatry were behavioral sciences, he prescribed the abandonment of traditional psychoanalytic language and the adoption of systems theory, and the creation of academic departments of psychoanalysis where "authoritative pronouncements and fuzzy formulations, isolation and inbreeding would at least be less possible."[47]

These psychiatric strictures reflected in part an ongoing debate among psychoanalysts and philosophers of science over the scientific status of psychoanalysis, which can be touched on only briefly here. Perhaps the most famous debate took place at New York University in 1958 while analysts were still celebrating the centennial of Freud's birth. It brought together philosophers such as Sidney Hook, Michael Scriven, Raphael Demos, and Adolf Gruenbaum, and the analysts Lawrence Kubie, Heinz Hartmann, and Jacob Arlow. The American analysts, reflecting in part the hard medical model of psychoanalysis, insisted on the scientific and empirical status of their observations. The philosophers tended to be heavily positivist, arguing the necessity of being able to "falsify" psychoanalytic propositions, in the tradition of the philosopher of science, Karl Popper. Much of the talk was at cross-purposes, the philosophers insisting on the necessity for highly precise criteria of verification and the analysts pleading for the validity of their admittedly imperfect, but closely detailed observations.

The philosophers' arguments on the whole, were more heated than the analysts'. Ernest Nagel, a philosopher of science at Columbia University, suggested that psychoanalytic propositions could not be verified by subsequent empirical data because of the vague and metaphorical nature of psychoanalytic language. It was all too easy to make the facts fit the theory after the facts had been ascertained. Moreover, analysts could differ in their interpretations of the same material. "I have little doubt myself that for every ingenious interpretation of a case, another one no less superficially plausible can be invented."[48] The "probative strength" of psychoanalytic observations was weak because the analyst directed "the course of the narrative." Data could be manufactured by the patient's previous knowledge, and there was no independent check on the accuracy of his memory. Without control groups it was impossible to confirm or deny psychoanalytic hypotheses. For instance, if an equal number of people underwent the same pathogenic experience posited by the psychoanalysts but did *not* become neurotic, the presumed universality of such psychoanalytic hypotheses would be disproved.

"As a set of hypotheses, . . . [psychoanalysis] was a great achievement fifty years ago; as no more than a set of hypotheses it is a great disgrace today," pronounced Michael Scriven, a philosopher from Swarthmore College. Without the psychoanalysts' claims to help most of their patients, "it is very difficult to see how they could possibly justify the removal of some ten million dollars a year from sick America. . . ."[49] These claims required controlled studies conducted by competent psychoanalysts with adequate follow-up of patients in order to answer such questions as whether or not psychoanalysis was more effective than self-help or talking to an untrained, neutral listener. Moreover, conflicting analytic views of what constituted a cure inevitably involved questions of value.

> Without any attempt to deal with the difficulties mentioned, how in the name of Roger Bacon could a psychoanalyst imagine that his own hopelessly contaminated, uncontrolled, unfollowed up, unvalidated, unformalized estimation of success has ever established a single cure as being his own work?[50]

Sidney Hook, a philosopher from New York University, propounded his favorite conundrum for psychoanalysts: How could you prove that a child did *not* have an Oedipus complex? Many normal children did not manifest the Oedipal phase, and this would seriously invalidate the universality of Freud's hypothesis and would suggest that the Oedipal phase was determined by social and cultural institutions.[51]

A few of the assembled philosophers were more kindly disposed. Philip Frank argued that many of the Viennese logical positivists, despite their demanding views of science, were sympathetic to psychoanalysis. John Hospers, associate professor of philosophy at Brooklyn College, suggested that the philosophers ignored the "vast amount of empirical detail" accumulated by the analysts as well as the complexities of analytic theory.[52] No single experiment could disprove a psychoanalytic hypothesis because its validity depended on context, on the accumulation of detail that confirmed or discomfirmed it.

Raphael Demos, the Harvard philosopher, argued that concepts of science should be based not on what philosophers think but on what scientists *do*. There was no "universal essence of science applying equally and in the same manner to all inquiries which claim the name of science," as Professor Nagel seemed to believe. In fact, there were sciences and sciences, not all of them predictive or propounding propositions testable in the laboratory, or subject to controls.[53]

Admitting the lack of conventional validation and the need for systematization, Heinz Hartmann insisted that psychoanalytic theory was based on more detailed, painstaking observations of single human subjects than those obtained by any other clinical method. He also argued that through the analysis of the analyst and the conception of counter-transference psychoanalysis had a method of combatting observational distortions. Moreover, to explain in physiological terms the field of psychoanalysis investigated would involve "hypotheses . . . considerably more tenuous and more speculative" than those of psychoanalysis.[54]

Lawrence Kubie insisted that free association was the only instrument for observing what goes on in the whole mind. Despite faulty validation techniques, it was not too difficult to demonstrate that an interpretation was probable, and, rarely, that it could be shown to be "adequate, unique, and necessary." Admitting that the analyst could not listen to a string of free associations without distorting them, he looked to recording techniques and computers to rectify the difficulty. Jacob Arlow insisted that psychoanalysis correlated and interpreted observed data like any other science, created consistent hypotheses, and made predictions on the basis of repetitive patterns of sequential relationships.[55]

In a lengthy review of the symposium the psychoanalyst Robert Waelder argued for a hierarchy of psychoanalytic hypotheses arranged in order of verifiability. Some could be confirmed from direct clinical experience, while others, less essential, were further removed from the data. The clinical data of psychoanalysis were based on the fact that the patient revealed himself more fully and frankly than in most other situations and that the analyst could observe the patterns of these complex revelations. He could then make interpretations about the relation of the data to other aspects of the patient's behavior and could modify these hypotheses as more material came to light. Beyond clinical observation and interpretation were clinical generalizations about an age group, a symptom, a character type, a family constellation, and so on. These were the three indispensable empirical foundations of psychoanalysis: clinical observation, interpretation, and generalization. Less directly relevant were clinical theories about such concepts as repression, defense, and regression, and then at a further level, metapsychology, and, finally, Freud's philosophy, none of which were essential for psychoanalysis.

Psychoanalysis resembled biology and the social sciences in its many closely linked variables, its constantly changing subject matter, and its often indirect and circumstantial evidence. Psychoanalysis proceeded with the same retrospective reasoning that applied in historical subjects, such as the theory of evolution or cosmology. Finally, Waelder argued, psychoanalysis had the advantage of making accessible what could be learned from empathy and introspection.[56]

Psychiatric authority, including psychoanalytic models of theory and therapy, were challenged in the 1960s by a number of developments that radically changed patterns of practice. Some psychiatrists saw the causes of nervous and mental disorder not in intrapsychic mechanisms but in "social

conditions—poverty, poor nutrition, discrimination, community breakdown . . . . A few argued that psychiatric disorders were merely socially
defined and stigmatized modes of deviant behavior. Society was sicker than
its mental patients.[57]

A Joint Commission on Mental Health and Illness, established by Congress to recommend a national psychiatric policy, had published its report in
1961. The Kennedy administration steered away from the report's focus on
the seriously mentally ill and focused on a community-based program that
inaugurated profound changes in the nation's psychiatric services.[58] Legisla-
tion to implement Community Mental Health Centers was passed in 1963 as
part of the social program of Kennedy's New Frontier, but inadequate financing drastically curtailed the original plans and the centers remained under-
funded and dependent on local support.

One of the commission's major concerns had been with the delivery of
mental health services. Drawing on Redlich and Hollingshead's pioneering
study of New Haven, *Social Class and Mental Illness,* and on later surveys, it
had concluded that community outpatient clinics were primarily patronized
by educated and psychologically minded people with higher incomes. Mid-
dle- and upper-class patients were diagnosed as neurotics and treated by
psychoanalysis and psychotherapy. Lower-class patients were more often diagnosed as schizophrenic and sent to state hospitals.[59] Services, including
psychotherapy, needed to be delivered to a wide public, and existing training
systems were judged ineffective for this purpose.

Other psychiatric critics charged that psychoanalysis counted few minor-
ities, black or Hispanic, among its patients.[60] Training programs in psychiatry
that emphasized psychoanalysis were thought to be preparing psychiatrists
for a highly restricted clientele while ignoring the far more serious problems
of the mass of psychotic patients.[61]

In cultivating an elite, meticulously trained profession, the psychoanalytic institutes may have succeeded too well. High fees, conspicuously normative pronouncements, lengthy training, a highly educated clientele all tended
to take from psychoanalysis its crusading aura, and to turn it into a symbol of
the psychiatric and social establishment.

At first, some psychoanalysts and academic departments of psychiatry
stayed aloof from the new community mental health centers, further reinforcing an upper-class and elitist image.[62] A 1987 national survey indicated
that 12 percent of the nation's psychiatrists were working in community
mental health centers, perhaps a reflection of the lower salaries they provided. Some 28 percent listed a medical school or university, state or federal
hospital, or a government agency as their primary practice setting, while for
58 percent, private practice remained the principal activity.[63]

Two issues distanced psychoanalysts from the community centers—the
psychoanalytic emphasis on intensive, individual psychotherapy and the insistence on a high level of training and expertise for therapists. For example,
residents who were trained at a major university medical center in the model
of psychoanalytic psychotherapy sought "interesting" patients who could be

treated by psychotherapy, and were less concerned with the psychotics or the addicts and alcoholics who appeared in increasing numbers at the institutions which became community mental health centers.[64]

The new centers often used minimally trained personnel as therapists, some of them from the patient's own communities. Justification for this included the presumably more effective delivery of services by someone who lived in a community and therefore was knowledgeable about it. Moreover, some research suggested that effective psychotherapy need not require extensive training.[65]

In some areas psychoanalysts were actively participating in community mental health centers, and some of them urged closer involvement in mental health clinics. Despite earlier findings to the contrary, new studies indicated that psychotherapy was successful with low-income patients, and one psychoanalytic outpatient clinic had success with a racially mixed group of blue-collar patients.[66] Robert Wallerstein, then psychoanalyst director of the Department of Psychiatry at Mt. Zion Hospital in San Francisco, reiterated the necessity of using carefully trained therapists and the importance of individual psychotherapy at the same time that he pointed to Freud's goal of therapy for the masses and urged a flexible approach to patients and a closer involvement in community mental health problems and institutions. Bernard Bandler urged psychoanalysts to return to an interest in the broad delivery of mental health services they had displayed during and after World War II.[67]

A clear picture of recent trends in psychiatric and psychoanalytic practice and their interrelation is not easy to draw. A number of surveys cannot be compared because they do not address the same issues, and so tentative conclusions must be derived from incomplete evidence.

The most notable changes have been in the treatment of the psychoses. One purpose of the Community Mental Health act was to see that patients were treated in their own communities, rather than in remote public hospitals. The dramatic depopulation of the state mental hospitals in the 1960s resulted from a combination of psychiatric idealists, eager to get rid of the old custodial hospitals, and fiscal conservatives eager to cut budgets. The state and county mental hospital population dropped from 559,000 in 1955 to 138,000 in 1980. One result was a large increase in private care. This included private in-patient care facilities subsidized by the government, including psychiatric hospitals, psychiatric units in public and private general hospitals, and, above all, nursing and board-and-care homes.[68] Elderly patients and many psychotics were relegated to the last two, housed there often without adequate supervision. Private psychiatrists treated a large group of psychotic patients, some of them Medicaid and welfare cases. In the early 1960s some 26 percent of the private psychiatrist' patients were psychotic. It has been estimated that in 1980 state hospitals provided 64 percent of all inpatient care, and that although stays were much shorter, the number of admissions also rose proportionately.[69]

Reflecting in part the new somatic orientation, drugs became an increasingly important part of both private and public psychiatric treatment. At first, some psychoanalysts had resisted drugs on grounds that these did not induce

personality change. Drugs could not "reproduce the effect of proper interpretation or reduce the need for it. They [could not] . . . restore sound
object relations, and therefore, [could] . . . have no really permanent, corrective effect upon the pathologic process." Despite such arguments some
dynamic psychiatrists welcomed drugs because they made patients more accessible to psychotherapy. By 1976 three-fifths of psychoanalysts "used medication for some of their patients."[70]

The once sharp distinction between "directive-organic" and "analytic
psychological" psychiatrists had broken down, according to Frederick Redlich's follow-up survey of psychiatry in New Haven in 1975, 25 years after
his original study. Psychiatric practice had become homogenized; the psychiatrist who did not prescribe drugs was the exception.[71]

Along with the increase in the use of drugs went an increase in the
amount of psychotherapy, indicating again the homogenization of practice as
well as the establishment of psychotherapy as a major modality of treatment.
By 1980, in general hospitals, public and private, and in private psychiatric
hospitals nearly 90 percent or more of the psychiatric patients, except for the
aged, were receiving individual psychotherapy and, to a much lesser extent,
family and group therapy. In state and county mental hospitals, the number
in individual therapy was much lower, 64 percent.[72] In community mental
health centers, a growing number of lower-class patients were treated by
psychotherapy. About 92 percent of the nation's health maintenance organizations provided some variety of individual dynamic psychotherapy; 62 percent provided behavior therapy; and 81 percent, group therapy.[73] In general,
couple and family therapy also were increasingly used. Probably much institutional psychotherapy was administered not by psychiatrists but by psychologists, social workers, and other mental health personnel. Half of the psychotherapy patients also were treated with medication.

At the same time that the use of psychotherapy increased, the role of
classical psychoanalysis as a therapy declined even among psychoanalysts.
Their practice became in effect far more flexible and eclectic. In the 1950s
they treated 43 percent of their patients with psychoanalysis. But in 1976,
they treated 30 percent with psychoanalysis and the rest with other forms of
individual psychotherapy. Analysts also were seeing patients less frequently,
administering drugs more, and doing both marital or couple therapy and
family therapy. Suitable patients were scarce, alternative forms of treatment
had proliferated, and the "one to one therapeutic relationship" had been
challenged by group and family therapists.[74] A national survey of private
psychiatrists published in 1975 indicated that less than a third classified
themselves as psychoanalysts. The majority of these devoted half or less than
half of their time to psychoanalytic patients, about the same proportion as in
1956.[75] In 1982 in a larger and more representative sample, psychiatrists
were treating 2 percent of their patients with psychoanalysis. They were
treating an even smaller number, less than 1 percent, with behavior therapy.[76] This suggests that behavior therapy probably received relatively less
attention in psychiatric training.

The Redlich survey that described the homogenization of practice also recorded a decline in the prestige of psychoanalysis. "An overwhelming majority of psychiatrists and psychologists" still regarded it as an important method, and an important theoretical foundation for psychotherapy. But only 45 percent of psychiatric residents saw it is an important tool versus its almost "universal acclaim" in 1950. It had practically "disappeared as a treatment modality in institutional settings." Moreover, its goal of insight and personality change had been largely replaced by the goal of relieving symptoms and returning patients to social functioning. The "predominant treatment technique employed a combination of individual, group and milieu therapies with an extensive use of drugs."

The psychiatric monopoly of psychotherapy had been broken, the Redlich survey noted, by other well-educated mental health professionals—chiefly psychologists and social workers; both had increased 700 percent in numbers since 1950. By 1980 psychologists in private practice provided as much outpatient treatment as psychiatrists, each profession supplying about one-third of the total for the nation, with another third provided by social workers or primary care physicians. There also were indications that psychologists were making inroads into the treatment of college-educated, middle- and upper-income patients. By 1980 there were 28,000 psychiatrists, 50,000 psychologists, and 300,000 social workers.[77] Along with these major changes in practice came a change in symptoms and problems. The most notable that Redlich observed was a large increase in alcoholism. But psychiatrists on the whole expressed little desire to treat alcoholic patients and had little contact with them or with drug addicts, the aged, or sociopathic patients. The other major increase was in the problems of children and adolescents, but again, psychiatrists treated relatively few of them and tended to refer them to other mental health specialists, presumably psychologists and social workers.[78] Psychoanalysts also believed that patients' symptoms had changed. There were "fewer good classical neurotics" and more "psychotics, borderlines, narcissistic characters, and patients with problems in development," as well as more with alcohol, drug abuse, and marital problems.[79]

Like the private psychiatrists in New Haven and like their analytic colleagues in the 1950s, analysts continued to treat an upper- and upper-middle-class, highly educated, largely white professional and managerial group of patients, which made up 66 percent of those in analysis. Many of them were mental health professionals. A survey edited by Judd Marmor in 1975 confirmed what other studies had shown, notably, that these patients often belonged to the "friends and supporters of psychotherapy," people with verbal and literary skills—writers, artists, those in entertainment and public relations, although the largest single contingent were physicians, many of them in training to be psychiatrists. Marmor noted that 77 percent of physicians seeking psychiatric treatment, 62 percent of writers and artists, 60 percent of college professors and instructors, 59 percent of social workers, and 56 percent of lawyers ended up with psychoanalysts. More engineers, for instance, were treated by non-analysts.[80]

The problems of these patients were serious. Some 83 percent of the analysts' patients suffered "moderate to severe functional impairment." Of the patients in analysis, 88 percent suffered from neuroses or personality disorders, and 3 percent from psychoses. Only 1 percent suffered from psychosomatic disorders, compared with 17 percent in the 1950s, an indication of the withdrawal of analysts from a field that once was important to them. The total proportion of analysts' psychotic patients, treated either by analysis or psychotherapy, remained at 23 percent in 1975, about what it had been in the 1950s. Most of their psychoanalytic patients were in treatment from three to five years, while patients they treated by other methods were seen for a shorter period of time.[81]

All the unresolved problems of psychotherapy research and of the cost and effectiveness of psychoanalysis were raised by the issue of insurance coverage for psychiatric services. Third-party payers—government and insurance companies—pushed a number of issues. Were patients in psychoanalysis "medically ill"? Was psychoanalysis cost effective in comparison with other treatment methods? Was it available to the needy individual? How predictable were costs given the frequency and length of treatment? The survey of psychoanalytic practice by the American Psychoanalytic Association, published in 1976, indicated that psychoanalytic patients were truly ill. But the outcome issue was harder to resolve. Data depended on the clinical judgment of the analysts, and compared with other treatment methods, "analysis does not fare well," the survey concluded. Because of the length of treatment, psychoanalysts faced the crucial challenge of formulating outcome measures "sufficiently sensitive to demonstrate the true cost-efficacy of analysis when compared with other treatment modalities" in order to gain insurance and government support.[82]

The increasing role of private psychiatric care made the insurance issue all the more important. By the mid-1970s the private sector was delivering 34 percent of all inpatient days and 86 percent of all outpatient visits in the United States. The number of people with some private insurance for outpatient psychiatry rose from 38 to 68 percent between 1965 and 1980. Unlimited mental health coverage seemed to level off at 7.5 percent of total medical benefits.[83]

However, a study of the Washington, D.C., area estimated that 3 percent of the psychiatrists' patients, presumed to be those in psychoanalysis, accounted for 19 percent of the mental health benefits. This area had one of the largest concentrations of psychoanalysts in the nation, and these patients were government employees with supplemental Blue Cross, Blue Shield coverage.[84]

In 1980 the Senate Finance Committee proposed to limit government support to therapies judged "safe and effective on the basis of controlled clinical studies which are conducted and evaluated under generally accepted principles of scientific research.[85] But precisely what principles were most appropriate for judging psychotherapies was, as we have seen, a major unresolved issue.

Nevertheless, beginning in 1980, mental health benefits in the Washington area were reduced and the number of outpatient visits limited to about 50. One result was an estimated decline of 7 percent in the total number of patients, a reduction of those in psychoanalysis or intensive psychotherapy, and a 10 percent decline in the patient hours of all psychiatrists, psycho-analysts and non-analysts alike, in the area.[86]

The American policy of drastically limiting the hours of therapy covered by insurance contrasted sharply with the policy in West Germany, where 200 hours of psychoanalysis or psychotherapy were covered by insurance pay-ments. German patients who had been in treatment used hospital facilities far less often than before their psychotherapy and far less often than did the general insured population.[87]

Although office-based practice still was the profession's "core activity," psychiatrists were working in a wider range of settings. Nationally, by the mid-1980s, nearly three-quarters of the psychiatrists primarily in private practice spent part of their time in a medical school or university, a private psychiatric hospital, a general hospital, or a community mental health cen-ter.[88]

Psychiatrists increasingly devoted time to community service. In Wash-ington, D.C., more than half of the members of the Washington Psychiatric Society were devoting at least 20 percent of their time to welfare patients.[89] Between 1963 and 1972 the majority of residents graduated from one psy-choanalytically oriented training program spent only about one-third of their time in private practice and the rest in public service psychiatry or academic institutions. And 78 percent of the residents trained at Harvard's Massa-chusetts Mental Health Center from 1912 to 1967 spent half or more of their time for at least a year "in a public or non-profit private institution," some of them as hospital superintendents, clinic or service directors, chairs of depart-ments of psychiatry, or personnel at the National Institute of Mental Health.[90] Two factors may account for this increasing public service employ-ment: the availability of public service jobs and the public service emphasis of the residency program. Another factor may well have been the heavy concen-tration of psychiatrists in particular areas, such as New England and New York, and consequent competition for private patients, making public ser-vice more attractive. Private practice also takes time to build, and residents tended to enter it some years after completing their training.

Whether the income of psychoanalysts still was above the income of the average psychiatrist in the 1980s remains undetermined because there have been no recent published national surveys of psychoanalytic incomes. But the income of psychiatrists in private practice, and thus presumably of medi-cal psychoanalysts, remained substantially higher than those employed by public institutions. Lowest incomes were for those who taught or who worked in community mental health centers, health maintenance organiza-tions, or independent clinics.[91] In 1982 incomes ranged from $113,102 in North Dakota, where psychiatrists were scarce, to $55,303 in Massachusetts, where they were heavily concentrated. The average fee had climbed to $70 an hour, and the average gross income of all psychiatrists was $82,000.

However, the average net income of those in private practice was $99,000. Psychiatrists earned more than general practitioners and pediatricians but less than surgeons and radiologists.[92] For psychotherapists and psychoanalysts who customarily charged by the individual patient hour, income depended on the number of patients in treatment and hourly fees. Recently in some areas, fees have ranged upward from $100 to $150 an hour or more.

By the 1980s the psychiatric fabric that had supported the increase of private psychoanalysis had changed dramatically. Competition from other mental health professionals had grown significantly. Psychotherapy was available in new settings often from social workers or psychologists. Alternative psychotherapies, chiefly behavioral, were developed, although the behavioral therapies continued to play a less important part in psychiatric practice and training. As early as 1965 there were at least 250 varieties of psychotherapy and the number was growing annually.

In 1980, psychoanalytic psychology and psychoanalytic psychotherapy, although less enthusiastically embraced than, say, in 1958, remained the most widespread and popular psychological theory and therapy among psychiatric residents. In one survey residents rated research, "training in psychoanalysis," and "personal analysis or psychotherapy" as the three most important aspects of their psychiatric training. A study in 1980 of 42 residents who had graduated by 1972 from the University of Illinois psychiatric institute reported that 29 had "sought psychoanalysis as therapy for themselves." Psychoanalytic psychotherapy still was the most popular non-biological therapy, and in 1980 was preferred by 61 percent of residents, a decline from 66 percent in 1976. In residency programs, interest markedly increased in community psychiatry, group and family therapy, and the treatment of alcohol and drug abuse. Perhaps the majority of graduates of NIMH-supported programs spent at least half their time in public-service psychiatry.[93]

Residents' overall approach in psychiatry was more strongly eclectic and increasingly biological, especially in the treatment of the psychoses. For "endogenous depression," behavior therapy was considered more valuable than individual psychotherapy, followed by group and milieu therapy. For depression and acute schizophrenia somatic therapy was the most highly ranked. A solid majority continued to accept a medical model of psychiatric illness. One survey of residents in the Washington, D.C., area not surprisingly indicated a more enthusiastic "psychodynamic" orientation.[94]

The eclectic nature of psychiatric teaching is indicated by the fact that in a large-scale survey of practitioners and educators in 1982, 99 percent agreed that a psychiatrist should know how to use "common psychopharmacological agents," while 94 percent agreed that providing "supportive psychotherapy with awareness of dynamic issues" was a necessary skill. Some 93 percent believed psychiatrists should know "genetic and dynamic formulations," psychodynamics, and character structure; another 87 percent believed they should know psychoanalytic psychotherapy; and 75 percent believed they should know about behavior modification. Thus, although the behavior therapies were gaining in importance, the basic approach still seemed to be a psychoanalytically inspired "dynamic" psychiatry.[95]

A national survey suggested that psychiatrist experts were equally eclectic. They regarded the major breakthroughs between 1970–80 to be in the fields of brain research and biological psychiatry, notably the discovery of neurotransmitters and receptors, and advances in psychopharmacology, including the use of lithium in treating mania and depression, and the confirmation of genetic components in the psychoses. But a large number also rated as important the development of brief psychotherapy, as well as cognitive, behavioral, and family therapy. Their list of major books included many that dealt with psychoanalytic theory—Otto Kernberg on object relations, Margaret Mahler on the psychological development of the infant, Heinz Kohut on narcissism. The two most important, however, were the new DSM III, and the *Comprehensive Textbook of Psychiatry,* which represented highly eclectic viewpoints.[96] Finally, there were indications of a reaction against the excessive use of drugs, a growing awareness of their side effects, and a new insistence on the usefulness of psychotherapy by clinical psychologists as well as psychiatrists.

In summary, analysts and private psychiatrists committed to psychotherapy shared a number of common developments. Both practiced in a variety of settings. Both prescribed drugs. Both were subject to the insurance restrictions on long-term psychotherapy. They continued to treat a largely middle- and upper-middle-class clientele. They faced competition for psychotherapy patients from other therapists, chiefly clinical psychologists, but also social workers and counselors. Both were increasingly using couple, family, or group therapy. They also were competing with alternative therapies outside the psychiatric spectrum. Both shared the disabilities of the antipsychiatry attacks of the 1960s.[97] Both also participated relatively little in the new community mental health centers. Both treated patients who were seriously impaired, although psychiatrists treated more psychotics than did the analysts.

But psychoanalysts faced particular issues of their own: the most important was to demonstrate that cost-effectiveness of their speciality, given the long duration and expense of psychoanalytic treatment. They also faced a decline in patients they deemed suitable for their technique, and used it less often with the patients they treated. They suffered, finally, from the mounting popular and professional attacks on Freud and on their specialty.

19

Popular Images of Controversy: Freud's Changing Reputation and the Psychotherapy Jungle

The popular press recorded most of the attacks on Freud and psychoanalysis that were launched on a large scale in the 1960s by feminists, revisionist scholars, and advocates of the new directions in psychiatry and psychotherapy. These assaults were in part reactions to the superhuman virtues ascribed to Freud and the excessive expectations of psychoanalysis that were rife in the early postwar years. Attention focused on psychoanalytic stereotypes of women, Freud's character, and the claims for psychoanalytic therapy, and moved on to the proliferation of psychotherapies, the new somatic style, and finally an eclectic synthesis.

Reasons for the public attention were not hard to find. Psychotherapy had become a major cultural force, and psychoanalytic notions of sex, aggression, dreams, and family relationships pervaded the organs of popular culture. The "friends and supporters of psychotherapy," which included large numbers of intellectuals and professional people, many of them patients, ensured a wide audience for new developments in therapy and for anything that affected the vogue of psychoanalysis and Freud's role as a cultural hero, particularly his personal life and character.

A headline in *Ms.* magazine in 1984 summed up two decades of popularized feminist criticism: "The Hundred Year Cover-up: How Freud Betrayed Women."[1] He had dismissed their stories of childhood rape and seduction as fantasies. He believed that woman's place was in the home; her career, motherhood; her greatest satisfaction, pleasing a man and bearing male children. Her motive for emancipation was simple penis envy.

In 1963 Betty Friedan launched the feminist attack by blaming Freud as the ultimate source of America's "Feminine Mystique." In her best-seller of the same title, she argued that Freudians held that women should find fulfillment in femininity and domesticity. This ideology which trapped countless American women had been elaborated by Freud's disciples and, above all, by popularizers in America's mass media. Freud saw women as "childlike dolls" whose nature was to be "ruled by man"; her degradation was "taken for granted"; her penis envy could be assuaged only by the birth of a male child. Education and careers "masculinized" woman and endangered her feminine role. This mystique resulted in a declining number of women entering the professions, despite more college and graduate degrees, and in an American birthrate overtaking India's. But perhaps most important, it was manifest in a pervasive malaise and discontent among women imprisoned in their prescribed roles of wife and mother. Some of them had sought psychoanalysis to cope with their troubles, only to feel even more enmeshed and desperate.

Friedan's argument testified to the extraordinary impact of psychoanalysis on the college-educated at the height of its popularity. Psychoanalysis, she argued, was effective. Freud was a true "genius," a "most perceptive and accurate observer of important problems of the human personality." But she also agreed with the psychologist Abraham Maslow that positive human growth and self-realization were as primary a need as sex.[2] She had absorbed the cultural criticism of the neo-Freudians, who attributed Freud's view of women to his "Victorian" attitudes and his peculiar sample of middle-class Viennese from a culture that repressed women's sexuality. Much that Freud took to be biological was in fact cultural in origins, and his views of women were an obvious example.

Finally, Friedan charged that psychoanalysis had become America's postwar secular religion, filling "the vacuum of thought and purpose that existed for many for whom God, or flag, or bank account were no longer sufficient . . . ." In fostering the pursuit of personal pleasure, psychoanalysis provided escape from a sense of responsibility, from the harsh reality of atom bombs, and from the "troubling questions of the larger world." It made private vice sinless and made suspect "high aspirations of the mind and spirit." Friedan was followed by far harsher critics, such as Kate Millet, who argued that Freud was "beyond question the strongest individual counterrevolutionary force" against women's liberation.[3]

By the 1970s popularizing feminists had classified Freud as a "male chauvinist pig." The critic Richard Gilman argued in the *New York Times Magazine* that although Freud's "great achievements" were unassailable, his "radical bias against women and the existence of that bias in the very texture of psychoanalysis came to seem indisputable."[4]

The feminist critique helped to revive the popularity of Karen Horney, who, *Ms.* magazine explained, was the brilliant "Psychiatrist Who Walked Out on Freud." She had dared to challenge the absurd views of women held by Freud and his Viennese disciple, Helene Deutsch. Horney had developed an alternative theory to penis envy, that is, womb envy: men felt inferior and envied women's capacity to give birth. Because she had questioned many of Freud's most cherished postulates, she had been disqualified as a training analyst by the New York institute, her revolt attributed to the penis envy of a castrating woman.[5]

Two views of one of Freud's most famous patients, the beautiful 18-year-old Dora, illustrate both the idealization of Freud and a severe feminist and methodological critique. The husband of her father's mistress had made advances to her which she had repulsed, and she suffered from a long litany of symptoms—migraine headaches, fits of nervous coughing, fainting spells, a complete loss of voice, depression. Her father brought her to Freud for treatment after a suicide threat. In an essay praising Freud's treatment of his patients, Donald Kaplan, a New York lay analyst, argued in *Harper's* in 1967 that Dora's "emotional blackmailing and tyranny were evident to Freud almost at once." During her treatment, Freud "exercised his finest ingenuity" to prove that she unconsciously envied her father's mistress and desired the man she had repulsed. Her symptoms were the result of her moral self-punishment for these unconscious desires. Kaplan concluded that Dora's "three months with Freud may have been the only experience with unimpeachable integrity in her long, unhappy life."[6]

Erik Erikson saw the case differently and suggested that Freud had failed to recognize the adolescent Dora's need to experience fidelity in the adults around her and to have a firm understanding of reality. Deception and sexual betrayal had been rife among most of the important people in her environment.[7] In 1974 the University of Chicago psychologist Salvatore R. Maddi argued that Freud exhibited egregious male bias and faulty methodology in his treatment of Dora. She was a "beleaguered, overwhelmed youngster caught in a fantastic web of corruption." Like the adults around her, Freud blamed her for her problems. He insisted that she must have been sexually excited by the man who propositioned her "because any healthy 14 year old girl would have been aroused by the embrace of an attractive, familiar male." Freud tried to convince her of her guilt "with all the manipulative weaponry of psychoanalysis." Her symptoms, Maddi argued, probably were caused by her high level of anxiety and her loneliness and disappointment rather than her fantasies. Freud's methods of interpreting Dora's dreams and associations were so diverse that he could read "any hypothesis" as the real meaning of her thoughts. Moreover, he assumed so many forms of resistance "that virtually any objection on the part of the patient can be interpreted as agreement on an unconscious level."[8]

Some analysts slowly have begun to revise their theories of women, largely under the impact of the feminist attack and the research of Masters and Johnson, who presented evidence refuting the analysts' insistence that women must experience vaginal orgasm to be sexually mature. A major reappraisal of women's sexuality by Mary Jane Sherfey appeared in the *American Journal of Psychoanalysis* in 1966.[9]

The sexual goals of the counter-culture of the 1960s probably went far beyond anything that Freud or most psychoanalysts would have found desirable. The orgiastic proclivities, the group sex, the varieties of promiscuity evident in Gay Talese's chronicle of the "sexual revolution," *Thy Neighbor's Wife,* might have been condemned by Freud as examples of immaturity in psychosexual development. Otto Fenichel tended to regard hypersexuality as neurotic, and so did other American psychoanalysts, as the reactions of Karl Menninger and Lawrence Kubie to the Kinsey reports suggest. The analysts, including Freud, have regarded "perversions" such as oral-genital contact as foreplay to affectionate heterosexual intercourse. The frequent recommendations of masturbation in the sex manuals of the 1960s and 1970s might have been seen as evidence of fixation and narcissism.[10]

Freud's own position on desirable sexual behavior remained ambiguous. In 1893 he wrote to his friend Wilhelm Fliess about the possibility of "free sexual intercourse with unattached young women" as a way of preventing neurasthenia in males only if there were "innocuous methods of preventing conception."[11] Beginning with his first essay, "Civilized Sexual Morality and Modern Nervousness," in 1908 and again in "Civilization and Its Discontents" in 1933, Freud truculently attacked the constraints of "civilized" convention which restricted intercourse to monogamous marriage. In 1933 he argued that a "single standard for sexual life for everyone disregards the dissimilarities, whether innate or acquired, in the sexual constitution of human beings." Whether he was referring to the strength of genital sexual impulses or partial impulses or to homosexuality is unclear. Only weaklings, he continued, submitted to all the requirements of civilized morality. Who were the courageous rebels he had in mind? Some of his own disciples? According to the English writer Vincent Brome, Lou Andreas Salome, who later analyzed Freud's daughter, Anna, had "led a life of sexual polyandry," sometimes indulging "more than one lover simultaneously."[12]

But Freud never specified precisely how he would change existing conventions, except for that possible hint in the letter to Fliess. He once wrote that after treatment in which conflicts over sexuality became conscious, a person could perhaps decide on a midway position between "living a full life and absolute asceticism." Any one who "has succeeded in educating himself to truth about himself is permanently defended against the danger of immorality, even though his standard of morality may differ in some respect from that which is customary in society."[13] He complicated the argument further by insisting that society required the restriction of children's sexuality as a prelude to the disciplining of adult sexuality, and that society also needed to utilize the sexual instinct to curb aggression.[14] Finally, something in the nature of sexuality itself, Freud speculated, prevented "full satisfaction." For many of those sympathetic to the counter-culture, organized psychoanalysis seemed a conservative institution, a bulwark of middle-class American sexual mores. The sexual revolution, which psychoanalysis had done much to further, had moved far beyond the reforms Freud probably had envisaged.

The idealizations of Freud and of psychoanalysis and the identification of psychoanalysis with the psychiatric establishment inevitably inspired disillusionment and disagreement. Popular journalism recounted the work of revisionist scholars who reassessed Freud's originality, his temperament, and the scientific status of his theories. Such revisions have been subject to heated debate, as the paladins of psychoanalysis battle their philistines.[15]

Much of the publicity centered around Freud's personal life and the degree of his originality. One of the first revisionists, Henri Ellenberger, a Swiss psychiatrist at the University of Montreal, tempered Freud's reputation for uniqueness and originality by placing him within a long tradition of exploring the unconscious by dynamic psychiatrists. Freud's originality was partly organizational. Breaking with official medicine, Freud inaugurated "dynamic schools with their official doctrine, their rigid organization, their specialist journals, their closed membership." Ellenberger challenged the received psychoanalytic wisdom, enshrined in Ernest Jones's biography, *The Life and Works of Sigmund Freud,* that Freud had been ostracized by medical colleagues and his work ignored. On the contrary, it was received favorably, with a mixture of "surprise and puzzlement." However, Ellenberger left Freud's originality and character intact.[16]

In the late 1960s a series of reassessments of the psychoanalytic movement began. The defections of Jung and Adler and the dissensions of the psychoanalysts had been notorious since the 1920s and had given rise to an unflattering vision of Freud as an intolerant autocrat. In *Freud and His Early Circle,* published in 1968, Vincent Brome, and English biographer, concentrated on the disputes, the jealousies over priority, which, according to a reviewer, were "at once comic, pathetic, and haunted with a sense of tragic inevitability." Brome described the perverse tendency among the analysts to attack those who disagreed with them both inside and outside the movement as exhibiting at best "resistance" because of their complexes and, at worst, serious mental disturbance, a polemical tendency reinforced by the psychoanalytic sensitivity to unconscious hostility. Brome did not attribute these disputes to Freud's "allegedly dictatorial attitude, or to exceptional instability" among the founders of psychoanalysis. Brome argued instead that the hostility of the world toward the psychoanalysts's sexual discoveries, their daring temperament as pioneers, and the lack of any way of objectively reconciling their differences made conflict inevitable.[17]

In 1974 Paul Roazen's *Freud and His Followers* placed Freud and the psychoanalytic movement in the context of the "human dramas" of its participants.[18] Based on interviews with more than 70 people who had known Freud, it offered new insights and a wealth of new information. Roazen revealed perhaps for the first time outside Freud's immediate circle that Freud had analyzed his own daughter, Anna, a major violation of orthodox therapeutic etiquette. Moreover, Freud was callous about the suicide of his troubled and brilliant disciple, Victor Tausk. Roazen's book about Tausk, *Brother Animal,* so enraged Kurt Eissler, the former head of the Freud Archives, that, not content with a review, he produced a tome in response. According to *Time,* Roazen in *Freud and His Followers* discredited the American vision of Freud as a healer and emphasized the lack of importance Freud placed on therapeutic success; Freud found in himself no "craving . . . to help suffering humanity." Roazen also described the drug-related death of Freud's American disciple Ruth Mack Brunswick, and the suicides of perhaps ten other early psychoanalysts. While maintaining Freud's greatness, Roazen described the close, often claustrophobic relationships of Freud's entourage and his role in their personal lives. On the whole Roazen's book was well received by non-psychoanalysts, but met with a chilly reception from members of the psychoanalytic profession, with the exception of Robert Coles.[19]

A more negative view of the psychoanalytic movement was taken by Frank Sulloway in *Freud: Biologist of the Mind,* published in 1979. A comprehensive analysis of the survivals of 19th-century biological presumptions embedded in Freud's theories, it also attacked the myth-creating penchant of his followers. "The standard version of Freud's struggles, as recounted by Freud and the Freudian historians, is heavily laced with legend and much of it is false," *Time* reported.[20] Freud was less original, isolated, and heroic than the legend claimed. For example, many of his ideas of infantile sexuality were anticipated by the contemporary sexologist Albert Moll; latency, bisexuality, and reaction formation came from his friend Wilhelm Fliess, whom his followers charged with being a crackpot. His "heroic" self-analysis did not play the role in his discoveries that had been claimed for it. As Ellenberger had argued, the notion of Freud as a beleaguered hero in a hostile world was equally false. On the whole, his work at first was favorably received by contemporaries who praised his "wealth of new ideas and often arresting and dazzling apercus."[21] It was only later, after psychoanalysis had become a sectarian movement, that opposition became fierce. None of this, Sulloway argued, detracted from Freud's greatness, but the myths so assiduously cultivated isolated and insulated psychoanalysts from the scientific world.

Jones's vision of Freud's domestic virtues and personality was challenged by a number of other studies also widely publicized. Jung told a disciple that Freud had had an affair with his sister-in-law, Minna Bernays; later, Peter Swales argued that on one of her vacation trips with Freud, he had arranged for an abortion for her. Freud's niece Judith Heller, who often had stayed with the Freuds, insisted that given the cramped domestic quarters of the Freud apartment an affair would have been difficult to carry on.[22]

Ernest Jones had suggested that Freud was neurotic, and Max Schur, who was Freud's personal physician and who worshiped him, embellished that image. Schur had been given uncensored access to Freud's letters to his friend Fliess, including letters omitted or heavily edited by Anna Freud and Ernst Kris in their published edition, which had included only what they believed was of "scientific" interest. Schur presented Freud as a "troubled and brooding" young man, "a Freud of moods and obsessions, a complaining, hypochondriacal Freud." Schur also saw Freud as stoical and heroic: when the Nazis came to Vienna, and Anna Freud suggested that it might be easier if they committed suicide, Freud asked her, "Why? Because they would like us to."[23]

Schur was the first to disclose that Fliess had bungled the nasal surgery of one of Freud's patients, Emma Ekstein, in a bizarre attempt to cure her neuroses. Jeffrey Masson, a Sanskrit scholar and former lay psychoanalyst, later noted that Freud blamed her repeated nosebleeds on hysteria rather than on the damage done when Fliess negligently had left half a meter of gauze in her nose during the surgery. Its removal by another physician caused a hemorrhage that could have killed her.

Masson, who became the focus of widely publicized charges, counter-charges, and legal battles, insisted that Freud had turned psychoanalysis away from the real world on a course that led to its "present-day sterility" when he ceased to believe that sexual abuse in childhood, usually by a father, was the cause of neurosis. To avoid the criticism of his medical colleagues, Freud blamed the child's own fantasies and sexual wishes. (Some have argued that Freud changed his mind because his siblings were neurotic and his own father might therefore have been implicated.) Masson's claims, first broached in a talk at Yale, resulted in his dismissal as project director of the Sigmund Freud Archives and a $150,000 settlement. He later completed an edition of the Freud-Fliess letters that made the full texts available for the first time. He was described by the journalist Janet Malcolm in the *New Yorker* as allegedly wanting to turn Freud's final home in London, the shrine at Maresfield gardens, into a place of "sex, women, and fun." Masson countered with a libel suit that is making its way through the courts.[24]

"Finding the Hidden Freud," a story illustrated by a cartoon of Freud as a recumbent Gulliver while Lilliputian scholars examined him, summed up the popular message of revisionist scholarship in *Newsweek* in 1981:

> Freud emerges from the scrutiny with his genius undimmed, but his portrait darkened: envious, often malicious, sometimes a pilferer of colleagues' ideas, a man who may have seduced his sister-in-law under his own roof. . . . The figure that steps from recent biographies is no longer the majestic prophet of the legend, but more like one of the neurotic egoists who might have frequented his own couch.[25]

However, *Newsweek* still found Freud a prodigious cultural influence. He had "charted the dark underside of civilized consciousness, a hellish 'unconscious' where even the most upright citizen harbors forbidden lusts and aggressions." He also had provided a world view. "His ideas about dreams, religion, creativity and the unconscious motivations underlying all human behavior are so pervasive that it would be difficult to imagine twentieth century thought without them."[26]

Perhaps the most extreme denigration of Freud came from a British writer who argued that Freud was a heavy user of cocaine and that therefore psychoanalysis was a product of his cocaine-stimulated imagination.[27]

By 1981 major elements of Jones's portrait of Freud had been questioned: his personal virtue, his originality, his scientific temperament. Some
of the reassessments merely carried further themes that Jones had suggested,
notably Freud's neuroticism. It is indicative of the place Freud and psychoanalysis occupied in America that in the mass magazines the new charges
were usually accompanied by psychoanalysts' rejoinders that, as *Newsweek*
was at pains to state, his monument was "secure." And in a withering account
of a particularly wooden psychoanalyst's New York practice, Janet Malcolm
in *The Impossible Profession* preserved a very real reverence for Freud's
achievements.

Not only Freud as a cultural figure but also psychoanalysis as a theory
and therapy were reexamined in the media, reflecting the professional debates. The dilution as well as the persistence of psychoanalytic therapy were
taken for granted in *Newsweek*'s "Finding the Hidden Freud" in 1981. Most
"mainstream" therapies operated in a "Freudian framework." But instead of
concentrating on the Oedipus complex, the modern psychoanalyst was

> apt to bear more on such worldly matters as work, intimacy, and success. In
> effect the therapist is less likely to ask about last night's dreams than to say,
> "What's new at the office?" and in place of the classic neutrality, he is likely to
> offer some considered advice on how to handle the boss or the boy friend.

In 1968 *Science Digest* recorded all the then-current discontents. Freudian
therapy was "inefficient, dogmatic, devoid of substantive research." Accepted
as a method of investigation, its therapy had not proven effective by any
"scientific test." Bruno Bettelheim was quoted as saying that the "major
theoretical structures of Sigmund Freud" were time-bound, "very shaky, very
dubious." The National Institute of Mental Health had found that psychoanalysis was the least used of 40 recognized therapies and reached only 2
percent of psychiatric patients. It was losing ground to "quick, cheaper therapies that can reach slum residents and low-income Americans who want
psychological help." Whereas in 1945 one of 17 psychiatric residents became
psychoanalysts, in 1968, only one of 20 did so. The psychoanalyst Robert
Lifton noted that the preferences of young psychiatric residents at Yale
exemplified the psychoanalytic crisis. The younger generation saw psychoanalysis as "part of the established order."[28] They were going into research in
"neuropharmacology, genetics, dream research and studies of brain function."
Finally, the community psychiatry movement was offering quick therapeutic
changes with drugs, direct suggestion, and conditioning, and was drawing on
guidance counselors, clergy, social workers, and teacher in the rehabilitation
process. The analysts were too busy with "endless ruminations and rhapsodiz-
ings, with variations on original analytic themes and theories." There was no
proof that long analyses were any better than short-term therapy. The analysts
answered their critics by arguing that one could change behavior and still leave
underlying problems unsolved. Moreover, thousands of patients could testify
to "considerable improvement" through psychoanalysis.

Eleven years later, in 1979, *Science Digest* summarized an examination of the scientific status of Freud's theories with the headline: "The Paradox of Psychoanalysis: Success Built upon Failures." The psychologists Seymour Fisher and Roger Greenberg argued that Freud's cases were largely unsuccessful and that he never produced evidence to show that psychoanalysis benefited the majority of his patients. Nor did he fashion an interlocking, comprehensive theory. Rather he had produced multiple individual theories which were often independent of each other. Freud's views of women were unsupported by evidence. Although there was some basis for the existence of erotic feelings toward the parent of the opposite sex and hostile feelings toward the parent of the same sex, the boy's superego, for example, grew not out of fear of castration but out of friendliness displayed by the father toward his son.[29]

In 1976, writing in the *New York Times,* the historian Christopher Lasch deplored the saturation of American popular culture by a debased, watered-down psychoanalysis. Americans had transformed Freud's modest goals for psychiatry into a new religion with a scientific priesthood, which purported to distinguish mental health from mental illness and illusion from reality. The Americans, especially the Adlerians and neo-Freudians, had renounced what was truly radical in Freud's thought, and had substituted a cult of personal health and fulfillment or else propounded panaceas for a sick society. The Freudian ego psychologists had stressed "not the insatiable appetites of the id as Freud did," but rather the ego's more genteel "search for identity and meaning."[30]

Freud was the "God That Failed" for the writer Dan Wakefield, who recounted his tribulations in an autobiography. While a student at Columbia University, he had begun psychotherapy with a member of the New York Psychoanalytic Society for serious episodes of depression. The distinguished literary critic Mark Van Doren had suggested in an English class that in our own time and culture "psychiatry was replacing God" as the instrument of personal transformation. Like others of his atheist generation of students at Columbia and former radicals who had given up Marx for Freud, Wakefield believed that sexual behavior was a "key factor" in "understanding and ameliorating the human condition."

His disillusionment reflected his own magical expectations for treatment, the unrealized "scientific" claims his analyst advanced, and a hostility toward his analyst which he believed to be mutual. After initial psychotherapy with one analyst, Wakefield, who had begun to suffer from impotence, began analysis with another physician, hoping for a more effective treatment and a radical personal transformation. He was to make no major decisions or life changes during his analysis and spent his four or five hours a week saying whatever came into his mind. He sought the magic key to his childhood in some early trauma and blamed his problems in part on his religious upbringing. He became sexually potent but his drinking grew more compulsive, to be followed by deepening depression and finally hallucinations. After five years he asked his analyst if he would get better after surviving this "ghastly torture." His analyst replied that psychoanalysis was a "medically scientific treatment with proven results, just as certain as setting a broken leg."[31] Wakefield called him a liar, left analysis, returned to his first therapist for what became a successful treatment, and finally returned to religion.

In addition to personal testimonials of disillusionment, popular accounts also emphasized the tendency to move away from classical analysis as well as the charge that it was ineffective. For instance, psychoanalysts were divided over how much solace to offer their patients. One psychoanalyst insisted that his colleagues were substituting for arduous psychoanalytic practice the presumably "easier" ways of psychotherapy, gratifying their patients' transference needs by, for instance, attending their weddings or plays. Orthodox analysts might disqualify patients for analysis by saying they were not analyzable and then take the easier road of therapy, while "liberals" could "see the transference ambiguity as an opportunity for a self indulgence which masks as experimentation." This lay analyst deplored the medical training of his colleagues which left them "scarcely versed in experimental method and the philosophy of science and practically illiterate about the grand issues of the Western cultural tradition." Other analysts argued that the classical position of neutrality protected both patient and analyst. The issue was crucial, conservative analysts believed, because neutrality was what separated Freudians "who seek slow, deep cures" from "therapists who simply want to make the patient feel better."[32]

Popularizations aired not only the charges of backsliding, inefficiency, and sacerdotalism, but also the controversy over congressional demands for better proof of the usefulness of psychotherapies in general. The president of the American Psychological Association countered that there were 100 therapies in the mainstream and that testing them would be more difficult than testing drugs. Hans Strupp, the veteran psychotherapy researcher, argued that, in fact, there were a number of studies, including Smith, Glass, and Miller's, which already had demonstrated the effectiveness of psychotherapy.[33]

Beginning in the 1970s and certainly by the 1980s popular articles indicated that psychotherapy had taken on a complex life of its own, through research and the development of brief and alternative therapies, some of them based on behaviorism or cognitive psychology. Short-term analytic therapies also were publicized, for example, the confrontational technique of Habib Davenloo, a professor of psychiatry at McGill University in Montreal. Some psychotherapy researchers endorsed his methods; others, including a number of psychoanalysts, remained skeptical.

Unlike classical analysis with its free associations, Davenloo's therapist directed the conversation, attacking the patient's defenses and forcing him to discuss the sources of his problems. The therapist also interpreted any transference immediately, attempting to point out similarities between the patient's reactions to the therapist and his other relationships. The *New York Times Magazine*'s account began with a quasi-miracle. A patient's phobias were so severe that he could not drive a car, take subways, planes, or elevators, or be alone in open spaces. He had been treated unsuccessfully for seven years by psychotherapists, and then at a phobia clinic. He was "completely cured" by Davenloo in 32 sessions. Although the symptoms were not targeted at all in Davenloo's therapy, they disappeared and the patient was still free of them four years later. The treatment had been videotaped so the techniques could be learned. The method offered "new hope" to thousands who otherwise might not get any kind of treatment.[34]

Another psychoanalyst, Aaron Beck, at the University of Pennsylvania, developed a cognitive therapy for depression, somewhat reminiscent of the Swiss psychologist Paul Dubois's early 20th-century method of persuasion. Beck believed that depressed patients saw things in a "completely negative way," blotting out positive experiences. The therapist showed the patient how he was reacting too negatively to ordinary events and how other interpretations of the same situations were possible. This technique, too, was successful, according to *Psychology Today*.[35]

By the 1970s guides were published to what had become the "psychotherapy jungle," with at least 130 recognizable varieties of "psychosocial" therapies. In a symposium in the *Saturday Review of Literature,* Morris Parloff, a psychotherapy researcher at the National Institute of Mental Health, wrote that the boundaries of treatment had become increasingly ambiguous: it was no longer reserved for the psychoses and neuroses but had taken on problems of "alienation and the meaninglessness of life." Therapy had assumed the roles of religion and science. He noted ironically that no school of therapy had ever withdrawn from the field "for failure to live up to its claims, and as a consequence all continue to co-exist." Where just after World War II there were primarily the mental hospital, the "snake pit," and the couch, there was now a whole range of therapies. Psychoanalysis had held a special fascination for novelists, playwrights, and moviemakers, and held almost undisputed sway in academia. There were four major schools—analytic, depth, or psychodynamic therapy; behavior therapy; humanistic therapy, oriented around human self-actualization; and transpersonal therapy, in which the patient aspired to be at one with the universe—as well as special therapies such as feminist therapy and primal scream. Most of them tended to be successful with two-thirds of their clients. But treatment was far from standardized.[36]

Where Parloff catalogued the new varieties of therapy, Jarl Dyrud, the associate chairman of psychiatry at the University of Chicago, argued that Freud's legacy remained the "best bet for dealing with emotional problems." Indeed, the "impending death of psychoanalysis" was one of its "oldest traditions." It had survived 75 years of putdowns from the scientific community and advocates of other therapies. Freud's method was the "only practical means of navigating through this stormy inner ocean of ideas and feelings." Although patients' complaints had changed from guilt and anxiety earlier in the century to today's "boredom and meaninglessness," the essential content of psychoanalysis—"its assumption that we can, with the analyst's aid, understand and alleviate our innermost conflicts—remains essentially what it was in Freud's day." Relying on medical analogy, he argued that psychoanalysts sampled the "stream of thought much as scientists sample the bloodstream for indications of health or sickness." Taking up the classical American postwar analytic posture, he argued that those who see psychoanalysis as a "revolutionary political and social force for good . . . are often dismayed to find that the main offering of psychoanalysis is a slow and often painful stripping away of illusion . . . a somewhat stoic but satisfying philosophy."[37]

In 1977 *Harper's Bazaar* published a breezy guide touting the wonders of short-term therapy and describing the situations when professional help might be necessary. "Maybe you've been nervous, screaming at the children. Perhaps your husband's been drinking a lot or behaving erratically. . . . " Frequent bouts of the blues that interfered with normal life, threats of violence or suicide, a child's problems with drugs or alcohol were all indications for therapy. Although Freud was the "father of modern psychotherapy," "classical psychoanalysis" had lost popularity not only because of time and expense but also because its effectiveness had been questioned and it was difficult to verify its results scientifically. The guide described most of the available therapies—Jungian, Adlerian, Masters and Johnson's sex therapy, operant conditioning, group therapy, guided meditation, psychodrama, and so on. Reminiscent of the advice of the 1920s, it warned that children who were "loners" might be more disturbed than those who were aggressive. The "losers" who seemed "goody goody" and did well in school might be "suppressing hostility which builds up inside and can surface very destructively later on."[38]

Mademoiselle also offered a guide, "How to Select Your Shrink." This too chronicled the wide variety of therapies including crisis intervention and hypnosis, and confirmed the swing away from long-term therapy, although classical psychoanalysis could be useful for those who felt the need for "radical change."[39] Thus, "classical" psychoanalysis remained a part of the popularized therapy scene. But it was also the most expensive and time-consuming, and therefore was used far less often than briefer methods.

The most extreme denigrations of psychiatry and psychoanalysis came not from journalists intending to inform but from the movies. Film had made both seem miraculous in what Krin and Glen Gabbard have called psychiatry's brief "golden age" from the late 1950s to the early 1960s. The movies began their attacks in the 1960s just when psychoanalysis was being widely questioned by psychiatrists. Where Freud had appeared as an almost Christ-like light-bringer in John Huston's movie about him in 1962, by the 1980s, in *Lovesick,* Freud was predicting that the future lay with a mix of psychology, religion, and chemistry. The movies seemed to argue that psychiatry and psychoanalysis had failed to solve social and individual problems, and thus psychiatrists were fallible or even inept and, often enough, corrupt or villainous. Psychiatry and psychoanalysis enforced social conformity, and the members of a psychoanalytic society in *Lovesick* were "stuffy, repressive, authoritarian types," more concerned with professional reputations and respectability than with their patients. Yet in the 1980s, in occasional films such as *Ordinary People,* the image of the humane, caring and successful psychotherapist appeared again.[40]

The rise of the new somatic psychiatry was welcomed as warmly in the magazines as psychoanalysis had been in its heyday. Seymour Kety, a Harvard psychiatrist, argued in the *Saturday Review* that serious mental illnesses resulted from "chemical, rather than psychological imbalances," and that in the majority of severe cases of schizophrenia and in a substantial number of manic-depressive illnesses, genetic factors played a "crucial causative role."[41] Perhaps the most sanguine claims were made in 1972:

> The biochemistry of the emotions is also coming into view, like a statue gradually taking form as the sculptor laboriously chips way at a block of material. We cannot yet say "depression—not enough adrenalin—just add a little more to his soup," or "anger, too much adrenalin—just take a couple of blocking pills," but we are on the verge.[42]

Journalists reported that "for too long psychiatry has ignored the fact that emotional disturbances are largely biochemical in nature," and that most emotional states were determined by brain chemistry. Instead of blaming parents or spending months or years ransacking the patient's past, psychiatrists now looked for physical causes and prescribed "highly effective medication."[43]

One case, reported in the *Washington Post* in the late 1980s, vividly illustrates the psychological versus somatic treatment controversy. A 41-year-old kidney specialist sued the psychoanalytic hospital Chestnut Lodge for not prescribing medication for his severe depression. For seven months be paced 18 miles a day up and down a locked ward, until his feet blistered and ulcerated; he stopped bathing and shaving. He claimed that he was treated only by intensive psychotherapy when "effective medication was available." The hospital's lawyers argued that he was "actually suffering from a narcissistic personality disorder for which drugs are not the appropriate treatment." His therapists at Chestnut Lodge hoped to "restructure" his personality which they thought would take three years, a process medication would interfere with. The patient's parents transferred him to another hospital after they had become alarmed at his deterioration; after three weeks of drug therapy he stopped pacing and was discharged nine weeks later. In an arbitration hearing, Gerald Klerman, then at Harvard Medical School, testified that the Lodge's treatment was "criminal . . . cruel and negligent." The doctor's agitated depression was something a first-year resident could have diagnosed and treated.[44]

But there were also serious doubts about some of the results of somatic psychiatry, particularly the over-use of tranquilizers and drugs, their ineffectiveness or their side effects, and the possibility of withdrawal symptoms. Lithium, for example, did not work with some patients, and the side effects could be devastating. The *New Yorker* ran a long series on the erratic course of the drug treatment of a woman in a New York public mental hospital.[45] In an autobiographical account of her breakdown, Barbara Gordon, a New York television producer, chronicled the ineptitude of a series of drug-prescribing psychiatrists and, by contrast, the sensitivity and insightfulness of a woman psychotherapist.[46] But the use of drugs was ubiquitous and genetic research continued to suggest partial but important underlying causes of serious mental disorders.

At the same time, dynamic psychotherapy, derived from psychoanalysis, continued to be an American psychiatric staple. American psychiatry and popular therapy remained, as it had begun, an eclectic synthesis. The psychiatrist who looked for "physical causes" instead of blaming parents also believed that "many of the insights of our great teachers, like Freud and Jung . . . are still equally valid today." Psychoanalysis worked for those with existential questions about "the value of life and work, the meaning of relationships, and the need to know more about the true self." For example, a man who failed to win an "important scientific award" became seriously depressed and could not function at work or in his marriage. Anti-depressant medication quickly relieved his depression. But the patient wanted to know why he continued to be severely disappointed at his failure to win the award. And for that problem psychotherapy was clearly indicated.[47]

A psychiatrist summed up the generally mixed approach of Americans who could comfortably combine somatic with psychotherapeutic treatment:

> For the first time in human history we have reliable ways of treating the symptoms of depression, and controlling the swings of manic-depressive illness and some of the symptoms of schizophrenia. We actually have the power to reset the neurotransmitter systems in the brain and get it thinking more or less right again.

But talk therapy also worked. He himself had become interested in psychiatry because he was fascinated by patients' stories and by the interactions between doctor and patient. "To me the amazing thing was not that psychotherapy sometimes fails, but that it EVER works. Those occasions when I said something to a patient and something changed seemed entirely unbelievable to me, giving evidence of the astonishing power of speech, of human contact." This psychiatrist chose not to enter the "monastic discipline of psychoanalytic training" but worked in an outpatient clinic where the most crucial question was "What kind of treatment works for whom?" And he concluded that despite all psychoanalytic theories, all the latest drug research, "when you actually have a patient sitting across from you, nothing is more important than intuition."[48]

For what problems was therapy recommended? By the late 1970s it had become so modish that *Vogue* published a cautionary tale in its therapy guide. A successful film editor who received a big promotion became depressed by the thought of her new responsibilities, and many of her friends recommended a therapist. But another friend, an experienced executive, suggested she first try her new job and then if she still felt depressed and confused to consult someone. In fact, she mastered the new job successfully and did not need a therapist. *Vogue* nevertheless recommended a therapist for a gamut of complaints: physical symptoms such as head or stomach aches, skin rashes without a physical basis; an inability to work or enjoy life; repetitive, self-destructive love relationships; unreasonable, persistent anxiety; constant nagging depression for which there is no reason; unreasonable fears that interfere with productive life; persistent, worsening sexual problems; unhealthy habit patterns such as overconsumption of food or alcohol or drug dependence; chronic feelings of helplessness or indecisiveness; and, finally, "the strong feeling that for whatever reason, one needs professional help" at a given time in one's life.[49]

Some of these complaints were the same as those voiced by Americans 60 or perhaps 100 years earlier: somatic symptoms without an apparent physical basis, anxiety, depression, drug or alcohol addiction, sexual problems, unreasonable fears, weakness and fatigue, indecisiveness and helplessness, the inability to work and enjoy life. Dr. George M. Beard, the neurologist who coined the term neurasthenia or nervous weakness, could have listed most of them in the 1880s. What was new were self-destructive relationships, a category which reflected psychoanalytic character analysis, and, most decidedly, the social legitimacy of seeking psychotherapy and the wide variety of available therapies. The popularizations revealed not only persistent problems but persistent preoccupations: the search for a flawless healer, which Freud once had seemed to be; the equally passionate search for a miraculous cure, which both psychoanalysis and somatic psychiatry had seemed to offer; and the persistent American tendency toward eclecticism.

20

The Crisis of American Psychoanalysis

The breakdown of the postwar dominance of the ego psychologists, the cumulative effects of criticism, particularly of clinical evidence, and the recent profound changes in psychiatry created the psychoanalytic crisis of the last decade. It is a crisis of clashing theories, competing modes of therapy, and uncertainties of professional identity.

Criticism inspired renewed attempts to verify psychoanalytic hypotheses and to document empirical observations of infancy and early childhood. Yet some of the conclusions derived from this research have provoked serious conflict with more traditional psychoanalytic views. The ego psychology synthesis of the postwar years was challenged by several opposing theories—hermeneutics and phenomenology, self-psychology, and object relations. Opposition by organized psychologists practicing psychotherapy has broken the medical and psychiatric cast of the American Psychoanalytic Association. Finally, psychoanalysts themselves have become acutely aware of their own professional crisis.

The crisis of theory began with the criticism on historical, clinical, and philosophical grounds of ego psychology, metapsychology, and Freud's logic and method.[1] Two stringent critics were the psychoanalytic psychologists George Klein and Robert Holt, among David Rapaport's most brilliant students at the Menninger clinic. Klein and Holt moved to New York University in the early 1950s, where Klein founded the Research Center for Mental Health. The center sponsored important psychoanalytic research, including the application of content analysis to psychoanalytic sessions.

Holt became increasingly disillusioned with Freud's methodology. In 1965, he analyzed appreciatively but critically Freud's "cognitive style," emphasizing Freud's unusual "tolerance for ambiguity and inconsistency," his penchant for hyperbole and for stating whatever he thought was a "law of nature" with "sweeping universalism and generality," his scientific penchant to "generalize from samples of one." Finally, he stretched the meaning of concepts. Freud expanded the meaning of sexuality from stimulation of the genitals and literal seduction in his earliest papers to include oral, anal, urethral, and voyeuristic partial drives, then the skin and all "sensitive internal organs." "Nothing of considerable importance can occur in the organism without contributing some component to the excitation of the sexual instinct," Freud argued.[2]

Freud also had committed serious logical errors: he had made extensive use of metaphor and other figures of speech at points of theoretical difficulty. Moreover, Freud had been "no paragon of self-criticism. He was unusually intolerant of outside critics . . . and analysts have faithfully copied him in this respect."

Holt and Klein repudiated metapsychology and ego psychology, arguing that both were based on drive theory, which in turn directly reflected outmoded 19th-century biological and neurological models. Metapsychology, with its economic theory of tension and discharge, was a substitute for neurophysiology and a product of Freud's philosophy of science which held that explanations expressed in terms of intention and meaning were not "scientific." The "drive reduction model" was more "appropriate to a rat than to a human being," Klein wrote.[3] Metapsychology was "moribund if not actually dead," and it was unlikely that the concept of the ego would "survive the general collapse," Holt asserted.[4] Finally, the thermodynamic model and its modern replacements were "irrelevant" to the clinical enterprise. Ego psychology was too abstract, and its reified terminology, such as ego, id, and superego, referred not to anything "even indirectly observable."[5]

However, the impetus for ego psychology, Holt argued, was important and had developed from two major sources. The first was a series of "virtually universal kinds of observations: the body image, the fact of death, the use of self-words, reflexive self-awareness, and the feeling that we are in control of some impulses but not of others."[6] A second source was Freud's attempt to create a scientific psychology and a structural theory of personality. The unusually abstract nature of the theories of ego psychologists such as Hartmann and Rapaport suggested the need for a more concrete psychology of the self, which some psychoanalysts already were developing.

Pursuing this bent, Klein defined clinical concepts in broadly phenomenological, existential terms: they involved primarily "meanings," "intentions," and "syntheses arising out of the crisis of an individual lifetime." It was

Freud's genius to bring back into psychology just such vital concerns, and psychoanalysis demonstrated the role of inner myth and fantasy in making objects and relationships significant.[7]

Most important, intentions, meaning, and purposes were just as "directly observable, and as specifiable as a neurological discharge," and in that sense just as "real." They could not be reduced to "impersonal models of stimuli, triggers, physiology, etc."[8] "The key factors, then, in the psychoanalytic clinical view of motivation are relational requirements, encounters, crises, dilemmas, resolutions, and achievements—not a hypothetical 'tension reduction.'"[9]

Although clinical concepts were just as theoretical as metapsychology, Klein argued, they were closer to the data of clinical observation and hence could be modified more systematically. At the time of his death in 1971 at the age of 53, Klein was working on a restatement of the fundamentals of psychoanalysis.[10] Klein's student and colleague, Roy Schafer, developed an "action language" based in part on the theories of the philosopher Gilbert Ryle, that attempted to eliminate the terms of metapsychology and to couch in "ordinary language" the transactions of the psychoanalytic clinical encounter.[11]

In 1985 Holt argued that even the clinical theory was a "sprawling mess." Its concepts still were "intermingled with metapsychological terms" such as id, ego, superego and as little subject to verification. "Analysts keep making new observations, which clash with existing formulations," he wrote. "Instead of trying to figure out what sampling or situational parameters make the difference, the tradition has been merely to say, in effect, "No, THIS is how it is. And the resulting contradiction is never resolved."[12]

More disturbing still was the fact that the raw data from patient sessions that were used to confirm clinical hypotheses could be equally compatible with the theories of rival schools, Freudian, non-Freudian, or even non-psychoanalytic. All of the rival theories "seem to be confirmed in clinical practice, but they cannot all be true."[13] The existence of "unconscious fantasies," a fundamental psychoanalytic concept, still was problematic; it was a simpler and more powerful explanation of many puzzling observations than alternative explanations, but based on clinical data, it remained only a hypothesis.

Holt argued that the genetic propositions of psychoanalysis could not be tested by psychoanalytic data because these did not establish causal connections in a controlled way. "It is hard to admit how little *proof* there is for any psychoanalytic hypothesis after all these years of use. . . . " The theory seemed clinically valuable and large parts of it had been adopted by intellectuals as "received knowledge." He concluded that "it would be an enormous loss to psychology if the great insights of psychoanalysis faded away without ever having had a chance to be converted into a real science, and a huge loss to society if it were deprived of the unique contribution to human welfare that clinical psychoanalysis at its best can make."[14] The strictures of Holt and Klein attacked primarily the psychoanalysts' lack of scientific precision and the explanatory difficulties of ego psychology but left intact the more positive functions that Hartmann and others had attributed to the ego.

Holt's rueful disappointment illustrates one aspect of the present crisis—an erosion of confidence in the objective, "scientific" nature of the psychoanalytic clinical encounter. This erosion was partly the result of Adolf Grünbaum's examination of the scientific credentials of psychoanalysis.

Grünbaum, a philosopher of science at Pittsburgh University, who had taken a minor part in the 1958 symposium on psychoanalysis and science at New York University, reexamined the disputed issues: Was psychoanalysis a science? Could its findings be justified or were they at best hypotheses, at worst unverified conjectures, products of the analyst's own presuppositions?

Against Karl Popper, the philosopher of science who insisted that psychoanalytic propositions could not be falsified and thus lacked scientific status, Grünbaum argued that Freud had a sophisticated notion of scientific method and frequently changed his mind in the light of new findings that contradicted his earlier views. Against the hermeneuticists who would construe psychoanalysis as solely a humanistic discipline concerned with unraveling the idiosyncratic meaning of subjective experience for the individual human being, Grünbaum defended Freud's view of psychoanalysis as an empirical science making generalizations about human psychology.

But he also concluded that the verification of psychoanalytic hypotheses by clinical evidence was fatally flawed logically and empirically. The logical flaw was that Freud's method of free association which provided the evidence not only for his theories of neurosis and sexuality but also for his analysis of transference, of dreams, and of parapraxes such as slips of the tongue or pen failed to prove causality. A chain of associations might show evidence of "thematic affinity" or "meaning connection" but this had no necessary relation to "cause." To assume anything else was to assume the classical fallacy of *post hoc ergo propter hoc,* that is, because *b* followed *a, b* must have caused *a.* The empirical flaw was that the clinical evidence was hopelessly tainted by the psychoanalyst's role in the therapeutic situation, by what Grünbaum once called the "suggestive, intimidating influence of the analyst."[15]

Grünbaum insisted that the chief argument Freud gave for the accuracy of data obtained from free association in the clinical situation was the evidence of cure. Grünbaum regarded this as Freud's central thesis of verification, what he called Freud's "tally argument," and he cited this passage: "After all his [the patient's] conflicts will only be successfully solved and his resistances overcome if the anticipatory ideas he is given tally with what is real in him. . . ." And he cited Freud's assertion that "under favorable conditions we achieve successes which are second to none of the finest in the field of internal medicine. . . . they could not have been achieved by any other procedure."[16]

By the 1930s Freud had given up his optimism about psychoanalytic cures, and with that, Grünbaum argued, he also gave up his chief method of verifying the truth of clinically based hypotheses. Moreover, recent research indicated that human memory, including adult recollections of childhood, was often inaccurate, malleable, and distorting. Moreover, these introspective productions would be expressed in language the patient found plausible, language suggested by the analyst's interpretations. So the patient's memories in therapy were thus doubly suspect.

After presumably destroying the scientific validity of the psychoanalytic enterprise by denying the possibility of verifying clinical hypotheses on the basis of what the patient said during the psychoanalytic hour, Grünbaum concluded in mollification:

> Future *extra*clinical evidence (e.g., epidemiologic or experimental findings) *may* turn out to reveal after all that Freud's brilliant intellectual imagination was quite serendipitous for psychopathology and other facets of human conduct, despite the clearcut failure of his clinical arguments.[17]

What was surprising about the reception of Grünbaum's argument was the number of prominent psychoanalysts who accepted some of his criticism. This contrasts sharply with the supreme confidence in the clinical enterprise of Jacob Arlow, Lawrence Kubie, and Heinz Hartmann at the New York University symposium on psychoanalysis and science. Some analysts tended to seize on Grünbaum's mollification and ignore his severe strictures. Psychoanalytic psychologists such as Holt, Morris Eagle, and Philip Holzman, traditionally more critical than many of their psychoanalytic colleagues, accepted much of Grünbaum's thesis.[18] But psychoanalytic psychiatrists such as Judd Marmor and Morton Reiser also accepted Grünbaum's contention that verification would have to come from extraclinical testing, or from the objective examination of recorded psychoanalyses. On the other hand, some analysts such as Robert Wallerstein have argued that psychoanalysts had long ago given up the view that successful psychoanalytic treatment depended on "correctly timed veridical interpretations."[19] Moreover, the telling emergence of surprising "circumstantial detail" in an analysis, detail previously not remembered by the patient and hardly imaginable in advance by the analyst, constituted one kind of useful clinical evidence. Suggestion by the analyst could be assessed and minimized. Grünbaum's recommended extraclinical testing of psychoanalytic propositions, although desirable, contained its own pitfalls of conception and method.

Whether in fact Grünbaum represented Freud's views of confirmation fairly is problematical. Freud appealed to wide varieties of evidence for the general propositions of psychoanalysis—observations of children, literature, myths and legends, anthropology, statistics, sometimes even psychological experiments.[20] And in the clinical situation he also appealed to fortuitous confirmation by outside evidence for the accuracy of memories, or the testimony of witnesses of early childhood events. His interpretations depended on their ability to "confer intelligibility on the data."[21]

The tally argument took on a new form as the result of some of the work of psychoanalytic researchers who, through predictions, believed they were able to confirm or disconfirm the "fit" and plausibility of rival psychoanalytic propositions. And their work has led to conclusions that have upset more orthodox psychoanalysts.

The objective scrutiny of recorded analyses, it was argued, would settle the question of contamination, of how much or how little was "suggested" to the patient in the analytic hour. Long before Grünbaum's criticism, several analysts, chiefly, perhaps, the psychoanalytic psychologist David Rapaport's colleagues and students Merton Gill, Lester Luborsky, and Klein's collaborator, Hartwig Dahl, inaugurated analytic research projects using audio and video recordings and transcripts to establish hypotheses about what went on in successful or unsuccessful treatment. Such judgments were usually made by "blind" raters who were presented with portions of the analytic transcript or process notes and who arrived at their conclusions independently of their colleagues and of the treating analyst.

At San Francisco's Mt. Zion Hospital, the psychoanalysts Joseph Weiss and Harold Sampson suggested a new theory of therapy and new techniques for overcoming disagreements over rival psychoanalytic hypotheses. They held that the degree to which the therapist fostered the patient's own unconscious plan of recovery governed the success of treatment. That plan involved testing in relation to the analyst the patient's "pathogenic beliefs." These were usually grounded in early relations with parents and were often "grim"—feelings of anxiety, guilt, shame, remorse. For example, the subject of the research, Mrs. C., a married social worker in her late twenties, came to treatment because she felt driven and unable to enjoy life, and because of sexual problems, primarily an inability to have orgasms during intercourse. She believed that she had deprived her parents and made them envious because she was better off; any assertion of independence would hurt their feelings, especially her father's.

Unconsciously she planned to test these guilt-provoking beliefs in relation to the analyst. She would show him that she was capable, strong, and independent without hurting his feelings or incurring his disapproval. Unconsciously she allowed repressed contents to emerge when she believed it became safe to do so.

Following Hartmann and the ego psychologists, Weiss and Sampson termed these complex unconscious operations the Higher Mental Functioning Hypotheses, as opposed to the Automatic Functioning Hypothesis, that is, the pleasure principle of Freud's early views that Rapaport had elaborated.

The Mt. Zion researchers believed that their findings supported the psychoanalytic theory of repression which Grünbaum had condemned as unscientific. He had argued that evidence for it was elicited by the analyst's suggestive influence. Their refuting evidence was the fact that Mrs. C. became aware of mental contents that the record showed the analyst had not suggested and that independent raters agreed had been repressed at the beginning of her treatment.[22]

The work of Weiss and Sampson was highly significant for a number of reasons. It argued for a more positive view of the patient's capacities. It suggested a systematic way for dealing with rival psychoanalytic hypotheses, for settling disputes when the "doctors disagree."[23] It asserted that some interpretive hypotheses could hinder treatment while others enhanced it, and that it was possible objectively to determine what kinds of interventions these were.

Weiss and Sampson began by predicting the clinical consequences of rival hypotheses and then had blind raters judge the course of therapy. Was the patient more or less anxious and in conflict after a given interpretation or after she had expressed previously repressed material? Those hypotheses that facilitated therapy were presumed to be truer than their alternatives, thus creating a new version of the "tally argument." But precisely at definitions of the clinical course, disagreements arose. The method depended on "predictions" of behavioral change, around which controversy had swirled among psychoanalysts.[24] Whatever the status of prediction, the Weiss-Sampson studies strongly indicated that analysts at least could agree on clinical judgments if these were presented as clearly stated alternative formulations. Hans Strupp, a major researcher in psychotherapeutic processes, argued that in the conception of "pathogenic beliefs," Weiss and Sampson were agreeing on quite different grounds with the therapeutic emphasis of the cognitive psychologists.[25] It also could be argued that this correcting of pathogenic beliefs had the same aim as the "corrective emotional experience" that Franz Alexander had posited as the basis of successful therapy. Other research also confirmed ways to measure the "accuracy and appropriateness of interpretations" and relate these to successful outcome, thus suggesting that specific techniques rather than general factors such as warmth and empathy were crucial.[26]

Although Weiss and Sampson insisted that they were merely adding to psychoanalysis, not taking any of it away, it also seemed possible to apply their ideas without resorting to explanations derived from many of the classical formulae of psychoanalysis, especially drive theory. The possible bypassing of traditional theories of treatment led to charges of the destruction of Freud's legacy by some conservative members of the profession in a ringing restatement of Freudian fundamentalism. One conservative argued that analyst-patient interactions were

more accurately expressed in terms referring to perceptions and activities of the body: touching, looking, smelling, holding, feeding, sucking, biting, shitting, penetrating, stabbing, slicing, mutilating, killing, fucking, etc. It is this order of speech, denoting infantile sexual and aggressive categories of action and experience, that are the common ingredients of interchanges between analyst and patient.

Thus, Weiss and Sampson were accused of ignoring aggressive and sexual drives and imposing a "plan" on the patient. They countered that how the unconscious mind functions is an entirely empirical question. It "cannot be settled by arguments or philosophical discussion, only by observation and research."[27]

One conclusion seems certain. The thrust of this extension of ego psychology was to emphasize the more positive assets and attributes of the patient and of unconscious processes than more traditional and especially earlier Freudian views. In the hands of some analysts such as Leo Rangell, ego psychology reinstated the concept of the "unconscious will" and gave a renewed emphasis to moral choice that had been absent for years from formal psychoanalytic theory, except as the expression of superego pathology. The therapeutic implications of ego psychology represent in part an inadvertent return to Adolf Meyer's emphasis on the patient's assets and positive abilities to cope, now given a new unconscious dimension.

Several other means were devised to test the validity of theoretical hypotheses as well as clinical inferences. Some psychoanalytic researchers were developing objective methods of assessing changes in patients over the course of individual therapy. Lester Luborsky and researchers at the University of Pennsylvania devised the "symptom context method" to discover the precise settings in which episodes of forgetfulness, migraine headache, or stomach pain, for example, occurred during therapy sessions. Independent judges agreed that the same context occurred in each of these symptoms. For stomach pain and migraine headache, feelings of helplessness supplied the immediately preceding context. For momentary forgetfulness, a threatening thought or a new attitude, cognitive difficulties, and guilt preceded the lapse. Both headache and forgetfulness also were preceded by a closer involvement with the therapist.[28]

Luborsky's group argued not only that it reliably discovered consistent factors preceding the onset of types of symptoms but that their method could verify "Freud's grandest clinical hypothesis, the transference." Again, independent judges were able to agree on a central and distinguishing relationship pattern for each patient, termed the Core Conflictual Relationship Theme or CCRT. This key pattern appeared consistently in relationships outside of therapy and also characterized the relationship to the therapist.[29] The CCRT became a crucial element in a new form of brief psychoanalytic psychotherapy, "supportive expressive therapy," based partly on work at the Menninger Foundation and which Luborsky codified in a treatment manual.

Luborsky also insisted that a good therapeutic relationship is more predictive of a successful outcome than the patient's "insight" or "understanding" of his difficulties or the independent qualities of either patient or therapist.[30] And this good relationship depends in considerable measure on shared values and background. Moreover, experienced therapists are more skilled at establishing a good relationship than inexperienced therapists. Some critics have argued that methods such as Luborsky's add nothing to what the clinician already knew, and Grünbaum suggested that Luborsky demonstrated only "consistency of character" and not the validity of the concept of transference.

Freud observed his own children in an attempt to gather evidence for his theories. Systematic observations of children, undertaken by several American psychoanalysts, challenged some cherished psychoanalytic assumptions, notably theories of the inevitable effects of early trauma. Central to David Rapaport's model of psychoanalysis as a systematic psychology was a view of the infant at the breast as the exemplar of drive and discharge, hunger and satiation. Psychoanalytic studies of actual infants vastly complicated that model. They attempted to lay the foundation for a view of childhood rooted less in theory and in reconstructions from the therapy of adults than in actual observation. In their work, Rapaport's emphasis on drives has given way to an emphasis on early relationships.

For instance, the mother's direct influence in the "pre-Oedipal" years played a critical role in the child's development, a role Freud ignored until quite late, but one that Melanie Klein early had regarded as decisive.[31] In the analysis of adults there was a growing emphasis on recapturing the texture of this early relationship.

The psychoanalytic researchers Margaret Mahler and Daniel Stern presented two contrasting versions of infancy, which nevertheless shared common ground in their reliance on direct observation and in some of their conclusions. They substantially enlarged the role of innate ego functions. Following Hartmann's general position, Mahler argued that the infant is endowed "with a striking capacity for adaptation to his environment."[32] And for Stern this endowment included the sense of an independent self from birth, with complex capacities for reality testing.

Mahler conducted her research in a special nursery equipped with a one-way mirror, where mother and infant could be observed in a naturalistic setting. She cross-checked the same half-hour segments of behavior described by participant observers aware of her theories with the observations of non-participant observers unacquainted with them. Conclusions were reached by "multiple, repeated, consensually validated observations and inferences." These were backed up by films and, at first, by psychological checklists, which later were found not to correlate well with the rapid shifts observed in actual behavior. She hoped to "strike an appropriate balance between free-flowing psychoanalytic observation and pre-fixed experimental design."[33] For Stern research involved not only ingenious original work on the mother-infant dyad but a whole new corpus of infancy studies, chiefly by non-psychoanalysts.

Both Mahler and Stern attempted to reconstruct the subjective experience of the infant during the preverbal period by inferences from observation. They argued for this approach against traditional analysts, who insisted that data should be backed by verbal memory and symptom change in therapy, and against developmentalists, who eschewed subjective data as irrelevant and unscientific. But subjective data, Mahler and Stern insisted, was the unique realm of psychoanalytic research.

Mahler's reconstructions were far closer to traditional psychoanalytic models than Stern's, but her insistence on direct observation of children marked an important departure, which a few other analysts also had attempted. She believed she had been sensitized to critical issues of the mother-child relationship because she remembered her own mother as cold and rejecting, preferring her younger sister. Born in Hungary in 1895, Mahler, a brilliant student, was trained as a pediatrician, studied at the Vienna Psychoanalytic Institute in the 1920s, and became the lover of her analyst, August Aichorn, a pioneer of the child guidance movement. She completed her training and attended the child analysis seminar of Anna Freud, whom she disliked. After emigrating to the United States in 1938, she became a friend of Benjamin Spock, America's most famous popularizer of Freudian child care. She had been introduced to Spock by Caroline Zachry, head of the bureau of child guidance of the New York City Board of Education and a close friend of Lawrence Kubie's. Spock had been analyzed for a year by Bertram Lewin and later by Sandor Rado, and sent Mahler her first American patient for child analysis.[34]

Like some other immigrants, Mahler at first met with an ambivalent reception from the New York Psychoanalytic Society. Kubie suggested she move to Elizabeth, New Jersey, where her husband worked, which she refused to do, settling finally on Central Park West, a favorite New York location for European analysts. In 1940 Kubie asked her to take over David Levy's seminar on child analysis at the New York institute at the height of Levy's involvement in the dispute over Karen Horney. Having obtained her New York medical license, she presumably was both acceptably medical and acceptably orthodox. This orthodoxy was reflected in her views of the very first months of life, which closely followed the models laid down by Freud and Sandor Ferenczi.[35]

Mahler believed her researches disclosed nothing less than the slowly unfolding "psychological birth of the human infant" from the initial, primitive narcissistic symbiosis with the mother that Ferenczi had posited. This psychological birth, which she termed separation-individuation, partly determined mental health throughout the life cycle.

Mahler's most intensive research started at the fourth or fifth month when the long process of psychological birth began, activated by a powerful innate drive toward "individuation."[36] In the first of four subphases, the differentiation of the child from the mother began. Then, children who developed "basic trust" were dominated by "curiosity and wonderment" and did not become excessively anxious around strangers. In a second phase, from 12 to 18 months, the child learned confidence and joy in his own functioning, exploring the physical environment in a peak of benevolent narcissism.

A third and crucial "rapprochement" subphase around the middle of the second year reflected her richest empirical data. Then the child needed the mother's love yet insisted on his or her own autonomy. The mother needed to be available emotionally yet gently encourage her child to be on his or her own. The child learned to give up delusions of grandeur and to realize that mother could be cross and still be good. At 21 months, the child found his optimal distance from the mother, learned to speak, and to use play for mastery; the child internalized rules, identifying with good, providing parents. In the fourth subphase, around age 3, the child achieved his "lifelong individuality" and the beginning of gender identity. Optimally, he learned give and take in relationships and to master ambivalence, not to reject a loved person because that person no longer provided satisfaction. To attain this "object constancy" the child needed to internalize a consistent emotionally positive "inner image of the mother" built on the trust and confidence that his needs were being met as early as the symbiotic phase. This relative object constancy and the attainment of self-esteem determined the child's mental health in the years before the Oedipus complex.[37]

In each subphase, the mother's behavior, including her unconscious fantasies about her child, played a crucial role, along with accidental events and the child's innate endowment. For instance, a mother's ambivalence toward her child, her intrusiveness, or her "smothering" could make initial differentiation more difficult. Her unresponsiveness during the rapprochement phase could lead to the child's desperate attempts to woo her and to be overconcerned with her whereabouts, leaving him or her insufficient energy and constructive aggression for developing ego functions.[38] Moreover, even where development seemed to be proceeding smoothly, events such as the child's illness or the absence of a parent could create apparently temporary quasi-neurotic difficulties.

Mahler preserved the traditional psychoanalytic framework of stages of psychosexual development, including the Oedipus complex and penis envy. She shared the general psychoanalytic belief that later pathology was rooted in early events and that neurotic outcomes could be prevented by early intervention. Prevention, she believed, could provide an answer "to major problems of our time," and perhaps partly because of this promise, the National Institute of Mental Health funded her work.[39]

At the same time, partly in cautious footnotes, she distanced herself from certain psychoanalytic assumptions. She noted that psychoanalytic investigators were "haunted" by the possibility of finding factors that could predict later development. The child's innate and "near-biological" endowment remained relatively unchanged. But other characteristics resulting from interactions with the "object world" such as "early identifications" and "defensive patterns" were "extraordinarily variable" and could shift massively at "crossroads of development."[40]

Mahler's research with normal mothers and infants modified assumptions about the consequences of early trauma in the first 15 months of life. Only severe, ongoing, and cumulative trauma were likely to result in a "proclivity to later, severe personality difficulties." Such was the case in only two or three of her sample of 38 children.[41] In her rejection of automatic predictability, in her use of disciplined group observation, her emphasis on unexpected and massive shifts in development, she broke with some of the traditional determinism of psychoanalysis that probably reflected habitual postdiction.

A psychoanalyst and professor of psychiatry at Cornell University Medical Center, Daniel N. Stern's most distinctive contribution to the theory of infant development, published in the 1980s, was his insistence that from birth we process our experiences in such a way that they "appear to belong to some kind of unique subjective organization we commonly call the sense of self":

> Even though the nature of self may forever elude the behavioral sciences, the sense of self stands as an important subjective reality, a reliable, evident phenomenon that the sciences cannot dismiss. How we experience ourselves in relation to others provides a basic organizing perspective for all interpersonal events.[42]

Some senses of the self were "essential to daily social interactions." These included agency, physical cohesion, continuity, affectivity, empathy with another person, the sense of creating organization, and transmitting meaning. If these were "severely impaired," normal social functioning would be disrupted and likely "lead to madness and great social deficit."[43]

Stern's archetypal infant possessed a complex, multifaceted, and emergent sense of self from the very beginning. This infant, "predesigned to be aware of self-organizing processes," was never symbiotically merged with the mother or confused between "self and other in the beginning or at any point during infancy," as Mahler had argued. Stern's infant developed a core self, a subjective self, and, after 15 months, a verbal self, and these co-existed throughout life, often outside awareness.[44]

Like Mahler, Stern expanded the infant's innate ego capacities. For instance, instead of assuming, as had Freud, that the pleasure principle preceded the reality principal, Stern argued that from the beginning the infant's ability to "deal with reality" was equal to his ability to deal with pleasure. Infants "have surprised us with their rich repertoire of immediately available or emergent mental functions": memory, perception, the capacity to translate perceptions experienced in one mode into another, such as things felt into things seen. For example, infants could "recognize by sight a distinctive nipple they had just sucked blindfolded."[45]

Stern rejected major psychoanalytic assumptions including stage theories derived originally from psychosexual development, in which particular issues such as orality, attachment, "autonomy, independence, and trust" predominated. These, he argued, were issues for the entire "lifespan." Even more important, he insisted that neurosis did not begin at "any one specific point or phase of origin in developmental time" and that there were no "relatively irreversible fixations." Rather, neurosis could begin at any point along the continuous developmental line of a clinical issue.

Psychoanalytic descriptions of earliest infancy, such as "delusions of merger or fusion, splitting, and defensive or paranoid fantasies," were really appropriate only to the period after language developed. These misapplications occurred because psychoanalysts had been too "pathomorphic" and too "adultomorphic"—that is, they had projected back into infancy observations about pathology more appropriate to adults and older children and inappropriately had attempted to find causes for this pathology in early experience.[46]

Stern stressed the mother's influence on behavior by what he called her mode of "selective attunement," that is, her mode of conveying which experiences were acceptable or unacceptable. This included which people to prefer, and the "degrees or types of emotional states" such as joy, sadness, or delight. Attunement, as well as verbalization, could create a "false self," that is, the "disavowal or repression" of parts of one's own subjective experience.[47]

At the same time, Stern also argued that the infant's genetic endowment was crucial, including temperament and tolerance for different kinds of stimulation. Individual biology dictated the limits of socialization. Parents could not bend the infant out of shape so he became "totally the creation of others' wishes and plans."

Many of Stern's hypotheses involved extrapolations about the inner states of infants from the rich data of recent observational studies. The question was whether the new infancy studies in fact supported Stern's arguments. Louise Kaplan, a student of Mahler's, insisted that the new data actually supported traditional psychoanalytic hypotheses.[48] Stern's emphasis on the self, his rejection of libido theory as a useless organizing principle for the earliest years of human development, his suggestion of a disavowed self, and his insistence that the personality is formed by interaction with early caretakers brought him closer to the interpersonal psychiatrists on the one hand and the new psychoanalytic self psychologists, such as Heinz Kohut, on the other.

The concern with self psychology of the last twenty years resulted partly from the conceptual criticism of metapsychology and partly from the views of integrative functions and non-conflictual spheres of the ego psychologists. Kohut's formal self psychology also represented dissatisfaction with the presumed therapeutic inefficacy of classical psychoanalysis. Gradually his views came to dominate the Chicago Psychoanalytic Institute and were taken up extensively by psychohistorians. There were other important influences on self psychology, among them Harry Stack Sullivan.

Sullivan rejected the reification of classical psychoanalysis—he found the superego, for instance, an indigestible, unscientific abstraction. For the "structures" of psychoanalysis he substituted "dynamisms," a term close to Rapaport's vision of a structure as a slowly changing psychological function. He placed anxiety at the core of his mature system, but here we will deal only with his views of the self. These represented a perpetuation of the war of the individual against society, of freedom and need against stricture and convention, that characterized the psychoanalytic stance of the 1920s. For Sullivan, the child's personality, particularly his crucial and determining experience of anxiety, was molded by the mother. She transmitted her anxieties to her child, based in part on what she believed to be socially desirable behavior. Gradually the child developed a "self system," consisting of good me, bad me, and not me, as the parent channeled behavior by tenderness or anxiety. In Sullivan's view the self system was primarily defensive and interfered, often unnecessarily, with the satisfaction of "needs."[49]

Heinz Kohut's self system derived from a different impetus. It represented a return to a psychoanalysis without causes, to the hermeneutics that Heinz Hartmann had repudiated. At the same time, Sullivan's and Freud's opposition between individual and society seemed to disappear in Kohut's theories, replaced by a sociological explanation for the emergence of a new social type, "tragic man," as opposed to the "guilty man, enmeshed in Oedipal struggles" of classical psychoanalysis. For Kohut, tragic man was the increasingly ubiquitous man with a self fundamentally flawed because of unempathic or pathological parents, in particular, the mother. In contrast to guilty man, the product of an over-heated, over-stimulated environment of family and servants, tragic man's early care givers are distant, indifferent, unable to reflect or respond to his needs; his family is small, his parents often absent. Or else, because of the small family and frequent changes of servants, the child is exposed without "effective relief" to the "pathogenic influence of a parent suffering from self pathology."[50] The distempers of the flawed self of tragic man are the narcissistic disorders of inadequate self-esteem or defensive overcompensation for it.

While traditional psychoanalysis might be effective as therapy and explanation for the neuroses of guilty man, self psychology was essential for the understanding and treatment of tragic man. And Kohut cited case after case in which dutiful, competent, traditional psychoanalysts had failed after years of treatment with patients his own system later had helped. Theory was important, Kohut insisted, because it influenced psychoanalytic practice, and he noted, for example, that Rank's theory of birth trauma had led to "single minded therapeutic preoccupation with separation anxiety."[51] Tragic man required an empathic analyst, who could become a therapeutic "self-object" for the patient, nurture his fractured self, help him discover his areas of competence, his goals and ideals, and thus his self-esteem.

Like Sullivan's theory, Kohut's was primarily environmentalist; not inner needs or drives, but interpersonal relations were determining:

> In the great majority of cases, it is the specific pathogenic personality of the parent(s) and the specific pathogenic atmosphere in which the child grows up that account for the maldevelopments, fixations, and unsolvable inner conflicts characterizing the adult personality.[52]

Like Stern, Kohut assumed the probable existence of a self from infancy and denied a period of symbiotic merger. The child's self was formed by relationships with what he called self-objects. In a sense the self-object is a human model with which the child and later the adult empathizes and identifies. Self-objects "serve functions which will later be performed by the individual's own psychic structure."[53] The child's first self-objects usually are his parents with their more highly developed psychic organization. The child experiences their feeling states as they transmit them by tone of voice and other ways "as if they were his own."[54] If parents empathize with the child's growing abilities, he will develop a healthy self-esteem. If he can merge with an idealized parent figure, he will develop viable goals and ideals. Kohut believed self-objects were necessary throughout life. "We need mirroring acceptance, the merger with ideals, the sustaining presence of others like us, throughout out lives. . . . "[55]

Like Fromm-Reichmann, Kohut regarded fixations on the drives or on Oedipal relationships as the product of pathology, of failure to establish a viable self. For example, not the oral drive but "how food giving is experienced" is crucial. If it were not empathic, the "joyful experience of being a whole, appropriately responded to self" disintegrated and the child retreated to a fragmented position, for instance, to "depressive eating."[56]

Although Kohut argued that aggression was a part of human nature, "rage and destructiveness" were not primary, original sins "requiring expiation," as Melanie Klein had assumed. Rather they were but a "fragment created by the breakup of a more comprehensive configuration." Moreover, the hostility patients displayed in transference was often a product of the analyst's interpretations that patients experienced as failures of empathy; it represented as well revivals of "reactions to empathy failures from self-objects in childhood."[57]

Kohut argued that psychoanalysis was not a science of "causes." Rather, psychoanalysis was a science of the "empathic-introspective immersion of the observer into the inner life of man."[58] It employed both empathy, defined as "vicarious introspection," and theorizing with scientific rigor to fit its data "into a context of broader meaning and significance." Kohut also believed that introspective data might someday be quantified.

Kohut's self psychology was essentially object relations theory in the sense that the self is formed by relations with others, notably the parents in the earliest years. And these relations are mediated not only by the actual behavior of parents and others, but also, and possibly more important, by how such persons and their behavior were perceived and experienced subjectively by the child, with its native endowment and temperament. These subjective perceptions of others became the child's "internal objects."

There was yet another strand that Kohut exemplified in his insistence on psychoanalysis as a search for meaning. One consequence of the repudiation of ego psychology and of Grünbaum's attacks on the scientific status of clinical observation was a revival of precisely the view that Hartmann had deplored, notably the phenomenological insistence that psychoanalysis dealt primarily with subjective experience, formulated as the patient's "narrative."

This represented a powerful European current, the hermeneutic bent, deriving from the German philosopher Wilhelm Dilthey via Jürgen Habermas and Paul Ricoeur. Ricoeur, for instance, argued that psychoanalysis, on the basis of the criticism at the New York University symposium in 1958, could not be a "scientific" enterprise in any positivist or behaviorist sense. Because its data derived from the linguistic dialogue between analyst and patient, it was a discipline of interpretation like history. At the same time Ricoeur was unwilling to reduce it to a hermeneutic exercise. It was not concerned with the construction of meanings that simply pleased patient and therapist. Rather, its status lay somewhere between traditional science and hermeneutics.

One recent American version of the hermeneutic strand interpreted the psychoanalytic encounter as the mutual construction of satisfying narratives, on the presumption that a narrative is a "deep structure" independent of medium. Donald Spence, a psychoanalytic psychologist, argued in 1983 that the narrative is always different from the order of events in "real life." The analyst does not, as Freud assumed, translate the patient's associations into underlying unconscious thoughts, but rather like an artist "is always choosing what to use of the patient's productions . . . and the language in which they should be expressed."[59] Historical truth could not and need not be sought for in psychoanalysis. For every narrative selected others could be found. Partly for this reason, Spence has argued that different forms of psychotherapy—Jungian, Freudian, Kleinian—might each "have a claim on the truth."

"As we jettison what remains of our metapsychology," Spence wrote, "we find ourselves seeing the clinical theory for what it is—and we start looking at the underlying evidence. Not very reassuring. In a very basic way, clinical theory rests on an archive of badly collected and mistakenly reported anecdotes that can never be checked because they were never written down. Thus our clinical archive is partly fictitious—it exists as a private narrative in the minds of all analysts." While undercutting the "objective" nature of clinical reconstruction, Spence at the same time insisted on systematic sampling, on collecting data from a large number of cases, and for making this accessible to outside investigators. Psychoanalysts needed to accumulate "honest archives, that are complete, cross-indexed and therefore generally usable . . . to build our theory on a range of cases rather than just one. . . ."[60] Thus he combined his argument for the subjective nature of the clinical encounter with a very American plea for a more rigorously "scientific" sampling of data.

Since the New York University symposium of 1958 in which a phalanx of Anglo-American positivist philosophers of science had denounced the analysts as "unscientific," American attitudes toward science changed. Some philosophers insisted that no single pattern characterized the scientific enterprise, that it was entirely individual and in a sense "lawless," without preconceived formulae. Perhaps, however, the most influential departure from the positivist stance was Thomas Kuhn's argument that what was "scientific" was decided by what any given community of scientists says it is; the nature of science was defined by the consensus of its practitioners. Changes in science occurred in sudden, culminating leaps. During a long period, the predominant model's inadequacies, contradictions, and problems were revealed. Unresolved difficulties proliferated. A period of crisis ensued. Then a new paradigm was devised that resolved these difficulties, and a new overarching consensus was reached. Then, puzzle-solving resumed in a scientific community on the basis of the new model which resolved the riddles of the older paradigm and carried out the implications of the new, in what Kuhn termed the "mopping up" operations of "normal science." Kuhn himself, however, piqued by the vague and expansive use of his terminology of "crisis" and "paradigm change" by everyone from scientists to historians and literary critics, revised his theory, discarding the notion of paradigm. He pointed rather to a "disciplinary matrix" and to "exemplars" which set the stage for the new solution of problems.[61]

Many psychoanalysts took comfort from Kuhn's first thesis, arguing that, like physicists, they represented a scientific community with their own standards of discipline and performance. They insisted that Freud devised one of the great changes of paradigm in the history of psychiatry. But precisely how differences of opinion among the various schools of psychoanalysis might be resolved was not an issue usually addressed in Kuhnian terms. Kuhn regarded disciplines such as psychoanalysis and psychology as pre-paradigmatic and thus pre-scientific in his earlier theory.[62]

A pervasive sense of crisis within the psychoanalytic profession has been characteristic of the last few years and began at the end of the 1960s.[63] Several institutes have had budget crises as the training fees declined with the number of students. The profession itself has been rapidly changing with the recent acceptance of non-medical candidates for institute training to practice psychoanalysis, a departure resulting in part from lawsuits brought by psychologists against the American Psychoanalytic Association. Some have perceived this acceptance of non-medical psychoanalysts as threatening the relationship of psychoanalysis to psychiatry.[64] Nationally four times more women than men and more non-medical than medical applicants have asked for training; the number of non-medical applicants has helped to stem the decline in the total number of students. Ultimately this trend could change the gender and background of the profession, bringing it closer to the European pattern and sharply restricting its identification with medicine.[65]

Divided into three major schools—traditional ego psychology, self psychology, and object relations theory (disregarding a large number of other viewpoints, humanistic and existential as well as Jungian and Alderian)—"mainstream" American Freudians have had to cope with a framework that has fractured severely since the waning of the dominance of ego psychology. Some have welcomed the divided vision as proof of energetic progress and have assumed that each view must contain some aspect of reality and can be clinically applied.[66] Perhaps the most comprehensive version of syncretism has come from the interpersonal psychiatrists of the William Alanson White Institute. On the basis of a broad definition of object relations, they have attempted to find common ground among theorists as different as Melanie Klein, Heinz Kohut, Harry Stack Sullivan, Heinz Hartmann, Otto Kernberg, and the British theorists H. Guntrip and D. W. Winnicott.[67]

Others have advanced a Freudian fundamentalism, much like the reaction to the Sampson-Weiss research, insisting on the validity of free association, which Lawrence Kubie once thought of as one of the most problematic and least researched aspects of psychoanalysis. They insist further on the critical role of sexuality, aggression, and childhood instinctual conflict in the creation of pathology. Self psychologists have watered down the hard truths of psychoanalysis. "One hears little, if anything, of internal intrapsychic conflicts, of anxiety, guilt, peremptory sexual impulses, unconscious struggles over latent preoedipal urges, aggression, forbidden perversions, fear of punishment, castration anxiety," Leo Rangell has argued.[68] This insistence on the importance of conflict and impulse is paired with an insistence on the scientific legitimacy of the clinical enterprise and the single case study. The domain of psychoanalysis is the subjective, the Yale psychoanalyst Marshall Edelson insisted in 1988; psychoanalysis is not suited to the study of actual events. Rather it is a science of the symbolic representation of "inner reality," of the "symbolizing activity of the mind." It is not parental behavior or childhood traumas or "disturbed object relations or traumatic events" that determine neurosis. Rather, it is the "complemental series," what the child does with these events in "constructing, responding to, revising or disposing of sexual wish-fulfillments," that determines the outcome.[69]

Most analysts would agree that their theories influence practice and technique. The proliferation of disparate theories and observations, some analysts have insisted, results from different analytic techniques, and therefore technique should be standardized. "It should be possible to decide on the degree of similarity and difference [in technique] and to evaluate how the differences that emerge may affect the data of observation and the theoretical conclusions that can be drawn from them."[70] But if Edward Glover's early study of British experience is any precedent, the actual practice of psychoanalysts, despite the appearance of uniformity in organization and training, is in fact highly diverse and individualistic.

Some ego psychologists linked their version of technique with a therapy that exacts "hard work" on the part of the patient, and scorned the gratifications received from the analyst, such as Kohut's nurturing. Leo Rangell observed:

> I still have patients who pursue with the analyst the intellectual journey toward insight, and reparation by that route, the path beyond the transference to the historical as well as the narrative, i.e., their personally distorted truths. These patients experience a liberation of energy, from the lifting and solving of unconscious conflicts, the "old fashioned way: they earn it!" With this comes a new freedom of having "choices," where this was not present before.[71]

What was perhaps most striking among some Freudians was the distancing from Freud. Jacob Arlow and Charles Brenner, pillars of ego psychology, for example, argued that psychoanalytic institutes are mired in a superannuated curriculum that stresses too much Freud's writings and the reworking of his case histories. They accepted the criticism of historians who argued that Freud created a myth of himself as a "lonely, isolated figure striving against overwhelming odds," thus fostering "an atmosphere in which heresy and orthodoxy flourished."[72]

A sense of modesty about the applications of psychoanalysis and a lively sense of its unresolved problems became more pervasive in the 1980s. First, attempts to make psychoanalysis a "general psychology" in the sense of Hartmann and Rapaport, that is, of aiming for a psychoanalytic "normal psychology," have diminished, although Mahler and Stern have provided perhaps the most important recent examples. Second, the applications of psychoanalysis have narrowed. Psychoanalytic psychotherapy is no longer much used directly as a technique for the psychoses, and psychoanalysis has been less frequently used to treat the compulsion neuroses, which Freud regarded as one of its preeminent domains. However, it is increasingly applied to a wide variety of character disorders, and has become increasingly refined and effective.[73]

The aims of therapy are narrower than in the expansive 1950s. Analysts no longer speak of cure or the elimination of conflict as they might have in the early years after World War II, or of resolving transferences, or even of completing analyses. Instead they speak of "changes, shifts, or compromise formations," a more favorable resolution of central conflicts, of understanding rather than "overcoming" resistances.[74] The retrieval of "old memories per se" is no longer a "principal goal." The "mirror analyst" has been downplayed in favor of an emphasis on both the "real relationship" of therapist and patient and a new examination of the therapist's own emotional relation with his patient, the "counter transference." Dreams are no longer, as they were for Freud, the "royal road to the unconscious." They are regarded as compromise formations like any other, and the analysis of transference and resistance, of character traits, and fantasies are as important as the analysis of dreams.[75]

Yet psychoanalysis remains the most carefully elaborated of the medical psychologies, and several departments of psychiatry of the top ten medical schools retain psychoanalysts as chairmen. A long succession of psychoanalysts have been elected presidents of the American Psychiatric Association. Moreover, more candidates are being trained and more patients treated than ever before, although the rate of growth has slowed.[76] Outside the United States, where positivist views of science hold less sway, psychoanalysis flourishes luxuriantly, especially in Europe and Latin America.

The current crisis of American psychoanalysis is in part the product of too great, too embarrassing a success. Psychoanalysis fostered the growth of psychotherapies which then proliferated independently into a variety of theoretical and practical systems.

What will remain of the resonance of psychoanalysis if its vocabulary is striped of its evolutionary biological language as well as its mythical beasts of instinctual energy, all the luxuriant attributes that have made it attractive to the literary "friends and supporters of psychotherapy"? Will translations into "ordinary language" have the impact of the death instinct, the id, the ego, the superego, and all the Freudian dramatis personae? Is ordinary language closer to the experience of the irrational and the compulsive than the poetic terminology of traditional psychoanalysis?

Finally, are the American modifications, even the mainstream orthodox ones, still Freud's psychoanalysis? Freud's own definitions of what constituted the bedrock of his science varied, but not greatly. The key concepts remained repression and resistance, the importance of sexuality and of the Oedipus complex, and transference. Freud regarded his science as an unfinished, but unified structure, "from which elements cannot be broken off at the caprice of whoever comes along."[77] In continuing to emphasize these three elements, orthodox American psychoanalysis has remained a highly conservative ideology and discipline. Perhaps the major exception has been modification of the central importance of the Oedipus complex and an emphasis on pre-Oedipal relations, along with a more positive view of the functions of the self.

Psychoanalytic orthodoxy was achieved after the early American reception of psychoanalysis had tamed much of Freud's theory, making it more optimistic, more moralistic. Then, the refugee analysts and their Americans disciples created a new, more stringent orthodoxy that was closer to Freud's views and indeed was often more rigidly Freudian than Freud had ever been. Ego psychology, the joint product of his European and American disciples, has been seen as a logical extension of Freud's thought, or by the Lacanians as an Anglo-American heresy that inculcated social conformity.

Despite a core conservatism, there have been profound modifications of psychoanalysis, and some of these resemble the first American interpretations. The emphasis on object relations and on the baleful effects of defective mothering may reflect American environmentalism, a significant departure from Freud's own emphasis on the innate impulses of the child. For much of its history, especially from the 1940s to the 1960s, American psychoanalysis held out far more therapeutic optimism than had Freud, although he had made his own quite optimistic pronouncements chiefly in the years before 1930. And there are signs of a renewed concern for moral values, for the conscience and the unconscious will in some recent ego psychologists. This is not the simple moralism of the period before World War I, but it is far removed from the almost entirely negative view of the superego entertained in the 1920s and from Lacan's distrust of the ego itself. Many of the empirical studies, of both infants and therapy, and many of the departures stemming from ego psychology, in stressing the innate capacities of the self, have suggested a more optimistic view of human nature than Freud's.

Thus, among mainstream American psychoanalysts, although the core of Freud's psychoanalysis remains intact, the emphases have shifted. In the downgrading of the interpretation of dreams, in the translation of the metapsychology into "ordinary language," and in the emphasis on the mother and on pre-Oedipal experience, Freud might no longer recognize the discipline as he had formed and practiced it.

Conclusion

What accounts for the extraordinary rise and pervasiveness of psychoanalysis in American culture? One obvious explanation is provided by the intrinsic qualities of Freud's system. No rival psychology has approached its sweep and dramatic interest, not gestalt psychology, not humanistic psychology, and not behaviorism in its many guises, despite the appeal of B. F. Skinner's operant conditioning with its engineered utopia. The boldness of the analytic vision, the intimacy and immediacy of its concerns—sex, family relationships, dreams, mistakes, hatred and love, lust and murder, even boredom—remain unparalleled except, as Freud well knew, in great literature. The literary qualities of psychoanalysis guaranteed its appeal to intellectuals. Its concerns could be discovered through the unique relationship of listener to client, freed to say whatever came to mind. It was possible to construct from applications of the analytic technique a systematic theory about all these untidy subjects. They are the stuff of what the British social anthropologist Ernest Gellner has described as the primary social mission of psychoanalysis, "pastoral care," the cure of souls under the aegis of science. But more is involved than either the subject matter of psychoanalysis or its role as a therapy. Freud's ambiguity about the application of his theories, his changing and sometimes contradictory views of sexuality and aggression, made it possible to deduce from psychoanalysis the orgastic flights of Wilhelm Reich or the ego psychology of Freud's daughter Anna, to reconcile psychoanalysis with Marxism or American liberal capitalism or European social democracy. Psychoanalysis could be seen in its early guise as an optimistic movement of sexual and cultural reform or, from the perspective of Freud's final papers, as a stoical and tragic vision of unending conflict. It could appeal to American optimism or to the lingering sense of tragedy tinctured with hope associated with elements of Judaism or survivals of Calvinism.

The intrinsic appeal of psychoanalysis underlies its development as a profession and as a cultural influence.[1] Psychoanalysis was transformed in the years from 1917 to 1940, from the calling of a self-chosen group of avant-garde psychiatrists and neurologists to a profession with its own institutions for training and certification, separate from medicine and psychiatry, yet with close ties to both. The American insistence on medical training came in part from the wish to attain the scientific authority associated with the medical profession, the prestige of which was rising in the years after World War I. Medicalization also can be seen as an attempt to foster a monopoly of practice by preventing the growth of self-appointed lay practitioners.

In the 1920s and 1930s an optimistic and highly diluted psychoanalysis was applied to mental hygiene, criminology, and education, where it tended to encourage more permissive approaches and at the same time enlarged the influence of new mental health professionals, social workers, guidance counselors, and, above all, psychiatrists. A core of "friends and supporters of psychotherapy," first recruited before World War I, expanded during the 1920s. Many of them were writers and journalists, and they were among the most active popularizers and proselytes for Freud's theories. Psychoanalysis also became part of a popular American *Kulturkampf* of cities against the hinterlands, of the new literature against the old, of the religion of science against outmoded tradition, of the modern attack on Victorianism against received standards of sexual behavior.

The formalization of training in psychoanalytic institutes was largely the creation of a new generation of recruits, some of them from well-to-do families and Ivy League medical schools, who had undergone systematic training in Europe or America. With the new institutes, and particularly with the influx of refugee analysts, came a hardening of Freudian orthodoxy, which replaced the loose eclecticism of some of the first Americans and led, as a counterweight, to the formation of formal neo-Freudian schools.

By the end of the 1930s psychoanalysis had won a minor place among the younger generation of neurologists and psychiatrists, and the development of psychosomatic medicine further strengthened the medical image of psychoanalysis. Psychoanalysis had a cadre of well-trained physicians, new educational institutions, and an increasingly systematized theory and therapy.

Partly because of the results of this successful professionalization, during the Second World War psychoanalysts often came to be in charge of psychiatric services in the military and demonstrated to a new generation of young physicians the apparent utility of Freud's theories in the treatment of the war neuroses. Although recovery often resulted from simple removal from combat, psychotherapy often took the credit. Army manuals and classification systems incorporated aspects of the psychoanalytic message often without identifying it.

In the years immediately after World War II, in the glow of wartime successes, and building on the utopianism of the mental hygiene movements of the 1920s, psychoanalysis furnished a major model of therapy and fostered one impetus for the reform of public hospital psychiatry. Psychoanalysis enjoyed an enormous, new, optimistic vogue, vastly expanding its therapeutic domain and its influence in medical schools and in the newly founded National Institute of Mental Health. Psychoanalysis seemed to promise in its psychological therapy a fundamental treatment for the neuroses and a promising approach and possibly a new psychotherapy for the psychoses and for psychosomatic illness.

After World War II, popularization reached an unprecedented peak in novels, films, and the press. Freud was lionized as the hero of modern liberalism, the founder of "modern" views of psychology, psychiatry, child raising, education, and sexuality. Surprising numbers of analysands, particularly writers, journalists, and movie stars described the successful psychoanalytic resolution of their personal tribulations. At the same time American and European refugee psychoanalysts developed an "ego psychology" that placed a new emphasis on internal controls over both sexuality and aggression and that attempted to make psychoanalysis a more systematic general psychology. This coincided with a time of increasing cultural and political conservatism. While some psychoanalysts were modifying psychoanalysis in the development of psychoanalytic psychotherapy, others were insisting on a "pure" psychoanalysis, more technically rigorous than Freud's own practice.

The optimistic promise and the sometimes incautious claims of psychoanalysis in the 1950s provoked a reaction. Rejecting the psychological emphasis of the psychoanalysts, a neo-somatic movement developed in psychiatry, even more optimistic than the American psychoanalysts. Alternative psychological therapies, most important, behaviorism, emerged, as well as a proliferating series of popular treatments, often an eclectic mix of psychoanalytic and other methods. The ministration of psychoanalytic psychotherapy escaped from the control of medical psychoanalysts, and in often diluted form was plied by new therapist recruits with highly varied training— psychologists, social workers, counselors, and guidance workers. In this sense psychoanalysis was partly undone by its own success. It became identified with the psychiatric establishment, with treatment for the well-to-do and with stereotypical norms of male and female. As psychoanalyses lengthened from one or two to five, eight, ten or more years, psychoanalysts themselves began to question the efficacy of psychoanalysis as a technique, and more of them began to practice psychoanalytic psychotherapy and to include drugs in their treatment. Growing criticism of psychoanalysis and a neo-somatic movement combined to create a decline of psychoanalytic influence in psychiatry. This was accompanied by reassessments of Freud as an historical figure, with attacks on his personal life and scientific integrity.

Perhaps to speak of a generalized "decline" of psychoanalysis in America may be mistaken, because, as Freud once observed, psychoanalysis is a "hydra" capable of sprouting new heads, for example, its alliance with some schools of literary and aesthetic criticism. But "decline" within psychiatry seems a relatively accurate description for a number of reasons. One of the unintended consequences of the American medicalization of psychoanalysis was that it became subject to the changing medical interpretations of what was both scientific and pragmatically effective. A major change in medical definitions of the scientific has been the eclipse of the single case method reported by a single observer, the very basis of psychoanalysis. It may generate hypotheses but scientific confirmation in medicine new seems to rest on controlled and, optimally, double-blind studies. But control groups of untreated patients for a process as lengthy as psychoanalysis probably are impossible. Moreover, controlled studies may be more appropriate to drugs or very specific procedures than they are to many of the highly complex, highly individual problems patients bring to psychotherapy.

As damaging as the changing definitions of what is "scientifically proven" has been the increase in the symptoms or disorders that can be treated by somatic means. Psychoanalysis began with the failures of the somatic style of the late 19th century in which Freud was trained, failures of conceptualization and therapeutic methods. Some of the first symptoms treated by the new "talking cure" were somatic—hysterical paralyses, for instance. These were followed by application to more strictly psychological symptoms, such as obsessions, compulsions, and phobias. For the next 40 years, psychoanalysts expanded the somatic and psychological symptoms they believed they could treat, if not by psychoanalysis, then by psychoanalytic psychotherapy. Beginning in the 1920s the range of treatable conditions was notably enlarged by including defects of character—patterns of self-defeating behavior, such as choosing a rejecting love object or the persistent courting of failure, and varieties of criminality and delinquency.

Between the two world wars, psychoanalysts applied their methods to chronic somatic illnesses for which adequate explanations and treatments were not then available—asthma, hypertension, peptic ulcers, and ulcerative colitis, for instance. The hope was that these illnesses would yield to psychotherapeutic treatment based on psychoanalytic observations and explanations of their origin. But here the psychoanalytic model relying on the reporting physician's account was rejected partly because of the claims and demands of medical specialists and academic psychologists for controlled observations. Most important, effective somatic interventions increasingly were applied to the psychosomatic diseases, rendering psychoanalytic approaches less relevant. However, as Morton Reiser has argued, a whole series of psychoanalytic observations about the course of these illnesses, their relation to the patient's life, and sometimes their effective treatment by psychotherapy remains unexplained. The very connections between mind and body may be more subtle, more intimately interactive than conventional medicine would allow.[2] Somatic breakthroughs also occurred in the control of symptoms in the psychoses, notably depression and elation, and to a lesser extent in the treatment of schizophrenia. The causes of these disorders remain largely unknown, although genetic disposition seems increasingly relevant as one factor. For both the traditional psychosomatic disorders and for symptoms of the psychoses, drugs have become more effective, thus narrowing the problems for which psychoanalysis seems appropriate.[3]

On the other hand, irreducible and expanding psychological and emotional problems persist for which psychotherapy and psychoanalysis may be more appropriate than somatic methods. What can somatic methods do for individuals whose problems are human relationships, unhappiness, feelings of inadequacy, who cannot maintain relationships although they wish to, who indulge repeatedly in the same self-defeating behavior, who cannot work effectively, or who fail for reasons they cannot understand? What drug will produce the aware, examined life, in which self-knowledge creates more effective control and functioning?

Are the medical and behavioral insistence on "objective" standards of treatment outcome appropriate for many of these problems? Are the feelings of patients and their therapists about the outcome of their treatment irrelevant, as some of the critics of psychoanalysis would argue? Is it really true that a subject cannot judge adequately his own state of sorrow or happiness? Or that a patient's therapist cannot assess the outcome of treatment? Or that patient and therapist together cannot judge the nature of the patient's progress? Psychological tests are indeed becoming increasingly refined. But can these highly complex states (including subtle changes in outlook and behavior) be objectively rated in a truly meaningful way? Psychotherapy, in its reliance on a human relationship, is closer to education and to parenting than to the procedures of medicine.[4]

A therapy for unsatisfactory human relationships, for diffuse unhappiness, represents a major expansion from the more circumscribed treatment of the neuroses by the early analysts. Such problems seem to be rife in affluent, modern Western societies. The very success of psychoanalysis in fostering the extraordinary vogue of psychotherapy suggests the ubiquity of these difficulties. Controlling anxiety, depression, and "problems of personal functioning" remain the most common goals patients bring to psychotherapy. And not "repressing" troubles but talking them out with a professional or an intimate has become the standard way of coping and one of Freud's unintended major cultural legacies.[5]

Part of the current difficulty of psychoanalysis has been its practitioners' insistence that it is a science within the context of medicine. But what kind of a "science" is it? Far more than medicine, psychoanalysis is an art and a skill, based on a structure of systematic theory for the therapist's guidance in the labyrinth of the patient's life and words. Its theories resemble those of some of the social sciences far more closely than they do the experimental sciences, except that the social sciences are not challenged to "treat" patients. Many of these issues of scientific "status" were exacerbated by the medical rhetoric and model psychoanalysts traditionally chose. Moreover, replicable results have been made acutely desirable by soaring medical expenses and third party payers' insistence on "cost effectiveness." That psychoanalysis is in a valid sense a science, that its procedures are not more artificial than the experiments of academic psychology, and that its concerns are truly significant has been argued by Marie Jahoda.[6] But that it should present adequate evidence for its therapeutic claims is a commonplace among recent evaluations by psychoanalysts themselves. Nonetheless, narrowly positivistic definitions of science, on the whole the dominant position in America, militated against granting the psychoanalytic enterprise scientific status.

Just as the success of somatic treatments circumscribed the psychoanalytic domain, so the changing symptoms that psychoanalysts believe they found in their patients have affected not only the theory and technique but the relevance of psychoanalysis. Psychoanalysis has changed in an intricate pattern of successes, failures, and highly individual departures in theory and therapy both formulating client needs and responding to them.

For many years American psychoanalysts claimed that their therapy was singularly effective. It is possible that this success was the result not only of initial enthusiasm but of a fit between a receptive patient population and the structure of psychoanalytic theory and therapy. The French sociologist Roger Bastide has suggested that patient and physician together formulate the symptoms in neurotic disorders.[7]

An impressionistic survey of case histories from 1917 to the 1950s and especially of the psychsomatic literature suggests a continuing fit between psychoanalytic theory and patient symptoms. However, one difficulty with this hypothesis is the fact that changes in analytic theory elicited supporting case histories, and it is probably impossible to escape from the structured bias of the observer or to recover raw "data" before an explanatory label was provided by patient-therapist interaction and the psychoanalytic vocabulary. For example, the growth of a massive concern with borderline patients coincided with the influence of ego psychology and the publications of Otto Kernberg and Heinz Kohut in the 1970s.[8]

The early successes of psychoanalytic theory may have rested not only on the enthusiasm of the practitioner but on a unique congruence between patients' needs and the structure of psychoanalytic theory and therapy. That fit reflected changing social norms and conditions internalized by different generational cohorts, with some variations by social class. The patients to be discussed here were born between about 1900 and 1930 and were treated between about 1920 and 1950 in clinics, public hospitals, and private practice. They ranged in age from the late teens to the forties. Their ailments included neuroses, psychosomatic illnesses, and, occasionally, psychoses. Their occupations ranged from skilled workers to upper-middle-class professionals, who made up the majority of patients.[9]

Their symptoms appeared at crucial stages of the life cycle: during the last years of high school; on leaving home for college or a job and thus separating from parents; during college or professional school; on beginning an occupation or losing a job; at engagements, marriage, pregnancy, or loss of a spouse. Thus family, sex, education, and occupation provided the social settings and the crucial events for the appearance of symptoms.

Sexuality and aggression, in that order, dominated psychoanalytic theory and therapy in the years from 1900 to the 1940s. The expression of sexual and aggressive impulses presumably was mediated by social norms, usually first transmitted by the family, and in Freud's theory encapsulated in the superego. Within the family the expression of these impulses was regulated along with the inculcation of stereotyped social roles. Psychoanalysis functioned as an unmasking psychology that exposed normatively forbidden impulses and encouraged their therapeutic verbal expression.

The social character and symptoms of some of the first generation of American patients were structured by the stringent late 19th-century American sexual code. In these patients, religious and social norms controlling sexuality, usually inculcated by mothers, were unequivocal. Typical symptoms were hysterias, anxiety neuroses, compulsions, impotence, frigidity, psychosomatic illness. After World War I, this traditional character survived most clearly among middle- and lower-middle-class patients, while for upper-middle-class patients, the religious elements of control were receding in importance, although there obviously was variation in each individual case.[10]

The older morality and its concomitant problems also survived to a surprising extent among the male patients, chiefly schizophrenics, whom Harry Stack Sullivan treated with such apparent success in the 1920s and early 1930s.[11] In the male social role, the analogue of sexual transgression was an intense fear of femininity and passivity, of being a "sissy." The pervasiveness of such anxieties seems clear from the psychiatrist G. V. Hamilton's study of the marriages of 200 high achievers in New York in the 1920s, all under 40 years of age. Although there was considerable rebellion against male stereotypes particularly among some artists and writers, the traditional masculine traits persisted as normative with remarkable tenacity. In the 1940s Franz Alexander's male patients seemed notably riven by conflicts over dependency needs, perceived as feminine, pitted against masculine wishes for competition and success. In many of his cases, a close-binding mother had made identification and competition with the father unusually difficult.[12]

There were also male patients for whom aggression and hostility provided serious problems because, once repressed, it then might break out in an impulse to punish oneself or people in authority. The accident-prone fracture patients of Flanders Dunbar in the 1930s are examples. On the surface, the men were casual about sexuality. But they deeply resented authority, and accidents often followed growing anger and sometimes acts of defiance. Aggression as a major difficulty also surfaced, as we have seen, in the "new woman" who began to appear in the case histories of the 1920s.[13]

What is surprising is how often in some of the American cases aggressive, competitive, and hostile feelings were just below the surface and how effective their therapeutic ventilation seemed to be, much as in the case of sexual feelings. Aggressive drives were conspicuous in many kinds of psychosomatic patients in addition to the accident-prone—sufferers from heart disease, hypertension, ulcers, and diabetes, for instance. Often very brief but seemingly effective therapy uncovered deep resentment of parents and especially of parental authority. These feelings were directed against strict, disciplinarian fathers, but also against mothers, particularly mothers whose ambitions had been frustrated and who interfered excessively in the lives of their children. Sometimes anger was directed toward parents who interfered with vocational choice, as in the case of a mother who tried to force her daughter to become a concert musician or who insisted her son follow the family business when he wished instead to become a doctor. Or it was directed toward parents who interfered with the choice of a spouse, to cite another common example, or who were simply considered too strict. Often aggressive feelings gave rise to guilt.[14]

This brief overview of selected cases from the 1920s to about the 1950s suggests two coexisting problems addressed by psychoanalysis. The first concerned sexuality, often connected with a complex Oedipal relationship to the mother or father and a traditional morality inculcated by either parent. The second problem to which attention was directed in the 1920s and 1930s was aggression against parents or against an authoritative parental tradition, and associated with a harsh internalized conscience, or superego.

In attempting to resolve conflicts over sexuality and aggression, the therapist often did not remain neutral, but became part of a new value system. The therapist sometimes sanctioned individual deviance from traditional patterns, encouraging patients to follow their own inclinations, or occasionally sanctioning realistic compromises with existing traditions. Modifying the superego, making it more tractable and realistic particularly in its regulation of sexuality, has been a major goal of psychoanalytic therapy since the 1920s. One of the chapters of Franz Alexander and Thomas French's text on *Psychoanalytic Therapy* was entitled "Alleviation of Rigid Standards." The therapist might give information about sexuality or legitimate the recognition of sexual or hostile feelings. Thus the therapist sanctioned the modified expression of normatively proscribed impulses.[15]

Developments within the family system also may account for what seems to have been a growing incidence of unresolved feelings of dependency upon the mother, for the increasingly problematic nature of aggression, and possibly for the emergence of a narcissistic character in the 1970s, flawed in its self-esteem.[16] Between 1890 and 1910 family size declined and one to three children remained the standard into the 1940s. More than ever, mothers assumed family authority and dominated child-rearing. Mothers also could use the aid of guidance literature and counseling professionals, purveying a popular "science" with often confusing and frequently changing fashions in professional advice. Increasingly, fathers, often absent, played a less authoritative role, and frequently in divorced families were little involved with their children. One might speculate that in self-conscious families guided by "expert" advice, disagreements may have been smoothed over with the new techniques of getting along, the "adjustment psychology" that began to be stressed in the 1920s and 1930s. This new emphasis on cooperation and adjustment became apparent not only within the family but also in the world of corporate and government bureaucracy. Both worlds were marked by the same ideals of individual adjustment within a group structure.

It seems likely that, as family size declined, emotional relationships within the family, particularly between mothers and children, both loving and hostile, may have become closer and more intense. The rise of psychoanalytic object relations theory emerged from precisely this long-term trend in family size and the growing role of the mother, and it focused primarily on early mother-child relationships. It became prominent in America in the immediate aftermath of the cult of devoted housewife and mother that Betty Friedan criticized as the Feminine Mystique of the 1950s. In one national symposium the British analyst John Bowlby argued then that children under three needed not group care but "*one* person whom they know and trust to mother them. And in the enormous proportion of homes that person has to be the mother. . . ."[17] Thus in the 1950s the psychoanalytic expert reinforced the maternal role.

In a highly suggestive study, Ilene Philipson has argued that the generation of 1940s and 1950s mothers, isolated in new suburban communities geographically distant from supporting kin, without meaningful work or adult companionship, with commuting husbands often absent, experienced unusual frustration and ambivalence about their maternal role. On the one hand were their felt needs and frustrations, on the other the normative cult of motherhood. One young mother observed, "I have a period of somewhat [sic] depression right now. I just don't think I'm getting anywhere . . . I feel I'm stagnating and it bothers me and I don't know why. . . . some women are quite lonesome. It's pretty frustrating to me."[18] Frustration, depression, anger, resentment, and, often enough, compensatory fulfillment through special closeness to their children were some of the ways these mothers reacted to their new historical circumstances.

These conflicting emotions could have produced inconsistent patterns of response to children's needs at crucial stages of their development, particularly when they were seeking greater autonomy. And this failed support, resulting from social conditions beyond the mother's control, could have created low esteem in their children, and compensating fantasies of grandiosity. The social patterns that created inconsistent mothering may underlie the narcissistic personality that became prominent in the 1970s among white middle-class patients.

The narcissistic character has been described as successful in work and superficially sociable, but at the same time unable to empathize with others or to sustain close relationships, a pattern possibly more predominant in men than women.[19] Blaming the mother for pathology seems to be a hallmark of much American psychoanalysis, perhaps because until very recently it has been a male-dominated profession, little sensitized to problems of gender.

Many analysts, both men and women, have insisted that they see more "borderline" and "narcissistic" patients than ever before. Patients so diagnosed were noted increasingly in the 1930s because they were far more difficult to treat than the neurotics who presumably were amenable to the enthusiastic uncovering methods of the first psychoanalysts. However, as Otto Kernberg has observed, no one knows whether there has been an actual increase of narcissistic patients, or simply that attention has been focused on them within the last few decades.[20]

Whether the rising divorce rate contributed to the increase of character and personality disorders is an open question. It may well have engendered less effective parenting, although authorities differ about the effects of divorce on children. Judith Wallerstein's ten-year study of a very limited upper-middle-class sample suggests that divorce can give rise not only to successful outcomes for some children but also, for others, to intense, persistent, and sometimes crippling emotional reactions—anger, resentment, and, above all, depression, loss of self-esteem, anxiety, and distrust.[21] Marriages have become more fragile perhaps because of higher expectations for sexual and personal fulfillment rather than a desire for secure affection, stability, or to fulfill an obligation to children. Remarriages yield other problems, such as how severely to discipline stepchildren, sexual tensions related to possibilities of incest, or relations to the natural parents.[22] With apparently growing family instability, peer groups have taken on an even more powerful social role, often subversive of traditional family authority, as children increasingly are raised with less direct parental involvement. The growth of single-parent households, often with mothers who have to work, may have created a whole series of additional problems: lessened parental control, guilty attempts to overcompensate for absence, greater distance between parents and children, fewer internalized controls in children. It is significant that Kohut's self psychology posits narcissistic characters malformed by inadequate or unempathic early mothering without a successfully compensating father figure, and asserts that the therapist's goal is to repair that early failure. This can be seen as a therapeutic response to both the over-close and the overly fragmented family constellations.

It is important to recall that psychoanalysis as a theory probed drives of sexuality and aggression within a close family system. The role of the therapist has been powerful because transference could mirror and thus help to resolve those intense, significant relationships. To be effective, Freud insisted, the relationship had to be positive. But perhaps with products of the fragmented family, psychoanalysis has been less successful, partly because of the large amount of hostility and underlying distrust patients bring to therapy, as if there had been no satisfactory models of love and closeness. The present lessened enthusiasm for psychoanalysis may reflect in part the partial passing of those close family relationships that once provided part of the basis for its special resonance in America. Nevertheless, psychoanalysis still provides perhaps the most important microscopic examination of a culture's emotional life that we possess, at least of its limited but influential patient sample.

While the psychoanalytic profession may be in a state of crisis, some of the tenets of depth psychology, a few of them far older than psychoanalysis and which psychoanalysis reinforced, are deeply embedded in American culture: the importance of early childhood and the influence of parents on children; the repetition in adult life of patterns formed in childhood; the existence of unconscious processes, particularly in the slips and errors of daily life; the role of trauma; and the importance of sexuality and sexual satisfaction and of aggression. Some of the early goals of psychoanalytic social reform have been realized: more ready acceptance of premarital relations and divorce, greater tolerance of masturbation and homosexuality, insistence on woman's sexuality and need for sexual fulfillment.[23] But on a public level there is hardly a sexual or aggressive impulse or practice which psycho-analysts might once have regarded as normatively repressed or perverse that does not flourish in literature or drama or movies, and, often enough in real life, in a progressive evisceration of what once might have been regarded as the "unconscious."

In psychiatry, psychoanalysis remains the most developed and systemat-ic medical psychology, its theories part of most standard texts, its personnel the most meticulously trained. Child-raising advice still is dominated by psychoanalytic professionals such as Benjamin Spock and T. Berry Brazelton. America, however, is no longer the only adopted homeland of psychoanalysis and its offshoots. France, to a lesser extent Germany, and parts of Latin America have enjoyed a Freudian vogue comparable to the American vogue of the 1950s. America remains the country of the earliest, widest, and most thoroughgoing applications. It has seen the most extensive attempts to codify and test psychoanalytic theories and techniques against actual, recorded clinical experience. Elsewhere, as in France, psychoanalysis has been interpreted in part as a linguistic and philosophical system, and among some Lacanians as a radically anti-institutional movement.[24]

Enough scholarly work has been accomplished recently to make possible a comparative perspective on the psychoanalytic movement. Everywhere the role of psychoanalysis as a therapy and its adoption by physicians were crucial for its initial success. In no country did psychoanalysis win a place solely as an intellectual ideology; thus its position within medicine has been central. Nevertheless, everywhere the role of intellectuals was the second most im-portant factor in Freud's reception. In England, for instance, the conversion of socially well-placed intellectuals, some of whom became psychoanalysts, helped to ensure a place for the practice of psychoanalysis by laymen.[25] If a layman with the talent and subsequent prestige of Walter Lippmann had become a psychoanalyst, matters might have turned out differently in Ameri-ca. However, the desire of American psychiatrists for medical and scientific authority might well have doomed such a possibility from the start. Where both well-placed medical specialists and important intellectuals with or without a therapeutic role took up psychoanalysis, its cultural impact was pervasive. That combination was noteworthy in America particularly after World War II, and in France beginning in the 1960s.

In every country intellectuals and physicians embraced psychoanalysis as contributing to a movement of psychiatric and sexual reform. In its early years, psychoanalysis held out the promise of a future free of neuroses through the reform of child-raising, education, and sexual mores. Psychoanalysis was part of a rebellion against a 19th-century code of sexual conduct, based on Judeo-Christian religious sanctions. Psychoanalysis was welcomed as an ideology of sexual liberation, seldom clearly defined, not only in America but in many other countries, including the Soviet Union during its period of official sexual freedom in the 1920s before the Stalinist crackdown.[26]

American psychoanalytic optimism was one enthusiastic variant of this generally utopian outlook. Psychoanalysis offered, Edith Kurzweil has written, a scientific "religion of humanity," a substitute for traditional faiths.[27] It has become, in a sense, a lay substitute for religion, and, as already noted, appealed as a system to American psychotherapists who often rejected the religion of their families of origin.[28]

Psychoanalysis was associated with reform in psychiatry, with a growing interest in psychotherapy and in the psychological understanding of the psychoses not only in America but also in Germany, England, and France. In both France and the United States, at different periods, it was associated with reform in the mental health systems.[29] Everywhere, psychoanalysis offered psychiatry a comprehensive etiological theory and a model of treatment. Psychoanalysts, especially in America, France, and Germany, developed a psychosomatic medicine that seemed at first to represent real hopes for the treatment of baffling chronic illnesses but whose relative failure ultimately damaged psychoanalytic prestige. Everywhere, psychoanalysis vastly increased the intrusive role of the "scientific" expert—the psychiatrist, the psychologist, and psychotherapeutic counselor—in fields where custom or religion once had held sway, as in child-raising and education, family and marital relations, social work and criminology.

Popularization also was universal, although at different times and in different ways. Much of the early favorable reception of Freud's work in Germany and Austria was in popular periodicals, although theologians, academics, and psychiatrists were still largely opposed. Freud told his early followers that his concepts of the suppression of instinct and overcoming resistance had established a connection with the "great cultural circles" and had aroused the interest of "all alert and educated people." He urged his Berlin disciple Karl Abraham to appeal to the public over the heads of the hostile medical profession.[30]

A close alliance of the media and the intellectuals characterized France's astonishingly rapid absorption of psychoanalysis in its Lacanian dispensation in the 1960s and 1970s. Even in Britain, where the first analysts themselves did not directly popularize, there was considerable attention given to psychoanalysis in magazines and newspapers.[31]

The issue of lay versus medical analysis surfaced in every country and led to frequent disputes. Eclecticism also was hardly an American monopoly. A hybrid psychoanalysis for many years characterized Britain's Tavistock clinic, France's movement of psychiatric reform, centering around the journal *L'Evolution psychiatrique,* and the psychotherapeutic movement in Germany into the early 1930s.[32] And everywhere, as in the United States, there also existed an orthodox Freudian phalanx.

Social theorists have suggested that psychoanalysis succeeded because it met profound needs in modern society. Morris Janowitz, the American sociologist, has seen psychoanalysis and its offshoots as humanizing agencies in medicine because of the insistence on the reality of subjective emotions and the importance of human relationships. For him it is a subtle and desirable agency of social control, because it reinforces the "autonomous ego." And he defines social control as the opposite of control by force. For Peter Berger, another American sociologist, psychoanalysis offers a welcome emphasis on the individual in a society growing ever more impersonal, in which work and personal identity are increasingly sundered.[33]

Ernest Gellner, the British social anthropologist, in a witty examination of psychoanalysis, sees human relations as the major source of anxiety in modern life, replacing in their pervasive impact the vagaries of nature that earlier societies attempted to propitiate. In the statusless society of modern governmental and corporate bureaucracies, as well as in personal life, human relationships determine happiness or failure. Psychoanalysis and its offshoots provide "pastoral care" for human relationships under the aegis of science, the current god of the modern world view, which otherwise remains cold and comfortless. And it offers, particularly for this violent century, a darker and far more realistic view of mankind than the denatured human nature of traditional academic psychology.[34]

Each of these explanations has a measure of cogency, but Gellner's is the most persuasive. Psychoanalysis has fostered the cure of souls in a scientific age. Its concentration on relationships has suited a world dominated by increasingly binding organizational structures. At the same time, its practice has been incompatible with authoritarian states, as its fate in the Soviet Union and Nazi Germany, as well as parts of Latin America, clearly demonstrate. But there are more specifically American resonances for psychoanalysis than its compatibility with democratic regimes. In its promise of augmenting individual potential, it has fitted neatly into the old American pattern of self-improvement and upward mobility. No longer the close "handmaiden" of psychiatry that it was in the 1950s, it must be seen now as one of the many modalities of psychotherapy, which has become a separate and vastly proliferating realm. In the parsimony of its interventions and, despite the formulaic quality of its theories, in its insistence on discovering the unknown pattern in the details of each individual case, psychoanalysis has protected individual autonomy and expressiveness, and has reinforced an older American tradition of individualism. Finally, its very lack of final definition and its ability to generate hypotheses, have meant that it could be applied imaginatively to a wide range of humanistic disciplines—art, social science, literature, all beyond the realm of therapy. At the same time, this very flexibility has meant a constant and reasonably systematic renewal of observation and theory in response to changing social conditions and patients' needs.

Abbreviations Used in Notes

Publications

AGP	*Archives of General Psychiatry*
AJI	*American Journal of Insanity*
AJO	*American Journal of Orthopsychiatry*
AJP	*American Journal of Psychology*
AmPsychol	*American Psychologist*
ANP	*Archives of Neurology and Psychiatry*
AP	*American Journal of Psychiatry*
BAPA	*Bulletin of the American Psychoanalytic Association*
BBS	*Behavioral and Brain Sciences*
BHM	*Bulletin of the History of Medicine*
BMC	*Bulletin of the Menninger Clinic*
BMSJ	*Boston Medical and Surgical Journal*
FJ	*The Complete Correspondence of Sigmund Freud and Ernest Jones* (Cambridge, Mass.: Harvard Univ. Press, 1993)
HCP	*Hospital and Community Psychiatry*
IJ	*International Journal of Psychoanalysis*
IJPsychiat	*International Journal of Psychiatry*
JACA	*Journal of the American Academy of Psychoanalysis*
JAMA	*Journal of the American Medical Association*

JAP	*Journal of Abnormal Psychology*
JAPA	*Journal of the American Psychoanalytic Association*
JCCP	*Journal of Consulting and Clinical Psychology*
JHBS	*Journal of the History of the Behavioral Sciences*
JHM	*Journal of the History of Medicine*
JME	*Journal of Medical Education*
JNMD	*Journal of Nervous and Mental Disease*
LHJ	*Ladies Home Journal*
MH	*Mental Hygiene*
NYSJM	*New York State Journal of Medicine*
NYT	*New York Times*
P	*Psychiatry*
PsyMed	*Psychosomatic Medicine*
Q	*Psychoanalytic Quarterly*
R	*Psychoanalytic Review*
SE	*The Standard Edition of the Complete Psychological Works of Sigmund Freud* (London: Hogarth Press and the Institute of Psychoanalysis, 1953–66)
SR	*Saturday Review*
SRL	*Saturday Review of Literature*

Manuscript Collections

AFP	Anna Freud Papers, Library of Congress
AMP	Adolf Meyer Papers, Johns Hopkins University
APSA	American Psychoanalytic Association Archives
APSAC	American Psychoanalytic Association Archives, Cornell-New York Hospital
BP	Abraham Arden Brill papers, Library of Congress
BibP	Grete and Edward Bibring papers, Francis A. Countway Library of Medicine, Boston
BernP	Siegfried Bernfeld papers, Library of Congress
COHC	Columbia University Oral History Collection
CP	V. F. Calverton Papers, New York Public Library
DLP	Mabel Dodge Luhan papers, Yale University Library
DP	Floyd Dell papers, Newberry Library, Chicago
FA	Freud Archives, Library of Congress
FAP	Franz Alexander papers, Chicago and Southern California Psychoanalytic Institute
FP	Otto Fenichel papers, Library of Congress
FW	Fritz Wittels Papers, New York Psychoanalytic Institute
GP	Maxwell Gitelson papers, Library of Congress
GrP	Ralph Greenson Papers, University of California, Los Angeles
HP	Ives Hendrick papers, Boston Psychoanalytic Institute
JelP	Smith Ely Jelliffe Papers, Library of Congress
JP	Ernest Jones Papers, British Psycho-Analytical Society Archives, London
KenP	Marion Kenworthy Papers, Cornell-New York Hospital
KP	Lawrence Kubie papers, Library of Congress
LAPSIA	Los Angeles Psychoanalytic Institute Archives

LewP	Bertram Lewin papers, Library of Congress
LP	David Levy Papers, Cornell-New York Hospital
MGP	Maurice Green papers, Cornell New York Hospital
MP	Millet Papers, Cornell-New York Hospital
NYPSIA	New York Psychoanalytic Institute Archives
RP	David Rapaport Papers, Library of Congress
SFIA	San Francisco Psychoanalytic Institute Archives
SP	Ernest Simmel papers, Los Angeles Psychoanalytic Institute Archives
WFA	William Alanson White Psychiatric Foundation Archives, Washington, D.C.
WMP	William Menninger Papers, Menninger Foundation, Topeka, Kansas
WP	Frankwood Williams papers, Cornell-New York Hospital

Notes

Introduction

1. Alfred Kazin, "The Freudian Revolution Analyzed," NYT Magazine, May 6, 1956, p. 22; *Time* 67 (April 23, 1956): 70–78; *Saturday Review* 39 (May 5, 1954).

2. Sir Peter Medawar, "Victims of Psychiatry," *New York Review of Books* (Jan. 23, 1975): 17; Frederick Crews, "Analysis Terminable," *Commentary* 70:1 (July 1980): 25–34.

3. David Evans Tanner, "Symbols of Conduct: Psychiatry and American Culture, 1900–1935" (Ph.D. Diss., University of Texas, Austin, 1981).

4. N. Hale, Jr., ed., *James Jackson Putnam and Psychoanalysis* (Cambridge, Mass.: Harvard Univ. Press, 1971), 89; Freud, "On the History of Psychoanalytic Movement," SE 14, p. 31, "The Question of Lay Analysis," SE 20, p. 250.

5. Freud, Preface to special issue of the *Medical Review of Reviews* 26 (March 1930): 103; "An Autobiographical Study," SE 20, p. 52.

6. Franz Alexander, *The Western Mind in Transition* (New York: Random House, 1960), 98–101.

7. John Demos, "Oedipus and America," *Annual of Psychoanalysis* 6 (1978): 23–39.

8. Kenneth Ludmerer, *Learning to Heal: The Development of American Medical Education* (New York: Basic Books, 1985), 83–84, 93; Paul Starr, *The Social Transformation of American Medicine* (New York: Basic Books, 1982), 113–14.

Chapter 1. The Great War: A Human Laboratory

1. William A. Brend, "Psychotherapy and War Experience," *Edinburgh Review* 233 (Jan. 1921): 57; Sidney I. Schwab, "Influence of War Concepts of Mental Diseases and Neuroses," *Modern Medicine* 2:3 (March 1920): 192, 197.

2. Elmer E. Southard, "Sigmund Freud: Pessimist," JAP 14 (1919–20): 198–214; J. C. Grey, "War Books of the Month," *Bookman* 47 (Aug. 1918): 658–60.

3. Marie Corelli, "The World's Greatest Need," *Good Housekeeping* 66 (Jan. 1918): 30–32; "War and Psychoanalysis," *New York Medical Journal* 104 (Dec. 1916): 1251; James J. Walsh, *Health Through Willpower* (Boston: Little, Brown, 1919), 267.

4. W. J. Toohey, "How We All Reveal Our Soul Secrets," LHJ 34 (Nov. 1917): 97.

5. *The Medical Department of the United States Army in the World War,* Vol. X, *Neuropsychiatry* (Washington, D.C., U.S. Government Printing Office, 1929), 1–3; Fred W. Parsons, "War Neuroses," *Atlantic Monthly* 123 (March 1919): 335–38; Mabel Brown and Frankwood Williams, *Neuropsychiatry and the War: A Bibliography with Abstracts* (New York: War Work Committee, National Committee for Mental Hygiene, 1918), 25.

6. Smith Ely Jelliffe and Charles Rockwell Payne, "War Neuroses and Psychoneuroses," *JNMD* 48 (1918): 389–90.

7. *Medical Department,* 3.

8. M. Allen Starr, "Shell Shock," *Scribner's Magazine* 64 (Aug. 1918): 183–87.

9. "Shell Shocked and After by an American Soldier," *Atlantic Monthly* 128 (Dec. 1921): 739.

10. Edward W. Lazell, "The Psychology of War and Schizophrenia," R 7:3 (July 1920): 225.

11. Tanner, "Symbols of Conduct" (Ph.D. Diss., University of Texas, Austin, 1981), 37; *Medical Department,* 3; Thomas W. Salmon, M.D., *The Care and Treatment of Mental Diseases and War Neuroses (Shell Shock) in the British Army* (New York: War Work Committee of the National Committee for Mental Hygiene, 1917), 29–30.

12. Salmon, *Care and Treatment,* 14.

13. Brown and Williams, *Neuropsychiatry,* 93–94, 97, 105. Tanner, "Symbols," ch. 2; J. Rogues de Fursac, "Traumatic and Emotional Psychoses, So-Called Shell Shock," AJI 75 (July 1918): 19–51.

14. Brown and Williams, *Neuropsychiatry,* 73, 211; Ernest Elmer Southard, "Shell Shock and After," BMSJ 179 (July 18, 1918): 73–93; "Special Discussion of Shell Shock Without Visible Signs of Injury," *Proceedings of the Royal Society of Medicine* 9 (1915–16), Sections of Psychiatry and Neurology, i–xliv.

15. Sidney I. Schwab, "The Influence of War on the Conception of Mental Disease and Neuroses," *Modern Medicine* 2:3 (March 1920): 194.

16. Southard, "Shell-Shock and After," 74; Lewellys F. Barker, "War and the Nervous System," JNMD 44 (1916): 1.

17. Smith Ely Jelliffe and Charles Rockwell Payne, "War Neuroses and Psychoneuroses," JNMD 48 (1918): 359–60, 367; Southard, "Shell Shock and After," 75; Introduction by Charles K. MIlls to Southard, *Shell Shock and Other Neuropsychiatric Problems* (Boston, W. M. Leonard, 1919), xv.

18. Clarence S. Yoakun and Robert M. Yerkes, *Army Mental Tests* (New York: Henry Holt, 1929), vii; Stewart Paton, "Mobilizing the Brains of the Nation," *Mental Hygiene* I (1917): 338; E. Stanley Abbott, "The Work of Psychiatrists in Military Camps," *AJI* 75 (1918–19): 457–67; John J. B. Morgan, "The Diagnosis of Potential

Neurosis," *Science Monthly* 4 (Jan. 1918): 84–89; Obituary, Pearce Bailey, AP 78, (1921–22): 704–7, and JNMD 56 (July–Dec 1922): 38–40.

19. Earl D. Bond, *Thomas W. Salmon, Psychiatrist* (New York: W. W. Norton, 1950), chs. 1–2, 6–7; Tanner, "Symbols," ch. 2.

20. Southard, "Shell Shock and After," 81–82; and Bailey in *Medical Department,* 295–96.

21. *Medical Department,* 295–97; Brown and Williams, *Neuropsychiatry,* 109; Tanner, "Symbols," 38–41.

22. *Medical Department,* 295; Earl D. Bond, *Thomas W. Salmon, Psychiatrist* (New York: W. W. Norton, 1950), 110; Tanner, "Symbols" 41–63.

23. Bond, *Salmon,* 111.

24. For the social creation of shell shock see Chris Feudtner, "Minds the Dead Have Ravished," *History of Science* 31 (Dec. 1993): 377–420. For the impact of psychoanalysis on British psychiatry as a result of the war, see Martin Stone, "Shellshock and Psychiatry," in *The Anatomy of Madness* (London: Tavistock Publications, 1985), 242–71.

25. Brown and Williams, *Neuropsychiatry,* 37, 43–44, 71, 73.

26. William Brown, "The Treatment of Cases of Shell Shock," *Scientific American Supplement* 86 (Dec. 7, 1918): 362–63; R. G. Rows, "Mental Conditions Following Strain and Nerve Shock," *British Medical Journal* 25 (March 1916): 441–43, 220–21.

27. G. Elliott Smith and T. H. Pear, *Shell Shock and Its Lessons* (2nd ed., Longmans, Green, 1917), ch. 3, esp. 73–75; review in AJI 75 (1917–18), 190–91.

28. Wilfred Trotter, *Instincts of the Herd in Peace and War* (2nd ed., New York: Macmillan, 1919), 82.

29. John T. MacCurdy, "War Neuroses," *Psychiatric Bulletin* (New York State Hospital Bulletin Series II) 2 (July 1917), vi–viii, 243–354, esp. 257, 349–51, and *War Neuroses* (Cambridge, Eng.: Cambridge Univ. Press, 1918), viii, 16, 85–86. MacCurdy defended psychoanalysis against charges of being a private "orgiastic religion" in "Ethical Aspects of Psychoanalysis," *Johns Hopkins Hospital Bulletin,* May 1915, pp. 169–73.

30. Salmon, *Care and Treatment,* 30; Bond, *Salmon,* 111–12.

31. Salmon, "War Neuroses," *Military Surgeon* 41 (Dec. 1917): 677–78, and *Care and Treatment,* 30; Bond, *Salmon,* 97.

32. Bond, *Salmon,* 111.

33. Sidney I. Schwab, "The War Neuroses as Physiologic Conservations," ANP I:5 (May 1919): 579, 627–28, and Discussion of Charles K. Mills, "Some Theoretical and Practical Aspects of Psychoanalysis," ANP 6:6 (Dec. 1921): 622.

34. Schwab, "War Neuroses," 627–28; Stanford Read, "A Survey of War Neuropsychiatry," *Mental Hygiene* 2 (1918): 361.

35. Freud, "Psychoanalysis and War Neuroses" (1919), in *Collected Papers* (London: Hogarth Press and the Institute for Psychoanalysis, 1957), 84, and "An Autobiographical Study," SE 20, p. 54.

36. Sandor Ferenczi et al., *Psychoanalysis and the War Neuroses* (London: International Psychoanalytical Press, 1921), 1–4, 24, 48, 58; Freud, "An Autobiographical Study," SE 20, p. 54. For the humanitarian role of psychoanalysis, see Jose Brunner, "Psychiatry, Psychoanalysis, and Politics," JHBS 27:4 (Oct. 1991): 352–65.

37. Ferenczi, *Psychoanalysis and War Neuroses,* 28–29, 43.

38. Feudtner, "Minds the Dead Have Ravished."

39. Bond, *Salmon,* 99, 104.

40. May Sinclair, *Ann Severn and the Fieldings* (London: Hutchinson, 1922); "Hospital

Aspect of the Nervous and Mental Shock of Battle," *Current Opinion* 59:2 (1915): 107; "Nerves and the War," *Scientific American* 112 (March 6, 1915): 214.

41. Edward William Lazell, *Psychoanalytic Review* 6:3 (1919): 350–52; Mary Jarrett, "The Home Treatment of Shell Shock," *Touchstone* 4 (1918): 110–15, 227–30, 321–28, 510–14.

42. Norman Fenton, *Shell Shock and Its Aftermath* (St. Louis: C. V. Mosby, 1926), 148–49.

43. Paris Singer, "Our War Work," *Touchstone* 3 (Aug. 1918): 371–80.

44. Frederick W. Parsons, "Shell Shock?," *Atlantic Monthly* 123 (March 1919): 336.

45. W. R. Houston, "The Amazing Effect of Shell Shock on Soldiers' Nerves," *Current History Magazine* of NYT 6 (May 1917): 340–45.

46. Of 21 articles about shell shock listed in the *Reader's Guide* from 1915 to 1921, about seven contained psychoanalytic conceptions whether identified as such or not.

47. Moses Allen Starr, "Shell Shock," *Scribner's* 64 (1918): 184.

48. NYT, Jan. 13, 1919, p. 10; Brown, "Treatment of Cases of Shell Shock," 362–63; W.H.R. Rivers, "Psychiatry and the War," *Science* n.s. 49 (April 18, 1919): 367–69; Rivers, "Psychology and the War," *Scribner's* 68 (Aug. 1920); Rivers, *Instincts and the Unconscious* (Cambridge, Eng.: Cambridge Univ. Press, 1920).

49. "A Warning Against the Effort to Forget Painful Experiences," *Current Opinion* 68 (May 1920): 656.

50. Stewart Paton, "Mobilizing the Brains of the Nation," *Mental Hygiene* 1 (1919): 338, and "Protecting Civilization," *Harper's* 148 (Jan. 1924): 168; Rivers, "Psychiatry and the War," 367–69.

51. NYT, June 16, 1918, sec. 6, p. 8; Elizabeth Meier, *A History of the New York School of Social Work* (New York: Columbia Univ. Press, 1954); catalogue, Pennsylvania School of Social Service, 1919–20, p. 20.

52. W. A. Neilson, "The Smith College Experiment in Training for Psychiatric Social Work," *Mental Hygiene* 3 (Jan. 1919): 61; Interview, Mrs. Everett Kimball, April 20, 1960, Smith College; Interview, Mary Jarrett, April 26, 1960, New York; *Bulletin,* Smith College School for Social Work, 1919–20; Everett Kimball, "A War Baby Grown Up," *Smith Alumnae Quarterly* (Feb. 1927): 146–51; Virginia Robinson, *A Changing Psychology in Social Case Work* (Chapel Hill: Univ. of North Carolina Press, 1930); Roy Lubove, *The Professional Altruist* (Cambridge, Mass.: Harvard Univ. Press, 1965).

53. White, *Thoughts of Psychiatrists on the War and After* (New York: Paul B. Hoeber, 1919).

54. Theodore Schroeder, "Determinism, Conduct and Fear Psychology," R 6 (Oct. 1919): 390.

Chapter 2. A New Generation of Psychoanalysts

1. Otto Kernberg, "Institutional Problems of Psychoanalytic Education," JAPA 34:4 (1986): 799–834; Michael Balint, "On the Psycho-Analytic Training System," IJ 29:3 (1948): 163–73, and "Analytic Training and Training Analysis," IJ 35:2 (1954): 157–62.

2. Eliot Freidson, *Professional Powers* (Chicago: Univ. of Chicago Press, 1986), 29, 63–64, 69–70, and *The Profession of Medicine* (New York: Harper and Row, 1970), ch. 4; William J. Goode, "Encroachment, Charlatanism, and the Emerging Professions: Psychology, Sociology, and Medicine," *American Sociological Review* 15 (Dec. 1960): 902–14; for psychiatry see Andrew Abbot, *The System of Professions* (Chicago: Univ. of Chicago Press, 1988), ch. 10.

3. Freud, "'Wild' Psycho-Analysis" (1910), SE 11, pp. 221–27.

4. Ralph Greenson, "The Origin and Fate of New Ideas in Psychoanalysis," IJ 50:4 (1969): 503–15.

5. Freud to Karl Abraham, Dec. 15, 1919, June 1, 1920, in Hilda Abraham and Ernst Freud eds., *A Psycho-Analytic Dialogue: The Letters of Sigmund Freud and Karl Abraham* (New York: Basic Books, 1965), 299–302; Freud, *Introductory Lectures* SE 16, p. 423, SE 17, pp. 166–68, 171–73.

6. Freud, Preface to *Medical Review of Reviews* 26 (March 1930): 103–4.

7. Eitingon, IJ 7:1 (Jan. 1926): 130–31; Edward Glover, "Introduction to the Study of Psycho-Analytical Theory," IJ 6:4 (Oct. 1930): 483; Jack Rubins, *Karen Horney* (New York: Dial Press, 1978), 128; Maxwell Gitelson, "On the Present Scientific and Social Position of Psychoanalysis," IJ 44:4 (Oct. 1963): 521–27.

8. Hilda C. Abraham and Ernst L. Freud, eds., *A Psychoanalytic Dialogue*, 300–305, 307–11, 314;

9. Frank Sulloway, *Freud: Biologist of the Mind* (New York: Basic Books, 1979), ch. 13.

10. H. V. Dicks, *Fifty Years of the Tavistock Clinic* (London: Routledge and Kegan Paul, 1970), 17–39.

11. Paul Federn and H. Meng, eds., *Das Psychoanalytische Volksbuch* (Bern: Huber, 1939).

12. Edouard Hitschmann, "A Ten Years' Report of the Vienna Psychoanalytic Clinic," IJ 13, parts 1–2 (Jan. 1932): 245–46; IJ (1920), 365; *The Lancet,* July 6, 1929, pp. 31–32; *Supplement to the British Medical Journal,* June 29, 1929, pp. 262–70. See the full discussion of the issue in Peter Gay, *Freud* (New York: W. W. Norton, 1988), 489–500.

13. *British Medical Journal Supplement,* June 29, 1929, p. 266.

14. Ernest Jones, *The Life and Work of Sigmund Freud* (New York: Basic Books, 1957), vol. 3, p. 44.

15. Freud to Jones, Sept. 25, 1924, in FJ, 552; see also pp. 288, 327, 416, 419, 551, 554; Lavinia Edmunds, "His Master's Choice," *Johns Hopkins Magazine* 40:2 (April 1988): 41–49; Daniel Goleman, NYT Magazine, March 6, 1990, p. 12. Ernest Jones, in *Freud,* vol. 3, pp. 105–6, reported that Frink never recovered, but he did, married a third time, and died in 1936.

16. Freud, "Group Psychology," SE 18, p. 99. Interview Erik Erikson, Tiburon, Calif., April 29, 1976. George Weiss, "Scientists and Sectarians: The Case of Psychoanalysis," JHBS 11:4 (Oct. 1975): 350–64.

17. For an insightful account of these tangled relationships and the surfacing of heretical views in orthodox theory see Paul Roazen, *Freud and His Followers* (New York: Alfred A. Knopf, 1971).

18. Rudolf Ekstein, "A Historical Survey on the Teaching of Psychoanalytic Technique," JAPA 8:3 (July 1960): 501; Bertram D. Lewin, "American Psychoanalytic Education," JAPA 10:1 (Jan. 1962): 123.

19. Susan Quinn, *A Mind of Her Own: The Life of Karen Horney* (New York: Summit Books, 1987), 238–39.

20. Ernst Simmel, "Zur Geschichte," *Zehn Jahre Berliner Psychoanalytisches Institut,* (Wien: Internationaler Psychoanalystischer Verlag, 1930), 7–12, 17; C. P. Oberndorf, "The Berlin Psychoanalytic Policlinic," R 13 (1926): 318–22. Sanford Gifford, "Remarks for Oral History Workshop, the History of Psychoanalytic Training, Berlin and Vienna, 1920–1938," ms., New York, Dec. 17, 1981.

21. Hanns Sachs, "Die Lehranalyse," *Zehn Jahre,* 53.

22. Ibid., 30.

23. Karen Horney, "Zur Organisation," *Zehn Jahre,* 49.

24. Therese Benedek, "Training Analysis, Past, Present and Future," IJ 50 (1969): 437–39. For the Berlin institute see the lively account in Gay, *Freud,* 459–64; Quinn, *A Mind of Her Own;* Perry Meisel and Walter Kendrick, eds., *Bloomsbury/Freud: The Letters of James and Alix Strachey 1924–1925* (New York: Basic Books, 1985).

25. Gregory Zilboorg, in "Aus Amerika," *Zehn Jahre,* 66–69.

26. Rudolph Loewenstein, COHC, 25.

27. Felix Boehm, IJ 5:4 (Oct. 1924): 489.

28. Dana to Williams, Nov. 26, 1926, WP.

29. *The Laws of New York,* 1926, pp. 1542–46; NYT, April 7, 1921, sec. 4, p. 4, mentions a proposal for the registration of psychotherapists, but this does not appear in the law passed May 17, 1926. See also NYT, Feb. 19, 1926, sec. 5, p. 3.

30. Williams to Freud, Nov. 5, 1926; Freud to Williams, Nov. 18, 1926, WP.

31. Gay, *Freud,* 490–92; NYT, May 25, 1927, sec. 6, p. 6. Jones, *Freud,* vol. 3, p. 293, noted, according to Ferenczi, that the New York legislature in the fall of 1926 passed a law on Brill's instigation declaring lay analysis illegal. But there is no record of such a law. I am indebted to Douglas Kirsner for information on this issue. See the discussions of lay analysis in IJ 7:1 (Jan. 1926): 129–35, 141–43; 8:4 (Oct. 1927): 559–60; 9:1 (Jan. 1928): 135–41, 151–56.

32. Jones to Brill, Nov. 7, 1930, JP; Smith Ely Jelliffe to Ernest Jones, Oct. 24, 1927, and Jones to Jelliffe, Dec. 21, 1929, Jan. 19, 1935, JelP; Jones to Brill, April 23, 1929, Oct. 17, 1930, Brill to Jones, Nov. 1, 1932, May 12, 1933, JP.

33. Freud to Williams, Dec. 22, 1929, trans. Dorian Feigenbaum; Freud to Jones, Aug. 30, 1926, in FJ, 604. Freud initially had refused to see Williams on grounds of fatigue; see Freud to Williams, Sept. 10, 1925, WP. For Freud's anti-American bias see Gay, *Freud,* 562–70.

34. Minutes of the New York Psychoanalytic Society, Feb. 29, 1929, Library of Congress.

35. Rado, COHC.

36. Minutes of the New York Psychoanalytic Society, Oct. 27, 1936, Library of Congress.

37. Abraham Kardiner, COHC.

38. Michael Balint, "On the Psychoanalytic Training System," IJ 29 (1948): 163–73.

39. Hanns Sachs, "Observations of a Training Analyst," Q 16:2 (1947): 157–68.

Chapter 3. Women, Character, and Anxiety

1. Ruth Fallenbaum, "The Borderline Rage" (Ph.D. diss., Wright Institute, 1983), ch. 6. For psychoanalysis as a general theory of the mind, see Chapter 13.

2. For a recent critical review of Freud's cases see Frank Sulloway, "Reassessing Freud's Case Histories," *Isis* 82:312 (June 1991), 245–75, Patrick Mahoney, *Freud as a Writer* (New Haven: Yale Univ. Press, 1987).

3. Edward Glover, "The Therapeutic Effect of Inexact Interpretation," IJ 12:4 (Oct. 1931): 399.

4. Quoted in A. A. Roback, *The Psychology of Character* (New York: Harcourt Brace, 1927), 45, ch. 4.

5. Freud, "The Sexual Theories of Children" (1908), SE 9, p. 218; "Three Essays on Sexuality" (1905), SE 7, pp. 219–21.

6. Karl Abraham, "Manifestations of the Female Castration Complex," IJ 3:1 (March

1922): 11; Helene Deutsch, "The Significance of Masochism in the Mental Life of Women," IJ 11:1 (Jan. 1930): 48–69, esp. 59.

7. See Sulloway, *Freud: Biologist of the Mind,* and the criticism of Sulloway by Paul Robinson in *Freud and His Critics* (Berkeley: Univ. of California Press, 1993).

8. What else can be the implication of Freud's statement "Thus a girl may refuse to accept the fact of being castrated, may harden herself in the conviction that she DOES possess a penis, and may subsequently be compelled to behave as though she were a man"? See "Some Psychical Consequences of the Anatomical Distinction Between the Sexes" (1925), SE 19, p. 253. He both explicitly rejected the equation of conventional role and biology yet also retained it and appealed once more to bisexuality in "New Introductory Lectures on Psycho-Analysis," SE 22 (1933), pp. 114–18.

9. Abraham, "Manifestations of the Female Castration Complex," 15, 9.

10. Helene Deutsch, "The Psychology of Women in Relation to the Function of Reproduction," IJ 6:4 (Oct. 1925): 405–18. For a comprehensive criticism of Deutsch's biologism, see Miriam J. Wimpfheimer and Roy Schafer, "Helene Deutsch's 'The Psychology of Women,'" Q 46 (1972): 287–318; for a sympathetic view based on Deutsch's case histories, see Brenda Webster, *Signs* 10:3 (Spring 1985): 553–71.

11. Zenia Odes Fliegel, "Feminine Psychosexual Development in Psychoanalytic Theory," Q 42 (1973): 385–408, and "Half a Century Later: Current Status of Freud's Controversial Views on Women," R 69:1 (Spring 1982): 7–27.

12. Paul Bousfield, "Freud's Complex of the Overestimation of the Male," R XII:2 (April 1925): 127–50; Ernest Jones, IJ 1:3 (1920): 324–28.

13. Beatrice Hinkle, "Arbitrary Use of the Terms Masculine and Feminine," R 7:1 (Jan. 1920): 15–30.

14. Horney, "The Flight from Womanhood," IJ 7:3,4 (July, Oct. 1926): 324–39, esp. 332.

15. Renate Bridenthal, "Beyond Kinder, Kuche, Kirche," *Central European History* 7:2 (June 1973): 148–66; Jill Stephenson, "Girls' Higher Education in Germany in the 1930's," *Journal of Contemporary History* 10:1 (Jan. 1975): 41–69.

16. Joan Riviere, "Womanliness as a Masquerade," IJ 10:3 (April–July 1929): 303–13; see Helene Deutsch, "The Significance of Masochism," IJ 11:1 (Jan. 1930): 59, and Horney, review of Deutsch in IJ 7:1 (Jan. 1926): 92–100.

17. For examples of how the mother's castration anxiety could create neuroses in her children, see Karl Abraham, "Manifestations of the Female Castration Complex," IJ 3 (March 1922): 27–29.

18. Freud, "Character and Anal Eroticism" (1908), SE 9, pp. 169–75.

19. Ernest Jones, "Anal Erotic Character Traits," originally published in JAP 13 (1918). Jones, *Papers on Psychoanalysis* (5th ed., Baltimore: Williams and Wilkins, 1943), 413–37.

20. Jones, "Hate and Anal Erotism in the Obsessional Neurosis," in Jones, *Papers on Psychoanalysis* (3rd ed., London: Bailliere, Tindall and Cox, 1923), 556–57, Abraham, "Contributions to the Theory of the Anal Character," IJ 4 (Oct. 1923): 400–418, esp. 404–5.

21. Karl Abraham, "The Influence of Oral Erotism on Character Formation," IJ 6:3 (July 1925): 247–58; Edward Glover, "Notes on Oral Character Formation," IJ 6:2 (April 1925): 131–54; abstract of Glover, "The Significance of the Mouth in Psycho-Analysis," IJ 6:1 (Jan. 1925): 57–59.

22. Abraham, "Character Formation on the Genital Level of Libido-Development," IJ 7:2 (April 1926): 213–22.

23. Franz Alexander, "The Castration Complex in the Formation of Character," IJ 4:1 (Jan. 1923): 11–42; Edward Glover, "The Neurotic Character," IJ 7:1 (Jan. 1926): 11–30.

24. Alexander, "The Castration Complex," 15.

25. For a devastating account of her analysis by Freud see Patrick Mahoney, "Freud as Family Therapist," in Gelfand, *Freud and the History of Psychoanalysis* (Hillsdale, N.J.: Analytic Press, 1992).

26. Anna Freud, *Psychoanalysis for Teachers and Parents* (Boston: Beacon Press, 1960), 32–33, 101–2. She was very aware of the consequences of child abuse, see p. 44.

27. Anna Freud, *The Ego and the Mechanisms of Defence* (New York: International Universities Press, 1946), 59–64, 155.

28. Ibid., 120–21.

29. Ibid., 128.

30. Ibid., 103–5.

31. Fenichel, *Rundbrief,* March 22, 1942, FP.

32. Compare Fenichel, *Outline of Clinical Psychoanalysis* (New York: W. W. Norton, 1934), with Fenichel, *The Psychoanalytic Theory of Neurosis* (New York: W. W. Norton, 1945), 464.

33. Seymour Fisher and Roger P. Greenberg, *The Scientific Credibility of Freud's Theories and Therapy* (New York: Basic Books, 1977), ch. 3.

34. Wilhelm Stekel, "The Psychology of Compulsory Disease," JNMD 73 (Dec. 1931): 600–626, esp. 617–18, 625–26.

35. *Zehn Jahre Berliner Psychoanalyitsches Institut* (Wien: Internationaler Psycho-analytischer Verlag, 1930), 17. The clinic also treated neurotic depression, manic-depressive, schizophrenic, and schizoid cases, psychopathy, and a few cases of epilep-sy, homosexuality, and neurasthenia.

36. Sandor Ferenczi and Otto Rank, *The Development of Psychoanalysis,* trans. Car-oline Newton (New York and Washington: Nervous and Mental Disease Publishing, 1925), 52, 55, 62; Max Eitingon, "Report of the Berlin Psycho-Analytical Policlinic," IJ 4:1–2 (Jan.–April 1923): 254, 258.

37. Freud, "Recommendations to Physicians Practicing Psycho-Analysis" (1912), SE 12, pp. 111–20.

38. Adolf Stern, "Psychoanalytical Experiences with Professor Freud," NYSJM 22 (Jan. 1922): 21–25.

39. In other respects Glover advocated some flexibility; see "Lectures on Technique in Psychoanalysis," IJ 8:3 (July 1927): 325.

40. Richard Sterba, "The Fate of the Ego in Analytic Therapy," IJ 15:2–3 (1934): 117–26.

41. Otto Fenichel, *Problems of Psychoanalytic Technique* (New York: Psychoanalytic Quarterly, 1941), 2–14, 27, 99.

42. Eitingon, "Report," IJ 4:1–2 (Jan.–April 1923): 264, 266.

43. Edward Glover, *The Technique of Psychoanalysis* (New York: International Uni-versities Press, 1955), 262, 264.

44. "Symposium on the Theory of the Therapeutic Results of Psycho-Analysis," IJ 18:2,3 (April–July 1937): 125–89, esp. 142–44, 139–40, 187–89.

45. Ferenczi and Rank, *Development of Psychoanalysis,* ch. 1, pp. 62, 65 passim.

46. Jessie Taft, *Will Therapy, Truth and Reality: Dr. Otto Rank* (New York: Alfred A. Knopf, 1945), esp. xiii, xiv. For a revealing and appreciative biography of Rank see James Lieberman, *Acts of Will: The Life and Work of Otto Rank* (New York: Free Press, 1985).

Chapter 4. Culture and Rebellion, 1912–1930

1. David Hollinger, "Ethnic Diversity, Cosmopolitanism and the Emergence of the American Liberal Intelligentsia," *American Quarterly* 27:2 (1975): 133–51; John C. Burnham, "The New Psychology: From Narcissism to Social Control," in John Braeman et al., eds., *Change and Continuity in American History in the 1920's* (Columbus: Ohio State Univ. Press, 1968). Henry F. May, *The End of American Innocence* (New York: Alfred A. Knopf, 1959); Fred Matthews, "The Americanization of Sigmund Freud," *Journal of American Studies* 1 (April 1967): 39–62, and "Freud Comes to America: The Impact of Freudian Ideas on American Thought, 1909–1917" (Master's Thesis, University of California, Berkeley, 1957). Stanley Coben, "The Assault on Victorianism in the Twentieth Century," *American Quarterly* 27 (Dec. 1976): 604–25, *Rebellion Against Victorianism* (New York: Oxford Univ. Press, 1991).

2. Randolph Bourne, *History of a Literary Radical and Other Essays* (New York: B. W. Huebsch, 1921), 62–65; Louis Filler, *Randolph Bourne* (Washington, D.C.: American Council on Public Affairs, 1943), 4–5; Floyd Dell, draft of a letter to George Bernard Shaw, Davenport, Iowa, 1908, DP; Sherwood Anderson, *Memoirs* (New York: Harcourt, Brace, 1942), 247–48.

3. Jack J. Spector, *The Aesthetics of Freud* (New York: McGraw-Hill, 1972), chs. 2 and 3, and Peter Gay, *Freud,* (New York: W. W. Norton, 1988), 313–23. Isador Coriat, *The Hysteria of Lady Macbeth* (Boston: Four Seas, 1920), x–xv; George Soule, "Realism as Confession," *New Republic* 8 (April 19, 1916): 63–64; George Thomas Tanselle (Floyd Dell), "Faun at the Barricades" (Ph.D. diss., Northwestern University, 1961), 248.

4. Tanselle, "Faun," 92; Walter Lippmann, *Preface to Politics* (New York: Mitchell Kennerly, 1913), 50–51; Floyd Dell, *Homecoming: An Autobiography* (New York: Farrar and Rinehart, 1933), 213; Dell, "The Science of the Soul," review of Jung's *Psychology of the Unconscious, The Masses* 8 (July 1916): 30.

5. Floyd Dell, *Intellectual Vagabondage* (New York: George H. Doran, 1926), ch. 5; Dell, *Women as World Builders* (c. 1913; Westport, Conn., Hyperion Press, 1976); Horace W. Frink, *Morbid Fears and Compulsions* (New York: Moffat, Yard, 1918), 135–36.

6. Joseph Freeman, *An American Testament* (New York: Farrar and Rinehart, 1936), 37, 246–47.

7. Quoted in Tanselle, "Faun," 190; Walter Lippmann, "Freud and the Layman," *New Republic* 2 (April 17, 1915): 10.

8. Interview, B. W. Huebsch, New York, May 15, 1960. NYT, March 2, 1913, sec. 5, p. 10; Mabel Dodge Luhan, *Movers and Shakers* (New York: Harcourt, Brace, 1933); Floyd Dell, "Speaking of Psycho-Analysis: The New Boon for Dinner Table Conversationalists," *Vanity Fair* 5 (Dec. 1915): 53.

9. Margaret Anderson, *My Thirty Years' War* (New York: Covici, Friede, 1930), 94, 41, 220; *Little Review* 7:4 (Jan.–March 1921): 23–24; Arthur Frank Wertheim, *The New York Little Renaissance: Iconoclasm, Modernism, and Nationalism in American Culture, 1908–1917* (New York: New York Univ. Press, 1976), 69–77; Hans Borchers, *Freud und die americanische Literatur 1920–1940* (Muenchen: Wilhelm Fink Verlag, 1987), 13–14.

10. Tanselle, "Faun," 253, 134; interview, Floyd Dell, Washington, D.C., June 18, 1960; Dell to Rabbi William Fineshriber, fall 1913, DP.

11. Walter Lippmann, *A Preface to Politics* (New York: Mitchell Kennerley, 1913), 85, 50–51, 162, 233; interview, Walter Lippmann, Washington, D.C., May 28, 1960;

Ronald Steele, *Walter Lippmann and the American Century* (Boston: Little, Brown, 1980); Frederick J. Hoffman, *Freudianism and the Literary Mind* (Baton Rouge: Louisiana State Univ. Press, 1957), 53–55; David E. Weingast, *Walter Lippmann* (New Brunswick, N.J.: Rutgers Univ. Press, 1949); Charles Budd Forcey, *The Crossroads of Liberalism* (New York: Oxford Univ. Press, 1961).

12. Lippmann, "Freud and the Layman," *New Republic* 2 (April 17, 1915): 9–10.

13. Alfred B. Kuttner, *New Republic* 2 (March 20, 1915): 182–83; Kuttner, "Sons and Lovers: A Freudian Appreciation," *New Republic* 2 (April 10, 1915): 255–57; Kuttner, "Nerves," in Harold E. Stearns, ed., *Civilization in the United States: An Enquiry by Thirty Americans* (New York: Jonathan Cape, 1922), 428–35.

14. Lippmann interview; Lippmann, *A Preface to Politics,* 84; review of Wilfred Trotter, *Instincts of the Herd in War and Peace, New Republic* 9 (Nov. 18, 1916): 16–18; review of C. G. Jung, *The Psychology of the Unconscious, New Republic* 7 (May 6, 1916): 22–23.

15. Floyd Dell, "The Science of the Soul," *The Masses* 8:9 (July 1916): 30; Max Eastman, "Revolutionary Birth Control," *The Masses,* 6:10 (July 1915): 21–22. William L. O'Neill, *The Last Romantic: A Life of Max Eastman* (New York: Oxford Univ. Press, 1978).

16. *The Masses* 9 (Oct. 1917): 22. Dell, "The Science of the Soul," *The Masses* 8:9 (July 1916): 30; review of A. E. Maeder, *The Dream Problem, The Masses* 8:6 (April 1916): 28.

17. James Oppenheim, "What Jung Has Done," *New Republic* 7 (May 20, 1916): 67–68; Oppenheim, *Your Hidden Powers* (New York: Alfred A. Knopf, 1923), 1, 37, 41.

18. Theodore Dreiser, "Neurotic America and the Sex Impulse," in Dreiser, *Hey, Rub-a-Dub-Dub* (New York: Boni and Liveright, 1920), 131–36, 141.

19. Floyd Dell, "How It Feels To Be Psychoanalyzed," undated ms., DP; Dell, *Homecoming,* 293–96; Otto Fenichel, *The Psychoanalytic Theory of Neurosis* (New York: W. W. Norton, 1945), 463–64.

20. Leslie Fishbein, "Freud and the Radicals," *Canadian Review of American Studies* 12:2 (Fall 1981): 175; Dell, *Homecoming,* 6, 23, 272–73; Alan Trachtenberg, ed., *The Memoirs of Waldo Frank* (Amherst: Univ. of Massachusetts Press, 1973), 6–7, 199–208; Max Eastman, *The Enjoyment of Living* (New York: Harper and Bros., 1948), 105–6, 124–25, 187, 243, 323–24.

21. Freeman, *Testament,* 403; interview, Joseph Freeman, New York, May 10, 1960; in interviews both Dell and Moritz Jagendorf, a friend of Andre Tridon's, insisted that the change was in attitudes, not personal conduct. But given Kinsey's findings, this could well have been truer for men than for women.

22. Freeman, *Testament,* 117.

23. Dell, *Homecoming,* 290–95.

24. Anderson, *My Thirty Years' War,* 4; Sherwood Anderson, *Notebook* (New York: Boni and Liveright, 1926), 21; Dell, *Intellectual Vagabondage,* 139, 171; Dell, *Moon Calf* (New York: Alfred A. Knopf, 1921), 387–89; Eastman, *Enjoyment of Living,* 124–25; Irving Howe, *Sherwood Anderson* (New York: William Sloan, 1951), 179.

25. Freeman, *Testament,* 236–7, 244–46; Tanselle, "Faun," 38; Dell, "How It Feels To Be Psychoanalyzed," 19.

26. Florence Kiper Frank, "Psycho-Analysis: Some Random Thoughts Thereon," *Little Review* 3 (June–July 1916): 15–17, and Frank, "The Psychoanalyst" R 4 (1917): 459.

27. Lippmann interview; Floyd Dell, "How It Feels To Be Psychoanalyzed," 5; Mabel Dodge Luhan, *Intimate Memories,* vol. 3: *Movers and Shakers* (New York: Harcourt Brace, 1936), 506.

28. Tanselle, "Faun," 243–48, 432, 20–24, 6, 45–47, 61–70, 134; Dell, *Homecoming,* 279–87, 291–95.

29. Dell interview; Dell, "How It Feels To Be Psychoanalyzed," 14–22.

30. Dell, *Homecoming,* 334; Dell, *Intellectual Vagabondage,* 242; Tanselle, "Faun," 245–49, 269, 255.

31. Dell, *Intellectual Vagabondage,* 248–49; Dell, *Janet March* (New York: Alfred A. Knopf, 1923), 250; Tanselle, "Faun," 259, 294, 315–16, 332, 255.

32. Interview, Malcolm Cowley, New York, May 14, 1960; Dell interview; Tanselle, "Faun," 380–87; Dell, *Love in the Machine Age* (New York: Farrar and Rinehart, 1930), 407, 141–42, 168, 179, 398, 99; *The Times of India* (Bombay), Nov. 25, 1930, clipping in CP.

33. Lois Palken Rudnick, *Mabel Dodge Luhan: New Woman, New Worlds* (Albuquerque: Univ. of New Mexico Press, 1984); for a useful account of Mabel's relationship to A. A. Brill, see Emily Hahn, *Mabel: A Biography of Mabel Dodge Luhan* (Boston: Houghton, Mifflin, 1977). Dodge Luhan, *Movers and Shakers,* 339–440, 505–6, 511–12; Van Wyck Brooks, *The Confident Years* (New York: E. P. Dutton, 1952), 476–77.

34. Mabel Dodge to Smith Ely Jelliffe, Jan. 7, 1916, DLP; Dodge Luhan, *Movers and Shakers,* 444, 506.

35. Undated postscript on a card, Mabel Dodge Luhan to Jelliffe, DLP.

36. Dodge Luhan, *Movers and Shakers,* 444, 506.

37. Ibid., 511.

38. Ibid., 468.

39. Brill to Dodge Luhan, Aug. 29, 1928, DLP.

40. O'Neill, *Last Romantic,* 55.

41. Eastman, *Enjoyment of Living,* xiii, 187, 490–494, 124; Eastman, "A Significant Memory of Freud," *New Republic* 104 (May 19, 1941): 694–95.

42. Eastman, *Enjoyment of Living,* 27, xiii, 187, 490–94, 124; "A Significant Memory of Freud," 693–95.

43. Eastman, *Enjoyment of Living,* 492; Freeman, *Testament,* 276; Waldo Frank, *In the American Jungle* (New York: Farrar and Rinehart, 1925), 89–91.

44. O'Neill, *Last Romantic,* 284.

45. Leonard Wilcox, "Sex Boys in a Balloon," *Journal of American Studies* 23:1 (1989): 7–26. See the Calverton papers in the New York Public Library for the problems of organizing the contributors to *Sex in Civilization,* along with press clippings of the reviews. Dell interview; Samuel Tannenbaum, "Sexual Abstinence and Nervousness," *American Journal of Urology* 9 (1913): 290–322; "Dr. Samuel A. Tannenbaum of New York City Recants," *Current Opinion* 72 (June 1922): 795; Samuel Schmalhausen and V. F. Calverton, *Sex in Civilization* (Garden City, N.Y.: Garden City Publishing, 1929); Clipping on the death of John Roach Stratton, *New York Telegram,* Oct. 30, 1929, CP.

46. Interview, Mauritz Jagendorf, New York, May 15, 1960; NYT, Nov. 23, 1922, p. 21; Nov. 28, 1922, p. 11; Burnham, "From Narcissism"; Bernard de Voto, "Freud in American Literature," Q 9 (1940): 236–45, and *Forays and Rebuttals* (Boston: Little, Brown, 1936), 224–25, 231–32.

47. Andre Tridon, *The New Unionism* (New York: B. W. Huebsch, 1913), 188, 192, 198; H. L. Mencken, *A Book of Prefaces* (New York: Alfred A. Knopf, 1917), 57; Andre Tridon, *Psychoanalysis and Love* (New York: Brentano's, 1923), 263; interview, B. W. Heubsch, New York, May 6, 1960.

48. Jagendorf interview.

49. Andre Tridon, *Psychoanalysis and Behavior* (New York: Alfred A. Knopf, 1923), 244, 247–50; Tridon, *Psychoanalysis, Its History, Theory and Practice* (New York: B. W. Huebsch, 1921), 121; C. P. Oberndorf, *A History of Psychoanalysis in America* (New York: Grune and Stratton, 1953), 175–76; Ernest Jones, Review of *Dream Psychology by Sigmund Freud, authorized translation by M. D. Eder, with Preface by Andre Tridon*, IJ 3 (1922): 114–15.

50. Tridon, *Psychoanalysis and Love*, 65, 80, 52–53, 103.

51. Tridon, *Psychoanalysis and Behavior*, 123–24.

52. Ibid., 244, 77; Joseph Wood Krutch, *The Modern Temper* (New York: G. P. Putnam's Sons, 1929), 1, 68.

53. Tridon, *Psychoanalysis and Behavior*, 247–49, 263–65; Tridon, *Psychoanalysis, Its History, Theory and Practice*, 135.

54. Tridon, *Psychoanalysis and Love*, 101; Tridon, *Psychoanalysis, Its History, Theory and Practice*, 244, 253.

55. Tridon, *Psychoanalysis and Love*, 112, 67–73.

56. Tridon, *Psychoanalysis, Its History, Theory and Practice*, 19, 239; Tridon, *Psychoanalysis and Behavior*, 282; *The Nation* 116 (Dec. 15, 1920): 694; *Survey* 47 (Oct. 15, 1921): 85.

57. See Ernest Jones to Freud, Jan. 26, 1922, in FJ, 456; see also FJ, 444, 455, 458; Jones, IJ 3 (1922): 114–15.

58. Quoted in Catherine Covert, "Freud on the Front Page: Transmission of Freudian ideas in the American newspaper of the 1920's" (Ph.D. diss., Syracuse University, 1975), 129.

59. NYT, April 23, 1922, p. 14.

60. NYT, Nov. 23, 1922, p. 21.

61. Max Bodenheim, *Current Opinion* 73 (Aug. 1922): 257–58; Helen McAffee, "The Literature of Disillusion," *Atlantic Monthly* 132 (Aug. 1923): 229–31; Stuart Sherman, "The Point of View in American Criticism," *Atlantic Monthly* 130 (Nov. 1922): 629–31; John Palmer, "H. R. Lenormand and the Play of Psychoanalysis," *Nineteenth Century* 100 (Oct. 1926): 594–602; John Farrar, "Sex Psychology in Modern Fiction," *The Independent* 117 (Dec. 11, 1926): 669–70; Dorothy Ross, "The New Psychology and the New History," in Stanley Elkins and Erik McKitrick, eds., *The Hofstadter Aegis* (New York: Alfred A. Knopf, 1974).

62. Walter Lippmann, *A Preface to Morals* (1929; New York: Beacon Press, 1960), 176–80.

63. Ibid., 302, 220–22, 6.

Chapter 5. Popular and Applied Psychoanalysis, 1917–1940

1. Ives Hendrick, *Facts and Theories of Psychoanalysis* (New York: Alfred A. Knopf, 1939), 249; interview, Gerald Pearson, Philadelphia, July 3, 1960; Charles Kadushin, *Why People Go to Psychiatrists* (New York: Atherton Press, 1969), 15; Robert Castel, *The Psychiatric Society* (New York: Columbia Univ. Press, 1982). John C. Burnham, "Psychology and Counseling: Convergence into a Profession," in Nathan O. Hatch, ed., *The Professions in American History* (Notre Dame, Ind.: Univ. of Notre Dame Press, 1988). For a negative and highly polemical view of Freud's impact on American culture see E. Fuller Torrey, *Freudian Fraud* (New York: Harper Collins, 1992). He blames Freud for American permissiveness and stresses the identification of radical politics and culture with psychoanalysis.

2. "Damage and Defense," *Time* 27:2 (May 25, 1936): 31–32.

3. J. Arthur Thompson, *The Outline of Science* (G. P. Putnam's Sons, 1937), 556–63; Sigmund Freud, "Psychoanalysis: Exploring the Hidden Recesses of the Mind," in *These Eventful Years* (New York: Encyclopedia Britannica, 1924), vol. 2, pp. 511–23. For some of the potboilers, see James Oppenheim, *Your Hidden Powers* (New York: Alfred A. Knopf, 1923); Joseph Ralph, *Psychical Surgery* (Los Angeles: Times-Mirror Printing and Binding, 1920); David Orr Edison, M.D., *Getting What We Want: How to Apply Psychoanalysis to Your Own Problems* (New York and London: Harper and Bros., 1921). For the Haldeman-Julius series see E. Haldeman-Julius, *The First Hundred Million* (New York: Simon and Schuster, 1928).

4. Jelliffe to Jones, Oct. 24, 1927, JP.

5. Harry Kerns to Frankwood Williams, June 6, 1923, Williams to Kerns, June 9, 1923, WP.

6. *The Occult Digest,* Oct. 1925, p. 50, FA; Peter M. Rutkoff and William B. Scott, *New School: A History of the New School for Social Research* (New York: Free Press, 1986); Frankwood Williams, quoted in Allan Harding, "Why Queer People Are Queer," *American Magazine* 97 (May 1924): 42–43; Clement Wood, *Sex in Psychoanalysis*, ed. E. Haldeman-Julius (Little Blue Book no. 800, Girard, Kansas, n.d.).

7. Catherine Covert, "Freud on the Front Page" (Ph.D. diss., Syracuse University, 1975), 247.

8. The evidence for this "cult" is largely anecdotal, often contained in the correction of "misinterpretations" by analysts; both psychiatrists and laymen thought it existed. See the discussion in Frederick J. Hoffman, *Freudianism and the Literary Mind* (Baton Rouge: Louisiana State Univ. Press, 1957), 32–33.

9. Percy Marks, *The Plastic Age* (New York: Century, 1924), 314.

10. Eugene O'Neill, *Strange Interlude,* in *Nine Plays by Eugene O'Neill* (New York: Modern Library, 1932), 515.

11. Joseph Jastrow, "The Freudian Temper and Its Menace to the Lay Mind," *Century* (Oct. 1929): 31, 29–38.

12. Grace Adams, "The Rise and Fall of Psychology," *Atlantic* 153 (Jan. 1934): 82–92; John Crowe Ransome, review of Freud, *Group Psychology,* SRL 1 (Oct. 4, 1924): 161.

13. Karl Menninger, "Psychiatry," in Harold Stearns, ed., *America Now* (New York: Literary Guild of America, 1938), 438; Travis Bogard, *Contour in Time: The Plays of Eugene O'Neill* (New York: Oxford Univ. Press, 1972), 346–47. Actually O'Neill wrote that too much Freud was read into his work and that only Jung interested him; see ibid., 345. David Sievers sees the Oedipus complex, "sexual suppression and frustration," dreams, and satires on psychoanalysis in a large number of Broadway plays of the 1920s; see Sievers, *Freud on Broadway* (New York: Hermitage House, 1955), chs. 3, 5, 6, 10.

14. Interview, Hilde Greenson, Santa Monica, Oct. 15, 1987.

15. See the seating list in FA; for the speeches, R 8:3 (July 1931): 237–50, 329.

16. Frankwood E. Williams, "Toward a Science of Man," *Survey* 64:3 (May 1, 1930): 123–25; "Psychoanalysis Comes of Age," *Survey* 68 (Nov. 15, 1932): 580. Ives Hendrick, *Facts and Theories of Psychoanalysis* (2nd ed., New York: Alfred A. Knopf, 1939). The psychologist Carney Landis argued that psychoanalysis was a form of psychological experiment, but that its metapsychology was mere speculative philosophy. See "Psychoanalysis and the Scientific Method," *Science* n.s. 93 (May 23, 1941): 486. Franz Alexander, "In Defense of Psychoanalysis," SRL 15 (Feb. 27, 1937): 9; Martin W. Peck, "Psychoanalysis and Humankind," *Survey* 4:3 (May 11, 1930): 127–30.

17. Dorothy Thompson, *Philadelphia Public Ledger,* March 11, 1923.

18. H. V. Kaltenborn, "A Talk with Dr. Freud, Psycho-Analyst," *Brooklyn Daily Eagle*, Dec. 18, 1921. See also Covert, "Freud," 129–30.

19. Havelock Ellis, "Tribute to Freud," *Forum* 76 (July 1926): 150–53. "In Freud's Death World Loses a Pioneer in Science of the Mind," *Science News Letter* 36 (Sept. 30, 1939): 221.

20. Interview, Moritz Jagendorf, New York, May 15, 1960.

21. "Intellectual Provocateur," *Time* 33 (June 26, 1939): 59–63.

22. *American Journal of Sociology* 45 (Nov. 1939); *Time* 31 (May 23, 1938): 61.

23. Bernard DeVoto, "Freud's Influence on Literature," SRL 20 (Oct. 7, 1939): 10–11.

24. John R. McMahon, "The Jazz Path to Degradation," LHJ 39 (Jan. 1922): 26, 71; review of *Sex in Civilization,* by John Langdon Davies, *New York Herald Tribune,* March 31, 1929, clipping in CP.

25. W. Beran Wolfe, "The Twilight," *American Mercury* 35: 140 1 (Aug. 1935): 393–94.

26. A thorough, sensitive discussion of changes in sexual attitudes and behavior in this period is Christine Clare Simmons, "Marriage in the Modern Manner, 1914–1941" (Ph.D. diss., Brown University, 1982); Mary Ware Dennett, *The Sex Education of Children* (New York: Vanguard Press, 1931), and *Who's Obscene* (New York: Vanguard Press, 1930), an account of Mrs. Dennett's trial for obscenity, with letters and testimony for and against.

27. Dennett, *Who's Obscene,* 103–6.

28. "Analyzing the Psychoanalysts," *Review of Reviews* 76 (Sept. 1927): 322–23.

29. Charles W. Burr, "Broken Minds of Youth," *Hygeia* 6 (Oct. 1928): 550.

30. *Weekly Review* 5 (July 16, 1921), 50–51.

31. George Matheson Cullen, *The Living Age* 31:1 (July 9, 1921): 103–8. S. T., "A Modern's Search in Science," *Century* 118 (May 1929): 90–95; "Meditations on the Death of Sigmund Freud," *Christian Register,* Oct. 5, 1939, pp. 567–70, FA. For the responses of religious leaders, see John C. Burnham, "The Encounter of Christian Theology with Deterministic Psychology and Psychoanalysis," BMC 49:4 (1985): 321–52; and Frances Arick Kolb, "The Reaction of American Protestants to Psychoanalysis, 1900–1950" (Ph.D. diss., Washington University, 1972); G. Allison Stokes, "Ministry after Freud: The Rise of the Religion and Health Movement in American Protestantism, 1906–1945" (Ph.D. diss., Yale University, 1981), 145, 152–58, and passim.

32. Editorial, *American Mercury* 11 (July 1927): 289.

33. Donald Slesinger, "Professor vs. Psychiatrist," *Survey* 59 (March 15, 1928): 762; Donald A. Laird, "Is Your Mind like an Iceberg," *Forum* 68:4 (Oct. 1922): 893; Eastman, *The Masses* 8:3 (Jan. 1916): 11; George S. Viereck, *Theodore Roosevelt* (New York: Jackson Press, 1919); William Bayard Hale, *The Story of a Style* (New York: B. W. Huebsch, 1920).

34. Quoted in Covert, "Freud," 148.

35. Franz Alexander, "Buddhistic Training as an Artificial Catatonia," R 18:2 (April 1931): 129–45; Lorine Pruette, "Some Applications of the Inferiority Complex to Pluralistic Behavior," R 9:1 (Jan. 1922): 35. Pruette wrote a biography of the psychologist G. Stanley Hall. Theodore Schroeder, "The Psychoanalytic Approach to Religious Experience," R 16 (1929): 376.

36. William Ernest Hocking, *Human Nature and Its Remaking* (New Haven: Yale Univ. Press, 1923), ix, 35–39.

37. Harvey O'Higgins, "Your Other Self," *Outlook* 150 (Nov. 1928): 1229.

38. Frankwood Williams, "Putting Away Childish Things," *Survey* 60 (April 1, 1928): 13; Martin W. Peck, "Psychoanalysis and Humankind," *Survey* 64 (May 1, 1930): 127–28.

39. For an insightful study of the Menningers, see Lawrence Friedman, *Menninger* (New York: Alfred A. Knopf, 1990); John C. Burnham, *Jelliffe: American Psychoanalyst and Physician and His Correspondence with Sigmund Freud and C. G. Jung* (Chicago: Univ. of Chicago Press, 1983); J. E. Carney, "The Psychoanalytic Education of the Dean of American Psychiatry," R 19:1 (Fall 1990): 71–87.

40. Karl Menninger, "Pseudoanalysis: The Peril of Freudian Verbalisms," *Outlook* 155:10 (July 9, 1930): 363, 397; Menninger, *The Human Mind* (New York: Alfred A. Knopf, 1930), 354.

41. Menninger, *Mind,* 117.

42. Ibid., 267.

43. Ibid., 364.

44. Menninger, "Mental Hygiene in the Home," LHJ (Nov. 1930): 101.

45. Menninger, *Mind,* 352. See Chapter 9, nn. 31–32.

46. Menninger, *Mind,* 369.

47. Karl Menninger, "The Quest for Happiness," LHJ (Feb. 1931): 96.

48. Abraham Myerson, AP 17:2 (Jan. 1938): 998–1001.

49. Menninger, *Man Against Himself* (New York: Alfred A. Knopf, 1938), 4, 420–21, 449–50. Some of Menninger's argument seems to be derived directly from Franz Alexander, "The Need for Punishment and the Death Instinct," IJ 10:2–3 (1929); 256–69.

50. Menninger, *Man Against Himself,* viii, 420–21.

51. Ibid., 436.

52. For the growth of college education and the professions see Stanley Coben, *Rebellion Against Victorianism* (New York: Oxford Univ. Press, 1991), chs. 2, 3.

53. Christine Mary Shea, "The Ideology of Mental Health and the Emergence of the Therapeutic Liberal State: The American Mental Hygiene Movement, 1900–1930" (Ph.D. diss., University of Illinois, Urbana, 1980), see especially chs. 5, 6; Theresa Richardson, *The Century of the Child: The Mental Hygiene Movement and Social Policy in the United States and Canada* (Albany: State Univ. of New York Press, 1989), applies a Foucaultian perspective.

54. The most expansive but critical assessment of psychoanalytic influence is Irving David Bernstein, *The Developmental Background of Psychotherapy* (New York: New York Univ. School of Education, 1934), 76–77, 112. The journal *Progressive Education* carried articles by psychoanalysts: Fritz Wittels, "Psychoanalysis for Teachers," 8 (1931): 238–41; Isador Coriat, "The Psychoanalytic Approach to Education," 3 (1926): 19–23; Frankwood Williams, "The Field of Mental Hygiene," 3 (1926): 7–13. Smiley Blanton and Margaret Gray Blanton, *Child Guidance* (New York: Century, 1927), 6, 7, 150–58, 167; and for perhaps the most often cited text see William Alanson White, *The Mental Hygiene of Childhood* (Boston: Little, Brown, 1919), xiv, 53, 61, 92, 112. For an early reflection of Freud's influence see Lewis Terman, *The Hygiene of the School Child* (New York: Houghton, Mifflin, 1914), 319–21.

55. Williams to Kerns, Feb. 8, 1924, WP.

56. "Harry Hopkins," *Fortune* 12:1 (July 1935): 62.

57. Frankwood Williams, *Soviet Russia Fights Neurosis* (London: George Routledge and Sons, 1934), 127–28, 134–39, 209–12, 237. Interview, Emily Martin, New York, May 8, 1960; interview, Bernard Glueck, Chapel Hill, North Carolina, June 2, 1960; "In Memoriam: Frankwood E. Williams, 1883–1936," Q 5:4 (Oct. 1936): 465–66.

58. Miriam Van Waters, *Youth in Conflict* (New York: Republic Publishing, 1926), x–xi. The daughter of an Episcopal priest, she held a Clark University doctorate in anthropology; see the biography *The Lady at Box 99* by Burton J. Rowles (Greenwich, Conn.: Seabury Press, 1962).

59. George Stevenson, *Child Guidance Clinics: A Quarter Century of Development* (New York: Commonwealth Fund, 1934), 65. For the lack of explicitly Freudian developmental content of popular child-raising literature see A. Michael Shulman, "The Freudianization of the American Child: The Impact of Psychoanalysis in Popular Periodical Literature in the United States, 1919–1939" (Ph.D. diss., University of Pittsburgh, 1972); for a typical eclectic view see Douglas Thom, *Everyday Problems of the Everyday Child* (New York: D. Appleton, 1927).

60. National Committee for Mental Hygiene, *Mental Hygiene Bulletin* 10:2–3 (Feb.–March 1932): 1; Frederick H. Allen, "The Evolution of Our Treatment Philosophy in Child Guidance," *Mental Hygiene* 14 (Jan. 1930): 1–11. The most insightful and comprehensive discussions of the mental hygiene movement in relation to education are Sol Cohen, "The Mental Hygiene Movement and the Development of Personality: Changing Conceptions of the American College and University, 1920–1940," *History of Higher Education Annual* 2 (1982): 65–101; Cohen, "The Mental Hygiene Movement, the Development of Personality and the School: The Medicalization of American Education," *History of Education Quarterly* (Summer 1983); Cohen, "The Mental Hygiene Movement, the Commonwealth Fund and Public Education, 1921–1933," in Gerald Benjamin, ed., *Private Philanthropy and Public Elementary and Secondary Education* (Rockefeller Archive Center Publication, 1979); Fred Matthews, "In Defense of Common Sense: Mental Hygiene as Ideology and Mentality in Twentieth Century America," *Prospects* 2 (Winter 1979): 459–516. See also Stevenson, *Child Guidance Clinics*, 232, 60–65, 122; Clements C. Fry and Edna Rostow, *Mental Hygiene in College* (New York: Commonwealth Fund, 1942). Harry Kerns to Frankwood Williams, Oct. 14, 1921, April 20, 1922, Jan. 26, 1923, Jan. 23, 1924, March 12, 1927, WP.

61. See Kathleen Jones's admirable study, "As the Twig Is Bent: American Psychiatry and the Troublesome Child, 1890–1940" (Ph.D. diss., State University of New Jersey, Rutgers, 1988). See esp. 295–302.

62. Margo Horn, *Before It's Too Late: The Child Guidance Movement in the United States 1922–1945* (Philadelphia: Temple Univ. Press, 1989), 60, 130, 101–2, 145–52.

63. Kathleen Jones, "As the Twig," 226, 287, 314–28. "Mama's Boys," *Time* 48 (Nov. 25, 1946): 80.

64. Carleton Ashburne, "The Educator's Response," *Mental Hygiene* 19 (1935): 47; Edward W. Homans, "Salvaging the Family," *Progressive Education* 3:4 (1926): 286.

65. Lawrence Cremin, *The Transformation of the School* (New York: Alfred A. Knopf, 1961), 210–12. See, for example, Fritz Wittels, "Psychoanalysis for Teachers," *Progressive Education* 8 (1931): 238–41; Floyd Dell, "Adolescent Education," ibid. 9 (1932): 472–81; Isador H. Coriat, "The Psychoanalytic Approach to Education," ibid. 3: 19–25; Frankwood Williams, ibid. 3, 7–13.

66. Morton Leavitt, "Dewey and Freud" (Ph.D. diss., University of Michigan, 1956), 175; Max Eastman, "A Significant Memory of Freud," *New Republic* 104:2 (May 19, 1941): 694; Lewis Feuer, "The Standpoints of Dewey and Freud: A Contrast and an Analysis," *Journal of Individual Psychology* 15–16 (1960): 119–36.

67. Sol Cohen, "In the Name of the Prevention of Neurosis: The Search for a Psychoanalytic Pedagogy in Europe, 1905–1938," in Barbara Finkelstein, ed., *Regu-*

lated Children/Liberated Children: Education in Psychohistorical Perspectives (New York: Psychohistory Press, 1979); Sol Cohen, "Psychoanalysis and Progressive Education in Europe: Susan Isaacs and the Malting House School, Cambridge, England, 1924–1927," ms., 4–5. Freud, "The Claims of Psychoanalysis to Scientific Interest" (1913), SE 13, p. 190.

68. Fritz Wittels, *Set the Children Free* (London: George Allen and Unwin, 1932), 232.

69. In an interview (Philadelphia, July 13, 1960), Gerald Pearson argued that permissiveness which came from Dewey's influence was important by the early 1930s and that the schools were too much concerned with personality development and not enough with whether children learned to work or not.

70. Interview, Peter Blos, New York, Nov. 10, 1977; interview, Erik Erikson, Tiburon, Calif., April 29, 1976.

71. Margaret Naumberg, *The Child and the World: Dialogues in Modern Education* (New York: Harcourt, Brace, 1928), 207–8, 211; Dalton B. Curtis, Jr., "Psychoanalysis and Progressive Education: Margaret Naumberg at the Walden School," *Vitae Scholasticae* 2:2 (Fall 1983): 339–59.

72. Benjamin Spock and Mary Morgan, *Spock on Spock: A Memoir of Growing Up With the Century* (New York: Pantheon Books, 1985), 43, 110–11, 112.

73. Caroline B. Zachry, "The Influence of Psychoanalysis in Education," Q 10:3 (1941): 431–44. "In Memoriam: Caroline B. Zachry, 1894–1945," Q 14 (1945): 392. For an example of the watered-down translation of such psychoanalytic conceptions as oral, anal, and genital stages and instinctive drives see Zachry, *Emotion and Conduct in Adolescence* (New York: D. Appleton-Century, 1940), 4–20.

74. Susan Isaacs, *Social Development in Young Children* (London: George Routledge and Sons, 1933), 416–24; D. E. M. Gardner, *Susan Isaacs* (London: Methuen Educational, 1969), 68, 73–74.

75. Isaacs, *Social Development,* 419:

76. Willi Hoffer, "Psychoanalytic Education," cited in Sol Cohen, "In the Name of the Prevention of Neurosis," 204; Rudolf Ekstein and Rocco L. Motto, "Psychoanalysis and Education—An Historical Account," in Ekstein and Motto, eds., *From Learning to Love to Love of Learning: Essays on Psychoanalysis and Education* (New York: Brunner/Mazel, 1969), 3–27.

77. See Chapter 13.

78. Zachry, "The Influence of Psychoanalysis in Education," 436, 442.

79. Sol Cohen, "From Badness to Sickness: The Mental Hygiene Movement and the Crisis in School Discipline," *Proteus* (Spring 1987), 9–14. For earlier summaries of the psychoanalytic influence see Lawrence Cremin, *The Transformation of the School* (New York: Alfred A. Knopf, 1961), 207–15, and Fred Kerlinger, "The Origins of the Doctrine of Permissiveness in American Education," *Progressive Education* 33:6 (Nov. 1954): 161–65.

80. Cohen, "From Badness to Sickness."

81. "Conference on Mental Factors in Crime," *Survey* 59 (Jan. 15, 1928): 490, 506; Frank Moore quoted in Virginia Robinson, *A Changing Psychology in Social Case Work* (Chapel Hill: Univ. of North Carolina Press, 1930), 66.

82. Scrapbook of Dr. Karl M. Bowman, who testified at the trial.

83. *Chicago Tribune,* July 30, 1924.

84. Covert, "Freud," 6; *Chicago Daily News,* Aug. 1, 1924.

85. Covert, "Freud," 8.

86. *Chicago Daily News,* July 29, Aug. 4, 1924.

87. *Boston Daily Advertiser,* Aug. 5, 1924.

88. The judge's opinion is quoted in Maureen McKernan, *The Amazing Crime and Trial of Leopold and Loeb* (Chicago: Plymouth Court Press, 1924), 378–79.

89. Covert, "Freud," 152–64.

90. Sheldon Glueck, "Mental Hygiene and Crime," R 19:1 (Jan. 1932): 31, 33.

91. Atwell Westwick, "Criminology and Psychoanalysis," Q 9:2 (April 1940): 280, 276. For an overview of some important psychoanalytic views of crime see John J. Fitzpatrick, "Psychoanalysis and Crime: A Critical Survey of Salient Trends in the Literature." *Annals AAPSS* 423 (Jan. 1978): 67–74.

92. Elizabeth G. Meier, *A History of the New York School of Social Work* (New York: Columbia Univ. Press, 1954), 63–69; Roy Lubove, *The Professional Altruist: The Emergence of Social Work as a Career* (Cambridge, Mass.: Harvard Univ. Press, 1965).

93. Grace F. Marcus, "The Status of Social Case Work Today," *Proceedings of the National Conference of Social Work* (1935), 128–30. A useful short summary is Gordon Hamilton, "Freud's Contribution to Social Work," in Howard J. Prad, ed., *Ego Psychology and Dynamic Casework* (New York: Family Service Association of America, 1958), 12–35, esp. 15, 19. For an overview of psychoanalysis and social work see Shirley Hellenbrand, "Freud's Influence on Social Casework," BMC 36 (1972): 407–18.

94. Interview, Mrs. Everett Kimball, Smith College, May 5, 1960; E. James Lieberman, *Acts of Will: The Life and Work of Otto Rank* (New York: Free Press, 1985), 273–75. The bulletins of the New York School of Social Work and catalogues of the Pennsylvania and Smith College schools document these trends. In interviews on June 20 and July 6, 1960, Phyllis Blanchard noted that the psychoanalytic influence in Philadelphia guidance clinics did not take hold until the late 1920s.

95. Virginia Robinson, *A Changing Psychology in Social Case Work* (Chapel Hill: Univ. of North Carolina Press, 1930), 35–37, 166, and *Supervision in Social Case Work* (Chapel Hill: Univ. of North Carolina Press, 1936), 57–60.

96. See the extensive correspondence in KenP.

97. Hellenbrand, "Freud's Influence on Social Case Work," 407–18.

98. Karl Menninger, *Love Against Hate,* 124.

99. John H. Preston, "D.D. vs. M.D., *Scribner's Magazine* 87 (May 1930): 554–59; George Draper, "Psychoanalysis: The Inward Eye," *Scribner's Magazine* 90 (Dec. 1931): 666–72; Andrew Abbott, *The System of Professions* (Chicago: Univ. of Chicago Press, 1988), Ch. 10, and "The Emergence of American Psychiatry" (Ph.D. diss., University of Chicago, 1982).

100. Interview, Margaret Mead, New York, May 16, 1960.

101. Ludwig Lewisohn, *The Island Within* (New York: Harper and Bros., 1929), 215–17, 248.

102. Hoffman, *Freudianism and the Literary Mind,* 282–83.

103. Lewisohn, *Up Stream, an American Chronicle* (New York: 1929), 145–47.

104. Lucien Cary, "How It Feels to be Psychoanalyzed," *American Magazine* 99 (May 1925): 29.

105. NYT, March 25, 1926, cited in Covert, "Freud."

106. Virginia Terhune Van de Water, "I Am Psychoanalyzed," *Century* 113 (Dec. 1926): 224–29.

107. "The Nervous Breakdown," *Fortune* 11:2 (April 1935): 84–86, 202–4. The article clearly indicated Adolf Meyer's dominance of the American psychiatric scene, but also dealt briefly with Adler, Jung, Freud, William Alanson White, Franz Alexander, Frankwood Williams, and Beatrice Hinkle and the major private sanitaria.

108. John Coignard, *Spectacle of a Man* (New York: Jefferson House, 1939); Lorine

Pruette, Review of *Spectacle of a Man, New York Herald Tribune,* June 13, 1937, p. 6, KP.

109. Coignard, *Spectacle,* 20, 31, 42.

110. Introduction to Freud, *Three Contributions* (4th ed., New York and Washington: Nervous and Mental Disease Publishing, 1930), xiii.

111. Interviews with: Frederick Lyman Wells, Boston, April 20, 1960; Bernice Engle, San Francisco, April 1, 1960; and Walter Lippmann, Malcolm Cowley, B. W. Huebsch, Joseph Freeman.

112. Simmons, "Marriage in the Modern Manner."

113. Freda Kircheway, *Our Changing Morality, a Symposium* (New York: Albert and Charles Boni, 1924); Ben Lindsey and Wainwright Evans, *Companionate Marriage* (New York: Boni and Liveright, 1927), and Lindsey, *The Revolt of Modern Youth* (New York: Garden City Publishing, 1925). *Recent Social Trends in the United States,* (New York: Report of the President's Commission on Recent Social Trends, 1933), vol. 1, pp. 418–20.

114. Friedman, *Menninger,* 82–84; Edith Kurzweil, *The Freudians: A Comparative Perspective* (New Haven: Yale Univ. Press, 1989), 23.

115. John B. Watson and K. S. Lashley, "Questions of Medical Opinion Relating to Sex Education and Venereal Disease Campaigns," *Mental Hygiene* 4:4 (Oct. 1920): 799–801. The only American exception was Horace W. Frink.

116. Menninger, *Man Against Himself,* 384.

117. The sex education movement, for example, retained most of the tenets of 19th-century "civilized" morality. See Bryan Strong, "Ideas of the Early Sex Education Movement in America, 1890–1920," *History of Education Quarterly* 12 (Summer 1972), 129–61.

118. Paula Fass, *The Beautiful and the Damned* (New York: Oxford Univ. Press, 1977), ch. 6; John d'Emilio and Estelle B. Freedman, *Intimate Matters: A History of Sexuality in America* (New York: Harper and Row, 1988), 256–60; Ellen K. Rothman, *Hands and Hearts: A History of Courtship in America* (New York: Basic Books, 1984), 285–300.

119. Michael Gordon, "From an Unfortunate Necessity to a Cult of Mutual Orgasm" in James M. Henslin, ed., *Studies in the Sociology of Sex* (New York: Appleton-Century-Crofts, 1971), 53–77; Simmons, "Marriage in the Modern Manner."

120. Katherine B. Davis, *Factors in the Sex Life of Twenty-two Hundred Women* (New York: Harper and Bros., 1929), 95–96, 56, 244–45, 331–32.

121. G. V. Hamilton, *A Research in Marriage* (New York: Albert and Charles Boni, 1929), 10, 17, 445, 468, 471. James Reed, *From Private Vice to Public Virtue* (New York: Basic Books, 1978), 335–36.

122. Lewis Terman, *Psychological Factors in Marital Happiness* (New York: McGraw-Hill, 1938), 222.

123. Robert L. Dickinson, *A Thousand Marriages* (Baltimore: Williams and Wilkins, 1931); Reed, *From Private Vice,* 143–93.

Chapter 6. Psychoanalytic Training: Young Americans Abroad

1. Jones to Hendrick, Dec. 11, 1935, HP; for the generation gap see John C. Burnham, *Jelliffe: American Psychoanalyst and Physician* (Chicago: Univ. of Chicago Press, 1983), 128–29; for the professional thrust see Burnham, "From Avant-gardism to Specialism," JHBS XV:2 (April 1979): 128–34.

2. Hendrick to Jelliffe, July 26, 1935, copy, HP.

3. Hendrick to Mother and Father, Sept. 6, 1928; Kubie to Glover, March 1, 1933, KP; Hendrick to Jelliffe, Jan. 16, 1933; Hendrick to Franz Alexander, March 25, 1932, HP.

4. Hendrick to Earnest Jones, Nov. 27, 1935, JP.

5. Kubie to Glover, March 1, 1933, KP.

6. Brill to Jones, June 6, 1933; Jones to Brill, July 15, 1932, JP.

7. Brill to Jones, June 6, 1933, JP.

8. Jelliffe to Hendrick, Jan. 23, 1934, HP.

9. Notebook, Reading 1916–1926, LewP.

10. Abram Kardiner, COHC.

11. Interview, Robert Cohen, Washington, D.C., Oct. 31, 1977.

12. Kardiner, COHC.

13. Freud to Leonard Blumgart, April 25, 1925, NYPSIA.

14. Smiley Blanton, *Diary of My Analysis with Sigmund Freud* (New York: Hawthorn Books, 1971), 36, 45, 62, 104, 117, 133.

15. Grinker to Jelliffe, Dec. 24, Oct. 7, 1933, JelP.

16. Zilboorg to Jelliffe, Feb. 3, 1929, JelP.

17. Sandor Rado, COHC.

18. John Murray to Jelliffe, Feb. 21, Nov. 12, 1930, JelP.

19. Sullivan to Jelliffe, May 20, June 1, 1928, JelP.

20. Hendrick to parents, Sept. 6, 1928, HP.

21. Ibid.

22. Hendrick to parents, Nov. 23, 1929, and March 3, 1930, HP.

23. "S. Rado's Lectures," Oct. 1926, Feb. 1927 (beginners), Berlin Psychoanalytic Institute, bound notebook, LewP.

24. Hendrick to parents, Sept. 23, 1928, HP.

25. Hendrick to parents, Oct. 6, 22, 1928, HP.

26. Hendrick to parents, Oct. 22, 1928, HP.

27. Hendrick to parents, March 3, 1930, HP.

28. Hendrick to parents, March 21, 1929, HP.

29. Hendrick to parents, Nov. 23, 1929, HP.

30. Hendrick to parents, July 7, 1930, HP.

31. Hendrick to parents, March 12, 1930, HP.

32. Hendrick to parents, April 15, 1930, HP.

33. Kubie to Glover, Feb. 17, 1932, KP.

34. Kubie to Glover, Feb. 17, 1932, Oct. 2, 1947, KP.

35. Frankwood Williams, "Finding a Way in Mental Hygiene," *Mental Hygiene* 14 (April 1930), 237.

36. Edward F. Denison and Alvin Slater, "Incomes in Selected Professions," *Survey of Current Business,* Oct. 1943, (Washington, D.C.: U.S. Dept. of Commerce), 16–20.

37. Hendrick to parents, Sept. 24, 1928, HP.

Chapter 7. The Depression, Schisms, Refugees, 1929–1942

1. Jones to A. A. Brill, Nov. 21, 1934, JP.

2. Ives Hendrick to Smith Elý Jelliffe, Jan. 16, 1933, JelP.

3. Brill, undated typescript, "History," notes that amendments to the constitution were accepted by the executive committee and passed on June 22, 1932, BP; Kubie

to Joseph Thompson, Jan. 4, 1926; Thompson to Kubie, Feb. 7, 1938; and Kubie to Thompson, Feb. 15, 1938, APSA.

4. Jelliffe to Brill, Feb. 17, 1930, copy, JelP.

5. Herman Nunberg to Siegfried Bernfeld, Oct. 26, 1934, trans. Cornelia Levine, BernP; Brill to Jones, June 7, 1923; Jones to Brill, Nov. 21, 1934; Brill to Jones, Dec. 8, 1934, JP.

6. Smith Ely Jelliffe to Karl Menninger, Feb. 24, 1933, JelP; Burnham, *Jelliffe,* 128.

7. John A. P. Millet, Autobiography, MP.

8. White to Jelliffe, April 11, 1933, JelP. Jelliffe helped a number of medical refugees; see David Krasner, "Smith Ely Jelliffe and the Immigration of European Physicians to the United States in the 1930's," *Transactions and Studies of the College of Physicians of Philadelphia,* Jan. 22, 1990.

9. Hendrick to Healy, Nov. 27, 1937, HP.

10. Carol Caton Schwartz, "Schools of Thought in Psychoanalysis: A Study in the Sociology of Knowledge" (Ph.D. diss., Yale Univ., 1969), 65.

11. Kubie to Glover, Feb. 17, 1932; Glover to Kubie, Nov. 11, 1930, KP.

12. Glover to Kubie, April 5, 1932, KP.

13. Kubie to Glover, Feb. 17, 1932; Glover to Kubie, Nov. 11, 1930, KP. These cases have been altered here to prevent identification.

14. Kubie, *Practical and Theoretical Aspects of Psychoanalysis* (New York: W. W. Norton, 1936).

15. Ibid., 103.

16. Jelliffe to Jones, Feb. 2, 1935, JelP.

17. Edwin F. Denison and Alvin Slater, "Incomes in Selected Professions," *Survey of Current Business,* Oct. 1943 (Washington, D.C.: U.S. Dept. of Commerce, Bureau of Foreign and Domestic Commerce), 16–20.

18. Harvey Brenner, *Mental Illness and the Economy* (Cambridge, Mass.: Harvard Univ. Press, 1973).

19. Benjamin Harris, "The Benjamin Rush Society and Marxist Psychiatry in the United States, 1944–1951," *History of Psychiatry* (London), in press; Daniel Benveniste, "Siegfried Bernfeld in San Francisco: A Dialogue with Nathan Adler," published in German translation in Karl Fallend and Johannes Reichsmayr, eds., *Siegfried Bernfeld in San Francisco* (Frankfort: Stroemfeld-Nexus, 1992).

20. Wittels to Bernfeld, Aug. 15, 1937, BernP.

21. Russell Jaccoby, *The Repression of Psychoanalysis* (New York: Basic Books, 1983); but see the recent reappraisals by Benjamin Harris and Adrian Brock, "Otto Fenichel and the Left Opposition in Psychoanalysis," JHBS 27 (1991): 161–63, and "The Rivalry of Wilhelm Reich and Otto Fenichel: The Psychopolitics of the Freudian Left Opposition, 1930–1935," BHM 66 (1992): 578–612. Fenichel's first wife noted that he was not a political activist, but was primarily a theoretician. Interview, Clare Fenichel, Los Angeles, Jan 22, 1985.

22. Ernest R. Mowrer, "A Study of Personal Disorganization," *American Sociological Review* 4 (Aug. 1939): 475–87; Paul O. Komora and Mary Augusta Clark, "Mental Disease in the Crisis," *Mental Hygiene* 19 (1935): 289–301.

23. Alexander to Jelliffe, May 6, 1932, JelP.

24. Jelliffe to Alexander, May 18, 1932, JelP.

25. Jelliffe to Wilhelm Stekel, May 26, 1927; White to Jelliffe, March 25, 1926, and Feb. 7, 1933, JelP.

26. Jones to Brill, July 15, 1932, JP; Jones, *Freud,* 3: 169.

27. Brill to Jelliffe, Sept. 9, 1931, JelP.

28. Jelliffe [?] to Dorian Feigenbaum, undated, JelP.

29. Feigenbaum to White, Sept. 12, 1931; Jelliffe to Feigenbaum, Nov. 10, 1931; Jelliffe to Feigenbaum, Nov. 14, 1931, JelP.

30. Jones to Brill, June 29, 1932, and Brill to Jones, Feb. 3, 1933, JP.

31. James Wands Riley, "Not Poppy nor Mandragora," R 15 (Oct. 1938): 500.

32. White to Jelliffe, Feb. 7, 1933, JelP.

33. Hendrick to Jelliffe, July 23, 1937, JelP; Jelliffe to Hendrick, June 30 and July 29, 1937, HP.

34. Jelliffe to Kubie, Jan. 12, 1934, and Kubie to Jelliffe, Jan. 26, 1934, JelP.

35. Brill to Jones, May 1 and 17, 1935, JP.

36. Brill to Jones, Nov. 11, 1935, JP.

37. Hendrick to Jones, Nov. 27, 1935, JP; Kubie to George S. Amsden, Nov. 28, 1934, KP; Jelliffe to Hendrick, May 24, 1935, HP. I have not found an indication of Schilder's reinstatement in the minutes of the New York Society, after the Jelliffe Committee's report was rejected. But see Hendrick to Jelliffe, Nov. 7, 1935, JelP, and Schilder's letter to Freud, Nov. 1, 1935, FA. For brief biographical information see Donald A. Shaskan and William L. Roller, eds., *Paul Schilder* (New York: Human Sciences Press, 1985).

38. Schilder to Freud, Nov. 1, 1935, and Freud to Schilder, Nov. 26, 1935, FA.

39. Brill to Jones, Dec. 11, 1935, JP.

40. Brill to Jones, March 5, 1938, JP.

41. Brill to Jones, March 5, 1938, JP.

42. Jones to Brill, Feb. 19, 1934, Sept. 25, 1933, JP.

43. See the excellent account of the refugees and particularly of Erik Erikson and Bruno Bettelheim by Lewis Coser, *Refugee Scholars in America* (New Haven: Yale Univ. Press, 1984), 42–82, and the overview of Laura Fermi, in *Illustrious Immigrants* (2nd ed., Chicago: Univ. of Chicago Press, 1971), ch. 6.

44. Interview, Erik Erikson, Tiburon, Calif., April 29, 1976.

45. Jones to Jelliffe, April 25, 1933, JelP.

46. Jones to Brill, Dec. 2, 1933, JP.

47. Brill to Jones, March 21, 1934, and Jones to Brill, March 7, 1934, JP.

48. Ann Bucholtz, "Appeal to All International Psychoanalysts," June 26, 1936, LewP.

49. See the reports and extensive correspondence of the Committee on Relief and Immigration in APSAC.

50. Bettina Warburg, Statement 1976, Summary of the Work of the Emergency Committee on Relief and Immigration of the American Psychoanalytic Association, APSAC.

51. Paul Federn to Jelliffe, stamped Oct. 11[?], 1938, JelP.

52. Jelliffe to Federn, Oct. 12, 1938, JelP.

53. "Refugee Physicians," *Time* 33 (Feb. 13, 1939): 38; Bettina Warburg to Carl Binger, Jan. 27, 1942, APSAC.

54. See the revealing account in Lawrence Friedman, *Menninger* (New York: Alfred A. Knopf, 1990).

55. A. A. Brill to Earnest Jones, May 12, 1933, JP.

56. NYT (June 20, 1934): 3:2.

57. IJ 16:2 (April, 1935): 244–45.

58. "Bulletin of Information to be Supplied Only to Psychoanalysts Who Wish to Emigrate to the United States," APSAC.

59. Walter C. Langer and Sanford Gifford, "An American Analyst in Vienna During the *Anschluss,* 1936–1938," JHBS 14 (1978): 37–54.

60. National Committee for Resettlement of Foreign Physicians, "Adjustment of 282 Emigre Physicians in Greater New York, March through August, 1945," APSAC.

61. Bruce Bliven, "Thank You, Hitler," *Reader's Digest* 32 (Feb. 1938): 81.

62. Freud to Reik, July 3, 1938, FA. See also Reik, *The Search Within* (New York: Farrar, Straus and Cudahy, 1956), 656–57, and *Fragment of a Great Confession* (New York: Farrar, Straus, Cudahy, 1949), 326; Jean-Marc Alby, *Theodor Reik* (Paris: Clancier-Guenaud, 1985), 115–19.

63. Reik to "Liebe gnaedige Frau," July 14, 1938, trans. Cornelia Levine, BernP.

64. Reik to Bernfeld, Feb. 14, 1939[?], June 10, 1938, trans. Cornelia Levine, BernP.

65. Reik to "Gnaedige Frau," July 14, 1938.

66. Reik, *The Search Within* (New York: Farrar, Straus and Cudahy, 1956), 656–57; Reik to Bernfeld, Feb. 14, 1939 [?].

67. Reik, *Listening with the Third Ear* (New York: Farrar, Straus, 1948), 17.

68. Ibid., 109.

69. Ibid., 109–10.

70. Ibid., 442–43.

71. Ibid., 125–26.

72. Reik, *Fragment of a Great Confession*, 22, 318–20.

73. SRL 41 (Jan. 11, 1958): 6.

74. "Analyst," *New Yorker* 24 (July 17, 1948): 19–20.

75. *Nation* 69 (Oct. 29, 1949): 424.

76. Interview, Helen Ross, Washington, D.C., Nov. 24, 1977.

77. George E. Gifford, ed., *Psychoanalysis, Psychotherapy and the New England Medical Scene, 1894–1944* (New York: Science History Publications, 1978), 334.

78. Interview, Franz Alexander, Cedars Sinai Hospital, Los Angeles, Sept. 28, 1960.

79. Alexander, *The Medical Value*, 13, 21.

80. Alexander, "Psychoanalysis Comes of Age," Q 7 (July, 1938): 303.

Chapter 8. The Second Psychoanalytical Civil War

1. IJ 21:1 (1940): 500–501; IJ 22:2 (1941): 188.

2. Carol Schwartz, "Schools of Thought in Psychoanalysis: A Study in the Sociology of Knowledge" (Ph.D. diss., Yale Univ., 1969), 109–10.

3. Susan Quinn, *A Mind of Her Own: The Life of Karen Horney* (New York: Summit Books, 1987). Compare Abraham Myerson's survey of opinion among psychiatrists and neurologists noted in Chapter 9 with the San Francisco *Chronicle*'s coverage of Freud's exile cited in notes 48 and 51 below.

4. Waelder to Fenichel, Aug. 13, 1938, FP, trans. Cornelia Levine.

5. Fenichel to Edward Bibring, Jan. 3, 1939, BibP.

6. Karl Menninger to Smith Ely Jelliffe, April 9, 1942, in Howard J. Faulkner and Virginia D. Pruitt, eds., *Selected Correspondence of Karl Menninger* (New Haven: Yale Univ. Press, 1988).

7. "Statement on the Situation in the New York Psychoanalytic Society and Institute," undated mimeograph, KP; Kubie, *Practical and Theoretical Aspects of Psychoanalysis* (New York: W. W. Norton, 1936), 102.

8. Minutes of the Special Meeting of the Council on Professional Training, New York, Feb. 26, 1939, APSA.

9. See the character portrait by Kubie's analyst, Edward Glover, in "Festschrift for Lawrence S. Kubie," JNMD 149:1 (July 1969): 5–18.

10. Kubie, "Relation of the Conditioned Reflex to Psychoanalytic Technique," ANP 32 (1936): 1137; "Physiological Approaches to the Problem of Anxiety," PsyMed 3 (1941): 263.

11. Kubie to Smith Ely Jelliffe, Jan. 18, 1935, copy, LP.

12. Kubie to Robert P. Knight, May 13, 1960; Kubie to David Rapaport, July 11, 1958; Kubie to Roy Grinker, Sept. 10, 1954; Grinker to Kubie, Sept. 14, 1954, KP. To Anna Freud he wrote, "I have become increasingly troubled by the extent to which metapsychological concepts have displaced Freud's earlier concepts of a continuous, unstable, dynamic interaction among conscious, preconscious and unconscious processes." Kubie to Anna Freud, June 4, 1954, KP.

13. Autobiographical manuscript, "Wrestling with the Man," FW.

14. Fritz Wittels to Siegfried Bernfeld, Dec. 31, 1941, trans. Cornelia Levine, BernP.

15. Sandor Rado, Oral History, Columbia University; Brill to Jones, Feb. 29, 1936, JP.

16. See the poll of student reactions to institute courses for 1939 and 1940 in the Levy papers. For Rado's difficult character see the ms. autobiography of John A. P. Millet, one of his colleagues at the Columbia Institute, MP.

17. Smiley Blanton, *Diary of My Analysis with Sigmund Freud* (New York: Hawthorn Books, 1971), 67.

18. David Levy to Lawrence Kubie, April 17 and 29, 1940; Lawrence Kubie to David Levy, May 2, 1940; and "Discussion of Dr. Rado's paper by Dr. Fedor [*sic*]," LP.

19. Henry A. Murray to Franz Alexander, May 19, 1940, AP.

20. Menninger to Otto Fenichel, Feb. 18, 1940, in Faulkner and Pruitt, eds., *Selected Correspondence of Karl A. Menninger,* 325.

21. Lawrence Friedman, *Menninger,* ch. 5.

22. Quinn, *A Mind of Her Own,* 330–31.

23. Lawrence S. Kubie, *Practical and Theoretical Aspects of Psychoanalysis: A Handbook for Prospective Patients and Their Advisers* (New York: W. W. Norton, 1936), 95.

24. Ibid., 110–11.

25. Ibid., 112–13.

26. Kubie to Glover, Nov. 2, 1939; Kubie to Glover, March 1, 1933, and Sept. 1, 1938, KP.

27. Kubie to David Levy, Nov. 17, 1939, LP.

28. "To the President of the New York Psychoanalytic Society," signed Fritz Wittels, March 13, 1940, LP.

29. Kubie to Wittels, March 20, 1940, LP.

30. Quinn, *A Mind of Her Own,* 339–40.

31. Ibid., 339–48.

32. A typed draft titled "Statement on the Situation in the New York Psychoanalytic Society and Institute," undated, but probably 1941, KP.

33. David Levy to Leonard Blumgart, July 8, 1941, Levy to Philip R. Lehrman, March 16, 1942, LP.

34. Interview, Nolan D. C. Lewis, Maryland, May 17, 1977; Alexander to David Levy, April 16, 1942, LP. Marianne Horney Eckardt, "Historical Notes on the Founding of the American Academy of Psychoanalysis," *Forum of the American Academy of Psychoanalysis* 25:2 (Summer 1981): 28–9.

35. Franz Alexander to David Levy, March 25, April 16, 1942; and Levy to Alexander, March 31, 1942, LP.

36. Interview, Frances Deri, Feb. 3, 1963, LAPSIA.

37. Karl Menninger to Ernst Simmel, Aug. 22, 1939; Robert P. Knight to Karl

[Menninger] and Ernst Simmel, March 16, 1940; Ernst Simmel to Robert P. Knight, March 25, 1940; Robert Knight to Karl Menninger and Ernst Simmel, March 28, 1940; Karl Menninger to Robert Knight, March 29, 1940; Simmel to Robert Knight, April 5, 1940, SP.

38. Minutes, Committee on Certification, Dec. 7, 1940, SP.

39. Interview, Ralph R. Greenson, Dec. 9, 1962, pp. 1–2, LAPSIA.

40. Fenichel to Edward Bibring, Sept. 1, 1938, BibP. Simmel had to ask for help to finance a trip to the Boston meetings in 1942 because patients owed him money and because he had cut down his practice to prepare for an internship. See Simmel to Jacob Kasanin, April 27, 1942, SP. Frances Deri at one time thought she might have to give up analysis and prepare for another activity; see Deri interview.

41. Robert Waelder to Otto Fenichel, Aug. 16, 1939, Rundbrief, July 10, 1942, FP.

42. Fenichel to Edward Bibring, Jan. 3, 1939, BibP.

43. Alexander to Bernfeld, Dec. 18, 1936, and May 24, 1939, BernP.

44. Karl Menninger to Joseph C. Solomon, Nov. 19, 1940, LAPSIA.

45. Bernfeld to Anna Freud, Nov. 23, 1937, trans. LAPSIA.

46. Menninger to Bernfeld, Jan. 28, 1938, BernP.

47. San Francisco *Chronicle, This World,* June 28, 1938, pp. 7–8, and cover; *Chronicle,* June 5, p. 1; June 6, p. 2; June 7, pp. 4, 10.

48. For Freud, see *Chronicle,* June 5, p. 1; June 6, p. 2; June 7, pp. 4, 10; *This World,* June 12, pp. 7–8; for the Psychiatrists, see June 6, p. 7; June 7, pp. 1, 4; June 8, pp. 1, 4; June 9, p. 5; June 10, p. 18.

49. Simmel, Banquet Speech at the Tenth Year Celebration of the Psychoanalytic Study Group of Los Angeles, Oct. 5, 1945, GrP.

50. Bernhard Berliner interview, Nov. 19, 1975, SFPIA.

51. Freud to Simmel, trans., quoted in "A Plan for a Psychoanalytic Institute in Southern California," SP, and LAPSIA.

52. For an excellent account of these issues, see Albert Kandelin, "California's First Psychoanalytic Society," BMC 30 (1966); Charles Tidd to David Brunswick, Nov. 6, 1939, "Psychoanalytic Institute Foundation, Prospectus," and Simmel, "The Development of the Plan of a Psychoanalytic Institute of Los Angeles"; David Brunswick to Lawrence Kubie, Oct. 13, 1939; Simmel to Karl Menninger, Dec. 5, 1939, SP.

53. Deri interview.

54. Karl Menninger to Glen Myers, Oct. 29, 1940; Atwell Westwick to Menninger, July 23, 1940; Simmel to Menninger, Dec. 2, 1940; Staub to Menninger, Jan. 12, 1941; Menninger to Staub, Jan. 23, 1941, LAPSIA.

55. Simmel to Karl Menninger, Aug. 7, 1941; Report by Albert Kandelin, "Santa Barbara Socialization Institute"; interview, Ernst Lewy, Feb. 24, 1963, LAPSIA; Staub to Franz Alexander, Dec. 8, 1940, AP.

56. Earl Warren to C. B. Pinkham, May 22, 1941, courtesy Daniel Benveniste, and *California and Western Medicine* 54:6 (June 1941): 160, courtesy Virgil Hancock.

57. Simmel to Ernst Lewy, Oct. 5, 1943, SP.

58. Simmel to Dr. Lucie Jessner, Oct. 26, 1946, SP.

59. May Romm to Ernst Simmel, Nov. 29, 1941; Charles Tidd to Simmel, Dec. 1, 1941; Joachim Haenel to Simmel, Dec. 3, 1941. Simmel countered their arguments in a letter of Dec. 6, 1941, addressed to prospective charter members, FP.

60. Bernfeld to Simmel, July 23 and Aug. 8, 1941, SP.

61. Jacob Kasanin to Otto Fenichel, Feb. 17, 1942, FP; Simmel to Robert Knight, March 3, 1942; copy or draft of letter to Robert Knight, April 12, 1943, unsigned but clearly by Simmel, SP.

62. San Francisco Psychoanalytic Society, Minutes of the Meetings Held on March 8, April 25 and 26, 1942, FP.

63. Fenichel, Rundbrief, July 10, 1942, p. 10, FP.

64. Bernfeld to Kasanin, June [11?] 1942; Kasanin to Bernfeld, June 9, 1942; Simmel to Karl Menninger, July 21, 1942, copy, SP; Emmanuel Windholz to Otto Fenichel, June 6, 1942, FP.

65. Interview, Claire Fenichel, Los Angeles, Jan. 22, 1985.

66. Fenichel, Rundbrief, July 14, 1945, FP. As a Marxist who attributed a vital role to social forces, Fenichel opposed the ultra orthodox who wished to ascribe everything to the Oedipus complex. See Rundbrief, March 22, 1942, FP. See also Chapter 7, n. 21.

67. Levy to Franz Alexander, March 31, 1942, and Alexander to Levy, March 25 and April 16, 1942, LP; Simmel to Kubie, Nov. 14, 1942, SP.

68. Minutes of the Forty-fourth American Psychoanalytic Association Meetings, May 17–20, 1942, p. 11, SP.

69. Lionel Blitzsten to Otto Fenichel, April 28, 1942, FP.

70. Kubie to Leonard Blumgart, Nov. 9, 1942, copy, SP.

71. At the time of the vote the San Francisco society had not yet been formally recognized, so that, as Rado argued, five of seven societies had accepted the amendment. But its members had not been canvassed for the Topeka vote on grounds that they had their own constituent society. Had this occurred, they would have defeated the proposal in the Topeka society. And they did vote against it as a constituent society. See Menninger to Rado, Nov. 19, 1942, SP.

72. Simmel to Karl Menninger, Nov. 16, 1942, SP.

73. Ernst Simmel to Ernst Lewy, Aug. 20, 1942, trans. anon., SP.

74. Simmel to Menninger, Nov. 16 and 2, 1942; Menninger to Simmel, Nov. 17 and 27, 1942, SP.

75. Menninger to Rado, Nov. 19, 1942, SP.

76. Menninger to Fenichel, Nov. 17, 1942, FP.

77. Menninger to Rado, Nov. 19, 1942, copy, SP.

78. John A. P. Millet, "The American Academy of Psychoanalysis, History of Its Foundation and Progress, 1956–1966," MP.

79. Grete [?] Bibring to Edward Glover, June 13, 1942, BibP.

80. Program of the meetings of the American Psychoanalytic Association, May 1942, SP.

81. Kubie to Glover, Nov. 17, 1942, and Nov. 20, 1940, KP.

82. Kubie to Edward Glover, Nov. 17, 1942, KP.

Chapter 9. Psychoanalysis and Psychiatry, 1917–1940

1. Harry Stack Sullivan, *The Interpersonal Theory of Psychiatry* (New York: W. W. Norton, 1953), 20–32, esp. 21–22, 314.

2. Gerald Grob, *Mental Illness and American Society 1876–1940* (Princeton, N.J.: Princeton Univ. Press, 1983), ch. 10.

3. Bernard Sachs, AP 91 (Sept. 1934): 356–57; for the focal infection craze and Greenacre's investigation, see H. A. Cotton, "The Etiology and Treatment of the So-Called Functional Psychoses," AP 79 (Oct. 1922): 157, and James Leiby, *Charity and Correction in New Jersey* (New Brunswick, N.J.: Rutgers Univ. Press, 1966), 220–23.

4. Andrew Abbott, *The System of Professions* (Chicago: Univ. of Chicago Press, 1988), ch. 10.

5. Leland Hinsie, *Concepts and Problems of Psychotherapy* (New York: Columbia Univ. Press, 1937), 18.

6. Dept. of Commerce, Bureau of the Census, *Patients in Hospitals for Mental Disease, 1935,* p. 34, lists 38.8% of psychoneurotic patients discharged from state hospitals as recovered and 43.3% as improved.

7. Dexter M. Bullard, "Experiences in the Psychoanalytic Treatment of Psychotics," Q 9 (1940): 493–504.

8. Franklin G. Ebaugh and Charles A. Rymer, *Psychiatry in Medical Education* (New York: Commonwealth Fund, 1942), 121, 194. The Murray quote is on p. 87.

9. Ibid., 186–88, 191–94, 380–82.

10. In 1924–25 out of a total of 46 articles in the *American Journal of Psychiatry,* five were concerned with psychological factors in nervous and mental disorder and four of these were psychoanalytic. A year later, psychoanalysts published six articles in the same journal. The American Medical Association's *Archives of Neurology,* originally founded to counter Smith Ely Jelliffe's editorial policies for the *Journal of Nervous and Mental Disease,* became increasingly favorable.

11. Elmer Klein, "Psychologic Trends in Psychiatry since 1900," AP 85 (Sept. 1928): 273–88, quote on 284.

12. J. H. Cooper, "Psychotherapy," *Journal of the Kansas Medical Society* 21:1 (Jan. 1921): 1–5.

13. For example, in 1925 the *Index Medicus* listed 32 articles on psychoanalysis, 17 on psychotherapy; in 1927, 93 on psychoanalysis and 52 on psychotherapy.

14. Douglas Thom, "Psychotherapy in Private Practice," AP 90 (July 1933): 77–85, for other papers on psychotherapy see 33–76, 86–96.

15. R. W. Lissitz, "A Longitudinal Study of the Research Methodology in the *Journal of Abnormal and Social Psychology,* the *Journal of Nervous and Mental Disease, and the American Journal of Psychiatry,*" JHBS 5 (July 1969): 248–55. However, see Ives Hendrick on trait studies, "The Analysis of Personality, a Survey of Psychologists' Experiments," AP 85 (Nov. 1928): 535–63.

16. Leland Hinsie and Siegfried Katz, "Treatment of Manic Depressive Psychoses," AP 88 (July 1931): 149–51, 131–83; Hinsie in the Symposium on the Relation of Psychoanalysis to Psychiatry, AP 91 (Mar. 1935): 1109–10, and papers by Ross McClure Chapman and Harry Stack Sullivan and discussion, in ibid.

17. Hinsie, in ibid.

18. Symposium on Psychotherapy, AP 90 (Nov. 1933): 659–98.

19. AP 91 (March 1935): 1133.

20. Ebaugh and Rymer, *Psychiatry in Medical Education,* ch. 4, and survey of medical school catalogues by Wilma Wake in the National Library of Medicine in possession of the author.

21. Ebaugh and Rymer, *Psychiatry in Medical Education,* 194, 191.

22. Ibid., 408–9.

23. Ibid., 193.

24. Leland Hinsie, *Concepts and Problems of Psychotherapy* (New York: Columbia Univ. Press, 1937), 136.

25. Ibid., 26–30.

26. Ibid., 137.

27. Carney Landis in ibid., 16, 155–69.

28. Robert P. Knight, "Evaluation of the Results of Psychoanalytic Therapy," AP 98 (Nov. 1941): 438–39.

29. Myerson to Kubie, Dec. 23, 1937, KP.

30. Abraham Myerson, "The Attitude of Neurologists, Psychiatrists and Psychologists Towards Psychoanalysis," AP 96 (1939): 623–41, quote on 630.

31. Kurt Eissler, "On: 'The Attitude of Neurologists, Psychiatrists and Psychologists towards Psychoanalysis,'" Q 10 (1941): 297–319.

Chapter 10. Teachers of Psychiatry, Psychosomatic Medicine

1. Typescript, dated Nov. 20, 1947, AMP.

2. Franklin G. Ebaugh and Charles A. Rymer, *Psychiatry in Medical Education* (New York: Commonwealth Fund, 1942), 6; for a stimulating comparison of Meyer's views and psychoanalysis, see Ruth Leys, "Types of One: Adolf Meyer's Life Chart and the Representation of Individuality," *Representations* 34 (1991): 1–28. See also the articles on Meyer by Theodore Lidz, David Henderson, and Franklin Ebaugh in AP 123 (Sept. 1966): 320–36.

3. Adolf Meyer, *Psychobiology,* compiled and edited by Eunice Winters and Anna Mae Bowers (Springfield, Ill.: Charles C. Thomas, 1957), 76.

4. Bertram Lewin, "Dr. Meyer," Oct. 1, 1918, LewP.

5. Meyer, Typescript, "Fourth Year Course, Eleventh Meeting, Notes on the Discussion of Thursday," Dec. 18, 1924, pp. 11–12, 16–17, AMP.

6. Wendell Muncie, *Psychobiology and Psychiatry: A Textbook of Normal and Abnormal Human Behavior* (St. Louis: C. V. Mosby, 1939), 123.

7. Lewin to Kubie, Feb. 20, [1923 or 1924], typescript, LewP.

8. See Meyer, "Fourth Year Course," 16.

9. Meyer, *Psychobiology,* 133.

10. Edward A. Strecker and Franklin G. Ebaugh, *Practical Clinical Psychiatry* (Philadelphia: Blakiston, 1931), 375.

11. Ibid. (1925 ed.), 251, 282; (1931 ed.), 306–8.

12. Sullivan, "Tentative Criteria of Malignancy in Schizophrenia," AP 8 (March 1928): 763; see the brilliant study of Sullivan by Helen Swick Perry, *Psychiatrist of America* (Cambridge, Mass.: Bellknap Press of Harvard Univ., 1982).

13. Sullivan, "Modified Psychoanalytic Treatment of Schizophrenia," AP 11 (Nov. 1931): 540.

14. Sullivan to White, June 14, 1930, WFA; White to Chapman, Nov. 21, 1922, cited in Arcangelo d'Amore, ed., *William Alanson White, The Washington Years, 1903–1937* (Washington, D.C.: National Institute of Mental Health, 1976), 78–79.

15. *Current Biography* (1942 ed.), 813–14.

16. Edward J. Kempf, *The Autonomic Functions and the Personality* (New York and Washington: Nervous and Mental Disease Publishing, 1918).

17. Sullivan, "Peculiarity of Thought in Schizophrenia," AP 5 (July 1925): 58, 82.

18. Sullivan, "Research in Schizophrenia," AP 9 (Nov. 1, 1929): 553–67, esp. 564; "Tentative Criteria," 766.

19. Sullivan to White, Oct. 6, 1928, WFA.

20. Sullivan, "Modified Psychoanalytic Treatment of Schizophrenia," 534.

21. Ibid., 540.

22. Sullivan to White, April 27, 1926, WFA.

23. Gerald Grob, *From Asylum to Community* (Princeton, N.J.: Princeton Univ. Press, 1991), 140.

24. Sullivan to White, June 13, 1934, WFA.

25. Harold Lasswell, Kurt Lewin. Confidential Memo, undated, probably 1936, WFA.

26. W. A. White Psychiatric Foundation, Circular letter to all Trustees and the

directors of the Washington School of Psychiatry, Sept. 21, 1937, signed H. S. Sullivan, WFA.

27. See "History of Washington School of Psychiatry," in folder marked "Publicity, 1947–1948." By 1947–48 there were 302 students of whom 117 were medical doctors; see also A. A. Brill to Sullivan, Sept. 2, 1937, WFA.

28. For subscribers, see annual report of the Publications Committee, 1945, WFA.

29. Thomas R. Henry, "New Type of Psychiatry," Jan. 22, 1939, *Washington Sunday Star,* part 2. Clipping File, WFA.

30. "Doctor Warns Nation of General Paranoia," *New Haven, Conn. Register,* June 3, 1940, Clipping File, WFA.

31. Robert C. Powell, "Helen Flanders Dunbar and a Holistic Approach to Psychosomatic Problems, I," *Psychiatric Quarterly* 49:2 (Spring 1977): 133–52, and "II," ibid. 50:2 (Summer 1978): 144–57; Erich Wittkower, "Studies on the Influence of Emotions on the Functions of the Organs," *Journal of Mental Science* 81 (July 1935): 540–50; Chase Patterson Kimball, "Conceptual Developments in Psychosomatic Medicine, 1939–1969," *Annals of Internal Medicine* 73 (1970): 306–16; Harold I. Kaplan, and Helen S. Kaplan, "An Historical Survey of Psychosomatic Medicine," JNMD 124 (1956): 546–48; Howard S. Liddell, "The Origins of *Psychosomatic Medicine,*" PsyMed 24 (1962): 10–12.

32. Ernst Kretschmer, *Physique and Character,* trans. W.J.H. Sprott (New York: Harcourt, Brace, 1925), 29–30, 34–35; George Draper, *Disease and the Man* (London: Kegan, Paul, Trench, Trubner, 1930), 25–26, 83–84, 204–8, 236. Alvarez cited in Edward Weiss and Spurgeon O. English, *Psychosomatic Medicine* (Philadelphia: W. B. Saunders, 1943), 242.

33. Smith Ely Jelliffe and Elida Evans, "Psoriasis as an Hysterical Conversion Symbolization," *New York Medical Journal* 104 (Dec. 2, 1916): 1077–84. Jelliffe to C. G. Jung, Aug. 28, 1932; Jung to Jelliffe, Aug. 27, 1932, JelP.

34. Flanders Dunbar, *Psychosomatic Diagnosis* (New York: P. B. Hoeber, 1943), 650–53; Dunbar, *Mind and Body* (New York: Random House, 1947), and *Emotions and Bodily Changes* (New York: Columbia Univ. Press, 1935), xi, 422–23, 429. Her later, judicious assessments are in *Psychiatry and the Medical Specialties* (New York: McGraw-Hill, 1959).

35. Dunbar, *Emotions and Bodily Changes,* 429–30; Sanford Gifford, "Felix Deutsch, a Biographical Sketch," ms.; Felix Deutsch, ed., *The Psychosomatic Concept in Psychoanalysis* (New York: International Universities Press, 1953).

36. H. F. Dunbar et al., "The Psychic Component of Disease," AP 93 (Nov. 1936): 651; Dunbar, *Psychosomatic Diagnosis,* 225.

37. Dunbar, *Psychosomatic Diagnosis,* 655, 690–91, 177; Dunbar, *Mind and Body,* 137, 172, 254, 260.

38. Franz Alexander, "The Logic of Emotions and Its Dynamic Background," IJ 16:4 (Oct. 1935): 399–413; Alexander, "The Influence of Psychological Factors on Gastrointestinal Disturbances," Q 3 (Oct. 1934): 501–39. For criticism of Dunbar, see Alexander, *Psychosomatic Medicine* (New York: W. W. Norton, 1950), 72–73.

39. Franz Alexander, *The Medical Value of Psychoanalysis* (New York: W. W. Norton, 1932), 204.

40. Ibid., 193, 197.

41. Ibid., 203, 197–201.

42. Alexander, *Psychosomatic Medicine,* 51–52. For an example of the stronger somatic emphasis see the discussions of Therese Benedek's work on the ovarian cycle in ibid., 216–62.

43. Weiss and English, *Psychosomatic Medicine* (1957 ed.), 431–39; Maurice Greenhill and Samuel Kilgore, "Principles of Methodology in Teaching the Psychiatric Approach to Medical House Officers," PsyMed 12 (Jan.–Feb. 1950), 44.

44. Leon J. Saul, "Psychogenic Factors in the Etiology of the Common Cold and Related Symptoms," IJ 19 (1938): 451–70.

45. Weiss and English, *Psychosomatic Medicine* (1943 ed.), 13–14.

46. Theodore M. Brown, "Alan Gregg and the Rockefeller Foundation's Support of Franz Alexander's Psychosomatic Research," BHM 61 (1987): 178.

47. *The Josiah Macy, Jr. Foundation, 1930–1955. A Review of Activities* (New York: 1955), 52, 10, 63–70.

48. Sir William Osler, *The Principles and Practice of Medicine* (14th ed., New York: Appleton Century, 1942), 1–2.

Chapter 11. World War II: Psychoanalytic Warriors

1. Gerald Grob, "World War II and American Psychiatry," *Psychohistory Review* 19 (Fall 1990): 41–69; Grob, "The Forging of Mental Health Policy in America: World War II, to New Frontier," JHM 42:4 (Oct. 1987): 410–46.

2. Grob, *From Asylum to Community,* 13; William Menninger, "Psychiatric Experience in the War, 1941–1946," AP 103 (March 1947): 577–78; Rebecca Greene, "The Role of the Psychiatrist in World War II" (Ph.D. diss., Columbia Univ., 1977), introduction, 32.

3. For a summary of different theories see Edwin G. Zabriskie and Louise Brush, "Psychoneuroses in War Time," PsyMed 3 (July 1941): 295–329; Abram Kardiner, "The Neuroses of War, *War Medicine* 1 (March 1941): 219–26, and *The Traumatic Neuroses of War* (New York: Paul B. Hoeber, 1941).

4. For psychiatric views of selection, see Greene, "Role of the Psychiatrist," 34–35, 64–74, 81–87.

5. Ibid., ch. 3, and pp. 384, 429–34.

6. Arthur O. Hecker et al., "Psychiatric Problems in Military Service during the Training Period," AP 99 (July 1942): 33–41; Nolan D. C. Lewis and Bernice Engle, *Wartime Psychiatry: A Compendium of the International Literature* (New York: Oxford Univ. Press, 1954), ch. 3.

7. Albert J. Glass, ed., *Neuropsychiatry in World War II,* vol. 2: *Overseas Theaters* (Washington, D.C.: Office of the Surgeon General, 1973), 460–62.

8. Interview, John P. Spiegel, New York, Nov. 12, 1977.

9. Ibid.

10. Leo Bartemeier, Lawrence Kubie, Karl Menninger, John Romano, and John C. Whitehorn, "Combat Exhaustion," JNMD 104 (1946): 358–89, 489–525. Interviews with John Spiegel and Norman Reider suggest that the appointment of analysts by other analysts occurred; however, Norman Brill, who worked with William Menninger in the Surgeon General's office, noted that this was not the basis for Menninger's appointments. A. Eisendorfer in *War Medicine* 5:3 (March 1944): 146, cited an article by Col. R. D. Halloran, the first chief of neuropsychiatry in the Surgeon General's office, and noted that he "placed qualified neuropsychiatrists, preferably with psychoanalytic training" in charge of psychiatric clinics at reception and replacement training centers. However, Halloran in AP 100 (1943): 14–20, only mentions the appointment of neurologists, psychoanalysts, and physicians from state hospitals and guidance clinics.

11. Greene, "Role of the Psychiatrist," 482–87; Kubie to Brigadier General Edward S. Greenbaum, Aug. 4, 1943, and to Arthur H. Ruggles, Sept. 27, 1943, KP.

12. S. Ferenczi et al., *Psycho-analysis and the War Neuroses* (London, Vienna, New York: International Psycho-Analytical Press, 1921), 18–19, 23–25, 52.

13. Grinker to Maxwell Gitelson, July 15, 1943, GP.

14. Carl Binger, "Winged Foot, with an Achilles Heel," NYT *Book Review*, Sept. 9, 1945, pp. 3, 29.

15. George Gifford, ed., *Psychoanalysis, Psychotherapy and the New England Scene 1894–1944* (New York: Science History Publications, 1978), 397–99.

16. Albert J. Glass, ed., *Neuropsychiatry in World War II*, vol. 1: *Zone of the Interior* (Washington, D.C.: Office of the Surgeon General, 1966), 280; Roy Grinker and John Spiegel, *War Neuroses* (Philadelphia: Blakiston, 1945), 78–105.

17. Grinker and Spiegel, *War Neuroses*, 80.

18. Ibid., 87.

19. Ibid., 101.

20. Ibid., 101–2, 60–62.

21. Ibid., 117.

22. Ibid., 4.

23. Ibid., 11.

24. Ibid., 114.

25. Glass, ed., *Neuropsychiatry in World War II*, 2: 8–9, and "Psychotherapy in the Combat Zone," AP 110 (April 1954): 725–31.

26. Alfred O. Ludwig, Review of *War Neuroses*, AP 103 (July 1946): 140–41.

27. George E. Gifford, ed., *Psychoanalysis, Psychotherapy and the New England Scene*, 400.

28. Glass, ed., *Neuropsychiatry in World War II*, 2: 650.

29. Ibid., 656–73.

30. Ibid., 671–73.

31. Ibid., 15, 636, and Glass, "Psychotherapy in the Combat Zone," 727.

32. Louis L. Tureen in Frederick Hanson, ed., *Combat Psychiatry, Bulletin of the U.S. Army Medical Department*, Vol. 9, Supplemental Number (Nov. 1949), 120, and Glass, ed., *Neuropsychiatry in World War II*, 2: 119, 137, 636. For the problem of abreaction and the use of sedation, see Leo H. Bartemeier et al., "Combat Exhaustion," JNMD 104:5 (Nov. 1946): 499–510.

33. Glass, ed., *Neuropsychiatry in World War II*, 2: 120; Hanson, *Combat Psychiatry*, 39–42, 451; NYT (Aug. 24, 1943), 21:5.

34. Roy Grinker and John Spiegel, "Brief Psychotherapy in War Neuroses," PsyMed 6 (April 1944): 123–31, esp. 125; Glass, ed., *Neuropsychiatry in World War II*, 2: 779.

35. Glass, ed., *Neuropsychiatry in World War II*, 2: 783–85, 62.

36. Ibid., 127.

37. Karl Menninger to Jean Menninger, May 25, 1945, WMP.

38. Gifford, *Psychoanalysis, Psychotherapy and the New England Scene*, 396–99.

39. Glass, ed., *Neuropsychiatry in World War II*, 1: 54.

40. Interviews, John Spiegel, New York, Nov. 12, 1977; Norman Brill, Los Angeles, Oct. 7, 8, 1986.

41. Interview, Hildi Greenson, Oct. 9, 1988.

42. Ralph Greenson, "Practical Approach to the War Neuroses," BMC 9:6 (1945): 196–97.

43. Charles A. Sarlin and Martin A. Berezin, "Group Psychotherapy on a Modified Analytic Basis," JNMD 104 (Dec. 1946): 611–67; Robert A. Cohen, "Military Group Psychotherapy," MH 31 (Jan. 1947): 99, 94–102; Giles W. Thomas, "Group Psychotherapy," PsyMed 5 (1943): 166–80; Howard P. Rome, "Military Group Psycho-

therapy," AP 101 (1945): 494–97; Louis A. Schwartz, "Group Psychotherapy in the War Neuroses," ibid., 498–500; Samuel B. Hadden, "Post-Military Group Psychotherapy with Psychoneurotics," MH 31 (Jan. 1947): 89–93.

44. "Neuropsychiatry for the General Medical Officer," MH 29 (Oct. 1945): 642.

45. Gerald N. Grob, "Origins of DSM-1: A Study in Appearance and Reality," AP 148 (April 1991): 421–31.

46. William Menninger, "Revised Psychiatric Nomenclature Adopted by the Army," MH 30 (July 1946): 456–76; William Menninger, "Lessons from Military Psychiatry for Civilian Psychiatry," MH 30 (Oct. 1946): 578–79.

47. Menninger, "Revised Psychiatric Nomenclature," 458–61.

48. Cited in Glass, ed., *Neuropsychiatry,* 2: 898.

49. Ibid., 136, 131–35. For a general discussion of conflict between the civilian and military role of the psychiatrist, see David J. Flicker, "Army Psychiatric Literature, Factors in Interpretation," AP 98 (May 1942): 795.

50. Grinker and Spiegel, *War Neuroses,* 66–67, 70; Malcolm W. Farrell and John W. Appel, "Current Trends in Military Neuropsychiatry," AP 101 (July 1944): 12–13; Paul Hoch, "Psychopathology of the Traumatic War Neuroses," AP 100 (July 1943): 124–26.

51. John W. Appel, in Glass, ed., *Neuropsychiatry in World War II,* 1: 390–91.

52. William Menninger, "Psychiatric Experience in the War," in Bernard H. Hall, ed., *A Psychiatrist for a Troubled World: The Selected Papers of William C. Menninger, M.D.* (New York: Viking, 1967), 2: 532.

53. Samuel P. Hunt, "Analysis of Neuroses Developing after Combat in Four Individuals with Outstanding Combat Records," PsyMed 8 (July–Aug. 1946): 258–70.

54. Sarlin and Berezin, "Group Psychotherapy," JNMD 104 (Dec. 1946), 611–67.

55. Grob, *From Asylum to Community* (Princeton, N.J.: Princeton Univ. Press, 1991), 14–16; Greene, "Role of Psychiatrist," 32, 420–21, 532; Glass, ed., *Neuropsychiatry in World War II,* 2: 1002, 761–73.

56. Edward A. Strecker and Kenneth E. Appel, *Psychiatry in Modern Warfare* (New York: Macmillan, 1945), 48.

57. William Menninger, "Psychiatry and World War II," in *A Psychiatrist for a Troubled World,* 531; Norman Q. Brill and Gilbert W. Beebe, *A Follow-Up Study of War Neuroses, U.S. Veterans Administration Medical Monograph* (Washington, D.C., 1955), 258.

58. Brill and Beebe, *A Follow-Up Study,* 116, 234–35, 256–61; Menninger, "Psychiatric Experience in World War II," 531.

59. Telephone interview, Judd Marmor, Los Angeles, Oct. 10, 1985.

60. Edwin A. Weinstein in Hanson, ed., *Combat Psychiatry,* 19.

61. For example, the Engle and Lewis compendium of wartime psychiatric literature includes very few articles about behavior therapy, but a substantial number about psychoanalytic psychotherapy.

62. Strecker and Appel, *Psychiatry in Modern Warfare,* 7–8, 37–39; Edward A. Strecker and Franklin G. Ebaugh, *Practical Clinical Psychiatry* (Philadelphia: P. Blakiston's Son, 1925–57).

63. Strecker and Appel, *Psychiatry in Modern Warfare,* 26, 35.

64. Strecker, "Psychoanalytic Perspectives," AP 100 (Jan. 1944): 516–19.

65. *The Nation* 161 (Dec. 1945): 602.

66. Grob, *From Asylum to Community,* 18–22; Grob, "World War II and American Psychiatry," *Psychohistory Review* 19 (Fall 1990): 41–69.

67. For the political views of the psychoanalysts in the late 1960s, see William E. Henry, *The Third Profession* (San Francisco: Jossey-Bass, 1971), ch. 5.
68. William C. Menninger, "Lessons from Military Psychiatry for Civilian Psychiatry," MH 30 (Oct. 1946): 571–89, esp. 576–85.
69. NYT (Nov. 2, 1946), 18:3.
70. Greene, "The Role of the Psychiatrist in World War II," 506.
71. William Granatir, "Psychotherapy and National Health Insurance," AP 131 (March 1974): 267.
72. Greene, "Role of the Psychiatrist," 511.
73. Walter Alvarez, "Psychosomatic Medicine That Every Physician Should Know," JAMA 135:11 (Nov. 1947): 707.
74. Seymour Vestermark, "Training and Its Support under the National Mental Health Act," AP 106 (Dec. 1948): 416.
75. NYT (Feb. 15, 1946), 29:1.
76. Grob, "The Forging of Mental Health Policy," 422–25.
77. The rise of psychosomatic medicine and psychoanalysis can be charted from listings in the *Index Medicus*. In 1947 there were about 161 articles on psychosomatic medicine and 137 on psychoanalysis. By 1965 the balance had shifted to an estimated 420 on psychoanalysis and 288 on psychosomatic medicine.

Chapter 12. The Subculture of the Psychoanalysts

1. Robert Knight to William Menninger, Jan. 15, 1949, APSA; Simmel to George Gero, May 5, 1943, SP. Otto Fenichel to Ralph Greenson, Nov. 5, 1944, GrP; for the national demand, see Robert Knight, "To Whom It May Concern," Nov. 26, 1945, and Charles Tidd to Robert Knight, Jan. 28, 1947, APSA. By 1951 there were 500 members of the American Psychoanalytic Association and 700 candidates in training, Robert Knight to Roy G. Formwalt, 1951, Folder, APA, GI Bill of Rights (1951), APSA.
2. JAPA, Bulletin 5 (March 1949): 3–4.
3. William Menninger, "Remarks on Accepting Nomination for the Presidency," May 26, 1946, APSA.
4. The committee on widening membership categories argued that the personal analysis should continue to be required and that the existing rules be retained. BAPA 6 (March 1950): 8. Menninger had broached the membership issue in his acceptance speech in Chicago; see "Remarks on Accepting Nomination for Presidency"; Robert S. Bookhamer to Robert Knight, Dec. 9, 1946; Paul Holmer to Bertram D. Lewin, Dec. 10, 1946; and "Resolution of the Boston Psychoanalytic Society," June 25, 1946, APSA.
5. Ives Hendrick to William Menninger, Dec. 31, 1948, APSA.
6. Bertram Lewin to William Menninger, May 22, 1948; Menninger to Lewin, May 24, 1948, LewP.
7. Robert Knight to William Menninger, Jan. 15, 1949, APSA.
8. For the impetus of Freud's followers to ensure orthodoxy by rigid training standards, see Siegfried Bernfeld, "On Psychoanalytic Training," Q 31 (Oct. 1962): 467; Bertram Lewin and Helen Ross, *Psychoanalytic Education in the United States* (New York: W. W. Norton, 1960), 34–38.
9. Robert Wallerstein and Rudolph Ekstein, *The Teaching and Learning of Psychotherapy* (New York: Basic Books, 1958), 69.
10. Joan Fleming and Therese Benedek, *Psychoanalytic Supervision* (New York: Grune and Stratton, 1966), 15.

11. New psychoanalytic societies included: Southern California, 1950; Western New England, with headquarters at Stockbridge, 1951; New Orleans, 1953; Psychoanalytic Association of New York and Michigan Psychoanalytic Association, 1955; Western New York, 1956; Cleveland and Seattle, 1957; Pittsburgh and New Jersey, 1959; Westchester, 1960. See John A. P. Millett, "Psychoanalysis in the United States," in Franz Alexander et al., eds., *Psychoanalytic Pioneers* (New York: Basic Books, 1966), 563.

12. Stanley Cobb to Lawrence Kubie, Oct. 18, 1932, KP.

13. Leo Bartemeier, "The Contribution of Psychiatry to Psychoanalysis," AP 101 (Sept. 1944): 205–9. Freud had consecrated this rhetoric by observing that "Psychoanalysis stands to psychiatry more or less as histology does to anatomy: in one, the outer forms of organs are studied; in the other, the construction of these out of the tissues and constituent elements." *General Introduction to Psychoanalysis* (Garden City, N.Y.: Garden City Publishing, 1943), 226–27; SE 16, p. 255.

14. Ives Hendrick, "Presidential Address: Professional Standards of the American Psychoanalytic Association," JAPA 3 (Oct. 1955): 580–82.

15. David Levy to Franz Alexander, April 6, 1938, LP.

16. Gerald Grob, *From Asylum to Community: Mental Health Policy in America* (Princeton, N.J.: Princeton Univ. Press, 1991), ch. 5 and p. 104.

17. Gitelson to Ives Hendrick, Jan. 6, 1955; David Brunswick to Ives Hendrick, Jan. 20, 1955; and Hendrick to Brunswick, Feb. 22, 1955, GP. The correspondence in 1954–55 between Hendrick and Arthur P. Noyes, president of the American Psychiatric Association, and related letters, APSA.

18. Hendrick, "Presidential Address," 580–82, 561–62.

19. Compare Bernard Bandler, "The American Psychoanalytic Association and Community Psychiatry," AP 124 (Feb. 1968): 1037–42, with Gitelson, "The Identity Crisis of American Psychoanalysis," JAPA 12 (July 1964): 451–76.

20. Interview, Frances Gitelson, Stanford, Calif., Oct. 3, 1977.

21. Kubie, "The Pros and Cons of a New Profession: A Doctorate in Medical Psychology," *Texas Reports: Biology and Medicine* 12 (1948): 125–70. The essence of Kubie's plan was carried out at the University of California, Berkeley, but foundered on the issue of the ability of its graduates to prescribe medication, which medical doctors opposed.

22. Spurgeon English to Gitelson, Dec. 13, 1954, GP. Obituary, Maxwell Gitelson, AP 122 (Oct. 1965): 469–70.

23. Katz to Gitelson, July 12, 1955, GP.

24. Gitelson to Bertram Lewin, April 16, 1958, LewP. Gitelson interview.

25. Anna Freud to Maxwell Gitelson, June 7, 1964, GP.

26. Hendrick, "Presidential Address," 585.

27. Robert Knight to Bertram Lewin, May 5, 1945; Lewin to Knight, May 8, 1945, APSAC.

28. David Levy, "Chairman's Address," in *Changing Concepts of Psychoanalytic Medicine* (New York: Grune and Stratton, 1956), 2. This anniversary volume describes the history, curriculum, and research of the Columbia Psychoanalytic Institute.

29. Ralph Kaufman to Ives Hendrick, April 18, 1953, APSA.

30. Robert Waelder to Gitelson, Sept. 20, 1955; Gitelson to Charles Tidd, Sept. 14, 1955, GP.

31. Anna Freud to Grete Bibring, Sept. 17, 1954, Feb. 17, 1955; Copy of letter to Anna Freud, unsigned, Feb. 23, 1955, BibP.

32. Mortimer S. Edelstein to Ives Hendrick, May 3, 1955, APSA.

33. Hendrick to William Barrett, March 2, 1955, APSA.

34. Robert Morse to Ives Hendrick, undated [1955], APSA.

35. JAPA 3 (1955): 344, cited in Reuben Fine, A History of Psychoanalysis (New York: Columbia Univ. Press, 1979), 137.

36. Harry P. Laughlin, "The Academy Movement," John A. P. Millet, "The Academy Movement," both mss., AAPSA. Marianne Horney Eckardt, "Organizational Schisms in American Psychoanalysis," ms., courtesy Dr. Eckardt.

37. Cited in Eckardt, "Organizational Schisms," 23.

38. Eckardt, "Historical Notes on the Founding of the American Academy of Psychoanalysis," Forum of the American Academy of Psychoanalysis 25:2 (Summer, 1981): 28–29, and John A. P. Millet, "Psychoanalysis in the United States," in Franz Alexander et al., eds., Psychoanalytic Pioneers, 571, 575–76; Millet, "The American Academy of Psychoanalysis: History of Its Foundation and Progress (1956–1966)," ms., AAPSA.

39. Copies of letters from the American Academy of Psychoanalysis to Dr. Boyd, Jan. 9, 1959; John A. P. Millet to all members of the American Psychoanalytic Association, Nov. 24, 1959; Millet to Dr. Boyd, Nov. 30, 1959, APSA.

40. See the piquant correspondence in Jules H. Masserman, A Psychiatric Odyssey (New York: Science House, 1971), 180–96; Lloyd E. Blauch, acting assistant commissioner for Higher Education, Dept. of Health Education and Welfare, Office of Education, to Gitelson, June 17, 1955, GP; Burness Moore, "The American Psychoanalytic Association: Its Janus Posture," JAPA 24 (1976): 263.

41. Manual for Training Analysts, Sept. 1, 1957, GP.

42. Lewin and Ross, Psychoanalytic Education, 53. I am indebted to Nancy Chodorow's revealing study of early women analysts for this perspective.

43. Joan Fleming to Bertram Lewin, Jan. 21, 1957, LewP.

44. Robert Holt and Lester Luborsky, Personality Patterns of Psychiatrists (New York: Basic Books, 1958), 1: 37–43, 47–59, 75–76, 287, 341–42.

45. William E. Henry, The Public and Private Lives of Psychotherapists (San Francisco: Jossey-Bass, 1973), 216. The analysts in this sample were from a variety of schools— Freudian, Jungian, Adlerian, and so on.

46. Lewin and Ross, Psychoanalytic Education, 76–77.

47. This is based on a small systematic sample in response to a questionnaire by the author; 21 psychiatrists out of 65 and 24 psychoanalysts out of 67 listed in 1973 on rosters of their respective organizations responded, while 19 psychiatrists out of 58 and 21 of 76 psychoanalysts responded who had been listed as members in 1958.

48. William E. Henry et al., The Fifth Profession (San Francisco: Jossey-Bass, 1971), 30–33.

49. Ibid., 22, 31–38, and Henry, Public and Private Lives, 80.

50. Lewin and Ross, Psychoanalytic Education, 109–14.

51. Henry, The Fifth Profession, 108, 118–20, 125, 128, 132–34.

52. Lewin and Ross, Psychoanalytic Education, 109–14.

53. Ibid., 145–46. H. Abelove, "Freud, Male Homosexuality and the Americans," Dissent 33 (Winter, 1986): 59–69; Smiley Blanton, Diary of My Analysis with Freud (New York: Hawthorn Books, 1971), 55.

54. Henry M. Fox et al., "Applicants Rejected for Psychoanalytic Training," JAPA 12 (Oct. 1964): 692–716, esp. 685; Marcia B. Nunes, "Professional Culture and Professional Practice: A Case Study of Psychoanalysis in the United States" (Ph.D. diss., Northwestern Univ., 1984), 219–20; Robert Knight, "The Present Status of Organized Psychoanalysis in the United States," JAPA 1 (1953): 197–221.

55. "Psychoanalytic Curricula—Principles and Structure," JAPA 4 (1956): 151; Rudolph Ekstein, "A Historical Survey on the Teaching of Psychoanalytic Technique," JAPA 8 (1960): 507.

56. Lewin and Ross, *Psychoanalytic Education*, 136.

57. Holt and Luborsky, *Personality Patterns*, 1: 318.

58. Ibid., and n. 72.

59. Lawrence Kubie, "The Didactic or Preparatory Analysis," BAPA 5 (Sept. 1949): 57; Nunes, "Professional Culture" 232–33, 251–52, 254; Rudolph Ekstein, "A Historical Survey on the Teaching of Psychoanalytic Technique," JAPA 8 (July 1960): 508–9.

60. Training Analysts' Seminar, June 1957, GP.

61. Nunes, "Professional Culture," 230–32.

62. Lewin and Ross, *Psychoanalytic Education*, 99–100; Holt and Luborsky, *Personality Patterns*, 42–44.

63. Howard W. Potter et al., "Problems Related to the Costs of Psychiatric and Psychoanalytic Training," AP 1131 (May 1957): 1013–19 and "Toward Unification of Training in Psychiatry and Psychoanalysis," AP 108 (Sept. 1951): 192–97.

64. Potter et al., "Problems," 1014.

65. Lewin and Ross, *Psychoanalytic Education*, 404–8; Nunes, "Professional Culture," passim.

66. Siegfreid Bernfeld, "On Psychoanalytic Training," 479, 457–82.

67. Nunes, "Professional Culture," 169–70, 183, 288, 298.

68. Otto F. Kernberg, "Institutional Problems of Psychoanalytic Education," JAPA 34 (1986): 799–834, quotation on 806.

69. Alfred Namnum, "Trends in the Selection of Candidates for Psychoanalytic Training," JAPA 28 (1980): 419–37.

Chapter 13. Psychoanalytic Ego Psychology

1. "Understanding and Explanation," in Hartmann, *Essays on Ego Psychology* (New York: International Universities Press, 1964), 377, 384, 386; for a carefully reasoned defense of psychoanalysis as a science, see Hartmann, "Psychoanalysis as a Scientific Theory," in ibid., 318–50, and Hartmann, Ernst Kris, and Rudolph M. Loewenstein, "The Function of Theory in Psychoanalysis," in Rudolph M. Loewenstein, ed., *Drives, Affects, Behavior* (New York: International Universities Press, 1953), 15–37.

2. Hartmann, "Understanding and Explanation," 391–92.

3. Robert Holt, "The Current Status of Psychoanalytic Theory," *Psychoanalytic Psychology* 2:4 (1985): 292.

4. Roy Schafer, *A New Language for Psychoanalysis* (New Haven: Yale Univ. Press, 1976), 59–60.

5. David Rapaport, *The Structure of Psychoanalytic Theory*, in Sigmund Koch, ed., *Psychology: A Study of a Science*, vol. 3 (New York: Grune and Stratton, 1959), 102. At the same time, Rapaport by no means espoused a return to traditional values as a panacea. See for instance his criticism of O. Hobart Mowrer in Merton Gill, ed., *The Collected Papers of David Rapaport* (New York: Basic Books, 1967), 458–59.

6. "Notes on the Theory of Aggression," in Heinz Hartmann, Ernst Kris, and Rudolph Loewenstein, *Papers on Psychoanalytic Psychology*, Psychological Issues 4:2, Monograph 14 (New York: International Universities Press, 1964), 69.

7. Elisabeth Young-Bruehl, *Anna Freud* (New York: Summit Books, 1988), 213–14.

8. Heinz Hartmann, *Psychoanalysis and Moral Values* (New York: International Uni-

versities Press, 1960), 43–44, 88; Hartmann, "Psychoanalysis and the Concept of Health," IJ 20:3–4 (July–Oct. 1939): 313.

9. Hartmann, Kris, and Loewenstein, "Notes on the Theory of Aggression," in Hartmann et al., *Papers on Psychoanalytic Psychology*, 71–74; Rapaport, "The Autonomy of the Ego," in Gill, ed., *Collected Papers of David Rapaport*, 364.

10. Anna Freud, *Normality and Pathology in Childhood* (New York: International Universities Press, 1965), 8.

11. Ibid., 55.

12. Ibid., 7–9.

13. Ives Hendrick, *Facts and Theories of Psychoanalysis* (New York: Alfred A. Knopf, 1939), 146, 324–29.

14. Ernst Kris to Lawrence Kubie, June 22, 1954, KP.

15. Compare Hartmann, *Die Grundlagen der Psychoanalyse* (Leipzig: Georg Thieme, 1927), 47, 168–69, with Hartmann, *Psychoanalysis and Moral Values*, 43–44. See also N. Hale, "From Berggasse 19 to Central Park West," JHBS 14 (1978): 299–315.

16. Hartmann, "The Psychiatric Work of Paul Schilder," R 31 (1944): 287–98.

17. Ruth S. Eissler and K. R. Eissler, "Heinz Hartmann: A Biographical Sketch," BMC 28:6 (Nov. 1964): 289–301.

18. Anna Freud considered Hartmann her professional older brother or half-brother; see H. Stuart Hughes, "The Advent of Ego Psychology," in Hughes, *The Sea Change: The Migration of Social Thought, 1930–1965* (New York: Harper and Row, 1975), 201, an admirably lucid essay on Hartmann.

19. Rapaport to Ruth Monroe, Oct. 29, 1952, RP.

20. Hartmann, *Ego Psychology and the Problem of Adaptation* (New York: International Universities Press, 1958), 81, 23.

21. Ibid., 13–14.

22. Ibid., 16–19.

23. Ibid., 8.

24. See George S. Klein, "The Emergence of Ego Psychology," R 56 (1969–70): 511–25.

25. Hartmann, *Ego Psychology*, 16.

26. Hartmann et al., "Notes on the Theory of Aggression," 59.

27. Leo Rangell, "The Scope of Heinz Hartmann," IJ 46 (1965): 14.

28. Heinz Hartmann et al., "Notes on the Theory of Aggression," 71.

29. Ibid., 74.

30. Hartmann, "Comments on the Scientific Aspects of Psychoanalysis," in Hartmann, *Essays on Ego Psychology*, 310–13.

31. Ibid., 302–3.

32. Ibid., 302, 313.

33. Rapaport, *The Structure of Psychoanalytic Theory*, in Koch, ed., *Psychology*, 3: 101–3, 133–34.

34. Ibid., 134, 81.

35. Merton Gill, "In Memoriam, David Rapaport, 1911–1960," JAPA 9:4 (Oct. 1961): 755; John Gedo, "Kant's Way," Q 42:3 (1973): 409–34.

36. Gill, "In Memoriam," 757.

37. Rapaport to Kubie, July 17, 1958; Kubie to Rapaport, July 11, 1958, RP.

38. Rapaport to Ruth Monroe, Oct. 29, 1952, RP.

39. Rapaport to Merton Gill, Sept. 21, 1953; Rapaport to Lawrence Kubie, June 24, 1949. RP.

40. For an insightful study of his career at Menninger's, see Lawrence Friedman, *Menninger's* (New York: Alfred A. Knopf, 1990), ch. 9.

41. Frank Fremont Smith to Robert Knight, Nov. 19, 1951; Rapaport to Smith, Aug. 23, 1951, Dec. 16, 1959, RP.

42. Ives Hendrick to Ruth Eissler, Feb. 23, 1953, RP.

43. Rapaport to Merton Gill, June 30, 1953, RP.

44. Robert R. Holt, "The Past and Future of Ego Psychology," Q 44:4 (1975): 571.

45. Rapaport to Lawrence Kubie, July 17, 1958, RP.

46. Rapaport, *The Structure of Psychoanalytic Theory,* in Koch, ed., *Psychology,* 3: 76, 84.

47. Ibid., 63.

48. Rapaport, "The Autonomy of the Ego," in Gill, ed., *Collected Papers of David Rapaport,* 365.

49. Holt, "The Past and Future of Ego Psychology," 571.

50. See n. 33.

51. For an earlier less complete attempt to construct a psychoanalytic model, see "The Conceptual Model of Psychoanalysis," in Gill, ed., *Collected Papers of David Rapaport,* 405–29.

52. Rapaport, *Structure,* 68–71.

53. Ibid., 93–97, 81.

54. Henry Murray to David Rapaport, Feb. 6, 1960, RP.

55. Rapaport, *Structure,* 68–73, 81.

56. Ibid., 93.

57. Ibid., 140–41.

58. Ibid., 144.

59. Rapaport to Bergman, July 17, 1953, RP.

60. Rapaport to Bergman, March 11, 1959, RP.

61. Rapaport, *Structure,* 152.

62. Ibid., 158.

63. Rapaport to Bergman, Oct. 8, 1957, RP.

64. Bettelheim to Rapaport, July 9, 1952, RP.

65. Rapaport to Bettelheim, July 19, 1952, RP.

66. See Chapter 20 and Charles Brenner, "Metapsychology and Psychoanalytic Theory," Q 49 (1980): 189–213.

67. Jacob Arlow and Charles Brenner, *Psychoanalytic Concepts and the Structural Theory* (New York: International Universities Press, 1964), 7.

68. Charles Brenner, *The Mind in Conflict* (New York: International Universities Press, 1982), 7.

69. Ibid., 109.

70. Ibid., 22.

71. Ibid., 124.

72. See Chapter 20.

73. Brenner, *The Mind in Conflict,* 114.

74. Ibid., 143–46, 92, 97–99, 172–73.

75. Ibid., 213.

76. For a cogent criticism of Freud's theories of the superego, see Eli Sagan, *Freud, Women and Morality* (New York: Basic Books, 1988).

77. Brenner, *The Mind in Conflict,* 132.

Chapter 14. The Rise of a Psychoanalytic Psychiatry

1. Eugene B. Brody, "Continuing Problems in the Relationship between Training in Psychiatry and Psychoanalysis," JNMD 136 (Jan. 1963): 60; Bernard Bandler, "The

American Psychoanalytic Association and Community Psychiatry," AP 124 (Feb. 1968): 1041; E. L. Caveny and E. A. Strecker, "Subsequent Nation-wide Effects of World War II Navy Psychiatric Training Program," AP 109 (Jan. 1953): 481–84. James L. Grisell, "U.S. Army Psychiatric Training Program: Subsequent Nation-wide Effects," ANP 77:2 (Feb. 1957): 218–22. Henry A. Davidson, "The Structure of Private Practice in Psychiatry," AP 113 (July 1956): 42. August B. Hollingshead and Frederick C. Redlich, *Social Class and Mental Illness* (New York: John Wiley and Sons, 1958), 145.

2. The new postwar emphasis is best described by Gerald Grob, "Psychiatry and Social Activism: The Politics of a Speciality in Post War America," BHM 60 (1980): 477–501.

The estimate of psychotic symptoms in psychoanalytic practice combines figures for these presenting "symptom clusters": schizophrenic, paranoic, depressive; see David A. Hamburg et al., "Report of Ad Hoc Committee on Central Fact Gathering Data of the American Psychoanalytic Association," JAPA 15:4 (Oct. 1967): 853. For a decreasing emphasis on the hospitalized patient, see Charles Watkins and Edward Knight, "Undergraduate Psychiatric Education as Reflected in Final Examinations," AP 116:1 (July 1959): 57. For the role of psychoanalysis in hospitals in 1944, see Robert P. Knight, "The Relationship of Psychoanalysis to Psychiatry," typed ms., SP. For the tendency of psychoanalytically trained psychiatrists to concentrate on office treatment of the neuroses, see Anita K. Bahn et al., "Survey of Private Psychiatric Practice," AGP 12 (March 1965): 300–301.

3. Seymour D. Vestermark, "Training and Its Support under the National Mental Health Act," AP 106:6 (Dec. 1948): 416–19; Bertram S. Brown, "The Life of Psychiatry," AP 133:5 (May 1976): 489–90. For the problems this posed for institutes see Helene Deutsch, *Confrontations with Myself* (New York: W. W. Norton, 1973), 183.

4. Wendell Muncie and Edward G. Billings, "A Survey of Conditions of Private Psychiatric Practice Throughout the United States and Canada," AP 108 (Sept. 1951): 171–72. John Maciver and Frederick C. Redlich, "Patterns of Psychiatric Practice," AP 115 (1959): 692–97.

5. Gerald Grob, *From Asylum to Community,* 32–43.

6. Sidney Levin and Joseph J. Michaels, "The Participation of Psychoanalysts in the Medical Institutions of Boston," IJ 43:3 (May–June 1961): 271–77; Joseph J. Michaels, "The Psychoanalyst in the Community," JAPA 5 (May 1949): 4–6; M. R. Kaufman, "The Role of Psychoanalysis in American Psychiatry," BAPA 6 (1950): 1.

7. Robert R. Holt and Lester Luborsky, *Personality Patterns of Psychiatrists* (New York: Basic Books, 1958), 1: 74–75. Median income was $10,700, and one in 10 was making more than $20,000. William E. Henry et al., *Public and Private Lives of Psychotherapists* (San Francisco: Jossey-Bass, 1973), 204.

8. Lorrin M. Koran, ed., *The Nation's Psychiatrists* (Washington, D.C.: American Psychiatric Association, 1987), 122.

9. Leonard I. Pearlin and Gerald S. Klerman, "Career Preferences of Psychiatric Residents," P 29 (Feb. 1966): 62–64.

10. Lawrence S. Kubie, "A Pilot Study of Psychoanalytic Practice in the United States," P 13 (1950): 227–46, 231–32. Henry et al., *Public and Private Lives of Psychotherapists,* 148.

11. Maciver and Redlich, "Patterns of Private Psychiatric Practice," 693.

12. For the social background of patients, see H. Aronson and Walter Weintraub, "Social Background of the Patient in Classical Psychoanalysis," JNMD 146 (Feb. 1968): 98–102; August Hollingshead and Frederick C. Redlich, *Social Class and Mental Illness,* 268–69.

13. Gerald Grob, *Mental Illness and American Society, 1875–1940* (Princeton, N.J.: Princeton Univ. Press, 1983), 300–308, and Grob, *From Asylum to Community*, 175–79. For issues in psychiatric research see Seymour Fisher and Susan Bender, "A Program of Research Training in Psychiatry," AP 132 (Aug. 1975): 821–24. For problems of lobotomy research see the admirable study by Jack Pressman, "Uncertain Promises: Psychosurgery and the Development of Scientific Psychiatry in America, 1935–1955" (Ph.D. diss., Univ. of Pennsylvania, 1986).

14. John Paul Brady, "Publication Trends in American Psychiatry," AP 116 (June 1962): 1071, 1069–77; Gerald Grob, personal communication, Aug. 22, 1989. For a view of psychoanalysis in relation to the "nature-nurture" controversy, see E. Fuller Torrey, *Freudian Fraud* (New York: Harper Collins, 1992).

15. Van Buren O. Hammett, "A Consideration of Psychoanalysis in Relation to Psychiatry Generally, circa 1965," AP 122 (July 1965): 42–54, quote on 46; Henry et al., *Public and Private Lives of Psychotherapists*, 62.

16. Myron R. Sharaf and Daniel J. Levenson, "The Quest for Omnipotence in Professional Training," P 27 (May 1964): 146.

17. Sherwyn M. Woods, "A Course for Medical Students in the Psychology of Sex," AP 125 (May 1969): 1509–10; Robert R. Holt and Lester Luborsky, *Personality Patterns of Psychiatrists* (New York: Basic Books, 1958), 1: 66–69; Henry et al., *Public and Private Lives of Psychotherapists*, 10.

18. "Psychodynamics as a Basic Science," in *Psychoanalysis of Behavior: Collected Papers of Sandor Rado* (New York: Grune and Stratton, 1956), 168, 167–72.

19. Jacob Arlow, *The Annual Survey of Psychoanalysis*, 1, 1951, p. 21; Ralph Greenson, "The 'Classical' Psychoanalytic Approach," in Sylvano Arieti, *American Handbook of Psychiatry* (New York: Basic Books, 1959), 2: 1403.

20. M. Ralph Kaufman, "The Teaching of Psychiatry to the Nonpsychiatrist Physician," AP 128 (Nov. 1971): 610–16, esp. 611.

21. See Robert P. Knight, "Evaluation of the Results of Psychoanalytic Therapy," AP 98 (Nov. 1941): 434–46.

22. Karl Menninger, *The Vital Balance* (New York: Viking, 1963), 73.

23. Sandor Rado, "Graduate Residency Training in Psychoanalytic Medicine," AP 105 (July 1946): 113.

24. Rado, "Psychodynamics as a Basic Science," AJO 16 (July 1946): 409.

25. John C. Whitehorn, "Report on Second Ithaca Conference on Psychiatric Education," AP 110 (Aug. 1953): 81–83.

26. Gerald Grob, "Psychiatry and Social Activism," BHM 60 (1986): 483–84. This gives a clear, comprehensive account of GAP's approach and activities.

27. "Public Psychiatric Hospitals," GAP Report no. 5 (April 1948), 14–15.

28. "Report on Medical Education," GAP Report no. 3 (March 1948), 10.

29. For Felix and the policies of NIMH see Grob, *From Asylum to Community*, ch. 3.

30. Gerald Grob, "The Forging of Mental Health Policy in America: World War II to New Frontier," JHM 42:4 (Oct. 1987): 416–17.

31. National Clearing House for Mental Health Information, U.S. Department of Health, Education and Welfare, U.S. Public Health Service Publication no. 1528, "Mental Health Research Grant Awards. Fiscal Years 1948–1963." The $3,966,376 figure is the author's estimate based on an assessment of the listed research projects. For training, see U.S. National Institute of Mental Health, Public Health Service Publication no. 966, Roger L. Robertson and Eli A. Rubinstein, "Training Grant Program, Fiscal Years 1948–1961," 2, 20, 55; U.S. Dept. of Health, Education and

Welfare, U.S.P.H.S. Publication no. 603, "Training Program of the National Institute of Mental Health, 1947–1957."

32. *Research in the Service of Mental Health,* Report of the Research Task Force of the National Institute of Mental Health (Rockville, Md.: National Institute of Mental Health, 1975), 315–16.

33. Maya Pines, "The Foundations' Fund for Research in Psychiatry," AP 140 (Jan. 1983): 4.

34. "Training in Psychiatry: The Preclinical Teaching of Psychiatry," GAP Report No. 54 (1962), 22.

35. Daniel H. Funkenstein, "The Problem of Increasing the Number of Psychiatrists," AP 121 (March 1965): 861.

36. American Psychoanalytic Association, Newsletter 14, no. 5 (Jan. 1962).

37. Clyde H. Ward, "Psychiatric Training in University Centers," AP 111 (Aug. 1954): 126.

38. "Training in Psychiatry," GAP Report Number 54 (Oct. 1962), 15.

39. Hammett, "A Consideration of Psychoanalysis," 42.

40. Joan B. Woods et al., "Basic Psychiatric Literature as Determined from the Recommended Lists of Residency Training Programs," AP 124 (Aug. 1967): 217–24.

41. Morton L. Enelow, "Psychoanalysis and Training Residents in Psychiatry at Tulane Medical School," JACA 10:1 (Jan. 1982): 137–45.

42. George E. Daniels and Lawrence C. Kolb, "The Columbia University Psychoanalytic Clinic," JME 35 (1960): 164–71.

43. Arthur P. Noyes and Lawrence C. Kolb, *Modern Clinical Psychiatry* (6th ed., Philadelphia: W. B. Saunders, 1963), 360–63, 500–510.

44. *Diagnostic and Statistical Manual of Mental Disorders* (2nd ed., Washington, D.C.: American Psychiatric Association, 1968), 39. DSM II in fact considerably modified DSM I to conform to the International Classification of Diseases-8, adopted by the World Health Organization in 1966.

45. Myrna M. Weissman and Gerald L. Klerman, "Epidemiology of Mental Disorders: Emerging Trends in the United States," AGP 35 (June 1978): 706.

46. Menninger, *Vital Balance,* 33.

47. Ibid., 75.

48. Ibid., 2.

Chapter 15. Expanding Applications of Psychoanalysis

1. Leo Stone, "The Widening Scope of Indications for Psychoanalysis," JAPA 2 (1954): 593, 567–94.

2. E. D. Wittkower and Z. J. Lipowski, "Recent Developments in Psychosomatic Medicine," PsyMed 28 (Sept.–Oct. 1966): 723.

3. E. D. Wittkower, "Twenty Years of North American Psychosomatic Research," PsyMed 22 (July–Aug. 1960): 309.

4. Bernard B. Raginsky, "Psychosomatic Medicine: Its History, Development and Teaching," *American Journal of Medicine* 5 (Dec. 1948): 859–60.

5. Jack Ewalt, "Psychosomatic Problems," JAMA 126:3 (Sept. 16, 1944): 152; "Postgraduate Education in Psychosomatic Medicine," JAMA 132:9 (Nov. 2, 1946): 518; Walter Alvarez, "Psychosomatic Medicine That Every Physician Should Know," JAMA 135:11 (Nov. 15, 1947): 704–8; Edward A. Strecker, "Psychosomatics," JAMA 135:18 (Aug. 30, 1947): 1520–21.

6. Interest in psychoanalysis preceded the interest in psychosomatic medicine in the

Index Medicus: 112 vs. 44 references in 1941. The references to psychosomatic medicine, however, grew steadily—from 90 in 1945 to 161 in 1947 and 194 by 1950. Interest continued through the 1950s, and by 1975 underwent a precipitous decline to 11, and was 36 and 28 respectively in 1980 and 1985. These figures are based on yearly counts from 1941 to 1956 and counts every five years from 1960 through 1985.

7. Saul, "The Relation to the Mother as Seen in Cases of Allergy," *Nervous Child* 5 (1946): 332.

8. Lucie Jessner et al., "A Psychosomatic Study of Allergic and Emotional Factors in Children with Asthma," AP 114 (1958): 890.

9. C. H. Rogerson, D. H. Hardcastle, and K. Duguid, "A Psychological Approach to the Problem of Asthma," *Guy's Hospital Report* 85 (1935): 289–308, esp. 299, 308.

10. Franz Alexander, *Psychosomatic Medicine* (New York: W. W. Norton, 1950), 139.

11. Leon Saul, "The Relation to the Mother," 333–34.

12. Alexander, "Clinical vs. Experimental Approaches in Psychodynamics," PsyMed 3 (July 1941): 333, and *The Western Mind in Transition* (New York: Random House, 1960), 162–63.

13. Fred Brown, "A Clinical Psychologist's Perspective on Research in Psychosomatic Medicine," PsyMed 20 (May–June 1958): 174–80.

14. Alexander, *Psychosomatic Medicine,* 134–35; George H. Mohr et al., "Family Dynamics in Early Childhood Asthma," in Henry I. Schneer, ed., *The Asthmatic Child* (New York: Harper and Row, 1963), 112–14; Margaret Gerard, "Bronchial Asthma in Children," *Nervous Child* 5 (1946): 331; The mother's attitude is conspicuous by its absence in Otto Fenichel's more orthodox and far less environmentalist discussion of asthma in *The Psychoanalytic Theory of Neurosis* (New York: W. W. Norton, 1945), 250–52, 321–23.

15. Hyman Miller and Dorothy Baruch, "Psychosomatic Studies of Children with Allergic Manifestations," PsyMed 10 (Sept.–Oct. 1948): 275–78, and "Maternal Rejection," in Harold A. Abramson, ed., *Somatic and Psychiatric Treatment of Asthma* (Baltimore: Williams and Wilkins, 1951), 632–54; Jeanne Block et al., "Clinicians' Conceptions of the Asthmatogenic Mother," AGP 15 (Dec. 1966): 610–18.

16. Alexander, *Psychosomatic Medicine,* 140–41, and "The Development of Psychosomatic Medicine," PsyMed 24 (1962): 25.

17. Margaret Gerard, "Bronchial Asthma in Children," 331; Leon Saul, "The Relation to the Mother," 332; Thomas French and Franz Alexander, *Psychogenic Factors in Bronchial Asthma,* Psychosomatic Medicine Monographs, no. 1 (Washington, D.C.: National Research Council, 1941).

18. Melitta Sperling, "The Role of the Mother in Psychosomatic Disorders in Children," PsyMed 11 (1949): 377–85.

19. Melitta Sperling, "A Psychoanalytic Study of Bronchial Asthma," in Schneer, ed., *Asthmatic Child,* 156–58.

20. Peter H. Knapp, "The Asthmatic Child and the Psychosomatic Problem of Asthma," in ibid., 234–55, esp. 239; Peter H. Knapp et al., "Personality Variations in Bronchial Asthma," PsyMed 19 (Nov.–Dec. 1957): 445–85, esp. 460–64.

21. Lawrence Kubie, "Psychosomatic Process," in Felix Deutsch, ed., *The Psychosomatic Concept in Psychoanalysis* (New York: International Universities Press, 1953), 79; Bernard Bandler, "Some Conceptual Tendencies in the Psychosomatic Movement," AP 115 (July 1958): 36–43.

22. Roy Grinker, *Psychosomatic Research* (New York: W. W. Norton, 1953), 15.

23. Peter Knapp et al., "The Context of Reported Asthma during Psychoanalysis,"

PsyMed 32 (March–April 1970): 182, 167–88; "Unconscious Affects," *Psychiatric Research Reports* 8 (1958): 55–74; Knapp and Claus Bahnson, "The Emotional Field," PsyMed 25 (1963): 460–83.

24. George L. Engel and Arthur H. Schmale, Jr., "Psychoanalytic Theory of Somatic Disorder," JAPA 15 (1967): 350, 344–65.

25. See Chapter 18.

26. E. Pumpian-Mindlin, "Changing Concepts of Therapy in a Veterans Administration Mental Hygiene Clinic," AP 113 (June 1957): 1095–99.

27. Leland E. Hinsie, "The Treatment of Schizophrenia: A Survey of the Literature," *Psychiatric Quarterly* (Jan. 1929): 5–39, esp. 9–16, and Hinsie, *The Treatment of Schizophrenia* (Baltimore: Williams and Wilkins, 1930); W. K. McKnight, "Historical Landmarks in Research in Schizophrenia in the United States, AP 114 (April 1958): 873–81; Loren R. Mosher and Samuel J. Keith, "Research on the Psychosocial Treatment of Schizophrenia: A Summary Report," AP 136 (May 1979): 623–31.

28. Eugene B. Brody and Frederick C. Redlich, eds., *Psychotherapy with Schizophrenics* (New York: International Universities Press, 1952), 11.

29. Ibid., 35, 22, 26, 11–12, 31–34.

30. Arieti, *American Handbook of Psychiatry* (1959), 493.

31. John Rosen, *Direct Analysis* (New York: Grune and Stratton, 1953), 4.

32. Rosen incorporated the work of Melanie Klein and Bertram Lewin on the oral phrase in ibid., 145, 61, 150, 66, 97–99, 150.

33. Kurt Eissler, "Remarks on the Psycho-analysis of Schizophrenia," IJ 32:3 (1951): 143.

34. Frieda Fromm-Reichmann, *Psychoanalysis and Psychotherapy* (Chicago: Univ. of Chicago Press, 1959), 163–64, 210, 292.

35. Fromm-Reichmann, "Notes on the Development of Treatment of Schizophrenics by Psychoanalytic Psychotherapy," P 11: (1948): 265.

36. Herbert Weiner, "Schizophrenia: Etiology," in Alfred M. Freedman et al., eds., *Comprehensive Textbook of Psychiatry* (2nd ed., Baltimore: Williams and Wilkins, 1975), 1: 877.

37. Leo Stone, "Two Avenues of Approach to the Schizophrenic Patient," JAPA 3 (Jan. 1955): 145.

38. Frieda Fromm-Reichmann, *Principles of Intensive Psychotherapy* (Chicago: Univ. of Chicago Press, 1950), 178.

39. Frieda Fromm-Reichmann in Brody and Redlich, eds., *Psychotherapy with Schizophrenics,* 100.

40. Fromm-Reichmann, "Psychotherapy of Schizophrenia," AP 111 (Dec. 1954): 412.

41. Frieda Fromm-Reichmann, "Discussion of Dr. K. R. Eissler's Remarks on the Psycho-analysis of Schizophrenia," IJ 32:3 (1951): 238–39.

42. Fromm-Reichmann in Brody and Redlich, eds., *Psychotherapy with Schizophrenics,* 101–2.

43. Fromm-Reichmann, *Psychoanalysis and Psychotherapy,* 203.

44. See n. 40.

45. Fromm-Reichmann, *Principles,* 32–35, 194.

46. See the sensitive appraisals of her life and work by Robert Cohen, Hilde Bruch, and others in P 45 (May 1982): 89–136.

47. Alfred H. Stanton and Morris S. Schwartz, *The Mental Hospital* (New York: Basic Books, 1954), 200–203, 69–71, 98–100, 199.

48. Ibid., 9, 6.

49. Ibid., 85–88.

50. Ibid., 104.

51. Ibid., 98–99.

52. Robert Knight, "The Relationship of Psychoanalysis to Psychiatry," ms., SP, p. 6.

53. Paul E. Feldman, "Inquiry into the Use of Psychotherapy for Hospitalized Schizophrenics," AP 118 (Nov. 1961): 405–9.

54. Stone, "The Widening Scope," 592–93.

55. Roy Grinker, "Neurosis, Psychosis and the Borderline States," in Freedman et al., eds., *Comprehensive Textbook,* 845–50, esp. 849.

56. Melita Schmideberg in Sylvano Arieti, *American Handbook of Psychiatry* (1959), 399–413; Edward R. Shapiro, "The Psychodynamics and Developmental Psychology of the Borderline Patient: A Review of the Literature," AP 135 (Nov. 1978): 1305–15; The most succinct descriptions are John G. Gunderson and Margaret T. Singer, "Defining Borderline Patients," AP 132 (Jan. 1975): 1–10; J. Christopher Perry and Gerald L. Klerman, "Clinical Features of the Borderline Personality Disorder," AP 137 (Feb. 1980): 165–73.

57. Ruth Hedy Ann Fallenbaum, "The Borderline Rage" (Ph.D. diss., Wright Institute, 1983), 70. For an exploration of the borderline concept from the point of view of treatment and with a useful historical summary, see John G. Gunderson, *Borderline Personality Disorders* (Washington, D.C.: American Psychiatric Press, 1984); and for examples of pathogenic parenting see James S. Grostein et al., *The Borderline Patient,* vol. 2 (Hillsdale, N.J.: Analytic Press, 1987).

58. Otto Kernberg, *Borderline Conditions and Pathological Narcissism* (New York: Aronson, 1975), 234–35, 73, 129, 227–28. For a critical review see Arnold J. Mandell, "Psychoanalytic Narcissism Projected," JNMD 166 (April 1979): 369–73.

59. Kernberg, *Borderline Conditions,* 312, 134, 260.

60. Franz Alexander, "Current Problems in Dynamic Psychotherapy in Its Relationship to Psychoanalysis," AP 116 (Sept. 1959): 322–23. See also Alexander and Thomas French, *Psychoanalytic Therapy* (New York: Ronald Press, 1946); and Alexander, *Psychoanalysis and Psychotherapy* (New York: W. W. Norton, 1956).

61. William E. Henry, *Public and Private Lives of Psychotherapists* (San Francisco: Jossey-Bass, 1973), x, 3, 78–79, 137, 204, 215–17, 223–31.

62. Lewis Wolberg, "Methodology in Short-Term Therapy," AP 122 (Aug. 1965): 139.

63. Judd Marmor, "Recent Trends in Psychotherapy," AP 137 (April 1980): 415.

64. Sifneos, "Individual Short-Term Dynamic Psychotherapy," *American Journal of Psychotherapy* 38: 4 (Oct. 1984): 474, 477; Sifneos, *Short-Term Dynamic Psychotherapy* (New York: Plenum Medical, 1979).

65. Robert S. Wallerstein, *Forty-two Lives in Treatment* (New York: Guilford Press, 1986), 631–40, 653–746, esp. 700–734.

Chapter 16. Popularization, 1945–1965

1. Dorothy Freeman,"The Psychoanalytical Joy Ride," *Nation* 171 (Aug. 26, 1950): 183–85, with comments by Frederick Wertham and Gregory Zilboorg; *Nation* 171 (Sept. 2, 1950): 205–9 and (Oct. 28, 1950): 399–401.

2. In my sample of 53 popular articles of varying length, there were 8 in 1943; 26 in 1944; 9 in 1945; 5 in 1946; 0 in 1947.

3. "A Returned Flier," "Give Us a Break," *Woman's Home Companion* 71 (Oct. 1944): 27.

4. Ibid.

5. William Menninger, "The Mentally or Emotionally Handicapped Veteran," *Annals of the American Academy of Political and Social Science* 239 (May 14, 1945): 23.

6. *Time* 43 (May 29, 1944): 44.

7. Albert Q. Maisel, "They're Beating Battle Breakdown," *Science Digest* 16 (Sept. 1944): 30; *Hygeia* 23 (Aug. 1945): 600.

8. *Newsweek* 23 (April 17, 1944): 93; Marjorie Van de Water, "Soldiers Wounded in Mind," *Science NL* 45 (April 22, 1944): 263–69.

9. John Hersey, "A Short Talk with Erlanger," *Life* 19 (Oct. 2, 1945): 118, 109–22; *Science NL* 46 (July 29, 1944): 78.

10. NYT (May 17, 1944): 36:2; Albert Deutsch, "Dramatic Effects of 'Truth Serum,'" *Science Digest* 20:4 (Oct. 1946): 65–7.

11. See n. 10.

12. See n. 9 above.

13. Kyle Crichton, "Repairing War-Cracked Minds," *Colliers* 114 (Sept. 23, 1944): 54; "Guilt Neurosis," *Newsweek* 23 (May 29, 1944): 69.

14. William C. Menninger, "The Promise of Psychiatry," NYT *Magazine* (Sept. 15, 1945): 10.

15. *Science Digest* 11:4 (April 1942): 48–49.

16. Axel Madsen, *John Huston* (Garden City: Doubleday, 1978), 70; John Huston, *An Open Book* (New York: Alfred A. Knopf, 1980), 122–26.

17. Arline Britton Boucher, "They Learn to Live Again," *Saturday Evening Post* 216 (May 27, 1944): 20, 105–6; "Acting Out Your Worries," *Newsweek* 29 (March 3, 1947): 50–1; for pentothol catharsis, see Deutsch, "Dramatic Effects of 'Truth Serum,'" 65, and "Man Given Nursing Bottle," *Science News Letter* 51 (March 1, 1947): 135; *Newsweek* 23 (May 29, 1944): 68; for catharsis in general, "Spit It Out, Soldier," *Time* 42 (Sept. 13, 1943): 60.

18. William C. Menninger, "An Analysis of Psychoanalysis," NYT *Magazine* (May 18, 1947): sec. 6, pp. 12, 49–50.

19. Ibid.; Brigadier General Elliot D. Cooke, *All But Me and Thee* (Washington, D.C.: Infantry Journal Press, 1946), 13–14.

20. Menninger, "An Analysis of Psychoanalysis," 12.

21. "Psychiatry and World War II," in Menninger, *A Psychiatrist for a Troubled World,* vol. 2 (New York: Viking Press, 1967), 513–14.

22. Roy Grinker and John Spiegel, *War Neuroses* (Philadelphia: Blakiston, 1945), 136, 78.

23. Francis Sill Wickware, "Psychosomatic Medicine," *Life* 18 (Feb. 19, 1945): 49–56.

24. George Engel, "Can Your Emotions Kill You?," *Reader's Digest* 112 (April 1978): 133–36; K. Kiesler, Jr., "Your Personality Can Be a Matter of Life or Death," *Today's Health* 51 (Feb. 1973), 16–19.

25. "What's on Your Mind," *Science Digest* 24 (Nov. 1948): 37.

26. Constance Foster with Spurgeon O. English, "Health Is What You Make It," *Parents' Magazine* (May 26, 1947): 87; D. Hartwell, "Is Your Personality Killing You," *Colliers* 30 (Nov. 1948): 37; "Your Emotions Can Make You sick," *Better Homes and Gardens* 23 (June 1945): 8, 23; "Mostly in the Mind," *Time* 50 (Oct. 6, 1947): 48.

27. *Time* 61 (Jan. 26, 1953): 39.

28. *Science Digest* 24 (Nov. 1948): 37.

29. Lucy Freeman, "Your Mind Can Make You Sick," *Science Digest* 24 (June 1954): 46.

30. *Time* (Oct. 6, 1947): 49; Irma Hewlett, "News about Asthma," *Parents'* 22 (Feb. 1947): 36; Constance Foster, "A New Approach to Health," ibid. 21 (Jan. 1946): 28–29.

31. "When Mind's the Matter," *Newsweek* 32 (Dec. 13, 1948): 46.

32. Smiley Blanton, "Best Prescription I Know," *Science Digest* 81 (Dec. 1952): 64–67.

33. Frederick Wertham, "Freud Now," *Scientific American* 181 (Oct. 1949): 50–54.

34. *Saturday Review* 39 (May 5, 1956): 9.

35. W. H. Auden, "Sigmund Freud," *New Republic* 127 (Oct. 6, 1952): 16–17, 31.

36. Robert S. White, *Scientific American* 201 (Sept. 1959), 267–71.

37. Francis Sill Wickware, "Psychoanalysis," *Life* 22 (Feb. 3, 1947): 98.

38. See n. 35.

39. Crane Brinton, "Freud and Human History," SR 39 (May 5, 1956): 8; Lawrence Kubie, "Freud and Human Freedom," ibid., 36–37.

40. "The Explorer," *Time* 67 (April 23, 1956): 76.

41. Ibid.

42. A. Michael Sulman, "The Freudianization of the American Child" (Ph.D. diss., Univ. of Pittsburgh, 1972), 115–16, 108, 121; Alice Payne Hackett, *70 Years of Best Sellers, 1895–1965* (New York: R. R. Bowker, 1967), 12.

43. Saul Pett, "Freud's Big Accomplishment," *Chicago Sun Times* (April 9, 1956), and Robert S. Kleckner, "Seek to Take Sex Stigma from Freud," ibid. (April 22, 1956).

44. Brendan Gill, *New Yorker* 29 (Oct. 10, 1953): 153; *Time* 70 (Oct. 14, 1957): 74; *Time* 62 (Oct. 19, 1953): 120–30; SRL 36 (Oct. 24, 1953): 32–34; *Scientific American* 189 (Nov. 1953): 101–4; *Newsweek* 46 (Sept. 19, 1955): 94–95; *Time* 66 (Sept. 19, 1955): 60–64.

45. *New Yorker* 32 (April 28, 1956): 34; *Time* 70 (Oct. 14, 1957): 71–74; Franz Alexander, SR 40 (Nov. 2, 1957): 18–19; Hans Meyerhoff, "Freud the Philosopher," *Commentary* 25 (Jan. 1958): 62–67.

46. Eric Fromm, "Freud, Friends, and Feuds," SR 41 (June 14, 1958): 11–13, and Jacob Arlow, "Truth or Motivations? Toward a Definition of Psychoanalysis," ibid., 14, 54.

47. Leonard Engel, "A Science Milestone," *Science Digest* 35 (June 1954): 81–85, "An Analysis of Sigmund Freud," NYT *Magazine* (Oct. 4, 1953): 12, 20, 22.

48. "Three Men," *New Yorker* (April 28, 1956): 34–35.

49. New York *Herald Tribune,* May 2, 1956, FA; *Newsweek* 47 (May 14, 1956): 74, 76. For Bailey's denunciation of Freud's influence on psychiatry see Chapter 16.

50. Alfred Kazin, "The Freudian Revolution Analyzed," NYT *Magazine* (May 6, 1956): 22.

51. SR 39 (May 5, 1956): 12.

52. Geoffrey Gorer, "Are We 'By Freud Obsessed,'" NYT *Magazine* (July 30, 1961): 5.

53. Robert S. White, *Scientific American* 201 (Sept. 1959): 267.

54. Ernest Havemann, "Unlocking the Mind in Psychoanalysis," *Life* 42 (Jan. 28, 1957): 119.

55. *Time* 67 (April 23, 1956): 76.

56. See David Hendin, "How to Pick a Psychoanalyst," *Science Digest* 75 (Jan. 1974): 10–14; Fritz Redlich and June Bingham, "What a Psychiatrist Does," *Science Digest* 34 (Aug. 1953): 61–63.

57. Lawrence J. Friedman, *Menninger* (New York: Alfred A. Knopf, 1990), 206.

58. Axel Madsen, *John Huston* (Garden City: Doubleday, 1978), 164; Ralph Green-

son to Rudolph Loewenstein, Feb. 19, 1958, GrP. For an account of the filming, see John Huston, *An Open Book* (New York: Knopf, 1980), 295–305.

59. Leo Rosten, *Captain Newman* (New York: Harper, 1956), 23, 29; Krin Gabbard and Glen O. Gabbard, *Psychiatry and the Cinema* (Chicago: Univ. of Chicago Press, 1987); Irving Schneider, "Images of the Mind: Psychiatry in the Commercial Film," AP 134 (June 1977): 613–20.

60. Nancy Lynch, "A Walk in a Dark Room," *Mademoiselle* 45 (Oct. 1957): 98; Philip Wylie, "What It's Like To Be Psychoanalyzed," *New Orleans Item, American Weekly* section (Oct. 21, 1956), FA.

61. Lucy Freeman, *Fight Against Fears* (New York: Crown, 1951), 248–49.

62. Lynch, "A Walk," 148.

63. Stanley H. Cath, "Narcissism and the Use of the Word 'Shrink,'" BMC 39 (May 1975): 209–21; Charles Winick, "The Psychiatrist in Fiction," JNMD 36 (1963): 43–57; Frederick C. Redlich, "The Psychiatrist in Caricature," AJO 20 (1950): 560–71.

64. Charles Kadushin, *Why People Go to Psychiatrists* (New York: Atherton Press, 1969), esp. 7, 11–7, 37–42, 134–37, 154–55, 266–73, chs. 3–6.

65. "The New Vienna—New York's Beehive of Psychiatry," *Newsweek* 57 (May 29, 1961): 57–58.

66. Freeman, *Fight,* 58.

67. Sid Caesar, "What Psychoanalysis Did for Me," *Look* 20 (Oct. 2, 1956): 48–49; Philip Wylie, "What It's Like To Be Psychoanalyzed."

68. Ernest Haveman, "Where Does Psychology Go from Here?," *Life* 42 (Feb. 4, 1957): 77.

69. Hannah Lees, "How I Got Caught in My Husband's Analysis," *Good Housekeeping* 145 (Nov. 1957): 80.

70. Freeman, *Fight,* 145–46; Lynch, "A Walk," 148.

71. Freeman, *Fight,* 49.

72. Ibid., 45, 167, 228–32.

73. Ibid., 84, 87, 122, 123, 139, 235–36.

74. For an insightful comparison of the novel with Frieda Fromm-Reichmann's descriptions of the therapy, see Jeffrey Berman, *The Talking Cure: Literary Representations of Psychoanalysis* (New York: New York Univ. Press, 1985), 154–76.

75. Hannah Green (Joanne Greenberg), *I Never Promised You a Rose Garden* (1964: New York: Holt, Rinehart and Winston, 1969), 27, 114, 122, 217.

76. Ibid., 122.

77. Ibid., 227.

78. "Analyzing the Analyst," *Newsweek* 64 (Oct. 12, 1961): 106; Ernest Havemann, *Life* 42 (Jan. 27, 1957): 123–24; Robert S. White, "Discussions of the Scientific Validity of Psychoanalysis, and of Freud, the Moralist," *Scientific American* 201 (Sept. 1959): 272; Nancy Lynch, "A Walk in a Dark Room," 151.

79. Freeman, *Fight,* 83; Lynch, "A Walk," 151.

80. *Newsweek* 48 (Dec. 3, 1956): 96–97; Karl Stern, "Religion and Psychiatry," *Commonweal* 49 (Oct. 22, 1948): 30–33; *Newsweek* 48 (Dec. 3, 1956): 96; *Newsweek* 50 (Aug. 4, 1947): 56–58; Frances Arick Kolb, "The Reaction of American Protestants to Psychoanalysis 1900–1950" (Ph.D. diss., Washington Univ., 1972), esp. chs. 8, 9; A. Rosenberg, *Freudian Theory and American Religious Journals 1900–1965* (Ann Arbor: UMI Research Press, 1980). For an insightful discussion of Norman Vincent Peale and Smiley Blanton, see Donald Meyer, *The Positive Thinkers* (New York: Doubleday, 1965). For a long look at the influence of psychoanalysis on American Protestants, see the illuminating articles by Sonya Michel, "American Conscience and

the Unconscious: Psychoanalysis and the Rise of Personal Religion 1906–1963," *Psychoanalysis and Contemporary Thought* 7:3 (1984): 387–421, and John Burnham, "The Encounter of Christian Theology with Deterministic Psychology and Psychoanalysis," BMC 49:4 (1985): 321–52.

81. Nancy Chodorow concluded that women analysts trained in the 1920s to the 1940s held relatively conventional views of their own domestic role while being supportive of careers for women; see "Seventies Questions for Thirties Women," in *Feminism and Psychoanalytic Theory* (New Haven: Yale Univ. Press, 1989), 202–12.

82. Freeman, *Fight,* 151, 219.

83. "The New Vienna—New York's Beehive of Psychiatry," 59.

84. Dorothy Barclay, "Trousered Mothers and Dishwashing Dads," NYT *Magazine* (April 28, 1957): 48.

85. Associated Press, undated note, AMA clinical meeting, Las Vegas, Nev., GrP; Greenson, "How Much Do We Know about Jealousy," *Look* 19 (Aug. 9, 1955): 84; Barclay, "Trousered Mothers."

86. Harold M. Vorth, "Some Effects of Freud's Personality on Psychoanalytic Theory and Technique," IJPsychiat 10:4 (Dec. 1972): 59.

87. See the contrasting views of Karl Menninger, "What the Girls Told," SR 36 (Sept. 26, 1953): 21, 30, 31, and Norman Reider, *San Francisco Chronicle, This World* (Sept. 13, 1953): 15.

88. C. C. Burlingame, AP (June 1948): 811–12; A. H. Hobbs and R. D. Lambert "An Evaluation of Sexual Behavior in the Human Male," ibid., 758–64.

89. Alfred C. Kinsey et al., *Sexual Behavior in the Human Male* (Philadelphia: W. B. Saunders, 1948), 181, 206–7; *Sexual Behavior in the Human Females* (Philadelphia: W. B. Saunders, 1953), 582–83.

90. Karl Menninger, "What the Girls Told," SR (Sept. 26, 1953): 35.

91. Ibid., 31.

92. For an account of the controversy with the psychoanalysts by one of Kinsey's researchers, see Wardell B. Pomeroy, *Dr. Kinsey and the Institute for Sex Research* (New York: Harper and Row, 1972), 70, 288–89, 296–99, 304, 367–68. Sidney Margolin, Review of *Sexual Behavior in the Human Male,* Q 17:2 (April 1948): 265–72. Therese Benedek, Review of *Sexual Behavior in the Human Female,* Q 23:2 (April 1954): 272–79. See n. 72 and Lawrence Kubie, "Psychiatric Implications of the Kinsey Report," PsyMed 10:2 (March–April 1948): 97–106; for the Rockefeller Foundation's decision not to fund further sex research by Kinsey's group, see Vern L. Bullough, "The Rockefellers and Sex Research," *Journal of Sex Research* 21:2 (May 1985), 122–23. For Kubie's support as well as reservations about Kinsey, see draft of letter not sent to George Corner, Sept. 12, 1956; also Kubie to Alan Gregg, June 16, 1948; Kubie to Mr. and Mrs. Max Lerner, June 5, 1950, KP.

93. Ronald Bayer, *Homosexuality and American Psychiatry* (Princeton: Princeton Univ. Press, 1987), 21–28.

94. Charles Socarides, in "A Symposium: Should Homosexuality Be in the AA Nomenclature?," AP 130 (Nov. 1973): 1212. This debate succinctly presents the clashing views. For an earlier discussion, see Richard Green, "Homosexuality as a Mental Illness, with Critical Evaluations," IJ Psychiat 5:5 (May 1968): 77–126.

95. Lawrence Kubie, "Psychiatric Implications of the Kinsey Report"; Edmund Bergler, *New York Herald Tribune* (May 2, 1956), FA; Robert E. Gould, "What We Don't Know about Homosexuality," NYT *Magazine* (Feb. 24, 1974): 13, 51, 56.

96. See, for example, Richard C. Friedman, *Male Homosexuality: A Contemporary Psychoanalytic View* (New Haven: Yale Univ. Press, 1988).

Chapter 17. The Decline of Psychoanalysis

1. Carl Degler, *In Search of Human Nature* (New York: Oxford Univ. Press, 1991), ch. 9; Bertram S. Brown, NIMH director, foresaw the possibility of correcting genetic defects, "blood or urine tests for the presence of mental disease or a predisposition to it," and more effective drug treatment for mental illness in "The Federal Mental Health Program: Past, Present and Future," HCP 27:7 (July 1976): 513.

2. Seymour Fisher and Roger P. Greenberg, *The Scientific Credibility of Freud's Theories and Therapy* (New York: Basic Books, 1977), 334, 341. The best results were obtained in psychosomatic cases; see 322.

3. For a thoughtful discussion of some of these issues see Donald W. Fiske et al., "Planning of Research on Effectiveness of Psychotherapy," AGP 22 (Jan. 1970): 22–32.

4. Joel Yager et al., "Professional Characteristics of Psychiatric Residents Trained at the UCLA Neuropsychiatric Institute, 1956–1975," *Journal of Psychiatric Education* 3 (1979): 75; Samuel Ritvo, "Psychoanalysis as Science and Profession," JAPA 18 (1971): 7–9; the percentage of NIMH funding for psychoanalytic research projects declined from 11 percent in 1957–61 to 6 percent in 1972–73. See Julius Segal, ed., *Research in the Service of Mental Health* (Rockville, Md.: National Institute of Mental Health, 1975), 315–16. For the counseling professions, see John C. Burnham, "Psychology and Counseling," in Nathan O. Hatch, ed., *The Professions in American History* (Notre Dame, Ind.: Notre Dame Univ. Press, 1988).

5. Eugene B. Brody, "Continuing Problems in the Relationship between Training in Psychiatry and in Psychoanalysis in the U.S.A.," JNMD 136:1 (Jan. 1963): 58–67. Melvin Sabshin, medical director of the American Psychiatric Association, estimated that in 1985 there were 23 chairmen of departments of psychiatry who had been trained as psychoanalysts, half the number of earlier years; see the remarks of Melvin Sabshin at the symposium, "Psychoanalysis and American Psychiatry," Feb. 23, 1985, St. Mary's Hospital, San Francisco. The ten medical schools are Yale, Columbia, North Carolina, Cornell, Stanford, Washington University, St. Louis, University of California, San Francisco, University of California, Los Angeles, Chicago, and Pennsylvania.

6. Sol Garfield and Allen E. Bergin, *Handbook of Psychotherapy and Behavior Change* (New York: John Wiley and Sons, 1986), 9, 158.

7. For the view of a psychoanalyst that the level of criticism had not changed in 20 years, see Jerome M. Levine, "Through the Looking Glass: An Examination of Some Critiques of Psychoanalysis," JAPA 15 (1967): 207.

8. For the attempts to bring psychiatry closer to medicine, see Gerald Grob, *Mental Illness and American Society, 1875–1940* (Princeton, N.J.: Princeton Univ. Press, 1973), 283–86; Richard A. Schwartz, "Psychiatry's Drift Away from Medicine," AP 131 (Feb. 1974): 129–33.

9. Hiram Johnson, "Psychoanalysis: Some Critical Comments," AP 113 (July 1956): 36–40.

10. Percival Bailey, "The Great Psychiatric Revolution," AP 113 (Nov. 1956): 387–406, esp. 391–95, 402.

11. Leo H. Bartemeier, "Presidential Address," AP 109 (July 1952): 4–5; Robert T. Morse, "A Serious and Little Recognized Deficit in Postwar Psychiatric Residency Training," AP 115 (April 1959): 899–904; Henry Davidson, Symposium, "The Image of the Psychiatrist," AP 121 (Oct. 1964): 331–32; Henry Davidson, "The Structure of Private Practice in Psychiatry," AP 113 (July 1956): 42–44; Jules Masserman et al.,

"Philosophy and Methodology in the Training of 500 Psychiatric Residents," AP 106 (Nov. 1949): 363–64.

12. John C. Whitehorn, "The Meaning of Medical Education in Our Society," AP 109 (Aug. 1952): 87–88.

13. See Chapter 3 and Ives Hendrick et al., "Symposium on the Evaluation of Therapeutic Results," IJ 29:1 (1948), 23–24.

14. C. P. Oberndorf, "Results with Psychoanalytic Therapy," AP 99 (Nov. 1942): 381.

15. BAPA 4:2 (May 1948).

16. Kubie to Glover, Oct. 2, 1947, KP.

17. Edward Glover, *The Technique of Psychoanalysis* (New York: International Universities Press, 1955), 345–50. See Chapter 3.

18. D. J. Kiesler, "Some Myths of Psychotherapy Research and the Search for a Paradigm," *Psychological Bulletin* 65 (Feb. 1966): 112, 121–23; Kenneth Colby argued that chaos reined in all the existing paradigms of psychotherapy—psychoanalytic, learning theory-based, or existential, in "Psychotherapeutic Processes," *Annual Review of Psychology* 15 (1964): 347–48.

19. Peter G. Denker, "Results of Treatment of Psychoneuroses by the General Practitioner," presented to the Section of Neurology and Psychiatry of the Academy of Medicine and the New York Neurological Society, April 9, 1946, NYSJM 46:2 (1946): 2164–66.

20. "Symposium on Therapy of the Psychoneuroses," ANP 57 (1947): 503–12.

21. Kubie, "Some Unsolved Problems of Psychoanalytic Psychotherapy," *Progress in Psychotherapy 1956* (New York: Grune and Stratton), 93–101.

22. Kubie, "Some Unsolved Problems," 89, 93.

23. C. P. Oberndorf et al., "Symposium on the Evaluation of Therapeutic Results," IJ 29:1 (1948): 14–15, 10–12, 21. For Greenacre's investigation of focal infection surgery see chapter 9, note 3.

24. BAPA 4:2 (May 1948): 23–24. The final report of the committee in 1966 reverses the order of these concerns, arguing that information about practice was sought first, when in fact assessment of therapeutic results was the original impulse. See David Hamburg et al., "Report of Ad Hoc Committee on Central Fact Gathering," JAPA 15 (1967): 843.

25. H. J. Eysenck, "The Effects of Psychotherapy: An Evaluation," *Journal of Consulting Psychology* 16 (1952): 319–24, and "The Effects of Psychotherapy," IJPsychiat 1 (1965): 322–23, 319, 102, 135–36. For a history of psychotherapy and psychotherapy research see Donald K. Freedheim, ed., *History of Psychotherapy. A Century of Change* (Washington, D.C.: American Psychological Association, 1992).

26. Eysenck, "The Effects," IJPsychiat 1 (1965): 108–21.

27. Ibid., 136–37.

28. Mary Lee Smith, Gene V. Glass, and Thomas I. Miller, *The Benefits of Psychotherapy* (Baltimore: Johns Hopkins Univ. Press, 1980), 1–3. The philosopher Clark Glymour explicitly rejected Eysenck's position, insisting that it was indeed possible to test psychoanalytic hypotheses with clinical evidence; see "Freud, Kepler, and the Clinical Evidence," in Richard Wollheim, *Freud: A Collection of Critical Essays* (Garden City: Anchor Books, 1974).

29. Lester Luborsky, "A Note on Eysenck's Article, 'The Effects of Psychotherapy: An Evaluation,'" *British Journal of Psychology* 45 (1954): 129–31, and H. J. Eysenck, "A Reply to Luborsky's Note," ibid., 132–33.

30. Elizabeth Zetzel, IJPsychiat 1 (1965): 144–50, esp. 147–48.

31. Lawrence Kubie, IJPsychiat 1 (1965): 175–78, esp. 176.

32. Carney Landis, "Statistical Evaluation of Psychotherapeutic Methods," in Leland Hinsie, *Concepts and Problems of Psychotherapy* (New York: Columbia Univ. Press, 1937), 155–69, esp. 159, 168; Denker, "Results of Treatment of Psychoneuroses by the General Practitioner," 2164–66.

33. Eysenck, *Decline and Fall of the Freudian Empire* (New York: Viking, 1985), 70–71.

34. A. E. Bergin, "The Effects of Psychotherapy," *Journal of Counseling Psychology* 10 (1963): 244–50; useful summaries of the controversy from a pro-psychotherapy point of view are in Smith, Glass, and Miller, *Effects of Psychotherapy;* D. H. Malan, "The Outcome Problem in Psychotherapy," AGP 29 (Dec. 1973): 719–29, esp. 722; J. Meltzoff and M. Kornreich, *Research in Psychotherapy* (New York: Atherton Press, 1970). For the behaviorist view, including Eysenck's defense of his handling of incomplete psychoanalytic treatment and spontaneous remission, see Eysenck, *Decline and Fall,* ch. 3; and S. Rachman and G. T. Wilson, *The Effects of Psychological Therapy* (London: Pergamon Press, 1980). For a balanced review of problems of psychotherapy research, see R. Bruce Sloane et al., *Psychotherapy versus Behavior Therapy* (Cambridge, Mass.: Harvard Univ. Press, 1975), ch. 2.

35. S. Rachman, *The Effects of Psychotherapy* (New York: Pergamon Press, 1971), ch. 3.

36. Joseph Wolpe, "The Prognosis in Unpsychoanalysed Recovery from Neurosis," AP 118 (July 1961): 35–39; Bergin, "The Effects of Psychotherapy," 244–50.

37. R. Bruce Sloane et al., *Psychotherapy versus Behavior Therapy,* 9.

38. Eysenck, *Decline and Fall,* 88–89. For an overview, including application to the psychoses, see H. J. Eysenck and S. Rachman, *The Causes and Cures of Neuroses* (San Diego, Calif.: Robert R. Knapp, 1965). Many of the first outcome studies of behavioral techniques lacked control groups.

39. Sloane et al., *Psychotherapy vs. Behavior Therapy,* 213–14.

40. Useful descriptions of patients' presenting difficulties and the problems of diagnosis and classification occur in Hans H. Strupp et al., *Patients View Their Psychotherapy* (Baltimore: Johns Hopkins Univ. Press, 1969), and in Sloane et al., *Psychotherapy vs. Behavior Therapy,* 2–4 and passim.

41. For a survey of a lifetime of psychoanalytic practice see John Gedo, "A Psychoanalyst Reports at Mid-Career," AP 136 (May 1979): 625–26.

42. Malan, "The Outcome Problem," 720.

43. A. Karush et al., *Psychotherapy in Chronic Ulcerative Colitis* (Philadelphia: W. B. Saunders, 1977); S. Orgel, "Effects of Psychotherapy on the Course of Peptic Ulcer," PsyMed 20 (1958): 117–25.

44. See the lucid discussion of this issue in Malan, *A Study of Brief Psychotherapy* (Springfield, Ill.: Charles C. Thomas, 1963), 43–65.

45. Sloane et al., *Psychotherapy vs. Behavior Therapy,* intro. and ch. 1; Frederick R. Hine et al., "Effectiveness of Psychotherapy: Problems of Research on Complex Phenomena," AP 139 (Feb. 1982): 204–8.

46. Malan, "The Outcome Problem," 728.

47. Edwin R. Wallace IV, "The Scientific Status of Psychoanalysis: Review of Gruenbaum's *The Foundations of Psychoanalysis,*" JNMD 174:7 (July 1986): 383.

48. See the useful discussion in Fisher and Greenberg, *Scientific Credibility of Freud's Theory and Therapy,* ch. 9.

49. Paul Meehl, *Clinical vs. Statistical Prediction: A Theoretical Analysis and Review of the Evidence* (Minneapolis: Univ. of Minnesota Press, 1954), 4.

50. For a thoughtful study of the problem of psychotherapy research see Thomas E. Schacht and Hans H. Strupp, "Evaluation of Psychotherapy," in Kaplan, *Comprehensive Textbook of Psychiatry,* vol. 2 (3rd ed., Baltimore: Williams and Wilkins, 1980), 1473–80. Stanley D. Imber: "Then and Now: Forty Years in Psychotherapy Research," *Clinical Psychology Review* 12 (1992): 199–204; Irene Elkin et al., "National Institute of Mental Health Treatment of Depression Collaborative Research Program," AGP 46 (1989): 971–82.

51. Lester Luborsky, "Comparative Studies of Psychotherapies," AGP 32:8 (Aug. 1975): 1000; Sol L. Garfield and Allen E. Bergin, *Handbook of Psychotherapy and Behavior Change* (New York: John Wiley and Sons, 1986).

52. Garfield and Bergin, *Handbook of Psychotherapy and Behavior Change,* 17, 62, 202. See also Jean Endicott and Robert L. Spitzer, "Evaluation of Psychiatric Treatment," in Harold I. Kaplan et al., *Comprehensive Textbook of Psychiatry* (3rd ed., Baltimore: Williams and Wilkins, 1980), 3: 2391–409.

53. C. R. Rogers, "The Necessary and Sufficient Conditions of Therapeutic Personality Change," *J. Consult. Psychol.* 21:2 (1957): 95–103; J. D. Frank, "The Dynamics of the Psychotherapeutic Relationship," P 22 (1959): 17–30; Garfield and Bergin, *Handbook of Psychotherapy and Behavior Change,* 185, 171–72; Lester Luborsky et al., "Do Therapists Vary Much in Their Success? Findings from Four Outcome Studies," AJO 56:4 (Oct. 1986): 501–12.

54. Robert S. Wallerstein, Review of David H. Malan, *Toward the Validation of Psychotherapy,* JAPA 27 (1979): 276–79, and "The Current State of Psychotherapy," JAPA 14 (1966): 218, 209–23.

55. Donald J. Kiesler, "Some Myths of Psychotherapy Research and the Search for a Paradigm," *Psychological Bulletin* 65:2 (1966): 110–14. Irene Elkin et al., "NIMH Treatment of Depression Collaborative Research Program," AGP 42 (March 1985): 305–16.

56. Hinsie, *Concepts and Problems,* 10, 167–69; Eugene Ziskind, "How Specific Is Psychotherapy?," AP 106: 4 (Oct. 1949): 285–91.

57. Luborsky et al., "Comparative Studies of Psychotherapy," AGP 32 (Aug. 1975): 1005, 995–1008.

58. Jerome D. Frank, "Therapeutic Components of Psychotherapy," JNMD 159:5 (1974): 325–42. For a brief autobiographical note, see P. E. Dietz, ed., *Jerome D. Frank, Psychotherapy and the Human Predicament* (New York: Schocken Books, 1978), xv–xx.

59. Jerome D. Frank, *Persuasion and Healing* (Baltimore: Johns Hopkins Univ. Press, 1961), 35 and passim; Frank, "Psychotherapy: The Restoration of Morale," AP 131:3 (March 1974): 271–74; and Frank et al., "Why Patients Leave Psychotherapy," ANP 77:3 (1957): 283–84.

60. Judd Marmor, "Recent Trends in Psychotherapy," AP 7:4 (April 1980): 409–15, and "Limitations of Free Association," in Marmor, *Psychiatry in Transition* (New York: Brunner/Mazel, 1974), 265–67.

61. Malan, *A Study of Brief Psychotherapy,* vi, ch. 13.

62. Robert S. Wallerstein, *Forty-two Lives in Treatment* (New York: Guilford Press, 1986), 66–71, 119–81.

63. Otto Kernberg, "Summary and Conclusions," BMC 36:2 (1972): 181–98, "Summary and Conclusions of Psychotherapy and Psychoanalysis, Final Report of the Menninger Foundation's Psychotherapy Research Project," IJPsychiat 11 (March 1973): 62–103.

64. Wallerstein, *Forty-two Lives,* 515–16, 682–734.

65. Smith, Glass, and Miller, *Benefits of Psychotherapy*, 183–84.

66. Ibid., 187.

67. Ibid., 3–4.

68. Ibid., ch. 2, 46–50.

69. Ibid., 125.

70. Nathan G. Epstein and Louis A. Volk, "Research on the Results of Psychotherapy," AP 138:8 (Aug. 1981): 1027–35.

71. Leslie Prioleau et al., "An Analysis of Psychotherapy vs. Placebo Studies," with peer commentary, BBS 6 (1983): 276, 279, 284, 290.

72. Ibid.

73. Garfield and Bergin, *Handbook of Psychotherapy and Behavior Change*, 50; Morris B. Parloff, "Placebo Controls in Psychotherapy Research," JCCP 54 (1986): 79–87.

74. Sol Garfield, Comment, BBS 6 (1983): 292.

75. BBS 6 (1983): 275; H. J. Eysenck, "An Exercise in Megasilliness," and Smith, Glass, and Miller's Reply, AmPsychol (May 1978): 517–19.

76. Roger B. Greenberg, BBS 6 (1983): 294.

77. Morris Eagle, BBS 6 (1983): 288; Morris B. Parloff: "Psychotherapy Research Evidence and Reimbursement Decisions," AP 139:6 (June 1982): 721–22.

78. Hartvig Dahl, BBS 6 (1983): 287. For a critical discussion of the placebo issue, see Morris B. Parloff, "Frank's 'Common Elements' in Psychotherapy," AJO 56:4 (Oct. 1986): 521–30.

79. Sol L. Garfield, "Issues and Methods in Psychotherapy Process Research," JCCP 58:3 (1990): 273–80. Hans H. Strupp et al., "The Nonspecific Hypothesis of Therapeutic Effectiveness: A Current Assessment," AJO 56:4 (Oct. 1986); Luborsky, "Do Therapists Vary Much in Their Success?," AJO 56:4 (Oct. 1986); Parloff, "Frank's 'Common Elements'"; Strupp, "Psychotherapy: Research, Practice and Public Policy," AmPsychol 41:2 (Feb. 1986): 120–30; Morris B. Parloff, "Can Psychotherapy Research Guide the Policymaker," AmPsychol 34:4 (April 1979): 296–306.

80. Gavin Andrews, BBS 6 (1983): 286.

81. Michael Shepherd, BBS 6 (1983): 302.

82. Richard C. Simons, *Newsletter of the American Psychoanalytic Association* 22:2 (Summer 1988): 10.

83. Henry M. Bachrach et al., "On the Efficacy of Psychoanalysis," JAPA 39:4 (1991): 871–916.

Chapter 18. A Diminishing Psychoanalytic Realm

1. Alvan Feinstein, *Clinical Judgment* (Baltimore: Williams and Wilkins, 1967), 23–24.

2. Fred Brown, "A Clinical Psychologist's Perspective on Research in Psychosomatic Medicine," PsyMed 20:3 (May–June 1958): 175–76.

3. Kenneth Purcell, "Critical Appraisal of Psychosomatic Studies of Asthma," NYS-JM 65:3 (Aug. 15, 1965): 2103.

4. M. C. Harris, "A Study of Behavior Patterns in Asthmatic Children," *Journal of Allergy* 27 (1956): 312–23, "Is There a Specific Emotional Pattern in Allergic Disease?," *Annals of Allergy* 13 (1955): 654–61; Nicholas J. Gross, *Bronchial Asthma* (New York: Harper and Row, 1974); Edward C. Neuhaus, "A Personality Study of Asthmatic and Cardiac Children," PsyMed 20:3 (1958): 185; Marvin Margolis, "The Mother-Child Relationship in Bronchial Asthma," JAP 63:2 (1961): 361–62. Dennis

Leigh and Edward Marley, "A Psychiatric Assessment of Adult Asthmatics," *Journal of Psychosomatic Research* 1 (1956): 128–36; Edward Kelly and Barbara Zeller, "Asthma and the Psychiatrist," *JPsychosom Res* 13 (1969): 394–95; A. K. Zeally, "Bronchial Asthma: A Problem Attributable to Sampling When Establishing Its Psychopathology," *Psychotherapy and Psychosomatics* 19 (1971): 37–46; Kenneth Purcell, "Childhood Asthma: The Role of Family Relationships, Personality and Emotions," in Anthony Davids, ed., *Child Personality and Psychopathology: Current Topics,* vol. 2 (New York: John Wiley, 1975), 120–21, 125, 128, 131–32.

5. E. H. Freeman et al., "Psychological Variables in Allergic Disorder: A Review," PsyMed 26 (1964): 543–71. In Herbert Weiner's comprehensive bibliography on asthma in his *Psychobiology and Human Disease* (New York: Elsevier, 1977), there were approximately 34 psychoanalytic books and articles from 1951 to 1964 and 7 from 1964 to 1977. Kelly and Zeller, "Asthma and the Psychiatrist," 386.

6. Weiner, *Psychobiology,* 250, 254, 257, 223, 294–98, 268–70; Kelly and Zeller, "Asthma," 388.

7. Herbert Weiner, "From Simplicity to Complexity (1950–1990): The Case of Peptic Ulceration," PsyMed 53 (1991): 467–90.

8. Weiner, *Psychobiology,* 294–98; Peter H. Knapp et al. strongly reiterated the psychoanalytic position in "Psychosomatic Aspects of Bronchial Asthma," in Earle B. Weiss and Maurice S. Segal, eds., *Bronchial Asthma: Mechanisms and Therapeutics* (Boston: Little, Brown, 1976), 1055–80, esp. 1063, 1068, 1071–72; see also Lawrence Deutsch, "Psychosomatic Medicine from a Psychoanalytic Viewpoint," PsyMed 28 (1980): 653–702, esp. 690–94; Weiner, "Contributions of Psychoanalysis to Psychosomatic Medicine," JACA 10:1 (Jan. 1982): 27–46.

9. Hans Selye, *The Stress of Life* (New York: McGraw-Hill, 1978): Harold G. Wolff, *Stress and Disease* (Springfield, Ill.: Charles P. Thomas, 1953), 39–45, 122.

10. David Hamburg, "A Perspective on Coping Behavior," AGP 17 (Sept. 1967): 277–84; Thomas W. Miller, "Advances in Understanding the Impact of Stressful Life Events on Health," HCP 39:6 (June 1988): 615; John J. Schwab, "Psychosocial and Epidemiological Concepts in Medicine," in Sylvano Arieti, ed., *American Handbook of Psychiatry,* (New York: Basic Books, 1974), vol. 4; 583–607; T. R. Holmes and R. H. Rahe, "The Social Readjustment Rating Scale," *J. Psychosom Res.* 11 (1967): 213–18.

11. John C. Nemiah, "Denial Revisited: Reflections on Psychosomatic Theory," *Psychotherapy and Psychosomatics* 26 (1975): 144; Margaret Thayer Singer, "Psychological Dimensions in Psychosomatic Patients," *Psychotherapy and Psychosomatics* 28 (177): 21–22; John Gunderson and Sanford Gifford, "Cushing's Disease," *Perspectives in Biology and Medicine* 13:2 (Winter 1970): 210–17.

12. Meyer Friedman and R. H. Rosenman, *Type A Behavior and Your Heart* (New York: Alfred A. Knopf, 1974); Z. J. Lipowski, "Consultation-Liaison Psychiatry: An Overview," AP 131:6 (June 1974): 623. Dartmouth Symposium on "Current Trends in Psychosomatic Medicine," *Int. J. Psychiat. in Med.* 5:4 (1974): 309–611.

13. Howard M. Spiro, *Clinical Gastroenterology* (2nd ed., New York: Macmillan, 1977), 250–51; McGhee Harvey, *Principles and Practice of Medicine* (New York: Appleton, Century, Crofts, 1976), 1659. Other citations are available from the author.

14. Leo H. Criep, *Clinical Immunology and Allergy* (2nd ed., New York: Grune and Stratton, 1969), 259.

15. Stanley Cheren and Peter H. Knapp, "Gastrointestinal Disorders," in Harold I. Kaplan and Benjamin Saddock, eds., *Comprehensive Textbook of Psychiatry* (Baltimore: Williams and Wilkins, 1980), 2: 1868; Aaron Karush et al., *Psychotherapy in Ulcerative*

Colitis (Philadelphia: W. B. Saunders, 1977), 140. For a recent claim of successful psychoanalytic psychotherapy, see Charles C. Hogan, "Inflammatory Disease of the Colon," in C. Philip Wilson and Ira L. Mintz, eds., *Psychosomatic Symptoms* (Northvale, N.J.: Jason Aronson, 1989).

16. Peter H. Knapp, "Current Theoretical Concepts in Psychophysiological Medicine," in Alfred M. Freedman et al., eds., *Comprehensive Textbook of Psychiatry,* 1631–37; Morton Reiser, "Converging Sectors of Psychoanalysis and Neurobiology," JAPA 33 (1985): 11–34, "Changing Theoretical Concepts in Psychosomatic Medicine," in Sylvano Arieti, ed., *American Handbook of Psychiatry* (New York: Basic Books, 1974), 477.

17. For the inroads of neo-somaticism on psychological therapy for schizophrenics see W. Carpenter and T. McGlashan, "The Treatment of Acute Schizophrenia without Drugs: An Investigation of Some Current Assumptions," AP 134 (Jan. 1977): 14–20.

18. Eli Robins and Samuel B. Guze, "The Establishment of Diagnostic Validity in Psychiatric Illness: Its Application to Schizophrenia," AP 126 (Jan. 1970): 983–87, and S. B. Guze et al., "Diagnosis and Prognosis in Schizophrenia," AGP 42 (1985): 15–25; Seymour Kety, "The Concept of Schizophrenia," in Murray Alpert, ed., *Controversies in Schizophrenia* (New York: Guilford Press, 1985), 9.

19. Gerald Klerman, "The Advantages of DSM-III," AP 141 (April 1984): 539–42.

20. Heinz E. Lehmann, "Schizophrenia: Clinical Features," in Alfred M. Freedman et al., *Comprehensive Textbook of Psychiatry* (Baltimore: Williams and Wilkins, 1975), 915.

21. J. E. Cooper et al., *Psychiatric Diagnosis in New York and London* (New York: Oxford Univ. Press, 1972); Michael Alan Taylor and Richard Abrams, "The Prevalence of Schizophrenia: A Reassessment Using Modern Diagnostic Criteria," AP 135 (Aug. 1978): 945–48; Jeffrey D. Blum, "On Changes in Psychiatric Diagnosis over Time," AmPsychol 33 (Nov. 1978): 1017–31.

22. "A Debate on DSM III," AP 141 (April 1984): 539–53.

23. See n. 22 and Ronald Bayer and Robert L. Spitzer, "Neurosis, Psychodynamics, and DSM III: A History of the Controversy," AGP 42 (Feb. 1985): 187. See also Robert I. Spitzer et al., "DSM-III Field Trials: I. Initial Interrater Diagnostic Reliability," AP 136 (June 1979): 815–17; Spitzer et al., "DSM-III: The Major Achievements and an Overview," AP 137 (Feb. 1980): 151–63.

24. Quoted in Bayer and Spitzer, "Neurosis, Psychodynamics, and DSM III," 190. For the St. Louis school's views of etiology, see Samuel B. Guze, "The Diagnosis of Hysteria: What Are We Trying To Do?," AP 124 (Oct. 1967): 491–98; Paul Chodoff, "The Diagnosis of Hysteria: An Overview," AP 131 (Oct. 1974): 1073–78; Myrna M. Weissman and Gerald L. Klerman, "Epidemiology of Mental Disorders," AGP 35 (June 1978): 705–13.

25. George E. Vaillant, AP 141 (April 1984): 544.

26. Seymour Kety and D. Rosenthal, Eds., *The Transmission of Schizophrenia* (Oxford: Pergamon Press, 1968), and Kety, "From Rationalization to Reason," AP 131 (Sept. 1974): 957–63.

27. Julius Segal, ed., *Research in the Service of Mental Health* (Rockville, Md.: NIMH, 1975), 64–65, 174–75. Some recent estimates place the concordance rate for schizophrenia in identical twins at 30 to 80%; see *Harvard Mental Health Letter* 8:12 (June 1992), 2.

28. See the thoughtful discussion of etiology by Herbert Weiner in Freedman et al., eds., *Comprehensive Textbook of Psychiatry,* 1: 866–890.

29. Arieti, "An Overview of Schizophrenia," AP 131 (March 1974): 243.

30. Otto Will, "Schizophrenia: Psychological Treatment," in Kaplan and Saddock, eds., *Comprehensive Textbook of Psychiatry*, 1217–40; Bertram P. Karon and Gary R. Vandenbos, *Psychotherapy of Schizophrenia* (New York: Aronson, 1981).

31. Robert Paul Liberman, "Schizophrenia: Psychosocial Treatment," in Kaplan and Saddock, eds., *Comprehensive Textbook of Psychiatry* (1985), 1: 724–34.

32. Freedman et al., eds., *Comprehensive Textbook of Psychiatry*, Vol. 1, 817.

33. Philip R. May, "Schizophrenia: Evaluation of Treatment Methods," in Freedman et al., eds., *Comprehensive Textbook of Psychiatry*, 1: 955–56.

34. John G. Gunderson et al., "Effects of Psychotherapy in Schizophrenia 2," *Schizophrenia Bulletin* 10:4 (1984): 564–612, but see also the critical discussion of these results in the same issue; Robert E. Drake and Lloyd I. Sederer, "The Adverse Effects of Intensive Treatment of Chronic Schizophrenia," *Comprehensive Psychiatry* 27:4 (July–Aug. 1986): 313–26; Robert S. Bookhammer et al., "A Five Year Follow-up Study of Schizophrenics Treated by Rosen's Direct Analysis, Compared with Controls," AP 123 (Nov. 1966): 602–4.

35. Sandra G. Boodman, "The Mystery of Chestnut Lodge," Washington *Post* Magazine, Oct 8, 1989; Gerald Klerman, "The Efficacy of Psychoanalysis and Psychoanalytically Oriented Psychotherapy," AP 146 (April 1989): 571; Linda Hilles, "Changing Trends in the Application of Psychoanalytic Principles to a Psychiatric Hospital," BMC 32:4 (July 1968): 210–11.

36. Alpert, ed., *Controversies in Schizophrenia*.

37. Seymour S. Kety, "From Rationalization to Reason," AP 131 (Sept. 1974): 961–62; Robert Paul Liberman, "Schizophrenia: Psychosocial Treatment," in Kaplan and Saddock, eds., *Comprehensive Textbook of Psychiatry* (1985), 1: 724–33.

38. Van Buren O. Hammett, "A Consideration of Psychoanalysis in Relation to Psychiatry Generally, Circa 1965," AP 122 (July 1965): 50, 42–54.

39. George Engle, "Some Obstacles to the Development of Research in Psychoanalysis," JAPA 16 (1968): 196, 200.

40. Maya Pines, "The Foundations' Fund for Research in Psychiatry and the Growth of Research in Psychiatry," AP 140 (Jan. 1983): 4, 9.

41. The degree of continuity is still an open question. Both Anna Freud and the non-psychoanalytic investigator Stella Chess have argued that neurosis in childhood does not necessarily mean neurosis in the adult. The most recent research suggests that in some children neuroses are continuous, but in others not, and the question now is what factors operate in each of these different outcomes.

42. Robert W. McCarley and J. Allan Hobson, "The Neurobiological Origins of Psychoanalytic Dream Theory," AP 134 (Nov. 1977): 1211; Seymour Fisher and Roger P. Greenberg, *The Scientific Credibility of Freud's Theories and Therapy* (New York: Basic Books, 1977), 63–74.

43. Paul Chodoff, "A Critique of Freud's Theory of Infantile Sexuality," AP 123 (Nov. 1966): 510, and see the evaluations of Chodoff in IJPsychiat 4:1 (July 1967): 49–61.

44. Morris Gelfman, "A Post-Freudian Comment on Sexuality," AP 126 (Nov. 1969): 651–57.

45. See the lucid discussion of these issues cited earlier by Zenia Odes Fliegel, "Feminine Psychosexual Development in Freudian Theory," Q 42 (1973): 385–409, and "Half a Century Later: Current Status of Freud's Controversial Views on Women," R 69:1 (Spring 1982): 7–28.

46. John E. Kysar, "The Two Camps in Child Psychiatry," AP 124 (July 1968): 103–

9; William S. Appleton, "Mistreatment of Patients' Families by Psychiatrists," AP 131 (June 1974): 655.

47. N. S. Lehrman, "Precision in Psychoanalysis," AP 116 (June 1960): 1097; Roy Grinker, Sr., "The Sciences of Psychiatry: Fields, Fences and Riders," AP 122 (Oct. 1965): 371, 373–76.

48. Sidney Hook, ed., *Psychoanalysis, Scientific Method and Philosophy* (New York: Grove Press, 1959), 50.

49. Ibid., 226–27.

50. Ibid., 249.

51. Ibid., 217–18.

52. Ibid., 336.

53. Ibid., 331.

54. Ibid., 6.

55. Ibid., 63, 58–59, 205.

56. Robert Waelder, "Psychoanalysis, Scientific Method, and Philosophy," JAPA 10 (1962): 617–37.

57. John R. Neill and Arnold M. Ludwig, "Psychiatry and Psychotherapy: Past and Future," *Am. J. Psychotherapy* 24:1 (Jan. 1980): 47.

58. Grob, *From Asylum to Community*, ch. 9; Joint Commission on Mental Illness and Health, *Action for Mental Health* (New York: Basic Books, 1961), 262–63, 265–68.

59. *Action for Mental Health*, 105.

60. Jerome Frank, *Persuasion and Healing*, 126–27.

61. Leon Eisenberg, "Developments in Psychiatric Postgraduate Training in the United States," *Social Science and Medicine* 7 (1973), 99–102. Lee Gurel, "Some Characteristics of Psychiatric Residency Training Programs," AP 132 (April 1975): 371. Phil Brown, *The Transfer of Care* (London: Routledge and Kegan Paul, 1985), 66; Anita K. Bahn et al., "Private Psychiatric Practice," AGP 12 (March 1965): 295–302.

62. Bernard Bandler noted that although an "extraordinary number" of psychoanalysts were active in community psychiatry, the American Psychoanalytic Association remained aloof: "The American Psychoanalytic Association and Community Psychiatry," AP 124 (Feb. 1968): 1037–42. In Los Angeles, participation was considerable; see Joseph B. Kopecs, "Psychoanalysis Today," AGP 18 (Feb. 1968): 161–68. However, Larry R. Faulkner and James S. Eaton, Jr., pointed to a rift between academic departments and community mental health centers in "Administrative Relationships between Community Mental Health Center, and Academic Departments of Psychiatry," AP 136 (Aug. 1979): 1040–44, and Lawrence Kubie's hostility to community psychiatry and his emphasis on thorough, individual treatment are clear in an interview in the *Baltimore Sun* (July 13, 1969), C: 1, 4.

63. Lorin M. Koran, ed., *The Nation's Psychiatrists* (American Psychiatric Association, 1987), 80–81.

64. Melvin Sabshin, "The Anti Community Mental Health Movement," AP 125 (Feb. 1969), 1005–11, and see the thinly disguised study of the Massachusetts Mental Health Center by Donald Light, *Becoming Psychiatrists* (New York: W. W. Norton, 1980), 330–35.

65. Jerome D. Frank, "New Therapeutic Roles," in Bert H. Kaplan et al., eds., *Further Explorations in Social Psychiatry* (New York: Basic Books, 1976), 111–29. Phil Brown, *The Transfer of Care* 68–69; Hans H. Strupp et al., *Patients View Their Therapy,* (Baltimore: Johns Hopkins Press, 1969), 119.

66. Nettie N. Terestman et al., "Blue Collar Patients at a Psychoanalytic Clinic," AP 131 (March 1974): 261–66.

67. Bandler, "The American Psychoanalytic Association and Community Psychiatry"; Robert S. Wallerstein, "The Challenge of the Community Mental Health Movement to Psychoanalysis," AP 124 (Feb. 1968): 1049–56.

68. Brown, *The Transfer of Care,* ch. 6; Leona L. Bachrach, "General Hospital Psychiatry," AP 138 (July 1981): 879–87.

69. Howard H. Goldman and Neal Adams, "Deinstitutionalization: The Data Demythologized," HCP 34:2 (Feb. 1983): 131.

70. Quoted in John R. Neill and Arnold M. Ludwig, "Psychiatry and Psychotherapy: Past and Future," *American Journal of Psychotherapy* 34:1 (Jan. 1980): 45; Sydney E. Pulver, "Survey of Psychoanalytic Practice 1976," JAPA 26 (1978): 621.

71. Fritz Redlich and Stephen R. Kellert, "Trends in American Mental Health," AP 135 (Jan. 1978): 26.

72. Anne K. McCarrick et al., "National Trends in Use of Psychotherapy in Psychiatric Inpatient Settings," HCP 39:8 (Aug. 1988): 835–41.

73. David L. Cheifetz and Jeffrey C. Salloway, "Patterns of Mental Health Services Provided by HMO's," AmPsychol 39:5 (May 1984): 498; Koran, ed., *Nation's Psychiatrists,* 101; McCarrick et al., "National Trends," 837.

74. Pulver, "Survey of Psychoanalytic Practice," 621.

75. Judd Marmor, *Psychiatrists and Their Patients* (Washington, D.C.: American Psychiatric Association, 1975), 4–6.

76. Koran, ed., *Nation's Psychiatrists,* 101–2.

77. Carl A. Taube et al., "Patients of Psychiatrists and Psychologists in Office-Based Practice: 1980," AmPsychol 39:4 (Dec. 1984): 1435–47; Jeffrey D. Blum and Fritz Redlich, "Mental Health Practitioners," AGP 37 (Nov. 1980): 1247–53. Neill and Ludwig, "Psychiatry and Psychotherapy: Past and Future," 39–50; Morton G. Wagenfeld et al., *Public Mental Health* (Beverly Hills: Sage Publications, 1982), 150.

78. Fritz Redlich and Stephen R. Kellert, "Trends in American Mental Health," AP 135 (Jan. 1978): 22–28. Marmor, *Psychiatrists and Their Patients,* 108.

79. Pulver, "Survey," JAPA 26 (1978), 620.

80. Marmor, *Psychiatrists and Their Patients,* 36–37, 102.

81. Marmor, *Psychiatrists,* 41–47, 68–75. John Gedo, "A Psychoanalyst Reports at Mid-Career," AP 136 (May 1979), 646–49.

82. Pulver, "Survey," JAPA 26 (1978): 625–26.

83. Steven S. Sharfstein et al., "The Impact of Third-Party Payment Cutbacks on the Private Practice of Psychiatry," HCP 35:5 (May 1984): 479.

84. Marmor, *Psychiatrists and Their Patients,* 137–38.

85. E. Marshall, "Psychotherapy Faces Test of Worth," *Science* 207 (Jan. 1980): 35–36; Morris B. Parloff, "Psychotherapy Research: Evidence and Reimbursement Decisions," AP 139 (June 1982): 718–27; Boris Astrachan and Steven S. Sharfstein, "The Income of Psychiatrists: Adaptation during Difficult Economic Times," AP 143 (July 1986): 885–87.

86. Sharfstein et al., "The Impact," 478–81; Edwin Hustead et al., "Reductions in Coverage for Mental and Nervous Illness," AP 142 (Feb. 1985): 181–86.

87. Steven S. Sharfstein, "Third-Party Payers: To Pay or Not to Pay," AP 1350 (Oct. 1978): 1187.

88. Koran, *Nation's Psychiatrists,* 79–84; Wayne S. Fenton, "Trends in Psychiatric Practice, 1965–1980," AP 141 (March 1984): 346–51.

89. Steven S. Sharfstein et al., "The Impact," 478–81.

90. Marvin A. Scharfman and Gary J. Grad, "Outcomes of Psychiatric Residency Training during the Past Decade," and Carl Salzman et al., "Alumni of the Massa-

chusetts Mental Health Center Residency Training," AGP 33 (April 1976): 431–35, 421–23.

91. Koran, *Nation's Psychiatrists,* 118–31.

92. Ibid., and Astrachan and Sharfstein, "The Income of Psychiatrists," AP 143 (July 1986): 885–87.

93. Joel Yager et al., "Professional Characteristics of Psychiatric Residents Trained at UCLA Neuropsychiatric Institute," *Journal of Psychiatric Education* 3:1 (1979): 72–85; Carlyle H. Chan and Boris M. Astrachan, "The First Postresidency Position: Correlations with Training Program Characteristics," ibid. 9 (1984): 82; David Dean Brockman and Joanne Marengo, "Outcome Study of Psychiatric Residents at the University of Illinois Neuropsychiatric Institute (1959–1972)," ibid. 5:1 (Spring 1981): 27–31.

94. William Coryell, "The Organic-Dynamic Continuum in Psychiatry," AP 139 (Jan. 1982): 89–91; John F. Greden and Jorge I. Casariego, "Controversies in Psychiatric Education," AP 132 (March 1975): 270–73.

95. Donald G. Langsley and Marc H. Hollender, "The Definition of a Psychiatrist," AP 139 (Jan. 1982): 82–83.

96. Gordon D. Strauss et al., "The Cutting Edge in Psychiatry," AP 141 (Jan. 1984): 38–41.

97. Norman Dain, "Critics and Dissenters: Reflections on Anti-Psychiatry in America," JHBS 25:1 (Jan. 1989): 3–25.

Chapter 19. Popular Images of Controversy

1. Carol Tavris, "The Hundred-Year Cover-up: How Freud Betrayed Women," *Ms.* 12 (March 1984): 78. There were also important Freudian feminists, among them Juliet Mitchell and Nancy Chodorow, but they drew less attention in the popular press.

2. Betty Friedan, *The Feminine Mystique* (1963; New York: Dell, 1974), 97, 13, 16, 37–38, 95, 115, 305–8.

3. Kate Millet, *Sexual Politics* (Garden City: Doubleday, 1970).

4. Richard Gilman, "The FemLib Case Against Sigmund Freud," NYT *Magazine* (Jan. 31, 1971): 10; "Liberating Women from Freud," *Time* 109 (Jan. 17, 1977): 67; Catherine Bigwood, "The Tyranny of the Male Therapist," *Harper's Bazaar* 104 (July 1971): 52–53; Suzanne Gordon, "Helene Deutsch and the Legacy of Freud," NYT *Magazine* (July 30, 1978): 23.

5. Rona Cherry and Lawrence Cherry, "Karen Horney, the Psychiatrist Who Walked Out on Freud," *Ms.* 3 (June 1975): 112–16, 120.

6. Donald M. Kaplan, "Freud and His Own Patients," *Harper's* 235 (Dec. 1967): 105–6.

7. Erik Erikson, "Reality and Actuality," JAPA 10 (1962): 454–57, 459–61.

8. Salvatore R. Maddi, "The Victimization of Dora," *Psychology Today* 8 (Sept. 1974): 91–100. For a brilliant reappraisal of Freud and Dora, see Hannah H. Decker, *Freud, Dora and Vienna 1900* (New York: Free Press, 1991).

9. Mary Jane Sherfey, "The Evolution and Nature of Female Sexuality in Relation to Psychoanalytic Theory," JAPA 14 (1966): 28–128.

10. For examples of the popular application of psychoanalytic principles to the "perversions," see Morton Hunt, *Sexual Behavior in the 1970's* (New York: Dell, 1974), 302–3; for psychoanalytic attitudes toward masturbation, see Paul Robinson, *The Modernization of Sex* (New York: Harper and Row, 1976), 65; Otto Fenichel, *The Psychoanalytic Theory of Neurosis* (New York: W. W. Norton, 1945), 243–44.

11. Freud then believed that neurasthenia was caused by masturbation. He also noted that men who had been "seduced by women at an early age" had escaped neurasthenia but implied that syphilis and gonorrhea were the consequence of recourse to prostitutes; see Freud to Fliess, Feb. 8, 1893, in Jeffrey Moussaieff Masson, ed., *The Complete Letters of Sigmund Freud to Wilhelm Fliess, 1887–1904* (Cambridge, Mass.: Harvard Univ. Press, 1985), 44, 41; Martin Gross, *The Psychological Society* (New York: Random House, 1978), 166.

12. "Civilization and Its Discontents" (1930), SE 21, p. 105. Vincent Brome, *Freud and His Early Circle* (New York: William Morrow, 1967), 69.

13. Freud, *Introductory Lectures on Psychoanalysis* (1917), SE 16, p. 434.

14. "Civilization and Its Discontents," 112. For the development of Freud's views on sexuality and society, see Timothy McCarthy, "Freud and the Problems of Sexuality," JHBS 17 (1981): 332–39.

15. For example, Paul Robinson's criticism of Sulloway, Masson, and Gruenbaum in *Freud and His Critics* (Berkeley: Univ. of California Press, 1993). Robinson sees in these critics a neo-positivism and a rejection of the relativist positions enshrined in "modernism" and recent literary criticism.

16. Henri Ellenberger, *The Discovery of the Unconscious* (New York: Basic Books, 1970), 418–20, 455, 463.

17. J. W. Burrow, SR 51 (June 1, 1968): 31.

18. Paul Roazen, *Freud and His Followers* (New York: Alfred A. Knopf, 1974).

19. Albert Schwartz, *New Republic* 172 (March 1, 1975): 28; Robert Coles, *New Yorker* 51 (July 14, 1975): 96–98; *Newsweek* 85 (Jan. 13, 1975): 67.

20. *Time* 114 (July 30, 1979): 51.

21. Frank Sulloway, *Freud: Biologist of the Mind* (New York: Basic Books, 1979), 451.

22. *Time* 95 (Jan. 12, 1970): 41; interview, Judith Bernays Heller, Berkeley, Calif., June 20, 1970; *Newsweek* 98 (Nov. 30, 1981): 64.

23. SR 55 (July 29, 1972): 52–53; see also emphasis placed in the Jones biography on "The Foibles of Sigmund Freud," *Time* 66 (Sept. 19, 1955): 64.

24. Jeffrey Masson, *The Assault on Truth* (New York: Farrar, Straus and Giroux, 1984): Masson, ed., *Complete Letters of Sigmund Freud to Wilhelm Fliess;* NYT (June 21, 1991): A9:1.

25. *Newsweek* 98 (Nov. 30, 1981): 64.

26. Ibid.

27. E. M. Thornton, *The Freudian Fallacy* (New York: Dial, 1984); *Village Voice Literary Supplement* (June 1984): 14.

28. John Leo, "Psychoanalysis Heads for Its Own Couch," *Science Digest* 64 (Nov. 1968): 58–63; Lawrence Galton, "After Fifty Years—an Analysis of Analysis," NYT *Magazine* (Feb. 12, 1961): 11, 73–74, 77.

29. *Science Digest* 86 (Sept. 1979): 49–53.

30. Christopher Lasch, "Sacrificing Freud," NYT *Magazine* (Feb. 22, 1976): 11.

31. Dan Wakefield, *Returning: A Spiritual Journey* (New York: Doubleday, 1988), 175–76, 170, 106–8, 115–17, 159, 165, and "My Six Years on the Couch," NYT *Magazine* (Dec. 20, 1987): 32.

32. Donald Kaplan, "Psychoanalysis: The Decline of a Golden Craft," *Harper's* 234 (Feb. 1967): 45; "How Kind Can the Analyst Be?," *Time* 119 (March 8, 1982): 87.

33. "Psychotherapy Faces Test of Worth," *Science* 207 (Jan. 1980): 35, 590.

34. "A New and Controversial Short-Term Psychotherapy," NYT *Magazine* (Nov. 21, 1982): 58, 60, 63, 102–3.

35. Aaron Beck and Maria Kovacs, "A New Fast Therapy for Depression," *Psychology Today* 101 (Jan. 1977): 94–95.

36. Morris Parloff in "The Psychotherapy Jungle: A Guide for the Perplexed," SR 3 (Feb. 21, 1976): 14.

37. Jarl Dyrud in ibid., 22–26.

38. *"Bazaar's* Guide to Psychotherapy," *Harper's Bazaar* 110 (Sept. 1977): 228–62.

39. Rosemary Blackmon, "Psychotherapy: How to Select Your Shrink," *Mademoiselle* 180 (Nov. 1974): 176–77, 214.

40. Krin Gabbard and Glen O. Gabbard, *Psychiatry and the Cinema* (Chicago: Univ. of Chicago Press, 1987), 151.

41. Seymour Kety, "It's Not All in Your Head," SR (Feb. 21, 1976): 28–32.

42. Michael Halberstam, "Can You Make Yourself Sick?" *Today's Health* 50 (Dec. 1972): 28.

43. "New Ways to Heal Disturbed Minds." *U.S. News and World Report* 80 (Feb. 16, 1976): 33–36; Ellen Switzer, "Who Needs Therapy?," *Vogue* 169 (Dec. 1979): 302.

44. Sandra G. Boodman, "The Mystery of Chestnut Lodge," *Washington Post Magazine* (Oct. 8, 1989): 18–24, 39–43. I am indebted for this reference to Dr. Richard R. Palmer.

45. Susan Sheehan, *Is There No Place on Earth for Me?* (Boston: Houghton, Mifflin, 1982).

46. Barbara Gordon, *I'm Dancing as Fast as I Can* (New York: Harper and Row, 1979).

47. Switzer, "Who Needs Therapy?," 302.

48. David Hellerstein, "The Making of a Psychiatrist," *Science Digest* 94 (April 1986): 71, 78, 79.

49. Switzer, "Who Needs Therapy?," 283; "How to Know When Someone in Your Family Needs a Psychiatrist," *Better Homes and Gardens* 44 (March 1966): 38.

Chapter 20. The Crisis of American Psychoanalysis

1. Freud referred to his formal attempts at psychological theory as his metapsychology. Perhaps the most famous examples were chapter 7 of *The Interpretation of Dreams,* the papers on metapsychology of 1915, his later papers on the "structural theory" of ego, id, superego, and anxiety. These later papers formed the basis for ego psychology. See Chapter 13.

2. Robert R. Holt, "Freud's Cognitive Style," *American Imago* 22 (Fall 1965): 173–75, 167–70.

3. George S. Klein, "Two Theories or One," BMC 37:2 (March 1973): 107–8.

4. Robert R. Holt, "The Past and Future of Ego Psychology," Q 44 (1975): 173.

5. Robert R. Holt, "The Current Status of Psychoanalytic Theory," *Psychoanalytic Psychology* 2:4 (1985): 292.

6. Holt, "Past and Future of Ego Psychology," 562–63.

7. Klein, "Two Theories," 103–4, 112–14.

8. Ibid., 116, 122.

9. Ibid., 108.

10. George Klein, *Psychoanalytic Theory: An Exploration of Essentials* (New York: International Universities Press, 1976).

11. Roy Schafer, *A New Language for Psychoanalysis* (New Haven: Yale Univ. Press, 1976).

12. Holt, "Current Status," 305.

13. Ibid., 302.

14. Ibid., 306, 296, 311.

15. Adolf Grünbaum, "Precis of *The Foundations of Psychoanalysis: A Philosophical Critique,*" BBS 9 (1986): 226.

16. Ibid., 222.

17. Adolf Grünbaum, *The Foundations of Psychoanalysis: A Philosophical Critique* (Berkeley: Univ. of California Press, 1984), 189.

18. Philip Holzman, "Psychoanalysis: Is the Therapy Destroying the Science?," JAPA 33 (1985): 737–40, 764; Morris Eagle, *Recent Developments in Psychoanalysis* (New York: McGraw Hill, 1984), 157, 171. Although Reiser argued that "ultimate validation" would have to come from extraclinical findings, reliable evidence in fact could be derived from the psychoanalytic process from new methods such as recording analyses and refining clinical hypotheses, but the contrast with Arlow's general confidence remains striking. See Reiser, BBS 9 (1986): 255–56; Judd Marmor, "The Question of Causality," in ibid., 249.

19. Robert Wallerstein, "Psychoanalysis as a Science: A Response to the New Challenges," Q 55 (1986): 431–47. For a thoughtful assessment of scientific issues in psychoanalysis and for the use of prediction, see Benjamin B. Rubenstein, "The Problem of Confirmation in Clinical Psychoanalysis," JAPA 2 (1980): 397–417.

20. Freud cited experimental studies in *New Introductory Lectures on Psychoanalysis,* SE 22, pp. 22–23. Freud noted that "the way to find out something about mother love can be only through statistical examination . . ." in Herman Nunberg and Ernst Federn, eds., *Minutes of the Vienna Psychoanalytic Society* (New York: International Universities Press, 1974), 118.

21. F. Cioffi in Commentary on Grünbaum, *Foundations,* BBS 9 (1986): 230. Grünbaum's thesis was examined by a variety of psychoanalysts, philosophers, psychologists on 228–66.

22. Joseph Weiss et al., *The Psychoanalytic Process* (New York: Guilford Press, 1986), 340.

23. The classic demonstration of the inability of clinicians to agree on interpretations of the same set of interview data is Philip D. Seitz, "The Consensus Problem in Psychoanalytic Research," in Louis A. Gottschalk and Arthur A. Auerbach, *Methods of Research in Psychotherapy* (New York: Appleton, Century, Crofts, 1966), 209–25.

24. Robert Waelder, "Psychoanalysis, Scientific Method, and Philosophy," JAPA 10 (1962): 627–28; Peter H. Knapp, "Short-Term Psychoanalytic and Psychosomatic Predictions," JAPA 11 (1963): 245–79.

25. Hans Strupp, Remarks at Conference on Structural Change in Psychoanalytic Psychotherapy, San Francisco, Feb. 28–March 1, 1987.

26. Jacques P. Barber and Lester B. Luborsky, "Psychotherapy Research," in L. K. George Hsu and Michel Hersen, *Research in Psychiatry* (New York: Plenum Medical Book, 1992), 351.

27. Remarks of Maurice G. Marcus, Symposium on Control Mastery Theory, San Francisco, Nov. 16, 1985; Weiss and Sampson, *The Psychoanalytic Process,* 40.

28. Lester Luborsky and Arthur H. Auerbach, "The Symptom-Context Method," JAPA 17 (1969): 91–98.

29. Lester Luborsky et al., "A Verification of Freud's Grandest Clinical Hypothesis: The Transference," *Clinical Psychology Review* 5 (1985): 231–46.

30. Lester Luborsky, "Evidence to Lessen Prof. Grünbaum's Concern about Freud's Clinical Inference Method," BBS 9 (1986): 247–49.

31. For a cogent analysis of Freud's attitude toward the mother, see Madelon Sprengnether, *The Spectral Mother* (Ithaca: Cornell Univ. Press, 1990).

32. Margaret S. Mahler et al., *The Psychological Birth of the Human Infant* (New York: Basic Books, 1975), 5.

33. Ibid., 17, 15.

34. Paul E. Stepansky, ed., *The Memoirs of Margaret Mahler* (New York: Free Press, 1988), 4–5, 68–69; Benjamin Spock and Mary Morgan, *Spock on Spock: A Memoir of Growing Up with the Century* (New York: Pantheon Books, 1985), 108–11.

35. Stepansky, *Mahler,* 102–5.

36. Mahler, *Psychological Birth,* 206, 39.

37. Ibid., x, 118–9.

38. Ibid., 43–44, 77–82, 101, 109–10, 118–19, 206.

39. Stepansky, *Mahler,* 149–52.

40. Mahler, *Psychological Birth,* 200 n. 3.

41. Ibid., 203.

42. Daniel Stern, *The Interpersonal World of the Infant* (New York: Basic Books, 1985) 6.

43. Ibid., 7.

44. Ibid., 7–10, 71.

45. Ibid., 239, 47–48, 98.

46. Ibid., 10, 19, 23, 257.

47. Ibid., 229–30, 208, 210–11.

48. Louise Kaplan, *Contemporary Psychoanalysis* 23:1 (1987): 27–42.

49. Harry Stack Sullivan, *The Interpersonal Theory of Psychiatry,* Helen Swick Perry et al., eds. (New York: W. W. Norton, 1953), 10, 17, 39–41, 44, 53, 160–70.

50. Heinz Kohut, *The Restoration of the Self* (New York: International Universities Press, 1977), 277.

51. Ibid., 101.

52. Ibid., 187.

53. Jay R. Greenberg and Stephen A. Mitchell, *Object Relations in Psychoanalytic Theory* (Cambridge, Mass.: Harvard Univ. Press, 1983), 353. Their lucid discussion of Kohut's theories has informed this one.

54. Kohut, *Restoration,* 86.

55. Kohut quoted in Mitchell and Greenberg, *Object Relations,* 370.

56. Kohut, *Restoration,* 81.

57. Ibid., 124, 115.

58. Ibid., 302–3, 308.

59. Donald Spence, "Narrative Persuasion," *Psychoanalysis and Contemporary Thought* 6:3 (1983): 460, and *Narrative Truth and Historical Truth: Meaning and Interpretation in Psychoanalysis* (New York: W. W. Norton, 1982).

60. Spence, "Narrative Persuasion," 477–78.

61. Paul K. Feyerabend, *Against Method: Outline of an Anarchistic Theory of Knowledge* (Atlantic Highlands: Humanities Press, 1975), 10–15, ch. 1; for an overview of theories see Frederick Suppe, ed., *The Structure of Scientific Theories* (Urbana: Univ. of Illinois Press, 1969); Thomas Kuhn, *The Structure of Scientific Revolutions,* with postscript (Chicago: Univ. of Chicago Press, 1977).

62. For applications of Kuhn's later theory, see Vann Spruiell, "Kuhn's 'Paradigm' and Psychoanalysis," Q 52 (1983): 353–63, and "The Future of Psychoanalysis," Q 58 (1989): 1–28; Henry M. Bachrach et al., "On the Efficacy of Psychoanalysis," JAPA 39 (1991): 873.

63. For an insightful assessment of the Americanization of psychoanalysis and a sense of crisis, see Benjamin Brody, "The Present Status of Psychoanalysis: An Addendum to Dr. Arieti," IJPsychiat 8:3 (Sept. 1969): 630–39.

64. James Bule, "Psychoanalysis," *American Psychological Association Monitor* 19:2 (Feb. 1988): 1, 14; Melvin Sabshin, "Psychoanalysis and Psychiatry: Models for Potential Future Relations," JAPA 33 (1985): 473–91, esp. 480.

65. Sam Hoch, *San Francisco Psychoanalytic Institute and Society Newsletter* 39 (April 1990): 14; Arnold Cooper, "The Future of Psychoanalysis: Challenges and Opportunities," Q 59 (1990): 177–96.

66. Samuel Perry et al., "The Psychodynamic Formulation," AP 144 (May 1987): 543–50.

67. Greenberg and Mitchell, *Object Relations.*

68. Leo Rangell, "The Future of Psychoanalysis: The Scientific Crossroads," Q 57 (1988): 328.

69. Marshall Edelson, *Psychoanalysis: A Theory in Crisis* (Chicago: Univ. of Chicago Press, 1988), 19, 163.

70. Jacob Arlow and Charles Brenner, "The Future of Psychoanalysis," Q 57 (1988): 10.

71. Rangell, "The Future of Psychoanalysis," 337.

72. Arlow and Brenner, "The Future of Psychoanalysis," Q 57 (1988): 5, 10, 8.

73. Robert Michels, "The Future of Psychoanalysis," Q 57 (1988): 169–70; personal communication, Sanford Gifford.

74. Edward M. Weinshel, "How Wide Is the Widening Scope of Psychoanalysis and How Solid Is Its Structural Model?," JAPA 38 (1990): 275–96.

75. Ralph Greenson, *The Technique and Practice of Psychoanalysis,* vol. 1 (New York: International Universities Press, 1967), 206–24; Arlow and Brenner, "The Future of Psychoanalysis."

76. Michels, "The Future of Psychoanalysis," 167–68.

77. "On the History of the Psychoanalytic Movement" (1914), SE 14, p. 16; "Two Encyclopedia Articles" (1923), SE 18, p. 247; "New Introductory Lectures" (1933), SE 22, pp. 138, 143; "Psychoanalysis" (1934), SE 20, p. 267.

Conclusion

1. John Burnham, "The Influence of Psychoanalysis upon American Culture," in Jacques Quen and Eric Carlson, eds., *American Psychoanalysis: Origins and Development* (New York: Bruner/Mazel, 1978).

2. Morton Reiser, "Converging Sectors of Psychoanalysis and Neurobiology," JAPA 33:1 (1985): 11–33.

3. However, recent studies suggest that placebos may be almost as effective as antidepressant drugs and that psychotherapy can create changes in energy consumption in the brain. See *Harvard Mental Health Letter* 9:6 (March 1993): 6.

4. For an important assessment of these issues, see Hans H. Strupp, "Psychotherapy," Am Psychol 41:2 (Feb. 1986): 120–30.

5. Lester Luborsky, *Principles of Psychoanalytic Psychotherapy: A Manual for Supportive-Expressive Treatment* (New York: Basic Books, 1984), xv; for the burgeoning of talk treatment and the declining the role of religion, see Joseph Veroff et al., eds., *The Inner American: A Self Portrait from 1957 to 1976* (New York: Basic Books, 1981), 14–16, chs. 7, 9, 10. For subjective clinical judgment in drug-induced personality change and its effects on diagnosis, treatment, and ethics, see Peter D. Kramer, *Listening to Prozac* (New York: Viking, 1993).

6. Marie Jahoda, *Freud and the Dilemmas of Psychology* (Lincoln: Univ. of Nebraska Press, 1977), 10–11, 14–19, 57–58, 154–58.

7. Roger Bastide, *The Sociology of Mental Disorder* (New York: David McKay, 1972).

8. Ruth Hedy Ann Fallenbaum, "The Borderline Rage: Theory, Practice, and Change in Psychoanalytic Psychotherapy" (Ph.D. diss., Wright Institute, Berkeley, Calif., 1983), 32, 37, 98–99.

9. These cases appeared in psychoanalytic journals and texts, and many of them were drawn from the psychosomatic literature.

10. See the cases in Flanders Dunbar, *Mind and Body* (New York: Random House, 1947). For the related problem of hysteria as a socially determined symptom, see Edward Shorter, "Paralysis: The Rise and Fall of a 'Hysterical' Symptom," *Journal of Social History* 19 (Summer 1986): 549–82; Roberta Satow, "Where Has All the Hysteria Gone?," R 66:4 (1979): 463–77. For a psychoanalytic view, see Alan Krohn, *Hysteria: The Elusive Neurosis* (New York: International Universities Press, 1978), ch. 4.

11. See Chapter 10.

12. See the cases in Franz Alexander et al., *Psychoanalytic Therapy: Principles and Application* (New York: Ronald Press, 1946), 118–19, 125–26, 247–48, 320–24, 148–54.

13. Flanders Dunbar, *Psychosomatic Diagnosis* (New York: Paul B. Hoeber, 1943), 217–19, 222–25, 246–47; see Chapter 3.

14. Dunbar, *Mind and Body,* 108–10; Tamara K. Haraven, "The History of the Family," *American Historical Review* 96:1 (Feb. 1991): 123.

15. Alexander et al., *Psychoanalytic Therapy,* ch. 13; Thomas French and Franz Alexander, *Psychogenic Factors in Bronchial Asthma,* Psychosomatic Medicine Monographs 4 (National Research Council 1941), 37, 56.

16. For the dependency issue, the cases of Franz Alexander illustrate often enough the growing role of the mother and a relatively uninvolved father. See, for example, Alexander, *Psychosomatic Medicine: Its Principles and Application* (New York: W. W. Norton, 1950), 133.

17. Ilene Philipson, "The Social Production of Personality: A Case Study of Narcissism" (Ph.D. diss., Univ. of California, Santa Cruz, 1981), 90.

18. Ibid., 106.

19. Ibid., 137.

20. For the classic discussion of narcissism from a different perspective, see Christopher Lasch, *The Culture of Narcissism* (New York: W. W. Norton, 1979).

21. Judith Wallerstein and Sandra Blakeslee, *Second Chances: Men, Women, and Children a Decade after Divorce* (New York: Ticknor and Fields, 1989), xvii, 4–8, 13–15, 23, 25, 50–51, 55.

22. Andrew J. Cherlin, *Marriage, Divorce, Remarriage* (Cambridge, Mass.: Harvard Univ. Press, 1981), 81–83, 87–92; Veroff et al., eds., *The Inner American,* 536.

23. Cherlin, *Marriage,* 16, 26–36, 53, 74–81.

24. Sherry Turkle, *Psychoanalytic Politics* (New York: Basic Books, 1978).

25. Gregorio Kohon, *The British School of Psychoanalysis* (New Haven: Yale Univ. Press, 1986); Judith Hughes, *Reshaping the Psychoanalytic Domain* (Berkeley: Univ. of California Press, 1989): Edith Kurzweil, *The Freudians: A Comparative Perspective* (New Haven: Yale Univ. Press, 1989).

26. Jean Michel Palmier, "La Psychanalyse en Union Sovietique," in Roland Jaccard, ed., *Historie de la psychanalyse* (Paris: Hachette, 1982), 383–84, 206, 214–16.

27. Kurzweil, *The Freudians,* 34.

28. William E. Henry et al., *The Fifth Profession* (San Francisco: Jossey-Bass, 1971), 48–51, 57, 66–67.

29. Turkle, *Psychoanalytic Politics,* 143, 262.

30. Kurzweil, *The Freudians,* 40: Hannah S. Decker, *Freud in Germany* (New York: International Universities Press, 1977); Herman Nunberg and Ernst Federn, eds., *Minutes of the Vienna Psychoanalytic Society,* vol. 3 (New York: International Universities Press, 1974), 147.

31. Dean Rapp, "The Reception of Freud by the British Press," JHBS 24 (April 1988): 191–201.

32. Geoffrey Cocks, *Psychotherapy in the Third Reich: The Goering Institute* (New York: Oxford Univ. Press, 1985), 26–27, 313–49, 240–41; Henri Vermoul and Andre Meylan, *Cent ans de psychiatrie* (Paris: Editions du Scarbee, 1969), 17–44; Henry Ey, "Psychiatrie et psychanalyse," *L'Evolution psychiatrique* 1957 (3): 473–87; Ernest Jones, *The Life and Work of Sigmund Freud,* vol. 3 (New York: Basic Books, 1957), ch. 9.

33. Peter Berger, "Towards a Sociological Understanding of Psychoanalysis," *Social Research* 32 (1965): 26–41; Morris Janowitz, *The Last Half Century* (Chicago: Univ. of Chicago Press, 1978), 424–26.

34. Ernest Gellner, *The Psychoanalytic Movement or the Coming of Unreason* (London: Granada Publishing, 1985). Janowitz, *Last Half Century,* 424.

Index